A Guide to the Nests, Eggs, and Nestlings of North American Birds
Second Edition

A Guide to the Nests, Eggs, and Nestlings of North American Birds

Second Edition

Paul J Baicich

and

Colin J O Harrison

Illustrations by
Andrew Burton, Philip Burton and Terry O'Nele

Egg Photographs by
F Greenaway and Clark Sumida

ACADEMIC PRESS
San Diego   London   Boston   New York   Sydney   Tokyo   Toronto

AP Natural World is published by
Academic Press
525 B Street, Suite 1900, San Diego
California 92101–4495, USA

Academic Press Limited
24-28 Oval Road, London NW1 7DX, UK

ISBN: 0–12–072831–1

Library of Congress Cataloging-in-Publication Data
Baicich, Paul J.
A guide to the nests, eggs, and nestlings of North American birds
by Paul J. Baicich, Colin J.O. Harrison.
p. cm.
Includes bibliographical references (p.   ) and index.
ISBN 0–12–072831–1 (pbk. : alk. paper)
1. Birds – Nests – North America.   2. Birds – Eggs – North America.
3. Birds – North America.   I. Harrison, Colin James Oliver. II. Title.
QL675.B163   1997
598.1564'097–dc21   96–47959
CIP

A catalogue record for this book is available from the British Library

First published as Harrison C, *A Field Guide to the Nests, Eggs and Nestlings of
North American Birds*, Collins, 1978.

Typeset by LaserScript, Mitcham, Surrey
Printed in Great Britain by Butler and Tanner Ltd, Frome, Somerset
97 98 99 00 01 02 EB 9 8 7 6 5 4 3 2 1

Contents

Color plates

The color plate section appears between p. 222 and p. 223.

Nestlings

All nestling plates are painted by Philip Burton

1. Loons, grebes, shearwaters, storm-petrels, gannets, pelicans, cormorants, and Anhinga
2. Herons, spoonbills, ibises and storks
3. Whistling-ducks, swans, and geese
4. Ducks
5. Ducks
6. American vultures, hawks, eagles, caracaras, and falcons
7. Guans and grouse
8. Typical gamebirds
9. Rails, galllinules, coots, Limpkin, and cranes
10. Shorebirds
11. Shorebirds
12. Gulls, terns, and skimmers
13. Jaegers, gulls, and auks
14. Doves, cuckoos, owls, and trogons
15. Goatsuckers, swifts, hummingbirds, kingfishers, and woodpeckers
16. Songbirds

Eggs

17. Loons, shearwaters, and gannets
18. Grebes, storm-petrels, cormorants, and Anhinga
19. Pelicans, herons, ibises, spoonbills, and storks
20. Bitterns and herons
21. Swans
22. Branta and gray geese
23. Gray geese, whistling-ducks, and wood and dabbling ducks

Please begin here

The nesting of birds is one of the most interesting aspects of their lives, but it is also the period at which they are most vulnerable. It would be unfortunate if the publication of this work resulted in harm to birds and their young. It may be a pity to begin a book with a plea or a warning to the reader, but we feel that we should make these comments at the very start.

During the latter part of the nineteenth century, when collecting all kinds of natural objects became almost a mania, nesting birds suffered heavily from the attention of egg collectors. The bright and varied colors of egg-shells, their hard form and clean surfaces made them convenient objects to collect. Apart from curiosity there was little reason for such collecting other than a desire, in some instances, to add to our knowledge of birds. This knowledge is now at a stage where little can be added except by careful and controlled scientific study, with any collecting required done under license. *There is no longer any justification for the random, unofficial collecting of birds' eggs by amateurs, and the casual destruction of nests and nestlings, such as occurred in the past in some rural areas, was not justified at any time.*

A more immediate danger to nesting birds at the present time, and one to which even the most well-meaning bird enthusiast may subject them, is unwise disturbance. The bird is a creature which normally evades its enemies by flying or running away. When incubating eggs or brooding young, it is tied to one place. If a predator of some kind does attack, then it is better that the parent bird should survive and nest again, and so the bird generally leaves the nest to the attacker. Under natural conditions the predator that finds the nest will destroy it, and probably search there again, and it is therefore safer if the bird does not return. Unfortunately, the bird cannot discriminate between a harmful predator and an inquisitive human, so a clumsy inspection of a nest when a bird is sitting might cause a bird to desert the nest and its contents completely.

Birds are particularly likely to desert in the early stages of laying and incubation. In addition, when the young of songbirds are growing feathers but still within a few days of being ready to leave the nest, they may leave it prematurely if the nest is touched. This is another device which is designed to save something from a predator, but it may result in most of the brood being lost. If large seabird colonies or similar assemblies are disturbed, harm may come to eggs or young in the ensuing panic. Once the nests are exposed, birds such as gulls will quickly move in to take eggs and young. Disturbance is at its worst in colonies of birds such as pelicans and some terns where disturbance may result in a whole colony deserting and failing to nest for that season.

In addition to all this the slight disturbance of twigs, leaves or grass, necessary to see into a nest, may be sufficient to indicate to a sharp-eyed predator the presence of a previously hidden nest. In addition, lingering near a nest may prevent the birds returning and cause eggs and young to become fatally chilled.

The basic rules for studying nesting birds, therefore, are as follows: *disturb as little as possible; preferably examine nests only when the owners are absent; be as quick as possible; and at all times exercise the greatest care and caution, remembering that a little carelessness can bring about the accidental destruction of nest and brood.* (For nest-finding technique and more on field behavior, see the section on this subject at the end of the Introduction.)

There are laws in the US and Canada prohibiting the collecting of eggs and nests and protecting nestlings (for example, the Migratory Bird Treaty Act of 1918). Anyone hoping to study nesting birds must take care that he or she knows and complies with these laws.

In most of the field guides to birds that are now available, the reader is offered information which assists in the identification of a bird, and some information is given on the habits of the bird and the type of surroundings in which it will be found. This book is intended to supplement the standard field guide by providing additional information on the breeding biology of the species within the area covered. Birds tend to show more variation in their breeding than might be expected, and the information is less easily summarized than are the data on species identification. In this book the basic information on the nesting cycle has been given, necessarily brief in view of the number of species involved, along with the habitat and nest-site, the appearance of nest, eggs, and young, the season of breeding, information on incubation, and details on care of the young.

We earnestly hope that this work will help in broadening the knowledge and appreciation of birds as living creatures, and not be an incentive to the pointless acquisition of eggs (or nests) as petty trophies. If there is a need now it is to study the breeding cycle as a whole, to link breeding success with particular habitat associations, and to be able to document successful breeding to the independence of the fledged young.

It is not possible to prepare a work of this kind without the help of existing sources of reference. Any worker in this field must gain a temporary advantage by building on the labors of earlier workers, adding his or her own contribution to theirs, and hope that by so doing he or she will enable those that follow to build still further. Bird students investigating the habits of North American species must pay tribute to the energies of Arthur Cleveland Bent, who for over 40 years compiled the life histories of these birds as published by the Smithsonian Institution, even though the investigators may have reservations about the way the information was presented. We are grateful not only to him through his *Life Histories of North American Birds*, but also to the multitude of other individuals who over the last half-century have made their contributions, large and small, in various books and ornithological journals, and steadily increased our knowledge of North American birds.

Moreover, much about the life histories of these birds is currently being compiled and re-presented in the *Birds of North America* (BNA) species accounts, jointly sponsored by the Academy of Natural Sciences and the American Ornithologists' Union. This expanding series (now numbering about 240 treatments) of modern, authoritative references is designed to replace the classic Bent series.

Besides the books and journals, there were significant other sources for the material in this book. These included specimens of eggs and nests, photos of eggs, nests, and young; nest record cards, and other original sources. All these efforts, including a number of important books listed in Selected Bibliography at the end of this volume, give us the basis for a serious synopsis of the breeding biology of North American birds.

We are very grateful to the staff of the American Museum of Natural History, British Museum (Natural History), Cornell Laboratory of Ornithology, Delaware Museum of Natural History, National Museum of Natural History (Smithsonian), Patuxent Wildlife Research Center of the Biological Resources Division of the USGS (formerly of the US Fish and Wildlife Service), and the Western Foundation of Vertebrate Zoology for access to their libraries and/or collections.

There were many people who gave us countless little pieces of information from their notes, or other forms of kindly assistance. Among those are some who deserve particular mention: Robert S. Berman, Jim Berry, Tim Brush, Gregory S. Butcher, Gene Hess, Cindy Lippincott, James D. Lowe, Thomas E. Martin, Terry McEneaney, Alan Poole, Noble S. Proctor, and Michael P. Walters.

Our editor, Andy Richford, gave us encouragement, and he certainly made the production of this book a task that otherwise would have been much more difficult.

And last, but by no means least, our very grateful thanks to the artists and photographers. Dr. Philip Burton painted the color plates of young birds and supplied line drawings for the introduction; Mr. Andrew Burton illustrated most of the nests; and Ms. Terry O'Nele supplied sketches of some of the nests and nestlings and did the cover artwork. Among our egg photographers were Mr. F. Greenaway, who took almost all of the egg photographs, and Mr. Clark 'Sam' Sumida, who photographed over two dozen others.

How to use this book

The information given in this book is intended to add to that already available in ordinary field guides to North American birds. A previous version of this book was written by Colin Harrison and was published in 1978; this current form of the book represents an expanded and more detailed improvement. It is intended to serve as a guide to the breeding biology of North American nesting birds. It covers the North American region from the Arctic to the southern boundary of the United States. The area includes Alaska, Canada, the contiguous United States and (in an exception to the usual treatment of North American avifauna) Greenland. We have followed in the main the 1983 American Ornithologists' Union Checklist and its recent taxonomic modifications.

The **Contents List** at the beginning gives a list of bird families and subsidiary groupings arranged in this sequence. The color plates of nestlings and of eggs are not necessarily in the exact same sequence. Though the names and taxonomic relations within each page of the plates are up-to-date, the order of the plates reflects the family order accepted when the first version of this book was written.

The **Introduction** gives the background necessary to use the information that occurs under each heading in the main text on any particular species. The sections deal with habitat and nest-site, nest, breeding season, eggs, incubation, nestlings, and the nestling period. Within the introduction each of these is treated in turn, giving the meaning of some of the terms used, and the general background of each section, including the scope and limitations of the information on each bird.

The information in the Introduction is intended to be read before the book is used, but the first immediately practical part is the section containing three **Identification Keys:** It is not possible, in the case of birds' nests, eggs, and young, to give keys which will enable the reader to identify rapidly a particular species unless the bird in question has well-marked peculiarities setting it apart from most others. It has, however, been possible to provide keys to nests, to eggs, and to young which may enable the user to narrow rapidly a meaningful search to a limited number of species, which he or she can then limit still further by reference to the plates and text. Since it is usually necessary to take a number of factors into consideration, cross-references to the other two keys are given in each key.

The **Main Text** is in the form of a systematic list. Each section begins with a general note on the family or species group, giving the general information common to the whole group of birds, and then each species is dealt with in turn, the available information being given in slightly abbreviated form. The families and groups may be traced from the index or the contents list at the beginning, while individual species can be traced from the indexes to common and scientific names at the end of the book.

The **Illustrations** consist of color plates and black-and-white drawings in the text. The *Nestling Plates* are grouped together between p. 222 and p. 223 and show young birds at the nestling stage. These plates usually show a view of young birds from the side. There is often a close similarity between the nestlings of related species and, apart from some distinctly-patterned downy chicks, in most instances single typical examples representative of a small group of species are shown. Some black-and-white figures of *Down Patterns* of chicks, mostly seen from above, have been included in the text section. These supplement the color plates, and they assist in the identification of downy young which are more often observed from above as they attempt to hide by crouching. A few other, side-view, *Nestling Sketches* are also provided.

The *Egg Plates* are also in a section between p. 222 and p. 223, and they show examples of almost every species in the volume. A few are omitted – primarily rare species, some recent taxonomic splits, or species that breed on the extreme limits of the region covered. Eggs may vary and in most cases it has only been possible to show a single example, although in some instances more than one is included and may indicate the range of variation rather than the typical single example. In the other instances, however, the degree of variation is indicated on the caption pages and can be further checked with the text. The caption pages also give the general information on the eggs and nest-site for each group.

The color plates, used in conjunction with the keys and text, should make it possible to identify most eggs and young.

There are also black-and-white drawings distributed in the text serving as *Nest Illustrations*. They have been chosen to show the typical nests of the various groups of birds, and also the more striking and more readily identifiable of the exceptional nests which some birds make. It was not thought necessary to show nest structure normally concealed in cavities (with the exception of one example, that of Gila Woodpecker, Figure 70).

Introduction

The scope of the book

This book covers the bird species found breeding in North America, from the Arctic to the southern boundary of the continental United States (omitting such areas as Baja California, the Gulf of California, and the Bahamas, but including Greenland).

In the main text, the basic information on the breeding cycle of each species has been summarized. For species with a wide distribution many of the statements found in literature concerning the nesting refer to particular limited areas, and statements concerning nest-material, nest-site, egg pattern, and other aspects of nesting which may be true for a particular region may not hold good for the entire range of the species. As a result some of the information given here is necessarily more generalized and less dogmatic than that found in works referring to more circumscribed areas.

In some cases there is also uncertainty and doubt about the information now available, and in such instances this has been indicated by a question mark in the text. The text also gives a clearer picture of the gaps in our knowledge of this part of the lives of many species. It is just possible that in some instances the information was available somewhere, but has been overlooked; but undoubtedly in many cases there is a real lack of information. These uncertainties, gaps, and unknown elements all present challenges and opportunities to the field ornithologist – professional and amateur alike.

The influence of past egg-collecting is apparent in that nest and eggs have usually been described, although some collectors took the eggs without commenting on the appearance of the nest. However, information on the incubation period and the appearance of the nestlings is often lacking; and the period when the young are in the nest, and more especially the period between leaving the nest and final independence, are very poorly documented.

Some of the information common to all the species within a family or species group has been summarized under a general heading at the beginning of that group, and it is therefore advisable, when checking information on a species, to look also at the information under this more general heading. *However, in the cases where a family or group is represented by only one or two species, it was not considered necessary to repeat information which would also appear under the species concerned.*

For each species, information has been arranged in what seemed to be a natural sequence – nest habitat, nest-site, nest, breeding season, eggs, incubation, nestling, and nestling period – to give in the space available an overall picture of this part in the bird's life cycle.

The introductory notes which follow here give the general background information on each of these stages in the cycle, explain some of the terms used, and indicate where caution is necessary in interpreting the information given. One point that will become apparent from the following notes is that even with a considerable knowledge of nests and eggs or nestlings the variation in these is such that it is not always possible to identify a species with absolute certainty from its nest and eggs or nestlings. In many cases the only sure identification lies in recognizing the adult bird itself, and it must be understood that a guide to nests, eggs, and nestlings does not always provide a guaranteed means of recognizing the bird species involved.

Nest habitat, nest-site, and breeding system

To begin with, we indicate the typical habitat in which breeding occurs, and the type of sites in which the nest will be found. If the species is particularly restricted in range in North America (e.g., western Alaska, southeast Arizona, south Florida, or south Texas), that is indicated in this section of the species' treatment. Species that have nested only once or only a few times in the area (e.g., Whooper Swan, White-eared Hummingbird, Eared Trogon, Mexican Crow, Flame-colored Tanager, or Brambling) are included, as are a very few species whose breeding is currently presumed (e.g., wild Muscovy Duck, Eurasian Dotterel, or Shiny Cowbird).

We know that each species of bird is limited to some extent in its distribution by the surroundings, or habitat, which it is prepared to tolerate. Each species treatment includes some details on the habitat requirements. When breeding occurs there are further limitations imposed by the site and nest materials it will accept. Each species therefore has a typical nest-site and nest structure. Most, however, show some degree of tolerance in adjusting to slightly less suitable sites, the tolerance varying considerably from one species to another. This can create problems in identification of the nests of the more adaptable species. For example, the American Robin's nest is usually in the branches of a tree or shrub, but it is adaptable and if the necessity arises it may place its nest on a cliff ledge or the ledge of a building, or even on the ground. (Height of the nest is usually mentioned in the species' treatments in this book.)

The site is not, therefore, a certain clue to the species, although it does indicate the probable occupier. Another problem of identification arises when birds use the old nests of other species. Owls and falcons may use old nests of larger birds such as crows; a cavity in a tree, such as a woodpecker hole, may have a succession of very different tenants; House Sparrows, House Finches, and wrens will use Cliff Swallow nests; and, perhaps oddest of all, the Solitary Sandpiper, although a shorebird, will utilize old nests in trees, such as those of thrushes, for its nesting. If there is evidence of an old nest being reused one therefore needs to see the bird to be sure which species is nesting there.

Finally, breeding systems are often mentioned at the beginning of species treatments, with non-colonial monogamy otherwise assumed for the species. Variations are emphasized; for example, if the species is colonial or if mating includes polygamy, or if the rearing of young involves cooperative breeding.

Nest and nest-building

This part of the species' treatment covers the type of nest, contents, structure, and sometimes who builds the nest, how long it takes, and the size.

A difficulty that all birds have to overcome is that their future offspring must spend a period of time as an egg. The egg requires warmth and continual protection from predators. The variety of nests that have evolved represent partial success in meeting these requirements. Thus, nests may form platforms that lift the eggs to a safer site, structures that hide the eggs from view, and/or insulated cavities that shelter the eggs from rain and cooling winds and allow the body heat of the parent bird to be used to best advantage.

In spite of their considerable diversity we can recognize a limited number of obvious types of nest. Some species build no nest at all. The only evidence of nesting might be a shallow hollow made by the bird's breast in the soft substrate. Such birds usually nest on flat open places, or on rock ledges, or occupy hollow cavities in tree or rocks. Examples of these within our region are the goatsuckers, owls, falcons, and kingfishers.

Most of the birds nesting in more open places line their shallow scrapes with material of some kind, the quantity varying, even in one species, from almost nothing to a very substantial layer. Most of these birds build by an indirect method called sideways-throwing. From the time that the site is chosen, either of the pair picks up nest material or small objects and throws these back to either side or beneath itself. Such items therefore gradually move towards the nest-site and accumulate there. The sitting bird performs a similar action called sideways-building, pulling in such items and tucking them alongside it. The resultant nest depends almost entirely on the material at hand near the nest, and on the degree of disturbance experienced by the birds. The need to use nearby material results in shorebirds like Piping Plovers lining scrapes with tiny pebbles. The fact that increased disturbance can cause a bird to add more material to the nest is of value in the instance where a bird on a less suitable site, perhaps damp and cold, reacts to increased discomfort by increased building activity which in turn produces a thicker nest and more effective insulation for the eggs and brooding bird. This type of building occurs widely in ducks, game-birds, cranes, loons, shorebirds, and most terns and auks.

Ducks and geese make this type of nest, but add to it an insulating inner layer of down from the breast of the female. Within the above groups, some species build more elaborate nests by this method. For example, swans pile up heaps of plant material by sideways-throwing and sideways-building.

Most of the other types of nests are built by birds carrying material directly to a site, and the type of nest is determined to some extent by the size and rigidity of the pieces of nest material used. Birds using lax plant material – for example, grebes with pondweed, cormorants with seaweed, and kittiwakes with mud and grass – build a solid platform or mound with a small hollow in the top for the eggs, the nest being usually consolidated by the trampling of the birds.

Birds using rigid twigs usually build in trees and may produce no more than a thin platform. When the twigs are put in place, a small lateral quivering of the bill while it is still holding the twig helps to work the latter into the existing structure. For example, pigeon nests show this type of construction in its simplest platform stage. Continual additions to nests of this type, such as often occur where nests are re-used in subsequent seasons, produce very bulky structures. Even with the simpler twig nests there is usually some evidence of a tendency for birds, in the later stages of nest-building, to select thinner and finer material which can be used as a lining and may shape an inner cup in which the eggs will lie.

Most of our birds build cup-shaped nests. The material used is usually fairly pliable and the bird sits in the structure as it builds, placing material, pulling in loose ends and tucking them into the existing framework to one side or the other and gradually producing the typical round shape. As the softer lining is added the bird shapes the cup to its own body, sitting in it with bill and tail uplifted, rotating a little, pressing with chin and under-tail coverts, and flexing bill and tail downwards to consolidate the rim. It also pushes backwards with the feet, enlarging the lower cup a little, and the final structure fits snugly around the sitting bird leaving room for the eggs beneath it.

Domed nests with side entrances are much less common, with only a few species of larger birds using them (e.g., Black-billed Magpie and Yellow-billed Magpie with thin roofs to the nests, and Monk Parakeet with a solid twig structure) and about a dozen smaller species (e.g., Verdin, American Dipper) building solid structures in trees or bushes, on a ledge, in a crevice, or on the ground.

Another uncommon type of nest is the suspended, pensile nest. This may be a cup slung between twigs to which it is bound at the rim. The Acadian Flycatcher's nest in a horizontal fork tends towards this type, and more typical examples are the nests of vireos and some orioles. The nests of kinglets are cups often hanging below a conifer branch and bound on either side to drooping twigs. Some orioles build an elongated pensile bag with an entrance at the top where it is either bound to more than one twig or hangs from a single loop. The Bushtit makes a similar long hanging nest with an entrance at the top but slightly to one side. This nest is peculiar in that it is spiders' webs which bind it together and create an elastic container which the bird stretches downward as it builds.

Spiders' webs are used as nest material by a number of small birds, especially when the nest is made of small fragmentary material or must be balanced on a large support, as in some of the wood warblers, the wood-pewees, and the gnatcatchers. It probably shows its greatest potential, however, in the delicate cups of the hummingbird nests.

Various birds may incorporate mud or wet woodpulp or leafmold into the nest structure to bind and shape it. This may be found in some crows, blackbirds, and thrushes. The phoebes ensure the safety of their nests on the ledges and small supports that they use, by building up their cups with mud pellets and plant material. Some swallows use mud extensively, building up nests of mud and plant fiber pellets placed like bricks in a wall, bonded by jabbing the tongue through the wet material, and built up into fine structures that can be stuck to vertical surfaces. These swallow and phoebe nests must be sheltered from the rain.

The swifts also require adhesives for their nests but create it themselves, using saliva which sticks the material of the nest together. This kind of nest is developed to a high degree in the Chimney Swift, which breaks off short dead twigs while in flight and glues them to a vertical surface – usually the inside of a chimney wall – and to each other to form a strong half-cup.

Although birds show definite preferences for materials when nest-building, there is a tendency to use whatever is most readily available, and there may be a noticeable variation in the nest structures of a single species. Because of this, it may make nest identification more difficult. Obvious examples of this are the seaweed nests made by cormorants on cliffs and the twig nests they may construct in trees; herons may use reeds or stems of tall marsh plants instead of twigs. More striking differences may be apparent in the nests of species using the sideways-throwing method of building, depending on the amount of material present in the vicinity of the nest.

Provided that they fulfill certain criteria, apparently unlikely man-made materials may be used. Numerous examples give testimony for acceptable substitutes for twigs, dead leaves, branches, and other natural elements regularly used in nest-building: a Warbling Vireo nest built almost entirely of tissues; a Chihuahuan Raven nest built completely of barbed wire; a colony of Double-crested Cormorants that used a sunken vessel to supply their nests with pocketknives, men's pipes, hairpins, and ladies combs; the regular use of multicolored yarn (Baltimore Oriole), paper (Blue Jay), and rags (Northern Mockingbird) for nests in suburban areas; Ospreys which used cast-offs such as bath towels, old shoes, bottles, fishnets, and metal cans in their nests; a Bullock's Oriole that had green Easter-basket grass and monofilament line integrated into the nest; a Blue Grosbeak nest made almost entirely from newspaper; a Western Kingbird nest with a large collection of cigarette butts and filters; a nest of Canyon Wrens built entirely of supplies gleaned from nearby offices, including paper clips, fasteners, matches, toothpicks, and rubber bands; and the regular use of plastic insulation and cellophane as a probable substitute for snakeskin in the nests of some flycatchers and titmice.

Humans can confuse birds when we build a series of identical compartments or divisions in a row, such as occur on some buildings, shelving, or where a ladder rests against a wall. A bird is not adapted to cope with such repetition, which does not occur in the wild. If it selects one such compartment as a nest-site it is likely to become confused and build a series of nests to varying degrees of completion in adjacent identical compartments, and to lay eggs in more than one of these.

In this book, the size of the nest (i.e., outside diameter, inside diameter, height, and depth) is indicated mostly for the larger, non-passerine birds. This is not done for the passerines, except where the nest is exceptional (e.g., a domed structure).

Breeding season

Birds in temperate regions usually breed in spring and early summer. The urge to breed appears to be controlled by endocrine gland secretions which in turn are affected by the increasing day-length in the early part of the year. Temperature and food availability also appear to have some immediate control on the breeding behavior of birds and can cause variation in the date of commencement of breeding from one year to another. The actual date of commencement of breeding differs from one species to another, and it has been suggested that the hatching of the young is timed to coincide with the period when the necessary food supply is most readily available.

Since the start of the breeding season differs from species to species and year to year only a very general indication of it can be given. It often differs from one part to another within a species' range, usually starting earlier in the south and west. *In the main text references to 'south' or 'north' in the sections on breeding seasons refer to those parts of a species' breeding range within our area.* In the most northerly species, nesting on the arctic tundra, breeding must await the summer thaw, and in cold summers no breeding may take place.

In the case of some birds, such as seabirds, where there may be a long period of colony-visiting and display before actual breeding starts, we have indicated the period of egg-laying in the section on the breeding season in order to provide a basis for comparison with more typical groups.

There is a human tendency to note the beginning but not the end of things, and while we often know when breeding starts we have little information on when the cycles finish. There are a number of factors that may affect such calculations. Theoretically it is easy to calculate how long the laying, incubation, and nesting period of a single brood would take to complete, and we have indicated the number of broods known for the species. However, species respond differently to a nesting failure. Although in a few species a failure may finish breeding attempts for the year, in others a replacement clutch will be laid and the whole cycle may occur, but at a later date. Where several broods are involved, these may be spaced, or may overlap to a point where the male is feeding the young of one brood while the female is already incubating the eggs of the next one. In addition, where there are several broods, replacements may occur more rapidly if one is lost; and so it is difficult to predict firmly the stage of the breeding cycle at any particular date. In any event, the season ends with what is for most species the least well-documented part of the breeding cycle. This is the interaction between parents and increasingly independent young. Therefore, do not be surprised to see such phrases as 'usually ends by,' or 'probably ends by' to qualify the end of the breeding season which we may surmise from the end of peak parental care of young and the absence of further nesting.

The breeding season usually terminates in late summer or autumn, followed by migration or the molt of feathers of the parents. Some resident species continue producing broods until late in the season. Energetically, birds may be ready to breed again after the autumn molt, and it appears to be the decreasing day length which inhibits them from doing so. Very occasionally, during periods of abnormally fine weather, individual pairs of some species may attempt to breed.

Clutch size

The clutch is the grouping of eggs laid by a bird and incubated by it at one time. The number of eggs in a clutch may vary with the species. Some species, sometimes referred to as determinate layers, have a fixed clutch size and will produce just that number of eggs and no more. Pigeons with two eggs are usually an example of this. Many other species of birds tend to vary the number of eggs a little above or below an average figure, and some appear to continue laying until they have a comfortable number which satisfies the sitting birds, and if eggs are removed they may lay more to make up the number. Birds of the latter type are known as indeterminate layers, and if eggs are constantly removed they may lay a very large number. The domestic hen is an example, since under natural conditions it may be satisfied with a clutch of about six eggs but can be induced to lay many more.

A widely distributed species may show variation of clutch size within its range. In the smaller songbirds there is a consistent tendency for the size of the clutch to increase from south to north. It is suggested that this is related to the fact that the northern birds have a longer summer day in which to find food for a larger brood. This is, of course, offset by the shorter breeding season and possibly fewer broods than more southerly birds.

Also, in many species there is a tendency for the clutch size to be reduced in renesting attempts. (This reduction in clutch size seems to be true both for species that are normally single-brooded, and those that are multi-brooded.)

It has been suggested that clutch size is determined by the number of young that a pair of birds can successfully rear. Other factors which have been thought to affect clutch size are the number of eggs that the female is physically capable of producing at one time; the number of eggs that a bird can successfully cover and warm when incubating; and the need to save energy for renesting following a nest failure. In addition there appears to be some correlation between the size of the clutch and the survival rate and likely length of life of the average individual of the species.

Egg shape

Eggs show a wide range of small individual variations in shape, but only four main shapes are usually recognized. The nomenclature proposed by F. W. Preston (1953, 'Shapes of birds eggs' *Auk*, Vol. 70[2]:160–182 and summarized in the Introduction to Volume I of Palmer's *Handbook of North American Birds*, 1962) is a convenient one for this purpose. At one extreme is the *elliptical* shape, elongated with equally rounded ends and broadest about the middle. A long, normal, and short form of each shape are recognized, and in the case of the elliptical egg a very short version of the shape would be spherical. The *subelliptical* egg is again rounded at the ends but a little more elongated, tapering more towards the rounded ends, with the broadest part nearer one end than the other. The *oval* egg has the typical egg shape, rounded and largest at one end, and tapering distinctly towards a narrower end. The term 'ovate' is sometimes used for this. The last shape is the *pyriform*, with the larger end distinctly blunt and rounded, and tapering to a narrower point at the other end. This type of egg is sometimes called 'pear-shaped,' but the taper is more even than that of a pear. Two special types that one might like to add to these four are the 'spherical' shape already mentioned, sometimes approached but rarely achieved, and a shape sometimes found in grebe eggs which may have a marked taper towards both ends, producing

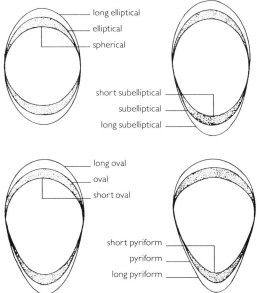

Figure 1. Egg shapes.

what is perhaps a special instance of the subelliptical sometimes referred to as 'biconical.'

Egg size

In addition to varying slightly in shape, eggs also vary individually in size, not only between clutches, but also between one egg and another within the clutch itself. The measurements we have given in the text are averages of length and breadth. If one takes a large sample of eggs and measures them, there are likely to be variations ranging up to ten to twelve per cent or more on either side of the average measurements. This must be taken into account when attempts are made to use comparative measurements in identifying eggs.

Eggs of abnormal size occasionally occur, usually single ones in a normal clutch. Exceptionally large ones are unusual in wild birds, but dwarf or runt eggs appear at intervals. These may be tiny yolk-less examples produced when an egg is formed around a small piece of loose tissue, and since they do not hatch they may be found in a nest when a brood has left. They are likely to be more spherical than normal eggs, thick-shelled, and often rough-surfaced.

Eggshell color

The shells of most eggs are partly translucent, and when in the nest and complete with their contents they tend to appear darker and deeper in color than the empty shells that appear in collections. Allowance must be made for this when looking at the color plates of the eggs. Apart from this, eggs kept away from the light show little color change save that a fine pinkish flush apparent on some newly-laid eggs such as pigeons' eggs disappears fairly rapidly. This pink tint is due to a fugitive pigment that is rapidly destroyed.

In spite of the considerable range of tints apparent on eggshells, only two kinds of pigment, in addition to the fugitive one mentioned above, appear to be present in the eggshells under consideration. One is a blue or greenish-blue pigment. When present this occurs through the whole shell structure, so that the basic shell is either white or some shade of blue.

The other pigment is a variably-tinted one that may appear as brown, red, or black, or intermediate shades of these. When it tints the whole shell it is normally only present in the thin surface covering. For example, small quantities of superficial brown color make the white shell appear yellow or buff and the blue shell green or olive. This pigment also produces the shell markings. In the gamebirds such markings are present only on the surface with the superficial tint, but in most other families these markings are applied at intervals as the shell is formed and occur at varying depths within the shell. Because the shell is partly translucent, and (when in very thin layers) partly transparent, markings such as these show through a thin layer of shell, if near the surface. Markings that are black, red, or brown may appear gray, pink, or buff on white shells, in varying degrees of paleness according to their depth; and if the shell is blue, may appear in shades of purple, lilac, and mauve.

If the eggs of a species are patterned, they are likely to show considerable minor variation within certain limits. In illustrating the eggs it has usually been possible to show only one of a species and an effort has been made to select a typical 'average' type, although a species may have several distinct types of pattern. Where more than one egg can be shown, these have been selected to give some idea of the range of variation rather than the average type. It must therefore be remembered that if only one or a few eggs of two related species have been seen, and appear very different, either may have an unusual variety which may be almost indistinguishable from eggs of the other species. Therefore, one must be very cautious of identifying species from their eggs.

Each individual female usually lays eggs of consistent color and pattern, but some species show fairly consistent variations within clutches. For example, clutches of eggs of some crows and of House Sparrows often have one or two eggs which are much paler and less patterned than others in the same clutch.

For many species the color and pattern of the eggs appear to form a camouflage concealing them from potential enemies. The almost invisible eggs of Piping Plovers and Least Terns on shingle beaches are a good example of this, and it can be assumed that this is true in a number of other instances. Species whose eggs show great individual variation are more difficult to explain, but we know that birds come to recognize the color and pattern of eggs in a particular clutch, and it has been suggested that the very variable pattern and color of Common Murre eggs allows the parent bird to recognize its own egg among the others on the bare ledge or cliff.

The eggs of birds nesting in dark cavities or holes are usually pale blue or white, and this probably helps to ensure that the bird can locate them easily. (Moreover, there may be no selection for camouflage involved.) Where species derived from a group with patterned eggs take to closed nests or holes, the eggs tend to be pale but to retain some pattern. Examples of this are the eggs of Rhinoceros Auklets and Atlantic Puffins among the auks; and the sparsely speckled or unmarked eggs of titmice, some wrens and sparrows, and the American Dipper, might be further instances.

Abnormal eggshell color

There is always a likelihood that abnormally colored eggs will appear from time to time. This is usually due to some genetic or physiological peculiarity of an individual bird affecting its entire egg production. It usually takes the form of a failure to produce some part of the normal pigmentation. For example, if the superficial pigment is absent, an egg normally buff or olive may appear uniform white or blue. An absence of blue can produce a white egg, and may have surprising effects on a patterned egg, where spots which normally appear as black or dark brown may appear buff or red when the blue is lost. Other variations occasionally encountered are replacement of black by brown or red, or of brown by red; and there may be an increase of pigments to produce very heavily marked or dark eggs, or, the other extreme, a total loss of color.

These abnormal colors have been recorded more frequently for some species than for others, but might potentially occur in most species; and we have not attempted to deal with them in describing eggs in the text. An excessive attention was paid to them during the heyday of egg-collecting, but they are mainly of interest in providing clues to shell pigmentation in species whose eggs are camouflaged and are assumed to be so colored in order to escape the notice of predators. In these species abnormally colored eggs should be more conspicuous, and it is of interest to see to what extent they survive to hatch in comparison with the normally colored eggs.

Incubation

The embryo requires constant warmth if it is to develop inside the egg. This is provided by the body warmth of the parents, usually from the underside, where in most species special bare 'brood patches' are present during the breeding season. Exceptions are the waterfowl and the pelicans, cormorants, darters, and gannets. The last provides heat from the webs of its feet, covering the egg with these before settling on it.

The incubation period is the time between the onset of incubation and the hatching of a single egg; but unless the eggs are marked as they are laid and closely watched as they hatch this period is difficult to determine. There are other factors that may cause this period to vary and we have therefore given an incubation period which refers not to the individual egg but to the sitting bird, being the period during which a bird incubates and hatches its eggs. Eggs are usually laid at intervals of one to two days. If the parents begin to incubate when the first egg is laid, the young may hatch at equivalent intervals, and there will be nestlings of varying age and size in the nest. If the proper incubation is delayed until the last egg is laid, the earliest eggs will have been present for some days and may have received some intermittent warmth and undergone some development. The eggs in such a clutch normally hatch in fairly rapid succession, but the precise period of incubation will differ from one egg to another.

In the very early stages of development of the embryo, lack of warmth will delay further progress but is not apparently harmful. Later in incubation a period of chilling may prove fatal. Striking exceptions here are the eggs of storm-petrels which appear to be adapted to possible periods of neglect and can undergo a period of days without incubation during the normal period and still hatch. This is presumably a safeguard in species where the adults change places only at long intervals. There is also some evidence that in ordinary songbirds cold conditions may prolong incubation to some extent, and perhaps add a day or two to the normal period without necessarily harming the young bird.

During incubation the eggs are frequently stirred and turned by the brooding birds. This is said to be necessary for the development of the embryo, although eggs have hatched successfully after being embedded in nest material in such a way that they could not be moved. It also seems that this stirring may be useful in some species for ensuring that the egg, at hatching, is resting in the position in which the chick can most easily emerge.

The part played by the sexes in incubation varies in different species from equal sharing to one sex doing all the incubating. The attentiveness may vary from a constant covering of the eggs by some species to a tendency in others, chiefly those of hotter climates, to leave the eggs uncovered for varying periods.

Hatching

The chick may be in vocal contact with the outside world a day or two before it emerges from the egg. It will make calls to which the parent responds, and may become silent in response to an alarm call from the parent. In some gamebird species, in which the developing chick before hatching pushes its bill through the membrane into the air space in the egg, it begins to make clicking noises. These appear to produce a response from within the other eggs of the clutch; this results in 'synchronous hatching,' that is, at or very near the same time. Therefore, eggs laid days apart hatch within hours, a useful device where all young need to leave a nest once their down has dried.

The nestling's typical position at hatching is resting on its back or left side, with the head lying on the breast and the bill turned to one side and tucked under the right wing. The bill is usually equipped with a small hard excrescence on the tip of the upper mandible – the egg-tooth. This is often white, and visible on the bill of the newly-hatched young bird, but drops off after a while. A few birds show a similar tooth on the tip of the lower mandible as well.

The chick in the egg is very limited in its movements but is able to raise the bill so that this egg-tooth at the tip comes into contact with the shell and pushes up a small 'pip' – a break in the structure. Some chicks move very little, but as they attempt to bring the head up to a more comfortable position, and continue the bill-raising movement, they make a diagonal break extending from their right to left and up towards the larger end of the egg. At the same time convulsive straightening movements put pressure on the ends of the already weakened shell, and sooner or later it breaks in half and releases the chick.

Chicks of some species are able to move more easily within the shell, and with a series of small movements they gradually turn over inside it, pipping it as they go,

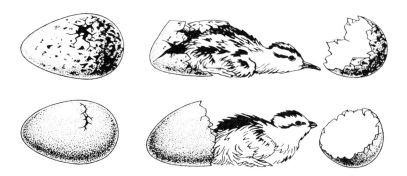

Figure 2. Breaking out of the egg.
Top: by rupturing shell after chipping rough hole (Whimbrel). *Bottom:* by turning in shell and making line of weakness producing two neat pieces (Gray Partridge).

and making a complete circle. This causes the shell to separate into two neat parts.

The time taken to escape from the shell may vary from a matter of minutes in the case of small songbirds to one or two days in the case of some larger species. The parent birds may help a little, possibly inadvertently, by pecking at the broken edge of the shell. Once the young bird has emerged, the adult either breaks and eats the shell fragments, or more usually carries them away and drops them some distance from the nest. Were they to remain at the nest, they might betray it to passing predators. Birds such as gamebirds, whose young leave the nest soon after hatching, may not bother to remove the shells.

Young birds may retain the egg-tooth for some days, or in some instances a week or two after hatching, the period varying with the species.

The nestling

There are two main types of nestling. One is the down-covered chick which is active soon after hatching and able to leave the nest if necessary. This type of nestling is called *precocial,* or sometimes the term 'nidifugous' is used. The other type is exemplified by the typical songbird nestling, hatched naked, blind, and helpless, and wholly dependent on its parents. This type of nestling is called *altricial,* or sometimes 'nidicolous.' These are convenient categories, but are not wholly exclusive since the precocial young have varying degrees of dependence on the adults, and may remain in the nest for some days before leaving it.

The appearance of the young bird at the nestling stage is not always well-documented. This may be due in part to a commendable reluctance of ornithologists to disturb the nesting bird unduly in order to examine the young closely. In this book we have tried to provide as good a description as possible of this early stage in the development of the bird.

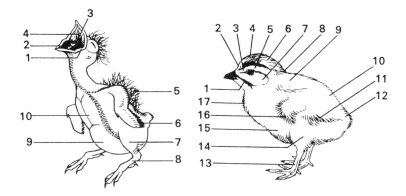

Figure 3. Nestling types.
Left: naked altricial nestling. l. gape flanges, 2. tongue, 3. tongue-spurs, 4. palate, 5. down filaments, 6. wing quills, 7. thigh, 8. tarsus, 9. belly, 10. breast.
Right: downy precocial chick. l. moustache streak, 2. forehead, 3. lores, 4. forecrown, 5. eyestripe, 6. hindcrown, 7. ear-coverts, 8. nape, 9. mantle, 10. back, 11. flank, 12. rump, 13. tarsus, 14. thigh, 15. belly, 16. wing, 17. upper breast.

Figure 4. Stages in growth of an altricial nestling: a House Sparrow. Stages – 36 hours, 4 days, 6 days, 8 days, 10 days.

Figure 5. Stages in growth of a precocial nestling: a Gull-billed Tern.
Stages — 30 hours, 9 days, 20 days.

The colors of bills, legs, bare skin, and irides, which change as the nestling grows, are the most poorly documented of all. In illustrating downy young and nestlings the artist has, where direct information was not available, deduced probable colors from preserved material or from juvenile birds. Unless confirmatory information is also given in the text, the colors shown in the plates should be treated with some caution.

The written descriptions of the nestlings deal basically with the appearance of the birds in the earliest stages of their nestling lives. However, some of the changes in the nestlings are dealt with under the next section in the species' treatment, the 'Nestling Period.'

Nestling period

This is the period during which the young bird is dependent on its parents for its survival. For our purposes in this book, the nestling period includes time spent in the nest (brief for precocial birds), nest departure, first flight, and feeding dependency.

During the earlier part of this period the young bird is still unable to control its own body temperature and must rely on the adults to brood it and keep it warm. It relies on the parents for food in most species, and also for protection from, or warning against, predators.

For many species with altricial young, the pattern is one in which the young are hatched blind, with little or no down, and unable to control their temperature, and spend a period in the nest developing. During this time they are brooded by the parents to keep them warm; the one not brooding brings food. Gradually the young become more active and aware of their surroundings. They grow feathers and become able to keep themselves warm. Finally they leave the nest and follow the parents, still being fed by them for some weeks, but gradually becoming increasingly neglected by them and learning to fend for themselves. Some precocial young are fed for the first few days of their lives, and all rely on the adults for warmth and warning of danger even though they may feed themselves. Even when they do not feed the young, adults may indicate where the food is to be found.

Although only two main types of nestling have been referred to, a more precise classification has been proposed by Margaret M. Nice (1962, Development of behavior in precocial birds *Transactions of the Linnaean Society of New York*, 8:1–211). For the present range of families, the categories under this system would be as follows:

Precocial. (Eyes open, down-covered, leaving nest in a day or two.)
  (a) follow parents, but find own food. Swans, geese, ducks, grouse, plovers, sandpipers, snipe, avocet, stilt, phalaropes.
  (b) follow parents, and are shown food. Grouse, typical gamebirds, oystercatchers, plovers.
  (c) follow parents, and are fed by them for varying periods. Loons, grebes, cranes, rails, oystercatchers, snipe.

Semi-precocial. (Eyes open, down-covered, stay at or near nest although able to walk.)
  Jaegers, gulls, terns, auks, goatsuckers.

Semi-altricial. (Down-covered, unable to leave nest.)
  (a) eyes open. Petrels, herons, bitterns, ibises, spoonbills, birds of prey.
  (b) eyes closed at first. Owls.

Altricial. (Eyes closed, little or no down, unable to leave nest.)
  Pelicans, gannets, cormorants, Anhinga, pigeons, parakeets, cuckoos, swifts, hummingbirds, kingfishers, woodpeckers, and songbirds (Passerines).

The young of some species may remain with the parents after achieving independence, and the family party may not break up until nesting occurs in the following spring. A few are exceptional in that the young may stay and assist with the next nesting. For many young, however, the final break with the parents occurs at migration or during the autumn molt.

The roles played by the respective parents vary from one species to another. This may vary from sharing of duties, to independent roles for each, and to complete neglect by one or the other. Intensive observation has revealed that in a variety of species, ranging from grebes to some songbirds, the parents may divide the brood between them as soon as they leave the nest, and one adult will accept full responsibility for feeding some of the young, but will neglect others of the brood or even behave aggressively towards them, these being the responsibility of the other parent.

The severing of contact between adults and young is a gradual process and not a sudden one triggered off at the same instant in all individuals, and so the period of days quoted as the nestling period is necessarily an approximate period rather than a precise one.

Nest-finding techniques and field behavior

Discussing effective nest-finding techniques and appropriate field behavior could fill many pages of this Introduction. Suffice it to say that many articles have been written on the subject, including the discussion of the ethics of nest observation. We only intend to outline some basic points and warnings here.

Clearly, familiarity with the *field marks, vocalizations, habits,* and *habitat preferences* of North American birds is extremely important. Your favorite field identification guide should deal with the first three of these elements, and help you with the fourth, habitat, which is also included in this book. You should also learn *when* the various species are nesting in your area, a variable discussed in general in this book, but which can often be more accurately assessed through sources on the birds of the state, province, or region in question.

Figure 6. Typical methods of feeding young.
a, Pelican, taking food directly from throat; **b,** hawk, (accipiter) young are fed at first on small morsels taken from larger prey; **c,** dove, young are fed on semi-liquid food, placing bill crosswise in that of adult; **d,** gull, young fed on regurgitated food; **e,** vireo, adult places food into bill of young; **f,** finch, adult regurgitates food and places it into bill of young.

The *different times* in the nesting cycle should be approached differently by the bird student. The following hints are particularly helpful for studying woodland passerines. Nests located *during construction* provide the best lessons and give the best estimates for nest success; the earlier nests are found, the more thoroughly they can be studied. This is the time to follow nest-building adults, if they are carrying nesting materials. It may also be easy during this time (the early part of the season) because vegetation may not be fully leafed out, making the task of following nest-builders simpler. Mapping the male's position – and singing – around the territory can often reveal the general area for probable nest sites. (Once the suspected nest-site has been identified, back off; early disturbance in nest building can induce abandonment.) It is often difficult to find a nest *during egg-laying*, since the female may visit the nest only when she lays an egg. Nest visitation usually does become more frequent, however, with more eggs in the nest. For the period *during incubation*, females may seem to 'disappear,' but males may actually increase their singing. Additionally, females may have a call note upon departing a nest. Males of some species may also guard the nest. Finding nests during the *nestling period* may be the easiest. Both parents can be bringing food and removing fecal sacs. The nestlings may be heard begging for food, either in the nest or once they have left. As previously mentioned, watching the young up to independence may be more difficult than you might think; accurate dates for independence are missing for many species. Knowledge of the possibility of *double-clutching* is also helpful in studying nesting birds. Some birds may begin with a new nesting within 8–10 days after the first young have fledged. The female may also begin renesting while the male is still tending to the first brood. Be aware of that possibility, also.

Thomas E. Martin and Geoffrey R. Geupel have outlined a number of helpful warnings for minimizing human-induced mortality in nest observation (1993, Nest-monitoring plots: methods for locating nests and monitoring success, *Journal of Field Ornithology,* **64** [4]:507–519). If you are involved in any nest surveying (see the next section in this Introduction for details), these suggestions are particularly important, and they deserve summary here:

When attempting to locate nests –
1. Listen for distress calls by adults and do not stay in the area if they continue for more than a few minutes.
2. Do not approach a nest when any potential nest predator, particularly a visually-oriented predator (e.g., corvid), is present.
3. Minimize physical disturbance to the area around the nest.
4. Do not get close to nests during nest-building; birds will abandon if disturbed prior to egg-laying.

When approaching nests –
1. Check the nest from as great a distance as possible. Use your optics for observation.
2. Disturb the birds and area as little as possible. Approach the nest via different paths on subsequent visits; broken stems or flattened grasses can become a cue for possible predators. Never leave a dead-end trail to the nest; always assume that a predator is watching.
3. Be quick and accurate during any data-driven nest checks. Minimize the time spent near the nest, since your presence may attract visually-oriented predators and since the more time spent at the nest the more scent is left for olfactory-oriented predators.
4. Minimize the number of observers visiting the nest (no photographers).
5. Use a pen or stick to check nests to prevent human scent from being left on or near a nest.

To this we could add the following general warnings –

1. Flagging or other visible markers can often increase the risk of predation.
2. Observations in severe weather – cold, rain, or heat – can increase the danger to the eggs and nestlings.

Finally, when going into the field, people studying birds may normally bring binoculars, field identification guides, and perhaps notebooks. Additional equipment for nesting study may differ slightly from the usual field gear. You may wish to bring a small hand mirror (to look into nests above your head or into larger cavities); a telescoping pole (available from window-washing or swimming-pool-supply outfitters) on which to attach a mirror is helpful; a small flashlight for additional illumination is another useful aid.

Nest recording and monitoring schemes

There are numerous ways in which nesting information can be collected and used by bird enthusiasts to further the knowledge of North American birds. We will mention just a few.

The development of state, county, or provincial breeding-bird atlases is an ongoing effort in many locations. Atlasing is an important activity, measuring the presence of breeding birds from location to location and mapping them out on a broad scale. Finding active nests is the very best way to verify the presence of breeding birds during atlasing. Even properly identified off-season nests can be used in confirming the presence of a particular species in breeding-bird atlas work. Atlas work should be appreciated for its significant conservation applications, especially identifying important habitats for land-use planning, determining the possible impact of human activities on bird distribution, and documenting the location of rare species and associated habitats. To find out about the status and location of current atlas work, contact the North American Ornithological Atlas Committee, PO Box 157, Cambridge, VT 05444–0157.

An excellent project is the North American Nest Record Program (NRP) run by the Cornell Laboratory of Ornithology. Since 1965, the laboratory has collected over 300 000 cards documenting the nesting of almost 600 species throughout North America. Participants in the program fill out a 4×6 inch card for each nest found, including information for dates, altitude, location, habitat, nest height, number of eggs and/or young, and nest activity during each visit. Important information is thus collected and a picture of breeding activity and success is formed. (For more information, write North American Nest Record Program, Cornell Laboratory of Ornithology, 159 Sapsucker Woods Road, Ithaca, NY 14850.) There are also some states and regional nest record schemes in the US and Canada.

The national Breeding Biology Research and monitoring Database (BBIRD) is another project that deserves attention. Designed to set up uniform field protocols for breeding bird research, the project since 1992 has collected data on nest success and associated vegetation for over 25 000 nests in over 23 states. Nest monitoring in BBIRD is used to measure breeding productivity in micro-habitats and across broad geographic regions. What is also important here is the use of standard vegetation sampling methods to examine habitat requirements by nesting birds. (For more information write to National BBIRD Coordinator, Montana Cooperative Wildlife Research Unit, University of Montana, Missoula, MT 59812.)

Some other creative projects dealing with nesting are species-specific or family-specific. These have included projects involving tanagers, thrushes, other forest birds, or various cavity-nesters run by the Cornell Laboratory of Ornithology (Bird Population Studies, Cornell Laboratory of Ornithology, 159 Sapsucker Woods Road,

Ithaca, NY 14850) and those involving Purple Martins (Purple Martin Conservation Association, Edinboro University of Pennsylvania, Edinboro, PA 16444.) Other nest-monitoring projects, for example those dealing with bluebirds or those dealing with colonial waterbirds, are arising on the local level with increasing frequency.

New information

Readers will notice that in a number of instances in the text, we have stated that 'no information' or 'little information' is available on some aspect of the nesting of a species, or that the information in the text is uncertain and therefore qualified by a question mark. We sometimes will also draw attention to missing information by stating outright that the incubation period or age at flight, for example, is 'unknown' for one or another species. It is possible, indeed sometimes likely, that this information is known to someone who has not realized that it was not more widely available. It is also possible that we overlooked some available, though perhaps obscurely published, information. In any case, we would be delighted to hear from anyone who feels that they possess facts which would help to make the next edition of this work more complete. Please write: Paul J. Baicich, PO Box 404, Oxon Hill, MD 20750, USA or Colin J. O. Harrison, 19 Kennington Road, Kennington, Oxford OX1 5NZ, UK.

Identification keys

This section has three keys as follows:

It should, in theory, be possible to identify the bird involved from either the nest and its site, or the eggs, or the young one. In fact this is more difficult than might be expected. In some instances the same type of nest, eggs, or young may be shared by several species; while at the other extreme there is always the possibility of a nest in an unusual site, or of an egg of abnormal color or markings, or with markings absent when they should be present.

It is therefore not possible to offer a key or series of keys which will enable the certain identification of any species in this way; and what has been done here is to group nests, eggs, and young in a series of fairly simple subdivisions which should help to narrow down considerably the number of possibilities, and enable the user to refer to likely species, or groups of species, much more rapidly.

With this end in view the various categories have been kept as simple as possible. A capital letter has been assigned to each nest type, a number to each egg type, and a lower-case letter to each type of young with, in some instances, a second letter to indicate whether a nestling is downy (d) or naked (n). In the lists of species or groups of species in each category, the letters and numbers in brackets following each name indicate the information from the other lists of categories. A question mark indicates lack of information.

For example – the information (8,cn) after 'waxwings' in the nests in category 'C.' Smaller cup nest in tree or shrub,' indicates that the egg is blue or gray-blue marked with brown, black, or gray, and that the young have a red or pink mouth and are naked. The entry (A,1) after the name of the American Dipper in the section on young, in smaller cup nests, with unpatterned yellow or orange mouths indicates that the nest is domed and the egg unmarked and white.

To trace the birds in the main text the species are indexed under both common and scientific names at the end of the book, and the list of groups of birds and the order in which they are arranged appears on pp. 5–6.

Finally it should be mentioned that a check with the current literature on distribution will sometimes reveal that only one of a group of species is present in a particular region and may also help substantially to reduce the list of possibilities.

Categories used in the keys

Nests

A. Domed nest.
B. Suspended nest, hanging, or pensile between forked twigs.
C. Smaller nest (up to *c.* 9–10 in. diameter) in tree or bush.

D.   on ground or in herbage layer (including reedbeds).
E.   in hole, cavity, crevice or burrow in ground, rocks, or buildings.
F.   in hole, cavity, or crevice in tree.
G. Mud nest, or saliva and debris nest, stuck to buildings, rocks, or similar site.
H. Cup nest on ledge of rock or building.
I. Larger nest in tree.
J.   on rock ledge or rocky island.
K.   by or in water.
L. Little or no nest, on mossy branch, in tree hole, or in cavity above ground.
M.   in burrow, hole, or cavity on or near ground.
N.   on rock ledge or rocky island.
O.   on the ground, usually near or by water.
P.   on open ground.
Q.   in growing herbage.
R.   on the ground under trees or shrubs.

Eggs

UNMARKED
1. White or cream.
2. Blue or greenish.
3. Buff or olive-buff.

SCRIBBLED, SCRAWLED, OR WITH LONG STREAKS
4. Scribbled, scrawled, or with long streaks.

SPECKLED, SPOTTED, OR BLOTCHED
5. White or creamy, marked with red or reddish-brown.
6.   brown, black, or gray.
7. Blue or gray-blue, marked with red or reddish-brown.
8.   brown, black, or gray.
9. Yellowish or pale buff, marked with red or reddish-brown.
10.   brown, black, or gray.
11. Olive, marked with reddish-brown, brown, olive-brown, black, or gray.
12. Greenish, marked with red or reddish-brown.
13.   darker green or olive.
14.   brown, olive-brown, black, or gray.
15. Pinkish or purplish, marked with red or reddish-brown.
16.   brown, black, or gray.
17. Deep buff, marked with brown, black, and gray.

Young nestlings and chicks

a. In smaller cup nest, mouth patterned.
b.   mouth unpatterned, yellow or orange.
c.   pink or red.
d. In unlined cavity in tree, bank or ground, nestling naked.
e. In larger nest on tree or ground, nestling naked.
f. Larger nestling with coarse, hairy down; usually sparse.
g. Larger downy nestling with plain white, gray, buff, or light brown down.
h.   yellowish or greenish down.
i.   down without pattern but with variation in overall dorsal coloration.

j.   Larger downy nestling with down boldly striped on head and usually over body, feet lobed.
k.   Larger downy nestling with down mainly striped or mottled, short seedeating bill, bare legs.
l.   Larger downy nestling with down mainly striped or mottled, short seedeating bill, downy legs.
m.   Larger downy nestling with down mainly striped or mottled, bill slender and longer.
n.   Larger downy nestling with down spotted or mottled, feet webbed.
o.   dark brown or blackish, feet unwebbed.
p.   three toes webbed.
q.   all four toes webbed.
r.   Nestlings with unwebbed toes patterned two in front, two behind.
s.   Nestlings with toes having two front digits fused for much of their length.
t.   Nestlings with toes having two back digits pivoted forward to present four forward toes.
u.   Nestlings with all four toes webbed.

Key I. Nests

A. DOMED, WITH ENTRANCE HOLE AT SIDE
Monk Parakeet (1,rn); Northern Beardless-Tyrannulet and Great Kiskadee (5,6,?d); Rose-throated Becard, suspended from twig (5,6,9,10,15,16,?); magpies (8,10,11,cn); Verdin (7,?); some wrens (1,5,6,9,10,15,17,bd,cd); American Dipper, ledge or niche by water (1,bd); Arctic Warbler, on ground (5,bd); Ovenbird, on ground (5,6,?); Olive Sparrow, on ground (1,cd); meadowlarks, on ground (5,?d); House Sparrow (6,cn).

B. SUSPENDED NEST, HANGING FROM SINGLE SUPPORT, OR SLUNG BETWEEN FORKED TWIGS
Acadian Flycatcher (6,?d); Rose-throated Becard, domed suspended nest (5,6,9,10, 15,16,?); Bushtit (1,?d); kinglets, slung under conifer branch (6,9,bd); vireos (1,6,bd); orioles (4,8,16,cd).

C. SMALLER CUP NEST (UP TO C. 9–10 IN. DIAMETER) IN TREE OR SHRUB
Smaller herons and egrets (2,g); Solitary Sandpiper, using other birds' nests (5,9,m); Marbled Murrelet, hollow in moss or lichens on a branch (11,14,n); most doves (1,f); cuckoos (1,2,a,f,r); most hummingbirds (1,g); most flycatchers (1,4,5,6,9,15,16,bd); most jays (6,8,10,11,14,16,cn); most thrushes (2,7,15,bd); kinglets (6,9,bd); gnat-catchers (7,an); Wrentit (2,?n); mockingbirds and thrashers (2,5,7,15,bd); waxwings (8,cn); Phainopepla (6,cd); shrikes (6,10,14,bd,cd); many warblers (1,5,6,8,9,10,cd); tanagers (7,8,cd); grosbeaks (1,2,5,6,cd); sparrows and buntings (1,2,4,5,6,7,8,cd); blackbirds and grackles (4,8,16,cd); cowbirds, parasitic in other birds' nests (2,6,cd); most finches (1,2,4,5,6,8,cd).

D. SMALLER CUP NEST ON GROUND OR IN HERBAGE LAYER, INCLUDING TALL HERBAGE GROWING IN WATER
By or in water. Smaller herons and egrets (2,g); rails (5,9,11,15,17,o); American Coot (10,o); blackbirds and grackles (4,8,16,cd).
Not necessarily near water. Common Ground-Dove (1,f); some hummingbirds (1,g); Yellow-bellied and Willow Flycatchers (1,5,6,?d); larks (6,10,14,a); some thrushes (2,7,15,bd); wagtails and pipits (6,10,16,bd,cd); many warblers (1,5,6,cd); Red-faced Warbler and Painted Redstart (5,6,bd); sparrows and buntings (1,2,4,5,6,7,8,cd); longspurs (4,6,8,9,10,11,14,16,cd); Dickcissel (2,?); Bobolink, blackbirds and grackles (4,8,16,cd).

E. SMALLER CUP NEST IN HOLE, CAVITY, CREVICE, OR BURROW, IN GROUND, ROCKS, OR BUILDING

Rock Dove (1,f); Cordilleran and Pacific-slope Flycatchers (1,5,?); some swallows (1,bd); White Wagtail (6,bd); some titmice (1,5,6,bd); some wrens (5,6,9,15,?); Townsend's Solitaire (5,6,9,10,?); American Pipit (6,cd); Northern Wheatear (2,bd); starlings (2,bd); Prothonotary and Canada Warblers, and waterthrushes (5,6,9,10,cd); sparrows (6,cn); rosy-finches (1,cd); Snow Bunting (7,8,cd).

F. SMALLER CUP NEST IN HOLE, CAVITY, OR CREVICE IN TREE

Yellow-bellied, Cordilleran and Pacific-slope Flycatchers (1,5,6,?d); Violet-green and Tree Swallows, and Purple Martin (1,?); titmice (1,5,6,bd); nuthatches (5,6,9,bd); Brown Creeper (5,bd); Bluebirds (2,?); starlings (2,bd); Prothonotary and Lucy's Warblers (5,6,9,?); sparrows (6,cn).

G. MUD NEST, OR SALIVA AND DEBRIS, STUCK TO BUILDING, ROCK, OR SIMILAR SITE

Swifts (1,cn,o,t); phoebes (1,5,6,cd); Barn, Cliff, and Cave Swallows (5,6,bd).

H. CUP NEST ON LEDGE OF ROCK OR BUILDING

Rock Dove and Spotted Dove (1,f); phoebes (1,5,6,cd); Canyon Wren (6,?); American Robin (2,bd); Townsend's Solitaire (5,6,9,10,b); juncos (5,6,cd)

I. LARGER NEST IN TREE

Pelicans (1,e,g,u); cormorants (1,2,e,g,q,u); Anhinga (1,2,e,g); Magnificent Frigatebird (1,e); larger herons and egrets (2,g); Wood Stork (1,g); Roseate Spoonbill (5,6,g); Glossy and White-faced Ibises (2,o); White Ibis (8,10,14,o); birds of prey (1,5,9,g); Osprey (5,6,9,10,g,r); Crested Caracara (3,5,9,17,g); some falcons, using old nests of other birds (5,9,15,g); Plain Chachalaca (1,k); Limpkin (10,11,g); Bonaparte's Gull (6,10,11,14,n); Brown Noddy (5,9,15,g); Great Horned, Barred, Spotted, Great Gray, and Long-eared Owls, on old nests of other birds (1,g,r); ravens and crows (6,8,14,cn); Brown Jay (5,cn), Pinyon Jay (5,7,12,?n); Clark's Nutcracker (6,14,?n or ?d).

J. LARGER NEST ON ROCK LEDGE OR ROCKY ISLAND

Northern Gannet (1,g,u); cormorants (1,2,e,g,q,u); larger herons and egrets (2,g); hawks and eagles (1,5,6,g); Osprey (5,6,9,10,g,r); Crested Caracara (3,5,9,17,g); many gulls (2,4,6,8,10,11,14,17,n); Thayer's Gull (6,10,11,p); kittiwakes (6,10,11,14,i); Brown Noddy (5,9,15,g); crows and ravens (8,14,cn).

K. LARGER NEST BY OR IN WATER

Loons (11,17,o); grebes, small nest in Pied-billed (1,3,g,j); pelicans (1,e,g,u); cormorants, occasionally (1,2,e,g,q,u); Magnificent Frigatebird (1,e); larger herons and egrets (2,g); Bittern (3,h); Roseate Spoonbill (5,6,g); Glossy Ibis (2,o); White Ibis (8,10,14,o); swans (1,2,g); Snail Kite (5,g); Northern Harrier (1,6,g); Osprey (5,6, 9,10,g,r); Crested Caracara (3,5,9,17,g); cranes (9,10,11,12,14,i); Limpkin (10,11,g); Forster's and Black Terns (6,10,11,14,17,n); Brown Noddy (5,9,15,g).

L. LITTLE OR NO NEST, IN TREE HOLE, OR CAVITY ABOVE GROUND

Some ducks, usually with down (1,2,3,n,p); California Condor (12,g); vultures (5,6,9,12,g); American Kestrel (5,15,g); Budgerigar and Canary-winged Parakeet (1,d,r); many owls (1,g,r); trogons (1,d,r); kingfishers (1,d,s); woodpeckers (1,d,r).

M. LITTLE OR NO NEST IN BURROW, HOLE, OR CAVITY ON OR NEAR GROUND

Storm-petrels (1,g,p); mergansers (3,p); California Condor (1,2,g); vultures (5,6,9, 12,g); Razorbill (1,4,5,6,9,10,14,15,16,p); guillemots (6,14,p); Xantus's and Ancient

Murrelet, Dovekie, auklets and puffins (1,2,3,4,6,8,10,11,14,17,g,i,p); Barn, Great Horned, Spotted, and Burrowing Owls (1,g,r); kingfishers (1,d,s).

N. LITTLE OR NO NEST, ON ROCK LEDGE OR ROCKY ISLAND
Northern Fulmar (1,g); some geese (1,g,h); California Condor, in cave or recess (1,2,g); vultures, in cave or recess (5,6,9,12,g); falcons (3,5,9,15,g); some terns (4,6,8,10,11,14,17,n); Razorbill and murres (1,2,4,5,6,7,8,9,10,11,14,15,16,17,p).

O. LITTLE OR NO NEST, ON THE GROUND, USUALLY NEAR OR BY WATER
Loons (11,17,o); Masked Booby (2,g,u); pelicans (1,e,g,u); geese (1,g,h); some ducks (1,2,3,n,p); Northern Jacana, on plants in water (4,m); oystercatchers (6,10,14,m); Black-necked Stilt and American Avocet (10,m); some plovers (6,10,m); most sandpipers, snipe, and phalaropes (5,6,9,10,11,12,13,14,m); jaegers (10,11,14,17,p); many gulls (2,4,6,8,10,11,14,17,n); terns (4,6,8,10,11,14,17,n); Sooty Tern (5,9,15,n); Black Skimmer (6,n).

P. LITTLE OR NO NEST, ON OPEN GROUND
Peregrine Falcon, rarely (5,9,g); ptarmigan (6,10,16,l); Himalayan Snowcock (3,k); Chukar (9,k); Wild Turkey (6,10,k); most plovers (6,9,10,11,m); some sandpipers (5,6,9,10,15,14,m); jaegers (10,11,14,17,p); Marbled Murrelet, rarely (11,14,n); Kittlitz's Murrelet (10,11,g,i); Snowy Owl (1,g,r); Poor-will, Pauraque and nighthawks (6,9,15,i).

Q. LITTLE OR NO NEST, IN GROWING HERBAGE
Some ducks (1,2,3,n,p); some grouse (1,3,6,10,16,17,l); some gamebirds (1,3,9,k); some sandpipers and phalaropes (5,6,9,10,11,12,14,m); Short-eared Owl (1,g,r)

R. LITTLE OR NO NEST, ON THE GROUND UNDER TREES OR SHRUBS
Some ducks (1,2,3,n,p); vultures (5,6,9,12,g); woodland grouse (1,3,6,9,10,11,16,l); gamebirds, quail, Wild Turkey (1,3,5,6,9,10,k); Long-eared and Short-eared Owl (1,g,r); some goatsuckers (1,6,9,15,16,g,i).

Key 2. Eggs

To assist further with identification, the eggs in the various color categories have been subdivided according to size – **small**, up to about crow size or to 40 mm., **medium**, from crow to Turkey Vulture size or 40–70 mm., and **large** at 70+ mm.

Unmarked eggs

1. WHITE OR CREAM
Large. Northern Fulmar (N,g); Northern Gannet (J,g,u); pelicans (I,K,O,e,g,u); swans (K,g); geese (N,O,g,h); California Condor (L,M,N,g); White-tailed and Bald Eagles (I,J,g); Razorbill and murres (M,N,p).
Medium. Grebes (K,g,j); cormorants (I,J,K,e,g,q,u); Anhinga (I,e,g); Magnificent Frigatebird (I,K,e); Wood Stork (I,g); some ducks (L,M,O,Q,R,n,p); Mississippi Kite, hawks (I,g); Plain Chachalaca (I,k), Ruffed Grouse (R,l); Lesser Prairie-Chicken (Q,l); auklets and puffins (M,p); Greater Roadrunner (C,a,f); owls (I,L,N,P,Q,R,g,r); Belted Kingfisher (M,d,s).
Small. Storm-petrels (M,g,p); most doves (C,f); Budgerigar and Canary-winged Parakeet (L,d,r); Monk Parakeet (A,r); anis (C,e); smaller owls (L,M,g,r); Poor-will (P,R,g); swifts (G,c,o,t); hummingbirds (C,D,g); trogons (L,d,r); kingfishers

(L,M,d,s); woodpeckers (L,d,r); *Empidonax* flycatchers (B,C,D,E,F,?d); phoebes (H,cd); some swallows (E,F,bd); occasionally Mexican Jay (C,cn); Plain and Bridled Titmice (E,F,bd); Bushtit (B,?d); Dipper (A,bd); some vireos (B,bd); Swainson's, Worm-eating and Bachman's Warblers (C,D,?d); some sparrows (C,D,cd); Olive Sparrow (A,cd); Indigo, Lazuli, and Varied Buntings (C,cd); rosy-finches (E,cd); Lawrence's Goldfinch (C,cd).

2. BLUE OR GREEN
Large. Mute Swan (K,g); California Condor (L,M,N,g); some large gulls (J,O,n); murres (N,p).
Medium. Masked Booby (O,g,u); cormorants, rarely (I,J,K,e,g,q,u); Anhinga (I,e,g); herons and egrets (C,D,I,J,K,g); Glossy and White-faced Ibises (I,K,O,o); some dabbling, diving, and sea ducks (L,M,O,Q,R,n,p); some gulls (J,O,n); Dovekie and Parakeet Auklet (M,p).
Small. Green Heron and Least Bittern (C,D,g); *Cocsyzus* cuckoos (C,a,f,r); anis, rarely (C,e); Sedge Wren (A,?); some thrushes (C,D,H,bd); Wrentit (C,?n); Catbird and Crissal Thrasher (C,bd); European Starling and Crested Myna (2,bd); Lark Bunting (D,?); Black-chinned Sparrow (C,?); Lazuli and Varied Buntings (C,cd); Dickcissel (D,?); Blue Grosbeak (C,cd); Shiny and Bronzed Cowbirds (–,cd); American and Lesser Goldfinches (C,cd).

3. BUFF OR OLIVE-BUFF
Medium. Grebes, nest-stained (J,g,j); American Bittern (J,h); some dabbling and sea ducks (L,M,O,Q,R,n,p); Crested Caracara (I,J,K,g); Prairie Falcon (N,g); Himalayan Snowcock (P,k); some grouse (Q,R,l).

Scribbled, scrawled, or with long streaks

4. SCRIBBLED, SCRAWLED, OR WITH LONG STREAKS
Large. Razorbill and murres, occasionally (M,N,p).
Medium. Some gulls, occasionally (J,O,n); some terns, occasionally (N,O,n); Xantus's Murrelet, Rhinoceros Auklet, and puffins, occasionally (M,p).
Small. Northern Jacana (O,m); *Myiarchus* flycatchers, streaked finely (C,bd); Chihuahuan Raven, fine longitudinal streaking (I,cd); California, Canyon, and Abert's Towhees, Vesper and Lark Sparrows, occasionally (C,D,?); Longspurs (D,cd); Bobolink, blackbirds (C,D,cd); orioles (B,cd); Evening Grosbeak, House Finch, and Crossbill (C,bd-cd).

Speckled, spotted, or blotched

5. WHITE OR CREAMY, MARKED WITH RED OR REDDISH-BROWN
Large. Vultures (L,M,N,R,g); Golden Eagle (I,J,g); Razorbill and murres (M,N,p).
Medium. Roseate Spoonbill (I,K,g); kites, hawks, Crested Caracara, Osprey (I,J,K,g,r); falcons (I,N,P,g); rails and gallinules (D,o); Sooty Tern (O,n); Brown Noddy (I,J,K,g).
Small. Merlin and American Kestrel (I,L,N,g); small rails (D,o); Western, Stilt, Upland and Spotted Sandpipers and Woodcock (O,P,Q,m); Solitary Sandpiper (C,m); some flycatchers (B,C,D,E,F,H, bd,cd); Rose-throated Becard (B,?); Barn, Cliff, and Cave Swallows (G,bd); Brown Jay (I,cn); Pinyon Jay (I,?n); some wrens (A,E,bd,cd); most titmice (E,F,bd); nuthatches (F,bd); Brown Creeper (F,bd); Arctic Warbler (A,bd); Townsend's Solitaire (E,H,?); Brown, Long-billed, and Bendire's Thrashers (C,?); most warblers (A,C,D,E,F,cd); Painted Redstart (D,E,bd); sparrows and

buntings (C,D,cd); Painted Bunting (C,cd);Yellow-headed Blackbird (D,cd); meadowlarks (A,?d); redpolls (C,cd).

6. WHITE OR CREAMY, MARKED WITH BROWN, BLACK, OR GRAY
Large. Vultures (L,M,N,R,g); Golden Eagle (I,J,g); Razorbill and murres (M,N,p).
Medium. Roseate Spoonbill (I,K,g); hawks and Osprey (I,J,K,g,r); ptarmigan (P,l); Ruffed Grouse (R,l); oystercatchers (O,m); golden-plovers and Black-bellied Plover (P,m); some larger sandpipers (O,P,Q,m); some gulls (J,O,i,n,p); Bonaparte's Gull (H,n); most terns (N,O,n); Black Skimmer (O,n); guillemots, Ancient Murrelet and puffins (M,p).
Small. Most plovers (O,P,m); some sandpipers and phalaropes (O,P,Q,m); Least and Black Terns (K,O,n); goatsuckers (P,R,g,i); Rose-throated Becard (B,?); some flycatchers (A,B,C,D,bd,cd); larks (D,a); Cliff Swallow (G,?); Clark's Nutcracker (H,?n,?d); Green Jay (C,c); most titmice (E,F,bd); nuthatches (F,bd); Winter, Canyon, and Rock Wrens (A,E,H,?,bd); kinglets (B,C,bd); Townsend's Solitaire (E,H,?); White Wagtail and pipits (D,E,bd,ce); Phainopepla (C,cd); shrikes (C,bd,cd); most vireos (B,bd); many warblers (A,C,D,E,F,cd); Red-faced Warbler (D,bd); grosbeaks (C,cd); sparrows and buntings (C,D,cd); Shiny and Brown-headed Cowbirds (–, cd); crossbills (C,bd-cd); European sparrows (A,E,F,cn).

7. BLUE OR GRAYISH-BLUE, MARKED WITH RED OR REDDISH-BROWN
Large. Murres (N,p).
Small. Pinyon Jay (H,?n); Verdin (A,?); gnatcatchers (C,ad); some thrushes (C,D,bd); Mockingbirds and most thrashers (C,bd); tanagers (C,cd); California, Canyon, and Abert's Towhees, Savannah and Tree Sparrows, Snow Bunting (C,D,cd).

8. BLUE OR GRAYISH-BLUE, MARKED WITH BROWN, BLACK, OR GRAY
Large. Murres (N,p).
Medium. White Ibis (I,K,o); some gulls, rarely (J,O,n); some terns, rarely (N,O,n); Xantus's Murrelet (M,i,p).
Small. Some jays (C,cn); magpies (A,cn); crows and ravens (H,I,cn); waxwings (C,cn); Olive Warbler (C,cd); tanagers (C,cd); some sparrows and buntings, Smith's Longspur (C,D,cd); Bobolink, Rusty and Brewer's Blackbirds (C,D,cd); orioles (B,cd); some finches (C,cd).

9. YELLOWISH OR PALE BUFF, MARKED WITH RED OR REDDISH-BROWN
Large. Vultures (L,M,N,R,g); cranes (K,g,i); Razorbill and murres (M,p).
Medium. Kites (I,g); Osprey (I,J,K,g,r); Crested Caracara (I,J,K,g); some falcons (I,N,P,g); Blue and Spruce Grouse (Q,l); rails and gallinules (D,o); golden-plovers and Black-bellied Plover (P,m); some sandpipers (O,P,Q,m); Sooty Tern (O,n); Brown Noddy (I,J,K,g).
Small. Smaller rails (D,o); some sandpipers (O,P,Q,m); Solitary Sandpiper (C,m); Pauraque (P,R,i); kingbirds (C,bd);Rose-throated Becard (B,?); Brown-headed Nuthatch (F,bd); House and Cactus Wrens (A,E,?,cd); Townsend's Solitaire (E,G,?); Prothonotary and Blackpoll Warblers and waterthrushes (C,D,E,F,cd); Lapland Longspur (D,cd).

10. YELLOWISH OR PALE BUFF, MARKED WITH BROWN, BLACK, OR GRAY
Large. Cranes (K,g,i); Razorbill and murres (M,N,p).
Medium. White Ibis (I,K,o); Osprey (I,J,K,g,r); grouse (K,i); Limpkin (I,K,g); American Coot (D,o); oystercatchers, Avocet and Stilt (O,m); golden-plovers and Black-bellied Plover (O,P,m); some sandpipers (O,P,Q,m); jaegers (O,P,p); gulls (J,O,i,n,p); Bonaparte's Gull (I,n); most terns (N,O,n); Forster's Tern (N,n); Kittlitz's Murrelet (P,g,i); Ancient Murrelet (M,g); Puffin (M,p).

Small. Most plovers (O,P,m); some sandpipers and snipe (O,P,Q,m); Least and Black Terns (K,O,n); Rose-throated Becard (B,?); larks (D,a); Green Jay (C,?); magpies (A,cn); Marsh Wren (A,?); Townsend's Solitaire (E,H,?); Yellow Wagtail and pipits (D,cd); shrikes (C,bd,cd); Blackpoll Warbler, waterthrushes (C,D,E,cd); some longspurs (D,cd).

11. OLIVE, MARKED WITH REDDISH-BROWN, BROWN, OLIVE-BROWN, BLACK, AND GRAY
Large. Loons (K,O,o); cranes (K,g,i); murres (N,p).
Medium. Limpkin (I,K,g); some sandpipers (O,P,Q,m); jaegers (O,P,p); gulls (J,O,i,n,p); Bonaparte's Gull (I,n); many terns (K,N,O,n); Marbled Murrelet (C,P,n); Kittlitz's Murrelet (P,g,i); Xantus's Murrelet (L,i,p).
Small. Sora (D,o); Mountain Plover (P,m); some sandpipers and phalaropes (O,P,Q,m); some jays (C,cn); magpies (A,cn); some longspurs (D,cd).

12. GREENISH, MARKED WITH RED OR REDDISH-BROWN
Large. Black Vulture (L,M,N,R,g); Whooping Crane (K,g,i).
Medium. Common Gallinule (D,p).
Small. Semipalmated Sandpiper (O,Q,m); Pinyon Jay (I,?n).

13. GREENISH, MARKED WITH DARKER GREEN AND OLIVE
Godwits (D,m).

14. GREENISH, MARKED WITH BROWN, OLIVE-BROWN, BLACK, OR GRAY
Large. Whooping Crane (K,g,i); Razorbill and murres (M,N,p).
Medium. White Ibis (I,K,o); Oystercatchers, rarely (O,m); some sandpipers (O,P,Q,m); Parasitic and Long-tailed Jaegers (O,P,p); some gulls (J,O,i,n); Bonaparte's Gull (I,n); Arctic and Forster's Tern (K,N,O,n); Marbled Murrelet (C,P,n); guillemots and Xantus's Murrelet (M,p).
Small. Larks (D,a); some jays (C,cn); crows (I,J,cn); Clark's Nutcracker (I,?n,?d); Northern Shrike (C,bd,cd); some longspurs (D,cd).

15. PINKISH OR PURPLISH, MARKED WITH RED OR REDDISH-BROWN
Large. Razorbill and murres (M,N,p).
Medium. Some falcons (L,I,N,g); King, Clapper, and Virginia Rails (D,o); Sooty Tern (O,N); Brown Noddy (I,J,K,g).
Small. Pauraque (P,R,i); Rose-throated Becard (B,?); kingbirds (C,bd); House and Cactus Wrens (A,E,?,cd); Northern Mockingbird, occasionally (C,bd); Fieldfare, occasionally (C,D,bd).

16. PINKISH OR PURPLISH, MARKED WITH BROWN, BLACK, AND GRAY
Large. Razorbill and murres (M,N,p).
Medium. Some grouse (P,Q,R,l).
Small. Chuck-wills-widow (R,i); Rose-throated Becard (B,?); Olive-sided Flycatcher (C,?); Blue and scrub-jays (C,cn); Meadow Pipit (D,cd); McCown's and Smith's Longspurs (D,cd); Bobolink, Rusty and Brewer's Blackbirds (C,D,cd); orioles (B,cd).

17. DEEPER BUFF TO PALE BROWN, MARKED WITH BROWN, BLACK, AND GRAY
Large. Murres (N,p).
Medium. Crested Caracara (I,J,K,g); Greater Prairie-Chicken (Q,l); jaegers (O,P,p); some gulls (J,O,n); a few sea terns (N,O,n); Atlantic Puffin and Xantus's Murrelet (M,p).
Small. Sora (D,o); Black Tern (K,O,n); Marsh Wren (A,?).

Key 3. Young Nestlings and Chicks

a. IN SMALLER NEST, MOUTH PATTERNED
Larks, mouth yellow with three dark tongue spots (D,6,10,14); gnatcatchers, mouth yellow with two black spots on tongue (C,7); *Cocsyzus* cuckoos have ten white spots on palate (C,1,2), Greater Roadrunner (C,1) has red and white palate with two white spots at throat. *Cocsyzus* cuckoos and Gray Catbird have black edge to tongue tip.

b. IN SMALLER NEST, MOUTH UNPATTERNED, YELLOW OR ORANGE
(All are downy). Oystercatchers (C,7); flycatchers (A,B,C,D,E,F,G,1,4,5,6,9,15,16); swallows (E,F,G,1,5,6); titmice (E,F,1,5,6); Winter Wren (A,1,5,6); American Dipper (A,1); Arctic Warbler (A,5); kinglets (B,C,6,9); thrushes (C,D,E,F,H,2,7,15); mockingbirds and thrashers (C,2,5,7,15); White Wagtail (E,6); shrikes (C,6,10,14); European Starling (E,F,2); Red-faced Warbler and Painted Redstart (D,E,5,6); vireos (B,1,6); Red Crossbill? (C,4,6,8).

c. IN SMALLER NEST, MOUTH UNMARKED, PINK OR RED
Downy young. Swifts (G,1); Cactus Wren (A,1,5,6,9,10,15); Yellow Wagtail and pipits (D,E,6,10,16); Phainopepla (C,6); shrikes (C,6,10,14); most warblers (C,D,E,F,1,5, 6,8,9,10); tanagers (C,7,8); grosbeaks (C,1,2,5,6); sparrows and buntings (C,D,H,1, 2,4,5,6,7,8); Olive Sparrow (A,1); longspurs (D,4,6,8,9,10, 11,14,16); blackbirds (C,D,4,5,6,8,16); orioles (B,4,8,18); cowbirds (–,2,6); finches (C,1,4,5,6,8); rosy-finches (E,I).
Naked Young Swifts, early stage (G,1); jays (C,6,8,10,11,14,16); magpies (A,8,10,11); crows and ravens (I,J,8,14); waxwings (C,8); European sparrows (A,E,F,6).

d. IN UNLINED CAVITY IN TREE, BANK OR GROUND, NESTLING NAKED
Most parakeets (A,L,1); trogons (L,1); kingfishers (L,M,1); woodpeckers (L,1).

e. IN LARGER NEST ON TREE OR GROUND, NESTLING NAKED
Pelicans (I,K,O,1); cormorants (I,J,K,1,2); Anhinga (I,1,2); Magnificent Frigatebird (I,K,1); anis (C,1,2).

f. LARGER NESTLING WITH COARSE, HAIRY DOWN; USUALLY SPARSE
Cocsyzus cuckoos (C,2); Greater Roadrunner (C,I); doves (C,D,E,H,1).

g. LARGER DOWNY NESTLING WITH PLAIN WHITE, GRAY, BUFF, OR LIGHT BROWN DOWN
White. Masked Booby (O,2); Northern Gannet (J,1); pelicans (I,K,O,1); some herons and egrets (C,D,I,J,K,2); Wood Stork (I,1); Roseate Spoonbill (I,K,5,6); California Condor, first down (L,M,N,1,2); Turkey Vulture (L,M,N,R,5,6); White-tailed Kite, pinkish-buff tint on back; hawks, sometimes tinted gray, buff and brown; Golden Eagle, sometimes with gray tips (I,J,1,5,6); falcons (I,L,N,P,3,5,9,15); Brown Noddy, drab white or with greyish-brown on upper parts (I,J,K,5,9,15); many owls (L,M,N,P,R,1).
Gray. Western and Clark's Grebes (K,1,3); Northern Fulmar (M,I); some storm-petrels (L,I); some cormorants (I,J,K,1,2); some herons and egrets (C,D,I,J,K,2); swans (K,1,2); Ross's Goose, Emperor Goose, and Brant (O,1); California Condor, second down (L,M,N,1,2); White-tailed Kite, second down (I,5,9); some hawks (I,J,1,5,6); Bald Eagle, first down (I,J,1); Peregrine Falcon and Merlin, buffish or brownish-gray (I,N,P,5,9,15); Ancient Murrelet, blackish (M,6,10); Kittlitz's Murrelet, gray and yellow (P,10,11); Elf Owl, sooty white (L,1); Burrowing Owl, grayish-white (M,1); Great Gray Owl (I,L,1); some hummingbirds (C,D,1).
Buff. Anhinga, buffish brown (I,1,2); Least Bittern, white below (C,D,2); Black Vulture (L,M,N,R,5,9,15), some kites, Harris's Hawk, White-tailed Eagle, grayish buff

(I,J,K,1,5,6,9); Crested Caracara, pinkish-buff (I,J,K,3,5,9,17); Barn Owl, buffish-cream second down (L,M,1); Hawk and Boreal Owls, buffish-white (L,1); Short-eared Owl (Q,R,1); Poor-will (P,R,1,6); Ruby-throated and Costa's Hummingbirds, yellowish (C,D,1).

Light Brown. Anhinga, buffish-brown (I,1,2); Great Blue Heron with gray, Tricolored Heron with gray and rufous, Black-crowned Night-Heron rufous or grayish (I,J,K,2); White-fronted and Barnacle Geese, brown and white (N,O,1); Snail Kite, grayish-brown second down, Rough-legged Hawk, grayish-brown first down, Harris's Hawk and Bald Eagle, second down (I,J,K,1,5,6); Osprey, brown and white (I,J,K,5,6,9,10); Crested Caracara (I,J,K,3,5,9,17); Limpkin (I,K,10,11); puffins, grayish-brown (M,1,3, 4,6,10,17); cranes (K,9,10,11,12,14).

h. LARGER DOWNY NESTLING WITH YELLOWISH OR GREENISH UNPATTERNED DOWN
American Bittern (K,3); some geese (N,O,1).

i. LARGER DOWNY NESTLING WITH DOWN WITHOUT PATTERN BUT WITH VARIATION IN OVERALL DORSAL COLORATION
Cranes (K,9,10,11,12,14); Kittlitz's Murrelet, gray and yellow (P,10,11); goatsuckers, (P,R,1,6,9,15,16).

j. LARGER DOWNY NESTLING WITH DOWN BOLDLY STRIPED ON HEAD AND USUALLY OVER BODY, FEET LOBED
Grebes (K,1,3).

k. LARGER DOWNY NESTLING WITH DOWN MAINLY STRIPED OR MOTTLED, SHORT SEEDEATING BILL, BARE LEGS
Plain Chachalaca (I,1); Himalayan Snowcock (P,3); typical gamebirds, quails, Wild Turkey (P,Q,R,1,3,5,6,9,10).

l. LARGER DOWNY NESTLING WITH DOWN MAINLY STRIPED OR MOTTLED, SHORT SEEDEATING BILL, DOWNY LEGS
Grouse (P,Q,R,1,3,6,9,10,16,17) .

m. LARGER DOWNY NESTLING WITH DOWN MAINLY STRIPED OR MOTTLED, BILL SLENDER AND LONGER
Northern Jacana (O,4); oystercatchers (O,6,10,14); Avocet and Stilt (O,10); plovers (O,P,6,9,10,11); sandpipers, snipe, woodcock, and phalaropes (O,P,Q,5,6,9,10,11,12, 13,14); Solitary Sandpiper (C,5,9).

n. LARGER DOWNY NESTLING WITH DOWN SPOTTED OR MOTTLED, FEET WEBBED
Most ducks (L,M,O,Q,R,1,2,3); Avocet, feet half webbed (O,10); most gulls (J,O,2,4,6, 8,10,11,14,17); Bonaparte's Gull (I,6,10,11,15); most terns (N,O,4,6,8,10,11,14,17); Forster's and Black Terns (K,O,6,10,11,14,17); Black Skimmer (O,6); Marbled Murrelet (11,14,C,P).

o. LARGER DOWNY NESTLING WITH DOWN DARK BROWN OR BLACKISH, FEET UNWEBBED
Loons, toes lobed (K,O,11,17); ibises, with white marks on head (I,K,2,8,10,14); rails, down black (D,5,9,11,15,17); gallinules, white sheaths on head at first (D,5,9,12); American Coot, orange on head at first (D,10).

p. LARGER DOWNY NESTLING, WITH DOWN DARK BROWN OR BLACKISH, THREE TOES WEBBED
Some storm-petrels (M,1); some diving and sea ducks (L,M,O,Q,1,2,3); jaegers (O,P,10,11,14,17); Brown Noddy (I,J,K,5,9,15); murres and Razorbill (M,N,1,2,4–11, 14–17); guillemots (M,6,14); Xantus's Murrelet, black and white (M,4,8,10,11, 14,17); Dovekie, auklets, puffins (L,1,2,3,4,6,8,10,17); Ancient Murrelet, grayish-black (M,6,10).

q. LARGER DOWNY NESTLING, WITH DOWN DARK BROWN OR BLACKISH, ALL FOUR TOES WEBBED
Cormorants (I,J,K,1,2).

r. NESTLINGS WITH UNWEBBED TOES PATTERNED TWO IN FRONT, TWO BEHIND
Osprey (I,J,K,5,6,9,10); parakeets (A,L,1); cuckoos (C,1,2); owls (I,L,P,Q,R,1); trogons (L,1); most woodpeckers (L,1).

s. NESTLINGS WITH TOES HAVING TWO FRONT DIGITS FUSED FOR MUCH OF THEIR LENGTH
Kingfishers (L,M,1).

t. NESTLINGS WITH TOES HAVING TWO BACK DIGITS PIVOTED FORWARD TO PRESENT FOUR FORWARD TOES
Swifts (G,1).

u. NESTLINGS WITH ALL FOUR TOES WEBBED
Boobies and gannets (J,O,2); cormorants (I,J,K,1,2); pelicans (I,K,O,1).

Loons (*Gaviidae*)

These birds breed on waters of the northern regions. They are unable to walk properly on land, and nest at the water's edge for easy access. However, falling water levels during incubation may leave the nest farther from the water's edge. More rarely nests are mounds of material in shallow water near the edge. Nest material is accumulated by sideways-building, and the nest may vary from a bare scrape to a mound of vegetation. The nest hollow is often damp. Nest may be reused from year to year. Young are precocial; downy, with a rather short stubby bill. They follow the adults in the water, and may be carried on the backs of swimming birds. They are tended by both parents, being fed on fish and Crustacea passed to them by the adults. When small they may hide in waterside vegetation if alarmed.

Red-throated Loon (*Gavia stellata*)   Figure 7, Plates 1, 17
Breeds on both large and small lakes, and small pools; in open or wooded situations. Nest usually on the shore at water's edge. Usually in solitary pairs but may be sociable with a number of nests near together, at times only a few yards apart.
Nest: A shallow scrape on a mound, with very variable nest material; or a heap of vegetable material, moss, etc., built up in shallow water near the bank. Built by both sexes. These nests may be built up higher if water rises. ***Breeding season:*** Late May or early June to September. Single-brooded. ***Eggs:*** Normally 2, rarely 1 or 3? Usually long subelliptical but variable. Often glossy, more so than in other loon species. Olive-buff, sometimes greenish or dark brown; marked with sparse blackish spots or blotches. 74 × 45 mm. ***Incubation:*** Eggs laid at 2-day intervals. Incubation by both sexes but mainly by female, usually beginning with first egg, but some young hatch

Figure 7. Red-throated Loon: typical bare scrape by water.

on same day. 24–29 days. **Nestling:** Precocial, downy. First down thick and short. Variable blackish-brown, blackish-gray, or paler grayish-brown on back; slightly paler on cheeks, throat, foreneck, upper breast and flanks; underparts pale gray. Sometimes quite mouse-gray overall. Pushed out by paler second down coat. Irides brown. Bill and feet dark gray. **Nestling period:** Young tended by both adults. Young will leave nest and swim after first day. First flight at about 6 weeks.

Arctic Loon (*Gavia arctica*)   Plate 17
Breeds in northwestern Alaska, near the coast in tundra habitat. Nest on a small island, sometimes on shore, on aquatic vegetation or very close to water.
Nest: A shallow scrape on a raised site, or with varying amounts of stems, roots, and mud, and at times a large heap; occasionally a raised heap of vegetation in shallow water. Built by both sexes. **Breeding season:** Begins in early June. Single-brooded. **Eggs:** Normally 2, sometimes 1 or 3. Subelliptical to long subelliptical, sometimes oval. Slightly glossy. Olive-brown, sometimes greenish or dark brown; with black spots, blotches or streaks. May tend more toward olive-brown than the eggs of Pacific Loon. 84 × 53 mm. **Incubation:** By both sexes, beginning with first egg. 28–30 days. **Nestling:** Precocial, downy. Down thick and short. Back, head and flanks dark brownish-gray, head and neck to upper breast pale gray, underparts grayish-white. Irides brown; bill dark gray. Legs and feet greenish-gray. **Nestling period:** Young tended by both adults. Adults may remain with young, which may feed themselves at about 5 weeks. First flight at 60–65 days.

Pacific Loon (*Gavia pacifica*)   Figure 8, Plate 17
Breeds in wooded or tundra lake country. Nest usually on a small island, sometimes on shore, on aquatic vegetation, or very close to water.
Nest: A shallow scrape on a raised site, or with varying amounts of stems, roots, and mud, and at times a large heap; occasionally a raised heap of vegetation in shallow water. Material added after first egg. **Breeding season:** Beginning early May in south of range, to mid-June in north. Single-brooded; replacement clutches usually have one egg. **Eggs:** Normally 2, sometimes 1. Subelliptical to long subelliptical, sometimes oval. Slightly glossy, olive-brown, sometimes greenish or dark brown; with black spots, blotches or streaks. 76 × 47 mm. **Incubation:** By both sexes, beginning with the first egg. 23–25 days. **Nestling:** Precocial, downy. Thick and short down is light brown on back, dark brown on sides of head and neck, whitish-gray on breast and belly. Irides brown. Bill dark gray. Legs and feet greenish-gray. **Nestling period:** As for other loons. Tended by both parents, which may fly some distance for food, bringing it back in the bill. Adults may remain with young, which may feed themselves at about 5 weeks. First flight at about 2 months.

Common Loon (*Gavia immer*)   Plate 17
Breeds on larger, deeper lakes in bare or wooded country; at varying altitudes. Nest-site is usually on a bare promontory, island or small island mound; usually on raised ground by the water's edge, more rarely on the edge of a reedbed, or on a muskrat house or mass of floating vegetation.
Nest: Usually a slight hollow scrape with little nest material, but in reedbed sites a large heap of vegetation may be assembled. Built by both sexes. Building continues during laying and incubation. Outside diameter: 24 in. or more; inside diameter: 16 in.; depth: 3 in.; height: 4 in. **Breeding season:** Late May or early June to September. Single-brooded. **Eggs:** Normally 2, rarely 1, very rarely 3 or 4. Elliptical oval to long oval. Slightly glossy with a slightly granular or rough texture. Olive-brown, sometimes more greenish; with a few small blackish spots, or larger blotches, or some-

Figure 8. Pacific Loon: at a site with plentiful material.

times immaculate. 90 × 57 mm. **Incubation:** By both sexes, beginning with the first egg. 29–30 days. **Nestling:** Precocial, downy. The darkest of the nestling loons. Down thick and short, blackish-brown, slightly paler on throat, foreneck, upper breast and flanks. Belly and lower breast gray-edged, becoming white. First down pushed out by second, paler down with the first attached to its tips. Irides dull reddish-brown. Bill light gray, becoming dark slaty or blackish towards the base. Legs and feet gray, blackish towards the outside. **Nestling period:** Young tended by both adults, but one adult more active and sometimes only one remains until the end of the period. Young may ride on parents' backs for first 2–3 weeks. May feed themselves after 6 weeks; fly at about 12 weeks.

Yellow-billed Loon (*Gavia adamsii*)
Breeds on bare arctic tundra, north of the tree-line. Nest usually on a raised site at the water's edge, a small mound in the water, or on a small island or peninsula; on a lake, large pool or large rivers.
Nest: Material usually scanty or absent, but the appearance of the mounds suggests an accumulation of muddy material. Hollow usually damp. Outside diameter: 15–40 in.; inside diameter: 9½–15 in.; depth: 3 in.; height: 3–13 in. **Breeding season:** Beginning June to early July, depending on a thaw. Usually ends by late August. Single-brooded. **Eggs:** Normally 2. Variably shaped; usually subelliptical. Like those of Common Loon but at times paler and more buff. 89 × 56 mm. **Incubation:** By both sexes, 27–29 days. **Nestling:** Like Common Loon. Down dark brownish-gray, but paler than that of Common Loon, with throat to upper breast and flanks paler still. Lower breast and belly white. Bill light horn-colored or even pale bluish-gray, dark basally and around nostrils. Legs and feet gray. Eyes dark brown. **Nestling period:**

Young brooded at nest or elsewhere on shore for first few days. Downy chicks ride on back of swimming adults. Fed by both adults. Time of first flight and full independence unknown.

Grebes (Podicipedidae)

They breed on freshwater lakes and sometimes rivers. The nests are accumulations of soggy, rotting plant material, in the water, often floating. Both sexes build, the material being carried to the nest by birds swimming from a little distance. It has been suggested that heat generated by rotting nest material assists incubation. The eggs are biconical in shape, thicker at the middle and tapering towards both ends. They are usually quickly covered with a layer of moist nest material by the bird when it leaves the nest, and during incubation become heavily stained brown or buff. The young are precocial, their down patterned in stripes. They follow the adults in the water, and may be carried on the backs of swimming adults. They are fed on fish and insects, and given feathers to help form pellets for casting up fishbones. Adults usually divide the brood between them.

Least Grebe (*Tachybaptus dominicus*)   Figure 10, Plate 18
Resident in southernmost Texas on lakes and pools of any size, and on quiet rivers and streams. Nest in water often several feet deep, anchored to growing plants, among tall water plants or in the open.
Nest: A mound of rotting aquatic vegetation with shallow nest hollow, anchored to plants. May be used for several successive broods. Building continues during incubation. Built by both. Foundation diameter: 14–24 in.; outside diameter at top of mound: 6–8 in.; height: 4–6 in. **Breeding season:** May nest at any time of year, usually mid-February to late September. 3–4 broods possible. **Eggs:** Usually 4–6, sometimes 2–7. Subelliptical to long elliptical or biconical. Smooth and white at first. 33×23 mm. **Incubation:** Eggs laid at 1–2-day intervals. Incubation by both sexes, beginning with first egg. 21 days. **Nestling:** Precocial and downy. Head mainly black with large tapering bare red patch on mid-crown, later covered with cinnamon down. Bare orange loral patch. Dark median stripe from chin, down throat to broaden on upper breast and divide to border white underside. Bordered on front of neck by conspicuous white stripes widening over throat to base of bill, with two narrow dark streaks from bill and lores. White stripe on side of neck turns upwards behind ear covert and terminates. Paired narrow white stripes on back of neck join on nape. Short white streak behind eye, and another above it, and tiny white median spot above bill. Pale neck stripes extend along brownish-black back. Bill pale with black tip and culmen, and broken black band near base. Irides dark brown. Feet gray. **Nestling period:** Young tended by both parents. Leave nest after hatching; usually carried on the back of one parent while the other brings food (insects). Nest used for resting and roosting in first two weeks. Young driven from nest but remain near and are visited by adults during incubation of next clutch. Time of first flight and full independence unknown.

Pied-billed Grebe (*Podilymbus podiceps*)   Figure 10, Plates 1, 18
Breeds on lakes and ponds, often very small, floodwaters, marshy borders of large lakes and rivers; exceptionally on quiet parts of estuaries. Nest usually floating in vegetation bordering open water.
Nest: A solid structure of rotting and green vegetation, with distinct nest hollow. Usually floating, anchored to growing plants; sometimes on the bottom in shallow water. Material added during incubation. Built by both sexes. Outside diameter:

Figure 9. Horned Grebe: c. 8–10 in. across; may be in open water or amid aquatic vegetation.

12 in.; height: 2–4 in. **Breeding season:** Begins about mid-March in south to mid-May in north. (In southern Florida it may nest throughout the year.) Single or double-brooded. **Eggs:** Usually 4–7, sometimes 2–10. Elliptical to subelliptical. Smooth and nonglossy. Almost white, tinted bluish or buff when first laid; later nest-stained. 44 × 30 mm. **Incubation:** Eggs laid daily, but occasional gap late in brood suggests more than 24-hour interval. Later clutches have longer intervals. Incubation by female at first, then shared, and by female only during period of hatching. 23 days. **Nestling:** Precocial and downy. Head pattern variable. Patches of bare yellowish skin on lores and crown; the latter soon replaced by rufous down. There is rufous color on hind-crown, loral region and eyestripe. Paired white stripes on back of neck meet at nape. Lateral white neck stripes meet on hind-crown, with extension to, or over, eyes. There is a variable double white chevron on forehead and fore-crown. Throat and sides of head are sparsely mottled with black, and thicker black speckling on lower neck and upper breast divides to border white underside. Four whitish stripes from the neck continue down the black back. Bill dark on culmen and tip with small dark marks around base. Iris dark brown. Feet and legs black becoming grayish or greenish. **Nestling period:** Young after hatching follow parents. While small they are carried for periods on parents' backs. Fed on insects at first. Later small fish. No information on fledging and age at independence.

Horned Grebe (*Podiceps auritus*)   Figures 9, 10, Plate 18

Breeds on large and small lakes and ponds, floodwaters, sloughs, wet marshes, and calmer river and stream backwaters; where vegetation is present. Often solitary, but with a number of nests near each other at times. Nests usually in small bays, with tall vegetation in the water providing cover.

Nest: A low mound of rotting aquatic vegetation built in shallow water, with a shallow nest hollow. Built by both sexes. Building continues during laying/incubation.

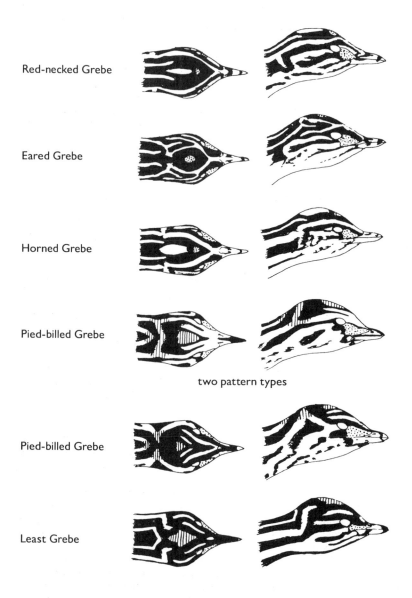

Red-necked Grebe

Eared Grebe

Horned Grebe

Pied-billed Grebe

two pattern types

Pied-billed Grebe

Least Grebe

Figure 10. Head patterns of grebe chicks from the side and from above. The pattern of throat and lower face tends to be variable, but the dorsal head pattern is usually diagnostic. Bare areas of colored skin are indicated by stippling.

Outside diameter: 12–14 in.; inside diameter: 4–6 in. **Breeding season:** Begins mid-May to July. Normally single-brooded, possibly occasional second brood. **Eggs:** Usually 4, occasionally 3–5, rarely 8; larger clutches in north of range. Long sub-elliptical or biconical. Smooth and white. 45 × 31 mm. **Incubation:** Eggs laid at *c.* daily intervals. Incubation by both sexes, with the female taking the major share; normally beginning about the third or fourth egg. Hatching spread over several days. 22–25 days. **Nestling:** Precocial, downy. Bare pinkish spot on crown. Longitudinally striped. Pale stripes on head and throat buff-tinted, on neck and back narrow and gray, and black stripes prominent, making appearance dark. Bill pinkish with two vertical black bands on upper mandible. Irides light gray. Feet dark gray. **Nestling period:** Little information. Young tended by both parents, but only a single adult sometimes apparent with older chicks. Estimated age at first flight 35–45 days.

Red-necked Grebe (*Podiceps grisegena*)   Figure 10, Plate 18

Breeds on freshwater lakes, lagoons, floodwaters, and calmer rivers; with some vegetation cover. Sometimes semi-colonial.
Nest: A low mound of rotting aquatic and waterside vegetation, floating and anchored by plants or built up in shallows with small hollow on top. Built by both sexes. Building continues during laying. Outside diameter: 24 in.; inside diameter: 6 in. **Breeding season:** Begins end of April to early June. Usually single-brooded. **Eggs:** Normally 4–5, more rarely 2–7. Variably shaped, long elliptical to subelliptical with biconical tendency. Smooth and white. 56 × 36 mm. **Incubation:** Eggs laid at 2-day intervals. Incubation by both parents, probably from first egg. 22–25 days. **Nestling:** Precocial, downy. Between white brow stripes crown is black, with small bare spot and narrow median white stripe. Pale neck stripes are dull and buffish, and dark stripes narrow on neck and poorly-defined on upper mantle. Back and sides of body unstriped, black stripes at side of neck broken about halfway, and pair of dark stripes bordering lower throat join to form a V. Center of underside white. Bare scarlet patches on lores and bare patch on crown. Irides olive-brown. Bill buffish with two vertical dark stripes. **Nestling period:** Estimated age at first flight 8–10 weeks. The brood and parents appear to remain together for a long period.

Eared Grebe (*Podiceps nigricollis*)   Figure 10, Plate 18

Breeds on open freshwater lakes, flood levels, pools, or river backwaters, with reed or vegetation cover. Usually nests colonially, often in close proximity. Nest usually in vegetation cover such as reeds.
Nest: A low mound of aquatic and waterside vegetation with a very shallow cup. Built by both sexes. Outside diameter: 12–14 in.; inside diameter: 5–6 in. **Breeding season:** Beginning from mid-April in south, late May and June in north. Double-brooded at times. **Eggs:** Normally 3–4, sometimes 5, rarely 2–8. Elliptical to sub-elliptical. Smooth and white at first. 44 × 30 mm. **Incubation:** Eggs laid at intervals of 24–28 hours. Incubated by both parents, beginning with first egg. 20–22 days. **Nestling:** Precocial and downy. With bare pink spots on lores and bare crown spot. The latter can change by flushing. Down darker than on other species, with stripes poorly-defined and broken. Upperparts, including back of head and neck, blackish; with narrow grayish, poorly-defined head and neck stripes and none on the back. Broken, irregular stripes on the sides of head and neck, a narrow inverted black V on sides of chin. Occasional dark central chin streak. Center of underside white, sides blackish with white flecks. Bill pinkish-flesh-colored or gray with two narrow black vertical bands, tip white. Feet gray, becoming red on lobe edges. Irides dark brown. **Nestling period:** Young first tended by both parents, later the adults divide brood between them. Young feed themselves at 2 weeks, independent at 3 weeks. Age at first flight 45 days.

Western Grebe (*Aechmophorus occidentalis*)   Figure 11, Plate 18

Breeds on lakes and in sheltered inlets and bays of the coast. Nest built in tall plants, tule and reeds, growing in water on the edge of large stretches of open water. Breeds in colonies that may be large, with hundreds of nests at times, all fairly close together. Nests on dry land where water has receded after breeding began.

Nest: A solid mound of rotten vegetation, built up from the bottom in shallow water, or floating, anchored to plants, in deep water. Usually well concealed by growing plants. Outside diameter: 18–25 in.; inside diameter: 7–9 in. **Breeding season:** Begins early June. Usually ends by late August. Single-brooded. **Eggs:** Usually 3–4. Long elliptical to subelliptical. Smooth but not glossy. Greenish or buffish when first laid, becoming white, then nest-stained. 58 × 39 mm. **Incubation:** Eggs laid at daily intervals. Incubation by both sexes beginning with the first egg. 23 days. **Nestling:** Precocial and downy. Triangular bare spot on crown orange, becoming red during excitement; bare loral spot orange. Color of down almost uniform; dull gray above, pale gray to whitish below and on face. Faint indication of pattern visible on close examination. Bill black. Legs and feet dark gray with greenish lobes. Identical to Clark's Grebe at hatching, though by 10–15 days a black crown color begins to show. **Nestling period:** Young leave nest at hatching, carried on parents' back and tended by both parents. At nests on dry land young are transported to water under wings of female. First flight at 9–11 weeks.

Clark's Grebe (*Aechmophorus clarkii*)

Breeds on lakes and in sheltered inlets and bays of the coast. Nest built in tall plants, tule, and reeds, growing in water on the edge of large stretches of open water. Breeds in colonies that may be large, with hundreds of nests at times, all fairly close together. Nests on dry land where water has receded after breeding began.

Nest: A solid mound of rotten vegetation, built up from the bottom in shallow water, or floating, anchored to plants, in deep water. Usually well concealed by growing plants. **Breeding season:** May begin mid-May. Usually ends by late August. **Eggs:** Usually 3–4. Long elliptical to subelliptical. Smooth but not glossy. Greenish or buffish when first laid, becoming white, then nest-stained. 58 × 39 mm. **Incubation:**

Figure 11. Western Grebe: two downy young on the back of an adult; black crown color can be visible by 10–15 days of age.

Eggs laid at daily intervals. Incubation by both sexes beginning with the first egg. 23 days. **Nestling:** Like Western Grebe at hatching, though feet pink in some individuals, and between 20–50 days feathering appears snow white. **Nestling period:** Young leave nest at hatching, carried on parents' back and tended by both parents. At nests on dry land young are transported to water under wings of female. No information on later part of nestling period.

Shearwaters (Procellariidae)

Northern Fulmar (Fulmarus glacialis)   Plates I, 17
Breeds on cliffs with suitable ledges, or on similar sites on rock outcrops or cliff at times some miles from the sea. More rarely on level tops of cliff stacks, or islands, or level ground on the shore, preferring a slight rise but needing some shelter at the site. **Nest:** A bare rock ledge or slight hollow in a softer substrate. The hollow may contain a few small stems or fragments. **Breeding season:** Mid- to late May, until late September, but adults may be present on the breeding ledges at intervals from November onwards. Single-brooded, with no replacements. **Eggs:** Usually 1, rarely 2 reported. Usually subelliptical. Dull white with a slightly rough texture. 74 × 50 mm. **Incubation:** By both adults in spells of about 4–5 days. 55–57 days. **Nestling:** Altricial and downy. Down long and thick, short and close on crown and chin. In first down, head, neck and underparts white, with a triangular pale blue-gray vent patch. Upperparts pale blue-gray. In second down upperparts are darker gray; and head, chin and throat become a similar gray; and white breast and underside are slightly tinted gray. Bill and legs gray at first, turning black in first week. **Nestling period:** Young brooded, and fed usually once a day at first but at longer intervals later, both parents taking part. The chick can eject oil, as adults do, from the moment of hatching onwards; and at first even the parents must approach with caution. 46–51 days in nest.

Manx Shearwater (Puffinus puffinus)
Breeds in small numbers in Newfoundland on offshore islands or mainland cliff slopes, in turf slopes or rocky screes and boulders. Elsewhere it may breed in colonies, sometimes very large.
Nest: A burrow in turf or soil or a natural crevice among rocks. Burrow excavated by both sexes and usually over 3 ft. long, but sometimes only half that length. Usually some material, plants and feathers present. **Breeding season:** In northwestern Europe begins early May. Single-brooded. **Eggs:** Only one. Subelliptical to oval. White, non-glossy. 61 × 42 mm. **Incubation:** By both sexes, in spells of 1–4 days, more rarely 5–6. Sitting bird apparently fed by mate, at night, 52–54 days. **Nestling:** Altricial and downy. Down thick, soft and long over most of bird; shorter on lores, chin, and around eyes. First down dull brown to gray-brown. A broad grayish-white band from chin down to center breast then dividing down either side of belly. Mid-belly and other parts gray-brown. Second down darker but similar to first. **Nestling period:** Brooded for first week, then only fed nightly by parents. Parents desert at about 59–62 days; chick remaining in burrow for c. 14 days more before leaving.

Storm-Petrels (Hydrobatidae)

Small seabirds with poor powers of movement on land, and reluctant to come to land. Nest in a burrow or natural crevice on island, mainland shore, or mountain, coming to site only by night. Often colonial nesters. Nest material very variable in quantity; accumulated at mouth of burrow by sideways-throwing and sideways-building and gradually moved down burrow. They produce only a single egg, not replaced if lost; and incubate in long spells, sometimes continuously for several days at a time. There may be long intervals between feeds for the young. The nestlings are downy, with usually two successive down coats, one attached to the tips of the next, which in turn is attached to tips of first feathers. They become very fat, larger, and heavier than the adults. They take regurgitated food from the bill of the parent, and they are usually finally deserted by the parents, and remain in the nest, emerging at night to exercise as the feathers grow and losing weight during this period. They usually leave for sea alone at night.

Fork-tailed Storm-Petrel (*Oceanodroma furcata*)

Breeds on offshore islands, on turf in the open or among trees; also among talus. Nests in colonies.
Nest: A burrow in turf, or rarely a deep natural hole among rocks. Some plant debris may accumulate at nest. Excavated by both sexes. Usually up to 3 ft. long and 18 in. below the surface, with an entrance 2½–3½ in. in diameter. **Breeding season:** Begins early to late June. Single-brooded. **Eggs:** Single egg. Elliptical to short subelliptical. White, nonglossy, often with wreath of tiny reddish specks around large end. 33 × 25 mm. **Incubation:** By both sexes, changing over at night. Egg may remain unattended for days at a time (contributing to long incubation period). 46–51 days. **Nestling:** Altricial and downy. First down blackish-brown above, gray below, with chin and lower face bare. Second down thicker, gray above, pale gray below. **Nestling period:** Chicks usually brooded 3–5 days; tended by both adults; begin exploring outside of burrow several nights before first flight, which is usually at 51–61 days.

Leach's Storm-Petrel (*Oceanodroma leucorhoa*)   Plates I, 18

Breeds on offshore islands on turf or rocky slopes, usually bare sites, but will use wooded islands. Nests in colonies.
Nest: A burrow excavated in soil, in soft ground, usually 1–3 ft. long and angled but in some instances up to 6 ft. with several pairs in separate nest-chambers; or natural cavity in fallen rocks, under boulders or buildings, or ruins. Burrow excavated by male in three nights and a day. Some plant debris accumulated in nest. **Breeding season:** Late May to October. Single-brooded. **Eggs:** Single egg. Elliptical to subelliptical, blunt-ended. White; non-glossy; usually with a zone of fine reddish spots at the larger end. 33 × 24 mm. **Incubation:** By both sexes, each taking an unbroken spell of about 4–6 days, changing at night. 41–42 days. **Nestling:** Altricial and downy. First down bluish-gray, long and soft, slightly paler on underside. Around eyes, lores, chin, and spot on hind-crown nearly bare. Replaced by second down, blackish and as long as first, and a little thicker on more exposed part. Skin around eyes blue-gray. Bill pale with black tip, darkening in first fortnight. Legs and feet gray or dull pinkish-flesh-colored. **Nestling period:** Eyes closed when first hatched. Brooded by one parent for first 5 days, then tended at irregular intervals. Eyes open at *c.* 15 days. Deserted when large and fat at *c.* 40 days. Lives on fat reserve and exercises at night, leaving for sea at 63–70 days.

Ashy Storm-Petrel (*Oceanodroma homochroa*)

Breeds on offshore islands in fallen rocks, rock walls, or burrows along California coast. Nests in colonies.
Nest: A natural cavity among piled rocks or a burrow. Occasionally a lining of plant debris present. **Breeding season:** Apparently prolonged. Eggs found from mid-May to mid-August. Nestlings found into December. Single-brooded, though may replace egg. **Eggs:** Single egg. Elliptical to short subelliptical. White, non-glossy, often with

a wreath of tiny reddish-brown specks around large end. 30 × 23 mm. **Incubation:** Incubation by both sexes, changing over at night. 42–59 days. **Nestling:** Altricial and downy. Both down coats brownish-gray. **Nestling period:** Young do not leave until fully feathered. The wide range is from 66 to 119 days.

Black Storm-Petrel (Oceanodroma melania)
Breeds in vicinity of Santa Barbara Island, California, in rocky cliff faces.
Nest: On ground, in cracks under boulders, in rock crevices or in abandoned burrows (about 3 ft. in length) of other species (often those of Cassin's Auklet). Occasionally some lining, but usually no materials used. **Breeding season:** Breeds May to December. **Eggs:** One egg. Elliptical to subelliptical. Dull white, sometimes with wreath of dark reddish or lavender spots at larger end. 37 × 27 mm. **Incubation period:** No information. **Nestling:** Altricial and downy. Long, thick, grayish-brown down, slightly darker above than below. **Nestling period:** No information.

Boobies and Gannets (Sulidae)

Masked Booby (Sula dactylatra)
Has nested on Florida's Dry Tortugas on a sandy island. Usually nests in island colonies in tropical waters.
Nest: A shallow scrape on the ground, cleared of twigs. **Breeding season:** Begins as early as January. **Eggs:** Usually 2, sometimes 1. Oval to long subelliptical. Chalky, pale-blue or white. 66 × 45 mm. **Incubation:** By both adults for about 43 days. **Nestling:** Altricial, with sparse yellowish-white down over gray, sometimes slightly pinkish skin. Bill and feet are gray. By three weeks bird is down-covered. **Nestling period:** Although 2 eggs usually hatch, seldom is more than a single young reared. Chick brooded continuously by both adults until it is nearly a month old, then left alone for long periods while parents are foraging. Young first fly at 115–120 days; cared for 30–60 days post-fledging.

Northern Gannet (Morus bassanus)   Plates I, 17
Breeds mainly on islands, usually with steep cliffs, nesting on the more level top or upper slopes, more rarely on large cliff ledges of islands or coasts. In colonies, often very large, with nests a bill-stab apart.
Nest: A rounded mound of material, mostly seaweed, but plants, feathers and other debris also used. Relieving birds may bring in seaweed during incubation period and this is added to heap by both birds with elaborate ceremony. Shallow nest hollow on top. Larger nests are up to 18 in. in diameter and 5 in. high. **Breeding season:** Normally from early April, but May farther north in range. Single-brooded. **Eggs:** Usually 1, very rarely 2. Long subelliptical. Dull chalky-white outer layer of irregular thickness, in places showing the bluish shell beneath. Outer layer may become stained buff or brown, and may flake away to reveal the underlying shell. 82 × 49 mm. **Incubation:** By both sexes. There are no brood patches and egg is covered by webs of feet, one over the other, then the bird resting on top. 43–45 days. **Nestling:** Altricial and downy. Skin black. At first sparsely covered with short pale creamy-white down tapering to hair-like tips. This is replaced by longer white down, woolly in appearance which spreads over the whole body but is short on throat and sparse around base of bill, eyes, and on forehead. Bill grayish. Irides dark brown. Legs and feet dark gray. **Nestling period:** Young fed by both parents, taking regurgitated food from inside the gullet. Tended for 13 weeks, then neglected for about 10 days before leaving for the sea. At sea cannot fly until after c. 1 week.

Pelicans (*Pelecanidae*)

American White Pelican (*Pelecanus erythrorhynchos*)　　　　Plate 19

Breeds on low, preferably bare, islands, in large shallow lakes. Also on islands in shallow coastal areas of Texas. Nests in colonies.

Nest: Usually a large mound of earth and debris, 2–3 ft. across and *c.* 1 ft. high, with a central, unlined hollow. Sometimes just a slight depression in the ground. Occasionally nests on floating tule island. Built by both over 3–5 days. *Breeding season:* Begins early April in south to late May or early June in north. Usually ends by late August. *Eggs:* Usually 2, sometimes 1. Elliptical to long subelliptical. Dull white with thick uneven chalky layer outside, becoming scratched and stained. 87 × 56 mm. *Incubation:* Incubation by both sexes. 29–36 days. *Nestling:* Semi-altricial. Naked and pinkish-flesh-colored at hatching, but covered with thick white down within 10 days. Pouch and bill grayish-white. Irides white. Feet pale yellow. *Nestling period:* Young hatch at intervals and differ in size. Tended by both parents. Brooded at nest for 2–3 weeks and fed mainly on liquid food. Can stand up at 3 weeks. Subsequently they leave and huddle in groups visited by adults for feeding only. Fly at *c.* 7–10 weeks.

Brown Pelican (*Pelecanus occidentalis*)　　　　Plates 1, 19

Breeds usually on small coastal islands. Nest on the ground or less frequently on bushes or low trees (e.g., mangroves).

Nest: The structure depends on material available nearby. May be a scrape with rim of soil and debris and some feathers for lining, or a similar structure built into a large mound; or a more elaborate platform of sticks woven into branches and heaped with sticks, reeds, straw, and grass. Male brings material, female builds. Outside diameter: 18–24 in.; height: 4–5 in., sometimes to 10 in. *Breeding season:* Variable in different years and different colonies; but on average may begin mainly March to April with some eggs from February to July. Single-brooded, but lost clutch replaced, possibly by single egg only. *Eggs:* Usually 3, sometimes 2. Long subelliptical. Dull white with thick uneven chalky layer becoming scratched and stained. 75 × 50 mm. *Incubation:* Eggs laid at intervals of 2 or more days. Incubation by both sexes. 28–30 days? *Nestling:* Semi-altricial. Naked, skin reddish, turning black. Coat of white down by 10–12 days. Pouch and bill pale gray. *Nestling period:* Young tended by both parents. Eyes open at 2 days. Leave nest at *c.* 6 weeks, huddle together if on ground, or clamber around arboreal nests. Fly at *c.* 9 weeks, but continue to be fed by parents. Age at independence unknown.

Cormorants (*Phalacrocoracidae*)

Fish-eating birds of sea-coasts and fresh waters, nesting on ledges, trees, bushes, or on the ground. Coastal nests may be simple seaweed heaps with hollow tops, but at inland sites may be larger twig structures with finer linings. Material may be carried to the nest in flight from a distance. At change-over during incubation the incoming bird may bring nest material. Young birds take food by reaching well into the parent's gullet, or pick up disgorged food. Young regurgitate food if alarmed.

Great Cormorant (*Phalacrocorax carbo*)　　　　Figure 12, Plates 1, 18

Breeds on higher parts of rocky cliff ledges, on the ground on islands, or rarely in low trees. Usually nests colonially.

Nest: On sea-coasts and offshore islands a heap of seaweed and sticks; sometimes a

Figure 12. Great Cormorant: left, stick nest (inland site), c. 2 ft. across; right, seaweed nest (coastal site), c. 1½–2 ft. across.

more solid structure of sticks, lined with long leaves, grasses, or water plants. Various other debris may be incorporated. Male brings most of material while female builds. Outside diameter: 20–24 in., sometimes to 36 in.; height: 3–4 in., sometimes to 12 in. **Breeding season:** Beginning early April in south, to early June in north. Single-brooded. **Eggs:** Usually 3–4, sometimes 5, rarely 6. Subelliptical. Pale blue shell with an uneven chalky-white outer layer, mostly concealing undershell, but becoming scratched and stained. 65 × 40 mm. **Incubation:** Eggs laid at about 2-day intervals. Sitting usually begins with the first egg, but serious incubation not until most are laid. By both sexes. 28–29 days. **Nestling:** Altricial. Naked at first with blackish-brown skin, but down appears within a week. Thick, dark brown down, blacker on head and neck, basally pale. Sparse on throat. Absent around eyes, and on lores and chin. Bill pale-flesh-colored, darkening later. **Nestling period:** Young tended by both adults. Eyes closed for first 4–5 days. In very hot weather adults may bring water to the chicks. Young remain in nest for c. 5 weeks but can leave and return when younger. They are fledged at 50–60 days, but take 11–12 weeks to become independent. Young regurgitate food if alarmed.

Double-crested Cormorant (*Phalacrocorax auritus*)   Plate 18

Usually breeds on larger water on small islands or islets, isolated rocks or trees standing in water; or in trees in remote swamps, or on cliff ledges overlooking water. 6–150 ft. up. Usually nests colonially.

Nest: A structure of twigs, plant debris and various coarse rubbish, with a finer lining. Nests thin and shallow in first year. Structure will be very modest if on ground, larger if in tree. Relined and used in subsequent seasons. Foundation built by male, which then brings material while female builds in 4 days. Male adds material throughout nesting. Outside diameter: 24 in.; inside diameter: 9 in.; depth: 4–6 in.; height: 4–9 in. **Breeding season:** Variable in different years and different seasons. In general begins early March in south to mid-June in north, but eggs recorded in Florida from late December to late October. Single-brooded, but lost clutch may be replaced. **Eggs:** Usually 3–4, sometimes 2–7, exceptionally 9, but possibly from two birds. Long subelliptical. Pale blue shell with uneven chalky outer layer, becoming stained. 51 × 38 mm. **Incubation:** By both sexes, beginning with third egg, or occasionally earlier. 25–29 days. **Nestling:** Altricial and naked on hatching. Skin brownish turning blackish-purple. Thick, short black woolly down begins to appear at 6 days, complete by 14 days. **Nestling period:** Eggs hatch over 2–7 days. Young tended by both parents. Eyes open at 4–5 days. Young active by 9–10 days. At 14 days not brooded but sometimes shaded. Feathering begins at 16 days, complete at 6–7 weeks. At 3–4 weeks young wander from nest but return to be fed. Fly at 5–6 weeks but can dive before this. After 7 weeks can accompany adults. Independent at 10 weeks.

Neotropic Cormorant (*Phalacrocorax brasilianus*)   Plate 18

Breeds by freshwater lakes and ponds, and on coastal islands. Nests usually in trees or bushes growing in water, or on bare ground or rocks. 3–20 ft. up. Nests in colonies.

Nest: A rough cup or bulkier structure of small sticks, lined with stems and coarse grass. Male brings material, female builds. Outside diameter: 15 in.; height: 4–6 in. **Breeding season:** Reported nesting 11 months of the year, but concentrated May–August. Single-brooded? **Eggs:** Usually 4, sometimes 3–6. Long subelliptical. Pale blue shell with uneven chalky outer layer, becoming stained. 55 × 34 mm. **Incubation:** Little information. *c.* 25 days. **Nestling:** Altricial and naked at hatching. Skin blackish-gray. Later covered with blackish down. **Nestling period:** Young hatch over several days and differ in size. Tended by both parents. Age at independence estimated at *c.* 84 days.

Brandt's Cormorant (*Phalacrocorax penicillatus*)   Plate 18

Breeds on offshore, rocky islands. Nest on the ground, usually on a slope towards the top of an island or ridge, avoiding perpendicular cliffs. Nests colonially, often in company with other cormorant species and seabirds.

Nest: A circular drum, made mostly of seaweed, sometimes with grass or moss, or exceptionally sticks. Built by both sexes, male bringing most material and female building. Material brought throughout incubation period. May be re-used in subsequent season. Outside diameter: 19–22 in.; inside diameter: 10 in.; depth: 4 in.; height: 5½–7 in. **Breeding season:** Begins late March in south to early May in north. Single-brooded. **Eggs:** Usually 4, sometimes 3–6. Long subelliptical. Shell pale blue with uneven chalky outer layer becoming stained. 61 × 38 mm. **Incubation:** By both sexes; beginning with first egg? 30? days. **Nestling:** Altricial. Hatched naked, with black skin. Later covered with down, gray and paler on underside, mottled white on underside and wings. **Nestling period:** Tended by both adults. Little further information.

Pelagic Cormorant (*Phalacrocorax pelagicus*)   Plate 18
Breeds on ledges and in niches of rocky coastal cliffs and islands, usually among the highest cliffs. Nests colonially.
Nest: A heap of seaweed, plant debris and other material if available. Built by both sexes, one (male?) collecting most of material. May be used in successive season (until 5–6 ft. high). **Breeding season:** Begins late April in south to early July in north. Single-brooded; but lost clutch replaced, although usually smaller, 2–3 eggs. **Eggs:** Usually 3–5, sometimes 7. Long subelliptical. Shell pale blue with uneven chalky outer layer, becoming nest-stained. 59 × 37 mm. **Incubation:** By both sexes, beginning with first egg. 26–28 days. **Nestling:** Altricial, hatched naked, skin blackish-gray. Later covered with down; sooty-gray with paler thighs. **Nestling period:** Tended by both adults. 49–62 days.

Red-faced Cormorant (*Phalacrocorax urile*)
Breeds on cliff ledges or structures overlooking water on islands from the Aleutians into southcoastal Alaska. Usually among the wider rock shelves projecting from low cliffs. Nest colonially.
Nest: Large heap of seaweed, plants, and shed feathers, and any nearby rubbish; with distinct nest hollow. The neatest of cormorant nests. Outside diameter: 16–20 in.; depth: 3 in.; height: 6 in. **Breeding season:** Begins mid-May. Single-brooded, but lost clutch replaced. **Eggs:** Usually 3–4. Long elliptical to long subelliptical. Shell pale blue with uneven chalky outer layer, becoming stained. 61 × 37 mm. **Incubation:** By both sexes. 21? days. **Nestling:** Altricial. Hatched naked with dark purplish-brown skin, white at base of lower mandible. Soon becomes downy. Down dusky-brown with grayish tips, mottled white on underside and with large white spot on outer thighs. **Nestling period:** Tended by both adults; thought to fly at 60 days.

Darters (*Anhingidae*)

Anhinga (*Anhinga anhinga*)   Plates 1, 18
Breeds by fresh, brackish, or salt water; still or slow-moving. Often in colonies and with colonies of other waterbirds. Nests in trees or bushes, 4–20 ft. up.
Nest: Built of twigs, or nest of other bird, such as a small egret, used. Nest lined with leafy twigs. Nests tend to be small. The male brings material which the female incorporates. Outside diameter: 18–20 in.; height: 6 in. **Breeding season:** Throughout the year in Florida. Shorter period beginning in April farther north. **Eggs:** 3–5, rarely 2. Subelliptical to long subelliptical. Shell bluish with an outer chalky-white layer of irregular thickness. 52 × 35 mm. **Incubation:** Eggs laid at intervals of 1–2 days. Usually both sexes incubate. Rare instances of male incubating and rearing alone. 25–28 days. **Nestling:** Altricial and naked. Skin yellowish-buff. Rapid growth of thick, short down, from gray to buff-brown to white. Irides dark. Bill dark. Legs and feet yellowish-buff. **Nestling period:** Both sexes tend young. After 2 weeks young will leave nest if disturbed and try to return later. Young regurgitate food if alarmed.

Frigatebirds (*Fregatidae*)

Magnificent Frigatebird (*Fregata magnificens*)
Breeds colonially on Dry Tortugas off south Florida and previously on Marquesas Keys, on top of low bushes or mangroves, at times on ground, or in taller trees.

Nest: A loosely built, frail platform of sticks and twigs, lined occasionally with dry grasses. Material collected by male; nest built mainly by female. Outside diameter: 10–15 in. **Breeding season:** May begin mid-September to late May, but probably more likely to begin between February and May. Single-brooded. **Eggs:** Normally 1, rarely 2. Elliptical to subelliptical. Dull white and thin-shelled. 68 × 46 mm. **Incubation:** By both sexes, about 50 days. **Nestling:** Altricial and naked. Soon the nestling acquires white down. **Nestling period:** Brooded by both. Fed by both adults. Fully feathered at 140 days, but unable to fly until 149–207 days after hatching. Young fed by female for an additional 4 months.

Bitterns and Herons (Ardeidae)

Long-legged, long-billed wading birds; rather awkward at perching in trees. In spite of this, nests are often in trees or bushes. In such sites they are of twigs; while ground nests in reedbeds are of reeds. The twig nests are often thin, but are added to annually and may become very large. There is little lining. Nest-building is simple, consisting largely of laying the twig on the existing structure and working it in with lateral quivering bill movements. The male usually brings twigs to the female on the nest, and she builds them in, twig presentation being accompanied by some ritual display. The young are downy, with bristling down on the crown, giving a typical shock-headed appearance. Adults bring food in the crop and are induced to disgorge it by the young seizing the bill of the adult in its bill. The adult regurgitates and the young may take the food directly from the parents' bill or, particularly in the case of larger items, and when the young are larger, will pick up disgorged food from the nest. The young disgorge food when alarmed.

American Bittern (Botaurus lentiginosus)   Plates 2, 20
Breeds in marshy areas of tall vegetation – cattails, bulrushes, or reeds; sometimes in wet swales; but has also bred in drier areas of tall grasses. Will use similar habitats on brackish or tidal marshes. Nest on the ground or raised slightly on platform of thick vegetation, usually 3–8 in. above water. Nests singly, but males may be polygamous, with several females nesting separately within territory.
Nest: A pile of reeds, sedges, or similar plant material available nearby. Pile 6–10 in. high and 12–16 in. across. Built by female alone. **Breeding season:** Variable. Usually begins late April to May and ends by late July. Apparently single-brooded. **Eggs:** Usually 2–5. Elliptical to short subelliptical. Buffish-brown to deep olive-buff. Smooth or slightly glossy. 49 × 37 mm. **Incubation:** First four eggs laid at daily intervals, with 2-day interval for the fifth. Incubation by female alone, beginning with first egg. 24–29 days. **Nestling:** Semi-altricial and downy. Down yellowish-olive, darker above. Bill pinkish-flesh-colored with dark tip. Eyes light olive. **Nestling period:** Young tended by female only. Eggs hatch over several days and young differ in size. Young leave nest after c. 2 weeks and are tended nearby. Age at first flight and at independence not known.

Least Bittern (Ixobrychus exilis)   Figure 13, Plates 2, 20
Breeds in freshwater marshes. Nest usually in dense stand of Typha or Scirpus, or similar growth; about a foot above water and near open water. Exceptionally in a low bush or tree, or on the old nest of another bird. Usually nests singly, but several adjacent pairs may occur in suitable areas.
Nest: Usually on a base of dried plants bent down, or natural base. Of dead and live stems forming a platform (with a radiating appearance) with shallow hollow, round to oval, c. 6–10 in. across and 5–6 in. high. Material may radiate from nest center.

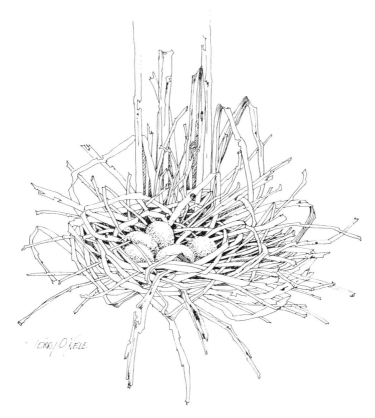

Figure 13. Least Bittern: c. 6–10 in. across; platform of radiating dried plants found among live stalks.

Both sexes build, but the male is more active. ***Breeding season:*** Variable over the wide range. Begins about mid-March in south, to early June in the north of range. Usually ends by late July. Probably double-brooded. ***Eggs:*** Usually 4–5, rarely up to 7. Elliptical. Pale bluish to pale greenish. Smooth and non-glossy. 31 × 24 mm. ***Incubation:*** Eggs usually laid at daily interval. Incubation by both sexes, beginning with second egg. 16–19 days. ***Nestling:*** Semi-altricial and downy. Down long; buff above and white below. Bill and legs pink; eyes dark. ***Nestling period:*** Young tended by both parents. They show bittern alarm posture at 3–4 days. Can leave nest at 4–5 days, but return to be fed for up to 3½ weeks. Early moves may be due to disturbance. Normally leaves at *c.* 13–15 days. First flight at 25 days.

Great Blue Heron (*Ardea herodias* – Includes Great White Heron,
A. h. occidentalis)   Plates 2, 19
Breeds by fresh or salt water. Nests usually built in tall trees, or sometimes in bushes, on ledges of cliffs or rock outcrops, or on the ground in tule beds or elsewhere. Up to 130 ft. Great White Heron usually in mangrove trees. Nests colonially.
Nest: A large flat platform of twigs. Thin and small when newly built, but old nests are added to seasonally, becoming very bulky. Nest hollow lined with leaves, grass,

fine twigs, and other plant material. Male brings material; female builds over 3–14 days. Outside diameter: 25–40 in. **Breeding season:** Information is inadequate but breeding appears to begin in November to December in Florida. Very extended in Great White Heron. Elsewhere from early March to April. Usually ends by early July. Single-brooded. **Eggs:** Usually 4, sometimes 3–7. Oval to long oval, long elliptical or subelliptical. Pale greenish-blue. Smooth or slightly rough, and non-glossy. 64 × 45 mm. **Incubation:** By both sexes. 25–29 days. **Nestling:** Semi-altricial and downy. Down on upperparts and flanks long, and on the crown down has long bristle-like tips, and stands up to produce a bristling wig. It is sparser on sides of back and mid-belly; absent around the eyes and on lores, chin, throat, and back of neck. Upperparts dark grayish-brown, side pale gray, underside white. Crown is smoky-gray with fine white tips. Bill relatively short and blunt at first. On Great White Heron down is white. **Nestling period:** Young tended by both parents. Always one adult present for first 3–4 weeks. Young fly first at c. 60 days, leave nest at 64–90 days.

Great Egret (Ardea alba)   Plates 2, 20
Breeds near fresh or salt water, in woodlands, and thickets. Nests in trees of woodland and cypress swamps, often high up (60–80 ft. recorded, but 15–40 ft. more usual); in mangroves or nearby trees on saltwater keys; in willow thickets of glades, or waterside thickets of rivers and streams; and in Texas in tule and the scrub of dry islands. Nests singly or in colonies of varying size, large at times, often with other heron species or with Wood Storks.
Nest: A large flat platform (with a diameter of about 2 ft.) or bulkier re-used structure, similar to but thinner and frailer than those of Great Blue Heron. Of sticks, twigs and tule stems; lined with smaller twigs and plant material. Building or repair begun by male, later male brings material and female builds. **Breeding season:** In general may begin in late December in Florida, to mid-April in north of range; but varies in different years, probably with weather or water levels. Probably single-brooded. **Eggs:** Usually 4–5, sometimes 3–6. Elliptical to subelliptical. Pale greenish-blue. Smooth and non-glossy. 56 × 41 mm. **Incubation:** By both sexes, 23–26 days. **Nestling:** Semi-altricial and downy. Down long and white with fine silky tips. Stiffer on crown producing crest; sparse on neck and underparts, absent from around eyes, on lores, chin, throat, back of neck, and central upper breast. Bill pink on hatching, then yellow. Legs and feet gray-green, becoming gray. Bare facial skin blue-gray, becoming yellow. Irides off-white. **Nestling period:** Both parents tend young. Young begin feathering at one week, mostly complete by 4–5 weeks. At 3 weeks leave nest for branches and return to be fed. By fourth week fed away from nest. Fly short distances by 5 weeks, fly with adults at 6–8 weeks.

Snowy Egret (Egretta thula)   Figure 14, Plate 20
Breeds in wide range of sites by fresh or salt water. Nests in trees, including cedar swamp and mangroves, in willows and buttonbush, in Prickly Pear and Huisache on dry Texas islands, and in Phragmites reeds, tule, and bulrushes in more open marshes. Nests in trees may be up to 30 ft. from ground, but usually at 5–10 ft. Very sociable, nesting in colonies, at times in thousands, and often with other heron species.
Nest: A shallow structure, elliptical and rather flat; of thin twigs, heavier in the foundations and thin in the lining. Building begun by male, continued by female, male bringing material over 5–7 days. Outside diameter: 12–24 in. **Breeding season:** Commencement variable, but usually begins late March in south, to mid-May in north. Probably single-brooded. **Eggs:** Usually 3–4, sometimes up to 6. Elliptical. Greenish-blue. Smooth and non-glossy. (Very similar to the next two species). 43 × 32 mm. **Incubation:** Eggs laid on alternate days. Incubation by both sexes,

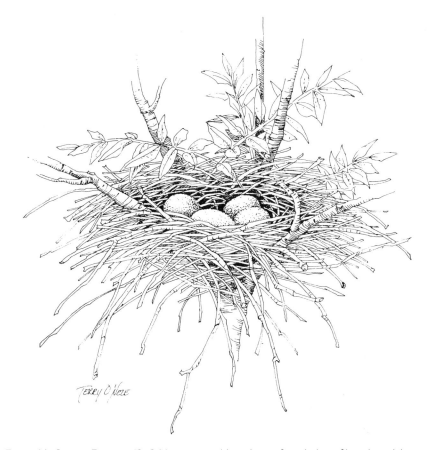

Figure 14. Snowy Egret: c. 12–24 in. across; thin twigs on foundation of heavier sticks.

beginning with first egg. 20–24 days. **Nestling:** Semi-altricial and downy. Down long and fine on head. Down white. Bill and feet pale yellow; skin light green. **Nestling period:** Young tended by both parents. Food dropped on to nest for first few days, later young grasp adult bill. Young leave nest for branches at 3–4 weeks.

Little Blue Heron (*Egretta caerulea*)   Plate 20
Breeds by fresh, brackish or salt water; in open by lakes, pools, marshes, or streams, and by overgrown woodland pools and dense Florida hummocks. Nest in trees, usually low down, or in shrubs. 8–15 ft. up. Nests colonially, often with other species where it tends to be on outskirts of colony.
Nest: Variable in shape and size, usually flat and elliptical with slight central hollow. Usually of sticks, lined with finer twigs, but some reeds and grass may be present. Female builds and male brings material over 3–5 days. Outside diameter: 16–20 in.; height: 6–8 in. **Breeding season:** Begins late March to early April in south, to mid-April farther north. Usually ends by mid-September. Single-brooded. **Eggs:** Usually 3–5, rarely 2–6. Elliptical to subelliptical. Pale greenish-blue. Smooth and

non-glossy. (Very similar to eggs of Snowy Egret and Tricolored Heron.) 45 × 33 mm. **Incubation:** Eggs usually laid on alternate days. Incubation by both sexes. 22–24 days. **Nestling:** Semi-altricial and downy. Down sparse on underside, longer on top of head. On hatching, down very pale gray with tawny tips on head, later down white. Bill pinkish-gray, becoming yellow. Mouth pale orange. Legs and feet gray, becoming greenish-yellow. Irides pale gray to white. **Nestling period:** Hatching takes 3–5 days. Regurgitated food dropped in nest at first; then young take bill of parent. Begins feathering by 1 week, mostly feathered by 12 days. Young can leave nest by 12 days. By 17 days young spend much time on branches near nest. Usually return for food, but parents will visit young on branches. By 30 days young make short flights. Independent probably by 35–49 days.

Tricolored Heron (*Egretta tricolor*)   Plates 2, 20

Breeds mainly near salt water. Nest 2–12 ft. up in mangrove or buttonwood, in thickets of tidal marshes, willow thickets or bulrushes of fresh marshes; on Texas island sites in dry thickets, large cane and prickly pear; and on bare coastal islands in grasses and herbage. Highly sociable, nesting in colonies, sometimes of thousands; often with other heron species.

Nest: A shallow structure, round or oval and *c.* 1–1½ ft. across, with a hollow several inches deep; of slender twigs with a lining of finer twigs, grass, and plant stems. Female does most of building, male bringing material. **Breeding season:** Begin mid-March in the south to early May in the north. Single-brooded. **Eggs:** Usually 3–4, sometimes up to 7. Usually elliptical. Greenish-blue. Smooth and non-glossy. (Very similar to previous two species.) 45 × 33 mm. **Incubation:** By both sexes. 21–25 days. **Nestling:** Semi-altricial and downy. At hatching down dark gray on head, neck, back and wings, with longer tawny down on head, and white on foreneck, underside, and thighs. Later head down brownish-red, and neck and back brownish-gray. Bill dark gray. Legs and feet pinkish-gray becoming gray-green. Irides off-white. **Nestling period:** Young tended by both parents. Feathering begins at 4–5 days, complete at *c.* 4 weeks. Young begin to climb from nest at 11–17 days but still fed on nest. By 24 days fed away from nest and tend to form social groups with young of their own species.

Reddish Egret (*Egretta rufescens*)   Plate 20

Breeds in coastal areas by salt water, in mangroves or in drier thickets of coastal islands. Nests at heights of up to 15 ft., or on the ground. Nests in colonies where possible.

Nest: A platform of thin sticks, stems, roots, and similar material; with little or no lining. On the ground may be a more solid structure of dry grass with a deep nest hollow. Both sexes appear to collect material and build; building continues through egg-laying. Outside diameter: 12–26 in.; inside diameter: 10–12 in.; depth: 3–4 in.; height: 8–10 in. **Breeding season:** Usually occurs in late winter in Florida, and spring in Texas; but eggs have been found in both areas in early April. **Eggs:** Usually 3–4, rarely up to 7. Elliptical to short subelliptical. Pale greenish-blue. Smooth, non-glossy. 50 × 36 mm. **Incubation:** By both sexes. 25–26 days. **Nestling:** Semi-altricial and downy. Down long on top of head, sparse under body. Smoky gray on body, grayish cinnamon on head and neck. Legs, feet, and bill dark olive. **Nestling period:** Short flights can be made at 28 days, flies well at 46 days. Continues to be fed by both parents another 2–3 weeks.

Cattle Egret (*Bubulcus ibis*)   Plate 20

Breeds in a variety of sites, usually near water. Nest often in large trees, not necessarily by waterside; or in small trees or bushes, growing in water or reedbeds; or in dense

reedbeds or on small rocky islands. Usually 6–13 ft. up, but as high as 30 ft. up. Nests in colonies; often together with other small heron species. (Typically located lower than that of Little Blue Heron, but higher than Snowy Egret or Tricolored Heron.)
Nest: A shallow structure of varied material; twigs, sticks, dead reeds, or other handy vegetation. Smaller twigs are used for lining. Male usually brings material and female builds over 3–6 days. Building will continue through incubation. Outside diameter: 10–18 in.; height: 3–9 in. **Breeding season:** Variable, beginning late March to mid-April. Nesting usually synchronized within a colony. Usually ends by mid-September. Usually single-brooded. **Eggs:** Usually 4–5, rarely 3–6. Elliptical to subelliptical, usually blunt-ended. Smooth, non-glossy. Very pale blue or whitish-blue. (Usually the palest of the heron eggs.) 46 × 34 mm. **Incubation:** By both sexes. Intermittent incubation from the first egg. 21–25 days. **Nestling:** Semi-altricial and downy. Down white, with fine tips, stiff and upright on the crown. Bill and loral skin greenish-yellow. Legs and feet reddish buff. Irides yellowish-white. **Nestling period:** Young tended by both parents. Hatching interval produces variation in size of young in nest. Fly at 40 days and possibly not independent until *c.* 60 days.

Green Heron (*Butorides virescens*)   Figure 15, Plate 20

Breeds by water in many habitats; in marshes on tussocks, muskrat houses, or even duck blinds at varying heights in trees by fresh or salt water, including aerial roots of mangroves; in shrubs and thickets by water and along ditches, and in woods and orchards away from water. 10–30 ft. up, sometimes higher. Either solitary or in small groups.

Figure 15. Green Heron: c. 12–18 in. across; some nests may be much flimsier than this example.

Nest: Varies in structure from small flimsy platform when new, to bulky structure re-used in successive seasons. Of twigs, reeds, and vines, with lining absent or of similar but finer material. Male builds or relines nest and displays to attract female. Later male brings material and female builds. Building proceeds for *c.* 4 days before first egg is laid. Some material added until after hatching. Outside diameter: 8–12 in.; inside diameter: 4–5 in. **Breeding season:** Begins late April (earlier in south) to early May. Usually ends by late June. Often single-brooded, sometimes double-brooded. **Eggs:** Usually 4–5, sometimes 3–6. Elliptical to subelliptical. Pale greenish-blue or more green. Smooth, non-glossy. 38 × 29 mm. **Incubation:** First three eggs laid at 2-day intervals, others at one-day intervals. Incubation by both sexes. 19–21 days. **Nestling:** Semi-altricial and downy. Down thin, thicker on back and bushy on head. Smoky-gray, paler below. **Nestling period:** Young tended by both parents. Eyes open at hatching. Brooding continuous for first week. Young able to move about by third day and show bittern alarm posture at 5 days. Can climb by 1 week, and clamber and jump about in trees by 16–17 days. Fly at 21–23 days, and fly with adults at 25 days. Probably independent at 30–35 days.

Black-crowned Night-Heron (*Nycticorax nycticorax*)   Plates 2, 20
Breeds in a wide variety of sites near fresh, brackish, or salt water; in all types of trees, bushes, and thickets, from near ground level to *c.* 150 ft. up; and in marshes in *Phragmites*, cattails, grass tussocks, and *Scirpus*. Nests in colonies, often with herons or other waterbirds.
Nest: Variable, according to available material. Usually a platform with shallow hollow, of twigs, reeds, and similar material. Material often tends to radiate from nest center. Foundation usually heavier, with a finer lining. Male begins building, later brings material for female which builds but may also collect over 2–5 days. Outside diameter: 24 in.; height: to 18 in. **Breeding Season:** Variable. Beginning in winter in south Florida to early April in the north. Usually single-brooded. **Eggs:** 3–4, sometimes 5. Elliptical to subelliptical. Pale greenish-blue, sometimes more green, or wholly blue. Smooth and non-glossy. 53 × 37 mm. **Incubation:** Eggs laid at *c.* 2-day intervals. Incubation by both sexes, beginning with first egg. 24–26 days. **Nestling:** Semi-altricial and downy. Down sparse with long silky tips, stiff and bristly on crown, producing a crested appearance. Absent about eyes, on lores, chin, throat, lower hind-neck, and mid and side belly. Down rufous-brown above, with pale tips forming crest on head, and white on thighs. Later grayish-brown above, darker and more rufous on head and neck. Bill gray. Legs and feet gray-green. Irides grayish or greenish becoming amber. **Nestling period:** Young tended by both parents. Feathering begins at *c.* 12 days, complete in *c.* 4 weeks. Young begin to leave nest at 2–3 weeks, returning to be fed. By 4 weeks fed away from nest. Fly at 6 weeks.

Yellow-crowned Night-Heron (*Nyctanassa violacea*)   Plate 20
Breeds by salt and fresh water. Nests in mangroves or adjacent trees, and elsewhere in trees and bushes at varying heights from near ground level to over 50 ft. Nests singly or in colonies, often small, sometimes with other heron species.
Nest: Usually a stout structure of heavy twigs, lined with finer twigs, rootlets and sometimes leaves. Both adults help build and material is added until young are present. Outside diameter: 20–46 in. **Breeding season:** Variable. Usually begins about March in south to late April in north of range. Timing along Atlantic coast dependent on crab emergence. Probably ends by late July. Single-brooded. A lost clutch may be replaced. **Eggs:** Usually 2–4, sometimes up to 6. Elliptical. Pale greenish-blue. Smooth and non-glossy. (Very similar to previous species.) 51 × 37 mm. **Incubation:** By both sexes. *c.* 21–25 days. **Nestling:** Semi-altricial and downy. Down fine and grayish, forming conspicuous long crest on head. Bill brownish and greenish.

Leg, feet, and loral skin greenish-yellow. Irides deep yellow. **Nestling period:** Fed by both parents. Leave nest at 30–42 days.

Ibises and Spoonbills (*Threskiornithidae*)

Long-legged, long-billed wading birds. Able to perch in trees. Nest on the ground in marshes and reeds, or build nests in trees, the latter quite strongly and competently built although the birds are clumsy on perches. Twigs are fixed by insertion followed by a small lateral shake. The young feed by taking regurgitated food from the throat of adults. When ground nests are used, and possibly elsewhere, young tend to wander from the nest before they can fly.

White Ibis (*Eudocimus albus*)   Figure 16, Plate 19
Breeds near water, fresh, brackish or salt; nesting on low trees or shrubs growing in or by water, and in palmetto. Also nests farther west in prickly pear, and in *Scirpus*, or long grasses on the ground. Nests in colonies, often with herons and other water-birds. Nest sites tend to be low (though up to 15 ft.), and at times on ground of crowded tree colonies.
Nest: A platform of dead sticks, fresh twigs with leaves and other plant material from nearby. Usually some green leaves in the lining. More sturdy and deeply cupped than nest of most waders. Female does most of building but both sexes collect material. Outside diameter: 10–24 in. **Breeding season:** Variable, beginning late March to

Figure 16. White Ibis: c. 10–24 in. across; nest site tends to be low and size very variable.

mid-May, but eggs have been found in Florida up to mid-August. *Eggs:* Usually 3–4. Subelliptical to long subelliptical. Pale buffish, bluish or greenish, variably marked with speckling, spots and irregular blotches of light to dark brown, smaller markings fairly evenly distributed, but blotches, where present, sometimes concentrated at larger end. Smooth and non-glossy. 58 × 39 mm. *Incubation:* By both. Begins with completion of clutch. 21–23 days. *Nestling:* Semi-altricial and downy. Down on head, neck, upper breast and wing, but rest of body almost bare. Skin dull pink to gray. Black down on head; longer smoky-brown down on neck and wings. Narrow white line in front of eye. Facial skin grayish, and two pink gular patches. Bill pink with broad black bands at base, middle and tip; or only two bands. Irides light brown. Later bare parts grow a straggly woolly down; upper parts appear smoky-gray, underside white. *Nestling period:* Tended by both. Young leave nest at *c.* 3 weeks. Fly at *c.* 5 weeks.

Glossy Ibis *(Plegadis falcinellus)*   Plates 2, 19

Breeds by water, fresh, brackish, or salt; or in marshes. Up to 10 ft., on top of low trees and shrubs growing in water or on the ground in cordgrass (*Spartina*). Nests in colonies, often with herons or other waterbirds.

Nest: A substantial shallow structure of sticks, twigs, and dried plant material, with cupped and well-lined egg cavity. Built by both in *c.* 2 days, with the male adding considerably during incubation and nestling period. *Breeding season:* Begins March to late May. Single-brooded. *Eggs:* Usually 2–4, sometimes 1–5. Subelliptical. Dull blue or greenish-blue. Darker than heron eggs. 53 × 37 mm. *Incubation:* By both sexes, but mainly by female which sits at night and part of day. 21 days. *Nestling:* Semi-altricial and downy. Down long and sparse dull black with white patches on crown and white bars on throat; absent on lores. Bill pink with black bands at base, middle, and tip. Feet yellowish. *Nestling period:* Young tended by both parents. One parent always present for first 5 days. At 2 weeks young move out to ends of branches but return to nest to be fed. By 6 weeks young fed by parent away from nest, but can fly a little and feed themselves. At 7 weeks they accompany parents. At ground colonies it is likely that adults feed young other than their own once they have left nest.

White-faced Ibis *(Plegadis chihi)*

Breeds in sloughs and freshwater marshes; uncommon in salt marshes. Mainly in *Scirpus*, tule or *Phragmites*. Nests in colonies, often with herons or other waterbirds. Nest may be placed on floating vegetation, or supported up to 6 ft. above water.

Nest: A rather well-formed platform of old reeds, tules, twigs, and lined with grass. Built by both sexes over 2–10 days. *Breeding season:* Begins mid-April. Usually ends by mid-July. Single-brooded. *Eggs:* Usually 3 or 4, sometimes 2–7. Subelliptical. Deep greenish-blue, 51 × 36 mm. *Incubation:* By both sexes. 21–22 days. *Nestling:* Semi-altricial and downy. Dull black down with white patches on the back of crown. Face skin pink. Bill pale-flesh-color, black at the tip and at base, with black band at middle. Legs pink. *Nestling period:* Young tended by both parents. Young will leave nest at 10–12 days but unable to fly. At least 28 days (as much as 49 days) before first flight.

Roseate Spoonbill *(Ajaia ajaja)*   Plates 2, 19

Breeds in mangroves of Florida, and elsewhere uses trees by or in water if available; in bushy scrub of dry coastal islands in Texas. 6–15 ft. up. Sometimes in *Scirpus*, or on the ground in mixed colonies where tree sites are not available. Nests in colonies, often with herons or other waterbirds.

Nest: A bulky structure of sticks and twigs, with a lining of finer material such as leaves. Male brings material and female usually does the major share of the building. Outside diameter: 16 in.; inside diameter: 7 in.; depth: 2 in. **Breeding season:** May begin November in Florida, April in Texas. Single-brooded. Will replace lost clutch. **Eggs:** Usually 2–3, sometimes 4. Subelliptical. White, with fine speckling and numerous small smudged blotches of reddish-brown or light buffish-brown; larger markings often concentrated in a zone about the larger end. Shell with roughly granular surface. Non-glossy. 65 × 44 mm. **Incubation:** Eggs laid at 2–3-day intervals. Incubation by both sexes. 23–24 days. **Nestling:** Semi-altricial and downy. First down short and white. Bill, legs, and feet and bare skin black. After *c.* 1 week second down grows thicker, longer and woolly. Feet pink. **Nestling period:** Young tended by both parents. When older they begin to leave nest for branches, returning to be fed. They leave finally at 5–6 weeks, being fed nearby until *c.* 8 weeks, when they learn to fly and are progressively neglected by adults.

Storks (*Ciconiidae*)

Wood Stork (*Mycteria americana*)   Figure 17, Plates 2, 19
Breeds in trees by fresh or brackish water, usually in stands of trees growing in water. Prefers large cypress, but will also use smaller trees where necessary, including red mangroves and buttonwoods on creeks. Nests often close together and at varying heights from a few feet above water to tree-tops. Usually in tree-tops, 50–80 ft. up. Nests in colonies.
Nest: A rather thin platform of sticks with a lining of some finer twigs and leaves. Built by female, male bringing material over *c.* 3 days. Outside diameter: 18–36 in.;

Figure 17. Wood Stork: *c.* 18–36 in. across; often nesting in cypress trees.

height: 5 in. **Breeding season:** Variable; affected by altered hydrocycles. Usually beginning December to January. Single-brooded. **Eggs:** Usually 3–4, rarely 5. Elliptical to subelliptical. Creamy-white, with a finely granular surface. 68 × 47 mm. **Incubation:** Eggs laid at 1–2-day intervals. Incubation by both sexes, beginning with first egg. 28–32 days. **Nestling:** Semi-altricial. On hatching, naked, with coarse, hairy down on wings. By two weeks becomes covered with thick woolly white down. Skin whitish. Bill short and thick, yellow. Legs and feet very pale yellow. Irides and skin around eye pale bluish-white. **Nestling period:** Young tended by both parents. Unless weather is bad young brooded for first week only, but for first 5 weeks one parent always on guard against bands of non-breeding birds which destroy eggs and young. Parents bring and disgorge water over young on hot days. Young leave nest and make short flights at 50–55 days, but return to nest for feeding and roosting until 75 days old. Age of final independence unknown.

Swans, Geese, and Ducks (Anatidae)

Medium-sized to large waterfowl living and feeding mainly in the water and nesting at its edge. Nest among swans a large heap of plant material accumulated by sideways-throwing and sideways-building; among geese and ducks usually a scrape lined with down and breast feathers from the female. The location may be an open site or cavity, but material is usually accumulated by sideways-throwing and sideways-building (particularly among geese) or with the female sitting on the site pulling in and placing material; the male in the water with his back to her, passing material back for the female (among swans). The precocial, downy young are brooded on nest or shore. Young of swans and geese generally remain with adults until the next season; young of ducks are normally tended only by the female until independent.

Fulvous Whistling-Duck (Dendrocygna bicolor)   Plates 3, 23
Prefers more open areas but breeds in similar sites to the next species. Usually in tall vegetation such as tule, reeds, and grasses, in swampy places or by water; rarely in tree cavities. 4–30 ft. up.
Nest: The foundations usually consist of bent-down stems and other plant material from nearby may be added. No down lining. **Breeding season:** Begins early April. Period prolonged. Single-brooded. **Eggs:** 8–16. Often several females lay in same nest and large numbers may occur. Short elliptical to short subelliptical. White to creamy-white, and may become nest-stained to shades of buff. Smooth and non-glossy or slightly glossy, the surface finely pitted. 53 × 39 mm. **Incubation:** By both adults, the male possibly playing a major role. 28 days. **Nestling:** Precocial and downy. Small, long-necked and long-legged. Down very pale. Light grayish above and whitish below. A few individuals may be silver-gray and white. Pale gray stripe up hind-neck terminating at short lateral stripe to ear-covert, forming 'T' at back of head. White stripe from base of bill up to and around nape. Cap darker gray. White on hind edge of wing. Bill dark gray and legs dark olive. **Nestling period:** Young tended by both parents. Fly at 55–63 days.

Black-bellied Whistling-Duck (Dendrocygna autumnalis)   Plates 3, 23
Breeds in swampy or cultivated areas, and in woodland by lakes and ponds in southernmost Texas, southern Arizona, and central Florida. Nest in a cavity inside a tree, or in a large fork, or on the ground (e.g., ricefields), concealed in tall herbage such as grasses, reeds or bulrushes. 8–30 ft. (usually lower end). Will use nest-box. Not necessarily near water.

Nest: A platform of bent-down stems, with some nearby plant material where available. Tree nests are unlined. No down is present. Cavity depth of *c.* 2 ft. Entrance hole ranges from 4×5 in. to 7×12 in. *Breeding season:* Late April (in Texas) to mid-October, occasionally to late November. Will replace lost clutches. *Eggs:* Usually 8–12, sometimes up to 18. Short elliptical. Glossy or glossless, with a finely pitted surface. White to creamy-white. 52×39 mm. *Incubation:* By both sexes. 27–28 days. *Nestling:* Precocial and downy. Small, with long neck and legs. Down pattern conspicuous. Blackish-brown above and yellow (sometimes bright) below and on neck and face. A dark stripe up the hind-neck terminates at a narrow lateral band extending towards the bill. Above this a band of yellow from the base of the bill extending back to, and around the nape; cutting off a dark cap on which is a small pale forehead streak extending back to the eye. There is yellow on the sides of the breast, hind-edge of the wings, a rounded patch on the thigh, and another on each side of the lower back. Bill dark brownish-gray with paler lower mandible. Legs olive-yellow. *Nestling period:* The young are tended by both parents. Young fly at 2 months; both parents stay with young for 4 more months.

Tundra Swan (*Cygnus columbianus*)   Plate 21

Breeds on tundra near water, beginning while snow is still present. Nests usually built on an islet or at the water's edge, or as a floating mass in water, but land sites may be used before melting snow has surrounded them with water. Pairs nest singly. *Nest:* A conspicuous mound of moss, grass, dead leaves, and other plant material, with a distinct central hollow. Built by both sexes. Outside diameter (at base): *c.* 4–6 ft.; inside diameter: *c.* $1\frac{1}{2}$ ft.; height: *c.* 2 ft. *Breeding season:* Begins late May to June. Single-brooded. *Eggs:* Usually 5, sometimes 3–7. Clutch smaller in colder seasons. Subelliptical. Creamy-white. Smooth and slightly glossy with a finely granular texture. 107×68 mm. *Incubation:* Behavior as for Trumpeter Swan. 32 days. *Nestling:* Precocial and downy. Pale grayish-white with some indication of darker patterning; and white on underside. Bill flesh-pink with darker tip and edges. Down extends less far laterally than on Trumpeter Swan. Legs dull pink. *Nestling period:* Similar to that of Trumpeter Swan, though age of first flight unclear.

Whooper Swan (*Cygnus cygnus*)

Breeds in arctic and subarctic on lakes of varying size, or by other waters. In our area it is a very rare nester, found in the western Aleutians (and perhaps formerly in west Greenland). Nests usually built at water's edge on an islet or at a raised area. Pairs nest singly. Usual site may be used for a number of years. *Nest:* A conspicuous heap of moss, grass, dead leaves, and other plant material. Large white down tufts and small feathers present in nest hollow. Built by both sexes. Outside diameter (at base): 3–6½ ft.; height: 20–28 in.; depth: 2–8 in. *Breeding season:* Usually May to June, though may begin earlier due to early thaw. *Eggs:* Usually 5–6, occasionally 4–8. Subelliptical to long elliptical. Creamy-white, slightly glossy with a finely granular texture. 113×72 mm. *Incubation:* Eggs laid on alternate days. By female, beginning with completion of clutch, with male on guard. 35–42 days. *Nestling:* Precocial and downy. Grayish-white above, a little darker on head and nape; white on underside. On lores extends to posterior end of nostril. Bill flesh-pink with darker tip. Legs and feet grayish. *Nestling period:* Young tended by both parents. Fly at *c.* 90 days. Remain with adults through autumn or winter.

Trumpeter Swan (*Cygnus buccinator*)   Plates 3, 21

Breeds on the edges of large inland waters. Nest on the water's edge, or on a muskrat house. Birds nest in scattered pairs.

Nest: A large heap of nearby plant material, with some white down and small feathers. Male brings material; female builds. Building continues during the incubation period. Outside diameter (at base): 5–11 ft.; inside diameter: 10–16 in.; height: 18 in. **Breeding season:** Begins late April to early May. Single-brooded. **Eggs:** Usually 5, sometimes 2–9. Clutches smaller in colder seasons. Subelliptical to long subelliptical. Creamy-white to pale yellowish. Smooth, slightly glossy with slightly granular surface texture. 111 × 72 mm. **Incubation:** Eggs laid at 2-day intervals. Incubation by female alone, beginning with completion of clutch, but male may occasionally sit on eggs. Eggs are covered with nest material if left. 33 days. **Nestling:** Precocial and downy. Down pale grayish-white, darker on lower nape, shoulders and wings; underside white. Bill flesh-pink with gray tip and edges. Feet pale orange to pale pink. A pale phase has down white, bill pinkish, feet approaching yellowish. **Nestling period:** Young may leave nest and feed by first day. Young protected by both parents. They find their own food, aided by parents pulling up and breaking up water plants but much of the food is insects taken from the plants. Young show aggressive behavior at 29 days. Fly at 90–122 days. Young stay with adults until the following spring.

Mute Swan (*Cygnus olor*)   Figure 18, Plates 3, 21

Introduced populations of this Old World bird well-established on the East Coast, less so on the Great Lakes. May breed on any waters, large or small, fresh or brackish, and in swamps and drainage ditches. Usually solitary, aggressive pairs; but semi-domesticated birds may nest colonially, in close proximity to each other. Nest usually at the water's edge on land or small islands, or built in shallow water in reedbeds.

Figure 18. Mute Swan: c. 4–5 ft. across at base; heap of plant material is very large.

Nest: A large heap of plant material with a raised hollow at the center. A small amount of down. Usually begun by male, later joined by female. Outside diameter (at base): 4–5½ ft.; inside diameter: 15–18 in.; height: 20 in. **Breeding season:** Begins mid-April to May. Single-brooded. **Eggs:** 5–7, exceptionally 4–12. Smooth, slightly glossy, slight granular texture. Some almost white, but more often with a pale blue-gray or blue-green tint. Subelliptical to long elliptical. 113 × 74 mm. **Incubation:** Eggs laid on alternate days. Incubation beginning with last egg or a little earlier; by female mainly, with shorter periods by male. 34–38 days. **Nestling:** Precocial and downy. Gray and white morphs occur. Down is white, though grayer and browner in gray morph or whiter and approaching yellowish in white morph. Bill and feet are dark gray or black in gray morph, light brown in white morph. **Nestling period:** Young stay on the nest for a day or two; then follow parents. Protected by both adults. Small young are carried on the backs of the adults. Young feed themselves but female pulls up and breaks up plants and roots. Independent by *c.* 4 months.

Pink-footed Goose (*Anser brachyrhynchus*)   Plate 23
Breeds in eastern Greenland, preferring ledges of gorges, cliffs, and rock outcrops, or riverbanks, large hummocks, and river islands; but occasionally on open tundra. Breeds in colonies. Nest-site may be used repeatedly in successive years.
Nest: A shallow scrape lined with plants, mosses, lichens, and down. Down tufts brownish-gray with or without paler centers. Feathers gray with pale tips. **Breeding season:** Begins late May. Single-brooded. **Eggs:** Usually 3–5, sometimes up to 7. Shape variable, elliptical to oval. Creamy-white, smooth with fine granular texture. 80 × 54 mm. **Incubation:** Eggs laid at daily intervals. Incubation by female alone, with male on guard; beginning with completion of clutch. 25–28 days. **Nestling:** Precocial and downy. Color variable but usually brown above, including crown of head and around eye, and whitish below, suffused with greenish-yellow. Pale wing-bar, spot below wing, and area under eye greenish-yellow. Some individuals may lack yellow tint. Stout bill dark gray with pinkish nail. Legs dark gray. **Nestling period:** Tended by both parents; leaving nest-site for vicinity of water as soon as down is dry. Begin to feather at 4 weeks, fledged at 8 weeks, but remain with adults until following season.

Greater White-fronted Goose (*Anser albifrons*)   Figure 19, Plates 3, 23
Breeds on tundra on islands in rivers, or raised places in bogs. Pairs tend to nest in close proximity to each other.
Nest: Shallow scrape, with lining of local vegetation, down, and some feathers. Built by female only. Down tufts pale gray; and feathers usually larger than those of other geese in region and more variably colored than those of most geese. **Breeding season:** Begins late May to early June. Single-brooded. **Eggs:** 5–6, rarely 4–7. Elliptical to subelliptical. Smooth, slightly glossy. Creamy-white. 79 × 52 mm. **Incubation:** Eggs laid every second day. Incubation by female only, with male on guard; beginning at completion of clutch. 22–27 days. **Nestling:** Precocial and downy. Brown above; grayish-white or yellowish below. Forehead, face, throat, and front of neck yellowish-white with dark streak from bill to eye. Pale bar across wing. Bill gray with dull yellowish-brown nail; legs and feet gray. **Nestling period:** Young leave nest in 1–2 days; tended by both adults. Fly at 42–49 days. Remain with adults until next season.

Snow Goose (*Chen caerulescens* – Including Blue Goose morph)   Plates 3, 23
Breeds on tundra, on open grassy areas by freshwater lakes. More rarely, in Greenland, on mountain slopes or ledges. Nests often in loose colonies.

Figure 19. Greater White-fronted Goose: c. 12 in. across; local vegetation, down, and some feathers.

Nest: A hollow on the ground, often in taller vegetation, lined with plants and dried grasses, and built up at the rim with an inner lining of small white feathers and pale gray down. Built by female alone. **Breeding season:** Begins mid-June. Single-brooded. **Eggs:** Usually 4–7. Elliptical to subelliptical. Smooth with a fine granular texture. White to creamy-white. 79 × 52 mm. **Incubation:** By female only, male remaining nearby. 22–25 days. **Nestling:** Precocial and downy. Very variable. Blue morph nestling has down dusky olive-green, lighter below and blacker on head and back, with a small yellow patch under chin. Legs and feet blackish; bill blackish with whitish nail. White morph has upperparts and hind-neck yellowish-brown, with dark patch over crown and small dark streak through eye. Remainder of head, neck and underparts golden greenish-yellow. Dark patch on thigh and flank, and some yellow on wings. Legs and feet gray. Bill gray with yellowish-brown nail. **Nestling period:** Young led from nest to water's edge soon after hatching. Guarded and brooded by parents. Fly at 42–50 days. Remain with adults until the following spring.

Ross's Goose (Chen rossii)

Breeds on small islands and islets in lakes in Canadian high arctic tundra. Nests in colonies on the ground in the open or among dwarf shrubs.

Nest: A hollow lined, thickly at times, with vegetation from nearby; often built up with a thick rim several inches high. Lined with white down after eggs are laid. **Breeding season:** Begins early June. Single-brooded, no replacement of lost clutches. **Eggs:** Usually 3–4. Later clutches usually smaller. Elliptical to subelliptical. Smooth with fine granular texture. White. 70 × 47 mm. **Incubation:** Eggs laid at 1½-day intervals. Incubation by female alone, beginning with last egg. Eggs are covered when the nest is left. 21–23 days. **Nestling:** Precocial and downy. Down very thick, with some longer silky tips. Down color varies widely, from almost white to dark gray, to yellow, or greenish, or blackish-yellow. The color is darker on the back and lower nape, with a dark mark through the eye and often a small dark patch on the crown. Legs greenish. Bill black with a pink nail. **Nestling period:** Young hatch almost simultaneously. They leave the nest a few hours after hatching, following the adults, and defended by them. They swim well from the first and can dive. They grow rapidly, and feather between three and six weeks old. Fly at 40–45 days. They remain with the adults until the next spring, not leaving until incubation begins.

Emperor Goose (*Chen canagica*)   Plate 22
Breeds on the coastal tundra, by lagoons, on the shore, or on low coastal or estuarine islands in western Alaska. Nest on the ground. Pairs nest sociably.
Nest: A hollow thickly lined with grass and plants to form a substantial structure, with inner lining of small feathers and down. **Breeding season:** Begins mid-May. Single-brooded. **Eggs:** 3–8, usually 5–6. Elliptical to subelliptical. White to creamy-white. Smooth with a finely granular texture. 78 × 52 mm. **Incubation:** By female only, guarded by male. 24–25 days. **Nestling:** Precocial and downy. Down pale gray, darker above and on head; darkest around eye. White area around bill. Paler below. Short and wide bill black with pale nail. Legs blackish. **Nestling period:** The young soon leave the nest and follow the parents. They grow quickly and feather within a few weeks. Fly at 50–60 days. They remain with the adults until the following spring.

Brant (*Branta bernicla*)   Plates 3, 22
Breeds on coastal tundra, usually by lakes, or on islands of coast or deltas. Also along river valleys, uplands with herbage, and on stony shores of the north.
Nest: A hollow in the ground, often lined and built up with moss and lichens, particularly on stony sites; with a thick inner lining of down. Down tufts brownish-gray with whitish centers, like Common Eider down but smaller. **Breeding season:** Begins early to mid-June. Single-brooded. **Eggs:** Usually 3–5, sometimes 2–8. Elliptical to subelliptical, often long. Smooth and slightly glossy. Creamy-white to yellowish. 71 × 47 mm. **Incubation:** By female alone, the male standing guard. Usually 23–24 days, at times 22–26 days. **Nestling:** Precocial and downy. Down on upperparts drab gray; underside pale gray with darker bases, and with white on chin and upper breast. Head and neck pale with darker gray crown patch, dark patch on lores, and streak through eye. Whitish mark on hind-edge and tip of wings, and on body below wings. In the dark Pacific race the upperparts are a darker gray and a gray cap on the head extends down to cover the dark eye mark. Bill and legs blackish-gray. **Nestling period:** Young are tended by both parents. Will leave the nest within a day, and are agile and active. They are usually led to the shore by the adults. They swim and dive well when small. Fly at 40–50 days. Will remain with the adults until the next spring.

Barnacle Goose (*Branta leucopsis*)   Plates 3, 22
Breeds in northeastern Greenland in arctic valleys on ledges of cliffs and rocky outcrops overlooking rivers or marshes; occasionally on low estuarine islands. Can be up to 300 ft. above base of cliff. Sociable, nesting in small colonies.
Nest: A hollow with little plant material, but quantities of down and some feathers. Down tufts are dark gray with whitish centers; darker than those of Pink-footed Goose, grayer and smaller than Common Eider's. Nest re-used in subsequent years. **Breeding season:** Begins late May to early June. Single-brooded. **Eggs:** 4–6, sometimes 2–9. Elliptical to subelliptical. Non-glossy with slight granular texture. Creamy-white. 77 × 51 mm. **Incubation:** By female only, with male on guard. Beginning with completion of clutch. 24–25 days. **Nestling:** Precocial and downy. Back olive-gray, and underside white, with a pale olive-gray area on upper breast. Head and neck whitish with an olive-gray crown patch, dark distinctive streak from bill

to eye, and brownish wash on nape. Small white areas on back and tip of wing and below wing. The whitish down has pale grayish bases. Bill and legs blackish. **Nestling period:** Young leave nest almost immediately and descend to the vicinity of water. Tended by both adults. Fledged in 7 weeks, but remain with adults.

Canada Goose (Branta canadensis)   Plates 3, 22

Breeds in a great variety of habitats from forest to open plains and prairie, inland and coastal marshes, muskeg and tundra. The nest is usually by water, and preferably on an islet, or a muskrat or beaver house, but frequently in waterside herbage or among trees. Rarely it may be on a raised site, a rock ledge, tree-stump, broken tree-trunk, or even the large old nest of a large raptor.
Nest: A hollow, lined with a variable amount of plant material, including twigs and plant stems, and at times built up into a substantial structure. It has an inner lining of down and some feathers. Down tufts large, grayish-brown with white centers and pale tips. Outside diameter: 16–25 in.; inside diameter: 7–9 in.; depth: 4 in. **Breeding season:** Variable through the range. May begin late April in south or west, early to mid-June in the north. Single-brooded. **Eggs:** Usually 5–6, occasionally 2–11. Elliptical to subelliptical. White to creamy-white. Smooth and non-glossy. Size varies with the different-sized races and may average 87 × 58 mm. in large races, 72 × 48 mm. in small races. **Incubation:** By female alone, with male on guard. 25–30 days. **Nestling:** Precocial and downy. Very variable. Down greenish-brown above, and on distinctive crown-cap and nape; greenish-yellow below, and on forehead, face and neck; with yellow on front and back edges of wings, and on body below wings. In some northwestern races – e.g., *fulva, minima, occidentalis,* and *taverneri* – the down may be less yellow, whitish below and olive above, with a dark mark across the eye. Bill dark blue-gray. Legs and feet blue-gray or greenish. **Nestling period:** Young tended by both adults. Flying at *c.* 9 weeks. Young remain with adults until the following spring.

Muscovy Duck (Cairina moschata)

Non-feral population breeds rarely along the lower Rio Grande along the river, by woodland resacas, or pools. Nest is in a cavity in the trunk or larger limbs of a tree, or a natural hole. (9–60 ft. up in the Neotropics.) Nest-boxes are also used. Males mate promiscuously.
Nest: Usually a bare cavity in trees, but sometimes on ground in dense waterside vegetation. Lined with down. **Breeding season:** Possibly beginning in mid-June, extending into late August, although starting in April in nearby Mexico. **Eggs:** Usually 8–9. Subelliptical to oval. Moderately oval. White or greenish-white. 63 × 47 mm. **Incubation:** By female alone. 35 days. **Nestling:** Precocial and downy. Down brown above and over back of neck and head. Face and underparts yellow. Thin, dark stripe from eye to nape. Relatively long tail. Pairs of wing-spots and dorsal patches yellowish. Bill gray-brown. Legs yellowish-gray. **Nestling period:** Little information. Young tended by female alone. Flight at *c.* 70 days.

Wood Duck (Aix sponsa)   Plates 4, 23

Breeds near woodland streams and pools. Nest is in a cavity in the trunk or larger limbs of a tree, a natural hole or old hole of a larger woodpecker. 3–60 ft.up. More rarely in a similar site in a building such as a barn. Nest-boxes are also used. Entrance hole *c.* 4 in. diameter.
Nest: A bare cavity, unless previously used by another bird or a mammal as a nest. No material other than already present, save for a lining of white down. **Breeding season:** Begins early March in south to early May in north. Usually ends by mid-

July. Usually single-brooded, though second broods are not uncommon. *Eggs:* Usually 8–10, sometimes 6–15. Subelliptical to oval. Smooth and fairly glossy. White or creamy-white. (See Hooded Merganser.) 52 × 40 mm. *Incubation:* By female alone. 28–32 days. *Nestling:* Precocial and downy. Down dark blackish-brown above and over head. Small whitish rear edge to wing, and whitish spot on either side of lower back. Face and underparts grayish-white to yellow. Dark, well-marked line from eye to nape. Relatively long tail. Bill bluish-gray with reddish-brown nail. Legs dark gray, feet yellowish and grayish. *Nestling period:* Within one day, young climb up to nest entrance and drop unaided in response to female's call, following her to water. Young tended by female alone. Fly at 56–70 days.

Green-winged Teal (*Anas crecca*)   Plates 4, 24
Breeds on islands in lakes, the edges of lakes, lagoons, and sloughs. Also on higher ground at a little distance from water. The nest is on the ground, well concealed in long grass or under bushes or low trees.
Nest: A hollow lined with dry grass and other plant material; and with a lining of small feathers and down. Down tufts small and very dark with white centers. Down added during incubation. Inside diameter *c.* 5½ in.; depth *c.* 3½ in. *Breeding season:* Begins early to mid-May in the south, to early June in the north. Single-brooded. *Eggs:* Usually 10–12, sometimes 6–18. Elliptical to short subelliptical. Smooth. Dull white, cream-colored, creamy-buff, or very pale olive-buff. 46 × 32 mm. *Incubation:* By female alone, beginning with completion of clutch. 23–24 days. *Nestling:* Precocial and downy. Down pattern like that of the Mallard, but with a second dark streak from the rear of the ear-coverts to the base of the bill, parallel to the eyestripe; and the longer filaments of down tinted warmer buff-brown. Appears 'square-headed.' Bill, legs, and feet are grayish-brown. *Nestling period:* Young tended by female only. They are led to the nearest water a few hours after hatching. Become independent at *c.* 23 days. Fly at *c.* 44 days.

American Black Duck (*Anas rubripes*)   Plate 23
Breeds near water, favoring woodland lakes and streams, tidal or freshwater marshes. Nest usually on the ground on an isolated islet, or high ground near open water or marsh. Rarely in an old hawk or crow nest high in a tree.
Nest: A hollow of grasses, leaves, and other debris. The lining is mixed with female's down (similar to Mallard's but pale centers are less conspicuous). Down accumulates as incubation advances. Outside diameter: *c.* 18 in.; depth 3–4 in. *Breeding season:* Begins mid-March. Single-brooded. *Eggs:* Usually 8–10, sometimes 6–15. Elliptical to subelliptical. Smooth with rather waxy surface. Green, greenish-buff, yellowish-buff, creamy with a green tinge. (See Mallard.) 59 × 42 mm. *Incubation:* By female alone. 26–28 days. *Nestling:* Precocial and downy. Down plumage like that of the Mallard but darker above, the dark color also extending farther down on to breast and flanks. Dark marks on the head by the ear-coverts and bill, sometimes more obvious and forming a dark stripe occasionally coalescing with the dark eyestripe. Bill brownish-gray. Legs yellowish-brown. *Nestling period:* As for the Mallard; the young being tended by the female only, leaving the nest within a few hours of hatching and being led to water.

Mottled Duck (*Anas fulvigula*)
Breeds in dense cover by marshes, freshwater ponds, brackish or salt meadows, canals, and brushy fields, or rice fields. Nest usually on or near the ground, though may be in cordgrass or under bush.
Nest: A hollow in ground, filled with grasses, weeds, and leaves. Rim of cavity lined

with female's brown down. Outside diameter: 11 in.; inside diameter: 6 in.; depth: $1\frac{1}{2}$–$3\frac{1}{2}$ in. **Breeding season:** Begins pairing in January or February (much earlier than American Black Duck). Usually into June, though as late as August. Single-brooded. **Eggs:** Usually 8–11, sometimes 5–12. Elliptical to subelliptical. Creamy-white to greenish-white. (See Mallard.) 55 × 41 mm. **Incubation:** By female alone. 25–28 days. **Nestling:** Precocial and downy. Similar to American Black Duck, but somewhat lighter-colored or brighter-colored, and the dark head markings are more restricted and paler. Bill brownish-gray. Feet are dark grayish-brown or blackish. **Nestling period:** Tended by female. Leave nest when less than 1 day old. Capable of limited flight at 60 days, but probably not until 70 days.

Mallard (Anas platyrhynchos)   Plates 4, 23

Breeds near any type of fresh water, in a variety of habitats, though may be far from water. Nest usually in cover on the ground, among tall vegetation, grasses, bushes, etc., and on small islands; or in raised sites in tree crotches or holes, in old nests of large birds, on buildings and ruins.
Nest: A hollow lined with plant debris, leaves, grass, etc., the lining mixed with down and feathers. Down tufts are brown, with paler centers and tips. Down covers eggs before incubation and when bird is away from the nest. Outside diameter: 11–12 in.; inside diameter: 6–7 in.; depth: 4 in. **Breeding season:** Usually March onwards, but feral populations breed at various times through year from February to late autumn. Probably single-brooded normally, but feral birds may have second brood. **Eggs:** Normally 10–12, occasionally 7–16. Elliptical to subelliptical, fairly short. Smooth, waxy rather than glossy. Usually very pale green or blue-green, sometimes creamy with green tinge, buffish-green, or almost blue. (Eggs of Mallard, American Black Duck, Mottled Duck, Northern Pintail, Northern Shoveler, and even Redhead can be very similar.) 58 × 41 mm. **Incubation:** By female alone; beginning with completion of clutch. 26–29 days. **Nestling:** Precocial and downy. Dark brown above and buffish-yellow below. Dark streak from bill through eye to nape, dark mark at rear of ear-coverts, otherwise sides of head and sides and front of neck yellow. Yellow wing-bar and patches at sides of back and sides of rump. Bill dark olive-brown. Legs and feet grayish-brown. **Nestling period:** Young take to water soon after hatching; mostly tended by female alone. Fledged at c. 7–8 weeks.

Northern Pintail (Anas acuta)   Plates 4, 24

Breeds by freshwater lakes, pools, sloughs, and lagoons; usually with drier margins. Usually sociable, nesting near each other. Nest in low vegetation and relatively open areas, sometimes near water; or on islands; occasionally well away from water.
Nest: A hollow, exposed or concealed in low vegetation; lined with plant material, down and some feathers. Down tufts longish, light brown with pale centers, like Northern Shoveler's. Outside diameter: $7\frac{1}{2}$–14 in.; inside diameter: 7–$8\frac{1}{2}$ in.; height: 3–7 in. **Breeding season:** Begins mid-April in south, to late May or early June in north. Probably ends by late July. Single-brooded. **Eggs:** Usually 7–9, rarely 6–12. Subelliptical to oval, occasionally long. Variable, yellowish-cream to greenish or bluish. (See Mallard.) 54 × 37 mm. **Incubation:** By female only, beginning with completion of clutch. 25–26 days. **Nestling:** Precocial and downy. Like that of Mallard but light brown above with the longer filaments creamy-buff, light markings paler, underparts grayish-white, and foreneck brownish to grayish-buff. Light patch on side of back sometimes extending towards rump. Cheeks white with light brown patch, eyestripe white and continuing down side of nape to breast. Light brown line through eye, ill-defined towards nape. Appears 'square-headed.' Bill light gray. Legs and feet brownish-gray or greenish-gray. **Nestling period:** Young tended by female, but male usually present. Fledging at c. 7 weeks.

Blue-winged Teal (*Anas discors*)   **Plate 24**
Breeds by small waters – pot-holes, ponds, sloughs, and marshes – in prairie and
forest regions. Nest on the ground, usually near water and well concealed in herbage. Sometimes semi-colonial in good habitat.
Nest: A hollow, lined with dry grass and nearby vegetation, with an inner lining of
down. Nearby cover often arched over nest. Down tufts drab brown, larger, and
lighter than that of Green-winged Teal, with large whitish centers. Built over 2–7
days. Down added during laying. Outside diameter $7\frac{2}{3}$ in.; inside diameter: $5\frac{1}{3}$ in.;
depth: $2\frac{1}{4}$ in.. **Breeding season:** Begins early May in south, to early June farther
north. Single-brooded. **Eggs:** Usually 8–12, sometimes 6–16. Elliptical to subelliptical. Smooth and slightly glossy. Dull white, creamy-white, or with pale olive tint.
47×33 mm. **Incubation:** Eggs laid at daily intervals. Incubation by female alone,
beginning with last egg. 23–24 days. **Nestling:** Precocial and downy. Down brown
above and creamy yellow below, with small yellow patches on either side above the
thigh and towards the rump. Rear edge of wing yellow. Sides of face yellow with dark
eyestripe from bill to nape, sometimes broken just in front of eye, and with short dark
streak on ear-coverts. The forehead is narrow and yellow. Bill olive-brown. Legs
grayish-yellow. **Nestling period:** Young tended by female alone. They are led to water
soon after hatching. They grow and feather rapidly, flying at 35–49 days.

Cinnamon Teal (*Anas cyanoptera*)   **Plate 24**
Breeds near shallow water, by pools, lake edges, or swamps, favoring areas where
tule is present. The nest may be in cover by the water's edge, or at some distance.
Usually very well concealed, deep in growing herbage, or in marsh or waterside
plants on the ground.
Nest: A hollow, usually with a slight lining of grass and plant material, but nests in
marsh vegetation may be built up above water level as more substantial structures.
The nest is lined with down. Down tufts like those of Blue-winged Teal. Down added
into incubation. Outside diameter: $6\frac{1}{2}$–$9\frac{1}{2}$ in.; inside diameter: $4\frac{1}{2}$–6 in.; depth:
$2\frac{1}{2}$–$3\frac{1}{2}$ in. **Breeding season:** Begins mid-April in south to early May farther north.
Usually ends by mid-August. Single-brooded. **Eggs:** Usually 8–12, sometimes 5–14.
Elliptical to subelliptical or oval. Smooth and slightly glossy. White, creamy-white,
creamy-buff, or warm buff. 48×35 mm. **Incubation:** By female alone, but male may
maintain contact. 24–25 days. **Nestling:** Precocial and downy. Down pattern like
that of Blue-winged Teal, but color a little more olive above and a brighter yellow
below and on face. Bill olive-gray (grayer than Blue-winged Teal). Legs grayish-
yellow. **Nestling period:** Young tended by female or by both parents. Young are led
to water soon after hatching. They swim well and escape predators by diving and
hiding. Fly at *c.* 7 weeks.

Northern Shoveler (*Anas clypeata*)   **Plates 4, 24**
Breeds by still or sluggish fresh water with vegetation at the edges; by shallow or
overgrown pools, marshes, bogs, sloughs, or slow creeks. Nest on the ground, in an
open site but sheltered by some grass or growing vegetation; usually but not invariably near the water, and on a dry site.
Nest: A hollow lined with plant material, down, and some feathers. Down tufts
brown with light centers like those of Northern Pintail. Down added during incuba-
tion. Outside diameter: $8\frac{2}{3}$ in.; inside diameter: $5\frac{1}{2}$ in.; height: $3\frac{2}{3}$ in. **Breeding
season:** Begins late March in south to early June in north. Single-brooded. **Eggs:**
Usually 8–12, sometimes 7–14. Elliptical to subelliptical. Smooth. Creamy-buff to
olive-tinted. (See Mallard.) 52×37 mm. **Incubation:** Eggs laid on successive days.
Incubation by female alone, beginning with the last egg. Males remain nearby.
26 days. **Nestling:** Precocial and downy. Like Mallard, but darker above with the

longer filaments reddish-buff and light patches paler and less conspicuous. No light wing-bar. Face warm buff to dusky and foreneck grayish-buff. Underparts grayish-white tinged with yellow. Bill proportionally large with upper mandible brownish-gray and lower mandible approaching dull orange. Legs and feet yellowish-brown. **Nestling period:** Young tended by female alone. They are led to water soon after hatching. They are agile divers. Independent in c. 6–7 weeks.

Gadwall (Anas strepera)   Plate 23
Breeds by freshwater lakes, pools, or slow streams with waterside vegetation. Nest usually in thicker vegetation and tall plants near water, often using island sites. May breed in close proximity.
Nest: A hollow lined with plant material, down, and some feathers. Down tufts dark with small pale center and distinct pale tips. (Down darker and larger than that of American Wigeon.) Down added during incubation. **Breeding season:** Variable, beginning mid-April in south to early June in the north. Single-brooded. **Eggs:** Usually 8–12, rarely 7–16. Elliptical, subelliptical or sometimes oval; usually rather short. Cream-colored or tinted very pale green. Smooth and waxy. Very similar to that of American Wigeon. 54 × 39 mm. **Incubation:** By female alone; beginning with completion of clutch. 25–27 days. **Nestling:** Precocial and downy. Like Mallard but upperparts browner, and longer filaments warm buff. Paler stripe over eye and narrower dark eye-streak. Pale dorsal patches and other parts of plumage creamier, less yellow. Bill with brownish-gray upper mandible and dull yellowish lower mandible. Legs and feet yellowish-gray. **Nestling period:** Young tended by female only; being taken to water almost immediately after hatching. c. 7 weeks.

American Wigeon (Anas americana)   Plates 4, 24
Breeds on lake islands or by lakes or rivers. The nest is on the ground, often at some distance from water, concealed in tall herbage or in more open sites under low bushes or small trees. In northern forests nests may be in leaf-litter by a tree or bush.
Nest: A hollow lined with dry grass or other plant material. Well lined with down and feathers. Down tufts dark with indistinct pale centers and pale tips. (Down lighter and smaller than that of Gadwall.) Down added into incubation. **Breeding season:** Begins early May in south to early June in north. Single-brooded. **Eggs:** Usually 9–11, sometimes 6–13. Subelliptical to oval. Cream colored. Smooth and slightly glossy. Very similar to that of Gadwall. 54 × 38 mm. **Incubation:** Eggs laid on successive days. Incubation by female alone, beginning with last egg. 24–25 days. **Nestling:** Precocial and downy. Down drab brown above, with some longer buff-tipped filaments, the dark color extending around the foreneck and up over hind-neck and head. Partial or complete light eye-ring. Sides of head pale cinnamon buff. No ear-spot present. Brown-faced variant darker. Hind-edge of wing, patch at side of lower back, and most of underside cinnamon-buff. Bill brownish-gray. Leg color variable, though usually grayish. **Nestling period:** Young tended by female alone. Independent in c. 6–7 weeks.

Canvasback (Aythya valisineria)   Plate 25
Breeds in sloughs and marshes, and other fresh waters with growing vegetation. Nest frequently concealed in a clump of vegetation growing in water. Sometimes in more open sites in sedges, or hidden in tall waterside plants.
Nest: Usually a substantial cup of stems and plant material, well lined with down. Down light grayish-brown with indistinct pale centers, darker than that of Redhead. Outside diameter: 18–20 in.; inside diameter: 8 in.; depth: 4 in. **Breeding season:** Begins mid- to late May. Single-brooded. **Eggs:** Usually 7–9. (Eggs of Redhead and

Ruddy Duck may also be present.) Eggs elliptical to subelliptical or oval. Pale dull green, bluish-green, olive-green, or grayish-olive. Smooth and slightly glossy. 63 × 45 mm. *Incubation:* By female alone. 24–27 days. *Nestling:* Precocial and downy. Like larger and paler Ring-necked Duck, but longer and wedge-shaped bill apparent at early stage. Down dark brown above and over back of neck and head. Underside and face yellow. Hind-edge of wings and spots at sides of lower back yellow. Pale tip to olive-gray bill, and nail at tip narrow (broad on Redhead). Legs and feet brownish-gray. *Nestling period:* Young tended by female only. They begin feathering at 5 weeks. Fly at 10–12 weeks.

Redhead (Aythya americana)   Plates 4, 24

Breeds by fresh water, usually in the taller vegetation (especially bulrushes) bordering lakes and sloughs, occasionally in more open sites in similar areas. Nest on the ground.
Nest: In drier sites a hollow sparsely lined with plant material, and in damper sites a substantial cup. There is an inner lining of down. Down tufts very pale, grayish-white, paler than that of Canvasback. Outside diameter: 16 in.; inside diameter: 8 in. *Breeding season:* Begins late April in south to early June in north. Single-brooded. *Eggs:* Usually 10–15. Difficult to determine since eggs are often laid in nests of other birds including other duck species (e.g., Canvasback, Mallard, Cinnamon Teal), and nests may contain a mixture of eggs. Eggs elliptical to sub-elliptical. Smooth and glossy. Greenish to very pale olive or olive-gray. (Larger and glossier than eggs of Mallard.) 61 × 43 mm. *Incubation:* By female alone. 24 days. *Nestling:* Precocial and downy. Down very pale, light brownish-olive above and over back of neck and head. It is the most yellow of North American ducklings. Underside and face yellow, with slightly warmer buff tint on unpatterned face. Bar on hind-wing and two patches at each side of lower back buffish-yellow. Nail at tip of dark gray bill is broad (narrow on Canvasback). Legs dark gray. *Nestling period:* Young tended by female alone. Brood often moved to site with deeper water than that preferred for nesting. Fly at 56–73 days.

Ring-necked Duck (Aythya collaris)   Plate 24

Breeds by fresh water, preferring smaller waters of ponds, sloughs, and marshes, often in or near woodlands. Nest in herbage on the ground near or by water, or in clumps of tall plants or tussocks in shallow water. Frequently in damp sites.
Nest: A hollow lined with grass and plant material. In wet places the material may be built up into a substantial cup. Building accompanies laying. Nest is lined with down. Down tufts warm medium brown with whitish centers. *Breeding season:* Begins late May to early June. Single-brooded. *Eggs:* Usually 6–12. Elliptical to sub-elliptical. Smooth and slightly glossy. Very pale olive, grayish-olive, or greenish. Similar to eggs of Lesser Scaup. 58 × 41 mm. *Incubation:* By female alone, though male may remain in vicinity and accompany female through incubation. 26 days. *Nestling:* Precocial and downy. Like small and darker Canvasback. Very dark brown above and over back of neck and head. Underparts, face and forehead yellow, brighter on face. Hind-edge of wing and two bold and extensive spots on either side of lower back yellow. Bill brownish-gray (with nail size between Redhead and Canvasback). Legs olive-gray. *Nestling period:* Young tended by female only. Fly at 49–56 days.

Greater Scaup (Aythya marila)   Plate 24

Breeds by fresh water on open ridges and tundra, often using lake islands. Frequently sociable with many pairs together. Nest in fairly open sites, with little or no cover.

Nest: A hollow lined with nearby vegetation, down and feathers. Down tufts dark sooty-brown with indistinct pale centers. **Breeding season:** Beginning from end of May to mid-June. Single-brooded. **Eggs:** 6–15, occasionally 17. Elliptical to subelliptical. Smooth but non-glossy. Pale greenish to olive-gray. 63 × 43 mm. **Incubation:** By female alone, remaining on nest for long periods. 24–28 days. **Nestling:** Precocial and downy. Down dark blackish-brown over much of body. Breast and belly creamy-yellow, upper breast buffish-brown. Sides of head faintly buffish with dark poorly-defined eye-streak and indistinct darker streak bordering yellowish throat. Bill dark blackish-brown with greenish sides and pale tip. Legs and feet olive-gray or blackish. **Nestling period:** Young tended by female, but male present at times. Independent in 5–6 weeks.

Lesser Scaup (Aythya affinis)   Plates 4, 25
Breeds by freshwater ponds, sloughs, and creeks, or on lake islands. Nest on the ground, usually near water in grass or waterside plants (e.g., bulrushes), exceptionally in vegetation growing in water.
Nest: A hollow, usually sparsely lined with plant material, and with an inner lining of down and some feathers. Down tufts dark brown with indistinct pale centers. **Breeding season:** Begins early May in south to mid-June in north. Single-brooded. **Eggs:** Usually 8–12, sometimes 6–15. Elliptical to subelliptical. Smooth and slightly glossy. Pale olive or greenish, to olive-buff. Similar to eggs of Ring-necked Duck. 58 × 40 mm. **Incubation:** By female alone. Male sometimes remains in vicinity into incubation. 26–27 days. **Nestling:** Precocial and downy. Like Greater Scaup, but face generally paler and more yellow. Down dark blackish-brown above, over much of head and upper breast. Lower breast and belly creamy-buff. Sides of face buffish and throat yellowish; with narrow dark (and usually well-marked) stripe through eye from bill to nape, and indistinct stripe across ear-coverts. Bill blackish-brown with pale tip. Legs and feet blackish. **Nestling period:** Young tended by female alone. Soon after hatching they are led to water. They feed mainly on insects. They dive well from an early age. Fly at 45–50 days.

Common Eider (Somateria mollissima)   Figures 20, 21, Plates 5, 26
Breeds on coast, or offshore islands, or on lakes or rivers near the sea. Usually on exposed sites. Nest a hollow selected by female reluctantly accompanied by male. Sociable, often nesting in colonies.
Nest: A hollow lined with nearby plant material or seaweed. Inner lining of copious down and feathers. Down tufts a light grayish-brown with ill-defined pale centers and palish tips. **Breeding season:** Begins late May in south to mid- or late June in north. Single-brooded. **Eggs:** 4–6, sometimes 3–10. Shape variable, elliptical to subelliptical, sometimes oval. Smooth, slightly glossy. Pale green, olive, grayish or bluish, rarely buffish. 77 × 52 mm. **Incubation:** By female alone, sitting closely and leaving only rarely for short periods. 24–27 days. **Nestling:** Precocial and downy. Like other eiders, almost uniform mostly grayish-brown. Paler on lower breast. A broad buffish or brownish-gray stripe from the lores, over the eye to the nape and a similar tint on the chin. A darker streak through the eye. Bill bluish-gray (with pink nail) and legs olive to gray. **Nestling period:** Young led to water and tended by female, sometimes accompanied by female without young. Young very active and independent. Broods scatter and join up to form larger groups. Independent at c. 60–75 days.

King Eider (Somateria spectabilis)   Figure 21, Plate 26
Breeds on lakes and pools of tundra regions, usually near the sea, in solitary pairs.
Nest: A shallow hollow in grass or heather stems, with little plant lining, but thick

Figure 20. Common Eider: c. 16 in. across; down in inner lining is thick.

down and some feathers. Down tufts sooty-brown, darker than Common Eider's, with indistinct pale centers; and occasional whitish tufts. **Breeding season:** Begins mid-June to mid-July. Single-brooded. **Eggs:** 4–7, occasionally 3–8. Subelliptical. Smooth, slightly glossy. Pale olive. 66 × 44 mm. **Incubation:** By female alone. 22–23 days. **Nestling:** Precocial and downy. Olive-brown above, lighter than Common Eider, whitish-buff below. Sides of head pale buffish with narrow dark streak through eye to nape. Chin, throat and breast whitish-buff. Bill bluish-pink to olive-gray. Legs olive-gray. **Nestling period:** Young tended by female alone. Young of several broods tend to group together, attended by only some of the females, or by one only. First flight estimated at 30–50 days.

Figure 21. Four duckling eiders (*left to right*): King Eider, Common Eider, Steller's Eider, Spectacled Eider.

Spectacled Eider (*Somateria fischeri*)   Figure 21, Plate 26

Breeds by pools on coastal marshes of tundra uncommonly in northwestern and western Alaska. Nest is set on a drier site, a small islet, or ridge or tussock by the water. The nest is often concealed in herbage.

Nest: A hollow lined with moss and plant debris from nearby, with inner lining of soft down and small feathers. Down tufts medium brown with slightly paler but inconspicuous centers. Down added as incubation advances. **Breeding season:** Begins early June. Single-brooded. **Eggs:** Usually 5–7, sometimes 3–9. Elliptical to subelliptical. Smooth, slightly glossy. Green, bluish-green, or olive-buff. 65 × 45 mm. **Incubation:** By female alone. 24 days. **Nestling:** Precocial and downy. Down dark brown, with underside paler and grayer. Large dark spectacle mark around eye. (As young develops, a buff-colored area forms around this spectacle. The spectacle may also appear bi-colored, crossed by a streak.) Down extends on to the base of the bill. Bill, legs and feet bluish-gray or blackish. **Nestling period:** Young tended by female alone. First flight at 50–53 days.

Steller's Eider (*Polysticta stelleri*)   Figure 21, Plate 26

Breeds on level tundra by freshwater pools or lagoons in parts of western and northern Alaska, often where deep water is present offshore. Nest may be on a slight rise or along a pond margin.

Nest: A hollow lined with some nearby plant material, down and some feathers. Down tufts very dark brown with occasional white tufts. **Breeding season:** Begins mid-June to mid-July. Single-brooded. **Eggs:** 6–8, occasionally 10. Short subelliptical. Smooth but non-glossy. Pale yellowish-olive, greenish, or olive-buff. 61 × 42 mm. **Incubation:** By female alone. Period unknown. **Nestling:** Precocial and downy. Down dark brown above, grayish on belly. Small buffish ring round eye and narrow streak from eye toward nape, and buffish chin. Bill blackish-brown; legs olive-gray. **Nestling period:** Young tended by female alone. Birds may join to form larger groups.

Harlequin Duck (*Histrionicus histrionicus*)   Plates 5, 26

Breeds on swift-flowing northern rivers, nesting, sociably at times, on rocky islands in rivers or in sheltered sites on the banks. Nest on the ground, usually concealed in thick shrub cover.

Nest: A hollow lined with a little plant material and with down and feathers. Down tufts light brown with pale centers. **Breeding season:** Begins mid-May to early July, usually in early June. Single-brooded. **Eggs:** Usually 6–8, occasionally 3–9. Elliptical to subelliptical. Smooth, slightly glossy. Pale creamy to pale buff. 58 × 42 mm. **Incubation:** By female alone, beginning before the last egg is laid. 27–33 days. **Nestling:** Precocial and downy. Down blackish-brown above, white below. Sides of head and throat white, crown of head down to below eyes dark brown with small white patch above and before each eye. A whitish patch on wing and either side of back and one above the thigh. A relatively long and pointed tail. Bill and legs dark gray. **Nestling period:** Young tended by female only, but the male occasionally present at first. Young can fly in 40 days.

Oldsquaw (*Clangula hyemalis*)   Plates 5, 25

Breeds in northern forest and tundra; on open tundra, often by pools, and on lake islands. Nest concealed in low vegetation or sheltered by rocks.

Nest: A hollow, lined with a little nearby plant material, down, and feathers. Down tufts dark grayish-brown with paler centers. **Breeding season:** Begins late May in south, to June in north. Single-brooded. **Eggs:** Usually 5–9, occasionally 5–11. Subelliptical to elliptical, sometimes oval. Smooth. Yellowish or with faint olive tint, or more greenish. 53 × 38 mm. *Incubation:* By female alone. Male nearby at first. 23–25 days. *Nestling:* Precocial and downy. Brown with golden tips above, grayish-white below with dusky-brown upper breast-band. Cream spot on lores, whitish behind, pale patch above and below eye. Some pale face-marks may be absent in individuals. Pale down has brownish bases. Bill and legs dark gray or bluish-gray. *Nestling period:* Tended by female alone. Young are led to the sea soon after hatching. They swim and dive well from the first. Some broods may combine. Independent in *c.* 5 weeks.

Black Scoter (Melanitta nigra)   Plates 5, 25
Breeds by freshwater lakes and pools on coastal marshes and higher open ground. Nest usually close to water, or on an island, in a slightly sheltered site.
Nest: A hollow lined with a little plant material, down, and some feathers. Down tufts medium-sized; dark brown with paler centers. *Breeding season:* Begins mid-June. Probably ends by mid-September. Single-brooded. *Eggs:* 6–9, occasionally 5–10. Subelliptical. Smooth and slightly glossy. Pale creamy to creamy-buff. 65 × 45 mm. *Incubation:* By female alone on completion of the clutch. 27–31 days. *Nestling:* Precocial and downy. Down mainly dark brown with whitish lower breast and belly; and white cheeks and throat. Appears more round-headed than other duckling scoters. Bill blackish with reddish-brown nail. Legs dark olive-brown or dark grayish-olive. *Nestling period:* Young tended by female alone. Independent at 6–7 weeks.

Surf Scoter (Melanitta perspicillata)   Plate 25
Breeds by ponds, lakes, and rivers in wooded, boggy, and tundra areas. Nest at times away from water; in wooded areas sheltered by low branches of conifers, in more open areas under bushes or in grasses.
Nest: A hollow lined with grasses and other plants and with an inner lining of down. Down dark brown with whitish centers and tips. *Breeding season:* Begins mid-June. Single-brooded. *Eggs:* 5–7, occasionally up to 9. Subelliptical to oval. Smooth and non-glossy. Creamy-white to pinkish-buff. 62 × 43 mm. *Incubation:* By female only. 28 days. *Nestling:* Precocial and downy. Like that of Black Scoter, but darker, and feathering extends in a wedge on to upper bill (cut off sharply in Black Scoter). Bill appears stout in side view. Down grayish-brown above and silvery-gray below. Cap black and cheeks, throat and chin brownish-gray. Upper breast brownish-gray. The darkest and least-patterned of all North American ducklings. Bill and legs blackish-brown. *Nestling period:* Young tended by female only. First flight at *c.* 8 weeks.

White-winged Scoter (Melanitta fusca)   Plates 5, 25
Breeds on islands or shores of freshwater lakes in wooded, bushy, or overgrown sites, or in concealed or bare sites in open tundra.
Nest: A hollow lined with nearby plant material, leaves or twigs, and with down and feathers. Down tufts larger than those of Black Scoter, dark brown with indistinct pale centers. *Breeding season:* Begins mid-June. Single-brooded. *Eggs:* 7–10, sometimes 6–11. Subelliptical. Smooth, non-glossy. Pale creamy to buff. 71 × 48 mm. *Incubation:* By female alone, beginning with the last egg. 27–28 days. *Nestling:* Precocial and downy. Down mainly dark brown above, grayer than Black Scoter. Cheeks, throat, and upper neck, and underside, white, separated by brownish-gray band across upper breast. Small white patches on upper wing and sides of rump. The most-patterned of the scoter ducklings. Bill and feet bluish-gray. *Nestling period:* Young tended by female alone, who tends to desert them for increasingly long periods. Young independent *c.* 4–5 weeks, fly at *c.* 6–7 weeks.

Common Goldeneye (*Bucephala clangula*)   Plates 5, 25
Breeds by lakes and rivers in forest country. Nest in natural cavities in trees or
stumps (often top snags), or in woodpecker holes; will also nest in nest-boxes.
Usually 6–60 ft. up.
Nest: No material other than that present, down, and some feathers added. Down
tufts grayish-white. **Breeding season:** Beginning early April in south, to June in
north. Probably ends by late August. Single-brooded. **Eggs:** 6–11, larger clutches
probably from two females. Subelliptical. Smooth. Bluish-green; bright at first but
fading. Like eggs of Barrow's Goldeneye. 60 × 43 mm. **Incubation:** Eggs laid at intervals of *c.* $1\frac{1}{2}$ days. Incubation by female alone; beginning on completion of clutch;
male remaining nearby. 27–32 days. **Nestling:** Precocial and downy. Down brownish-black above, almost white below with upper breast brownish-gray. Dark cap
extends just below eyes, but cheeks pale. Grayish-white on wing-bar, patches on
either sides of back and rump, and above thigh. Bill gray with reddish-gray nail.
(The bill is longer and squarer than Barrow's Goldeneye bill). Legs and feet yellowish-gray. **Nestling period:** Young scramble out of nest and drop unharmed. Tended
by female only. Able to fly at 51–60 days.

Barrow's Goldeneye (*Bucephala islandica*)   Plate 25
Breeds by lakes or rivers; including saline lakes in open country. Nest usually in a
natural cavity or woodpecker hole in a tree up to 50 ft. or more. Has used cavity in
roof of barn.
Nest: Only material already present in cavity, with significant down and some
feathers. Down tufts white. **Breeding season:** Begins mid-May. Single-brooded.
Eggs: 8–14. Elliptical. Smooth. Green or bluish-green. Like eggs of Common Goldeneye. 62 × 45 mm. **Incubation:** By female alone, beginning on completion of clutch.
30 days. **Nestling:** Precocial and downy. Like young of Common Goldeneye, but a
little larger with a larger-appearing head. Bill grayish with a reddish-gray nail. Bill
shorter, more tapering than that of Common Goldeneye with a much wider nail. Legs
and feet more greenish-gray than those of Common Goldeneye. **Nestling period:**
Tended by female. First flight estimated at 8 weeks.

Bufflehead (*Bucephala albeola*)   Plate 25
Breeds by freshwater lakes, ponds and rivers in wooded regions, and less frequently
in open muskeg with few trees. Nest usually in a Northern Flicker hole, occasionally
in a natural tree cavity (2–10 ft. up, though sometimes much higher); very exceptionally in a hole in a bank. Will use nest-boxes.
Nest: A cavity with the material already present, if any, and down and feathers. The
entrance is small $2\frac{1}{2}$–3 in. in diameter; the interior diameter is *c.* 6 in.; the depth is
10–14 in. Down tufts pale gray tinted purplish or brownish and with indistinct pale
centers. **Breeding season:** Begins mid-May in south to early June in north. Single-
brooded. **Eggs:** Usually 8–12, sometimes 7–16. Elliptical to oval. Smooth and
slightly glossy. Creamy-white, yellowish-cream and pale olive-buff. 51 × 37 mm.
Incubation: Eggs laid at 1–3-day intervals. By female alone, usually beginning with
last egg. 29 days. **Nestling:** Precocial and downy. Like a small Common Goldeneye.
Down brownish-black with white patch on cheeks and throat, and white lower
breast and belly. Breast-band sometimes poorly defined. Small white patch on hind-
wing and three more along each side of back, the foremost two sometimes forming
an irregular stripe. Bill dark gray with reddish-gray nail. Bill tapered much like Barrow's Goldeneye, but nail even smaller than Common Goldeneye's. Legs gray.
Nestling period: Young remain in nest 24–36 hours, coaxed out of cavity and led to
water by female. Young tended by female alone. Fly at 50–55 days.

Hooded Merganser (*Lophodytes cucullatus*)   Figure 22, Plate 26
Breeds by still or slow-moving fresh water, forest ponds and lakes, flooded forest, riverside swamps and streams. Nest in a cavity in tree or stump, exceptionally between tree-roots, in a fallen hollow log or a hole in a bank. Usually 15–20 ft. up. Will use nest-boxes and can enter a hole 3½ in. diameter.

Nest: A cavity with any material already present and a lining of down and some feathers. Down tufts very pale gray with centers a little lighter still. **Breeding season:** Begins late April. Single-brooded, but will replace lost clutch. **Eggs:** Usually 5–12. Short elliptical to short subelliptical. Smooth and very glossy. White. Much like eggs of Wood Duck, but slightly paler and larger. 54 × 45 mm. **Incubation:** By female only. 31 days. **Nestling:** Precocial and downy. Darkest of the mergansers and lacks face-stripes. Down brown on back, over head and on upper breast. Cheeks pale buffish-brown and throat white. Lower breast and belly white, white patch on hindwing, and two small white patches on each side of back. Bill slender and gray to light brown. Legs grayish-olive. **Nestling period:** Young tended by female only. Age of first flight estimated at 71 days.

Common Merganser (*Mergus merganser*)   Figure 23, Plate 26
Breeds by freshwater lakes or rivers, in wooded or, more rarely, open areas. Nest frequently in tree cavity, or in hole in bank, or cavity among boulders; will use nest-boxes. Usually 15–50 ft. up. Nest-site may be re-used annually.

Nest: Hollow, lined with nearby plants. Outside diameter: *c.* 12 in.; inside diameter: *c.* 7½ in.; depth: 4 in. No addition in tree cavities other than down. Down tufts large and pale gray. **Breeding season:** Beginning mid-March in south to early May in north. Usually ends by early June. Single-brooded. **Eggs:** 7–14, rarely 15. Elliptical to subelliptical, slightly long. Smooth and slightly glossy, creamy-white to yellowish. 66 × 46 mm. **Incubation:** Eggs laid on successive days. Incubation by female alone. 28–32 days. **Nestling:** Precocial and downy. Dark brown above and white below. Crown appears larger and rounder than that of Red-breasted Merganser. Sides of neck, nape and sides of head rusty rufous-tinted. Narrow whitish streak from bill below eye, and pale loral spot. White patch on wings and either side of rump; and white on fore and hind thigh. Bill dark brownish-gray with whitish nail. Legs yellowish-gray. **Nestling period:** Tended by female alone. Young said to remain in nest a day or two before leaving with female. Independent in *c.* 5 weeks.

Figure 22. Hooded Merganser chick: the least-boldly marked of the mergansers.

Figure 23. Common Merganser chick: dark cap and bill, light lower cheek, chin white.

Red-brested Merganser (Mergus serrator)   Figure 24, Plates 5, 26

Breeds by freshwater ponds, pools, and rivers, occasionally on coastal sites or off-shore islands. Nest is concealed under thicket or in cavity among rocks or tree-roots, more rarely hollow in bank, or in burrow, or pile of driftwood, or under low tree branches.

Nest: A hollow lined with nearby plant material, down, and some feathers. Down tufts darker gray than Common Merganser's, brown-tinged, with pale centers and palish tips. Outside diameter: 12–14 in.; inside diameter: 7–8 in. **Breeding season:** Begins early June. Single-brooded. **Eggs:** Usually 7–12, but up to 21 recorded. Elliptical to subelliptical. Smooth, but non-glossy to slightly glossy. Creamy-stone to greenish-buff. 66 × 45 mm. **Incubation:** By female alone, beginning with completion of clutch. 28–35 days. **Nestling:** Precocial and downy. Much like Common Merganser, but crown appears higher and angular. Brown above and white below. Crown dark brown, extending to just below eye, cheeks rufous, and throat white. Rufous spot before and above eye and white spot below it. White wing-bar, and white patches either side of back and rump. On bill, lower mandible is yellowish-brown, upper mandible grayish. Feet yellowish. **Nestling period:** Tended by female alone; broods tending to gather in larger packs with a single female. Flying by 59 days.

Ruddy Duck (Oxyura jamaicensis)   Plates 5, 26

Breeds on freshwater lakes, ponds, sloughs, and marshes, where open water is bordered by tall plants growing in water.

Nest: A partly floating structure attached to growing plants, well woven and built up above water level, with plants pulled together over it. Of reed stems, weeds, or other nearby plants, usually without down. Outside diameter: 8–16½ in.; inside diameter: 7–12 in. **Breeding season:** Begins late April in south to early June in north. Single-brooded. **Eggs:** 6–10, rarely to 20. Elliptical or short subelliptical. Rough and granular. Dull white. 64 × 42 mm. **Incubation:** By female alone, the male remaining nearby. 24 days. **Nestling:** Precocial and downy. Dark gray-brown above, white below. Dark cap; white line from nape to bill, below eye; and slanting dark line below this one separating it from the cheeks and throat which are white freckled with brown. Also a pale spot on either side of the back. Bill grayish-brown (lower mandible may be light) and distinctly spatulate with high bridge and narrow nail. Legs gray. **Nestling period:** This species and Masked Duck are unique among ducks in that the male remains and accompanies the brood. The young are clumsy on land but swim and dive well. Fly at 42–49 days.

Figure 24. Red-breasted Merganser chick: dusky cap and bill, cheek rufous, chin white.

Masked Duck (*Oxyura dominica*)

A rare breeder in ponds, usually small and always thickly vegetated, in southern Texas and possibly Florida. In a dense bed of reeds close to the water.
Nest: An elaborately built flat platform of green reeds, with little or no lining. **Breeding season:** April to November. **Eggs:** Usually 3–4, sometimes 2–6. Oval to subelliptical. Rough. Cream-colored, white, or pale bluish-white; smoother than those of the Ruddy Duck. 60 × 44 mm. **Incubation:** By female alone. Estimated at 28 days. **Nestling:** Precocial and downy. Dark gray-brown above, yellow below. Down notably long. Dark cap and cheek-stripe. Relatively long tail. Sides of head, hindneck, yellow-buff, as are pairs of spots on either sides of back and on sides of rump. Bill dark brown (lower mandible may be lighter), distinctly spatulate with wide brownish-red nail. Legs brownish-gray. **Nestling period:** Little information. Male assists female in caring for young.

American Vultures (*Cathartidae*)

Medium to large soaring birds, feeding on carrion. No nest built but protected sites such as tree or rock cavities used. May nest sociably. Two eggs laid by smaller species, one by large. Young are downy. Two down coats in California Condor, not certainly recorded for others. Young fed by regurgitation, taking the food directly from inside the adults' throats. Young mature slowly.

Black Vulture (*Coragyps atratus*)   Plates 6, 27

Breeds in secluded sites in wooded or open country. Nest on ledge in shallow cave or on low cliff or gully side, in hole under rock, in the cavity of a broken tree or tree-stump, or on the ground under a fallen tree or under thick vegetation. Usually up to 8 ft. up, rarely more than 15 ft. up. Nests singly or with several pairs near each other.
Nest: No nest is made. Birds may move the eggs about within the nesting area. **Breeding season:** Begins late January. Single-brooded but a lost clutch is usually replaced. **Eggs:** Normally 2, rarely 1, exceptionally 3. Subelliptical to blunt oval. Smooth and slightly glossy. Usually very pale gray-green, creamy-white or faintly buff; with sparse small blotches or spots of deep reddish-brown or light brown, faint lilac or purple, and occasionally a few large blotches. The markings sometimes concentrated at the larger end. 76 × 51 mm. **Incubation:** Eggs laid at 2-day intervals. Incubation by both sexes, beginning with first egg. 32–39 days. **Nestling:** Semi-altricial and downy. Down long, thick and creamy-buff, with a more reddish tint

on upperparts. Head bare. **Nestling period:** Young tended by both parents. They hatch at intervals and differ in size. They are active at 10 days. Brooded by both parents for first 6 weeks. First feathers at *c.* 17 days, but although full-grown at *c.* 6 weeks are still downy at 8 weeks, not feathered fully until 11 weeks. When younger they hide head and remain motionless when alarmed. At 8 weeks will leave nest cavity if on ground. At 10–11 weeks can fly a little and leave nest. When alarmed food is regurgitated. Dependent on parents for another 8–12 weeks.

Turkey Vulture (*Cathartes aura*)   Plates 6, 27
Breeds in a variety of habitats, but tends to select secluded and undisturbed sites. Nest may be in a cave or rock recess, or in unused building, or crevice in rocks, hollow log or stump, or on the ground in thick cover or a swamp. A dark site is preferred. Usually 0–20 ft. up. Where conditions are suitable several pairs may nest in proximity, but not contiguously.
Nest: No nest is built; but it is claimed that there may be some preparation of the site. **Breeding season:** Begins late January in south to mid-April in north. Single-brooded. **Eggs:** Usually 2, occasionally 1, rarely 3. Subelliptical to long subelliptical. Smooth and slightly glossy. White or creamy-white, sparsely or heavily marked with spots and small to medium, or rarely large, blotches of reddish-brown, dark brown, and faint purple, often concentrated at the larger end. Larger markings often combined with overall fine spotting or speckling of similar color. 71 × 49 mm. **Incubation:** By both sexes. Sitting birds leave reluctantly. 37–41 days. **Nestling:** Semi-altricial and downy. Down long and white, head mainly bare, with blackish skin, and a little thin white down over crown. **Nestling period:** Young tended by both adults. Fed by regurgitation. Young have eyes open at hatching and are more active than typical hawks. Feather slowly between second and tenth week. Fly at *c.* 11 weeks.

California Condor (*Gymnogyps californianus*)   Plate 27
Breeds on mountainsides at 1500–4500 ft., once at 6500 ft. in a limited area of southern California. Nest in a cave on cliff-face, or cavity behind a boulder, or, rarely in a large tree cavity. Nest-site may be re-used, or several sites used alternately.
Nest: No nest is built. A narrow site floored with sand or fine detritus is usually chosen within the nest cavity. **Breeding season:** Begins mid-February. Young mature slowly and successful nesting takes 2 years. **Eggs:** Only one. Long subelliptical. Smooth and glossy surface with very fine elongated pits. White faintly tinted green or blue. 110 × 67 mm. **Incubation:** By both sexes. 42–50 days. **Nestling:** Semi-altricial and downy. Down of first coat white, head and neck bare; skin flesh-pink becoming yellowish. Second down gray and woolly, also extending to head and neck. **Nestling period:** Young one tended by both parents. Brooded continuously for 2–3 weeks, then only at night for next 3–6 weeks. Subsequently visited by parents for feeding once a day. Feathers slowly between seventh and twenty-second week. Young may leave nest at *c.* 5 months, but may not be able to fly for another two months. Flies well at 10 months but may rely on feeding by parents until the following summer.

Kites, Hawks, Eagles, and Allies (*Accipitridae*)

Raptors, varying in size from large to small, and hunting live prey or scavenging. Nests are large cups of twigs and various debris; on trees, rock ledges, or on the ground. Leafy twigs may be added to the lining during incubation. Eggs are usually rather rounded, often slightly rough-textured, white or with brown blotchings, and frequently stained by leafy nest linings. The young hatch at intervals and vary in size; and the smallest may die of starvation or be killed and eaten by the older ones if food is short. The young are downy, with two down coats, and relatively helpless at first. As they grow they perform bouts of wing-flapping and practice seizing objects. They may leave the nest for nearby branches and return at times before the first real flight. They rely on the parents for food for a period after leaving the nest, while they learn to hunt, but information on this is relatively incomplete.

Osprey (*Pandion haliaetus*)   **Figure 25, Plates 6, 31**
Breeds near water on lakes, rivers, estuaries, and coasts. The nest-site usually on a tree-top or rocky outcrop overlooking a stretch of water. Sometimes on ruins, pilings, low bushes, or the ground on undisturbed sites; and artificial sites (e.g., cartwheels, on poles) may be used. Up to 60 ft. Solitary at times, but in colonies in suitable areas. Males polygamous on occasion, with two females nesting nearby.
Nest: A massive accumulation of sticks and debris including various man-made materials, re-used and added to in successive years. The cup lined with finer material, stems, and grasses. Both sexes build, the male tending to bring material and the female to incorporate it. **Breeding season:** Begins late March in south (as early as early December in Florida), to early June in north. Single-brooded. **Eggs:** Usually 3, rarely 2–4. Shortish subelliptical. Slightly glossy. Creamy to yellowish, spotted, and blotched variably with chestnut-red to dark brown, some pale grayish markings. 61 × 46 mm. **Incubation:** By both sexes, beginning with the first egg; female taking the greater part and being fed by the male. 32–33 days. **Nestling:** Semi-altricial and downy. First down short and thick. Mottled smoky-brown above and creamy-white below. A sandy-buff streak down the central back and on the head. Second down

Figure 25. Osprey: c. 3–5 ft. across; height is variable, from 1–10 ft.

similar above but dorsal streak whitish; and speckled with brown tips on pale under-side. Bill dark gray. Feathering begins at *c.* 3 weeks. **Nestling period:** Young varying in size and the smallest may die if food is scarce. They become active at *c.* 2 weeks. For *c.* 40 days female remains at nest brooding, feeding, and tending young; male brings food. Young feather towards end of this period; pick up food after *c.* 42 days; fly first at 51–59 days. Young depend on parents for at least 10–20 additional days.

Hook-billed Kite (*Chondrohierax uncinatus*)

An uncommon breeder in woodlands of the lower Rio Grande Valley of Texas. Nest in a tree *c.* 20–35 ft. up and often far out on a branch.

Nest: A shallow-cupped nest of dried sticks and twigs. Built by both sexes. **Breeding season:** Begins April–May. Single-brooded. **Eggs:** Usually 2. Elliptical. Unglossed white blotched with irregular spots of chocolate brown. 45 × 37 mm. **Incubation:** By both sexes. Period unknown. **Nestling:** Precocial and downy. Born with eyes open. Down rather long, white with reddish tinge on crown and upperparts, including wings. Beak and iris black, cere greenish-yellow. **Nestling period:** Little information. Young tended by both parents.

Swallow-tailed Kite (*Elanoides forficatus*)   Plate 28

Breeds in open or wooded areas, usually by fresh water. Nest in a tree in a clearing or on woodland edge. Usually situated well out on an upper branch, 60–100 ft. up. Several pairs may nest in close proximity.

Nest: A shallow cup of dead twigs broken off in flight; lined with Spanish Moss, more of which may be added during incubation. Nest *c.* 15–20 in. across by 12 in. deep. Cup 6 in. across by 4 in. deep. Built by both sexes over days, sometimes weeks. **Breeding season:** Begins early March in south, to early May in north. Usually ends by early June. Single-brooded. **Eggs:** Usually 2, sometimes 3, rarely 4. Shortish ellip-tical. Smooth, non-glossy or slightly glossy. White, marked, often heavily, with blotches of reddish-brown, usually varied in size and often distributed overall or sometimes concentrated at larger end. Large markings at times combined with pro-fuse minute speckling of similar color. 47 × 37 mm. **Incubation:** Mostly by female. 28 days. **Nestling:** Semi-altricial and downy. First down buffish-white. Second down darker on nape and breast. **Nestling period:** Young tended by female while male brings food. Young leave at 36–42 days; dependent on parents at least 2 weeks after leaving nest.

White-tailed Kite (*Elanus leucurus*)   Figure 26, Plate 28

Breeds in open country – cultivation, meadows and marshes – with scattered trees. Nest in a tree, usually near water, 12–60 ft. up. Several pairs may nest in nearby trees. Old nests of other birds may be used as nest foundation.

Nest: A loose but well-built twig structure, lined with dry grass, roots, Spanish Moss, and other plant material. For second broods a second nest is built on a different site. Nest built by female, but male may initiate building behavior. Outside diameter: *c.* 20 in.; inside diameter: *c.* 7 in. **Breeding season:** Begins mid-February. Probably ends early July. Sometimes double-brooded. **Eggs:** Usually 4–5. Short subelliptical. Smooth and non-glossy or slightly glossy. White or faintly buffish; very heavily mottled and blotched overall with deep reddish-brown, more concentrated towards the larger end, while ground color becomes buff-tinted. 42 × 33 mm. **Incubation:** By female only, the male remaining nearby and feeding the female. 28–30 days. **Nestling:** Semi-altricial and downy. First down is short, whitish tinged with pink-ish-buff on the back. Second down bluish-gray. **Nestling period:** Young tended by female, but all food brought by male and passed to female away from nest. Female

Figure 26. White-tailed Kite: c. 20 in. across; twig structure lined with grass and roots.

tears up food for first 24 days. Young fly at 35–40 days, but may return to nest to feed or brood. First brood young are tolerated until the second brood has hatched in a different nest.

Snail Kite (*Rostrhamus sociabilis*)   Plates 6, 28

Breeds in open marsh areas of the Everglades of southern Florida. Nest low in a bush or tree growing in the water, 3–15 ft. up, or on the ground in thick marsh grass or reeds. Pairs usually nest in a colony.

Nest: A loose structure of plant stems or twigs, lined with fine twigs and stems, leaves or sawgrass heads. Males do most of the nest-building. Outside diameter: 7–12 in.; depth: 1½–3½ in. **Breeding season:** Usually February–June; sometimes late November to early July; in wet years either parent may desert mate and young near fledging and probably re-mate. **Eggs:** Usually 3–4, sometimes 2. Elliptical to shortish elliptical. Smooth and non-glossy. White with usually an overall speckling and spotting of dull or dark brown, or reddish-brown, and with larger irregular blotching of the same color. Often markings concentrated in a zone around or at the larger end. Sometimes extensive pale blotching. 44 × 36 mm. **Incubation:** Begins generally after second egg. By both sexes. 27 days. **Nestling:** Semi-altricial and downy. First down buff, tinged with cinnamon on crown, wings, and rump. Second down thicker; dark grayish-brown. **Nestling period:** Young tended by both parents. Young leave the nest at 23–34 days. Able to feed themselves at *c.* 10 weeks of age.

Mississippi Kite (*Ictinia mississippiensis*)   Plate 28
Breeds in open pine forest and woodland bordering lakes and rivers of more open regions. In the Great Plains will use shelterbelts. In the west in scrub oaks or scattered trees. Nest in a fork or crotch of a tree, high up where possible but low in scrub oaks. Usually 30–135 ft. up. A number of pairs may nest in a loose colony.
Nest: Variable twig structures, small flimsy platforms to compact structures; usually irregular or oval. *c.* 14 × 11 in., and 5 in. deep. Cup shallow and lined with green leaves. **Breeding season:** Begins mid-March. Single-brooded; but a lost clutch will be replaced. **Eggs:** Usually 2, sometimes 1–3. Short elliptical to short subelliptical. Bluish-white. Smooth and non-glossy. 41 × 34 mm. **Incubation:** By both sexes. 30–32 days. **Nestling:** Semi-altricial and downy. Down whitish, tinged with buffish-brown on upperparts and nape. Lores grayish. Bill dull blue-gray, cere brownish-orange, gape light orange. Eyes grayish-brown. Legs and feet yellowish-orange. **Nestling period:** Young tended by both parents, bringing food (insects) to the nest. Small young are fed directly, older young have food disgorged on to nest. Young leave nest at *c.* 34 days. Rely on adults for food for several weeks afterwards. Fledged young are fed on the wing.

Bald Eagle (*Haliaeetus leucocephalus*)   Figure 27, Plates 6, 30
Breeds usually by lakes, large rivers, and on coasts. Nest a large, conspicuous structure on a site with a wide view; in a large tree, or on a rocky outcrop, or may be on the ground on islands. Usually close to water. Site usually re-used annually.
Nest: A massive structure of sticks and branches; the deep cup lined with grass, pine needles, and plant stems. Leafy twigs are added throughout the nesting period. With constant annual additions nests may become huge, sometimes ultimately *c.* 12 ft. high and 8½ ft. across. Typically, outside diameter: 6 ft.; inside diameter: 20 in.; depth: 4–5 in. **Breeding season:** Begins late autumn, early November, in Florida, to May in north. Single-brooded. **Eggs:** Usually 2, rarely 1–3, short subelliptical to short oval. Rough-shelled. White and non-glossy. 71 × 54 mm. **Incubation:** Eggs laid at several day intervals. Incubation by both sexes. 35–46 days. **Nestling:** Semi-altricial and downy. First down gray, slightly paler on head and underparts, almost white on chin and throat. Second down drab dark brown. **Nestling period:** Young tended by both parents. First hatched young frequently kills or starves the second. Feathers at *c.* 5 weeks. Leaves nest at 10–11 weeks, but may return to nest to feed and rest.

White-tailed Eagle (*Haliaeetus albicilla*)   Plate 30
Breeds by coasts, large rivers or lakes in southwest Greenland and at the end of the Aleutian chain in Alaska. Nests on the ground or a rock outcrop, to 65 ft. or higher. In solitary pairs, using several alternative nest sites within a territory.
Nest: A massive structure, built slowly and added to continually. Of branches and twigs, the cup lined with green plants, kelp, and leafy twigs. Smaller nests may be 1 ft. high and 3 ft. across. Both sexes build, the male tending to bring most material and the female incorporating it. **Breeding season:** Begins late March. Ends late July (Greenland). Single-brooded. **Eggs:** Usually 2, sometimes 1–3, rarely 4. Short subelliptical to elliptical. Slightly glossy. Dull white. 78 × 58 mm. **Incubation:** Eggs laid at 2–4-day intervals. Incubation by both sexes or by female alone, beginning with the first egg. Green branches for lining brought during incubation. 35–45 days. **Nestling:** Semi-altricial and downy. First down thin and long, creamy to grayish-buff, darker on wings and rump, paler on throat. Replaced at *c.* 3 weeks by second down; longer, coarse and woolly. Pale grayish-buff above, darker on sides and underside. Feathering begins at *c.* 30 days. **Nestling period:** Young brooded and tended closely by female for 2 weeks, female in attendance nearby for an additional 2 weeks; male bringing all food during this period. Young become active at *c.* 10 days, pick up

Figure 27. Bald Eagle: c. 5 ft. across; a new nest can be this size; it will be added to each year.

food at *c.* 35–40 days, move from nest at *c.* 56 days. No loss of smallest. They fly at *c.* 70 days, remaining near nest and relying on parents for food for an additional 35–40 days.

Northern Harrier (*Circus cyaneus*)   Plate 31

Breeds on meadows and open marshland, salt or fresh. Nest on the ground; usually in the shelter of taller vegetation, shrubs or grasses. The same area but not the same site may be re-used. Pairs associate in a loose colony at times. Males may be polygamous. **Nest:** On dry sites a thin layer of small sticks and reeds, lined with grass. On wet ground it is a larger and substantially thicker structure. Built mainly by the female. Outside diameter: 15–30 in.; inside diameter: 8–9 in.; depth: 2 in. **Breeding season:** Begins mid-March in the south to mid-May in the north. Single-brooded. Replacement clutches may be laid. **Eggs:** 4–6, rarely up to 12. Short subelliptical. Bluishwhite, rarely blotched with light brown; inside of shell green. 47 × 36 mm. **Incubation:** Eggs laid at intervals of 2 days or more. Incubation by female alone, beginning with second to fourth egg. 29–39 days. **Nestling:** Altricial and downy. First down mainly white with buffish on back and wings, and sides of head and neck, and a dark patch surrounding the eye. Second down buffish-brown above, becoming paler on the sides, and whitish below. Irides blue-gray. Cere and feet pinkish, turning yellow. **Nestling period:** Young closely brooded and fed by female for *c.* 2 weeks, the male bringing food and passing it to the female in mid-air. The young begin to feather at *c.* 14 days and this is complete in *c.* 35 days. During this period they leave the nest and hide in nearby vegetation, returning when the parent brings food. Very small young often die. Young fly at *c.* 37 days, at first remaining nearby while the adults bring food, later accompanying them. The point of independence varies from *c.* 45 days to *c.* 66 days. Males occasionally have 2 or 3 females but this forces the females to hunt too, with a greater likelihood of nest loss.

Sharp-shinned Hawk (*Accipiter striatus*)   Plate 28
Breeds in forest, or sometimes in groves of trees in more open country. Prefers thick cover and conifers when available. Nest in a tree, in a crotch or next to the trunk on a horizontal branch, 10–60 ft. up. Occasionally the old nest of a bird or squirrel used as a foundation; rarely nest is in a hollow of tree-trunk or a cliff crevice.
Nest: A large, well-built twig structure; lined with finer twigs and strips of bark, or with chips of bark. Nest usually newly built annually and not re-used. Outside diameter: 24–26 in.; inside diameter: 6 in.; depth: 2–3 in.; height: 6 in. **Breeding season:** Begins mid-April. Single-brooded. **Eggs:** Usually 4–5, rarely 3–8. Short subelliptical to elliptical. Smooth and non-glossy. Bluish-white; very variably marked with dark or light brown or reddish-brown, and rarely pale grey or lilac. Markings may be sparse large blotches, distinct zones, irregular large and small blotches, speckling, or ill-defined mottling; sometimes concentrated at the larger end. 38 × 30 mm. **Incubation:** By both sexes (beginning with last egg). 30–35 days. **Nestling:** Semi-altricial and downy. First down short; creamy-white or yellowish. Second down longer and pale purplish-buff to white, sometimes with some grey on the back. **Nestling period:** Young tended by female while male brings food and passes it to female away from nest. Eggs hatch over a short period. Young begin feathering at 14 days, fly at *c.* 23 days. Young dependent on adults for 21–28 days postfledging.

Cooper's Hawk (*Accipiter cooperii*)   Plates 6, 28
Breeds in forests, or in groves or trees along rivers, but also in low scrub of treeless area. The wooded area is often near the edge of a field or a water-opening. Nest in a tree, 20–60 ft. up. Nest usually near to the tree-trunk on a horizontal branch, but may also be built on the foundation of an old nest of bird or squirrel.
Nest: A broad, flat twig platform, lined just before laying with flakes and chips of bark. Bark and, more rarely, leafy twigs are added during incubation and may be several inches deep by hatching. The male does most of the building, although the female may undertake relining if an old nest is used. Outside diameter: 24–28 in.; inside diameter: 8 in.; depth: 2–4 in.; height: 6–8 in. **Breeding season:** Begins late February in south to late April in north. Single-brooded, but lost clutches will be replaced. **Eggs:** Usually 4, sometimes 5–6. Short subelliptical to elliptical. Smooth and non-glossy. White, tinged pale blue. Rarely with pale brown specks or a few tiny blotches. 49 × 38 mm. **Incubation:** Eggs laid every second day, with extra day interval between fourth and fifth egg. Incubation begins with third egg, by female alone, but male who brings food for female may cover eggs. 36 days (fifth egg takes 35 days). **Nestling:** Semi-altricial and downy. First down short, creamy-white. Second down short, silky and white. Eyes blue-gray, tinged brown at first. **Nestling period:** Young tended by female. Male brings food to female away from nest for first 3 weeks when female is brooding young. Later when female also hunts he takes food to nest. Young grow rapidly for first 17 days; then feather in next 3 weeks. Young become active and

feed themselves at 3 weeks. Young male leaves nest at *c.* 30 days, female at *c.* 34 days. For *c.* 10 days young return to nest for food. Young take *c.* 3 weeks to learn to hunt. Become independent at *c.* 8 weeks.

Northern Goshawk (*Accipiter gentilis*)   Plate 28
Breeds mostly in mature woodlands. Nest is in a tree; usually built by the bird, more rarely based on a nest of another species. Up to 75 ft. Old nest may be re-used and a series of alternative sites in the territory utilized. Larger nests may have an outside diameter of 3–4 ft. and a height of 18–35 in.

Nest: A large, shallow, untidy structure of dead twigs, lined with pieces of bark and leafy green twigs or bunches of conifer needles which are constantly renewed. Built mainly by the female. **Breeding season:** Begins in March in the south to mid-June in the north. Single-brooded. **Eggs:** 2–3, rarely 1–5. Short subelliptical. Non-glossy and rough-textured. Pale bluish-white. 59 × 45 mm. **Incubation:** Eggs laid at 3-day intervals. Incubation mainly or entirely by the female, fed by the male. 36–41 days. **Nestling:** Semi-altricial and downy. First down short, silky and thick above, sparser below, white. Second down longer and woollier; gray-tinged above and white below. Irides gray. Cere and feet light yellow. **Nestling period:** The female closely broods and feeds the young for 8–10 days, and after this remains nearby; the male bringing food. The young feather in 18–38 days. They tear up food from *c.* 28 days. The female brings leafy twigs for renewing the nest lining through most of the period. The young leave the nest to perch at *c.* 40 days, and fly at *c.* 45 days, after which the female also hunts. The young begin hunting at *c.* 50 days and are independent at *c.* 70 days.

Common Black-Hawk (*Buteogallus anthracinus*)   Plate 31
Breeds in riverine woodland near water along parts of the US–Mexican border from Arizona to Texas. Nest in a tree at very varied heights, from 15–100 ft. up, but often low. Nest may be re-used in successive years.

Nest: Often small at first, becoming very large with re-use. Of large sticks mixed with smaller twigs, stems and debris; lined with finer twigs and green leaves. Twigs are collected in flight. Leaved twigs added until young fledge. Built by both sexes. Outside diameter: *c.* 20 in.; inside diameter: *c.* 10 in.; height: 8 in. **Breeding season:** Begins early April. Usually ends by late July. Single-brooded. **Eggs:** One, sometimes 2, rarely 3. Short subelliptical to elliptical. With granular surface. Grayish-white, with small specks and blotches, or indistinct smudging of light brown or purplish-brown and faint purple. 57 × 45 mm. **Incubation:** By both. 38 days. **Nestling:** Semi-altricial and downy. Down whitish on head and breast but dull gray on back and head, throat, and sides of breast. Dark eye-patch prominent. Legs pinkish. **Nestling period:** Brooded by female, with the male bringing food through day 15, after which both parents hunt. Young leave nest at 43–50 days. Dependent on parents another 6–8 weeks.

Harris's Hawk (*Parabuteo unicinctus*)   Figure 28, Plate 31
Breeds in open areas, dry woodland, or scrub. Nest in a small tree, tall shrubby growth, or on a cactus, often low, from 5–30 ft. up. Nest in social units of up to seven individuals.

Nest: A variably sized platform, often compact but sometimes flimsy or bulky. Of sticks, twigs, plant stems and roots, lined with leaves, grass, bark, Spanish Moss and roots; and sometimes fur and animal bones. Built mainly by female. **Breeding season:** Usually begins early February. Prolonged activity, though concentrated April–June. Double- or sometimes treble-brooded. **Eggs:** Usually 2–4. Short sub-

Figure 28. Harris's Hawk: c. 18–24 in. across; in a Saguaro cactus in this case.

elliptical. Smooth and non-glossy. White or bluish-white. Sometimes with small irregular markings of pale brown or lavender gray. 53 × 42 mm. **Incubation:** By both parents, mostly by breeding female, but sometimes assisted by other members of group. Beginning with first egg. c. 31–36 days. **Nestling:** Semi-altricial and downy. First down light buff. Second down described as rich brown at 5–6 days, and also as buff becoming white. This might be due to fading. **Nestling period:** Breeding female stays at nest for first week; food delivered by breeding male and other group members. Young are well feathered and beginning to feed themselves at 17 days. Leave nest at c. 38 days to climb about. Fly at c. 45–50 days.

Gray Hawk (*Buteo nitidus*)   Plate 31
Breeds in or by riverine forest in southeast Arizona and the lower Rio Grande Valley in Texas. Nest usually in large tree (often a cottonwood), up to 90 ft. up; but may be in thorny mesquites at 35–40 ft. up. Nest often hidden in foliage.

Nest: Small and shallow, of twigs often freshly broken off, and lined with leafy stems. Outside diameter: 18 in. **Breeding season:** Begins late March. Single-brooded. **Eggs:** Usually 2, sometimes 1–3. Subelliptical. White or bluish-white. Usually unmarked, or rarely with a few tiny pale brown marks. 51 × 41 mm. **Incubation:** By female. 32–34 days. **Nestling:** Semi-altricial and downy. Down dull white below and on head, grayish-brown on back and wings, and a grayish-brown streak behind eye. Cere yellow. Irides brown. Bill black. Feet dull yellow. **Nestling period:** Little information. Fed by both adults. Flight estimated at 42 days.

Red-shouldered Hawk (Buteo lineatus)   Plate 28

Breeds usually in moist woodland. Nest in a large tree, usually in a large crotch; in Florida may use palmettos. Usually 20–60 ft. up. Old nests of birds or squirrels may be used as foundations.
Nest: A bulky twig structure, rather flat on top, lined with stems, leaves, lichens, and bark. Leafy twigs are added during nesting. Outside diameter: 18–24 in.; inside diameter: 8 in.; depth: 2–3 in.; height: 8–12 in. **Breeding season:** Begins late January in south (even earlier in southern California) to mid-April in north. Usually ends by late June. Single-brooded, but more than one clutch may be laid to replace lost clutches. **Eggs:** Usually 2–3, sometimes 4, rarely 5. Short subelliptical to elliptical. Smooth and slightly glossy. Dull white or with faint buff wash. Very variably marked in reddish-brown or dark brown, and rarely pale lilac. Markings bold to indistinct. Large to small blotches, spots, or specks. Larger markings often concentrated towards larger end. 55 × 43 mm. (Those of southern birds average little smaller). **Incubation:** By both sexes possibly mainly by female, fed by male. Beginning with first egg. 23–25 days. **Nestling:** Semi-altricial and downy. First down coat long, soft and silky, longest on head, white below and buffish-white above, with purplish-buff tint on back and wings. Darker down around eye; bill black; cere yellow. Second down coat thick and woolly. Pure white below, grayish-white above. **Nestling period:** Young tended by both adults. Young hatch over a period and vary in size. Inactive at first, becoming active at c. 10 days. Begin feathering at c. 2 weeks. Leave nest at 5–6 weeks.

Broad-winged Hawk (Buteo platypterus)   Plate 29

Breeds in forest. Nest in a tree, deciduous or coniferous, usually 18–90 ft. up but has occurred as low as 3 ft. Nest usually in a main crotch but, especially in conifers, may be next to the trunk on a horizontal branch. May take 3 weeks or more to build. Old nests of other birds or of squirrels may be used. Site usually used only once. Outside diameter: 14–21 in.; inside diameter: 6–7 in.; depth: 1–3 in.; height: 5–12 in.
Nest: A usually small and loose structure of twigs, sparsely lined with chips of bark and lichens, and with leafy twigs added during nesting. Built by both sexes but lined by female. **Breeding season:** Begins mid-April in south to late May or early June in north. Single-brooded. **Eggs:** Usually 2–3, rarely 4. Short subelliptical. Smooth and non-glossy. White usually marked with brown, buff, reddish-brown, purplish-brown, pale lilac, or gray; often with profuse tiny speckling and sparser larger irregular blotches. Sometimes almost unmarked. 49 × 39 mm. **Incubation:** Mostly by female. 28–31 days. **Nestling:** Semi-altricial and downy. First down short; buffish-white with gray bases, fading to white. Second down white. **Nestling period:** Young tended by both parents. Brooded by female for 1–2 weeks. Male provides most of food. Begin feathering at c. 2 weeks. Leave nest at 29–30 days, begin hunting at 37–46 days, but depend on adults until 50–56 days.

Short-tailed Hawk (*Buteo brachyurus*)

Breeds in forest, in or near a swamp, or in mangroves in Florida, south of the panhandle. Nest in a tree, 15–95 ft. up.

Nest: A large stick cup; lined with finer twigs, Spanish Moss and green leaves. Generally, the male gathers the material and the female arranges it. About 24–36 in. across and 6–12 in. deep. Fresh twigs with leaves added during incubation and brooding. **Breeding season:** Early March to early July. Single-brooded. **Eggs:** Usually 2, occasionally 1–3. Short subelliptical to oval. Smooth and non-glossy. Bluish-white to dull white, or with a buffish wash; unmarked or with sparse speckling or scattered scrawls or spots in pale buff or brown; or heavy irregular spotting and blotching of dark brown, often concentrated at one end. 53 × 43 mm. **Incubation:** By female. 34 days. **Nestling:** Semi-altricial and downy. Down white. **Nestling period:** At first, food brought by male, fed to young by female. Later, both provide food. Time of first flight and full independence unknown.

Swainson's Hawk (*Buteo swainsoni*)   Plate 29

Breeds in open country, usually nesting in scattered trees. Nest usually high in a tree, but when necessary in a low tree, on a giant cactus, on a ledge of a rock outcrop or embankment, and exceptionally on the ground. Usually 6–30 ft. up. Nests are usually re-used annually.

Nest: An often large and conspicuous structure of twigs and grasses, lined with bark, lichens, and plant material, and with leafy twigs added at intervals. Outside diameter: 21–28 in.; inside diameter: 8–9 in.; depth: 2–5 in. **Breeding season:** Begins early March in south to mid-May in north. Single-brooded. **Eggs:** Usually 2, rarely 3–4. Short subelliptical to elliptical. Smooth and non-glossy. White, sparsely marked with some dark brown or pale purplish blotches around larger end, or sparse tiny speckling in reddish brown or indistinct buff. 56 × 44 mm. **Incubation:** By both sexes, beginning with first egg. 28 days. **Nestling:** Semi-altricial and downy. First down thick; white with yellowish tint. Second down white. **Nestling period:** Young tended by both parents. Young hatch over several days and differ in size. Fly at *c.* 4–5 weeks.

White-tailed Hawk (*Buteo albicaudatus*)   Plate 29

Breeds in open country and low scrub in southern Texas. Nest on a low tree, large shrub, or the crown of a yucca; usually 4–15 ft. up. Usually on a slight rise and often visible for some distance. Nest re-used annually.

Nest: Large, increasing in size with annual rebuilding. Of twigs, often thorny, and grass tufts, lined with finer plant material, and leafy twigs added. Built by both sexes. Outside diameter: 26–36 in.; inside diameter: 11 in.; depth: 4½ in.; height: 18 in. **Breeding season:** Begins late January. Usually ends by late July. Single-brooded. **Eggs:** Usually 2, occasionally 1–3. Short subelliptical. White, unmarked or with some faint sparse specklings of pale brown or lavender. 59 × 47 mm. **Incubation:** By both. 31 days. **Nestling:** Semi-altricial and downy. Down short and yellowish-white with a warm brown tint on head and wings. The down on the head is long and silky. There is a blackish area around the eye. **Nestling period:** Fed by both. Young fly at 49–53 days.

Zone-tailed Hawk (*Buteo albonotatus*)

Breeds in broken or riverside woodland. Nest in a tree. Site and height vary, from 25–100 ft. up and from concealed to exposed. In deciduous (often cottonwoods) or coniferous trees, rarely in mesquite trees.

Nest: A bulky twig structure, lined with plant material and with leafy twigs added. **Breeding season:** Begins late April. Single-brooded. **Eggs:** Usually 2, rarely 1–3.

Short subelliptical. Smooth and non-glossy. White or bluish-white, exceptionally with a few fine brown spots. 55 × 43 mm. **Incubation:** By both. 35 days. **Nestling:** Semi-altricial and downy. Down grayish. **Nestling period:** Leave nest at 35–42 days; fly at 42–49 days. Adults continue to provide food for some weeks after fledging.

Red-tailed Hawk (*Buteo jamaicensis* – *Includes Harlan's Hawk*, *B. j. harlani*) Plate 28

Breeds in a wide variety of habitats. Nest normally in a tall tree often bordering open space or in an isolated, commanding position (usually 35–90 ft.); but low trees may be used if necessary, or large cacti in desert regions, and elsewhere ledges of rock outcrops or cliffs. Nest may be re-used annually.
Nest: A bulky structure of twigs with finer lining of stems and bark, and leafy twigs are added throughout the nesting period. Both sexes build. Outside diameter: *c.* 28–30 in.; inside diameter: *c.* 14–15 in.; depth: *c.* 4–6 in. **Breeding season:** Begins mid-February in south to early April in north. Single-brooded. **Eggs:** Usually 2–3, sometimes 4, rarely 1 or 5. Elliptical to short subelliptical. Smooth and non-glossy. White, sometimes with a faint buffish wash; sparsely or heavily marked with blotches of buff, pale reddish-brown, dark brown or purple. Markings often indistinct or combined with fine speckling. 59 × 47 mm. **Incubation:** By both sexes, but mainly by the female, fed by the male. 28–32 days. **Nestling:** Semi-altricial and downy. First down long, soft and silky above, shorter below, grayish or buffish-white. Second down shorter and woollier; white. **Nestling period:** Young tended by both parents. They are active from the second day; begin to peck at food at *c.* 1 week, begin feathering at *c.* 16 days. At *c.* 4 weeks may leave the nest for nearby branches. Feed themselves at 4–5 weeks from food brought by parents. Fly at *c.* 6 weeks. Learn to hunt by *c.* 3 weeks after leaving nest.

Ferruginous Hawk (*Buteo regalis*) Plate 29

Breeds in open country, including prairie grassland and shrubsteppe, using a tree where available and nesting high in it, but will also use low hillside bushes, a ledge of a rock outcrop or cliff, or among rocks on a hillside. 6–55 ft. up. Will use artificial nest platform. Nests are re-used annually.
Nest: A bulky structure becoming massive and high with constant re-use; of sticks, old bones, and similar debris, lined with grass, shredded bark, and horse or cow dung. Built by both. Outside diameter: 24–42 in.; height: *c.* 24 in. **Breeding season:** Begins mid-April. Probably ends by mid-July. **Eggs:** Usually 3–4, sometimes 5. Short subelliptical to elliptical. Smooth and non-glossy. White to bluish-white; finely and irregularly speckled and spotted or with additional sparser larger blotching in reddish-brown, medium brown, buffish-brown or light purple. Sometimes almost unmarked. Rarely with sparse faint scribbling. 62 × 49 mm. **Incubation:** By both sexes. 32–36 days. **Nestling:** Semi-altricial and downy. First down white, tinged gray on back and wings. Second down thicker; white. Bill gray; mouth pink. **Nestling period:** Young tended by both parents. Leave nest at 44–48 days.

Rough-legged Hawk (*Buteo lagopus*) Plate 29

Breeds in bare, open, and mountainous regions; or in open woodland. Nest usually on a ledge or rock outcrop in more open regions, or in a tree in wooded areas. On an outcrop or cliff, the nest is usually near the top. Nests may be re-used annually or several alternate sites may be used.
Nest: A bulky structure of twigs, lined with moss, grass, and other green plant material. New nests may be small but with re-use become very large and often very tall if supported at the side. **Breeding season:** Begins early May, possibly later farther

north. Single-brooded, no replacement clutches laid. Young from late clutches have poor chance of survival. **Eggs:** Usually 2–3, 5–7 in good lemming years. Short sub-elliptical to short elliptical. Non-glossy. White, very variably marked with blotches or streaks of chestnut-red and brown. 55 × 44 mm. **Incubation:** By both sexes or by female alone, beginning with first egg. 28–31 days. **Nestling:** Semi-altricial and downy. First down pale grayish-brown above, white below. Second down thicker, dark gray. **Nestling period:** Female broods the young closely and feeds them; the male bringing food. Later she remains nearby but does not hunt until the young are well feathered. Young vary in size and small ones may die and be eaten at c. 2 weeks old. Second down acquired at c. 10 days and feathers by c. 35 days. They fly at c. 41 days.

Golden Eagle (Aquila chrysaetos)   Plates 6, 30
Breeds in mountain regions. Nests on rock ledges of outcrops or cliffs, or in trees (10–100 ft. up), individuals using either or both. Several alternate sites within a territory are used.
Nest: New nests on ledges tend to be large but thin, those on trees are thicker; but both become massive with re-use. Building may occur at more than one site during a year. Nests are of thick branches, twigs, and stems of any kind, and are lined with leafy twigs or tufts of conifer needles, which may be added continually during the nesting period. Outside diameter: 2½–3 ft. for new nests, 5–6 ft. for old; height: 1½ ft. for new nests, 4–5 ft. for old. **Breeding season:** Begins early February in the south to late May to June in the north. Single-brooded. **Eggs:** Usually 2, sometimes 1, rarely 3. Short subelliptical. Non-glossy, white, usually spotted or blotched with brown, chestnut-red and pale gray; the two in a clutch often varying with one unmarked. 77 × 59 mm. **Incubation:** Eggs laid at 3–4-day intervals. Incubation usually by female alone, sometimes by both, beginning with first egg. 43–45 days. **Nestling:** Semi-altricial and downy. First down white or with pale gray tips. Second down thicker and woollier, white. Irides brown. Bill blackish. Cere and legs yellowish-white. **Nestling period:** Young are closely brooded by the female at first, brooding ceasing at c. 30 days, the young feathering at 30–50 days. Usually the smaller young one dies. The female feeds young on food brought by the male, continuing until c. 40 days when young feed themselves. Later both parents bring food. The young exercise and practice pouncing while on the nest at c. 50 days and fly at c. 63–70 days, but are weak on the wing for another 3 weeks.

Caracaras and Falcons (Falconidae)

Small to medium-sized raptors, usually capable of swift flight and capturing prey on the wing. They breed in solitary pairs or colonies. They make no nest, using a natural cavity or ledge, or the nest of another large bird. The Crested Caracara is an exception, feeding on carrion and building a large nest. The eggs are rather rounded and usually mostly, or entirely, chestnut-red in color. The young are downy, having two successive down coats before feathering. Within a brood young usually hatch at intervals, varying in size; and the smallest may die if food is scarce, but not through the aggression of other young.

Crested Caracara (Caracara plancus)   Plates 6, 32
Breeds in various habitats, though shows a preference for open brushland in central and south Texas, central Florida, and south-central Arizona. Nests may be in trees, usually concealed among branches, or palm fronds (especially Cabbage Palms in Florida), or on cacti; from 8–80 ft. up. In treeless areas nests may be on rock ledges

or under overhanging rocks, or on the ground in a secluded site such as a marsh island. Nests often re-used annually.
Nest: A large untidy structure, of sticks, plant stems, vines, briars, and weeds, unlined or lined with debris including dung and animal remains. Nest often bulky with re-use, and with a deep cup. **Breeding season:** January–September (Texas); December–August (Florida). Lost clutches are replaced. Double-brooded at times. **Eggs:** Usually 2–3, rarely 4. Short subelliptical to elliptical. Smooth and non-glossy or slightly glossy. White to pinkish-white, buff, orange-buff or purplish; marked with chestnut-red, reddish-brown or brown. Often so heavily speckled, mottled, blotched, or smeared as to obscure ground color which in most instances is tinted with profuse fine speckling. 59 × 46 mm. **Incubation:** By both sexes. c. 28 days. **Nestling:** Semi-altricial and downy. First down pinkish-buff? Second down similar but with dark rich brown on upper head, and patches on shoulders, thighs, and rump. **Nestling period:** Young tended by both parents. Fed on fragments torn from carcasses in typical falcon fashion. Age at first flight 42–56 days.

American Kestrel (Falco sparverius)   Plate 32
Breeds in open country, areas with scattered trees, or woodland edge. Nest in a hole, a natural cavity or crevice in a tree, a woodpecker hole, or a similar cavity in a building or a rocky or earth bank. Usually 9–32 ft. up. Rarely in the old nest of another bird. Will use nest-boxes.
Nest: A shallow scrape. No material added other than what is already present. **Breeding season:** Begins early March in the south to late May in the north. May be double-brooded. **Eggs:** Usually 4–5, sometimes 3–7. Short subelliptical to subelliptical. Smooth and non-glossy. White, creamy or pale pink, with minute speckling tinting the ground color pale buff or pink, with indistinct mottling or fine spotting and occasionally small blotches in reddish-brown or medium brown. Darker tint often concentrated towards one end. 35 × 29 mm. **Incubation:** Eggs laid at 2–3-day intervals. Incubation mostly by female, the male bringing food and occasionally assisting. 29–30 days. **Nestling:** Semi-altricial and downy. First down rather scanty, white. Second down thicker and creamy or yellowish-white. **Nestling period:** Young tended by both parents, being brooded and fed by female at first, the male bringing all food. Later both hunt. Young feed themselves at 20 days, leave nest at 30 days.

Merlin (Falco columbarius)   Plates 6, 32
Breeds in forest, in sparse woodland bordering open areas, in mountain areas, and open plain or prairie with scattered trees. Nest in large old nests of other birds in trees, in open tree cavities, on cliff-ledges or rocky hillsides, or on the ground. Usually 15–35 ft. up, though may be up to 60 ft. up.
Nest: Normally a bare hollow; but nests on the ground may have a plant lining apparently pulled in by the sitting bird; while old nests have their original material. **Breeding season:** Begins from early to mid-May. Usually ends by early July. Single-brooded. **Eggs:** Usually 5–6, occasionally 2–7. Short subelliptical to short elliptical. Smooth, non-glossy. Pale buff, usually obscured by a heavy sprinkling of red, purplish-red, or brown and often appearing wholly of the latter colors. 40 × 31 mm. **Incubation:** Eggs laid at about 2-day intervals. Incubation mainly by the female, beginning before completion of the clutch, the male bringing all food. 28–32 days. **Nestling:** Altricial and downy. First down, thinner and shorter, creamy-white. Second down longer and coarser, brownish-gray above, pale gray below, and white with gray bases on chin, throat, and belly. **Nestling period:** Young closely brooded by female in the early stages, the male bringing food but rarely feeding the young. Later both adults hunt. The young are mainly feathered by 18 days, and fly at 25–30 days. They remain nearby and take c. 6 weeks to become independent.

Aplomado Falcon (*Falco femoralis*)

A former breeder in grassland and scrub desert from south Texas to southeast Arizona. Uses the old nests of large birds such as Chihuahuan Ravens, which are usually in yuccas, mesquites or other low trees, at 7–25 ft. up.

Nest: No nest other than the material already present. **Breeding season:** Late February to October. Single-brooded. **Eggs:** Usually 2–3, rarely 4. Subelliptical to short subelliptical. Smooth and non-glossy. White to pinkish-white; profusely marked with speckling, spots, and blotches of light brown or chestnut-red. 45 × 35 mm. **Incubation:** By both sexes. 31–32 days. **Nestling:** Semi-altricial and downy. Down white. Eyes closed; cere bluish, legs and feet greenish-yellow. **Nestling period:** Tended by both parents. Fly at 28–35 days. Dependent on parents after leaving nest.

Prairie Falcon (*Falco mexicanus*)   Plate 32

Breeds in open regions, with rock outcrops or cliffs. Nest on a ledge under an overhang, or in a pothole or shallow cave in cliff face. Usually 30–40 ft. up, though may be up to 400 ft. up on cliffs. Sometimes old nests of other birds in such sites are used. Often several alternate sites used.

Nest: A scrape in any soft substrate, or any old nest material already present. **Breeding season:** Begins mid-April. Single-brooded. **Eggs:** Usually 4–5, occasionally 3–6. Subelliptical to short subelliptical. Smooth and non-glossy. White or pinkish-white, with very fine overall speckling and spotting of reddish-brown or brown, tinting ground color, and usually extensive but indistinct blotches or smears in buff, purplish-pink or light reddish-brown. Sometimes more heavily marked with small blotches of brown or reddish-brown and lilac; or almost uniform buff or pinkish-buff. Paler generally than most other falcon eggs. 52 × 41 mm. **Incubation:** Usually by female; male rarely assists, but feeds female. Incubation begins with first egg. 29–31 days. **Nestling:** Semi-altricial and downy. Both down coats white. Grayish around face. Bill gray. **Nestling period:** Young tended by both parents. They hatch over a period of days and differ in size. Quill feathers grow at *c.* 2 weeks. Young move about nest ledge at *c.* 30 days, leave nest at *c.* 40 days.

Peregrine Falcon (*Falco peregrinus*)   Plate 32

Breeds in a wide range of habitats. Nest normally on a ledge of a cliff or rocky outcrop; more rarely on a raised mound on the ground in bare open regions; or in the top of a hollow stump. Sometimes on ledges of large city buildings. Tends to return to the same site annually.

Nest: A hollow scrape with no material added to it. **Breeding season:** Begins in early March in the south to mid-May in the north. Single-brooded. **Eggs:** 3–4, sometimes 2–6. Short subelliptical to short elliptical. Smooth, non-glossy. Creamy or buff, very heavily marked and usually obscured by dense fine red or chestnut-red specklings, irregularly marked at times with pale patches and gray or purple blotches. 53 × 41 mm. **Incubation:** Eggs laid at 2–3-day intervals. Incubation by both sexes, but mainly by the female, beginning with the second to third egg, the male bringing food. 28–29 days for a single egg. **Nestling:** Semi-altricial and downy. First down sparse, short and creamy-white. Second down long and woolly, buffish-gray above and creamy below. Irides dark. Cere and legs pale gray. **Nestling period:** The female closely broods and feeds young for the first 14 days, but later leaves them more. For most of the period she feeds the young and the male brings food for all; but after the first period of intensive care he will feed the young if she is absent. Young begin to feather at *c.* 18 days, and exercise at 21 days. During the later period they tear up prey themselves. They fly at 35–42 days, but appear to be dependent on the adults for an additional 2 months.

Gyrfalcon (*Falco rusticolus*)   **Plate 32**

Breeds in open tundra regions and within the northern forest limits. Nest usually on a ledge of a cliff or outcrop, often of a river gorge; at times nests of other large birds are utilized on ledges, and more rarely in trees. Breeding frequency varies with weather conditions, and pairs appear not to breed every year.

Nest: A hollow scrape with no additional material, or an old nest of another bird such as Common Raven or Rough-legged Hawk. Ledge nests are usually under overhangs. The site is usually heavily stained with droppings. **Breeding season:** Begins May. Usually ends by late July. Single-brooded. **Eggs:** 3–4, sometimes 2–8. Short subelliptical to short elliptical. Smooth, non-glossy. Pale buffish or yellowish-white, rarely white; finely spotted with red or reddish-brown. 59 × 46 mm. **Incubation:** Eggs laid at *c.* 3-day intervals. Incubation usually by female alone, beginning with the first egg, and disturbance of the sitting bird may cause fatal chilling. The male rarely assists, but normally brings food. 35–36 days. **Nestling:** Semi-altricial and downy. Down thicker and short on the upperparts, thinner below, absent at the base of neck. White with a creamy tint. Irides dark. Cere and feet pale yellow. **Nestling period:** The female closely broods the young at first, feeding them; the male bringing food. Later both adults hunt and feed young. Young feather at 31–35 days, and fly at 46–49 days. The young remain nearby for another 4 weeks, relying on the adults for food, before becoming independent.

Guans (*Cracidae*)

Plain Chachalaca (*Ortalis vetula*)   **Plates 7, 33**

Breeds in wooded thickets in the lower Rio Grande Valley of Texas. Nest in a small tree, often in a clump near water. Nest well out on a branch, hidden in thick foliage, 5–25 ft. up. The nest is built from material plucked from branches within reach of the nest.

Nest: A small, frail platform, of twigs, lined with a few leaves. Outside diameter: *c.* 24 in. **Breeding season:** Early March to September. **Eggs:** Usually 3. Subelliptical to oval. Smooth but surface very finely granular. Non-glossy or slightly glossy. White, but often nest-stained. 66 × 53 mm. **Incubation:** By female alone, the male remaining nearby. 22–26 days. **Nestling:** Precocial and downy. Down cinnamon-buff with a black spot on forehead, a black reddish-tinted stripe over center of crown and nape; warmer cinnamon-buff with fine blackish mottling on sides of neck; cinnamon-buff and dark brown mottling on back; chin, throat, and belly white. Bill black. Legs and feet pinkish. **Nestling period:** Young, tended by both parents, leave nest for ground on day of hatching. Food is passed to them by adults and feeding continues for a long period, at least until young are half-grown. Adults roost on perches above ground, and young clamber and flutter up to roost with them, one under each adult wing. Wing feathers are well grown within the first few days, and young fly well at 3 weeks. The throat begins to become bare at *c.* 1 month. Young stay with adults and join flocks.

Partridges, Grouse, Turkey, and Quail (*Phasianidae*)

Gamebirds of open spaces, tundra, scrub, and woodland. Nest usually a hollow scrape on the ground, made by the female and relying on the camouflaged plumage of the female birds for concealment. The scanty nest lining is added by sideways-throwing and sideways-building. The part played by the male varies from full participation to relative indifference. Eggs are usually uniformly colored or finely marked, helping in concealment. In some species shells are very thick and hard. The chicks are precocial and very active, leaving the nest within a day of hatching. In some species the male assists in care and protection of young. They are led to places where food is available, and its position may be indicated by the pecking female, but the young pick it up for themselves. They are usually brooded by the adults. The down is usually long and fluffy on the body, shorter and closer on the head, and boldly patterned. Wing-feathers grow first and grow quickly while the young are still small. They can flutter some distance at a few days old. Parental care is not always effective and small young seem to be easily lost from larger broods. Broods tend to remain together until the following breeding season.

Himalayan Snowcock (*Tetraogallus himalayensis*)   Plate 32
Introduced to the Ruby and East Humboldt Mountains of Nevada (originating from Pakistan), this species breeds in alpine habitats, mainly in vegetated alpine turf and tundra in carved glacial cirques and ridges above 9300 ft. Nest on the ground, usually on the lee side of a rocky ridge using the shelter of a rock, boulder or tuft of scruffy grass.
Nest: A shallow scraping, usually in grass and sometimes with down feathers added. **Breeding Season:** From May to July, though may begin as early as March. **Eggs:** Usually 4–6, sometimes 7. Oval to long oval. Slightly rough, but moderately glossy. Pale grayish-tan to a rich reddish-buff with a tinge of gray or green. Spots or blotches of reddish-brown over entire surface. 65 × 45 mm. **Incubation:** By female, with male nearby. 28–31 days. **Nestling:** Precocial. Mottled with brownish-black and fulvous above, the crown darker with the black more defined down the center, with a blackish-brown eyestreak; a second dark line from the base of the bill dividing into two below the ear coverts; below, dull grayish-white. Legs and feet yellow; bill black; eyes brown. **Nestling period:** Young leave soon after hatching and are tended by both adults. Later the birds collect in large flocks.

Gray Partridge (*Perdix perdix*)   Figure 29, Plates 8, 32
Breeds on grassland, and the borders of scrub and cultivation. Introduced from Europe. Nest on the ground in tall grasses or growing crops or in the base of hedgerows or shrubs, or young trees; very rarely above ground in stacks.
Nest: A shallow hollow, usually sheltered by taller plants, and lined with dead grasses and leaves. Outside diameter: 6–12 in.; depth: $2\frac{1}{2}$–4 in. **Breeding season:** Begins mid-May to early June. Single-brooded. **Eggs:** 9–20, sometimes 8–23, larger broods probably from two females. Subelliptical to short oval or short pyriform. Smooth and glossy. Uniform shades of buff, brown or olive. 36 × 27 mm. **Incubation:** Eggs laid at 1–2-day intervals and covered with nest material until incubation. Incubation by female alone, with the male in close attendance, beginning on completion of clutch. 23–25 days. **Nestling:** Precocial and downy. Creamy-yellowish on underside; yellower on throat and sides of head. Crown light orange-buff with four longitudinal blackish lines usually broken into short streaks or spots and more rufous between middle pair. Black spots on broken lines around eyes and ear-coverts, nape, and neck. Mantle mottled. Back dark brown, rufous towards rump, with three pale cream longitudinal streaks breaking up flanks. Wings dark, rufous edged, with two pale bars. Legs and feet buffy-pink; bill light brownish-gray. **Nestling period:** Young hatch within a short period, and may leave the nest on the first day. They are tended and brooded by both parents. They grow quickly. Wing-feathers appear at 5–6 days; the young can flutter at 10–11 days, fly at 16 days, and feather by 28 days. They remain together until late winter or the following spring.

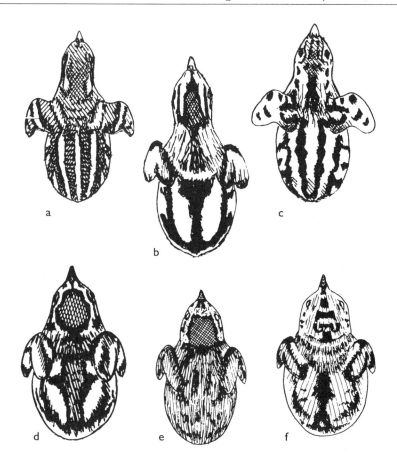

Figure 29. Dorsal patterns of downy chicks: **a,** Chukar; **b,** Ring-necked Pheasant; **c,** Gray Partridge; **d,** Willow Ptarmigan; **e,** Spruce Grouse; **f,** Greater Prairie-Chicken.

Chukar (*Alectoris chukar*)   Figure 29, Plates 8, 32

An Old World species, introduced in western North America, this species breeds mainly in sagebrush-grassland on hill slopes. Nest on the ground, usually under the shelter of a rock or shrub, or against a grass-tuft in more open sites.

Nest: A shallow hollow, with a variable, usually sparse, lining of nearby vegetation, leaves and stems. **Breeding season:** Begins March to early June. Single-brooded. **Eggs:** Usually 8–15, up to 20 at times. On some occasions at least the female produces two clutches at one period. Subelliptical. Smooth and glossy. Pale yellowish, buff or brown, with fine light red speckling; often heavily marked. 43 × 31 mm. **Incubation:** By the female only, on completion of the clutch. A separate additional clutch may be incubated independently by the male. 22–23 days. **Nestling:** Precocial and downy. Creamy-white below, more grayish on breast. Sides of head and thin streak over eye cream-colored, and blackish streak from eye to nape. Top of head light brown, dark-speckled; browner on nape. Back mottled blackish-brown with three dark-edged cream stripes down the back, the central one narrow, two shorter lateral ones, and one across each wing. Legs and feet yellow; bill brown. **Nestling period:** Young cared for by the adult that incubates them. Young fly when about 7–14 days old; chicks can fly 30–60 ft. when about 14 days old. The brood remains together and joins with others into larger groups in autumn.

Ring-necked Pheasant (*Phasianus colchicus*)   Figure 29, Plates 8, 34

Breeds in reedbeds, on waste ground among cultivation, hedgerows, scrub, and woodland. Introduced (from Asia) in cultivated regions. Males are polygamous and females nest alone. Nest normally on the ground in cover of tall plants, briers or shrubs; rarely on raised sites on stacks or overgrown ruins, or flattish old bird nests or squirrel nests in trees.

Nest: A shallow hollow, unlined or sparsely lined with nearby plants, grass, or dead leaves. **Breeding season:** Begins mid-April to early May. Single-brooded. **Eggs:** 7–15. Subelliptical. Smooth and glossy. Uniform olive-brown, sometimes more definite brown, or olive, or blue-gray. 46 × 36 mm. **Incubation:** Eggs laid on consecutive days. Incubation by female alone, beginning with completion of the clutch. 23–27 days. **Nestling:** Precocial and downy. Down varies in color, dark parts dark brown to rufous, pale parts creamy to rufous-buff. Rufous forms have less distinct pattern. Creamy-buff below, extending to sides of neck and forehead. Dark mark behind eye and narrow dark streak over it. Broad stripe over nape, rufous-centered and dark-edged. Back dark brown, with a pair of longitudinal broad pale cream stripes tending to terminate just before the tail-end. Wing rufous with pale edge. **Nestling period:** Young all hatch within a short period, and are tended by the female alone, led to food, and brooded. They can fly at 12–14 days. When the young are half-grown they tend to roost in trees at night.

Spruce Grouse (*Dendragapus canadensis*)   Figure 29, Plates 7, 33

Breeds in forest areas. Nest on the ground, well concealed, often under low branches and at the base of coniferous growth, or in brush, or in deep moss by or in spruce thickets. Males are promiscuous.

Nest: A slight scrape lined with a few twigs, stems or leaves from nearby. Inside diameter: 7 in.; depth: 3 in. **Breeding season:** Begins in mid-May. Usually ends by early September. Single-brooded. **Eggs:** Usually 7–8, sometimes 4–10. Subelliptical. Smooth and slightly glossy. Buff or pinkish-buff, finely speckled, spotted and with small irregular blotches; of dull reddish-brown or brown. Smaller markings often profuse and overall. 44 × 32 mm. **Incubation:** By female alone. 21–24 days. **Nestling:** Precocial and downy. Down pattern rather similar to that of ptarmigans but lacks distinctive dorsal pattern and feathered toes of latter. Young are pale whitish-buff below, yellowish-buff on head with chestnut-red patch bordered with black on crown tapering to nape, two black spots on forehead and irregular black line through eye. Back indistinctly mottled in buff and blackish-brown. **Nestling period:** Young leave nest after about 8 hours. Tended by female alone. Young begin growing wing feathers in few days, and can fly a little at 6–10 days. Feathered when half-grown.

Blue Grouse (*Dendragapus obscurus*)   Plates 7, 33

Breeds in montane forest. Nest on the ground, well concealed, near or under fallen logs, low tree branches or tree-roots; usually in a dry site, often near forest edge. Occasionally by solitary trees or bushes in the open. Males are promiscuous.

Nest: A shallow scrape lined with a little vegetation pulled in from around the site, and occasionally some feathers. Inside diameter: 6–7 in.; depth: 1–3 in. **Breeding season:** Begins late-April in south to late May in north. Usually ends by early

September. Single-brooded. *Eggs:* Usually 6–8, sometimes 7–12. Short subelliptical to oval. Smooth and slightly glossy or non-glossy. Very pale pinkish-buff or buff, with very fine speckling of reddish-brown or light brown, and with sparse irregular spotting. 50 × 35 mm. *Incubation:* Eggs laid at 12-day intervals. Incubation by female alone. 26 days. *Nestling:* Precocial and downy. Down pattern varies in color. Pale whitish-buff below, darker and grayer on upper breast. Upperparts heavily mottled in black, brown, and buff; the blackish markings tending to form two broken stripes on the lower back. Crown has a zone of warmer buff with broken transverse black markings. Neck of similar color with fine black mottling. Dark longitudinal mark and some mottling behind eye. Bill dark gray. *Nestling period:* Young tended by female alone. Young feed themselves from hatching, brooded and guarded by female. Can fly some way at 6–7 days, well at 2 weeks. Brooding ceases at *c.* 8–10 days. Brood moves from nest area to thicker cover. Young disperse by late summer.

Willow Ptarmigan (*Lagopus lagopus*)   Figure 29, Plates 7, 33

Breeds in zones of willow, birch, or juniper scrub, often in partially open and rather boggy places on tundra, or on more open areas in low, close, shrubby growth on rocks. Nests are often partly in the shelter of a small shrub or taller tuft of vegetation. *Nest:* A shallow hollow made by the female, lined at times with a sparse layer of grasses, moss, and heather stems. Inside diameter: 6–8 in.; depth: 3–4 in. *Breeding season:* Begins mid-May in south to early June in north. Single-brooded. *Eggs:* Usually 6–11, sometimes 4–17. Subelliptical. Smooth and glossy. Yellowish, or sometimes slightly reddish; heavily and irregularly blotched and mottled all over with dark chocolate-brown to reddish-brown. Markings very variable. 44 × 32 mm. *Incubation:* Eggs laid at intervals of 36–48 hours. Incubation by the female only, beginning with the next-to-last egg or complete clutch. The male remains nearby. 20–26 days. *Nestling:* Precocial and downy; the down extending to legs and feet but toenails bare. Down is pale sandy-buff below and on sides and extending to cheeks; throat a little paler, upper breast warmer. Crown of head chestnut-red with a blackish border, and patches of similar color on the ear-coverts. Pale sandy-buff streak from lores back over eye. Another pale streak breaks the ear-coverts to join broad pale patches on either side of a dark nape streak. The body pattern is irregular. A central dorsal stripe of warm or rufous-buff is bordered with irregular blackish bands, and broadens into a saddle on mid-back, with darker bands extending to the shoulders. There are irregular dark patches either side of the rump. The wings are rufous with black edges. The bill is dark. *Nestling period:* Young hatch in a short period, and are led away by female soon afterwards. The male helps to guard the young, which are brooded by the female but find their own food. Wing feathers grow quickly while the young are still small. They fly at 12–13 days. Though the young are independent at 8–10 weeks, the family remains together until late autumn and may group with others to form winter flocks.

Rock Ptarmigan (*Lagopus mutus*)   Plates 7, 33

Breeds on rocky arctic tundra and on high latitude zones of similar vegetation farther south. Nest a scrape in an open site, sometimes slightly sheltered by a plant tuft or rock. *Nest:* A rather bare hollow scrape, scantily lined with pieces of grass, plants, and a few feathers. Inside diameter: 6–7 in.; depth: 3 in. *Breeding season:* Begins late May to early June. Usually ends by late July. Single-brooded. *Eggs:* 5–10, sometimes 3–12. Subelliptical. Smooth and glossy. Tend to have paler ground color and darker markings than those of Willow Ptarmigan. Whitish to pale creamy-yellow with irregular blotching and mottling of dark chocolate brown. 43 × 31 mm. *Incubation:* Eggs laid at intervals of 1–2 days. Incubation by female alone, beginning with the next-to-last egg, the male remaining nearby. 24–26 days. **Nestling:** Precocial and downy; down extending over legs and feet to toe-nails. The pattern similar to that of Willow Ptarmigan but tending to be bolder, with conspicuous black zones edging the rufous and rufous-buff areas, and across the sides of the head. The pale parts lacking most of the yellow, and a more pale grayish-buff. Bill blackish. **Nestling period:** Young are tended by both parents at first; brooded by the female, guarded by the male, but finding their own food. Wing-feathers grow first and they can fly weakly at c. 10 days. In the latter part of the period the males tend to leave the family and flock together, joining unmated males. Females and young remain together, (though young actually independent at 10–12 weeks) joining with others later to form winter flocks.

White-tailed Ptarmigan (*Lagopus leucurus*)   Plates 7, 33
Breeds in alpine tundra areas of mountains, in or above stunted willows or spruce.
Nest: A shallow scrape usually lined with slight vegetation such as grasses which are pulled in to line the hollow. Inside diameter: 6 in.; depth: 1–2 in. **Breeding season:** Begins mid-June. Single-brooded. **Eggs:** Usually 4–7, sometimes 3–9. Subelliptical to long elliptical. Smooth and slightly glossy. Very pale warm buff to pinkish-buff with sparse but regular small spotting in dark brown; and very fine overall speckling. More sparsely marked than other ptarmigan eggs and resembling those of the Spruce Grouse. 43 × 29 mm. **Incubation:** Eggs laid at 1½-day intervals. Incubation by female alone, the male remaining nearby. 22–23 days. **Nestling:** Precocial and downy. Down colors paler than on other ptarmigans. Chestnut-red cap poorly defined with narrow margins. Forehead pale buff with broken dark markings, black streak behind eye, and throat whitish. Dorsal stripe tends to be indistinct, but this area is warmer buff, bordered and mottled with black, the rest of the back being mottled with buff, gray, brown, and black. Underparts grayish-white. Toes feathered. **Nestling period:** Brooded by female. Young tended by both parents, finding their own food. Can fly at c. 10 days. Broods remain together until the following spring.

Ruffed Grouse (*Bonasa umbellus*)   Figure 30, Plates 7, 33
Breeds in forest areas with some deciduous trees. Nest on the ground at the base of a tree or stump, under logs, bushes or brush piles. Males are promiscuous.
Nest: A shallow scrape, lined with any nearby plant material that can be pulled in, including dead leaves and pine needles. **Breeding season:** Begins early April in south to early May in north. Will replace lost clutches but with fewer eggs. **Eggs:** Usually 9–12, replacement clutches often c. 7. Subelliptical to oval. Smooth and moderately glossy. Creamy or ivory to very pale buff or pinkish-buff; often unmarked, sometimes with very fine speckling of brown. 40 × 30 mm. **Incubation:** Eggs laid at rate of 2 every 3 days. Incubation by female alone, beginning with last egg. 23–24 days, or longer in cold seasons. **Nestling:** Precocial and downy. Down pattern dark. From crown of head to rump reddish-brown, paler on the crown. Pale yellowish-buff on sides of head, breast and flanks, and underparts yellow to yellowish-white. There may be slightly darker markings on crown, and a black stripe extends from eye to nape. **Nestling period:** Young tended by female alone. Young leave nest soon after hatching. Feed themselves, brooded and guarded by female. Wings grow rapidly and young can flutter up to tree branches while small. Fly at 10–12 days. Broods begin to break up at c. 12 weeks.

Sage Grouse (*Centrocercus urophasianus*)   Plates 7, 34
Breeds in sagebrush areas. Nest on the ground, sheltered by shrubby growth. Males have communal display leks and are promiscuous. Females nest alone.

Figure 30. Ruffed Grouse: depression c. 10–12 in. across; shown amid leaf litter, incorporating the dry leaves into the nest.

Nest: A shallow scrape; bare or with a slight lining of nearby plants. **Breeding season:** Begins mid-March to early May. Probably few lost clutches are replaced. **Eggs:** Usually 7–8, sometimes up to 13. Subelliptical to oval. Smooth and moderately glossy. Pale drab olive to olive-buff; with profuse spots, specks and tiny blotches of dark brown. 55 × 38 mm. **Incubation:** By female alone. 25–27 days. **Nestling:** Precocial and downy. Down has general spotted pattern, mottled in black, brown, buff, and white. Head whiter with bolder spots and short stripes in black and brown over most of it. Two brownish, black-edged spots on foreneck. Upper breast buff mottled with black. Bill black. **Nestling period:** Young tended by female alone. Young leave nest as soon as down is dry, feeding themselves, and brooded and guarded by female. Brood moves to a moister site where feeding is better.

Greater Prairie-Chicken (*Tympanuchus cupido*)   Figure 29, Plates 7, 34
Breeds on open grassland and prairies. Nest on the ground in growing herbage, in the open or on the edge of marshes, bushes or scrub woodland. Males have a communal lek display and are promiscuous. Females nest alone.
Nest: A shallow scrape with a little of the surrounding vegetation pulled in as

lining, and may be concealed by overhanging plants possibly pulled over by birds. Inside diameter: 7–8 in.; depth: 2–3 in. **Breeding season:** Begins early April in south to late May in north. Usually ends by mid-September. Single-brooded, but will replace lost clutches. **Eggs:** Usually 12–14. Short subelliptical to short oval. Smooth and moderately glossy. Ground color in shades of buff, light ivory-buff to deep buff, very finely and minutely speckled and spotted in dark brown, sometimes almost or completely unmarked. 45 × 34 mm. **Incubation:** Eggs laid at a little more than 1-day intervals. Incubation by female alone, beginning a little before or after laying of last egg. 23–26 days. **Nestling:** Precocial and downy. Down pattern like that of Lesser Prairie-Chicken and Sharp-tailed Grouse, but with deeper color above. Mainly yellowish with a rufous-brown tinge above. Head with several black spots on crown and nape and some indication of a median crown stripe. Tiny black patch immediately behind eye, and row of three dark spots across ear-coverts. Upperparts marked with irregular black patches. Bill light brown with black along the upper edge. Feet yellowish. **Nestling period:** Young leave the nest after the first day, tended by female alone. Young brooded frequently during first week, less often after this. Become independent at *c.* 6–8 weeks.

Lesser Prairie-Chicken (*Tympanuchus pallidicinctus*)   Plate 34
Breeds on more arid grasslands in Texas panhandle and nearby states. Nest on the ground in grassy places, sometimes under shrubs. Males have a communal lek display and are promiscuous. Females nest alone.
Nest: A shallow scrape lined with grasses and with other plant material from nearby. **Breeding season:** April to June. Single-brooded. **Eggs:** Usually 11–14. Short subelliptical to short oval. Pale ivory-buff to ivory-yellow, with or without minute speckling. 42 × 32 mm. **Incubation:** Eggs laid at a little over 1-day intervals. Incubation by female alone, beginning a little before or after last egg. 23–26 days. **Nestling:** Precocial and downy. Down pattern like that of Greater Prairie-Chicken, but paler and less brownish above, without a median streak. **Nestling period:** As for Greater Prairie-Chicken.

Sharp-tailed Grouse (*Tympanuchus phasianellus*)   Plates 7, 34
Breeds in areas of mixed open grassland with woodland or scrub. Nest on the ground, usually near to or within tree or shrub cover, exceptionally in open sites, typically on the borders of open areas, usually partly or wholly concealed by tall herbage or bushes. Males have a communal lek display and are promiscuous.
Nest: A shallow scrape scantily lined with plant material pulled in from nearby. Inside diameter: 7–8 in.; depth: $2\frac{1}{4}$–4 in. **Breeding season:** Begins early April in south and west, to early May in north. Single-brooded. **Eggs:** Usually 10–13. Subelliptical to oval. Smooth and slightly to moderately glossy. Usually buff or slightly olive-buff, pinkish or warm buff; unmarked or with fine speckling and a few larger spots of dark brown. 43 × 32 mm. **Incubation:** Eggs laid at daily intervals. Incubation by female alone, beginning with last egg. 23–24 days. **Nestling:** Precocial and downy. Down pattern like that of prairie-chickens, but lacks the warmer tints above and is a yellowish color overall. There are small black marks along mid-crown and some spots on nape, and only one or two black spots on ear-coverts. Upperparts have irregular black patches or streaks. **Nestling period:** Young tended by female only. Young soon leave nest and are led by females to moister areas. Can fly a little at 10 days. Become increasingly independent in period from 10 days to 6–8 weeks, when broods disperse.

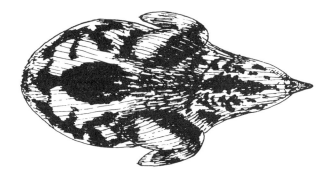

Figure 31. Dorsal pattern of downy chick: Wild Turkey.

Wild Turkey (*Meleagris gallopavo*)   Figure 31, Plates 8, 33
Breeds in more open deciduous forest, along forest edges and in clearings; and in more open and scattered woodland of drier regions. Nest on the ground. Usually by or under shrubby cover or against a fallen log or foot of a tree; occasionally among rocks or in an open site. Apparent sharing of nest by several females recorded. Males are polygamous and take no part in nesting.
Nest: A shallow hollow, sparsely lined with nearby vegetation or dead leaves. Inside diameter: *c.* 12 in. **Breeding season:** Begins mid-March. Single-brooded. **Eggs:** Usually 8–12, sometimes up to 20. Elliptical to oval. Smooth and glossy. Pale buff or yellowish, rarely white, heavily spotted and speckled overall with light to dark brown or purplish-brown, and rarely buff. 63 × 45 mm. **Incubation:** By female alone. 28 days. **Nestling:** Precocial and downy. Down pinkish-cinnamon on head and back, slightly lighter on upper breast and flanks. Crown and upperparts heavily spotted with dark brown. Sides of head and underparts pale pinkish-buff to yellowish. Throat white. Legs and feet buffy-pink; bill light brownish-gray. **Nestling period:** Young tended by female alone. Feed themselves and are brooded and guarded by adult. Wings grow rapidly and young can fly into trees at *c.* 2 weeks, and roost on branch with female. Broods remain together until winter.

Montezuma Quail (*Cyrtonyx montezumae*)   Plates 8, 34
Breeds in montane pine-oak and oak scrub. Nest on the ground, sometimes under a bush, and usually built into the side of a tuft of grass or herbage.
Nest: A scrape several inches deep, *c.* 5–6 in. across, among grasses, lined with grass and leaves, and with grass-stems worked together at the sides and pulled over at the top to form a closed cavity. Male may help to build? **Breeding season:** Begins late April, but actual nesting probably not until June. **Eggs:** Usually 6–14. Oval to sub-elliptical or short pyriform. Smooth and moderately glossy. White to creamy-white. 32 × 25 mm. **Incubation:** By female, with male on guard, but some records of males sitting. 25–26 days. **Nestling:** Precocial and downy. Down lacks a distinct dorsal pattern. Head pale cinnamon-buff with narrow black line from eye to nape. Light chestnut patch on crown and nape, tapering into forehead. Back and wings mottled brown and chestnut with some cinnamon-buff forming two indistinct pale streaks on upper back. Rear edge of wing yellowish. Grayish-white on underside. Whiter on throat. **Nestling period:** Young tended by both parents. Fed on insects and seeds, but gradually feeding themselves. Broods remain together and coalesce into larger groups in autumn.

Northern Bobwhite (*Colinus virginianus*)   Figure 32, Plates 8, 34

Breeds in a wide variety of habitats, but basically a species of scrub, scattered cover in grassland or cultivated areas, and on woodland edge. Nest on the ground, usually in low cover bordering an open space.

Nest: A shallow hollow, lined with plant material pulled in from nearby, and with growing plants pulled over to hide it. Both sexes build. **Breeding season:** Begins mid-March in south to late May in north. Single-brooded, possibly double-brooded in south. Lost clutches replaced. **Eggs:** Usually 12–16, sometimes 7–28. Short subelliptical to short oval or short pyriform. Smooth and slightly glossy. Dull white to creamy-white. 30 × 24 mm. **Incubation:** Eggs laid at a little over one-day intervals (14 eggs in 18–20 days). By both. 23–24 days. **Nestling:** Precocial and downy. Grayish-buff on underside. Sides of head yellowish-buff with blackish streak from eye to nape. Forehead rufous-buff, and crown and nape chestnut-red, deeper at edges, tapering on to forehead. Blackish streak from eye to nape. Broad chestnut-red band continues down middle of back, bordered with narrow creamy-buff stripes; and flanks mottled chestnut, blackish and buff. Some individuals show more rufous over all of back. Legs, feet, and bill buffy-pink. **Nestling period:** Young tended by both parents. In captivity male is known to take over brood while female re-nests. Feathers grow rapidly and young can fly when less than 14 days old. Before 21 days start to feed as covey. Feather in 4–8 weeks, and are full-grown in 2 months. Brood remains together until spring.

Scaled Quail (*Callipepla squamata*)   Plates 8, 34

Breeds in arid grassland, brush or desert, where some water is available. Nest on the ground usually under or sheltered by a shrub or herbage, but not usually in even herbage such as grass or grain.

Nest: A shallow scrape with a lining, often sparse, of nearby grasses or other plants. **Breeding season:** Season prolonged, may begin early March in south, although early May is more typical as in north. Rarely double-brooded. Breeding may be completely inhibited in dry seasons. **Eggs:** Usually 12–14, sometimes 9–16. Female may sometimes lay two clutches. In some instances two females lay in one nest. Subelliptical to oval. Glossy and smooth. Very pale creamy to pale ivory with very fine speckling in pale buffish- or reddish-brown. 33 × 25 mm. **Incubation:** Usually by female with male sometimes nearby. 22–23 days. **Nestling:** Precocial and downy. Down pattern like those of Gambel's and California Quails; but grayer on body, with almost white paired lines on back. Small grayish tuft where adult has crest. Forehead to crown, and sides of head, cinnamon-buff or pinkish-buff. Throat whitish. Elongated dark chestnut-red streak on rear edge of ear-coverts. Broad chestnut-red stripe from mid-crown to nape, with blackish edges, and bordered with narrow whitish stripe. On back paired blackish lines, joining on upper back, area between stripes mottled buff and chestnut. Dark stripe bordered by a pair of whitish stripes, and a blackish broken band along the flank. Flanks and breast grayish-buff becoming paler on underside. **Nestling period:** Young tended by both or either parent. Plumage grows rapidly and young can fly when half-grown. Male possibly takes over brood while female raises second brood. Young remain with adults and later join to form large coveys.

Gambel's Quail (*Callipepla gambelii*)   Plates 8, 34

Breeds in arid desert scrub. Nest on the ground at the base of the trunk of small tree or shrub, or under a low shrub, or fallen branches, or sheltered and shaded by a tall tuft of herbage.

Nest: A shallow scrape, variably lined with grasses or other plant material. **Breeding season:** Begins late April. Single-brooded, or double-brooded in good seasons. **Eggs:**

Figure 32. Dorsal patterns of downy chicks (*left to right*): Northern Bobwhite, California Quail, Mountain Quail.

Usually 12–14, sometimes 10–19. Oval to subelliptical or short pyriform. Smooth and slightly to moderately glossy. Pale creamy-buff with fine overall speckling, occasionally lacking, and sparser irregular spotting and blotching in light reddish-brown, buffish-brown or dark brown. More heavily marked than eggs of California Quail. 32 × 24 mm. **Incubation:** Eggs laid at 25–28-hour intervals. Incubation by female alone, with male nearby. 21–23 days. **Nestling:** Precocial and downy. Like pale California Quail. Forehead and sides of head pinkish-buff or paler; dark chestnut streak on hind ear-covert. Tiny topknot tuft. From mid-crown to nape broad band of chestnut-red bordered with black and with a pale cream band along the side. Upperparts pale pinkish-buff with four longitudinal dark brown bands on lower back, a single band and some dark blotches on upper back. Underparts pale grayish-buff. **Nestling period:** Young leave the nest upon hatching. Normally female broods young while male guards. Young feed themselves, mostly on insects, and grow rapidly (*c.* 3 months to rear brood). Young tended by both parents; but if conditions are good male may take care of young and female nest again; or after *c.* 4 weeks chicks may be left with other adults and the pair re-nest.

California Quail (*Callipepla californica*)   Figure 32, Plates 8, 34
Breeds in a wide range of habitats, from moister forest edges through chaparral regions to scrub desert; where bushy cover is combined with open areas of herbage. Nest usually on the ground; rarely in the nest of another bird in tree or shrub, or on suitable raised site formed by branches and creepers, or on tree stump.
Nest: A shallow hollow, usually lined with vegetation from nearby. **Breeding season:** Begins January in south to mid-May in north. Sometimes, possibly often, double-brooded, and lost clutches are replaced. **Eggs:** Usually 12–17, sometimes 6–28. Short subelliptical to short oval, or short pyriform. Smooth and glossy. Creamy-white to creamy-buff or yellowish; often with fine overall speckling, and with irregular spotting and blotching, often heavy, of golden-brown, buffish, or dull brown. Not as heavily marked as eggs of Gambel's Quail. 31 × 24 mm. **Incubation:** Eggs laid at a little more than 24-hour intervals, averaging five per week. Incubation normally by female with male nearby, but male may incubate if female dies. 21–23 days. **Nestling:** Precocial and downy. Down pattern like young Gambel's or Scaled Quail, but with yellower tint. Underside buffish-white. Sides of head and forehead, warm yellowish-buff; crown and nape rufous-brown with blackish edges, tapering

to point on forecrown, and bordered by pale creamy-buff stripe. Short black mark on hind-edge of ear-covert. Back dark brown with three broad longitudinal yellowish-buff stripes. Flanks and wings with broken pattern of dark brown and buff. **Nestling period:** Young very active soon after hatching. Tended by both parents, but often, perhaps regularly, female appears to leave male to tend young and re-nests to produce second brood. Young drop from raised nests without harm. Wing feathers grow rapidly, and young can flutter some way at 10 days. Broods may gather into flocks while young are still small.

Mountain Quail (Oreortyx pictus)   Figure 31, Plates 8, 34

Breeds on the edge of mountain woodland and scrub. Nest on the ground usually well-concealed; in herbage or shrubs at the base of large tree, under fallen pine branch, and under or in shrubby growth. It is usually near a pathway and at no great distance from water.
Nest: A shallow scrape, lined with plant material pulled in from nearby. **Breeding season:** Begins mid-March. Single-brooded, but lost clutches replaced. **Eggs:** Usually 7–10, large clutches of 19–22 eggs usually attributed to two females. Oval. Slightly glossy and smooth. Deep pinkish-buff to pale creamy; completely unmarked. 35 × 27 mm. **Incubation:** Mostly by female. 24–25 days. **Nestling:** Precocial and downy. Down pattern rather like that of Northern Bobwhite, but body color generally paler and markings blacker with larger mark on ear-coverts. Upperparts and head buffish-white, and underside grayish or yellowish-white. There is a broad chestnut-red stripe bordered, and in places marked, with black. It extends up the middle of the back, is narrow and blacker at shoulders, broad again on nape and hindcrown, and tapers to point on mid-crown. There is a black streak from the eye across the ear-coverts, broadening posteriorly. There is a chestnut and black patch on the inner wing, and a blackish band on the upper flanks. **Nestling period:** Young tended by both parents, or by either alone. Wings and other feathers begin rapid growth in first few days. Young are very active, feeding themselves, brooded and guarded by parents. Young fly at about 14 days.

Rails, Gallinules, and Coots (Rallidae)

Birds of swamp and waterside, usually long-legged and preferring to swim rather than fly. They nest in low vegetation, by or just in water. The nests are bulky cups; and material is carried to the site. Clutches are relatively large. There is evidence that occasionally eggs or young may be carried to another site nearby after disturbance of the nest. Downy young have a claw at the carpal joint of the wing.

Yellow Rail (Coturnicops novaboracensis)   Plate 35

Probably breeds over a wide area but nest rarely found. Where found nests are in sedge marshes or wet meadows, on the ground in drier portions of grassy vegetation, or sometimes among grasses or plant tufts in several inches of water.
Nest: A thick cup of plant material, concealed in a natural hollow with an overhanging tuft of vegetation or with grasses bent over to form a concealing canopy. 4–5 in. diameter, 1–1½ in. thick, with rather deep cup (c. 2 in.). Built by both, but finished by female. **Breeding season:** Probably begins May–June. Usually ends by late August. Single-brooded. **Eggs:** Usually 8–10. Subelliptical to oval. Slightly glossy and smooth. Warm buff; with sparse marking of fine spots and specks of light reddish-brown and lilac, usually mostly concentrated in a small cap or wreath at the larger end. Darker than eggs of Virginia Rail, paler than those of Sora. 28 × 21 mm. **Incubation:** By female. 16–18 days. **Nestling:** Precocial and downy. Down long and

glossy black. No bare patch on forehead. Bill pinkish-flesh. Feet grayish-brown. **Nestling period:** Tended by female. Young leave the nest within 2 days of hatching. Feed themselves at 5 days. Become independent in 3 weeks; fly in 35 days.

Black Rail (*Laterallus jamaicensis*) Plates 9, 35

Breeds on salt or brackish marshes and occasionally in inland freshwater marshes or wet meadows. Nest on the ground concealed in a tuft of grasses or *Salicornia*.
Nest: A neat, small and deep cup of grasses and sedges, overhanging adjacent grasses or plant stems being pulled and woven together to form a concealing canopy. Outside diameter: 4–5 in.; inside diameter: $3\frac{1}{2}$ in.; depth: $2\frac{1}{4}$ in. **Breeding season:** Begins as early as mid-March. Usually ends by mid-July. Single-brooded, though possibly double-brooded. **Eggs:** Usually 6–10, sometimes up to 13. Subelliptical to elliptical. Smooth and moderately glossy. White, or faintly tinted buffish or pinkish, with very fine speckling in reddish-brown and purple; mainly concentrated towards the larger end. 26 × 20 mm. **Incubation:** By both. 17–20 days. **Nestling:** Precocial and downy. Down black. **Nestling period:** Little information. Young leave nest within 24 hours of hatching.

Clapper Rail (*Rallus longirostris*) Plate 35

Breeds on salt, brackish, or fresh (in southwest) marshes. Nest on the ground, hidden in growing or dead herbage, or under a small bush; or raised above ground in a grass tuft or clump of rushes.
Nest: A bulky cup built up well above the ground in a concealed hollow. Of grasses and plant stems, lined with finer material. Growing plants are pulled over to form a canopy. Nest *c.* 7–10 in. diameter, 3–6 in. thick; with cavity 5–6 in. across and $1–1\frac{1}{2}$ in. deep. **Breeding season:** Begins mid-March to mid-April. Usually ends late August. Single-brooded but lost clutches replaced. **Eggs:** Usually 8–11, sometimes 4–14. Replacement clutches may be only 4–6. Subelliptical to long subelliptical. Smooth and glossy. Very pale buff, pinkish-buff or creamy-white. Sparsely spotted or blotched with dark reddish-brown or purplish-red, and paler purple or gray. The larger markings sometimes concentrated towards the larger end. 42 × 30 mm. **Incubation:** By both sexes. 20–24 days. **Nestling:** Precocial and downy. Down black, with a slight greenish gloss on upperpart, dull black on underside, and usually a little white down just below and behind the wings. **Nestling period:** Young tended by both parents. Leave nest soon after hatching. Can swim at 1 day. Independent of parents 35–42 days after hatching; fly at 63–70 days.

King Rail (*Rallus elegans*) Plate 35

Breeds in large freshwater marshes with rank vegetation. Nest on the ground in a grass tussock or waterside vegetation, or raised on plants growing in shallow water.
Nest: On dry sites a cup of grasses with growing stems pulled over to form a canopy. In wet site stems of plants are bent down to form a base and a substantial cup several inches thick is built up from plant material, and may be 6–18 in. up. Leaves are pulled over and interwoven to form a canopy. Nest *c.* 8–9 in. across, *c.* 1–4 in. thick. Nest built by both sexes. **Breeding season:** Begins early to mid-May. May be double-brooded in south. **Eggs:** Usually 8–11, sometimes 6–15. Subelliptical. Smooth and glossy. Creamy white or tinted very pale buff or pinkish-buff; with sparse spotting in dark reddish-brown and purple, and sometimes small blotches concentrated at the larger end. 41 × 30 mm. **Incubation:** By both sexes. 21–24 days. **Nestling:** Precocial and downy. Down short, thick and black. **Nestling period:** Young tended by both parents. Leave nest soon after hatching. First short flights about 63 days after hatching.

Virginia Rail (*Rallus limicola*) Plates 9, 35

Breeds on freshwater marshes or in rank vegetation in brackish areas bordering fresh water. Nest on the ground concealed in a grass tussock or waterside vegetation, or built up among plants on mud, or raised in tall vegetation in water.

Nest: A substantial cup, in a hollow, or built up well above water in a wet site, or suspended in bases of tall vegetation; of coarse grass, rushes, cat-tails, and similar material. *c.* 8 in. diameter, with cup 4–5 in. across and rather shallow. Leaves or stems are pulled over to hide the nest. Built by both over *c.* 7 days. **Breeding season:** Usually begins early April in south and west to mid-May in north. Usually end mid-July. May be double-brooded in some areas. **Eggs:** Usually 7–12. Subelliptical. Smooth and glossy. Creamy-white or faintly tinted buff or pinkish-buff; with sparse speckling, spotting, and a few small blotches of light to dark reddish-brown and pale gray or purple. Paler than eggs of Sora and Yellow Rail. 32 × 24 mm. **Incubation:** By both sexes, beginning before completion of clutch. 20 days. **Nestling:** Precocial and downy. Down long, thick, and rather coarse. Black with greenish gloss on back and bluish gloss on head. Sometimes a little white down under the wings. Bill longer than on Sora, pinkish at first, then orange-red, with a broad black band across the middle. **Nestling period:** Young tended by both parents. Young leave nest soon after completion of hatching. Active, swimming and diving at an early age. Food is given to young by adults for 14–21 days. Fly at 25 days.

Sora (*Porzana carolina*) Figure 33, Plates 9, 35

Breeds in marshes, sloughs, and wet meadows in fresh water, though sometimes in brackish areas. Nest raised in grass tussock or in bases of tall plants such as reed-mace or bulrushes, by water's edge or in water, sometimes in a more exposed site.

Figure 33. Sora: c. 7–9 in. across; raised above water level (c. 6 in.) usually in a grass tussock.

Nest: A substantial cup of dead reed-mace, sedges and grasses, with finer lining of grass and sedges. Outside diameter: *c.* 6 in.; inside diameter: 3 in.; depth: *c.* 2 in. Plants are pulled over to form a cavity and there may be a runway of nesting material leading up to it from the water. **Breeding season:** Begins late April in south to late May in north. Single-brooded. **Eggs:** Usually 8–12, sometimes 5–18. Subelliptical to oval. Smooth and glossy. Buff or olive-buff; with some minute dark speckling, and with sparse spots and small blotches of chestnut-red or light purple. Darker than eggs of Virginia and Yellow Rails. 31 × 22 mm. **Incubation:** Eggs laid on consecutive days. Incubation by both sexes beginning with first to third egg. 16–20 days. **Nestling:** Precocial and downy. Down long with fine silky tips. Black, with tip of upperparts glossed greenish. Tuft at apex of chin, of long and coarse, hair-like yellowish down. **Nestling period:** Young tended by both parents. Eggs hatch over several days. Young leave nest within 1–2 days of hatching, but may return for brooding at night. Can fly at *c.* 36 days.

Purple Gallinule (Porphyrula martinica) Plates 9, 35

Breeds in fresh marshes and by ponds, lakes, and rivers where tall dense waterside vegetation occurs. Nest on the ground in tall marsh herbage, or among plants growing in water, on branches of shrubs at water level, and exceptionally more open sites. **Nest:** A bulky cup of dead or green plant material, built up well above the water. May be up to 8 in. high and 8–10 in. across, with cup *c.* 3 in. deep. **Breeding season:** Begins early to mid-April. **Eggs:** Usually 6–8, sometimes 5–10. Subelliptical to oval. Smooth and slightly glossy. Pale creamy-buff to cream-colored, with speckling and fine spotting in dark reddish-brown and light purple. 39 × 29 mm. **Incubation:** By both. 20–25 days. **Nestling:** Precocial and downy. Down, thick and long, but scanty around bill and eyes. Black, glossy on the back, dull on the underside, and on crown, cheeks, and throat retains sheaths, appearing whitish and hair-like. Bill yellowish at base, black toward end with white tip. **Nesting period:** Young leave nest 1–2 days after hatching. Nonbreeders will help feed young; become independent at about 63 days.

Common Moorhen (Gallinula chloropus) Plates 9, 35

Breeds at the edge of fresh water of all kinds, from lakes and rivers to tiny marshes and ditches. Nest usually on the ground by water, or among plants in water, but sometimes above ground in thick shrubs or in large old nests of other birds in trees. Additional nests (brood platforms) may be built in territory, especially in marshy sites, and are used for brooding young. **Nest:** Usually a bulky platform of dead plant material and debris. Tall growing plants nearby are pulled over to conceal it. Built by both sexes, the male bringing most of the material. Outside diameter: 14–18 in.; inside diameter: 7–8 in.; depth: $2\frac{1}{2}$–3 in.; height: 8 in. **Breeding season:** Usually begins early to mid-May, though may be nearly a year-round breeder in Florida. **Eggs:** Usually 5–11, sometimes 2–21, but larger clutches may be from two females. Subelliptical. Smooth and glossy. Grayish-white to pale buff or greenish, with spots or small blotches or reddish-brown and blue-gray. 44 × 31 mm. **Incubation:** Eggs laid on consecutive days. Incubation by both sexes, and may begin at various times in the laying period. 19–22 days. **Nestling:** Precocial and downy. Down long and black with long fine tips except on head, skin shows light blue on crown, pinkish on nape. Bill red and orange with yellow tip, fading after *c.* 3 weeks to dull yellowish-green. Legs and feet blackish-olive. **Nestling period:** Young may hatch together or over a period, and stay in the nest for several days, tended by both parents. Young of earlier broods of same year may help to feed later ones. Young able to feed alone in 3 weeks, independent in 5 weeks, and can fly in 6–7 weeks. Tend to remain with adults for some period after.

American Coot (*Fulica americana*)   Plates 9, 36

Breeds on lakes, larger pools, and slower rivers, usually with waterside vegetation. Also in swamps with some open water and tall reeds or similar cover. Nest usually on the ground among reeds or growing vegetation in or by water, or at water level in branches lying in or hanging into water. Extra nests (brood platforms) may be built and used by young for resting.

Nest: A bulky cup of dead leaves and stems of waterside plants. Often well raised. Both sexes build, the male bringing most materials, the female building it in. Outside diameter: 14–20 in.; inside diameter: 7 in. **Breeding season:** Begins mid-April in south to mid-May in north. **Eggs:** Usually 6–9, sometimes 5–15. Subelliptical. Smooth and slightly glossy. Pale buffish-stone, fairly uniformly marked overall with specks and fine spots of dark brown and black. 49 × 34 mm. **Incubation:** Eggs laid on consecutive days. Incubation by both sexes, beginning early in the laying of the clutch, or with the first egg. 21–24 days. **Nestling:** Precocial and downy. Down thick and soft, with long, fine hair-like tips except on the underside. Grayish on underside, black on back and head. Reddish to orange waxy tips on down of neck, throat and front of head, yellow sheaths on down of mantle and wings. On larger young reddish tips and sheaths are lost and the bird is black above, and white on the throat, front of neck and belly. Bare crown reddish, blue skin over eyes. Bill reddish, white-tipped. Legs and feet blackish-gray. **Nestling period:** Young may hatch over several days. Tended by both parents. Usually brooded by the female and fed by male for first 3–4 days. Later young follow adults, and are brooded on nest or platforms. Adults tend to divide brood and feed certain young only. Young feed themselves by 1 month; independent at 8 weeks.

Limpkins (*Aramidae*)

Limpkin (*Aramus guarauna*)   Plates 9, 35

Breeds in marshes and swamp forests in Florida and into southern Georgia. Nest in sawgrass clumps, or on low trees, or bushes, overgrown with climbing plants; occasionally on a stump. Usually 5–8 ft. up, sometimes as high as 45 ft.

Nest: A loosely constructed saucer of plant stems, dead leaves, dead vines, and various plant material, including Spanish Moss. In sawgrass the blades of growing plants are incorporated. The fragile nest is usually resting on a substantial base of growing plant material. Building begun by male, finished by both. **Breeding season:** May be as early as November, more frequently January; usually April to July. Single-brooded. **Eggs:** Usually 4–8. Subelliptical. Smooth and slightly glossy. Pale creamy-buff or olive-buff, with spots and blotches of medium brown, dark brown, and pale gray or lilac. Markings mostly concentrated at the larger end. 59 × 44 mm. **Incubation:** By both sexes. Estimated at 25–27 days. **Nestling:** Precocial and downy. Down long, soft, and thick. Upperparts warm brown, paler on sides of head and on underparts. Almost white on chin. **Nestling period:** Young leave nest the day they hatch. Tended by both parents. Age of independence estimated at 2½ months.

Cranes (*Gruidae*)

Sandhill Crane (*Grus canadensis*)   Figure 34, Plates 9, 35

Breeds in north on open tundra near water, or on grassy flats with drier ridges; farther south in large marshes with some open water and areas of tall grasses or rushy vegetation. Nest on the ground. In north tends to be on low ridges and may be a dry hollow; but in water nests are large. More southerly nests usually in shallow

Figure 34. Sandhill Crane: c. 3–4 ft. across; the mound of materials rises c. 8 in. above the water-line.

water with vegetation, or on small islands, and screened by tall herbage or some shrubs.

Nest: A large heap of plant material thrown in from around site; with a slight central hollow; in dry sites may be only a hollow with a thin grass lining. Located 6–8 in. above water, with an outside diameter of 3–5 ft. **Breeding season:** Begins in January in Florida, April in mid-US to mid-May in north. Single-brooded. **Eggs:** Usually 2, sometimes 1, rarely 3. Subelliptical to long subelliptical. Smooth and moderately glossy. Pale to medium buff to olive-buff; spotted and blotched with light to medium brown or reddish-brown, and with paler purple and lilac. The markings often concentrated towards the larger end. 94 × 60 mm. **Incubation:** Eggs laid at intervals of two days. Incubation by both sexes. 30–32 days. **Nestling:** Precocial and downy. Dark brown on top of head, tapering to forehead; forehead and sides of face light buff, with a darker line under eye becoming a dark mark in front of eye. Diamond-shaped dark brown area on upper back, tapering on mid-back and expanding to diamond-shaped area on rump. Hind neck gray, throat whitish, underside grayish-white. Bill dull pinkish-flesh-color with dark tip. Irides gray. Legs and feet pinkish-flesh-colored, becoming gray. **Nestling period:** Young tended by both parents. Hatch c. 1 day apart. Leave nest soon after both hatched. Fed directly by adults at first, on small items; begin to feed themselves in second week. Wing feathers begin to grow at c. 16 days. Young fly at c. 70 days. Remain with adults to following year.

Whooping Crane (Grus americana) Plates 9, 35

Breeds in large marshes, open or with rank herbage, in Wood Buffalo National Park on the Alberta–Yukon border. Nest on the ground, often surrounded by shallow water where material has been gathered to form nest.

Nest: A heap of plant material thrown in from around site, c. 4–5 ft. across, and 8–18 in. high. Central nest depression slight. **Breeding season:** Begins late April. Single-brooded. **Eggs:** Usually 2, sometimes 1, rarely 3. Subelliptical. Creamy-buff to olive-buff or greenish; spotted and blotched and finely speckled with light brown or darker reddish-brown and paler purple and lilac. 100 × 63 mm. **Incubation:** By both sexes. 33–35 days. **Nestling:** Precocial and downy. Down cinnamon to light brown, darker brown or rufous-brown along middle of back and on rump. Paler and grayer on neck. Drab buffish-gray or brownish-white on underside. Bill brown at tip, pinkish-flesh-colored at base. Legs and feet brownish. **Nestling period:** Young tended by both parents. Leave nest within *c.* 1 day of hatching. Fly at *c.* $3\frac{1}{2}$ months. Remain with adults until following year.

Plovers (*Charadriidae*)

Short-billed waders, inhabiting drier terrain and water's edge, and nesting on open ground with vegetation very short or absent. The nest is a shallow scrape, but often placed where it commands a view of surrounding country. Eggs tend to be more rounded and less pyriform than those of typical waders. Usually 3 or 4 eggs in clutch. Young can run as soon as down is dry and may leave the nest quickly. Appear not to feed for first 24 hours. They crouch motionless when alarmed and may do so even when well grown.

Black-bellied Plover (*Pluvialis squatarola*)   Plate 36
Breeds in arctic tundra regions, usually on a slightly raised area or ridge giving a wide view. Nest on the ground.
Nest: A shallow hollow sparsely lined with moss or lichen fragments. Initiated by male, finished by both. Inside diameter: *c.* 6 in.; depth: *c.* $1\frac{1}{2}$ in. **Breeding season:** Begins late May. Usually ends by late August. **Eggs:** Usually 4, rarely 3. Oval to pyriform. Smooth but non-glossy or slightly glossy. Pale buff or grayish-stone, or sometimes tinged brownish, greenish, or reddish; variably spotted and blotched in black, and less frequently brown and pale gray. Marking tends to be concentrated towards the larger end, or in a zone around it. 52 × 36 mm. **Incubation:** By both sexes, but mainly by male. 27 days. **Nestling:** Precocial and downy. Down pattern like that of American Golden-Plover, but upperparts more grayish-buff and less golden. Markings larger and with more marbled effect. There is a bold white collar around nape. Legs and feet olive-gray; bill dark gray. **Nestling period:** Young first tended by both adults. Female deserts family at *c.* 12 days; male stays with chicks until fledging. Young independent just before or after first flight (*c.* 35–43 days, sometimes earlier).

European Golden-Plover (*Pluvialis apricaria*)
A local breeder in northeast Greenland, in dry tundra slopes with dwarf-shrub vegetation. Nest on the ground.
Nest: A shallow scrape, lined with a variable amount of mosses and other plant material, sometimes considerable. Inside diameter: $4\frac{1}{2}$–$5\frac{1}{2}$ in.; depth: 1 in. **Breeding season:** Begins June? Single-brooded. **Eggs:** Usually 4, sometimes 3. Pyriform or oval. Smooth and slightly glossy. Buff or sandy; heavily marked with blotches of blackish-brown or reddish-brown. Most heavily marked at larger end. Slightly larger than eggs of American Golden-Plover, and occasionally tinted reddish-brown or olive. 52 × 36 mm. **Incubation:** Laid at intervals of 2–3 days. By both sexes, but mainly by female. 28–31 days. **Nestling:** Precocial and downy. Down grayish-white on underside. Back, head, thighs, and wings are greenish-yellow or golden-yellow, finely mottled with black. On head mottled yellow patches with dark lines on crown, over eye, and from base of bill back to nape under eye, and pale streak below eye. Pale nape with irregular dark border. Indistinct pale stripe down each side of back. Wingtips white; dark stripe near fore- and hind-edges of upper wing. **Nestling period:** Young tended by both parents. Parents may divide brood. Fly at 25–33 days. Independent soon thereafter.

Pacific Golden-Plover (*Pluvialis fulva*)

Breeds on well-drained tundra areas, often on hillsides, ridges, or raised polygons in northwestern Alaska. Nests on the ground.

Nest: Similar to American Golden-Plover. Inside diameter: *c.* 4 in.; depth: *c.* ½ in. **Breeding season:** Begins early June. Probably ends by early August. Single-brooded. **Eggs:** Similar to American Golden-Plover, but ground color may average paler. **Incubation:** By both sexes, but mainly by female. 25 days. **Nestling:** Precocial and downy. Like American Golden-Plover, except that the yellow is brighter and more extensive, predominating over the black on the crown, back, and rump; distinct yellow wash covering broad white hindcollar, sides of face, neck, and chest. There is very little grayish-white anywhere, except in the patch under the eye, and on the chin, throat, and underparts. Reportedly, there are no white stripes down sides of back as in American Golden-Plover. **Nestling period:** Young tended by both parents. Estimated at 26–28 days.

American Golden-Plover (*Pluvialis dominicus*)   Plates II, 36

Breeds on drier tundra areas, often on uplands; where ground herbage is scanty, often only mosses and lichens. Nests on the ground in an exposed site giving a wide view.

Nest: A shallow scrape, unlined, or lined with a variable amount of plant material. **Breeding season:** Late May–July. Single-brooded. **Eggs:** Usually 4, sometimes 3–5. Pyriform. Smooth and slightly to moderately glossy. Buff, creamy-buff or ivory-yellow; heavily marked with spots and small blotches of black, and less frequently brown, and lighter shades of gray. Markings heaviest at or around the larger end. 48 × 33 mm. **Incubation:** By both sexes, but mainly by female. 26–27 days. **Nestling:** Precocial and downy. Down soft, with longer silky tips. Down grayish-white on underside. Back, head, thighs, and wings are greenish-yellow, finely mottled with black and with broken black patches of relic pattern. Indistinct white stripe down each side of back. Crown thickly mottled black, but hind-neck and nape pale, unmarked or with a few dark marks down middle. Thin dark line through eye. Pale stripe above and below eye, with dark borders, forms pale eye-patch. Forehead mainly yellow. **Nestling period:** Young tended by both parents. Adults may divide the brood between them but do not separate. Young fly at *c.* 21–22 days.

Mongolian Plover (*Charadrius mongolus*)

Has bred in western and northwestern Alaska. Nests in tundra regions on the ground not far from the high water line. In Asia nests in small colonies of 3–12 pairs. **Nest:** A slight depression in the ground, lined with dried leaves, seeds, stems, and grass. Sides of the nest lined with moss. **Breeding season:** Begins early June in Alaska. **Eggs:** Usually 3. Oval to pyriform. Cinnamon buff to olive-buff, finely spotted with dark brown and some gray, tending toward the larger end. 35 × 26 mm. **Incubation:** By both sexes. 24–25 days. **Nestling:** Precocial and downy. Sides of head, hindneck, and underparts white; a loral line, postocular streak, a spot beneath suborbital region, bar on sides of nape, and stripe down middle of nape, black; median portion of crown mottled black and cinnamon; back and rump irregularly but boldly marbled with black, cinnamon, and whitish. **Nestling period:** Young probably tended by both.

Snowy Plover (*Charadrius alexandrinus*)   Plate 36

Breeds on open areas of shingle or sand, frequently on or near the sea, but also on edges of saline lagoons or dry lake beds inland, and on areas of dry mud with scanty vegetation near brackish water. Nest is on the ground.

Nest: A hollow scrape; unlined or sparsely lined with fragments of plants and debris. Eggs are often partly buried. **Breeding season:** Begins from mid-March in south to early May in north. Often double-brooded. (Three broods in central California.) **Eggs:** Usually 3, sometimes 2 or 4. Shorter oval to pyriform. Smooth but non-glossy. Buff, or sandy, sometimes tinted olive; with irregular lines and fine spots in black and pale gray. Markings at times concentrated towards the larger end. 33 × 23 mm. **Incubation:** By both sexes. 24 days. Eggs in sandy sites are often partially buried when found if adults are disturbed. **Nestling:** Precocial and downy. Down pattern like that of Semipalmated Plover but back and crown light creamy-buff with blackish mottling. Dark nape edge to crown absent; and dark streak from bill to eye faint or absent. **Nestling period:** Leave nest soon after hatching. Tended by both. Fly at 27–31 days.

Wilson's Plover (*Charadrius wilsonia*)   Plates II, 36

Breeds on dunes, shingle beaches, or reefs. Nest on the ground in the open on sand and shingle; often by a piece of driftwood or some large object, or by grass tuft.
Nest: A shallow scrape, unlined or lined with fragments of shells and pebbles. **Breeding season:** Begins early April in south to early May in north. Single-brooded. **Eggs:** Usually 3, sometimes 2, rarely 4. Oval to short oval. Smooth and non-glossy to slightly glossy. Very pale creamy-buff to cream-colored. Heavily spotted and speckled and with more sparse small blotches and scrawls of black and pale gray. 36 × 26 mm. **Incubation:** By both sexes (males are the main nocturnal incubators). 24–25 days. **Nestling:** Precocial and downy. Down grayish-white on underside and face. Broad white collar round hind-neck. Forehead buffish-white. Back and upperparts of head pale buffish very heavily speckled with black. Paired irregular lines on crown. Narrow paired black lines down mid-back, joining on the lower back. Black line along flank to tail, bordering pattern. Black line along wing. **Nestling period:** Young tended by both parents. Leave nest soon after hatching. Fly at 21 days.

Common Ringed Plover (*Charadrius hiaticula*)   Plate 36

Breeds on islands of eastern Canadian Arctic, Greenland, and occasionally Bering Strait area of Alaska, on open areas of shingle, sand, or mud, most often on the seashore; but also on bare or shingly areas at higher altitudes. Nest is on the ground.
Nest: A shallow scrape on the ground; usually exposed, but often near or sometimes sheltered by plant tuft. Lining varies with the availability of nearby material, and varies from tiny pebbles and debris to plant material. **Breeding season:** Begins mid-June. **Eggs:** Usually 4, rarely 3 or 5. Shorter pyriform or oval. Smooth and glossless or slightly glossy. Color and markings very variable. Pale bluish-gray, grayish-buff, stone-buff, yellowish, or intermediate; usually marked with profuse blackish-brown and pale gray spots, sometimes with larger sparser black blotching or almost immaculate. 36 × 26 mm. **Incubation:** By both sexes, usually commencing before completion of clutch. 23–26 days. **Nestling:** Precocial and downy. Down pattern similar to that of Semipalmated Plover but ground color of back and head lighter. **Nestling period:** Young tended by both adults. Independent in *c.* 25 days.

Semipalmated Plover (*Charadrius semipalmatus*)   Figure 40, Plates II, 36

Breeds in dry arctic tundra, usually near water, on areas of sand, shingle, gravel, or similar rubble; also away from water on gravel tundra or thin turf.
Nest: A hollow scrape; unlined or lined with a little debris, pebbles or shell fragments from nearby. **Breeding season:** Begins early June in south to late June in north. Single-brooded, possibly double-brooded in south. **Eggs:** Usually 4, rarely 3–5. Shorter oval to pyriform. Smooth and slightly glossy. Buff, pale creamy-buff, or

olive-buff. Heavily spotted and blotched with black, and with finer spots and specks of black and pale gray. Markings sometimes more concentrated towards larger end, large blotches sometimes black and brown. Eggs consistently more heavily marked than those of Common Ringed Plover. 33 × 23 mm. **Incubation:** By both sexes but mainly by male. 23 days. **Nestling:** Precocial and downy. Down white on underside to throat; white collar circling neck. Upperparts of body and crown dark grayish-buff, buffer on the mantle and wings, finely mottled overall with spots and short streaks of blackish-brown. Forehead white, a dark band bordering upper edge of collar round nape from eye to eye, and dark line from eye to bill. Sometimes a black broken line along mid-crown. Dark line to hind-edge of collar, and partial paired dark lines on mantle, dark band along flank bordering back. Short dark band across upper fore-edge of wing and dark band along hind-edge. **Nestling period:** Young tended by both parents. Active, leaving nest soon after hatching, and finding their own food. Guarded and brooded by adults. Young fly at 22–31 days.

Piping Plover (*Charadrius melodus*)   Figure 35, Plate 36

Breeds on open sandy beaches, on the coast, larger inland (usually alkali) lakes, and river sandflats or gravel islands, often where there are scattered grass tufts. Nest on the ground.

Nest: A shallow scrape. Unlined or lined with fragments of shells, driftwood, or small pebbles. Sometimes found under grass tufts. Nest formed by both sexes. **Breeding season:** Begins late April on coast and late May inland, to late August. Single-brooded, but lost clutches replaced. **Eggs:** Usually 4, sometimes 3 in replacement clutches, exceptionally 5. Oval to pyriform. Smooth and non-glossy to slightly

Figure 35. Piping Plover: a shallow scrape or depression in the sand, in open areas or among sparse grass tufts.

glossy. Creamy or ivory, to very pale creamy-buff; finely speckled and spotted with black and gray, the markings usually denser at the larger end, smaller and more sparse elsewhere. 32 × 24 mm. **Incubation:** By both sexes. 27 days. **Nestling:** Precocial and downy. Down white below, and white collar round hind-neck. Back, and upperparts of head, speckled buff and grayish and spotted with blackish-brown. Forehead buffish-white, and the dark speckling on crown may form a dark chevron at center. Dark spots on wings and thighs. Bill, black; legs, orange. **Nestling period:** Young can walk within several hours of hatching. Tended by both parents, though female often deserts, leaving male to raise young. Fly at *c.* 30–35 days.

Killdeer (*Charadrius vociferus*)   Figures 36, 37, Plates II, 36

Breeds in a variety of open spaces, usually on short turf or on bare sandy or gravelly areas. Often around lakes, ponds, and rivers; also in meadows, pastures, on golf courses, airports, and similar areas of open turf; and on bare cultivated land, or bare stony ground, gravel road, and railroads, and rarely graveled roofs.

Nest: A shallow scrape, unlined or lined with nearby material – pebbles, woodchips, plant fragments, and any small debris – sparsely lining the cavity. Inside diameter: 5–7 in.; depth: 1–1½ in. **Breeding season:** Begins mid-March in south to early April in north. Sometimes double-brooded. **Eggs:** Usually 4, rarely 3–5. Pyriform to oval. Smooth, non-glossy to slightly glossy. Very pale buff or creamy-buff; heavily marked with specks, spots and blotches or scrawls of black, blackish-brown, and pale gray. Markings often overall, sometimes with a grouping of larger markings towards the larger end. 36 × 27 mm. **Incubation:** By both sexes (males are the main nocturnal incubators). 24–26 days. **Nestling:** Precocial and downy. Down white on underside, with white on lower half of face continuing as collar round hind-neck, separated from underside by a black chest band. Forehead whitish with black band across forehead between eyes, from eye to base of bill, and around upper edge of white collar bordering nape. Crown of head and back mottled finely in buff and grayish-brown, with short broken black band along mid-back, and black edges to back pattern. Elongated tail tuft blackish, and barred at base. **Nestling period:** Young tended by both parents. Young leave nest soon after hatching and are often led to nearby water. They are brooded and guarded by adults, but feed themselves. First fly at *c.* 40 days.

Figure 36. Killdeer: scrape *c.* 5–7 in. across, often in gravelly area; young dark breastband and white nape already present.

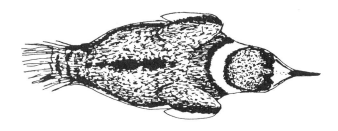

Figure 37. Dorsal pattern of downy chick: Killdeer.

Mountain Plover (*Charadrius montanus*)   Plate 36

Breeds on shortgrass prairie or arid high plains (generally dominated by Blue Gamma and Buffalo Grass), often in disturbed areas with large patches of bare ground. Nest on the ground in an exposed site or often next to a cow patty or large stone.

Nest: A shallow hollow, unlined, or lined with pieces of earth and plant material. **Breeding season:** Late April to early August. Double-brooded. **Eggs:** Usually 3. Female may lay two clutches in two nests, one after the other with the same or a different mate. Oval. Smooth and slightly glossy. Drab light olive, or olive-buff, rarely pinkish-buff; finely speckled, spotted, and scrawled with black and gray. 37 × 28 mm. **Incubation:** Eggs usually laid at 1–2-day intervals, exceptionally at longer intervals. By both sexes, or where more than one clutch laid, one is incubated by male alone, the other by female. 28–31 days. **Nestling:** Precocial and downy. Down whitish below, pale yellowish-buff on flanks and more definite but pale yellowish-buff on back and head. Collar round hind-neck, and forehead, unmarked. Remainder of upper head and back and wings heavily spotted and mottled with black spots, those on the crown forming broken lines at times, and heaviest on hind-crown. Pale eye-stripe and thin dark line from eye to dark mark on ear-coverts. **Nestling period:** Young will leave nest within hours of hatching. They are mostly tended by the single, incubating parent. Young can fly at least several hundred feet at 33–34 days.

Eurasian Dotterel (*Charadrius morinellus*)

A sporadic breeder in northwestern Alaska on tundra, bare hills, or mountains. Nest on the ground. Female often polyandrous, laying two or three clutches to be hatched and raised by different males.

Nest: A shallow hollow on the ground, unlined or sparsely lined with nearby vegetation. Started by female, finished by both. **Breeding season:** Begins June. Single-brooded, though will replace lost clutch. **Eggs:** Usually 3, sometimes 2, rarely 4. Oval. Smooth, non-glossy, or slightly glossy. Color variable, pale buff, at times yellowish, greenish, or reddish-buff; marked with large spots or heavy blotching of blackish-brown, sometimes reddish-brown, and sparse pale gray marks. Markings tending toward larger end. (Not unlike eggs of American Golden-Plover, though smaller.) 44 × 29 mm. **Incubation:** Eggs usually laid at 1–2-day intervals. Incubation usually by male alone, beginning with second egg. 23–29 days. **Nestling:** Precocial and downy. Down grayish-white on underside becoming creamy on breast. On back and crown yellowish-buff to sandy-buff, irregularly and heavily mottled in black and white. Sometimes two white streaks on lower back. Forehead white or pale buff with black line down middle. Conspicuous white crescent around hindcrown with black line below it extending forward to lores below eyes. Narrow dark line from bill through eye to nape. Broad streak over eye, ear-covert, and cheek white; and white collar with faint dusky mottling. Legs olive with yellowish joints. Bill lead-gray at hatching, soon turning to black. Irides dark brown. **Nestling period:** Young may remain in the nest for first day. Subsequently cared for mainly or entirely by male, the female rarely helping. First flight at 19–23 days, strong flights a week later.

Oystercatchers (*Haematopodidae*)

American Oystercatcher (*Haematopus palliatus*)   Figure 38, Plates II, 36

Breeds on open sites, on coastal beaches; among rocks, on islands, in dunes, or on shingle beds, occasionally on saltmarsh.

Nest: A shallow hollow, unlined or with pieces of dead plants, small stones, broken shells, or other debris. Often on a little mound, serving as a lookout. **Breeding season:** Begins early April in south, to June in north. Usually ends by early July. Single-brooded but lost clutches replaced. **Eggs:** Usually 3, rarely 2–4. Subelliptical to oval. Smooth and glossy. Yellowish with stone, grayish or buffish tints, more rarely greenish or brownish; variably marked, but usually boldly spotted, blotched or irregularly streaked with brownish-black markings which vary considerably in size. 56 × 39 mm. **Incubation:** By both sexes, usually but not invariably beginning with the last egg. 24–27 days. **Nestling:** Precocial and downy. Down dark grayish-black above, finely tipped and tinted with grayish-white and buff; white on the underside. A blackish band across the breast at lower edge of dark breast shield, and a dark line on flanks separating blackish back and white underside. A narrow dark line from eye to nape, along center of crown, two narrow longitudinal lines on back, and one across wing. Legs and feet light gray, irides brown. Bill dark with pinkish base. **Nestling period:** Young tended by both parents. They remain at the nest for 1–2 days. Some food is brought to them. Later they follow parents and pick up their own food, but may still be given some food. They can swim at an early age, and crouch motionless if alarmed. Independent in 34–37 days; but bill not fully developed for adult feeding until 8–9 weeks.

Black Oystercatcher (*Haematopus bachmani*)   Plate 36

Breeds on coastal sites, preferring rocky shores, promontories and islands. Nest a hollow on the ground in shingle or turf, or on bare rock.

Nest: A shallow hollow, unlined or with a variable amount of small pebbles, fragments of shell, driftwood or other debris. Where dead plant material is present a gull-like nest is accumulated by sideways-building. Mostly built by male. Same site

Figure 38. American Oystercatcher: c. 6–10 in. across; a shallow hollow with variable amounts of broken shells and other debris.

may be used in successive years. **Breeding season:** Begins late May to early June. Usually ends by late August. Single-brooded, but lost clutches replaced. **Eggs:** Usually 2–3. Similar to those of American Oystercatcher in shape, color and size. **Incubation:** By both sexes. 26–27 days. **Nestling:** Precocial and downy. Down pattern like that of American Oystercatcher, but darker on face and back. **Nestling period:** Young tended by both adults. Begin to take insects at 5 days and some shellfish by 30 days. Young active but do not follow adults until 3–5 weeks. Fly at *c.* 5 weeks. Apparently continue to receive food from parents for a long period.

Stilts and Avocets (*Recurvirostridae*)

Black-necked Stilt (*Himantopus mexicanus*)   Figures 39, 40, Plates II, 39
Breeds by fresh or brackish water in shallow areas of lagoons, or edges of lakes (including alkaline lakes) or flood waters; where water is of little depth or muddy. Usually nests in colonies. Nest is on plant tuft or tussock in water, or built up in very shallow water, or on mud by the water's edge. Conditions may vary through change of water level during nesting.
Nest: A shallow hollow; with very variable amount of nest material which may be a few scraps in dry sites or a built-up accumulation of plant debris in wet sites. Material may be added during incubation if water level rises. Outside diameter: 6–10 in.; inside diameter: 4 in. **Breeding season:** Variable; beginning mid-April to early May. Single-brooded. **Eggs:** Usually 4, often 3, sometimes 5. Subelliptical to oval. Smooth but only slightly glossy. Pale brownish-buff, variable but usually marked with small black spots and blotches and sometimes grayish markings. Very similar to those of American Avocet, but smaller and more marked. 44 × 31 mm. **Incubation:** By both sexes. 25–26 days. **Nestling:** Precocial and downy. Down white below and finely freckled with pale gray and pale buff above, grayer on neck. Thin broken blackish line along mid-crown. Thin line through the eye and fine mottling on the head. Broader, very broken double blackish line down middle of upper back terminating in a dark spot on lower back; and broken blackish line along each flank. Thin black line on fore-edge of wings. **Nestling period:** Young tended by both parents, running and feeding soon after hatching. Independent at 28–32 days.

American Avocet (*Recurvirostra americana*)   Figure 40, Plates II, 39
Breeds in open areas on the edges of salt or brackish lagoons, or on low islands, sands, or mudflats, or meadows by salt or brackish waters. Usually nests colonially. Nest in the open on bare dry mud or sand near the water's edge, or in short sparse vegetation.
Nest: A shallow hollow, lining often absent or very sparse, usually a little dead plant material. Nest material may be added if surrounding water rises. Inside diameter: 3–7 in. **Breeding season:** Begins mid-April in south, to mid-May in north. Single-brooded. **Eggs:** Usually 4, sometimes 3–5, rarely less. Subelliptical to oval. Smooth, but non-glossy or with slight gloss. Pale brownish-buff, very variably marked but usually with scattered small spots and blotches of black, and rarely some gray spots. Very similar to those of Black-necked Stilt, but larger and less marked. 50 × 35 mm. **Incubation:** By both sexes. 22–24 days. **Nestling:** Precocial and downy. Down soft and silky; white on underside and pale buffish-gray on back. Pattern variable and very broken. Thin dark mark from bill through eye. Thin broken line or mottling along mid-crown. Sparse black blotches indicate relict paired lines in mid-back; single mid-line on lower back and line along each flank. Bill short, slender and almost straight at first. Bill blackish, legs and feet gray with orange edges to webs. **Nestling period:** Young tended by both parents, running and feeding themselves soon after hatching. Independent in c. 6 weeks.

Figure 39. Black-necked Stilt: c. 10 in. across, with variable amount of material; this nest is a more elaborate example.

Jacanas (*Jacanidae*)

Northern Jacana (*Jacana spinosa*)   Plates 11, 35

Breeds rarely in southern Texas on marshes, lakes, and other areas of open water that are in part covered with floating plants which will support the birds. The nest is laid on a mass of floating plants, or on water hyacinths or lily pads, and is at water level, sometimes sinking slightly into the water when the bird is sitting. The male is smaller and duller in color than the female and the usual sex roles are reversed, the male incubating the eggs and caring for the young alone. Female polyandrous, with simultaneous males.

Nest: An often thin, damp layer of water plant material, or a few loosely-arranged stems, lying on plants floating on the surface. Built by female and added to during

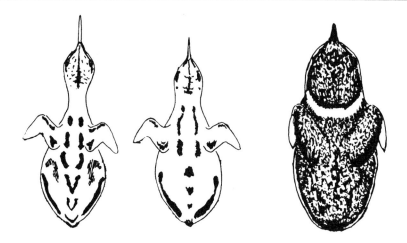

Figure 40. Dorsal patterns of downy chicks (*left to right*): Black-necked Stilt, American Avocet, Semipalmated Plover.

incubation. **Breeding season:** Begins late April. **Eggs:** Usually 3–4. Subelliptical to oval or sometimes elliptical. Smooth and highly glossy. Golden-buff to buff or golden-brown, heavily scrawled and scribbled overall with irregular patterns of thin black lines. 30 × 22 mm. **Incubation:** By male alone. 22–24 days. **Nestling:** Precocial and downy. Down white below and on sides of face. Crown of head orange-buff with a dark band extending on to crown from nape, and narrow black line from nape to eye on each side. There is a chestnut band down mid-back, with blackish edges, bordered by a pair of whitish-buff bands and outside these a dark brownish band along each flank with a blackish inner edge. Wings brown with pale tips and dark foreedges. Dark patch on thigh. **Nestling period:** Tended (but not fed) by male. Young can run and dive soon after hatching. The adult broods them under his wings, against the flanks, and may transport the young by gripping them against the flanks with closed wings, often with legs dangling. Mostly independent of male 28 days after hatching. First flight at 35 days.

Sandpipers, Phalaropes, and Allies (*Scolopacidae*)

Small to medium, long-legged wading birds, occurring in a variety of habitats, but usually by water. Nest usually a hollow in the ground. Nest-lining added by sideways-throwing and sideways-building, and there may be considerable variation according to the nature of the site and the material available nearby. Nests may be in bare, open sites or hidden in herbage. In the latter sites growing plants are usually pulled together over the nest, concealing it. The Solitary Sandpiper is an exception in habitually using an existing platform, usually the old nest of another bird, in a tree. Usually 4 eggs, pyriform or oval, cryptically colored and patterned. Young are downy and also cryptically colored and patterned. The patterns are rather like those of gamebird chicks. The dorsal pattern is basically a dark central stripe which may be split by a paler median band; and at either side one or two more dark stripes. The pattern becomes irregular, the central stripe varying in width along its length, and in the *Calidris* sandpipers and in the Common Snipe the dark bands are partly concealed by pale buff or white dots formed by specialized brush-tips to some down filaments, and the pattern is often not obvious.

The part played by the adults varies between species. In some cases both sexes incubate and care for young; but in the Pectoral Sandpiper the female does it all, while in the phalaropes sex roles are reversed and the male alone cares for eggs and young. In a number of instances the male plays a major role either in incubation or care of the young. It has been found that in some species the female may lay two clutches, one of which is incubated by the male; or may do so but involve two males, sharing incubation with the last male; or may initiate several such male-incubated clutches. The young are precocial and usually leave the nest as soon as the down is dry after hatching, being led away to better feeding by the adults. In most instances the young feed themselves, but are brooded and guarded by the parents. In such circumstances it is difficult to be sure of the point where independence is achieved.

Greater Yellowlegs (*Tringa melanoleuca*)   Figure 41, Plate 38

Breeds in muskeg country, along tundra/forest edge, and on high tundra. Nest on the ground in an open site, often on a slight ridge or hummock usually near a pool or open water. Nest often by a log or dead branch.

Nest: A shallow hollow in moss or dry peat, unlined or scantily lined with some grasses and dead leaves. **Breeding season:** Begins late May to early June. Single-brooded. **Eggs:** Usually 4. Pyriform to oval. Smooth and slightly glossy. Very pale creamy-buff or faintly olive, rarely pinkish-buff; speckled, spotted, and blotched with dark brown or purplish-brown, and pale purple or gray. Larger markings often concentrated at the larger end, and sometimes spirally elongated. 50 × 33 mm. **Incubation:** Probably by both sexes. 23 days. **Nestling:** Precocial and downy. Down pattern shows variations. Paler parts of plumage grayish-white with slight buff tint on back and sides. Dark pattern blackish-brown. Narrow dark line from bill through eye. Dark crown-patch with narrow line to bill, or smaller crown-patch with dark line from above eye on either side converging on hind-crown. Dark spot at rear of ear-coverts. Dark patch on nape. Three dark bands down back, the middle one broad and sometimes divided on lower back to produce pale median streak. Dark lateral patches on flanks join outer dorsal bands. Two small dark wing-patches. Bill black. Legs and feet yellowish-green. **Nestling period:** Young tended by both sexes. First flight at *c.* 18–20 days.

Lesser Yellowlegs (*Tringa flavipes*)   Plate 38

Breeds in drier sites than Greater Yellowlegs, sometimes by a muskeg, but more often in clearings or burnt-off areas in forest, with or without secondary growth; on thinly wooded hillsides; on grassy marshland in clearings. Nest on the ground in the open; but by a branch or log, or sometimes sheltered by a shrub. May nest in a loose colony.

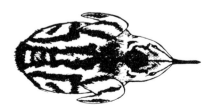

Figure 41. Dorsal pattern of downy chick: Greater Yellowlegs.

Nest: A shallow depression lined with a few dry leaves and grasses. Inside diameter: $3\frac{1}{2}$–4 in.; depth: *c.* $1\frac{1}{4}$–$1\frac{1}{2}$ in. **Breeding season:** Begins mid-May in south, to early June in north. Ends by August. **Eggs:** Usually 4, sometimes 3. Pyriform to oval. Very pale creamy-buff, or faintly tinted olive or greenish; speckled, spotted, and blotched, often profusely, with medium to purplish-brown, and pale purple or lilac. Larger markings sometimes concentrated at larger end. 42×29 mm. **Incubation:** By both sexes. 22–23 days. **Nestling:** Precocial and downy. Down pale grayish-white below and on neck and head; warm or pinkish-buff on back and wings. Pattern similar to that of Greater Yellowlegs; but crown-patch smaller, and dark lateral streaks over eyes more conspicuous. Broader black band across wings, and bolder band continuing along flanks to rump. **Nestling period:** Young tended by both sexes. Young leave nest soon after hatching, usually led by parents to nearest water. First flight at *c.* 18–20 days.

Wood Sandpiper (*Tringa glareola*)

Has bred in western and central Aleutian islands in Alaska in wet areas of tundra. Nest usually on the ground in a slightly raised site, in herbage or low shrubby growth.

Nest: A shallow depression lined with a few dry leaves and grasses. **Breeding season:** Begins early June. Single-brooded. **Eggs:** Usually 4, rarely 3. Pyriform to oval. Smooth and slightly glossy. Pale to very pale greenish to olive, or rarely pale olive-buff; blotched, speckled, or spotted, or coarsely scrawled, in blackish-brown or dark purplish-brown, and paler purplish-gray. Frequently with fairly plentiful small speckling, and more sparing small blotches or scrawls concentrated at or around the larger end. Blotches often show slight slanting elongation. 38×26 mm. **Incubation:** By both sexes, but mainly by female. Estimated at 22–23 days. **Nestling:** Precocial and downy. Down long and soft. Underparts white, with warm buff tips on sides. Upperparts warm pinkish-buff marked with blackish-brown. Dark cap leading to dark midline on forehead. Narrow line from top of bill through eyes to dark nape. Dark bands down back, broad irregular patch along lower flank to rump, and dark patch at top of leg. Dark line along wing. Bill dark gray. Legs proportionally long and olive-gray. **Nestling period:** Young leave nest when down is dry. Tended by both sexes at first, mainly or entirely by male later. First flight at 28 days.

Solitary Sandpiper (*Tringa solitaria*)   Plate 38

Breeds in northern forests, tundra-forest edge, muskeg country, and in mountain forest. Usually near open water, lake, or pool, in places where forest is open with scattered trees or broken cover. Nest is usually in a conifer in the old nest of a Rusty Blackbird, American Robin, or similar-sized bird, in a tree at almost any height, usually 3–36 ft. up.

Nest: The old nest of another bird species, no material other than that already present, though female Solitary Sandpiper may rearrange some materials. **Breeding season:** Begins late May to early June. Single-brooded. **Eggs:** Usually 4, sometimes 3. Pyriform to oval. Smooth and slightly glossy. Creamy, tinted very pale green, olive or buff; speckled, spotted and with a few blotches of purplish or reddish-brown, and pale lilac or purple. Markings often sparse except at or around the larger end. 36×26 mm. **Incubation:** By both sexes. *c.* 23–24 days. **Nestling:** Precocial and downy. Down grayish on head and underside, buffish-brown on upperparts. Small dark spot on hind ear-coverts. Blackish patch with browner center on hindcrown; fore-crown mottled brown with dark median streak from hind-crown patch to bill, and lateral streaks from patch to just above eyes. Nape mottled. Back with three dark bands. Dark mark on thigh and dark stripe along hindflank. Dark patches on wings. **Nestling period:** Little information. Young tended by both parents? Leave nest, probably dropping unaided, soon after hatching.

Willet (*Catoptrophorus semipalmatus*)   Plates 10, 38

Breeds usually near, or in flying distance of, salt, brackish, or fresh water. Nests in open places, coastal marshes, beaches, or islands: and inland in wet grassland by lakes, or short grass or bare ground by water. Nest on the ground, in the open on bare ground or in short grass, or by a plant tuft, or well-concealed in grass-tufts or low bushes. Pairs often nest near each other.

Nest: A shallow scrape, lined to a varying degree with grasses or other vegetation, or shells, or other debris in barer sites. Inside diameter: *c.* 6–7 in.; depth: 3 in. **Breeding season:** Begins mid-March in south to early June in north. Single-brooded. **Eggs:** Usually 4, rarely 5. Pyriform to oval. Smooth and moderately glossy. Very pale greenish, olive, buff, stone, or slightly pinkish-buff; finely speckled, spotted, and blotched with medium to dark brown, or purplish-brown, and pale gray or purple. Larger markings often concentrated at or around larger end. 55 × 39 mm. **Incubation:** By female during the day, male at night (occasionally at midday). 24–26 days. **Nestling:** Precocial and downy. Down buffish-white on underside. Head pale buff, whiter on throat. Dark stripe through eye. Dark brown mottled patch on crown with dark streak to bill. Nape mottled. Back grayish to buffish-brown, patterned with blackish-brown. Three dark stripes down back, the middle one divided down the mid-back to enclose a long pale streak. Flanks and wings with dark patches. **Nestling period:** Young tended by both parents, but deserted at fairly early stage. Age at first flight estimated at 28 days.

Wandering Tattler (*Heteroscelus incanus*)

Breeds in mountain areas above tree-line, by freshwater streams and pools. Nest in a level gravel bar or rocky site by water.

Nest: A shallow scrape lined with a variable amount of rootlets and other plant material. **Breeding season:** Begins early June? **Eggs:** Usually 4. Pyriform to oval. Smooth and slightly glossy. Very pale greenish or olive, spotted and blotched with medium to dark brown, and paler brownish-gray. Markings mainly concentrated at larger end. 43 × 32 mm. **Incubation:** By both sexes. 23–25 days. **Nestling:** Precocial and downy. Down whitish below, becoming pale bluish-gray on sides, back, and head. Dark line from bill through eye, but otherwise only a faint indication of a *Tringa*-sandpiper type pattern in darker brownish-gray on head and back. Bill blackish. **Nestling period:** Young tended by both parents at first, but later usually only one present. Young probably fly at *c.* 4 weeks.

Spotted Sandpiper (*Actitis macularia*)   Figures 42, 43, Plates 10, 38

Breeds by fresh water – pools, lakes, streams, dams, rivers, marshes, or floodwaters; in both open and wooded areas; and less frequently in open grassy areas away from water. At any altitude from tree-line to sea-level. May be semi-colonial. Females often polyandrous.

Nest: Nest a grass-lined depression on the ground, in growing herbage or low shrubby growth, or against plant-tuft, log, or driftwood in an open site. Built by both. Outside diameter: 4½–5 in. **Breeding season:** Begins mid-May in south to mid-June in north of range. Single-brooded. **Eggs:** Usually 4, rarely 3 or 5. But female frequently lays more than one clutch, often two and sometimes more, with different males. Eggs pyriform to oval. Smooth and slightly glossy. Creamy or pale creamy-buff; usually with fine profuse speckling and sparser, more random spots or blotches in blackish-brown, purplish-brown or reddish-brown, and pale gray or purple. 33 × 24 mm. **Incubation:** Where several clutches are laid, earlier clutches incubated by males alone, last by both sexes. 20–24 days. **Nestling:** Precocial and downy. Some down with long fine tips. Underside, bill to vent, white. Sides of head and forehead pale buffish, with dark streak from bill through eye to hind ear-covert.

Figure 42. Spotted Sandpiper: c. 4½–5 in. across; a grass-lined depression in ground, often against surrounding plants.

Figure 43. Dorsal pattern of downy chick: Spotted Sandpiper.

Upperparts finely mottled in buffish-brown and blackish-brown; long down having black tips. Broad dark band over mid-crown tapering to forehead and nape. Dark stripe down mid-back. Down of rump elongated to form long wispy tuft. **Nestling period:** Young tended by male alone or by both parents. Young have teetering action of adults from the first. Leave nest as soon as down is dry. Fly in c. 16–18 days.

Upland Sandpiper (*Bartramia longicauda*)   Plates II, 38

Breeds on open grassland, prairies, and meadows, usually by wet sites; and in clearings in spruce muskegs in north; but sometimes on dry areas. Nest in tall growing herbage. Often in loose colony.

Nest: A hollow, lined with grasses, leaves, or small twigs, the surrounding grass pulled over, concealing the nest. Inside diameter: *c.* 4–5 in.; depth: *c.* 2–3 in. **Breeding season:** Begins late April to early May. Single-brooded. **Eggs:** Usually 4, sometimes 3. Oval to subelliptical. Smooth and glossy. Very pale buff, creamy-buff or pale stone; finely speckled and spotted, and occasionally with a few small blotches of reddish- or purplish-brown, and pale gray or lilac. Larger markings tend to be concentrated at the larger end, and the ground color predominates elsewhere. 45 × 33 mm. **Incubation:** By both sexes. 21 days. **Nestling:** Precocial and downy. Down of underparts and throat whitish; of breast, neck and sides of head buff. Back and wings mottled blackish-brown and buffish-brown, with overall buff and white tips, producing a spotted pattern with a few irregular black markings. Elongated black patch on ear-coverts and on nape. White stripe through eye to hind-crown, bordering a crown-patch which tapers to dark line on forehead and shows dark border and streaks converging completely or incompletely on hind-crown, the remainder mottled buff and white. **Nestling period:** Young tended by both parents. Full-grown in *c.* 30 days, when they first fly.

Eskimo Curlew (*Numenius borealis*)   Plate 37

Very rare and almost extinct. May still breed in western Northwest Territories and perhaps northeast Alaska on barren grounds and tundra. Nest usually in an open site with a wide view.

Nest: A shallow hollow with a scanty lining of plant material. **Breeding season:** June. **Eggs:** Usually 4, rarely 3. Oval. Smooth, non-glossy to slightly glossy. Pale olive to pale buff; speckled, spotted and with small blotches of varying shades of brownish-olive or dark brown and pale purplish-grey; the markings tending to be concentrated towards the larger end. 51 × 36 mm. **Incubation:** No information. **Nestling:** Precocial. **Nestling period:** No information.

Whimbrel (*Numenius phaeopus*)   Figure 44, Plates II, 37

Breeds on wet tundra in hummock areas with grasses, cottongrass, and low heath scrub; on heathland and open areas in birch scrub. Nest on the ground in the open, often on a ridge or slight eminence.

Nest: A shallow hollow, sparsely lined with nearby plant material. Inside diameter: 4½ in.; depth: 1½ in. **Breeding season:** Begins mid-May. Usually ends mid-August. Single-brooded. **Eggs:** Usually 4, occasionally 3, rarely 5. Oval to pyriform, or subelliptical. Smooth and slightly glossy. Pale green or olive to deeper olive-buff or buff; blotched, and more sparingly speckled and spotted, exceptionally coarsely scrawled with olive-brown, shades of medium to dark brown, and sometimes blackish-brown. Most frequently with irregular small blotches; occasionally well distributed, sometimes more concentrated towards the larger end. 58 × 42 mm. **Incubation:** By both sexes. 27–28 days. **Nestling:** Precocial and downy. Down on upperparts pale buff, on underparts whitish-buff with warmer buff breast. Dark line from bill to crown and two dark brown bands over crown divided by a median buff streak. Dark line from eye to nape. Indistinct dark band down nape and four parallel dark stripes between wings. Large irregular dark patch around pale spot on lower back. Dark patch on flanks and dark hind-edge of flanks extending back to rump. Two small dark patches on wings. Bill short and straight at first. **Nestling period:** Young tended by both parents who divide brood between them. Young leave nest as soon as down is dry. Fly at 5–6 weeks.

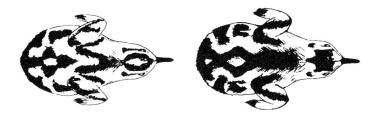

Figure 44. Dorsal patterns of downy chicks: *left*, Whimbrel; *right*, Hudsonian Godwit.

Bristle-thighed Curlew (*Numenius tahitiensis*)
Breeds only in western Alaska on drier rocky areas of upland tundra. Nest on the ground usually open site.
Nest: A shallow hollow in moss, unlined or sparsely lined with plant material. **Breeding season:** Begins mid-May? **Eggs:** Usually 4. Similar to those of Whimbrel, but more buff and less greenish; with large, bold markings. 60 × 42 mm. **Incubation:** By both. Estimated at 26 days. **Nestling:** Precocial and downy. Down pinkish-buff, paler below; with blackish-brown pattern like that of Whimbrel. Crown has a pale center, dark stripe from eye to nape is incomplete, and dark band on hind-flank does not meet tail mark. **Nestling period:** Cared for by both parents at least until they are over 3 weeks old; age of first flight estimated at 5–6 weeks.

Long-billed Curlew (*Numenius americanus*)   Plate 37
Breeds widely on open grassland, from wet meadows to dry prairie, often on uplands. Nest on the ground in flat area with short grasses.
Nest: A shallow hollow, variably lined with nearby grasses and other plant material and debris, the rim sometimes raised. In damp sites a substantial layer of material may be accumulated. Inside diameter: *c.* 8 in.; depth: *c.* 2 in. **Breeding season:** Begins late April to early May. Single-brooded. **Eggs:** Usually 4, rarely 5. Oval to pyriform. Smooth, non-glossy to slightly glossy. Pale greenish or olive; heavily speckled and spotted, and sometimes with small blotches or scrawls of medium to dark olive-brown and pale purplish-gray. 65 × 46 mm. **Incubation:** By both sexes. 27–28 days. **Nestling:** Precocial and downy. Down creamy-buff on back, wings, underside, and head, paler on throat; and warm buff on breast and flanks. The brownish-black pattern of head, back, and wings is basically similar to that of the Whimbrel, but the markings are narrow and more broken, producing a more mottled appearance. Bill at first pink with black tip. **Nestling period:** Young tended by both adults. Adults may divide the brood between them since a number of broods of two young are recorded. First flight at 32–45 days.

Hudsonian Godwit (*Limosa haemastica*)   Figure 44, Plates 10, 37
Breeds on wet tundra near water at northern forest limits, and on bogs and marshes within the forest edge. Nest on the ground in a dry site. Often under a small birch or willow, or on a grass tuft or a raised hummock.
Nest: A hollow sparsely lined with dry plant material. **Breeding season:** Late May to July. Single-brooded. **Eggs:** Usually 4, sometimes 3. Pyriform to long oval. Smooth and moderately glossy. Pale to deep olive or greenish; with faint and indistinct spots, blotches, and mottling in darker olive and gray; or with dark brownish spots or blotches concentrated at the larger end. 55 × 38 mm. **Incubation:** By both sexes. 22–23 days. **Nestling:** Precocial and downy. General down color very pale pinkish-

buff, or pinkish-gray, becoming whiter on sides of face, throat, and underside. Dark line from bill to eye. Forehead pale but squarish black patch on crown, with dark lateral spot at either corner on hind-crown, and narrow dark stripe down nape. Dark stripe continues down back, wider on shoulders; and on lower back widening to a lozenge shape with pale center. Two dark patches on wings, small one on foreflank, and dark band on hind-flank sometimes joining dorsal stripe at patch on rump. **Nestling period:** Young leave nest about 24 hours after hatching; can run, swim, and catch insects at about 48 hours. Young tended by both parents for about 10 days. Apparent tendency for adults to divide brood between them. Fully-feathered at about 30 days.

Bar-tailed Godwit (*Limosa lapponica*)   Plate 37
Breeds in swampy tundra, or marshes or shrubby tundra with pools bordering forest in western and northern Alaska. Nest on the ground, on a dry site on raised ridge or mound.
Nest: A hollow lined with fragments of nearby plant material. Inside diameter: *c.* 6–7 in.; depth: 3 in.; height 3–5 in. **Breeding season:** Late May to August. Single-brooded. **Eggs:** Usually 4, sometimes 3 or 2. Subelliptical, oval, or pyriform. Smooth and slightly glossy. Light to medium or olive brown, and paler gray. On shells with darker ground color markings are often indistinct, but on other markings are bold and may be evenly and fairly thickly distributed, or sparser and concentrated towards the larger end. 55 × 38 mm. **Incubation:** By both birds, mainly by male. 20–21 days. **Nestling:** Precocial and downy. Down pattern like that of other godwits but dark line from bill to crown, and lateral spot absent from hind-crown. Pale parts of back and head warmer buff, and underside drab, washed with buff. Legs, feet, and bill bluish-gray. **Nestling period:** Young tended by both parents. Reports of single adults may refer to divided broods. First flight estimated at 30 days.

Marbled Godwit (*Limosa fedoa*)   Plate 37
Breeds on prairies and meadowland, on wetter areas near water, usually in short grass. Nest on the ground. A number of pairs may nest in close proximity.
Nest: A shallow hollow, sparsely lined with dry grass. **Breeding season:** Begins mid- to late May. Single-brooded. **Eggs:** Usually 4, rarely 3, exceptionally 5. Oval or pyriform. Smooth and moderately glossy. Pale buff or olive; sparsely spotted and with small blotches and scrawls of dark brown and pale purplish-gray. 57 × 40 mm. **Incubation:** By both sexes. Estimated at 21–23 days. **Nestling:** Precocial and downy. Ground color pale buffish-brown. General appearance like that of Hudsonian Godwit, but face and belly whiter, dark head marking only begins on hind-crown with a separate lateral spot on each side, and the dark markings are browner. **Nestling period:** Little information. Young tended by both or one parent. Adults possibly divide brood between them.

Ruddy Turnstone (*Arenaria interpres*)   Plates 10, 37
Breeds on open ground, usually on a small island near shore, or along river or delta; on bare stony area, but also among rocks or in rank herbage which shelters nest. Also on barren high ground, often near a source of water. Nest on the ground. Some-times several near each other.
Nest: A shallow hollow; lining sometimes absent, or a variable lining of nearby vegetation, substantial at times. Inside diameter: $3\frac{3}{4}$–$4\frac{1}{2}$ in.; depth: 1–$1\frac{1}{2}$ in. **Breeding season:** Late May to early August. Single-brooded. **Eggs:** Usually 4, some-times 3, rarely 5. Oval to short pyriform. Smooth, slightly glossy. Very pale green, bluish-green, or light olive; usually irregularly blotched, spotted, and speckled with

drab brown, olive-brown or blackish-brown, and paler gray markings. Most frequently marked with small blotches, tending to be densest at the larger end. Sometimes more heavily freckled with smaller markings. Marking often variably elongated into streaks slanting across shell. 40 × 29 mm. **Incubation:** By both sexes, at first mainly by female, with increasing help from male, beginning with third egg. 21–23 days. **Nestling:** Precocial and downy. Down white on underside, dark grayish-buff at sides of upper breast. Forehead and area around eyes buffish-white. Crown and sides of head around eye-patch mottled pale buff and blackish-gray; and black streak from bill to eye. Nape whitish, slightly mottled. Back yellowish-buff with blackish-gray mottling, at times in an indistinct triple-stripe pattern. Wing blackish with pale edge. Legs and feet buffish-brown to pale yellow; bill bluish-gray. **Nestling period:** Young tended by both adults, the male taking major share. Eggs hatch over 2 days. Young leave nest one day after completion of hatching and follow adults to nearby wet area, but feed themselves. Fly at 24–26 days, when female usually leaves, but male may stay with brood an additional two weeks.

Black Turnstone (*Arenaria melanocephala*)   Plate 37
Breeds on coastal tundra or offshore islands. Nest on wet tundra, near small open waters in grassy places. The nest is on the ground in an open site. A number of pairs may nest in close proximity.
Nest: A shallow hollow lined with grasses. Inside diameter: $3\frac{1}{2}$–$4\frac{1}{2}$ in.; depth: 1–$2\frac{1}{2}$ in. **Breeding season:** May to July. Single-brooded. **Eggs:** Usually 4. Oval to short pyriform. Smooth, non-glossy to slightly glossy. Pale yellowish-olive to buffish-olive, or very pale greenish; marked with spots, small irregular blotches or scrawls, of buffish-olive, olive-brown and gray, sometimes poorly defined. There are also markings of blackish-brown, the darker markings tending to be limited to the larger end, the others more overall in distribution. 41 × 29 mm. **Incubation:** By both sexes. 21 days. **Nestling:** Precocial and downy. Down pattern darker, finer and more uniform than that of Ruddy Turnstone. Down thick and soft. White on belly and chin. Remainder of head, body, and wings finely and heavily spotted and speckled with black, pale gray and buffish-gray, to produce an overall effect of dark blackish-gray with a buffish tint in places. Upper breast dark gray. Blackish loral spot at base of bill. **Nestling period:** Young leave nest soon after hatching. Tended by both parents, with male deserting about a week before chicks fledge. Fledging begins at 23 days, though sustained flight may not occur until 28–30 days.

Surfbird (*Aphriza virgata*)
Breeds on rocky areas of mountains, above the tree-line in central Alaska and the Yukon Territory. Nests are in dry sites on rocky ridges with sparse vegetation, the nest in the open affording a wide view.
Nest: A shallow hollow with a thin lining of nearby plant material. **Breeding season:** Late May to July. **Eggs:** Usually 4. Pyriform. Smooth. Buff to pale buff; marked with spots and small blotches of buffish-brown, reddish-brown or dark brown, and paler purplish-gray, the markings usually concentrated at or around the larger end. 43 × 31 mm. **Incubation:** Probably by both sexes. Period unknown. **Nestling:** Precocial and downy. Down on underparts grayish-white, whiter on belly and throat; on upperparts finely mottled with buffish-white, warm buff, brown, and brownish-black. The crown is more heavily marked with black, the sides of the head and the forehead are buffish-white spotted and mottled in black. The back and wings are browner, and there is some white spotting on head and back. **Nestling period:** Little information. Young tended by both parents, but mainly by male?

Red Knot (*Calidris canutus*)   Plate 38
Breeds on barren ground at high or low altitudes, nesting on dry areas of bare stones
and rock, scree or bare earth with some scanty vegetation. Nest sometimes made
against a clump of vegetation.
Nest: A hollow lined thickly with lichens. **Breeding season.** June to August. Single-
brooded. **Eggs:** Usually 4, rarely 3. Oval to pyriform. Smooth, slightly glossy. Very
pale, green to greenish-olive; with small blotches, spots, specks and short streaks
or scrawls, in medium to dark brown and sparse purplish-gray. Markings usually
small and fairly evenly distributed. 43 × 30 mm. **Incubation:** By both sexes, male taking larger share. Beginning with last egg. 21–23 days. **Nestling:** Precocial and
downy. Down of underside white, throat sometimes buffish. Head cream-colored,
whiter or buffer. Broken blackish and buff patch on crown, dark line from bill to
crown, side of bill to eye, parallel low streak and dark irregular markings on ear-
coverts. Nape whitish. Back mottled warm or grayish-buff and blackish-brown,
finely dotted with creamy-white. Legs and bill yellow. **Nestling period:** Young tended
mainly by male; leave nest soon after hatching and gradually move to more heavily
vegetated area. Can fly at 18–20 days; independent soon thereafter.

Sanderling (*Calidris alba*)   Plates 10, 39
Breeds on the tundra, usually near the coast, on drier sites with areas of stones or
gravel scattered among clumps of low plants and herbage. Nest on the ground,
usually against a clump of vegetation and within sight of a marshy pond.
Nest: A neat deep cup well lined with dead willow leaves, or other plant material.
Breeding season: Begins late June to July. Single-brooded, but possibly two clutches
laid serially. **Eggs:** Normally 4, exceptionally 3. Pyriform to oval. Smooth and moderately glossy. Light olive or greenish; blotched, speckled, spotted or scrawled, with
dull olive-brown, and purplish-gray. Markings tend to be concentrated towards the
larger end, sparser towards the narrow end. 36 × 25 mm. **Incubation:** Eggs laid at
26–29-hour intervals. By both sexes, possibly mainly by female, beginning with
completion of clutch. 23–24 days. In some instances female may lay two clutches,
one being incubated by her, the other by the male; incubation of the first clutch
being delayed by 5–6 days. **Nestling:** Precocial and downy. Down on underside
white, tinted light buff on throat. On upperparts buff, mottled with black and finely
dotted with white. Black line from bill to crown, two from base of bill to eye; a few
black marks on cheeks. Bill gray with black tip. Legs and feet black to bluish-black or
greenish-gray. **Nestling period:** Young tended by both parents, but one appears to
take major part. Possibly only one present if two clutches are produced. Leave nest
soon after hatching. Fly at 17 days. Independent in 23–24 days.

Semipalmated Sandpiper (*Calidris pusilla*)   Plate 39
Breeds on grassy tundra, on areas of ridges and hummocks, usually near pools of
water; or on dunes. Nest usually in herbage, often partly concealed by a tuft of vegetation. Normally monogamous.
Nest: A shallow hollow, lined with grasses, moss and dead leaves. Constructed by
both. Inside diameter: 2–2½ in.; depth: 1½–2 in.; height: 2½–3½ in. **Breeding season:** Begins early June. Usually ends by mid-August. Single-brooded. **Eggs:** Usually
4. Pyriform to oval. Smooth and glossy. Very pale olive, greenish or buff; very heavily
spotted with reddish-brown, or more sparsely spotted, blotched or scrawled with
dark brown or purplish-brown, and pale purple or gray. Speckling sometimes elongated into tiny streaks. 30 × 21 mm. **Incubation:** By both sexes. 20–22 days.
Nestling: Precocial and downy. Down with long silky tips, but white-tipped (brush-
tipped) down shorter. Underparts grayish-white, slightly buff on upper breast.
Upperparts warm buff and blackish-brown in an ill-defined pattern, with areas of

fine white tips along the dark parts. Buffish-white face with pair of small dark marks by bill, and some on ear-coverts. A brown stripe over eyes, broadening towards nape, and between these the dark crown is bordered by a pair of whitish lines converging at nape. Dark crown is golden-brown at nape, has narrow point at forehead, and short paired white marks on mid-crown. Legs and bill black. **Nestling period:** Young led away from nest within hours of hatching. Tended by both parents. Become independent early, before able to fly. Fly at 16–19 days.

Western Sandpiper (*Calidris mauri*)   Plate 39

Breeds on raised and drier islands and ridges of heath tundra, surrounded by marsh areas and pools. Nest on the ground, usually under or partly hidden by a dwarf birch, heath, or other plant tuft. Normally monogamous. May nest in loose colony.
Nest: A shallow scrape formed by male, subsequently lined with lichen fragments and leaves, or other plant material. Inside diameter: 2–3 in.; depth: $1\frac{1}{2}$–3 in.; height: $2\frac{1}{4}$–4 in. **Breeding season:** Begins late May. Usually ends by late August. Single-brooded. **Eggs:** Usually 4, rarely 5. Pyriform to oval. Smooth and slightly glossy. Creamy-white to buffish or brownish; heavily speckled, spotted, and blotched with light to dark reddish-brown and purplish-brown and some faint grayish. The markings tend to be concentrated towards the larger end and often show spiral elongation. There may be a few blackish hair-lines or scrawls. 31×22 mm. **Incubation:** By both sexes, beginning with the next-to-last egg. 21 days. **Nestling:** Precocial and downy. Down whitish on belly and throat, and pale buff on breast. Cinnamon-buff on neck, sides of head and forehead. Blackish-brown crown patch, bordered by pale stripes from bill to hind-crown over eye. Paired pale marks on crown. Double dark marks at base of bill and dark markings on ear-coverts. Back, wings, and thighs mottled heavily in black, brown, and golden-brown, with an irregular pattern of pale buff tips on dark zones. Similar tips form the pale markings on the crown. **Nestling period:** Young tended by both parents. Leave nest soon after hatching, adults brooding and guarding the young. Young begin to fly and are independent at *c.* 17–18 days. Female may leave brood before this time.

Red-necked Stint (*Calidris ruficollis*)

Breeds on dry tundra or cottongrass bogs, or by water in high tundra in northwestern Alaska. Nest on the ground in a tussock or hidden in growing herbage.
Nest: A small hollow lined with dry willow leaves and similar material. **Breeding season:** Begins late May to July. Single-brooded. **Eggs:** Usually 4. Pyriform to oval. Smooth and slightly glossy. Yellowish-buff; heavily speckled and spotted with reddish-brown or reddish-buff, with markings often concentrated in a zone around the larger end. 32×22 mm. **Incubation:** By both sexes. Period not recorded. **Nestling:** Precocial and downy. Down whitish on underparts, but pale buff on breast. Neck, sides of head, forehead, and eye-stripe bordering crown are warm buff. Crown blackish, variegated with brown, and with dark line down forehead. Broad dark mark from bill to eye. Upperparts are mottled in black, brown, and warm buff (white or buff speckling is probably present, but lost on older young). **Nestling period:** Little information. Young tended by female only?

Least Sandpiper (*Calidris minutilla*)   Plates 10, 38

Breeds in wetlands of subarctic forests and tundra, particularly boggy places, with moss, grasses or sedges, usually close to water; sometimes on drier ridges or high ground. Nests in boggy sites usually on, or inside of a moss hummock or plant tuft. In drier sites usually by a heath-clump, shrub, or small tree.
Nest: A small hollow, lined with dead leaves, grasses, and stems. Construction

begun by male, finished by female. Inside diameter: $2\frac{1}{2}$ in.; depth: $1\frac{1}{4}$ in. **Breeding season:** Mid-May (in south) to August. Single-brooded. **Eggs:** Usually 4. Pyriform to oval. Smooth and glossy. Creamy, tinted pale greenish, buff or reddish; with fine speckling and spotting, often dense, or sparser spotting and small blotches, in dark or medium brown or purplish-brown, and pale purple. Speckling often elongated into tiny streaks. 29 × 21 mm. **Incubation:** By both, but mostly by male. 19–23 days. **Nestling:** Precocial and downy. Down whitish on underside, tinted buffish on upper breast and sides of head and forehead. Black streak from bill to eye, and short malar streak. Dark marks on ear-coverts. Pale area around eye; blackish crown tapering to base of bill. Sides of crown, hind-crown and nape warm orange-buff with a little black mottling and four incomplete lines of whitish down tips. Back and wings mottled black and warm golden-brown, patterned with bands of whitish down tips, forming a diagonal cross on mid-back. **Nestling period:** Young leave nest within 1 day of hatching, tended by both adults, with the male taking the major role. Fly at *c.* 15 days

White-rumped Sandpiper (*Calidris fuscicollis*)   Plate 39

Breeds on grassy or mossy tundra, from wet areas to dry eminences, but prefers wet, well-vegetated hummocks with persistent moisture. Nest on the ground, raised in a grass tussock, or moss hummock, in wet sites. Males mate promiscuously.
Nest: A shallow hollow, lined with dry grass, leaves and similar material. **Breeding season:** Begins early or mid-June. Usually ends by early August. Single-brooded. **Eggs:** Usually 4 eggs. Pyriform to oval. Smooth and slightly glossy. Buff; spotted and blotched with medium to dark reddish-brown, mainly concentrated at larger end, and showing distinct spiral elongation; or pale green with similar markings in dark olive-brown and gray. 34 × 24 mm. **Incubation:** Eggs laid at intervals of *c.* 30 hours. Incubation by female only, beginning with completion of clutch. 22 days from laying to hatching of last egg. **Nestling:** Precocial and downy. Down on belly and throat whitish; on breast, sides of head, forehead and eye-stripe pale buff to buffish-white. The forecrown is warm brown, with a blackish stripe over forehead to bill, and sides of crown mottled blackish. Back and wings are variegated with dull tawny-brown and black; crown and back being patterned with zones of white down tips. Legs and bill brown. **Nestling period:** Young tended by female only. Very active, leaving nest soon after hatching. Fly and are independent in *c.* 16–17 days.

Baird's Sandpiper (*Calidris bairdii*)   Plate 38

Breeds on tundra in dry areas with sparse grassy vegetation or low shrubby growth. Nest on the ground in fairly open site, or sheltered by a plant-tuft or rock.
Nest: A shallow hollow, sparsely lined with leaves and grasses, *c.* $2\frac{1}{2}$ in. across, *c.* 2 in. deep. **Breeding season:** June and July. Single-brooded. **Eggs:** Usually 4. Pyriform to oval. Smooth and glossy. Pale creamy-buff, or tinted pale buff, reddish or olive; with profuse speckling and spotting in reddish-brown and pale purple. Markings usually denser at the larger end and may be elongated. 33 × 24 mm. **Incubation:** By both sexes. 21 days. **Nestling:** Precocial and downy. Pale parts whiter than on other species. Underside, including breast, sides of face and forehead are white. Short dark malar streak and dark thin line through eye to blackish markings on ear-coverts. Blackish-brown crown has bordering white stripes converging on hind-crown and paired white marks on mid-crown. Back, wings, and thighs exceptionally dark, mainly black with some lighter brown on flanks and wings; heavily spotted with white down tips. Legs and bill dusky. **Nestling period:** Young tended by both parents for 5–7 days, after which male deserts. Fly at *c.* 20 days.

Pectoral Sandpiper (*Calidris melanotos*)   Figure 45, Plate 38

Breeds on grassy tundra of varying types, but at a dry site. Nest on the ground, usually concealed in grasses or under a bush. Males mate promiscuously.

Nest: A shallow hollow, usually well lined to form a definite nest of grass and leaves. Inside diameter: $3\frac{1}{2}$ in. **Breeding season:** Late May to July. Single-brooded. **Eggs:** Usually 4. Pyriform to oval. Smooth and slightly glossy. Very pale olive or stone; heavily marked with small blotches and spots in dark brown or purplish-brown, and pale gray and purple; the markings often concentrated towards the larger end and showing some spiral elongation. 37×25 mm. **Incubation:** By female alone. 21–23 days. **Nestling:** Precocial and downy. Down of underside, head, and forehead may be a warm orange-buff, or more whitish with warm buff on breast. Dark malar spot and thin black stripe through eye to hind-crown. Dark stripe down forehead from crown. Crown deep golden brown with blackish edges, and blackish median mark with paired white patches. Horseshoe-shaped pale buff stripe around hind and mid-crown, and broad brownish stripe from nape to above eye. Back mottled in warm golden-brown and black, with patterns of bands of whitish-buff down tips. **Nestling period:** Young tended by female alone. First fly at *c.* 23–25 days.

Purple Sandpiper (*Calidris maritima*)   Plate 38

Breeds on the tundra, from sea level to *c.* 1500 ft., on barer, more open, peaty ground with some low shrubby cover and herbage, from ridge-tops and summits to hill-sides and tops of dry shingle ridges. Nest on the ground in the open.

Nest: Nest a fairly deep hollow lined with dead leaves. Nest hollow formed by male. **Breeding season:** Begins mid-May to early June. Single-brooded. **Eggs:** Usually 4, sometimes 3. Subelliptical to oval and pyriform. Smooth and slightly glossy. Similar in appearance to Dunlin eggs but a little larger. Light to very pale olive, green or bluish-green; variably blotched, spotted, speckled or scrawled in drab, dark brown, or olive-brown, and some pale purplish-gray. Most typically blotched and with scattered smaller markings, tending to be sparser towards narrow end and largely concentrated towards larger end. Larger markings often show elongation and slant. 37×26 mm. **Incubation:** By both birds, but mainly by male. 21–22 days. **Nestling:** Precocial and downy. Down on underparts grayish-white with dark bases. On crown, ear-coverts and upperparts mottled yellowish-buff and blackish-brown with fine white dots. Forehead, forecrown, nape and sides of head otherwise light buff. Dark line from bill to crown, from side of bill above eye to nape, and short moustache streak. Legs olive-gray; bill dark gray. **Nestling period:** Young tended by male alone. Independent at *c.* 3–4 weeks.

Rock Sandpiper (*Calidris ptilocnemis*)   Plate 38

Breeds on tundra from sea-coast to hillsides and mountain ridges, like Purple Sandpiper. Nest on the ground in the open.

Figure 45. Crown pattern of downy chick: Pectoral Sandpiper.

Nest: A deep hollow lined with grasses and leaves; *c.* 3 in. across and *c.* 2 in. deep. *Breeding season:* Begins in early June. *Eggs:* Usually 4. Pyriform to oval. Smooth and slightly glossy. Pale green or olive; heavily spotted and blotched with medium to dark brown; usually concentrated at or around the larger end and sometimes showing spiral elongation. *Incubation:* Eggs usually laid at daily intervals. Incubation by both sexes. 20 days? *Nestling:* Precocial and downy. Down of underside, including breast, neck, and throat, pure white. Head warm buff on upperparts, paler on sides. Converging loral and malar stripes. Crown mottled and striped black and buff, with tapering black stripe to bill. Nape dull and mottled. Back, wings, and thighs warm golden-brown and buff, mottled with black and patterned with narrow bands of bold buffish-white down tips. Hour-glass pattern of mid-back, typical of calidrine sandpipers, often well defined. *Nestling period:* Young tended by both sexes, especially by male. Young leave the nest soon after hatching. First flight at *c.* 22 days.

Dunlin (*Calidris alpina*)   Plate 39

Breeds on tundra with pools, lowland grassy areas with similar water, or grassy coastal saltmarshes. Nest on the ground, often on a slight eminence. Often a number of pairs nest in some proximity.

Nest: A cup-like hollow in a grass tussock, lined with grass or leaves. Inside diameter: $3\frac{1}{4}$–4 in.; depth: 2–3 in. *Breeding season:* Begins late May to early June. Single-brooded, though there is evidence of sequential polyandry. *Eggs:* Normally 4, occasionally 2–6. Oval to short pyriform. Smooth and slightly glossy. Pale to very pale olive or greenish, or blue-green; blotched, spotted, or speckled with dark brown, olive-brown, and occasionally pale purplish-gray. Markings very variable. Small specklings tend to be profuse, larger blotching more sparing. Markings often concentrated towards the larger end where they may form a cap. Larger markings often slanting and elongated. 36×28 mm. *Incubation:* By both sexes. 21–22 days. *Nestling:* Precocial and downy. Down of breast tinted yellowish-buff, underparts white. Head yellowish-buff, paler on cheeks, and back yellowish-tawny; both patterned with blackish-brown, the dark parts of the back being finely dotted with pale buff. Head has dark line from top of bill to crown, and crown mottled dark blackish and yellowish-tawny. Dark streak from side of bill to eye, and small moustache streak. Nape dark; back mottled dark and light. Legs and bill dark gray. *Nestling period:* Female does most brooding for first few days. Both parents present at first, later only male may be apparent. Independent in *c.* 25 days; and flying at 18–24 days.

Curlew Sandpiper (*Calidris ferruginea*)

Breeds rarely in northern Alaska on open coastal lowland tundra. Nest on the ground on slightly raised areas, in low grasses and sedges. May nest semi-colonially?

Nest: A shallow scrape among low herbage, with little or no lining. *Breeding season:* Begins mid-June. *Eggs:* Usually 4, sometimes 3. Long oval to pyriform. Smooth and glossy. Light olive-green; blotched, spotted and very sparsely speckled with dark olive-brown, blackish-olive, or reddish-brown. Markings tend to be more concentrated at larger end and to show some slanting elongation. 36×26 mm. *Incubation:* By female alone, male leaving after egg laying. About 21 days. *Nestling:* Precocial and downy. Pattern similar to that of Dunlin, but paler and yellower upperparts, more rufous on wings, ear-coverts and crown. Forehead, sides of breast and upper breast yellowish-buff, lower breast and belly white. Narrow black streak through eye, widening on nape. Pale patch around eye with dark, lower edge. Blackish square crown patch, bordered by pale buff stripes converging on nape, with small pale spots; lighter mottled area on mid-crown and narrow dark line to base of bill. Bill blackish. Legs and feet purplish-gray. *Nestling period:* Little information. Young leave nest soon after hatching and are tended by female only.

Stilt Sandpiper (*Calidris himantopus*)   Plate 39
Breeds on open tundra, near marshy areas or shallow pools. Nest on the ground, among grasses, usually on slightly elevated, drier sites. May be partly sheltered by a plant tuft.
Nest: A shallow hollow, unlined or sparsely lined with a few dead leaves and grasses. **Breeding season:** Begins mid- or late June to August. Single-brooded. **Eggs:** Usually 4. Oval to pyriform. Very pale creamy-olive or creamy-buff; blotched or spotted with reddish- or purplish-brown, and paler purple; often concentrated at or around the larger end and sometimes tending to show spiral elongation. 36 × 25 mm. **Incubation:** Eggs laid at an average 36-hour interval. Incubation by both sexes, usually male by day, female by night. 19–21 days. **Nestling:** Precocial and downy. Typical calidrine sandpiper pattern. Underside white and breast buffish; sides of head pale buff; forehead and throat drab white. Short black loral and malar streaks. Crown black, mottled brown, with black tapering stripe to bill. White band formed by down tips around crown, converging on hind-crown. Nape mottled. Back and wings mottled in black and warm golden-brown and patterned with narrow lines of bold white down tufts. **Nestling period:** Young leave nest soon after hatching. Tended by both parents at first, later by male only. Young left alone by 14 days. Can fly at 17–18 days.

Buff-breasted Sandpiper (*Tryngites subruficollis*)   Plate 39
Breeds on dry tundra, preferring grassy areas, with drier raised ridges where nests may occur. Nest on the ground in an open site. Males may mate with several females.
Nest: A shallow scrape, sparsely lined with dry grasses, dead leaves or moss. Built by female. **Breeding season:** Early June to August. Single-brooded. **Eggs:** Usually 4. Pyriform to oval. Smooth and slightly glossy. Very pale creamy, tinted greenish or olive; heavily blotched and spotted with medium to dark brown, the markings tending to be concentrated towards the larger end, and often showing slight spiral elongation. 37 × 26 mm. **Incubation:** By female. 23–25 days. **Nestling:** Precocial and downy. Down whitish below and brownish-gray above. The back mottled with blackish-brown in an irregular pattern, the dark areas more profusely spotted with zones of white down-tips. Dark eye-stripes to nape; and grayish-buff stripes above these bordering a dark crown-patch with a poorly-defined short whitish chevron. Legs pale green. **Nestling period:** Male leaves breeding area before young have hatched. Young leave nest within 12 hours, and fly at 16–20 days.

Ruff (*Philomachus pugnax*)
Rare breeder in northwest Alaska in moist tundra area. Nest on the ground, concealed in herbage where this is tall enough. Males have communal displays on open ground and are promiscuous. Females nest alone nearby.
Nest: A grass-lined depression in meadow, marsh, or grass clump on more open tundra. **Breeding season:** Begins June. **Eggs:** Usually 4, rarely 3. Oval to pyriform. Smooth and slightly glossy. Light to very pale olive or green, with smallish irregular blotches, spots, specks, and rarely, short scrawls of medium to dark olive-brown or blackish-brown, and pale violet-gray. Heavier markings often concentrated around larger end. Looks similar to eggs of Long-billed Dowitcher. 44 × 31 mm. **Incubation:** By female alone. 20–21 days. **Nestling:** Precocial and downy. Resembles *Calidris* chicks, but entire upperparts buff. Down yellowish to pinkish-buff with black patterning on head and back, the black area speckled with fine buff spots. Crown with three bold black streaks broken by fine buffish mottling. Unmarked around eye but short dark streak on lores. Pattern of back and wings not obvious in irregular mottling of yellowish or pinkish-buff, and blackish-brown finely speckled with buff. Legs and feet deep olive-gray to reddish-gray. Bill dark gray. **Nestling period:** Young

soon leave nest. Tended by female alone. Fed by her on insects for several days, then feed themselves, but are guarded and brooded by female. First flight at 24–27 days.

Short-billed Dowitcher (*Limnodromus griseus*)   Plates 10, 39

Breeds in coniferous muskegs, usually on mosses or sedges and at the base of a small tree or dead sapling. Also in coastal tundra with low scrub vegetation.

Nest: A shallow hollow, a little above water level, lined with dry grasses, leaves, and small twigs; *c.* 4 in. across. **Breeding season:** Late May to early August. Single-brooded. **Eggs:** Usually 4. Oval to pyriform. Smooth and slightly glossy. Pale green-ish, olive, or buff; speckled, spotted, and blotched with dark brown and pale gray; the larger markings tending to wreath the larger end. 41 × 29 mm. **Incubation:** By both sexes. 21 days. **Nestling:** Precocial and downy. Sides of face, throat and breast are yellowish-buff, belly and chin whitish. Crown black with some brownish tips, taper-ing towards bill. Crown bordered by bold stripes over eyes, whitish by eyes and nape, otherwise buff. Black stripe from base of bill through eye to hind-edge of ear-coverts. Back and wings golden-brown with paired blackish-brown stripes down mid-back, and two short similar stripes along each side. Dark band and dark tips to wings. Bold white down tips border outer edge of paired dorsal stripes and occur along dark side stripes. **Nestling period:** Little information. Female takes little part in raising brood and may leave breeding grounds in late June.

Long-billed Dowitcher (*Limnodromus scolopaceus*)   Plate 39

Breeds in grassy tundra and wet meadows near open water (usually fresh), on tree-line edge, or with scattered trees in more open areas. Nest on the ground among grasses or sedges.

Nest: A hollow, sparsely lined with grasses and small leaves. **Breeding season:** Late May to August. Single-brooded. **Eggs:** Usually 4. Oval to pyriform. Smooth and slightly glossy. Pale greenish or olive. Speckled, spotted, and blotched with medium to dark brown, and purplish-gray. Markings tending to wreath the larger end. 42 × 29 mm. **Incubation:** By both sexes at first, later by male alone. 20 days. **Nestling:** Precocial and downy. Down pattern like that of Short-billed Dowitcher, but ground color of back and wings a deeper brown. **Nestling period:** Little information. Young tended by male alone, female leaving breeding ground early.

Common Snipe (*Gallinago gallinago*)   Figure 46, Plates 10, 38

Breeds in moist sites in a wide range of habitats at varying altitudes; in marshland, bogs, and swamps, moorland, grassland, waterside vegetation, and sometimes in saltmarsh. Nest on the ground usually concealed in a clump of herbage partly pulled over to hide the nest. Exceptionally on bare sites.

Nest: A shallow hollow lined with grass, sometimes with woven canopy. Outside diameter: *c.* 6 in.; inside diameter: *c.* 3 in.; depth: 1¼ in. **Breeding season:** Mid-April to August. Single-brooded. **Eggs:** Usually 4, sometimes 3. Oval to pyriform. Smooth and slightly glossy. Very pale to pale green or olive, or deeper olive-buff to buff; excep-tionally whitish-green. Marked with blotches, spots, specks and, more rarely, coarse scrawling, in dark brown, dark olive-brown, blackish-brown, reddish-brown and shades of gray or violet-gray. Markings often mainly small blotches, frequently rather sparing and often tending to be densest at the larger end. Sometimes with some blackish scrawling superimposed around the larger end. Blotches often irregu-lar, or may show slanting elongation. 39 × 28 mm. **Incubation:** By female only, begin-ning with third or fourth egg. 18–20 days. **Nestling:** Precocial and downy. Down thick and soft. Dark chestnut-red and blackish-brown with fine white spots. Under-parts pale tawny-buff with a pair of indistinct dark stripes down the front of the neck. Most of sides of head buffish-white, forming pale patch around eye, with warm buff patch on lower ear-coverts and streak from bill to over eye. Dark brown moustache streak, narrow dark streak from bill to eye. Dark patch on forehead separated from dark crown by pale transverse stripe. Rufous and blackish crown and nape patch bordered by pale stripe which constricts it over eyes. Pale streak across below eye. Mottling of body consists of median double dark streak with pale spots, and two pairs of lateral dark streaks with pale spots, but pattern is not obvious. Legs and feet deep olive-gray. Bill black, short and squat at first. **Nestling period:** Young tended by both parents. Leave nest as soon as down is dry. Apparently take food from parents' bills at first. Can fly at *c.* 19–20 days.

American Woodcock (*Scolopax minor*) Figures 46, 47, Plates 10, 38
Breeds in woodland sites, in low shrubby cover, or tall herbage, bordering clearings, in thickets or under scrub oaks or pines, or in open woodland with dead leaf cover on ground. Usually near a moist area. Nest on the ground. Male promiscuous, probably polygamous.
Nest: A hollow lined with dead leaves or other dry plant material from nearby. **Breeding season:** Begins early January to February in south, to early April in north. Usually ends by early June. Single-brooded. **Eggs:** Usually 4, occasionally 3–5. Oval to short oval or subelliptical. Smooth and moderately glossy. Very pale creamy-buff, buff, or creamy-olive; with spots, specks, and blotches of light brown to reddish-brown and pale gray. Markings often rather sparse and sometimes concentrated around the larger end. 38 × 29 mm. **Incubation:** By female only. 20–21 days. **Nestling:** Precocial and downy. Underparts pinkish-cinnamon, upperparts light brownish-buff. Dark brown crown-patch tapering forward to bill, narrowing on hind-crown and broadening on nape to extend along mid-back to tail and a dark band. Pale eye-stripes from the bill converge on the hind-crown as do the dark stripes through the eyes which join on the hind-edge of the ear-coverts with dark marks on the coverts. Dark bands along the sides from the shoulders meet the median band at the tail, and there is a dark band across the wing, and a thigh patch. Gray bill is short at first. **Nestling period:** Young tended by female alone, led from nest soon after hatching, grow rapidly, can fly a little at 14–15 days. At 25 days well grown and fly well.

Wilson's Phalarope (*Phalaropus tricolor*) Figure 48, Plate 39
Breeds on the edges of shallow, inland waters, where mixed-grass prairie (often by potholes) and grassy marshes with short vegetation are present, or by grassy muskeg. Nest on the ground, concealed by overarching grasses. Usually a number of pairs nest in close proximity. Usual sex roles reversed, larger brighter female displays, male incubates and tends young.

Figure 46. Downy chicks: *left*, Common Snipe, crown pattern; *right*, American Woodcock, dorsal pattern.

Figure 47. American Woodcock: a slight depression on the ground camouflaged among dead leaves.

Nest: A hollow lined with dry grasses in variable amounts, *c.* 3–4 in. across; with grasses pulled over to hide nest. In wet sites nests may be larger accumulations of grasses, moss, and twigs. Female lays eggs in bare scrape; male lines with vegetation over 3–4 days and builds canopy. **Breeding season:** Begins early to mid-May. Usually ends by mid-August. Single-brooded. **Eggs:** Usually 4, sometimes 3. Pyriform to oval. Smooth and slightly glossy. Creamy to ivory or pale creamy-buff; usually heavily and profusely marked with speckling, spotting, and blotching in blackish-brown or purplish-brown and sparse pale gray. 37 × 24 mm. **Incubation:** By male alone, with female nearby. 20–21 days. **Nestling:** Precocial and downy. Down buff on upperparts and across the breast, deepening to tawny-orange on crown, wings, and back. Underside is white. Crown lacks the large dark patch present in other phalaropes, and is buff with a narrow median line from forehead to hind-crown where it terminates at a narrow transverse line joining two elongated lateral spots to produce an anchor-shaped mark. Bold dark stripe from nape to tail, two dark lateral stripes from wings to rump along flanks, and dark patches on wings and thighs. Pattern sometimes more broken. **Nestling period:** Little information. Young tended by male alone, away from nest.

Figure 48. Crown pattern of downy chicks: *left*, Red Phalarope; *right*, Wilson's Phalarope.

Red-necked Phalarope (*Phalaropus lobatus*)   Plates 10, 39
Breeds on grassy or marshy ground by water or with some open pools, on marshy edges of lakes, low islands in rivers, or sometimes small offshore islands. Nest in a grass tussock near open water. As with other phalaropes, usual sex roles reversed. Female polyandrous.
Nest: A hollow, built into a grass tussock with grass lining and grass pulled together over the nest. Built by both sexes. **Breeding season:** Late May to August. Single-brooded. **Eggs:** Usually 4, sometimes 3. Oval to pyriform. Smooth and slightly glossy. Similar in color and pattern to those of Red Phalarope. 30 × 21 mm. **Incubation:** Eggs laid at 1–2-day interval. Incubation by male alone. 18–20 days. **Nestling:** Precocial and downy. Like that of Red Phalarope, but slightly buffier, less white in the orbital area, rear of crown darker, and bill finer and darker. Usually the streaking on the back is lighter and yellower; and dark streak from bill to eye absent but small spot may be present. Bill dark gray. Legs pale gray. **Nestling period:** Young tended by male alone; female sometimes present. Independent in 18–22 days.

Red Phalarope (*Phalaropus fulicaria*)   Figure 48, Plate 39
Breeds on level tundra with shallow pools and lagoons; or near coasts, or on offshore islands, where freshwater pools are present. Nest on the ground, usually on slightly raised site, a grass tussock, ridge or shingle-bank, or small island in water. Usually a number of pairs nest in a small colony. Sex roles reversed as in other phalaropes. Female polyandrous.
Nest: A shallow hollow, material varying from sparse plant fragment in an open site to a substantial structure of grass and leaves in a grassy site. In the latter site grasses usually pulled over to hide the nest. Made by male. **Breeding season:** Begins late June to early July, but may be late May in Alaska; ends in August. Single-brooded. **Eggs:** Usually 4, rarely 3. Oval to pyriform. Smooth and slightly glossy. Light olive, or green, or deeper olive-buff; with irregular blotches, spots and specks of black and blackish-brown, and scarce paler purplish markings. Irregularly scattered large blotches combined with profuse finer markings very typical. Larger markings often concentrated towards the larger end. 30 × 22 mm. **Incubation:** By male only. 19 days. **Nestling:** Precocial and downy. Down on underside grayish-white. Yellowish-white or yellowish-buff on neck and throat; and warm buff marked with black on upperparts, forming a triple streak pattern on back. Forehead warm buff. Black crown with slight buff mottling, bordered by yellowish eye-stripe. Dark streak across lores to eye, and dark spot on cheek behind eye. Indistinct dark band down nape. Back has dark central stripe, bordered by two buff ones, these bordered in turn by irregular dark band along flanks and upper wings, and black patch on thigh. Dark spots on fore-edge and tip of wing. Bill grayish-yellow and flattened along sides. Legs light gray. **Nestling period:** Young usually tended by male alone, although female may be present. Independent in 16–20 days.

Jaegers, Gulls, Terns, and Skimmers (*Laridae*)

This group of medium to large birds of coasts, open areas, marshes and inland waters is varied enough in breeding biology to be treated in three sub-groups: jaegers, gulls, and terns and skimmer.
   Jaegers: These predators and scavengers nest on open ground, often near the sea. The nest, often rather exposed, is a scrape with little or no lining, though sideways-building may be used to accumulate some material. Usually 2 eggs, brownish with dark spots. Incubation begins with the first egg, and the young hatch at intervals, showing difference in size. The young are downy, but not patterned. They may leave the nest after a few days, but remain in the parental territory.

Gulls: These scavenging birds nest on the ground near water, or on a ledge of cliff or rock outcrop, rarely in a bush or tree. Often nest in colonies. Nest material is carried to site, but sideways-building can occur at site. Amount of material is very variable and depends to some extent on the amount of excitement or discomfort at the site. Usually 2–3 eggs. Eggs cryptically colored, usually darker olive or buff in northern species, and much paler and more boldly marked in more southerly species. Young downy. Cryptically colored in variable, poorly defined patterns. Well brooded for first few days but capable of leaving nest after first day.

Terns and **skimmer:** Nests usually in colonies, with nests often only a bill-stab apart. More than one species of this group may be present in these colonies. The nest is usually a shallow scrape (though it may be a floating mass of materials or in a bush for a few species). Usually 1–3 cryptically colored eggs. Incubation by both birds, often beginning early in laying of clutch, and young may hatch at intervals of a day or two. Young downy. Upperparts usually patterned in blackish-brown on buff or gray. Pattern often broken but may show paired dorsal streaks. (In some species the tips of down are joined in bunches to give down plumage a spiky appearance.) The young, fed by both parents, may leave the nest after a few days. While observation can be difficult after the young are able to fly, they may be wholly or partly dependent on adults for some time (a month or more).

Pomarine Jaeger (*Stercorarius pomarinus*)   Plate 40

Breeds on swampy areas of level tundra. Less sociable in nesting than other jaegers. Nest on the ground.
Nest: A shallow hollow in moss, unlined or scantily lined. Built by both sexes. **Breeding season:** Begins mid-June. Single-brooded. Lost clutch sometimes replaced. **Eggs:** Usually 2, rarely 3. Subelliptical. Smooth and very slightly glossy. Ground color buff, olive, or warm brown; with spots and flecks of dark blackish-brown. 64 × 44 mm. **Incubation:** By both sexes. 26–28 days. **Nestling:** Semi-precocial and downy. Down thick and soft, with fine silky tips. Pale brown on upperparts, paler grayish-brown on the underside. Light and dark morphs may occur. Face may appear very dark gray-brown. Generally the darkest of the jaegers. Bill dark gray with black tip, relatively heavy and blunt. Legs dark gray. **Nestling period:** Young tended by both adults. Fly at *c.* 32 days. Become independent at 5–6 weeks.

Parasitic Jaeger (*Stercorarius parasiticus*)   Plates 13, 40

Breeds on tundra near sea level, or on barer hills or cliffs, on low shingly areas, or on offshore islands. Nest on the ground, often in a swampy area or near water.
Nest: A shallow depression, unlined or sparsely lined, in grass, heather, or moss. Built mostly by female. **Breeding season:** Begins late May or early June. Single-brooded. **Eggs:** Usually 2, sometimes 1. Subelliptical. Smooth and only slightly glossy. The ground color olive, greenish, dull buff, or brown; with spots or blotches, of dark brown, light brown, or gray. Markings are very variable, often sparse. Ground color rarely pale blue. 57 × 40 mm. **Incubation:** By both sexes, beginning with first egg. 24–28 days. **Nestling:** Semi-precocial and downy. Down thick and soft with fine silky tips. Down colors variable, generally warm dark brown, or blackish-brown; lighter and gray-tinted around eyes, on chin, central underside, and wing-tips. Light and dark morph may occur. Down remains on tips of first feathers. Lighter than Pomarine Jaeger, darker than Long-tailed Jaeger. Bill gray with dark tip, short though slenderest of the jaegers. Legs blue-gray. **Nestling period:** Young are tended by both adults. They may leave the nest-site after a few days but remain in territory. They fly at 27–33 days, are independent at *c.* 7–8 weeks.

Long-tailed Jaeger (*Stercorarius longicaudus*)   Plate 40
Breeds on tundra, bare stony flats, swamps and bogs bordering forests. Often at some
distance from the sea. Loose associations of scattered nests. Nest on the ground,
usually on a slight elevation.
Nest: A shallow hollow, unlined or with a few fragments, in peat or moss. Built
mostly by female? **Breeding season:** June. Single-brooded. **Eggs:** Usually 2, rarely
1–3. Subelliptical. Smooth and only slightly glossy. Olive-green to olive-brown, dull
buff, or pale green; with spots, blotches, or scrawls, of dark brown or pale gray,
mostly towards or around the larger end. 55 × 38 mm. **Incubation:** Eggs laid at $1\frac{1}{2}$–
2-day intervals. Incubation by both sexes, beginning with first egg. 23 days.
Nestling: Semi-precocial and downy. Down thick and soft with fine silky tips.
Usually palest and grayest of the jaegers. Sides of head and entire underside pale
grayish-brown. Dark gray bicolored (with black tip) bill has angle on lower mandible
mildest of the jaegers. Legs and toes pale blue, with webs pinkish. **Nestling period:**
Young hatch over a period. Tended by both adults. They may leave the nest after 2
days. They fly at *c.* 3 weeks. Independent at *c.* 5 weeks.

Laughing Gull (*Larus atricilla*)   Figure 49, Plate 41
Breeds on seacoasts; on saltmarshes, dunes, beaches, and shell and shingle ridges of
coast and offshore islands. Nest on the ground in colonies, often large, with nests in
close proximity. Nests in tall herbage, in beach grass, or among bushes if present.

Figure 49. Laughing Gull: c. 18 in. across; nest may be well constructed among beach
grasses (as in this case), or a mere hollow in the sand with a lining of grasses and sticks in the
open.

Nest: An accumulation of dry stems and plant material, thinner in drier or sandy sites and often substantial in wet sites, with a lining of thinner material. Built by both. Outside diameter: 18 in. **Breeding season:** Begins early April in south to late May in north. Single-brooded. **Eggs:** Usually 3, sometimes 2–4. Subelliptical to oval. Smooth and slightly glossy. Pale to very pale olive-buff, olive, greenish or buff; spotted, speckled, blotched, or scrawled with olive-brown to blackish-olive and paler gray or violet. Markings variable but usually small blotches or spots of fairly overall distribution. Occasionally larger markings concentrated at or around the larger end. 54 × 38 mm. **Incubation:** By both sexes. 21–23 days. **Nestling:** Semi-precocial and downy. Down long and soft. Down pale drab brown above tinted with cinnamon or warm brown. Underside a paler shade of the same with a warmer tint on the breast. Head, neck, and throat are boldly spotted and streaked in blackish-brown to dark brown, and the back heavily mottled with the same. **Nestling period:** Young tended by both parents. Continuously brooded or shaded at first. After a few days leave nest to run and hide in herbage. Begin flying at 38–50 days.

Franklin's Gull (*Larus pipixcan*)   Plate 41

Breeds in marshy and reed-grown areas on the shores of inland lakes or on large prairie marshes. Usually a large colony with nests close together. Nests built on floating vegetation held and anchored by growing stems of tall plants such as bulrushes (*Scirpus*).

Nest: A floating mass of dead plant material, built up 4–8 in. above water level and with a shallow nest cavity. Built by both. Outside diameter: 12–30 in.; inside diameter: 5 in. **Breeding season:** Begins early May to early June. Usually ends by early July. Single-brooded. **Eggs:** Usually 3, sometimes 2. Clutches of 4 possibly from two females. Subelliptical. Smooth and slightly to moderately glossy. Very pale to medium greenish, olive, olive-buff, or buff; spotted, speckled, blotched, or scrawled with olive, brown, blackish-olive, or black, and paler gray. Markings variable. Often a zone of heavier markings wreathing the larger end. 52 × 36 mm. **Incubation:** By both sexes. 24–25 days. **Nestling:** Semi-precocial and downy. Down has two color phases. In brown phase down is pale brown becoming more buff posteriorly and paling to white below, while the throat and breast are yellowish-buff. Back heavily mottled with dark brown, densest along the mid-back, and the head also mottled. A black patch at the base of the bill and a few dark spots on throat. The gray phase has the buff and brown tints replaced by similar shades of gray. **Nestling period:** Young tended by both parents. Can swim at 3 days. Fly at 28–33 days.

Little Gull (*Larus minutus*)   Plate 41

Breeds locally in northwestern Great Lakes area and along Hudson Bay on marshes, lakes with marshy edges, and shallow inland waters. Nests usually in colony, sometimes with other small gulls or tern species. Nests on tussocks of grass or rushes in water or marsh, or in shallow water among reeds and similar plants, or in open sites on low sandbanks or islands.

Nest: An accumulation of dead waterside plants, reeds, rushes, and sedges with a shallow cup. Built by both sexes. **Breeding season:** Late May to mid-July. Single-brooded. **Eggs:** Usually 3, sometimes 2, rarely 4–5. Subelliptical. Smooth and slightly glossy. Light olive-green, olive, or buff, sometimes very pale greenish or creamy. Buff eggs usually darkest. Finely and variably marked with specks, spots, and usually small blotches, of black, blackish-brown, or olive, and with paler shades of gray. Markings sometimes overall, but often sparse with a thicker zone around larger end. Blotching sometimes large and concentrated towards larger end. 42 × 30 mm. **Incubation:** First 2 eggs laid at intervals of 1–2 days, later at less than 1-day intervals. Incubation by both sexes. 20–21 days. **Nestling:** Semi-precocial and downy. Generally grayer and smaller than Black-headed Gull. Appearing less heavily marked. Down thick, soft, and fairly long, with fine silky tips. Down has blackish-brown bases but appears buffish-gray on the underside; and on the upperparts is dark grayish-buff with irregular inconspicuous patches of blackish-brown with buff tips. Bill dull pink with dusky tip. Legs grayish-pink. **Nestling period:** Young tended by both parents. Young fly at *c.* 21–24 days.

Black-headed Gull (*Larus ridibundus*)

Casual breeder in eastern Canada and rare breeder in northeast US. Nests in open sites by water on coast. On low coastal islands, sandhills, marshes, and edge of pools. Usually nests colonially or in the company of other gull species or terns.
Nest: A shallow scrape, at times on a raised site, with a variable accumulation of live and dead plant matter. Built by both sexes, though mainly by male, material being added over a long period. **Breeding season:** Begins mid-April to early May. Single-brooded. **Eggs:** Usually 3, sometimes 2, occasionally up to 6. Subelliptical. Smooth, and slightly to moderately glossy. Very variable, usually light olive, greenish or buffish, but may vary from pale whitish-blue to deep brownish-buff or brown. Marked with spots, blotches, scrawls, or rarely fine scribbling, in black, blackish-brown, olive-brown, or olive, and with fainter markings in shades of gray. Markings usually well-distributed overall, and often profuse, but sometimes sparse, and rarely absent. Often a zone of markings circling larger end. (Often similar-looking, though smaller, than eggs of Mew Gull.) 52 × 37 mm. **Incubation:** Eggs laid at daily intervals. By both sexes, beginning with first egg. 23–26 days. **Nestling:** Semi-precocial and downy. Down long and soft with fine silky tips. Upperparts dark buff, variably patterned with broken lines of blackish-brown. Underparts pale buff with dark brown bases producing some mottling. Throat rufous-buff. Some individuals may be generally pale buffish-gray. Bill dull pink with dark tip. Legs brownish-pink. **Nestling period:** Tended by both parents. Capable of leaving nest after a short period but remain nearby. Fly at 35–42 days.

Bonaparte's Gull (*Larus philadelphia*) Plates 12, 41

Breeds in muskeg-dominated conifer forests, often near lakes and rivers. In scattered pairs in woodland areas, usually nesting on flatter branches of spruce trees, 4–20 ft. up, or more.
Nest: A shallow cup of twigs, small sticks and a finer lining of grasses, mosses, and lichens. Built by both sexes. **Breeding season:** Begins mid-June. Single-brooded. **Eggs:** Usually 3, sometimes 2, rarely 4. Subelliptical. Smooth and slightly glossy. Very pale to medium greenish, olive, olive-buff, or buff; spotted, speckled, blotched, or scrawled with shades of olive-brown, blackish-olive, and dark brown, and paler gray or violet. Markings very variable, from fine overall speckling, to large blotching or scrawling mainly concentrated at or around larger end. 49 × 34 mm. **Incubation:** By both sexes, but chiefly by female? 24 days. **Nestling:** Semi-precocial and downy. Down yellowish-buff with blackish-brown mottling on upperparts and head. Breast pinkish-cinnamon. Flank and belly gray. Bill blue-black, dull pink-flesh color at base. Legs and feet buffish-pink with gray tint. **Nestling period:** Young begin to leave nest at end of 1 week. Tended by both parents.

Heermann's Gull (*Larus heermanni*) Plate 41

A few breeding records for the California coast. Normally nest in large colonies on rocky islands. Nest on the ground, in sand, or among rocks, sometimes nestled in bunchgrass.
Nest: A depression in sandy or rocky area lined with sticks and grass. In some places

a more complete nest made of sticks, dry grasses, and weeds among grass or reeds. Sometimes lined with feathers. Outside diameter: 10 in.; depth: 2½ in. **Breeding season:** May and June. Single-brooded. **Eggs:** 2–3. Subelliptical. Smooth and slightly glossy. Highly variable. Pearl gray, cream, or bluish, spotted or blotched with lavenders, browns, or olives. Faint wreaths at the larger end, or fine lines may occur. 59 × 43 mm. **Incubation:** By both birds. Estimated at 28 days. **Nestling:** Semi-precocial and downy. Short, thick down on the head, throat, breast, and flanks is pinkish-buff. Belly is white; back grayish-white mottled with dark gray. A few dark gray spots are on the top of the head. **Nestling period:** Little information. Tended by both parents.

Mew Gull (*Larus canus*)   Plate 41

Breeds on wet tundra, nesting on small islets or tussocks, or around lakes where low, scrubby conifers are present. Nest on the ground, or on a stump, or on the top of a spruce tree.

Nest: A shallow hollow with a variable accumulation of nearby plant material, varying according to site. Built mainly by female. In a tree a shapeless platform of plant material. **Breeding season:** Begins late May. Single-brooded. **Eggs:** Usually 3, sometimes 1–4. Subelliptical. Smooth and slightly glossy. Usually light olive, greenish, or buffish, but may vary from whitish-blue to deep brownish-buff. Very variably marked with spots, blotches, specks, or short scrawls, in brown, blackish-brown, black, and olive, with fainter gray markings. Markings may vary in distribution and intensity from unmarked shells to those with heavy overall pattern, but in general show an even distribution with a tendency, particularly on sparingly marked shells, for a heavier zone at the larger end. 57 × 41 mm. **Incubation:** By both birds, usually beginning with last egg. 22–27 days. **Nestling:** Semi-precocial and downy. Down long and soft, with silky tips. Upperparts pale buff to buffish-gray. Underparts buffish, yellowish, or whitish, darker at the sides. Pattern on head, neck, and back of spots or blotches of blackish-brown; spotted on head and forming broken irregular mottling elsewhere. Bill blue-gray with pink along cutting edge and at tip. Legs grayish-pink. **Nestling period:** Young leave nest in first day or two but remain nearby. Tended by both parents. Begin flying at *c.* 4 weeks, fly well at 5 weeks.

Ring-billed Gull (*Larus delawarensis*)   Plate 41

Breeds mainly at inland lakes, nesting on small islets or islands, isolated rocks, occasionally peninsulas or islands formed by floating vegetation in marshy areas of lakesides. Nests on the ground, usually on the higher parts of islands, often in the open but sometimes in sites protected by rocks or shrubs. Nests in colonies with nests often close together, sometimes in company with other waterbirds.

Nest: A hollow lined with a variable amount of material, often sparse. Dead plant materials, green weeds, feathers, and any available rubbish. On rock sites a pad of material a few inches thick. Built by both sexes. Outside diameter: 10–12 in.; inside diameter 6–9 in.; depth: 2 in.; height: 3–4 in. **Breeding season:** Begins early May in south to mid-June in north. Usually ends by early August. Single-brooded. **Eggs:** Usually 3, sometimes 2, very rarely 4. Subelliptical. Smooth and slightly glossy. Very pale to medium olive, olive-buff or deeper buff; spotted, speckled, blotched, or scrawled with olive-brown, brown, or blackish. Markings very variable in size and number, but small markings tend to be overall, larger ones sparse and concentrated at larger end. 59 × 42 mm. **Incubation:** By both sexes. 21 days. **Nestling:** Semi-precocial and downy. Down has two color phases. Brown phase has pinkish or reddish-buff on upperparts, paler below and whiter on breast; spotted with dark brown on head and neck, and faintly mottled dark brown on the back. The gray phase has pale smoke-gray ground color. Bill pinkish-brown. **Nestling period:** Young tended by both parents. Swim at an early age. Fed until able to fly (*c.* 35 days).

California Gull (*Larus californicus*)   Plate 41

Breeds mainly on prairie or alkaline lakes, on islands, usually with little vegetation. Nest on the ground, usually close to water, in the open or in short herbage. Usually nests in colonies, often in company with other waterbirds.

Nest: An accumulation of dead plant material, stems, feathers, and rubbish; making a largish cup built up a few inches from the ground. Built by both sexes. Outside diameter: 10–18 in.; inside diameter 7 in.; depth: 2 in. **Breeding season:** Begins early May in south to early June in north. Single-brooded. **Eggs:** Usually 3, sometimes 2, rarely 4–5 and these possibly from two females. Subelliptical. Smooth or very slightly granular in texture. Very pale olive to olive-buff, greenish or deeper buff; spotted, speckled, blotched, or scrawled in shades of olive-brown to blackish-olive, and paler gray or violet. Markings may be small and profuse, or very sparse and large, the latter often concentrated at the larger end. Rarely pale blue with or without pale violet markings. 68 × 46 mm. **Incubation:** By both sexes. 23–27 days. **Nestling:** Semi-precocial and downy. Down thick and soft. Pale buff, brighter on head and breast. Sparse dull black spotting on head. Back, wings, and throat mottled or indistinctly blotched with light gray. The markings become obscured as the young grow. Bill black with creamy-pink tip which is gradually lost. Legs and feet black, becoming grayish-pink. **Nestling period:** Young tended by both parents. Leave the nest and run around and swim at a few days old. Fly at 45 days.

Herring Gull (*Larus argentatus*)   Figure 50, Plates 12, 40

Breeds low in sand-dunes or on shingle, among rocks or on grass; or on ledges of sea-cliffs, cliffs, or edges of islands. On freshwater lakes inland. May nest on branches of conifers or roofs of buildings. Usually in colonies.

Nest: A usually large accumulation of grass, seaweed, and other plant material; in hollow. Built by both birds. Outside diameter: 12–24 in.; inside diameter 10 in.; depth: 3 in.; height: 5–10 in. **Breeding season:** Begins early May in south to mid-June in north. Usually ends by early August. Single-brooded. **Eggs:** Usually 2–3. Sub-elliptical. Smooth and non-glossy, or slightly glossy; and with finely granular surface. Very variable. Usually light olive, buffish, or greenish, but may vary from pale whitish-blue to deep brownish-buff. Speckled, spotted, and blotched, or rarely irregularly scrawled in black, blackish-brown, or dark olive. Markings vary from profuse overall markings, to sparse speckling or blotches; rarely unmarked.

Figure 50. Herring Gull chick: c. 2 days old.

Infrequently a zone of dark markings around larger end. Exceptionally creamy or pinkish with pink or reddish-brown markings. 70 × 48 mm. **Incubation:** Eggs laid at 2–3-day intervals. Incubation by both birds but mostly by female, beginning with first egg. 25–33 days. **Nestling:** Semi-precocial and downy. Down long and soft with fine silky tips. Upperparts and throat buffish-gray, lower throat buff, underside buffish-white. Head and throat marked with small numerous blackish-brown spots and small streaks forming a line of marks around eye, a series of blotches along mid-crown and nape, and streaks at sides of throat. Upperparts of body mottled with irregular patches of blackish-brown blotches. Bill black with pink tip. Legs and feet pinkish. **Nestling period:** Young tended by both parents. Brooded for first few days. Begin to fly at c. 6 weeks.

Thayer's Gull (Larus thayeri)

Breeds on northern Baffin Island and on other islands in arctic Canada and northern Greenland on cliffs, on rock ledges.

Nest: A bulky, fairly deep cup of moss and plant material. **Breeding season:** Begins early to mid-June. **Eggs:** Usually 2–3. Subelliptical to oval, approaching pyriform. Smooth and slightly glossy. Very pale to pale olive, olive-buff, or buff; spotted, blotched, or scrawled with olive-brown, brown, or black, and pale gray or violet. 74 × 49 mm. **Incubation:** c. 26 days. **Nestling:** Semi-precocial and downy. Closely resembling Glaucous Gull in tone (though sometimes darker and with a grayish tone around the base of the bill), Herring Gull in pattern (though with fewer head-markings). Bill grayish-pink or brownish-pink. Legs pinkish. **Nestling period:** Little information. Young tended by both parents. Chicks do not run from nest when alarmed, but become immobile like kittiwake young.

Iceland Gull (Larus glaucoides)   Plate 40

Breeds on eastern Baffin Island and Greenland on ledges of high cliffs and on low sandy shores.

Nest: A bulky cup of mosses and grasses. **Breeding season:** Begins late May. Single-brooded. **Eggs:** Usually 2–3. Subelliptical. Smooth or with fine granular texture. Pale to very pale olive, olive-buff, or stone; spotted, blotched, speckled, and sometimes scrawled with olive-brown to blackish-olive, and paler gray and violet. Size and density of markings varies but often a wreath of larger markings around the larger end. 69 × 48 mm. **Incubation:** Period not recorded. **Nestling:** Semi-precocial and downy. Down overall drab grayish-white, with brownish-gray spots on head and back, more distinct on the former. Like small Glaucous Gull, with fewer head-markings (especially around orbital area and lore) and slightly darker bill. Legs pinkish-brown. **Nestling period:** Little information. Tended by both.

Lesser Black-backed Gull (Larus fuscus)   Plate 40

Breeds uncommonly in western Greenland and perhaps eastern Canada on coastal islands and tops of cliffs, on shingle beaches, or on lake islands. In its main range it normally breeds in colonies but sometimes in small groups, depending on numbers and terrain. Nest on the ground.

Nest: A shallow hollow usually well lined with a variable accumulation of nearby plant material or seaweed. Built by both sexes. **Breeding season:** Possibly begins early May to mid-June. Single-brooded. **Eggs:** Usually 3. Sometimes 1 or 2. Subelliptical. Smooth, non-glossy, and very finely slightly granular in surface texture. Light olive-buff, olive, green, or buff, rarely very pale greenish-blue; sometimes deep buff or olive. Spotted, speckled, blotched, or rarely with short irregular lines and scrawls, in blackish-brown, black, olive-brown, and olive, with fainter gray or blue-gray markings. Markings usually well distributed over shell, rarely with a heavy zone around the larger end. 68 × 47 mm. **Incubation:** Incubation by both sexes. 25–29 days. **Nestling:** Semi-precocial and downy. Very much like Herring Gull in color and pattern, though may have heavy forehead spot. Bill and legs usually finer than Herring Gull. **Nestling period:** Tended by both parents. 35–40 days.

Western Gull (*Larus occidentalis*)   Plate 40
Breeds on islands and rocks offshore. Nests on the ground, at varying heights above the sea, sometimes in tideline debris, often in a sheltered hollow, niche, or crevice in rocks, at the base of a cliff, or sometimes on grassy slopes and high exposed rocks.
Nest: Nest an often bulky cup of dead grasses, plant stems, and other debris. Nests may be re-used in successive years. Built by both. Outside diameter: 13 in.; inside diameter 8 in.; depth: 2–4 in. **Breeding season:** Begins early May in south to early June in north. Probably ends by mid-August. Single-brooded, but lost clutches replaced. **Eggs:** Usually 3, often 2, sometimes 1, rarely 4. Replacement clutches usually 2. Subelliptical. Smooth or with slight granular texture. Non-glossy to slightly glossy. Very pale to medium olive or olive-buff; spotted, speckled, blotched, or scrawled, often heavily, with olive-brown to blackish-olive, and pale gray or violet. 72 × 50 mm. **Incubation:** Eggs laid at 2–3-day intervals. Incubation by both sexes. 24–29 days. **Nestling:** Semi-precocial and downy. Down drab grayish to buff, with some variegation, becoming paler below. Head and throat spotted and irregularly streaked with black. The back and rump are heavily spotted with blackish-brown. Bill black with dull pink tip. Legs and feet pinkish-brown. **Nestling period:** Young tended by both parents. Leave the nest at 2–5 days and hide nearby. Fly at 6–7 weeks. Are fed through 11–12 weeks.

Glaucous-winged Gull (*Larus glaucescens*)   Plate 40
Breeds on steep coastal cliffs and on rocky islands offshore. Nests on rock ledges, and in hollows and niches, sometimes sheltered by shrubs, or on open sites on rock or turf on top of islands. In large colonies or scattered pairs. Sometimes with other gull species and seabirds.
Nest: Well-made bulky cup of grasses, seaweed, feathers, fish-bones, and other debris. **Breeding season:** Begins mid-May to early June. Usually ends by early August. Single-brooded. **Eggs:** Usually 3, often 2, rarely 4. Subelliptical. Smooth or very slightly granular texture. Non-glossy or slightly glossy. Very pale olive or stone, or slightly deeper buff; marked overall with spots, small blotches, some speckling or scrawling, in medium to dark olive-brown, and blackish-olive, and pale markings in gray or violet. 73 × 51 mm. **Incubation:** By both sexes. 26–29 days. **Nestling:** Semi-precocial and downy. Down pattern like that of Western Gull but the general ground color is grayer and the dark markings of the back are less bold. **Nestling period:** Fed by both adults. First flight at 35–54 days.

Glaucous Gull (*Larus hyperboreus*)   Plate 40
Breeds usually in colonies, sometimes as single pairs. Nest on ledge of cliff, or on ground on small islands or at foot of cliff or rock outcrop.
Nest: An accumulation, frequently large, of moss and nearby plants, and seaweed. Sometimes the last alone. Usually built by both birds. The larger mounds may be as large as 48 in. across at the base, 18 in. across the top and 30 in. high. **Breeding season:** Begins late May to early June. Single-brooded. **Eggs:** Usually 2–3, sometimes 1–4. Subelliptical. Smooth and non-glossy, with a fine granular texture. Light olive or creamy-olive to buff; exceptionally bluish-white. Very variably marked with spots, blotches, specks, and occasionally thin scrawls, of black, blackish-brown, and olive-

Terry O'Neill

Figure 51. Great Black-backed Gull chick: c. 2 days old; note heavy legs and bill.

brown, and paler shades of gray. Markings are most frequently smallish and profuse, but sometimes a few large sparse blotches. Exceptionally pinkish varieties with reddish markings are known. 77 × 54 mm. *Incubation:* Eggs laid on alternate days. Incubation by both birds, beginning with first egg. 27–30 days. **Nestling:** Semi-precocial and downy. Similar in appearance to Great Black-backed Gull but dark markings on the back are paler and less well-defined. Also, many spots are within the orbital area. The heavy bill is pinkish-gray with yellowish tip in small young, much darker in large young. Legs pinkish-brown. **Nestling period:** Young tended by both parents. First flight at 45–50 days.

Great Black-backed Gull (*Larus marinus*)   Figure 51, Plate 40
Breeds in colonies or as single pairs. Nest on top of rock stack or island, or on ground on islands in lakes or estuaries.
Nest: A large accumulation of sticks, mosses, seaweed, grass, and some feathers. Built by both birds. Outside diameter: *c.* 20 in.; inside diameter *c.* 10 in.; depth: *c.* 2½ in. **Breeding season:** Begins mid-April. Single-brooded. **Eggs:** Usually 2–3, rarely 4? Smooth, non-glossy or slightly glossy; with a fine granular surface. Pale olive, olive-buff, or greenish, exceptionally pale whitish-blue or buff; marked with specks, spots, small blotches, or short scrawls of blackish-brown, olive, or olive-brown, and fainter gray or blue-gray markings. Markings usually more consistently smaller and evenly distributed in comparison with other large northern gulls. Pinkish variety known. 77 × 54 mm. **Incubation:** Eggs laid on alternate days. Incubation by both sexes, beginning before completion of clutch. 26–30 days. **Nestling:** Semi-precocial and downy. Down long and soft with fine silky tips. Upperparts and throat gray, slightly buffish; lower throat buffish; underside whitish. Many small blackish-brown spots and blotches on head, chin, and throat (though not usually in orbital area), and similar markings coalescing to form an irregular mottled pattern on back and rump. Darker than Glaucous Gull; usually lighter about the head than Herring Gull and with heavier bill. Bill dark blackish-purple with light tip. Legs and feet dull pinkish-gray. **Nestling period:** Young tended by both parents. Fed for *c.* 7 weeks at the end of which they begin to fly, and fly well within a week.

Figure 52. Black-legged Kittiwake: c. 1 ft. across, on cliff ledge.

Black-legged Kittiwake (*Rissa tridactyla*)   Figure 52, Plates 13, 42

Breeds on ledges of cliffs at varying heights, and in sea-caves. Normally in colonies.
Nest: A solid drum of grass, mud, moss, and seaweed, built up on some small projection or irregularity of rock face by continuous addition and firm trampling of material by both birds, the whole adhering to form a nest with a well-defined hollow. Outside diameter: 8–12 in.; inside diameter 6 in.; depth: 2 in. **Breeding season:** Begins mid-June. Usually ends by early August. Single-brooded. **Eggs:** Usually 2, rarely 1–3. Subelliptical, smooth, non-glossy. Pale, creamy, or very pale greenish, yellowish, stone, buffish, or olive; sometimes a warmer yellow or pinkish-buff. Very variably marked with specks, spots and blotches, of light brown, olive-brown, blackish-brown, and paler gray or blue-gray. Frequently some fine speckling, occasionally some irregular scrawling. Markings often sparing, and where heavy blotching occurs it tends to be concentrated in a zone around the larger end. 56 × 41 mm. **Incubation:** Eggs laid on alternate days. Incubation by both birds. 25–30 days. **Nestling:** Semi-precocial and downy. Down long with fine, silky tips. Head and neck, tips of wings, and edges creamy-white, glossy. Back grayish-brown mixed with some creamy-white. Underparts white. Down clings to tips of first feathers. Black bill may have pinkish tip. Legs dark gray. **Nestling period:** Young tended by both adults. Usually leave at *c.* 43 days, but period may vary from *c.* 35–55 days.

Red-legged Kittiwake (*Rissa brevirostris*)

Breeds in cliff in Aleutians and Pribilof Islands in Alaska, usually close to Black-legged Kittiwakes. Nest on a narrow ledge.

Nest: A cup of grasses, moss, seaweed, or other plant material, similar but somewhat smaller than that of Black-legged Kittiwake. **Breeding season:** Begins early June. Usually begins after nest-building of Black-legged Kittiwake has already started. Usually ends by mid-September. **Eggs:** Usually 1, sometimes 2, rarely 3. Subelliptical. Off-white, marked with lavender and brown, averaging lighter and less heavily spotted than Black-legged Kittiwake. 56 × 41 mm. **Incubation:** By both birds. 24–26 days. **Nestling:** Semi-precocial and downy. Down pure white. Bill whitish-gray, with darker upper mandible. Legs pinkish. **Nestling period:** Young tended by both adults. Fly at 38–48 days.

Ross's Gull (*Rhodostethia rosea*)   Plate 42
Has been found nesting in northern Canada and Greenland. In small colonies in boggy tundra or on an island in a tundra lake. Nest on the ground a few inches above the water.
Nest: A substantial, lined nest of dried grasses, sedges, twigs, willow leaves, lichens, or even mosses. Outside diameter: 6–7 in.; inside diameter *c.* 4 in. **Breeding season:** May-July. **Eggs:** Usually 3, sometimes 1–4. Subelliptical. Deep olive-green, with indistinct spotting of darker greenish-olive or brown, sometimes smears of chalky-white deposit. 42 × 33 mm. **Incubation:** By both, with female at night and male during the day. 21–22 days. **Nestling:** Semi-precocial and downy. Much like Sabine's Gull, but yellower and spots smaller and more numerous. Down long and mustard-yellow colored, rarely with fine a cinnamon-buff cast, with dark gray basal parts. Densely spotted and speckled with gray-black, mainly on forehead, nape, back, wing-pad, thigh, and crissum. Bill pink with dusky tip. Legs and feet pinkish-gray. **Nestling period:** Young tended by both adults. First flight at about 21 days.

Sabine's Gull (*Xema sabini*)   Plates 12, 42
Breeds on swampy tundra on small islands and raised areas, or on tussocks; or on coastal islands. Breeds sociably, sometimes in company with Arctic Terns. Nest on the ground, in grass, or on drier sites on bare ground.
Nest: A shallow hollow, lined with plant stems and nearby plant debris. Coastal nests may have seaweed and feathers. Inside diameter 5 in.; depth: 2 in. **Breeding season:** Begins early June. Single-brooded. **Eggs:** Usually 3, sometimes 2. Subelliptical. Smooth, slightly glossy. Shades of deep olive to buffish-olive, darker than most gulls' eggs. Indistinctly and variably marked with shades of olive-brown, sometimes widely distributed, sometimes mostly confined to a zone around the larger end. Some eggs paler greenish-olive with blackish-brown markings. 44 × 32 mm. **Incubation:** By both birds, probably beginning with first egg. 23–26 days. **Nestling:** Semi-precocial and downy. Down long and soft with silky tips. Underside buff, often white on mid-breast and belly. Upperparts deep brownish-buff mottled with black. Almost tern-like. Markings vary. Usually three lines of broken blotches over crown and broken line of spots under eye, and blotch on side of throat. Broken lines of black spots and blotches over back. Bill pink with grayish tip. Legs grayish-pink. **Nestling period:** Leave nest shortly after hatching and hide in vegetated shoreline. Taken by parents to water's edge. Fly at 20–25 days.

Ivory Gull (*Pagophila eburnea*)   Plates 13, 42
Breeds locally on Canadian arctic islands and Greenland in small colonies, on shores with shingle and boulders, or on ledges of cliffs; sometimes on similar sites inland.
Nest: A shallow hollow lined with moss, grass, lichen, and often some feathers, seaweed, and driftwood splinters. Built by both. Outside diameter: 18–24 in.; height: 6–9 in. **Breeding season:** Begins late June or early July. Probably ends by early

September. Single-brooded. **Eggs:** Usually 2, often 1, rarely 3. Subelliptical. Smooth, slightly glossy. Light olive to olive-buff, or buff; spotted and blotched, with blackish-brown, olive-brown, and olive, and paler markings in varying shades of gray. 61 × 43 mm. **Incubation:** By both birds beginning with second egg. 24–26 days. **Nestling:** Semi-precocial and downy. Down long with fine, hair-like tips. Down gray with white tips. Unpatterned. Whiter overall than Black-legged Kittiwake. Bill dark gray with pinkish or yellowish at the tip. Legs blackish. **Nestling period:** Chicks are mobile within a few days. Young tended by both parents. First flight at 28–35 days.

Gull-billed Tern (*Sterna nilotica*)   Figure 5, Plate 42
Breeds on sandy beaches of coasts and offshore islands, on shores of saline lagoons or shallow lakes, on bare sand, shell mounds, soil, or dry mud; in colonies with nests close together.
Nest: A shallow hollow in soft sand or soil, usually sparsely lined with grasses, seaweed, or nearby vegetation, or with shells and other debris. Built by both sexes. Outside diameter: *c.* 18 in.; inside diameter *c.* 4 in. **Breeding season:** Begins early May in south, early June in north. Usually ends by early August. Single-brooded.
Eggs: Usually 3, sometimes 2–5, larger number possible from two females. Subelliptical. Smooth and non-glossy, or very slightly glossy. Very pale creamy-buff to pale yellowish-buff; marked with spots, specks and blotches, usually small, of shades of dark brown, dark olive-brown or blackish-brown, and paler shades of gray. Markings usually evenly distributed, often profuse, rarely with a concentration around larger end. 49 × 35 mm. **Incubation:** Eggs laid at daily intervals. Incubation by both birds, beginning with third egg. 22–23 days. **Nestling:** Semi-precocial and downy. Down soft and long with fine, hair-like tips. Usually upperparts buffish-gray, patterned with blackish-brown. Forehead unmarked; three narrow irregular crown stripes, spots or short streaks on nape and behind eye. Pair of dark streaks along mid-back. Short streaks or spots at sides of mantle, along flanks and on upper wings. Rest of wings buff with whitish tip. Lower face whitish, throat light gray, and underside white. Down clings to tips of first feathers. A lighter type occurs lacking most markings. A third, rarer type with very dark throat, light brown upperparts, and a pale area around the eye has been identified. All types have fairly distinctive gull-like, thick orange bill. Legs usually brownish-pink. **Nestling period:** Young tended by both parents. Remain at nest for several days before leaving with parents. Fly a little at *c.* 4 weeks, well at *c.* 5 weeks. Young fed at least 2–3 months.

Caspian Tern (*Sterna caspia*)   Plates 12, 44
Breeds near coasts on sandy or stony beaches, on shores of large inland lakes, and on offshore islands. Nest on ground on bare sand, shell beach, or shingle. Usually in colonies, occasionally as single pairs.
Nest: A shallow hollow, unlined, or with a sparse collection of nearby plant debris. Built by both sexes. **Breeding season:** Begins early April in south to late May in north. Single-brooded, but will replace lost clutch. **Eggs:** Usually 2–3, rarely 1. Subelliptical. Smooth, non-glossy or very slightly glossy; sometimes with a finely granular or textured surface. Pale creamy to creamy-buff; marked with specks, spots, and rather small blotches of black, olive, brown, and pale gray. The markings are relatively small, usually finely and evenly distributed. Rarely odd large irregular blotches, sometimes at or around larger end. (See Royal Tern.) 64 × 45 mm. **Incubation:** By both birds, beginning with first egg. 26–28 days. **Nestling:** Semi-precocial and downy. Like Gull-billed Tern, but larger, usually paler, and with larger bill. Down soft and long with fine hair-like tips. Colors highly variable. Usually underparts white, sometimes buffish, and throat dusky. Upperparts dull buff or buffish-gray, with small blackish-brown markings, fewer than on Gull-billed Tern,

on back and wings, but not on crown and nape. Bill reddish-orange with dark near tip. Leg-color varies from gray to orange-pink. **Nestling period:** Young tended by both parents. After a few days young leave nest and hide in nearby cover. Fly at 25–30 days.

Royal Tern (*Sterna maxima*)   Plate 44

Breeds on coastal beaches, sand-bars and islands. Nests in close-packed, often large, colonies; sometimes in company with other tern species. Colony may desert if disturbed.

Nest: A shallow scrape, usually unlined. **Breeding season:** Begins early April in south to mid-May in north. Single-brooded. **Eggs.** Usually 1, rarely 2, the latter possibly from two females. Subelliptical to oval. Smooth and non-glossy. Creamy-white to ivory-yellow, very pale buffish or greenish and rarely deeper buff or pinkish-buff; thickly marked overall with specks, spots, and, less frequently, bold blotches and scrawls in black and gray, larger markings usually showing a blurred brown edge. (See Caspian Tern.) 63×45 mm. **Incubation:** By both sexes. 28–31 days. **Nestling:** Precocial and downy. Down stiff on head, long with fine tips on body. Like Caspian Tern, color very varied. Ground color varies from pale pinkish-cinnamon or pinkish-buff, paler on the underside, deepening through shades of buff to a dusky form in which down tips are blackish and forehead and throat may be black. On palest forms markings may be absent except for a few on rump and head; on buff forms there is heavy spotting over back, wings, flanks, head, and throat; and in dusky forms the markings are barely apparent. Bill, legs, and feet vary from yellowish-flesh to gray or black. **Nestling period:** Young tended by both parents. Active at one day old and after 2–3 days leave nest and combine in a creche flock that roams about near colony. Young are recognized and fed by parents. Leave creche and can fly at 25–30 days. Adults recorded feeding young about 7 months old in wintering areas.

Elegant Tern (*Sterna elegans*)

Breeds intermittently in southern coastal California in colonies with other terns. Nest on the ground at undisturbed, protected beaches and saltmarsh dikes, often within 20 yards of water.

Nest: A slight depression in sand. **Breeding season:** Begins April to early May through June. **Eggs.** Usually 1, rarely 2. Oval to subelliptical. Pinkish-buff to white; may be blotched with medium to dark gray or brown; some spotted. Similar-looking to those of Sandwich Tern. (See especially examples d and e on Plate 44). 53×38 mm. **Incubation:** Possibly around 20 days or more. **Nestling:** Semi-precocial. Down grayish-white with dark gray streaks about the nape and behind the eye. Bill pinkish; legs pinkish-gray. **Nestling period:** No information.

Sandwich Tern (*Sterna sandvicensis*)   Plates 12, 44

Breeds on or near the coast, on sandy or shingle banks, sand dunes, offshore sandbanks, and islands, and low rocky islands; or by lagoons near the sea. In colonies with nests near each other.

Nest: A shallow hollow, sometimes unlined, or sparsely lined with nearby material. Built by both sexes. **Breeding season:** Begins late April to early May. Single-brooded. **Eggs:** Usually 2, sometimes 1, rarely 3. Subelliptical. Smooth, slightly glossy. Pale yellow, yellowish-buff, or creamy-white. Very variably marked with spots, blotches, specks, and scrawls, of brown, blackish-brown, dark olive-brown, and paler gray. Great variation in size and distribution of markings. Large blotching frequently occurs, often concentrated towards larger end, occasional eggs show elongated, slanting markings, or blotches may show brownish blurring along one side. Smaller markings vary from profuse to very sparse. 51 × 36 mm. **Incubation:** Eggs laid at 2-day intervals. Incubation by both birds, beginning before second egg. 21–25 days. **Nestling:** Semi-precocial and downy. Down on head, neck, throat, back and, wings long and soft with fine tips, but groups of tips joined in one sheath, giving the down a clearly spiky appearance. On flanks and underside down is normal. Spiky down light buff to gray, with blackish down-bases showing, and black spots and mottling on crown of head, and black line along wings. Downy sides buffish-white. Bill grayish, sometimes with pinkish tone and/or black subterminal spot. Legs and feet gray tinged with blue, pink, or yellow. **Nestling period:** Young may hatch at intervals of up to 2–3 days. Tended by both parents. During second week young of colony tend to assemble, usually by water's edge, where they are fed by parents which recognize their own young. They fly at *c.* 22–28 days. Age of independence probably *c.* 4 months, perhaps longer (difficult to determine since the birds are on migration).

Roseate Tern (*Sterna dougallii*) Plate 43

Breeds on coastal sites; on sand, shingle banks, or low rocky shores or islands. Nests in colonies, often among other terns.
Nest: A shallow hollow, usually unlined, on rock or among shingle or shore plants. Built by both sexes. **Breeding season:** Begins early June. Single-brooded. **Eggs:** Usually 1–2, rarely 3. Subelliptical. Smooth, non-glossy. Light cream, or tinted yellowish, buffish or olive, or occasionally deeper olive or buff. Speckled, spotted, or blotched, or occasionally with short lines or scrawls, of blackish-brown, black, dark brown, or olive, and paler shades of gray. Markings very variable, often fine and rather profuse, sometimes more sparse. Occasionally a concentrated zone around the larger end.Usually with finer spots and sometimes more elongated than eggs of Arctic or Common Tern. 43 × 30 mm. **Incubation:** Eggs laid at 2–3-day intervals. Incubation by both birds, mainly by female, beginning early in laying of clutch. 21–26 days. **Nestling:** Semi-precocial and downy. Down resembles that of Sandwich Tern in that, except on breast and belly, the filament tips are joined in groups, giving the down plumage a spiky appearance. May appear in a buffy or gray morph. Breast and belly white. Upperparts gray tinted with warm buff, and speckled with blackish down bases and dark markings. Bill bluish to pinkish-gray with darker reddish-brown or darker gray tip. Legs and feet gray to pinkish-gray. **Nestling period:** Young tended by both parents. Usually fly at 27–30 days, but as early as 22 days.

Common Tern (*Sterna hirundo*) Figure 53, Plates 12, 42

Breeds on shingle and sand banks, usually coastal or by large inland lakes, sometimes in rivers; sand dunes; sandy or rocky coastal islands; or saltmarshes. Nest on the ground, occasionally on muskrat lodges or rafts of floating vegetation. Nests colonially.
Nest: A hollow, unlined, or variably lined with nearby plant material and odd feathers, built by female. **Breeding season:** Begins mid-May. Single-brooded. **Eggs:** Usually 2–3, rarely 4. Subelliptical. Smooth, non-glossy. Creamy, or tinted very pale yellowish, greenish, or olive; or light to deep buff or olive; very variably marked with blotches, spots, specks, and fine irregular lines of black, blackish-brown, dark to olive-brown, and paler shades of gray. Frequently irregular heavy blotching mixed with fine spots and specks; but markings may vary from sparse to profuse. Occasionally markings concentrated around larger end. Rarely pale bluish-white and very sparsely marked. (Similar to eggs of next two species.) 42 × 30 mm. **Incubation:** Eggs laid at 1–2-day intervals. Incubation by both birds, but mainly by female, beginning with first egg. 20–23 days. **Nestling:** Semi-precocial and downy. Down long and soft with fine, hair-like tips. Upperparts basically buff; patterned with blackish-brown, usually as spots on head, but forehead usually uniform. Larger dark blotching on back and wings broken along flanks but tending to form paired dark streaks down

mantle and back. Area round eyes buff with buff streak to bill, but chin white, upper lores and throat dusky blackish-brown, and rest of underside whitish. Legs and feet pink to yellowish-orange, rarely black. Bill orange with dark brown or black tip. **Nestling period:** Young tended by both parents. May leave nest after 3 days but return for brooding. They can swim at an early age. Begin flying at *c.* 28 days.

Arctic Tern (*Sterna paradisaea*)   Plate 42

Breeds on small rocky islands, near or off shore, on sand or shingle banks, sand dunes, or grassy slopes. Usually on coast, sometimes inland. Usually in colony, sometimes with other terns or other seabirds and seaducks.

Nest: A shallow hollow, often unlined or sparsely lined with nearby plant material and debris. Built by female. Outside diameter: 5 in.; depth: 1 in. **Breeding season:** Begins mid-May to early June. Single-brooded. **Eggs:** Usually 2, sometimes 3 or 1. Subelliptical. Smooth, non-glossy. Often shades of buff or pale greenish or olive, but may vary from bluish-white or creamy through to deep brown; exceptionally pink. Marking variable. Blotching, sometimes extensive, spots, specks, and sometimes short scrawls, in blackish-brown, black, or dark olive. (Usually similar to eggs of Common and Forster's Terns.) Sometimes a zone of heavy markings around larger

Figure 53. Common Tern: *top:* no nest material; *bottom:* with material nearby, *c.* 8 in. across.

end, or larger markings elongated and slanting in one direction. 40×29 mm. *Incubation:* By both birds. 20–22 days. **Nestling:** Semi-precocial and downy. Similar to that of Common Tern, but with two morphs (buff or gray), usually more heavily marked on the back, and the dusky blackish-brown of the throat usually extends to chin and forehead. **Nestling period:** Young tended by both parents. May leave nest soon after hatching but remain nearby. Can swim at 2 days. Fly at 19–22 days, but are fed by adults for a longer period.

Forster's Tern (*Sterna forsteri*)   Plate 42
Breeds on inland lakes and marshes, on floating masses of plant material held by growing stems of tall plants, tules, reeds, or sedges; or on floating logs, old muskrat houses, or occasionally old grebe nests; and on coastal or island sites on saltmarsh, using drifted tideline debris or short herbage.
Nest: An accumulation of plant material, varying according to that available at site, from scantily lined hollow to a neat cup. Built by both sexes. Outside diameter: 20–30 in.; inside diameter 7–8 in.; depth: $1–1\frac{1}{2}$ in. **Breeding season:** Begins mid-May to early June. Single-brooded. **Eggs.** Usually 2–3. Subelliptical to oval. Smooth and non-glossy. Very pale olive or greenish to light buff or olive-buff; heavily speckled, spotted, and blotched overall with dark brown, black, and pale gray. (Similar to previous two species.) 43×31 mm. **Incubation:** By both sexes. 23–25 days. **Nestling:** Semi-precocial and downy. Down varies in color from pale stone to cinnamon-buff or pinkish-buff, darkening to brown on the throat but not as dark as on the Common Tern. Underside similar but paler, almost white on belly. Upperparts spotted or streaked in blackish-brown, heavier on the back where it forms large irregular aggregations or longitudinal bands. **Nestling period:** Young tended by both parents. Remain in nest for a few days. Then run and swim actively. Fed by parents until able to fly.

Least Tern (*Sterna antillarum*)   Plates 12, 43
Breeds, usually in small colonies, on sand and shingle beaches on coast, or banks in estuaries and sand and gravel on river islands. Less frequently on other sites with gravel, such as parking lots, road shoulders, and roofs.
Nest: A shallow hollow, usually unlined, or sparingly lined with nearby plant material or small pebbles or shell fragments. Made by female. **Breeding season:** Begins May. Single-brooded, but replaces lost clutches. **Eggs:** Usually 2–3. Subelliptical. Smooth, non-glossy. Very pale, tinted olive or buff, or cream-colored, sometimes slightly warmer buff. Spotted, blotched, and speckled, in brown, blackish-brown, and shades of gray. Often finer dark markings are combined with larger pale gray ones. Markings variable but usually well distributed, often profuse; with occasionally some concentration towards larger end. Exceptionally slanting elongated blotches or streaks towards larger end. 32×23 mm. **Incubation:** Eggs laid on consecutive days. Incubation by both birds, usually beginning with second egg. 19–22 days. **Nestling:** Semi-precocial and downy. Down shorter than that of other terns, with fine hair-like tips. Sandy-buff on head and upperparts, with mottling of darker brown, sometimes showing three parallel streaks on crown, and paired dark streaks on back, or so irregular that pattern is not obvious. Underparts white, or tinted light sandy-buff. Bill flesh-gray with dark brown tip. Legs and feet dull pinkish-flesh-colored. **Nestling period:** Young tended by both adults. Can leave nest after 1 day but remain nearby. Fly at 19–21 days.

Aleutian Tern (*Sterna aleutica*)   Plate 43
Breeds on offshore islands, on raised dry areas, in open places in coastal Alaska. Nest on the ground, in colony, sometimes with Arctic Terns.

Nest: A hollow in moss, usually unlined. *Breeding season:* Mid-June to late August. Single-brooded, but may replace lost clutch. *Eggs:* Usually 2, rarely 1–3. Smooth and non-glossy. Yellowish or olive to yellowish-buff or olive-buff. Heavily and boldly blotched, with more sparse spotting or speckling in medium to dark brown and pale gray. Markings often elongated and tending to be concentrated at the larger end. 42 × 29 mm. *Incubation:* 20–23 days. *Nestling:* Semi-precocial and downy. Down light buff to grayish-buff on upper parts, blotched with black. Black on chin and throat extending to upper breast, unlike Arctic Tern, and breast otherwise white, shading into very dark gray on belly and flanks. *Nestling period:* Young stay near nest 2–3 days then move into surrounding vegetation. Fly at 25–31 days. Fed for 2 weeks post-fledging.

Bridled Tern (*Sterna anaethetus*)

Breeds in colonies, often with Sooty Terns and other seabirds. Rare breeder in Florida Keys (in Roseate Tern colony). Nest on the ground, well-hidden among broken rocks, rock cavities, cacti, small plants, or other vegetation. Sometimes on steep cliffside.

Nest: A slight depression. *Breeding season:* Late April to late July. *Eggs:* One egg. Oval to short pyriform. Pinkish-white or creamy-white, well-covered with small spots of varied shades of brown, gray, lavender, or violet. Similar-looking to eggs of Roseate Tern (see especially example b on Plate 43). Size varies, but averages 46 × 33 mm. *Incubation:* By both sexes, with changeover every 24 hours. 28–30 days. *Nestling:* Semi-precocial and downy. Down light gray to dark gray, usually tinged with buff. Underparts are grayish-white and throat is dark gray; the upperparts are more or less mottled with dark brown. *Nestling period:* Young tended by both adults. Leave nest after a few days and hide nearby. Fly at 55–63 days; independent in another *c.* 35 days.

Sooty Tern (*Sterna fuscata*)   Plate 43

Breeds on open beach in Florida's Dry Tortugas and rarely Texas, Louisiana, and southern Atlantic coasts. In large colony with nests close together. Birds apparently visit and select sites by night.

Nest: A shallow scrape. Unlined, but some nearby stones or leaves (of Bay Cedar at Dry Tortugas) may be pulled to edge of scrape. *Breeding season:* Traditionally began early April to early May, but now as early as February–March in Florida. Single-brooded, but lost clutch replaced. *Eggs:* Only one. Subelliptical. Smooth and non-glossy. White or tinted pink or more rarely buff. Usually profusely and finely spotted and speckled overall, or occasionally blotched, with deep reddish-brown and paler lilac. On some markings are sparse except for a concentration of bold dark blotches at or around larger end. Some larger markings show a blurred, paler edge. 50 × 35 mm. *Incubation:* By both sexes. Sitting periods variable but may be long at times, possibly several days. Change-over usually at night. 28–31 days. *Nestling:* Semi-precocial and downy. Down shortish and filaments may be grouped in sheaths as on Roseate Tern. Upperparts, head, throat, and neck speckled with grayish-white and gray-black. Buff tips to down may also be present. Underparts white. *Nestling period:* Young tended by both parents. Brooded during first week. Usually leave nest and hide when alone. Feathered at *c.* 30 days. Fly at 55–60 days. Young leave with adult male and may remain with him at sea for *c.* 3 weeks.

Black Tern (*Chlidonias niger*)   Figure 54, Plates 12, 43

Breeds on shallow, still waters, fresh or brackish, often with reedy vegetation or sloughs and swampy marshes. Nest either as heap of floating vegetation in water,

Figure 54. Black Tern: c. 8–10 in. across, on a heap of floating vegetation.

anchored by growing plants, or on mats of floating aquatic vegetation or heaps of
fallen herbage; on old muskrat houses, old grebe or coot nests, or floating driftwood;
or on firm ground among marshy herbage. Usually nests in small colonies.

Nest: In water a heap of water-plants and reeds, formed by material pulled together,
or rarely carried to the site, and lined with finer material. On firmer ground the nest
is a scrape with a sparse lining of pieces of reeds and other plant matter. Built by
both. Outside diameter: 4–10 in. **Breeding season:** Begins mid- to late May. Usually
ends by mid-July. Usually single-brooded. **Eggs:** Usually 3, sometimes 2–4. Oval to
short pyriform. Smooth and slightly glossy. Light buffish to brown, or pale yellowish
or creamy; with irregular spotting or blotching, often large, in black and brown,
frequently concentrated in a broad zone around the larger end. 34 × 25 mm.
Incubation: By both sexes, beginning with last egg. 20–22 days. **Nestling:** Semi-
precocial and downy. Down long and soft with fine silky tips. Upperparts warm buff
mottled with black and extending to throat and chin. Mid-breast grayish-white,
flanks and belly buffish-gray. Forehead, around base of bill, and patch around eyes
white. Double row of small irregular blackish blotches over crown, dark streak down
neck, double streak down mantle, broken line of blackish mottling along sides of
back and dark median streak ending in a blotch; and dark mottling on the upper
wings. Bill gray with pinkish base. Legs grayish-pink. **Nestling period:** Young tended
by both adults. Young can move about but remain on nest for *c.* 2 weeks, start to fly at
c. 3, are fully fledged at *c.* 4.

Brown Noddy (*Anous stolidus*)   Figure 55, Plates 12, 43

Breeds in our area only in Florida's Dry Tortugas, nesting on trees, shrubs, cacti, on
rocks or on the ground. Nests mostly built on raised sites up to 12 ft., in bush (Bay
Cedar at Dry Tortugas) or low tree. Usually in large colony, with nests fairly close
together.

Nest: A platform or shallow cup, of sticks, seaweed, and sometimes shells and coral
fragments in the lining. Re-used in subsequent years and may become substantial.
Built by both sexes. **Breeding season:** Begins early May. Single-brooded. **Eggs:** Only

Figure 55. Brown Noddy: c. 8 in. across, in Bay Cedar.

one. Subelliptical. Smooth and non-glossy. White or faintly tinted buff or pink, sparsely marked, mostly at the larger end, with specks, spots, and blotches of reddish-brown, and paler shades of lilac and purple. 52 × 35 mm. **Incubation:** By both sexes. 35–36 days. **Nestling:** Semi-precocial and downy. Several color phases. May be uniform drab whitish, or overall dark brownish-black, or dark with white cap, or mainly white with grayish-brown on back and wings, or other intermediate states. **Nestling period:** Young tended by both parents. Normally remain in nest until fledged but will leave nests in low sites at a young age when alarmed, and climb back later or be fed on the ground by parents. Fly at 40–44 days.

Black Skimmer (Rynchops niger)   Figure 56, Plates 12, 43

Breeds on large beaches, or low sandy islands offshore or in estuaries; rarely on saltmarsh. Usually in an open site. Nest on the ground in a loose colony.
Nest: A bare shallow scrape, unlined. Excavated by both. Inside diameter: 4–5 in.; depth 1–2 in. **Breeding season:** Begins early May in south to early June in north. Usually ends by mid-August. Single-brooded. **Eggs:** 2–5. Subelliptical to oval. Smooth and non-glossy. White to creamy-white, or faintly tinted buff; irregularly and boldly blotched, and with some sparse spots and specks, of black, blackish-olive, and shades of pale gray. Gray markings often numerous. 45 × 36 mm. **Incubation:** By both, beginning with first egg. 21–25 days. **Nestling:** Semi-precocial and downy. Down thick and soft. Pale vinous-buff, lightly mottled with dusky brown on back and faint mottling on head. Underparts white. Mandibles of reddish bill are of even length, adult bill only attained by fledging period. Legs dark dull red. **Nestling period:** Young tended by both parents. Fed on regurgitated food at first, later on whole fish. Young have mandibles of even length and can pick up food and catch insects; when alarmed young may dig themselves into hollows in the sand, kicking up sand which partly hides them. First flight at 23–26 days.

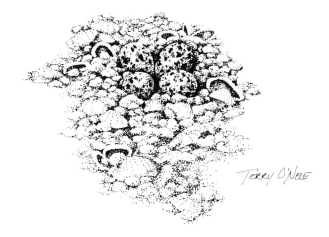

Figure 56. Black Skimmer: a bare unlined scrape, inside diameter c. 4–5 in.

Auks, Murres, and Puffins (*Alcidae*)

Medium-sized to small seabirds, living by diving for prey. Nest usually on shore at or near the sea, on rock ledges or in crevices or holes. Sideways-building is used but owing to sites nest material may be absent or very variable. Eggs are large for the size of the birds, and clutches of one or two. Young downy, and most are virtually altricial, remaining at the nest-site. They leave the nest and go straight to sea.

Dovekie (*Alle alle*)   Plates 13, 47

Breeds on or near sea-coasts, on cliffs, or steep hillsides farther inland in Greenland, rarely on islands in the Bering Strait area, and perhaps on northeastern Ellesmere Island in Canada, usually in large colonies. Nest in holes or crevices in rocks or among piled boulders at the foot of slopes.

Nest: An unlined hollow. **Breeding season:** Begins mid-June. Single-brooded. **Eggs:** Usually 1, rarely 2. Subelliptical. Smooth, non-glossy. Pale blue, normally immaculate, rarely marked with spots or scribbles of buffish-brown at the larger end. 48 × 34 mm. **Incubation:** By both sexes (12-hour shifts). 29 days. **Nestling:** Semi-precocial and downy. Down thick, soft and silky tipped. Blackish-brown, with paler brown on the underside (almost black when first hatched), and gray on mid-underside. Short and thick bill blackish. Legs and feet dark gray. **Nestling period:** Young tended by both parents. Brooded for up to a week. Later in period may come to entrance of hole and exercise wings while parents are present. Leaves nest at c. 3–4 weeks, usually going to sea accompanied by adults.

Common Murre (*Uria aalge*)   Plates 13, 46

Breeds on sea-coasts, on ledges of cliffs and on the level tops of isolated rock stacks, and on the slopes and tops of low rocky islands. Breeds colonially, with birds crowded very close together.

Nest: No nest material, egg laid on bare rock, sometimes on loose soil. Individually variable egg patterns may assist adults to identify eggs. **Breeding season:** Begins mid-May in south to mid-June in north. Single-brooded. **Eggs:** Only 1. Large and pyriform. Surface finely granular and roughened, non-glossy. Color and markings extremely variable. Ground color from white through shades of buff, brown, reddish, cream, blue, or green; immaculate or marked in shades of brown or black with variable combinations of dots, spots, blotches, or intricate scribbling; at times uniformly dark in color or with pale or dark central zones. 81 × 50 mm. **Incubation:** By both sexes (with shifts of 12–24 hours). Egg rests on the webs of the feet, covered by the belly feathers. 28–35 days, though sometimes to 45 days early in the season. **Nestling:** Altricial and downy. Down thick, with fine tips; short on underside, longer and coarser on head and neck. Black on head and neck streaked with white sheaths enclosing several filaments. Body sooty-brown above with some grayish mottling, and buffish-white underneath. Belly usually pure white. Feathers begin to show within a few days. Conical bill blue-gray with blackish tip. Mouth pale pinkish-flesh. Iris brown. Legs and feet yellowish-black. **Nestling period:** Young tended by both parents. Leave for sea at 18–25 days, only part-grown; accompanied, and cared for communally by adults until able to fly, about 39–46 days after hatching.

Thick-billed Murre (Uria lomvia)   Plate 45
Breeds on sea-cliffs and rock stacks, in similar sites to the Common Murre, but farther north; although sometimes in mixed colonies. Breeds in colonies, often large, with birds crowding very close together.
Nest: As for Common Murre. **Breeding season:** Begins early to mid-June. Single-brooded. **Eggs:** Only 1. Large and pyriform. Surface granular and roughened, non-glossy. Color and markings very variable. Ground color shades of white, cream, buff, reddish, greenish, or blue; marked with buff, brown, purplish, or black specks, spots, blotches, streaks, or scribbling. 80 × 50 mm. **Incubation:** By both sexes (with shifts of 12–24 hours). Eggs rest on the webs of the feet, covered by the belly feathers. 28–35 days. **Nestling:** Altricial and downy. Resembles that of Common Murre but shows more streaking, with white sheaths of head and neck more prominent and paler brown tips to down of back. Head sometimes with a tinge of buff. Belly mottled (normally white in Common Murre). Feathers begin to show after a few days. Bill slightly darker than that of Common Murre. **Nestling period:** Young leave nest at $\frac{1}{4}$ adult weight, at 16–30 days. Tended by parents (particularly male) for several weeks after leaving nest.

Razorbill (Alca torda)   Plates 13, 45
Breeds on sea-coasts, on cliffs or on low rocky or boulder-strewn shores. Nests colonially, usually in a crevice or niche, more concealed than the exposed ledges used by murres, or holes between or under boulders.
Nest: Normally no nest material, occasionally a few loose fragments accumulated. **Breeding season:** Begins early to mid-June in north. Single-brooded. **Eggs:** Usually 1, rarely 2. Subelliptical to oval. Surface finely granular and roughened, non-glossy. Very variable in color. Ground color varies from white through yellowish, buff and shades of brown, or sometimes reddish or greenish; variably speckled, spotted, scribbled, blotched, or banded with dark brown and/or black. The inner shell membrane is greenish. 73 × 47 mm. **Incubation:** By both sexes (with shifts of 12–24 hours). 25–36 days. **Nestling:** Altricial and downy. Down short and thick, with fine silky tips. Lores, forehead, and crown white; remainder of head, throat, back of neck blackish-brown with white tips. Upperparts and wings blackish-brown, tipped with pale buff above and on wings, white on mid-underside. Distinctive large and compressed bill black, mouth pale yellow. Iris brown. Legs and feet dark gray. **Nestling period:** Young tended by both parents. Brooded 5–10 days. Leaves nest at c. 18 days for sea, accompanied by an adult. Reaches independence several weeks later, perhaps at 3 months of age.

Black Guillemot (*Cepphus grylle*)   Plates 13, 47
Breeds on sea-coasts. Nest in a hole, under or among boulders, on low island, boulder beach, or base of a cliff; or in hole or crevice in cliffs. More rarely in hole in earth bank, or turf, or hole in building; or steep hillside near sea. Nests are in a colony, loose aggregations or scattered sites.
Nest: A hollow, normally unlined; sometimes with an accumulation of nearby debris. **Breeding season:** Begins early June in south to late June in north. Single-brooded. **Eggs:** Usually 2, often 1, sometimes 3. Shortish subelliptical. Smooth, non-glossy. White, sometimes lightly tinted with buff or bluish-green, marked with a mixture of various-sized spots and blotches of black and pale gray, or reddish-brown at times. The inner shell membrane is green. 58 × 40 mm. **Incubation:** By both sexes, beginning with first egg, sometimes with shifts at 1–4 hours. 29 days, though 21 to 39 days reported. **Nestling:** Semi-precocial and downy. Down soft, thick and with silky tips. Blackish-brown, slightly paler below. Bill slender, conical, and blackish. Mouth pink. Legs and feet dark brown. The down remains on the tips of the first feathers. **Nestling period:** Young tended by both adults, brooded for up to 5 days and leaving the nest at 34–40 days, fully fledged.

Pigeon Guillemot (*Cepphus columba*)   Plate 47
Breeds on rocky coasts and offshore islands. Nests in cliffs, talus slopes, piles of rocks and boulders on shores, and caves. Nest in a cavity under a rock, in a crevice or a similar cavity site. From the foot of a cliff to 200 ft. up. Nests are in a small to medium colony, loose aggregation, or isolated sites.
Nest: A natural hollow or slight concavity. Unlined, or tiny stones and other debris from immediately around site may be brought together to form a heap. **Breeding season:** Begins mid-May in south to mid-June in north. Usually ends by mid-August. Single-brooded. **Eggs:** Usually 2, sometimes 1. Similar to those of Black Guillemot in shape, color and markings. 61 × 41 mm. **Incubation:** By both sexes, beginning with first egg, with shifts at 2–4 hours but up to 17 hours. 28–32 days. **Nestling:** Semi-precocial and downy. Down soft and thick. Blackish-brown above, browner on underside. Gape and legs flesh-pink. **Nestling period:** Young tended by both parents and brooded for at least 3 days. After then, young may leave nest itself and move around and hide, but do not leave nesting cavity until fledging. May come to entrance to take fish from adults. Young fly and are independent at 29–39 days.

Marbled Murrelet (*Brachyramphus marmoratus*)   Plate 47
Nests found in Pacific coastal coniferous forest, up to 20 miles or more from sea, 22–248 ft. up an evergreen tree; near the trunk on a horizontal branch, sheltered but with direct access in flight; in Alaska rarely on ground. Probably re-used in successive years.
Nest: A thick pad of moss, consolidated with a ring of droppings around a hollow. **Breeding season:** Egg-laying begins in April, continuing to late June or early July. **Eggs:** Only 1. Long elliptical with bluntly rounded ends. Pale greenish-yellow or greenish-buff, with a thick spotting of dark brown, black and pale blue or gray. **Incubation:** By both sexes (change shifts at dusk); 27–30 days. **Nestling:** Semi-precocial and downy. Down long, soft, and thick, absent below eyes and around bill. Underside light buffish-gray, darker on flanks. Back and head yellowish-buff, the back mottled with black; head and neck with distinct black spots. Bill black. Legs and feet pinkish white to gray in front, black behind. Iris brown. **Nestling period:** Tended by both, with brooding for up to 3 days. Adults bring fish in bill. Young must fly to sea, appearing alone and independent 27–40 days after hatching.

Kittlitz's Murrelet (*Brachyramphus brevirostris*)   Plate 13
Breeds in Alaska at moderately high elevations (up to 6500 ft. but usually lower) on
mountains, near tops, regularly at some distance from the sea. Nest on scree slopes
above tree-line, where snow may still be present.
Nest. Egg laid on bare ground in slight concavity. No material, or possibly a few small
stones and fragments of moss pulled in. **Breeding season:** Begins late May to early
June. **Eggs:** Only 1. Fairly long elliptical with bluntly rounded ends. Olive, olive-buff,
or pale green, with specks, spots, and small blotches of light brown, dark brown, and
black. 60 × 36 mm. **Incubation:** By both sexes. Estimated at 30 days. **Nestling:** Semi-
precocial and downy. Down of body mainly medium gray, with blackish bases showing in places, and back suffused with buffish-yellow. Head and throat buffish-yellow
with black spotting, becoming gray on breast and pale gray on belly. Bill black. Legs
and feet pink at front, brownish-black at back. Nails black. Irides dark brown.
Nestling period: Tended by both. Young still at nest at 13 days; downy, with wing
quills showing. Age at first flight estimated at 24–29 days.

Xantus's Murrelet (*Synthliboramphus hypoleucus*)   Plates 13, 47
Breeds on rocky offshore islands in southern California in colonies. Nest in a cavity,
cliff crevice, cavity under rock, corner of a cave, or hollow under dense bush or agave
foliage.
Nest: A bare natural hollow, or a scrape on soft earth; with no lining. **Breeding
season:** Begins mid-March. Late eggs have been suggested as second broods, but
probably reflect extended breeding season (due to food supply) as in Cassin's Auklet.
Probably ends by mid-July. **Eggs:** Usually 1 or 2. Two eggs often differ in color. Long
elliptical. Smooth and moderately glossy. Pale blue, greenish, olive, buff or brown,
the last two sometimes darker. Speckled, spotted, blotched, or scrawled with brown
and paler purple. Smaller markings often fine and profuse, larger markings sparse
and may be concentrated at the larger end. 53 × 36 mm. **Incubation:** By both sexes.
Change-over at night (usually every 3 days). 34 days. **Nestling:** Precocial and downy.
Down thick and fine, and very dense on underparts. Sooty-black on upperparts,
including head down to lores and ear-coverts, with a small white mark above and
below eye. Remainder of underside, from throat downwards, white. Color pattern
similar to that of adult plumage. **Nestling period:** Young brooded for 1–2 days and
tended by both parents. Remain at nest for *c.* 2 days, then leave for sea at night, in
down plumage, and swim away with parents. Can swim and dive easily at this age.

Ancient Murrelet (*Synthliboramphus antiquus*)   Plate 47
Breeds on offshore islands, either treeless or forested, nesting in colonies. Burrows
into matted vegetation or soft soil, or uses old burrows of other species, cavities
under rocks, openings under tree roots, stumps, or fallen logs, crevices, or similar
sites.
Nest: A tunnel, sometimes 2–3 ft. long, with nest cavity at end, *c.* 5 in. across and 2–3
in. deep; often but not always lined with dry grass or leaves brought in from outside.
Breeding season: Appears to vary, beginning late April to mid-June. **Eggs:** Usually 2,
sometimes 1. Long subelliptical. Smooth and slightly to moderately glossy. Very pale
to medium creamy-buff or buff; evenly but not heavily marked with fine speckles and
spots, and with some small blotches of light to medium brown and paler purplish-
gray. The larger markings mainly of the last color. 61 × 39 mm. **Incubation:** By both
sexes, with night-time changeover every 2–5 days. 35 days. **Nestling:** Precocial and
downy. Down of upperparts, including head to lores and lower edge of ear-coverts,
black with a blue-gray tinge, and with a whitish patch on the hinder ear-covert.
Underparts white, tinged yellow. Bill dark with a light tip. **Nestling period:** Young
are brooded by both, but not fed in nest, for 2 days. At 2–3 days young leave burrow

at night and go to sea in response to calls of parents. They can swim well and are led out to sea away from breeding ground. Independence is at 42–65 days.

Cassin's Auklet (Ptychoramphus aleuticus)   Plates 13, 48
Breeds on offshore islands, often in large colonies. Nests in burrows dug in sandy soil, in turf or under rocks, cavities under rocks, crevices in rocks, driftwood piles, or any similar site. From sea level to c. 500 ft.
Nest: A burrow 2–6 ft. long, the nest cavity bare or with a nest of plant stems, twigs or any material that may be present near entrance to burrow. Both sexes dig burrow. **Breeding season:** Begins about mid-May in north, but in south appears prolonged, with burrows being excavated in January, eggs from March to July, and young from May to July. Usually ends by early August. **Eggs:** Only 1. Subelliptical. Smooth and non-glossy. White, frequently nest-stained. 47 × 34 mm. **Incubation:** By both sexes (with shifts at 24 hours). 39 days. **Nestling:** Semi-precocial and downy. Down varies from black to dark purplish-gray on back and from medium or pale gray to pale purplish-gray on underside. Absent from area around eye. Irides brown. Legs and feet pink with black claws at first; changing to blackish-gray by tenth day. **Nestling period:** Young brooded for 3–5 days and tended by both parents. Brooded for first 3–4 days. Adults visit burrow at night. Birds defecate at burrow entrance. Young bird's feathers begin to appear at 12–16 days. Wing exercise at entrance at 30–35 days. Young leaves burrow at 41–50 days, after which it is independent.

Parakeet Auklet (Cyclorrhynchus psittacula)
Nests on offshore islands with cliffs and rocky slopes on the periphery of coastal Alaska. Nest in turf-covered rock slopes where cavities and crevices occur, in crevices on cliff-face, among large boulders by shore, or under ledges. Breeds in loose groups or colonies, with nests sometimes scattered.
Nest: Eggs laid on a bare site, rock, or soil; or with nearby pebbles gathered together to line hollow. **Breeding season:** Begins mid- to late June. **Eggs:** Only 1. Subelliptical. Smooth with slight granular texture, non-glossy. Dull white, bluish-white, or rarely pale blue. 54 × 37 mm. **Incubation:** By both sexes. 35–36 days. **Nestling:** Semi-precocial and downy. Down blackish-brown on upperparts, back browner than head; underside paler and grayer. **Nestling period:** Young tended by both parents. Wing feathers developed rapidly. Young do not leave nest cavity until fully fledged. Age of first flight, 34–37 days.

Least Auklet (Aethia pusilla)   Plate 47
Breeds on rocky coasts and offshore islands on the periphery of coastal Alaska. Nest in crevice in rocks, among fallen boulders, on talus slopes, or similar sites. Usually nests in large colonies.
Nest: Egg laid on a bare site; no nest materials. **Breeding season:** Begins mid-May to late June. Usually ends by late August. **Eggs:** 1; oval to subelliptical. Smooth and non-glossy. White. 39 × 29 mm. **Incubation:** By both sexes. 31–36 days. **Nestling:** Semi-precocial and downy. Down brown above and pale grayish-brown below. **Nestling period:** Young brooded for about a week and tended by both parents. Fed on small crustaceans brought in throat pouch. Leaves nest at c. 4–5 weeks, at which time it is independent.

Whiskered Auklet (Aethia pygmaea)
Breeds in the central Aleutians, often in colonies with Least and Crested Auklets. Nest in crevice and holes in cliffs and talus.
Nest: Egg laid on a bare site; no nest materials. **Breeding season:** Begins mid-May. Usually ends by mid-August. **Eggs:** 1; oval, smooth and lusterless. White. 48 × 34 mm.

Incubation: By both sexes, with shift change at night. At least 35–36 days. ***Nestling:*** Semi-precocial and downy. Covered by a dense down, dark sooty above, lighter and more grayish on the abdomen. ***Nestling period:*** Young brooded for about a week and tended by both parents. Leaves nest at *c.* 39–45 days, at which time it is probably independent.

Crested Auklet *(Aethia cristatella)*   Plate 48

Breeds on rocky shores and offshore islands on the periphery of coastal Alaska. Nest in crevices or cavity among fallen boulders, on talus slopes, or similar sites. Nests colonially.

Nest: Egg laid on a bare site; no nest materials. ***Breeding season:*** Begins mid-May to late June. Usually ends by late August. ***Eggs:*** 1; oval. Smooth or very slight granular texture, non-glossy. White. 54 × 38 mm. ***Incubation:*** By both sexes. 34–41 days. ***Nestling:*** Semi-precocial and downy. Down brown above and pale grayish-brown below. ***Nestling period:*** Young brooded for about a week and tended by both parents, food brought in throat pouch. Young leave nest at 27–36 days at which time it is independent.

Rhinoceros Auklet *(Cerorhinca monocerata)*   Plate 48

Breeds on offshore islands. Nest in a burrow dug by birds in steep slope or on more level ground, often among tree roots or logs. (Underground nest-boxes have been successfully occupied.) Located from the shoreline to 400 ft. up. Nests in colonies.

Nest: A burrow 5–15 ft. long, or sometimes 4–20 ft.; *c.* 5 in. in diameter; sloping down at end to nest chamber *c.* 12 in. across and 6–8 in. high. Excavation by both sexes taking 1–2 weeks. ***Breeding season:*** Begins late April in south to early June in north. Single-brooded, but a lost egg may be replaced. ***Eggs:*** Only 1. Subelliptical to oval. Smooth and non-glossy. Often nest-stained. White, unmarked, or marked sparsely with scrawls and spots of pale purplish-gray and light brown, often confined to a zone around the larger end. 68 × 46 mm. ***Incubation:*** By both sexes, changing over at night. 39–52 days. ***Nestling:*** Semi-precocial and downy. Down dark grayish-brown, paler below. Bill dark gray. ***Nestling period:*** Young brooded for 4 days and tended by both. Young can move around soon after hatching. Comes to entrance to defecate. Fledges at *c.* 52 days (while still downy and only partly grown) after which it is probably independent.

Tufted Puffin *(Fratercula cirrhata)*   Plate 48

Breeds on rocky shores and offshore islands. Nest in a shallow burrow in the soil under turf, usually on the tops of islands, or in a rock crevice on a cliff or slope. Nests in colonies.

Nest: A burrow 2–6½ ft. long, with a hollow, usually well lined with dry grasses, feathers, and other material brought in from nearby; sometimes hollow unlined. Both sexes dig burrow. ***Breeding season:*** Begins late April in south to early June in north. ***Eggs:*** Only 1. Subelliptical to oval. Smooth and non-glossy. Dull white, often nest-stained; unmarked, or marked with sparse to profuse faint spots and scrawls in pale gray or purplish-gray and sometimes pale brown. 72 × 49 mm. ***Incubation:*** By both sexes. *c.* 44 days. ***Nestling:*** Semi-precocial and downy. Down long, soft and silky. Sooty-black above and sooty-gray below. ***Nestling period:*** Young tended by both parents. Young leave nest for sea when about half-fledged (as early as 38 days). Unable to fly but independent of parents. Fly at 49 days.

Atlantic Puffin *(Fratercula arctica)*   Plates 13, 48

Breeds on sea-coasts, on turf slopes on tops of cliffs. Cliffs with talus slopes, coastal hillsides, or the tops of islands down to sea-level. Nest in a burrow excavated by puffin, or in a hole among boulders or a natural crevice. Nests colonially.

Nest: A shallow hollow, a few feet (2–4) inside tunnel. Plant material and feathers are carried in, but not arranged systematically as a lining. Mostly excavated by male. **Breeding season:** Begins early June. Single-brooded. **Eggs:** Usually 1, rarely 2. Shortish subelliptical. Smooth, non-glossy. Usually white, but often with markings within the shell showing as faint brown or purplish blotches. Exceptionally shell buff or light brown with brown or purple blotches and spotting. 61 × 42 mm. **Incubation:** Usually by female alone, the male occasionally helping (shifts may occur at from 2–50 hours). 40–43 days. **Nestling:** Semi-precocial and downy. Down short on the face and long and soft with fine tips on the belly. Down buffish-brown to blackish-brown on upperparts. Down bases gray. Down on crown particularly fluffy. Mid-underparts white. Bill compressed and black or dark reddish-gray, lower mandible paler. Mouth pale pinkish-flesh-color. Iris brown. Legs and feet dark gray. **Nestling period:** Young brooded for up to 9 days and tended by both adults. Leaves for sea alone at night after 46–51 days, after which time it is independent.

Horned Puffin (*Fratercula corniculata*)   Plate 48
Breeds on rocky headlands and offshore islands. Nest a burrow in earth at varying heights from sea level; may also use crevices or cavities in rocks occasionally. Located from the shoreline to the crest of island cliffs. Often nests in large colonies. **Nest:** Nest in a tunnel 2–10 ft. long. Shallow nest hollow bare, or sparsely lined with dry grasses or other nearby plant material. Excavated by both sexes. **Breeding season:** Begins early June. **Eggs:** Only 1. Subelliptical to oval. Smooth and non-glossy. Dull white, often nest-stained; marked with faint spots or scrawls in pale gray or purplish-gray. 72 × 49 mm. **Incubation:** By both sexes. 40–42 days. **Nestling:** Semi-precocial and downy. Down long, soft and dense. Pale grayish-brown or darker brown above, paling to grayish-white or yellowish-white on belly. **Nestling period:** Young tended by both parents. Young leave nest when partly grown and feathered (as early as 38 days), unable to fly properly, but entirely independent of parents.

Pigeons and Doves (*Columbidae*)

Medium-sized bird nesting in trees or shrubs, or on rocks. Nest thin, sketchy, and platform-like. Some species will use nest of another species as a foundation for the nest. Material carried to the nest in the bill and added with small lateral quiverings of the bill as material is inserted. Male bringing material may land on back of female, and pass it to her over her shoulder. Clutch of 2, or sometimes 1, white egg. Eggs covered continually after first is laid. Male usually incubates by day, female by night, changing over in late afternoon. Young have sparse hairy down with bare skin showing through. The base of the bill is swollen and sensitive. They are fed by adults on a crop secretion for several days, then the amount of seed and plant material is increased. They take the food from inside the adult's bill. Young follow parents, or are visited and fed by them, after leaving the nest, but there is little information on this period and its duration.

Rock Dove (*Columba livia*)   Plate 50
A commonly introduced species which usually nests colonially. The wild form breeds in caves and crevices of sea-cliffs, gorges, or rock outcrops in the Old World. Domesticated form breeds on ledges on or in man-made structures, sometimes at or below ground level. Nest on a ledge or in a hole, often well inside the various major sites, in almost dark situations. Usually 10–30 ft. up, but may be as high as 100 ft. **Nest:** A scanty layer, at times almost absent, at others more solid, of fine stems, roots, twigs, etc., or in towns sometimes pieces of wire of similar appearance. Both sexes

build, but male usually brings material for female to incorporate. **Breeding season:** March or April to August or September. In urban situations may be longer. Double- or treble-brooded. **Eggs:** Normally 2, rarely 1. Subelliptical. Smooth and slightly glossy. White. 39 × 29 mm. **Incubation:** By both sexes, beginning with first egg. 17–19 days. **Nestling:** Altricial and downy. Down sparse and coarse, mainly yellow- ish with a slight reddish tint. Bill dull gray with pale, pinkish-flesh-colored tip. Legs and feet grayish-pink. **Nestling period:** Young are brooded continually at first, and fed by both parents. Later left alone more. After flying they are still fed by parents for a time. Independent in 30–35 days.

White-crowned Pigeon (*Columba leucocephala*)   Plate 50
Breeds in woodland, mangroves and low scrub in southern Florida. Nest in tree, or shrub, often low (up to 15 ft.), or in cacti. Nest often in fairly open site. Usually nests in colonies.
Nest: A platform of twigs, roots, and plant-stems. **Breeding season.** Mid-May through September. Double brooded. **Eggs:** Usually 2. Long elliptical to subelliptical. Smooth and fairly glossy. White. 37 × 27 mm. **Incubation:** By both sexes, with females during the night and males during the day. 14 days. **Nestling:** Altricial and downy. Down sparse and pale buff with bare blackish skin showing. **Nestling period:** Young tended by both parents. Young leave at 16–20 days, fed by both parents until 28–40 days.

Red-billed Pigeon (*Columba flavirostris*)   Plate 50
Breeds in woodland, or cultivated areas and open areas with patches of woodland or groves of trees in lower Rio Grande Valley of Texas; usually in semi-arid or arid areas but near water. Nest in a tree or shrub, or a horizontal tree branch, or in a dense tangle, 6–30 ft. up.
Nest: A shallow platform of twigs, sometimes with some finer stems, roots or grasses. *c.* 8 in. across by 2½ in. deep, and 1 in. depression. Built by both sexes. **Breeding season:** Mid-February to mid-August. Several broods. **Eggs:** Only 1. Long elliptical to subelliptical. Smooth and moderately glossy. White. 39 × 27 mm. **Incubation:** By both sexes. Probably 18–20 days. **Nestling:** Altricial and downy. Down coarse and sparse; dark. Skin reddish-brown. **Nestling period:** Young tended by both parents. Adults appear to remove the droppings of unfeathered young.

Band-tailed Pigeon (*Columba fasciata*)   Plate 50
Breeds in a variety of mountain and highland forests, particularly areas where oaks are plentiful. Nest in a tree or shrub, often standing above a small slope or precipice, and near a clearing. Often fairly low, 8–20 ft. up, occasionally much higher.
Nest: A typical shallow twig platform. Built by female, using material brought by male, in 2–6 days. **Breeding season:** Begins early March in south to early May in north. Prolonged. Probably several broods. **Eggs:** Only 1. Long elliptical. Smooth and fairly glossy. White. 40 × 28 mm. **Incubation:** By both sexes. 18–20 days. **Nestling:** Altricial and downy. Down sparse, coarse and white, with yellow skin showing. **Nestling period:** Young leave nest at about 25–30 days.

Eurasian Collared-Dove (*Streptopelia decaocto*)
An introduced bird, now in Florida and expanding. Breeds in partly urbanized or cultivated areas. Nest in a tree, often in an evergreen; rarely on a ledge on a building. Usually 10–40 ft. up.
Nest: A thin platform of fine twigs and plant stems. Built by female, using material brought by male. **Breeding season:** Almost year-round, excepting Autumn (usually

March to August). Triple-brooded, but up to 6 at times. **Eggs:** 2. Subelliptical. Smooth and moderately glossy. White. 30 × 23 mm. **Incubation:** By both sexes. 14 days. **Nestling:** Altricial and downy. Down a drab yellowish-white. Skin dark, but bill pale pinkish-flesh. **Nestling period:** Young tended by both parents. Fly at *c.* 18 days and leave nest area at *c.* 21 days.

Spotted Dove (*Streptopelia chinensis*)   Plate 50
Introduced from Asia and breeds along coastal southern California. This species is a bird of open woodland and of cultivated areas and human settlement where trees or shrubs are present. Nest on a tree or shrub (5–35 ft.), or on the ledge of a building. Often quite low.
Nest: A small saucer-shaped structure of small twigs, grass-stems and roots. **Breeding season:** May breed any time of year, but mostly from February through October. Double- or triple-brooded. **Eggs:** Usually 2. Elliptical to long elliptical or subelliptical. Smooth and glossy. White. 26 × 21 mm. **Incubation:** By both sexes. 14 days. **Nestling:** Altricial and downy. Down sparse and hair-like. **Nestling period:** Young leave nest at *c.* 10 days.

White-winged Dove (*Zenaida asiatica*)   Plates 14, 50
Breeds in semi-arid regions with scrub and thickets, woodland, and cultivated areas with trees. Nest in a tree or shrub. Often nests in loose colonies in mesquite thickets. Elsewhere nests singly or in loose groups. Nests may be 4–25 ft. up, but usually about 8–12 ft. up.
Nest: A shallow, thin platform of twigs, or occasionally weed-stems or grasses. Built by female, with material brought by male, in 2–10 days. **Breeding season:** Begins late March to early April. Prolonged. Double- or sometimes treble-brooded. **Eggs:** Usually 2. Elliptical to long elliptical or subelliptical. Smooth and glossy. Buff to creamy or white. 31 × 23 mm. **Incubation:** By both sexes, by female from mid-afternoon through night, male throughout most of day. 13–14 days. **Nestling:** Altricial and downy. Down long, straggling and sparse. Dull white tinged with buff. **Nestling period:** Young tended by both parents. Down mostly replaced by feathers in quill by end of first week. Leave nest at 13–16 days, begin flying at *c.* 15 days. When young safely flying, adults may breed again.

Mourning Dove (*Zenaida macroura*)   Figure 57, Plate 50
Breeds in a wide variety of habitats. Open woodland, cultivated areas with trees or shrubs, suburban gardens, semi-arid and arid areas within reach of water. Nest usually in a tree or shrub between 10–25 ft., often on the old nest of some other bird species; occasionally higher or even on a stump, exceptionally on a ledge of a building or on the ground.
Nest: A platform of twigs, sometimes with finer twigs as lining. Built by both over 2–4 days. **Breeding season:** Very prolonged. Begins December to February in south to late April in north. Double- or, treble-brooded, sometimes more. **Eggs:** 2. Elliptical to long elliptical or subelliptical. Smooth and slightly glossy. White. 28 × 22 mm. **Incubation:** First egg laid in evening, second on early morning of next day but one. Incubation by both sexes, the male sitting most of the day, the female at night. 14–15 days. **Nestling:** Altricial and downy. Down sparse and stringy, short and white; with yellowish skin showing through. **Nestling period:** Young tended by both parents, one usually present on nest most of the time. Young fledge at 13–15 days. Cared for until 25–27 days old.

Figure 57. Mourning Dove: c. 7–9 in. across; a frail-looking platform of twigs.

Inca Dove (*Columbina inca*)   **Plate 50**
Breeds in arid areas, and in cultivated places around human settlement, where trees
and shrubs are present. Nest in a tree or bush, on a fork of flattened limb, or on the old
nest of another bird species; on cacti, or occasionally on beams of open buildings.
Usually 8–20 ft. up. Nests may be re-used for subsequent nestings with small addition to the linings.
Nest: A small, compact, flat platform of thin twigs, stems, grass-roots, etc., sometimes lined with finer material. 2–5 in. across, 1–1½ in. high with shallow center
hollow. Built by both sexes, male carrying and female building. Usually takes *c.* 3
days. **Breeding season:** Often prolonged. Late February to October. Several broods
2–3, sometimes 4–5. **Eggs:** 2. Long elliptical to long subelliptical. Smooth and
glossy. White. 22 × 17 mm. **Incubation:** By both sexes. 13–15 days. **Nestling:** No
information. **Nestling period:** Young tended by both parents. Brooded for 7–9 days.
Young fledged at 14–16 days, becoming independent during an additional week.

Common Ground-Dove (*Columbina passerina*)   **Plate 50**
Breeds in open country with trees and shrubs, in cultivated areas and around
human habitation. Nest in a tree or shrub up to 25 ft., or rarely on the ground in
the shelter of a plant tuft or grasses.
Nest: A thin frail platform of fine twigs, grasses, stems, rootlets, and occasionally
feathers. *c.* 2½–4 in. across, with barely any central depression. **Breeding season:**
Usually prolonged, February to November. Several broods; 2–3, possibly 4. **Eggs:** 2.
Elliptical to long elliptical or subelliptical. Smooth and slightly glossy. White. 22 × 16
mm. **Incubation:** By both sexes. 13–14 days. **Nestling:** Altricial and downy. Down

coarse and sparse, hair-like and dull gray. *Nestling period:* Young can fly at 11 days. They are brooded or shaded by an adult for much of the time until well feathered.

White-tipped Dove (*Leptoptila verreauxi*)   Plate 50
Breeds in open woodland, forest edge, scrub, and cultivated areas with trees and thick bushes in southernmost Texas. Nest in a tree, shrub, or, sometimes, cactus, 3–25 ft. up, often low – about 3–6 ft. up or even to ground level.
Nest: A thick, slightly concave platform, variable in size and bulk but often substantial, more so than those of typical pigeons. Of twigs, or grasses and weed stems. Usually single-brooded. *Breeding season:* Early February into September, but mostly between April and August. *Eggs:* Usually 2, occasionally 1, rarely 3. Long elliptical to elliptical or long subelliptical. Smooth and slightly glossy. Dull white, to creamy or pale buff. 31 × 23 mm. *Incubation:* By both sexes. 14 days. *Nestling:* Altricial and downy. Down sparse and hair-like. Bill pinkish-brown, with black subterminal band and white tip. Eyes brown. *Nestling period:* Young tended by both parents. Young are brooded even when well feathered. Young leave nest at 10–12 days, and begin to feed themselves at *c.* 4 weeks.

Parakeets and Parrots (*Psittacidae*)

Birds of small to medium size, of tropical or subtropical origin. Nest usually in cavity, but in large stick-nest for Monk Parakeet. Eggs white, usually 2–6. Nestlings are usually naked, or with sparse white dorsal down, usually giving way to gray down and feathers. Usually brooded and fed by female, later by male. Young develop slowly and will remain with parents after fledging. The three species discussed are established in North America, though there are a number of other species, particularly in Florida and California, which may become established in the near future. The only North American native of this family, the Carolina Parakeet (*Conuropsis carolinensis*), is extinct.

Budgerigar (*Melopsittacus undulatus*)
Breeds in residential and suburban areas on the west coast of Florida. Introduced. Nests in man-made sites (including nest-boxes), rarely in natural cavities in dead pines, or in axils of Cabbage Palms.
Nest: No nesting material; eggs laid in cavity. *Breeding season:* Usually May through October, but may lay eggs throughout year. *Eggs:* 4–7. Elliptical, slightly glossy. White. 19 × 14 mm. *Incubation:* By female, fed by male. About 18 days. *Nestling:* Altricial. Flesh pink, grayish about the eyes and bill. Bill, pinkish-gray. Legs, light gray. Down, white. *Nestling period:* Young tended by both adults. Feathered at 21 days, fly at 30–36 days. Fully independent within a few days.

Monk Parakeet (*Myiopsitta monachus*)
Breeds in residential and suburban areas in Florida. Introduced. Nests in trees, on power poles, electrical substations, and other man-made structures. Nest is a communal structure with multiple units.
Nest: A bulky structure of sticks (often with thorns) and weed stalks. The entrance is usually toward the bottom of the structure. A two-chambered tunnel is used. A solitary nest may be as large as 3 ft. in diameter; communal nests much larger. Nests with up to 20 pairs have been recorded; those with 4–5 pairs more common. Individual interior compartment lined with a bed of twigs. *Breeding season:* Eggs possibly laid throughout year. *Eggs:* 5–8. Elliptical, slightly glossy. White. 28 × 22 mm.

Incubation: By female. 23 days. *Nestling:* Altricial. *Nestling period:* Young tended by both adults. Leave nest at *c.* 6 weeks.

Canary-winged Parakeet *(Brotogeris versicolurus* – Includes *B. v. chiriri)*

Breeds in suburbs commonly along southeastern Florida coast, less commonly around Los Angeles, California. Nest in a hollow limb or in tree cavity, or in dead fronds of palm trees.

Nest: No nesting material added, eggs laid in cavity. *Breeding season:* Early March to early August. *Eggs:* Usually 5–6, sometimes up to 9. Elliptical. White. 23 × 19 mm. *Incubation:* By female. About 26 days. *Nestling:* Altricial. Bill white. *Nestling period:* Young tended by both adults. Young leave at 7–8 weeks. Fed by adults for another 3–4 weeks.

Cuckoos, Roadrunner, and Anis *(Cuculidae)*

Medium-sized, mainly insectivorous birds. Often partly terrestrial. Tend to nest low. Nests often loose and poorly-made twig structures. Eggs pale blue or greenish-blue, with white outer layer in some species. Some species may occasionally lay eggs in nests of other individuals of the same species, or of cuckoos of other species, or other birds, foreshadowing brood parasitism. In anis a number of pairs may nest communally. Nestling naked or with sparse coarse down. Feathers grow rapidly, remaining in sheath until most of plumage is present, and breaking out when young leave nest. Young leave nest early, some time before they are able to fly properly.

Black-billed Cuckoo *(Coccyzus erythrophthalmus)*   Plates 14, 50

Breeds in deciduous woodland with shrubby vegetation. Also along shelterbelts. Nest in a tree or bush, on a fork or a horizontal branch, 2–15 ft. up, but usually low. At times almost on ground, partly concealed by tall herbage; exceptionally on a fallen log or in herbage on the ground.

Nest: A loosely-built cup, usually more substantial than that of Yellow-billed Cuckoo, rounded but with many projecting twig ends. Of twigs, grass, plant-stems, and seed-heads of weeds, lined with dried grass, leaves, flowering heads of trees and herbs and similar material. Outside diameter: 8 in.; inside diameter $3-3\frac{1}{2}$ in.; depth: $\frac{3}{4}-1$ in. *Breeding season:* Begins early to mid-May. Single-brooded. *Eggs:* Usually 2–3, rarely 4–5. Larger clutches may be from two females. Eggs are sometimes laid in nests of other cuckoos or other bird species. Elliptical to subelliptical. Smooth and non-glossy. Light blue, bluish-green, or light green. 27 × 21 mm. *Incubation:* Eggs are laid at irregular intervals. Incubation by both sexes, beginning with first egg. 10–14? days. *Nestling:* Altricial. Almost naked, skin black with sparse, coarse white hairs. These persist at tips of feather which follow. There is a complex pattern of white papillae inside the pinkish mouth. Tongue with black edges at tip. Gape grayish yellow. Feathers appear first as long quills, break later. *Nestling period:* Young tended by both parents. Hatch at intervals and differ in size. Adults bring insects carried in throat pouch and disgorge into mouth of nestling. Eyes open at 2–3 days. Young begin preening at 6 days, quill sheaths break at 7–9 days, and young leave nest and perch and climb on branches. Fly at *c.* 21–24 days.

Yellow-billed Cuckoo *(Coccyzus americanus)*   Plate 50

Breeds in open woodland, scrub, parkland, orchards and gardens. Nest in a bush or tree, 2–20 ft. up, in a crotch or on a horizontal limb, usually concealed in dense foliage.

Nest: A very loosely-built shallow twig platform, with rootlets, dry leaves, grass, and other debris; loosely lined with grasses, pine needles, flowering parts from trees and weeds, and mosses. Cup poorly formed, the nest small for the size of the bird with many projecting twigs; and eggs may be lost. *c.* 5–8 in. outer diameter, by $1\frac{1}{2}$ in. depth. **Breeding season:** Begins late March in south to late May in north. Single-brooded, or sometimes double-brooded in south. **Eggs:** Usually 3–4, sometimes 1–5. More may be from two females. Eggs occasionally laid in nests of other cuckoos or other bird species. Elliptical to subelliptical. Smooth and non-glossy. Light blue, greenish-blue or pale green, usually slightly greener than eggs of Black-billed Cuckoo. 30×23 mm. **Incubation:** By both sexes but mainly by female, beginning with first egg. 9–11 days. **Nestling:** Altricial. Almost naked with black skin, but some sparse, hair-like down also present. Feathers grow in sheath until young are covered with quills. Mouth deep pink; gape flanges grayish-yellow. **Nestling period:** Young tended by both parents. They hatch over a period; differ in size. Feather sheaths break to release feathers a day or two before young leave nest. Leave nest and climb on branches at 7–8 days; fly at about 21 days.

Mangrove Cuckoo (*Coccyzus minor*)   Plate 50

Breeds in mangroves and adjacent hardwood hammocks in southern and western Florida. Nest in mangrove tree, fairly low horizontal branch.
Nest: A shallow cup of dead twigs. **Breeding season:** Begins mid-May. Double-brooded. **Eggs:** Usually 2. Elliptical to subelliptical. Smooth and non-glossy. Pale blue, greenish-blue or pale green. 31×23 mm. **Incubation:** Estimated at 14 days. **Nestling:** Altricial. **Nestling period:** Little information. Young tended by both adults.

Greater Roadrunner (*Geococcyx californianus*)   Figure 58, Plates 14, 51

Breeds in arid desert areas. Nest usually in a low tree, shrubby thicket, or on cactus clump. 3–15 ft. up. Varies from well concealed to exposed. Rarely nest on ground in cover.
Nest: A compact cup of twigs or plant or grass stems, lined with leaves, grass, roots, and feathers, and with debris such as snakeskins, flakes of cattle dung, and seed-pods. Outside diameter: *c.* 12 in.; height: 6–8 in. **Breeding season:** May begin March, but more usually April. Single-brooded, possibly double-brooded at times. **Eggs:** Usually 3–6. Larger numbers may be from more than one female. Elliptical to sub-elliptical. Smooth and slightly glossy. White to creamy-white. 39×30 mm. **Incubation:** Eggs laid at irregular intervals. Incubation by both during the day, by male at night. Beginning with first egg. 20 days. **Nestling:** Altricial. Almost naked. Shiny black skin with sparse coarse whitish hairs followed by feathers in sheath. Mouth bright red with white upper palate, white hind-edges to tongue and white lump on either side of throat. Gape flanges pink. Legs and feet first dark, then blue-gray. Irides deep brown. **Nestling period:** Young tended by both parents. Hatch over long intervals, eggs and young in various stages may be present. Eyes open at 6–7 days. Feathers break sheaths at 10–14 days. Young probably leave nest at *c.* 11 days, before able to fly (17–19 days). Begin feeding themselves at *c.* 16 days.

Smooth-billed Ani (*Crotophaga ani*)   Plates 14, 51

Breeds in brush, or trees around farmland, brushy fields and scrublands in south Florida. In social groups with 3–4 females and 1 male often forming the core. (Com-munal nests with more than 1 laying female, however, is the exception rather than the rule in Florida.) Nest in a twig fork of tree or shrub, at times high. 6–30 ft. up.
Nest: Usually a loose mass of twigs, *c.* 12 in. across and 6 in. deep, with at times weed and vine stems and coarse roots; lined with green leaves which later wither. Fresh

Figure 58. Greater Roadrunner: c. 11–12 in. across; this fairly solid structure is in cactus.

green leaves and sometimes twigs may be added during incubation change-overs. **Breeding season:** March to December. **Eggs:** Usually 4–7 from one female. With several birds nests may have up to 29. Elliptical to subelliptical. Light blue to greenish-blue, thinly covered with a smooth and fairly glossy white layer, the blue color showing through at times to varying degrees. Rarely the white layer absent. The layer tends to become scratched and stained during incubation. 35 × 26 mm. **Incubation:** Eggs laid at 2-day intervals. Incubation by both sexes and all members of group. 12–15 days for particular eggs, but with large numbers eggs may be in layers in nest and the lower ones may not hatch. **Nestling:** Altricial and naked. Skin black. Sheathed pin-feathers grow rapidly in first few days. **Nestling period:** Young tended by both sexes and all of group. Eyes open at 3 days. Pin-feathers begun by 3 days. Sheaths breaking by 5 days, and young may leave nest if disturbed. Young leave nest at 10–11 days. May remain with adults and help with later broods.

Groove-billed Ani (*Crotophaga sulcirostris*)   Plate 51
Nest usually in a thick twiggy or tangled growth, often in thorny trees or shrubs, on the edge of an open area in south Texas. Nest is in a fork or among twigs. 2–25 ft. up, but usually below 10 ft. Nesting may be by a single pair or by up to four breeding co-operatively.
Nest: A conspicuous bulky cup of loose coarse twigs, lined with green leaves. Both sexes may carry and build, but often the female, or females, build and males bring material. Green leaves and sometimes twigs are added during incubation. Where several females lay successively, earlier eggs may be covered with leaves. **Breeding season:** Early May to mid-September. **Eggs:** Usually 4, sometimes 3–5, by one female, but up to 14 recorded from one nest with several females. Eggs like those of Smooth-billed Ani. 31 × 24 mm. **Incubation:** Eggs laid at 2–3-day intervals, usually at mid-day. All birds of both sexes appear to incubate, male usually incubating at night. 13–14 days for individual eggs. **Nestling:** Altricial and naked. Black skin. Rapidly

becomes covered with sheathed pin-feathers. **Nestling period:** Young tended by all birds of group. Brooded for first week. Sheathed feathers grow rapidly and burst from sheaths at *c.* 6 days. At 6 days young begin to leave nest and climb branches. Subsequently may roost out of nest. At 11 days can hop easily and make short flights. Young of earlier broods may help to feed later broods.

Barn Owls (*Tytonidae*)

Barn Owl (*Tyto alba*)   Figure 59, Plates 14, 49
Generally distributed, breeding in cavities in trees, buildings of all types, crevices in rocks, outcrops, cliffs, and quarries. Will use nest-boxes.
Nest: No nest material, but there may be a shallow hollow in existing debris, partly lined with owl pellets. **Breeding season:** May begin January in south to late February or March in north. Season prolonged. Often double-brooded. **Eggs:** Clutch variable,

Figure 59. Barn Owl: typical grouping of young of varied sizes and ages.

usually 4–7, occasionally 3–11. Long subelliptical to elliptical. Smooth but non-glossy. White. 42 × 33 mm. **Incubation:** Eggs laid at 2-day intervals, longer intervals at times. Female alone incubates, male bringing food. 32–34 days. **Nestling:** Altricial and downy. Unlike other owls has two down coats. First down white and short, sparse on the belly, covering legs to claws but absent on back of tarsus, also absent on sides of neck. Replaced in *c.* 12 days by a longer, thicker buffish-cream down, first down clinging to its tips. Down more sparse on lower legs and toes. Iris pale blue for first few weeks. Bill ivory. **Nestling period:** Young vary in size. Tended and fed by both parents; feathering between third and seventh week; flying at *c.* 60 days; independent in *c.* 10 weeks.

Typical Owls (*Strigidae*)

Small to medium-sized raptors; usually nocturnal. No nest made, but female may make scrape by revolving on her breast on nest-site. A few species may collect material, but information is very unsatisfactory. Eggs white, and are usually rounded. Clutch may be large, and, in some species regulated by food supply, being larger when food is plentiful. Incubation begins early in laying and young hatch at intervals, differing in size. The nestlings hatch with their eyes closed. Young covered in down, soon followed by first plumage of soft feathering, the first down persisting on the feather tips. If food becomes short, smaller young die. Young of larger owls appear slow in achieving complete independence, possibly slower than our present information suggests.

Flammulated Owl (*Otus flammeolus*)
Breeds in old montane pine woods, often in Ponderosa Pine and close to open area. Nest usually in a woodpecker hole, more rarely in a natural cavity. Occasionally will use nest-boxes. 8–39 ft. up.
Nest: An unlined cavity. **Breeding season:** Begins mid-May to early June. Usually ends by late July. Single-brooded. **Eggs:** Usually 3–4. Elliptical to short subelliptical. Smooth and slightly glossy. White. 29 × 26 mm. **Incubation:** By female, fed by male. 21–22 days. **Nestling:** Altricial and downy. Down thick and white. Bill, legs, and feet, pinkish-flesh-colored. Irides dark blackish-brown. Soon grayish-white barring develops on upperparts, white below. **Nestling period:** Female broods, male brings food through day 12, then both hunt for food. Young leave nest at 21–25 days. Brood separates into two parts, each tended by one adult. Independent of parents at 46–57 days.

Eastern Screech-Owl (*Otus asio*)   Figure 60, Plate 49
Breeds in woodlots, forests, swamps, parks, orchards, and suburban gardens. Nest in a natural cavity or old woodpecker hole. Will also use nest-boxes. 5–30 ft. up.
Nest: A cavity unlined apart from any material already present. **Breeding season:** Begins early March to May (earlier in south Texas). Usually ends by mid-July. **Eggs:** Usually 4–5, sometimes 3–7. Elliptical. Moderately glossy; white. 36 × 30 mm. **Incubation:** By female. 26 days. **Nestling:** Altricial and downy. Down thick and white, extending down toes to claws. Second downy plumage is olive to umber above, white below. **Nestling period:** Young brooded by female for first two weeks while male brings food. Young begin to feed themselves and cast pellets at *c.* 10 days, down replaced by downy feathering in second and third weeks. Young leave at 30–32 days. Remain dependent on parents for 8–10 weeks.

Figure 60. Eastern Screech-Owl: c. 17 days old, venturing outside of nest hole.

Western Screech-Owl (*Otus kennicottii*) Plate 49

Breeds in open woodlands, streamside groves, parks, deserts, and suburban areas. Nest in a natural cavity or old woodpecker hole, including those in cacti. Will also use nest-boxes. 6–30 ft. up.

Nest: A cavity unlined apart from any material already present. **Breeding season:** March to early June. **Eggs:** Usually 2–4, sometimes 5. Elliptical to spherical. Moderately glossy; white. 38×32 mm. **Incubation:** By female? 21–30 days. **Nestling:** Altricial and downy. Down thick and white, extending down toes to claws. **Nestling period:** Young tended by both. Fly at 28 days.

Whiskered Screech-Owl (*Otus trichopsis*)

Breeds in thick oak and oak-pine woods in southeastern Arizona and southwestern New Mexico. Nest in a tree, in a natural cavity or woodpecker (often Northern Flicker) hole, 17–23 ft. up.

Nest: An unlined cavity. Breeding season. Begins late April or early May. **Eggs:** Usually 3, sometimes 4. Elliptical to subelliptical. Smooth and slightly glossy. White. 33 × 28 mm. **Incubation:** No information. **Nestling:** Little information. Reportedly similar to Western Screech-Owl, though with a coarser plumage pattern and with smaller feet. **Nestling period:** Little information. Young will rely on adults for food after leaving nest.

Great Horned Owl (*Bubo virginianus*)   Figure 61, Plate 49

Breeds through a wide range of woodland habitat. Nest in a natural cavity in a tree, in a fork of a giant cactus, on a rock ledge, or in a rock or earth cave. Often in the old nest of a large bird in such sites. In some treeless regions on open ground.

Nest: An unlined cavity, or lined with any material already present. **Breeding season:** Begins late November or January in south to early April in north. Single-brooded, but lost clutch may be replaced. **Eggs:** Usually 2–3, sometimes 1–5. Sub-elliptical or short subelliptical to elliptical. Smooth and slightly glossy with slight granular texture. White. 56 × 47 mm. **Incubation:** Mostly by female, beginning with first egg. 26–35 days. **Nestling:** Altricial and downy. Down white. Bill gray. **Nestling period:** Young hatch over a period of days. Tended by both parents. Brooded by female for first 3 weeks with male bringing all food. Eyes open at *c.* 10 days. Young

TERRY O'NELE

Figure 61. Great Horned Owl: of varied ages, *c.* 30–36 days old; venturing out on branch.

leave the nest at $4\frac{1}{2}$–5 weeks, but do not fly well until 9–10 weeks. Rely on adults for food for a long period afterwards.

Snowy Owl (*Nyctea scandiaca*)   Figure 62, Plates 14, 49

Breeds in level, open country, on arctic tundra, or bare stretches of higher fells and mountains, or on islands. Nest on the ground; usually located on a slightly raised site with an extensive view around, often on a hummock, but at times on a large boulder or ledge of a crag.

Nest: A hollow scrape formed by the female, at times with some moss fragments and feathers. **Breeding season:** Begins mid-May to early June. Usually ends early September. Single-brooded; like other arctic breeders, may not nest in some years. **Eggs:** Clutch varies with food supply, usually 4–10, sometimes up to 15. Short elliptical or subelliptical. Smooth and slightly glossy. White. 57 × 45 mm. **Incubation:** By female only, beginning with first egg, the male bringing food. 32–37 days. **Nestling:** Altricial and downy. Down white, soft, short, and thick, extending down to the claws, but with bare patch on back of leg joint. Followed after 6–10 days by a first plumage of dark grayish-brown loose feathering which looks like down. Bill dark gray. **Nestling period:** Eggs hatch at 1–2-day intervals, a large clutch may hatch over 2 weeks. Female spends much time brooding, the male bringing food. When young are larger both adults hunt. Young leave the nest-site 3–4 weeks before they can fly. They fly well at *c.* 8–9 weeks but are still fed by adults.

Northern Hawk Owl (*Surnia ulula*)   Plate 49

Breeds in conifers and birch forests, often bordering marshes or other open areas. Nest in holes in trees, including old woodpecker holes; hollows at ends of broken tree-trunks; and old nests of large birds. 5–43 ft. up.

Nest: An unlined hollow or cavity. **Breeding season:** Usually begins in April or early May. Single-brooded, possibly two in good food years. **Eggs:** Usually 3–10, rarely 13, depending on food supply. Short elliptical to short subelliptical. Smooth and glossy. White. 40 × 32 mm. **Incubation:** Mainly by female, beginning with first egg, but the male may take some part. 25–30 days. **Nestling:** Altricial and downy. Down white with a yellowish-buff tint. **Nestling period:** Young tended by both parents. Leave at *c.* 23–27 days. Probably not fully independent until nearly 90 days.

Figure 62. Snowy Owl: c. 15–20 in. across; often on a raised site overlooking tundra.

Northern Pygmy-Owl (*Glaucidium gnoma*)

Breeds in forest, either in conifer or deciduous forest and often near forest openings. Nest in a natural hole or old woodpecker hole in a tree. Usually 8–20 ft. up.
Nest: An unlined cavity. **Breeding season:** Begins late April to early May. Single-brooded. **Eggs:** Usually 4–6, sometimes 3–7. Short elliptical to short subelliptical. Smooth and slightly glossy. White. 29 × 24 mm. **Incubation:** Eggs laid at 3–4-day intervals. Incubation may not begin until clutch is complete. 28 days. **Nestling:** Altricial and downy. Down whitish. **Nestling period:** Female broods young and feeds them on food brought entirely by male. Young leave nest at 29–32 days. Probably not independent until 50–60 days old.

Ferruginous Pygmy-Owl (*Glaucidium brasilianum*)   Plate 49

Breeds uncommonly in southern Arizona and southernmost Texas. In Arizona nests in old woodpecker holes in Saguaro cacti and cottonwoods. In Texas uses cavities in mesquite and ebony woodlands. 11–30 ft. up.
Nest: Usually no material added in cavity, though occasionally a few leaves or bits of leaves. **Breeding season:** Late March to late June. **Eggs:** Usually 3–4, occasionally 5. Elliptical to spherical. Smooth and slightly glossy to non-glossy. White. 29 × 24 mm. **Incubation:** By female, fed by male. 22–30 days. **Nestling:** Semi-altricial. Down white to slightly buffy-white. **Nestling period:** Both adults feed nestlings. Young fly at 27–30 days.

Elf Owl (*Micrathene whitneyi*)   Plate 49

Breeds in desert regions along much of the US–Mexican border. Nest usually in an old woodpecker nest in a Saguaro cactus or tree. Rarely in a natural cavity. 15–30 ft. up.
Nest: An unlined cavity. **Breeding season:** Mid-March to September. **Eggs:** Usually 3, sometimes 2–5. Elliptical. Smooth and slightly glossy. White. 27 × 23 mm. **Incubation:** By both sexes, probably beginning with the second egg. 21–24 days. **Nestling:** Altricial and downy. Down sooty-white. Grayish-yellow irides and horn-gray bill. **Nestling period:** Young tended by both parents. Leave nest at 27–33 days.

Burrowing Owl (*Speotyto cunicularia*)   Plate 49

Breeds on prairies and open grassy places (including golf courses and airports). Usually occupies holes of prairie-dogs, ground squirrels, badgers or armadillos, but will enlarge or modify these if necessary and will excavate their own burrows if others are lacking. Underground nest-boxes have been used successfully.
Nest: Usually a burrow sloping down for 1½–3 ft. and then level and *c.* 5–10 ft. long, *c.* 5 in. diameter, and with a nest chamber of 12–18 in. Nest chamber lined with debris – cow dung, stalks, feathers, grasses, bones, and any rubbish. This appears to be the only owl bringing material into a cavity. **Breeding season:** Begins late March in south (earlier in Florida population) to early May in north. Usually single-brooded. A lost clutch may be replaced by a smaller clutch. **Eggs:** Usually 5–6, sometimes 3–11. Elliptical, almost spherical at times, to short subelliptical. Smooth and glossy. White. 31 × 26 mm. **Incubation:** By female, fed by male, beginning with the first egg. 27–30 days. **Nestling:** Altricial and downy. Down sparse and grayish-white, on feather tracts only, with bare areas showing. **Nestling period:** Young tended by both adults. As the young mature they spend increasing time at the mouth of the burrow (starting at about 14 days), retreating into it when alarmed. Fledging is at *c.* 40–45 days.

Spotted Owl (*Strix occidentalis*)   Plate **49**
Breeds in conifer forests (usually old-growth) and forested canyons. Nest in a natural cavity in a tree, broken tree-top, more rarely in the nest of a large bird in a tree
or cave, or on a bare site in cave or on rocky slope. 33–163 ft. up.
Nest: An unlined cavity, or material already present in old nest. *Breeding season:*
Begins early April. Usually ends early June. Single-brooded, though may re-nest
after initial nest failure. *Eggs:* Usually 2, sometimes 3, rarely 4. Elliptical to short
subelliptical. Smooth but with slight granular texture, non-glossy or slightly glossy.
White. 50 × 41 mm. *Incubation:* By female, fed by male, beginning with first egg. 28–30
days. *Nestling:* Altricial and downy. Down pure white. *Nestling period:* Female feeds
the young on food brought by male. Young leave at 34–36 days, usually fly within
one more week. May be fed by both adults for 3 months.

Barred Owl (*Strix varia*)   Plate **49**
Breeds in forest over a wide area. Nest in a natural cavity in a tree-trunk or stub, or in
the nest of a large bird such as a hawk, or on an old squirrel nest. Occasionally in
nest-boxes. 15–30 ft. up. Very rarely on the ground.
Nest: An unlined cavity, or material already present on an old nest. *Breeding
season:* Begins late December in south to mid-March in north. Single-brooded but
lost clutches are replaced. *Eggs:* Usually 2–3, rarely 4. Elliptical, almost spherical at
times; to short subelliptical. Smooth and slightly glossy. White. 49 × 42 mm.
Incubation: By female only. 28–33 days. *Nestling:* Altricial and downy. Down thick
and soft; white. Second downy coat buffy and white. *Nestling period:* Young tended
by both parents. Brooded for the first 3 weeks. Eyes open at *c.* 7 days. Young may leave
nest for adjacent branches at 4–5 weeks. Fly at *c.* 6 weeks. Parental care extends
beyond 4 months.

Great Gray Owl (*Strix nebulosa*)   Figure **63**, Plate **49**
Breeds in conifer forests. Nests on the top of broken-off tree-trunks or on old nests of
other large birds. 15–50 ft. up.
Nest: An unlined hollow, or old nest of another species. *Breeding season:* Begins
late March. Usually ends by mid-July. Single-brooded. Nesting may not occur in
unfavorable years. *Eggs:* 3–5, sometimes fewer, but up to 9 in good years. Subelliptical, less rounded than those of most owls. Smooth and slightly glossy. White.
54 × 43 mm. *Incubation:* Eggs laid at variable intervals of 2–12 days. Incubation by
female only, beginning with first egg. 28–30 days. *Nestling:* Altricial and downy.
Down pale gray on upperparts, white on underpart. Irides yellowish-gray; legs and
feet pale yellow. *Nestling period:* Young hatch at different times and vary in size. The
female guards the young and feeds them on food brought by the male. The young
have eyes closed for first seven days; feather during 10–35 days; begin to leave the
nest at 3–4 weeks but do not fly well until 5 weeks. They are still fed by adults and
may remain together until about 4–5 months old.

Long-eared Owl (*Asio otus*)   Plate **49**
Breeds mainly in dense coniferous or mixed woodland, including riverine woodland
belts; exceptionally in open areas of scrub and marsh. Nest frequently in a large old
nest of another bird species, or a squirrel. Usually 10–29 ft. up, sometimes as high as
60 ft. up. More rarely on the ground sheltered by the base of a tree, or among low
shrubby growth.
Nest: The nest of another bird, but will occupy a natural tree cavity, squirrel nest, or
an unlined hollow on the ground. *Breeding season:* Begins early March in south to
mid-April in north. Usually single-brooded, occasional second broods in periods of

Figure 63. Great Gray Owl: c. 21–28 days old; in typical broken-off tree trunk site.

good food. **Eggs:** Usually 4–5, rarely 3–8. Short elliptical. Smooth, moderately glossy and finely pitted. White. 41 × 33 mm. **Incubation:** Eggs laid on alternate days. Incubation normally by the female only, beginning with first egg. 25–30 days. **Nestling:** Altricial and downy. Down fairly thick, short, and soft; white or ochre. Extending to the claws, with a bare patch on back of leg joint. Black feathering soon appears at base of bill. Belly striping evident after 10 days. **Nestling period:** Female feeds young with food brought by male. Often not all young are reared. Young leave nest at 23–24 days, fly at 30–40 days. Independent at c. 60 days.

Short-eared Owl (Asio flammeus)   Plates 14, 49

Breeds in open country, on plains, prairie, marshes, tundra, or dunes. Nest on the ground sheltered by tall grass, reeds, or bushes.

Nest: A shallow hollow, probably made by female, sparsely lined with weed stalks, grasses, etc. Diameter: 9–12 in. **Breeding season:** Begins early April sometimes. Usually ends by early June. Usually single-brooded, but double-brooded when food is plentiful. **Eggs:** Usually 4–8, rarely 3; up to 14 when food is plentiful. Short elliptical. Smooth, non-glossy or slightly glossy. White. 40 × 31 mm. **Incubation:** Eggs laid at 2-day intervals, occasionally longer. Incubation by female alone, beginning with first egg. 24–28 days. **Nestling:** Altricial and downy. Down thick, short, and soft, extending to the claws, with a bare patch on the back of leg joint. Creamy-buff to light warm buff on upperparts, with darker zone bordering mantle, white with a buff tinge on underside. **Nestling period:** Female broods and feeds young, the male bringing food. Young leave nest at 12–17 days, but do not fly until *c.* 10 days later.

Boreal Owl (Aegolius funereus)   Plate 49

Breeds in woodland, usually in conifers, and often near forest openings. Nests in holes in trees, natural cavities and old holes of woodpeckers; sometimes in artificial nest-boxes. 35–55 ft. up. **Nest:** An unlined cavity. **Breeding season:** Begins mid-April. Probably ends by early July. Usually single-brooded, possibly double-brooded at times. **Eggs:** Usually 3–6, sometimes 10 when food is plentiful. Short elliptical. Smooth, moderately glossy and finely pitted. White. 32×27 mm. **Incubation:** Eggs laid at 2-day intervals. Incubation by female alone, beginning with first egg. 26–36 days. **Nestling:** Altricial and downy. Down sparse, short, and soft; buffish-white on upperparts, white on underparts, extending down to claws. **Nestling period:** Young hatch at *c.* 1-day intervals and vary in size. The female broods the young for the first 3 weeks. Young leave nest at *c.* 30–36 days, occasionally longer.

Northern Saw-whet Owl (Aegolius acadicus)   Plate 49

Breeds in conifer or deciduous woodland, often in swampy areas. Nest usually in an old woodpecker hole, less often in a natural cavity. Occasionally will use nest-boxes. 14–60 ft. up. **Nest:** An unlined cavity, or material from old nests of other birds or mammals already present. **Breeding season:** Begins mid-March to mid-April. Usually ends by late June. **Eggs:** Usually 5–6, sometimes 4–7. Elliptical to short subelliptical. Smooth and non-glossy or slightly glossy. White. 30×25 mm. **Incubation:** Eggs laid at 1–3-day intervals. Incubation by female alone, probably beginning with the second egg. 26–28 days. **Nestling:** Altricial and downy. Down sparse and white. When eyes open, irides are brown. **Nestling period:** Young hatch at intervals, varying in size. Brooded by female; male brings food for first 3 weeks, then both hunt and feed. Eyes open at 8–9 days. Down replaced by downy feathers during second to fourth week. Leave nest at 27–34 days.

Goatsuckers (Caprimulgidae)

Medium-sized, nocturnal insect-eaters; highly modified with large mouths and weak feet. Ground-nesting, with no modified nest-site. The bird may roll the eggs under it when it settles. Clutches are of two eggs, with partially cryptic coloring, mainly concealed by the daytime brooding of the cryptically colored adults. Young are downy and protectively colored. Both eggs and young may be moved within the vicinity of the nest-site. The nestlings hatch with their eyes open. The young take food directly from the bills of the parents, seizing these in their own.

Lesser Nighthawk (Chordeiles acutipennis)   Plate 51

Breeds in open areas, such as deserts, dry washes, rocky areas, and scrubland. Nest on bare ground in sandy or gravelly site, though occasionally on roofs. **Nest:** No material accumulated. Nest on a bare open site. Eggs may be rolled a little distance, or young led to a new site, if frequently disturbed. **Breeding season:** Begins mid-April. Single-brooded. **Eggs:** 2. Long subelliptical to almost elliptical. White, creamy or faintly buff; very heavily marked with overall small speckling, spotting, or freckling of pale gray and dull dark brown or olive-brown, or occasionally whitish with pale gray mottling. 27 × 20 mm. **Incubation:** By female only. 18–19 days. **Nestling:** Semi-precocial and downy. Upperparts and head mottled in buff and brown. Underside buff, paler on mid-breast and belly. **Nestling period:** Young tended by both parents. Hatch at 24-hour interval. Can walk towards parents from soon after hatching. Well feathered at 12 days. Food regurgitated into bills of young by pumping movements. Young fly at c. 3 weeks.

Common Nighthawk (*Chordeiles minor*)   Figure 64, Plates 15, 51

Breeds in open areas, forest clearings, burnt-over areas, cultivation, barren rock, gravel, or beaches. Nest on bare ground, infrequently on stumps. Also nests on flat, graveled roofs of buildings.

Nest: No material accumulated. Nest is on a bare site. **Breeding season:** Begins late March to early April in south, to late May or early June in north. Single-brooded. **Eggs:** Usually 2. Long subelliptical to almost elliptical. Smooth and moderately glossy. Pale creamy-white to creamy; very heavily speckled, spotted, or freckled with pale gray or purplish-gray and dark olive-brown. Markings vary from mainly pale gray with sparse brown flecking to heavy overall brown mottling. 30 × 22 mm. **Incubation:** Eggs laid at 1-day interval. Incubation by female alone with male nearby. Beginning with first egg. 19 days. **Nestling:** Semi-precocial and downy. Down pale gray above, darker on chin, mid-throat and malar stripe. Upperparts and head mottled and marbled in pale and dark gray, with olive-buff tint on upper back and nape, and buff tint around base of bill. Bill pale gray at hatching, becoming darker gray. Legs and feet dull brown. **Nestling period:** Young tended by both parents; all brooding by female, and male bringing food. Feathers replace down during 10–20 days. Young begin making short flights at 23 days, begin feeding themselves at 25 days. Independent at c. 30 days.

Figure 64. Common Nighthawk: no nest materials; eggs laid on bare ground.

Antillean Nighthawk (*Chordeiles gundlachii*)

Breeds in Florida Keys and extreme southeast mainland of Florida, in open areas. Nest on the ground.

Nest: No material is added, nest on a bare site. **Breeding season:** Mid-April to mid-August. **Eggs:** Usually 1, sometimes 2. Long subelliptical to almost elliptical. Smooth and moderately glossy. Pale creamy-white to creamy; lightly speckled with medium gray to brownish. Paler and lighter marked than Common Nighthawk. 29 × 21 mm. **Incubation:** Begins with first egg. 20 days. **Nestling:** Semi-precocial and downy. Similar to Common Nighthawk, but with finer, more dispersed, paler gray to sooty gray markings interspersed with creamy to grayish-buff areas. **Nestling period:** Young tended by both parents.

Pauraque (*Nyctidromus albicollis*)   Plates 15, 51

Breeds in open woodlands, forest edge, and scrub on more level areas in southern Texas. Nest in the open on a bare site, usually at the foot of a low bush, sometimes partly hidden by it.

Nest: No material accumulated. Nest on bare ground. **Breeding season:** Begins early March. Single-brooded. **Eggs:** 2. Long elliptical to long subelliptical. Smooth, non-glossy, or slightly glossy. Pale pinkish-buff, variably but often heavily marked with specks, spots, or small irregular blotches in pale lilac, light reddish-brown, or light brown. 30 × 22 mm. **Incubation:** By both sexes. Period not recorded. **Nestling:** Semi-precocial and downy. Down long and soft. Forehead, crown and nape pinkish-buff; lores to ear-coverts brown. Back and rump brown with pinkish-buff band down middle. Chin and throat pale pinkish-cinnamon. Underparts pinkish-buff. **Nestling period:** Young tended by both adults. Adults feed young by inserting narrow tip of bill into the nestling gape and regurgitating insects from the parent's throat. Young can leave nest-site by hopping after parents at 2–3 days.

Common Poorwill (*Phalaenoptilus nuttallii*)   Plate 51

Breeds in open areas, on prairies, flats, or hillsides, or in scrub or scattered brush of semi-arid regions. Nest-site a bare open area, rock, gravel, or bare earth; usually shaded from strong sunlight by a bush or tuft of herbage.

Nest: No material accumulated, the site usually bare of herbage. **Breeding season:** Late March in south to late May in north. Usually ends by early September. Often double-brooded. **Eggs:** 2. Long elliptical to subelliptical. Smooth and slightly glossy. White or creamy-white with faint pink tint, unmarked or with a few faint small markings. 26 × 20 mm. **Incubation:** By both sexes, beginning with first egg. 20–21 days. **Nestling:** Semi-precocial and downy. Down warm buff, paler on underside. Bill black; feet gray-brown. **Nestling period:** Tended by both. Adults may move young frequently during nesting period. Fly at *c.* 20–23 days.

Chuck-will's-widow (*Caprimulgus carolinensis*)   Plate 51

Breeds in woodland, particularly mixed oak and pine woods. No nest is built and eggs are laid on the leaves or pine needles of open ground under the trees.

Nest: No material is accumulated. Eggs or young may be gradually moved from site. **Breeding season:** Begins early March in south to mid-May in north. Single-brooded but lost clutches are replaced. **Eggs:** 2. Elliptical or subelliptical. Smooth and moderately glossy. White, cream, or pinkish, mottled, blotched, and spotted with large areas of pale gray or purple, often faint; and with, unusually, sparser markings in dark or pale brown. 36 × 26 mm. **Incubation:** By both? Begins with first egg. 20 days. **Nestling:** Semi-precocial and downy. Down long and soft. Tawny-brown on the back and yellowish-tawny to yellowish-buff on the head and underside, becoming paler on throat and belly. Bill and gape grayish. **Nestling period:** Young have eyes open, but usually kept half-shut during day; and are active from first, moving in short hops if necessary. Can fly 50–150 ft. at 17 days. Cared for by female.

Buff-collared Nightjar (Caprimulgus ridgwayi)   Plate 51
Breeds uncommonly in rocky hillsides with fairly open stands of juniper and mesquite, and rocky canyon floors in desert and arid areas of southeast Arizona and southwest New Mexico. Nest on the ground.
Nest: No material accumulated, nesting among leaf-litter. **Breeding season:** Late May to mid-June. **Eggs:** 2. Elliptical to subelliptical. Smooth and slightly glossy. White or creamy-white with pale gray and brownish blotches. 27 × 20 mm. **Incubation:** Little information. Mostly by female? **Nestling:** No information. **Nestling period:** No information.

Whip-poor-will (Caprimulgus vociferus)   Plates 15, 51
Breeds in drier, more open woodlands, or near woodland edge. No nest is built. Eggs are laid on the ground in an open site under trees or under a bush, usually on a bed of dead leaves.
Nest: No material is accumulated. The movements of the birds may produce a slight hollow. **Breeding season:** Begins early May. Occasionally 2 broods. **Eggs:** 2. Long elliptical to subelliptical. Smooth and slightly glossy. White or creamy-white; with spots or small blotches of pale dull gray scattered overall, and occasional larger darker blotches and small spots and dots of warm brown. Rarely unmarked. 29 × 21 mm. **Incubation:** By female with occasional help from male. 17–20 days. **Nestling:** Semi-precocial and downy. Down long, soft, and silky. Cinnamon-buff on the back, pinkish-cinnamon on the breast, and light pinkish-cinnamon on head and underside. **Nestling period:** Young tended mainly by female with the male bringing food at night. Young are active from an early stage and will leave nest and crouch if disturbed. Fly at 14–20 days. Male will assume care of brood if female begins second clutch.

Swifts (Apodidae)

Small, insect-eating birds adapted for catching insects in the air. The bill is broad with a wide gape, and the legs are reduced since swifts rarely settle except at nestsites. Nest material is difficult to collect and is scanty. The nest is frequently glued together and to the site with a copious salivary secretion which hardens. Eggs are white and elongated. Young are fed directly with insects brought back by the parents in a pouch below the tongue.

Black Swift (Cypseloides niger)   Figure 65, Plate 52
Breeds in areas with cliff faces, on coasts or inland in canyons. Nests are in sheltered crevices or ledges under overhangs, but usually in a moist situation near some source of seepage, or by or behind a waterfall; or on a cliff face over a river or deep pool. Often 20–45 ft. up. Pairs nest in close proximity in a colony where conditions allow.
Nest: A small rounded cup of moss, fern or other plant material, with some mud but apparently no saliva, sometimes built up on a small projection. 3–8 in. across, 3 in. deep. **Breeding season:** Sometimes begins in May, but usually mid-June – September. Single-brooded. **Eggs:** Only 1. Long subelliptical or long oval. Smooth and non-glossy. White. 29 × 19 mm. **Incubation:** By both. 24–27 days. **Nestling:** Altricial. Naked when first hatched with bluish-black skin, eyes closed. Later covered with

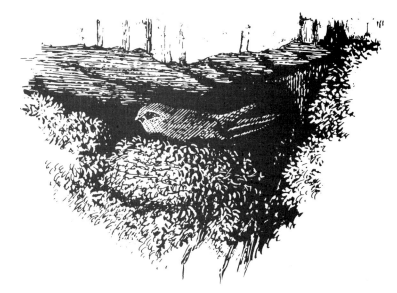

Figure 65. Black Swift: c. 3–8 in. across at wall; often on cliff wall or behind waterfall.

long soft blackish-brown down. **Nestling period:** Tended by both adults. Young fed at infrequent intervals, mainly at dawn and dusk. Young near fledging frequently exercise wings while clinging to nest. Fly at 45–49 days.

Chimney Swift (*Chaetura pelagica*)   Figure 66, Plates 15, 52

Breeds over a wide area where suitable sites are present. Nests are inside chimneys, in open well shafts, in open silos, on the inside of hollow trees, or exceptionally inside buildings. The nest is stuck to a vertical surface within a shaft, from just below the top aperture to 4–5 ft. above the bottom. One or two additional adults may help a nesting pair. May nest in colonies.

Nest: The nest is a shallow half-cup of short dead twigs broken off by the birds in flight and glued together and to the wall by saliva. There is no lining. Built by both sexes. It is 4 in. across where attached to wall. **Breeding season:** Begins mid-May. Single-brooded. **Eggs:** Usually 4–5, sometimes 3–6. Long subelliptical to long elliptical, blunt-ended at times. Smooth and moderately glossy. White. 20×13 mm. **Incubation:** By both sexes and any helpers. 19 days. **Nestling:** Altricial. Naked at hatching, later covered with the dark spine-like quills of the first plumage. Bill gray. Mouth pink. No gape flanges. **Nestling period:** Young tended by both adults and any helpers. Adults bring insects in throat pouch and disgorge directly into mouths of young. Young can climb and move from hatching onwards, but eyes not open until 14 days. May leave nest and cling to, and climb on, walls at 19 days, fly at 24–26 days, leave nest at 28 days.

Vaux's Swift (*Chaetura vauxi*)

Breeds where suitable sites are present in forested regions. Nests on the insides of hollow trees, or tree-stumps, less frequently in chimneys, in woodpecker holes, or inside buildings. Nest placed relatively low, near the bottom of a shaft or cavity (usually 6 in. to 6 ft. from the bottom, sometimes to 20 ft. up).

Figure 66. Chimney Swift: c. 4 in. across at chimney wall.

Nest: A small, narrow half-cup or hammock of dry twigs and conifer needles, glued together and lined with needles. **Breeding season:** Begins early May. Usually ends by late August. Single-brooded. **Eggs:** Usually 4–7, sometimes 3. Long oval to long sub-elliptical. Smooth and non-glossy. White or creamy-white. 18 × 12 mm. **Incubation:** By both sexes. 18–20 days. **Nestling:** Altricial. Naked at hatching, later covered with spine-like quills of first plumage. **Nestling period:** Young tended by both parents. Small young may starve in large broods. Young leave nest for wall that nest is built on at 20–21 days, but may not fly freely for an additional 7 days.

White-throated Swift (Aeronautes saxatalis)
Breeds on cliffs of mountain canyons, rugged foothills, and on sea-coasts where steep cliffs are present. Nests are in rock cracks and crevices; and exceptionally in holes of Rough-winged Swallows, or crevices in buildings. At heights of 10–195 ft. above the base of the structure. Breeds in small colonies.
Nest: Rounded cup of feathers, plant down, grass, bark, or wool, or any material that can be snatched from the air; glued together and to site. Shape may be modified in confined spaces. **Breeding season:** Begins early May. **Eggs:** Usually 4–5, sometimes 3–6. Long oval, long subelliptical or long elliptical. Smooth and non-glossy. White to creamy-white. 21 × 14 mm. **Incubation:** No information. **Nestling:** Altricial and naked. **Nestling period:** No information.

Hummingbirds (Trochilidae)

Tiny birds with hovering flight, taking nectar from flowers, and insects, on the wing. Nest a minute cup on a raised site, usually the upper surface of a plant stem or a twig. Made mainly of plant down and similar fine material, bound together and supported by spiders' webs. Web may be wound round structure by bird in flight. At times sites are re-used, several nests being built, one on the other, to produce an abnormally tall structure. Nest-building, incubation, and care of young are by female alone. Laying and incubation may begin before nest-lining is complete. Eggs white, elongated, and very large for the size of the bird. Incubation period long and variable. Young hatch with very little down. They have very short bills at first. Female inserts bill deep into mouth and throat of young and regurgitates food. Young may sit on nest edge and exercise wings 2–3 days before leaving nest.

Broad-billed Hummingbird (*Cynanthus latirostris*)
Breeds usually in smaller trees and shrubs along streams in wooded mountain canyons in southeast Arizona, southwest New Mexico, and southwest Texas. Nest built on to drooping or horizontal twig or stem, at times overhanging a stream. At heights of 4–12 ft.
Nest: A cup of stems, grasses, shreds of bark, and parts of dry leaves, bound together with spiders' webs and lined with white down. Sometimes decorated on the outside with bark, small dead leaves, or dry tree-blossoms, but not lichens. **Breeding season:** Mid-April to early August. Double-brooded. **Eggs:** Usually 2. Long elliptical to long subelliptical. Smooth and non-glossy. White. 13×8 mm. **Incubation:** No information. **Nestling:** Altricial and naked. **Nestling period:** No information.

White-eared Hummingbird (*Hylocharis leucotis*)　　　　　Figure 67
A rare breeder in southeast Arizona in mountain areas, in open woodland or clearings on mountainsides with shrubby growth. Nest built in fork of slender twigs of shrubs. At heights of 4–25 ft. (There have been reports from Mexico of nests – made mostly of moss – in woodlands on banks below 5 ft.)
Nest: A deep rounded cup, usually built almost entirely of plant down, bound with spiders' webs and with the outside decorated with flakes of lichens and occasionally odd tree-blossoms or green mosses. *c.* $1\frac{3}{4}$–2 in. diameter and $1\frac{1}{2}$–2$\frac{3}{4}$ in. deep.

Figure 67. White-eared Hummingbird: *c.* $1\frac{3}{4}$–2 in. across; built almost entirely of plant down.

Internal cup about 1 in. across and $1\frac{1}{8}$ in. deep. **Breeding season:** Probably April through May. **Eggs:** Usually 2. Long elliptical to long subelliptical. Smooth and non-glossy. White. 12 × 8 mm. **Incubation:** By female alone. 14–16 days. **Nestling:** Altricial. Naked skin black. Line of sparse, short down along mid-back. **Nestling period:** Young tended by female alone. Pin feathers sprout at 7–8 days. Eyes open at 9–10 days and feathers begin to break from sheath. Wing and tail feathers break out at 16 and 18 days. Young brooded until *c.* 18 days. Leave nest at 23–26 days. A young one seen fed by female at 40 days, although feeding itself by then.

Berylline Hummingbird (*Amazilia beryllina*)
A rare breeder in mountains of southeast Arizona. Nest in a variety of locations, from low shrubs and seed stalks to higher oaks, sycamores, and pines, usually 17–25 ft. up, but may be up to 45 ft. above the ground.
Nest: A cup covered with lichens and thin grasses, attached with spider webbing on the bottom, with often a 'streamer' of a few blades of grasses hanging below. **Breeding season:** Begins July–August. Double-brooded. **Eggs:** 2. Long elliptical to long subelliptical. White. 13 × 9 mm. **Incubation:** No information. **Nestling:** No information. **Nestling period:** Leave nest at *c.* 20 days.

Buff-bellied Hummingbird (*Amazilia yucatanensis*)
Breeds in lowland on woodland edge or in shrubby thickets in south Texas. Nest in a small tree or shrub, usually by open space. The nest usually saddles a small horizontal or drooping twig, 3–8 ft. up.
Nest: A cup of plant and bark fibers, tiny leaves, and lichens, mixed with plant down, bound together with spiders' webs, lined with fine plant down; the outside decorated with shreds of bark, lichen flakes, and dry tree-blossoms. **Breeding season:** April to mid-August. **Eggs:** Usually 2. Long elliptical to long subelliptical. Smooth and non-glossy. White. 13 × 9 mm. **Incubation:** No information. **Nestling:** Altricial and naked. **Nestling period:** No information.

Violet-crowned Hummingbird (*Amasilia violiceps*)
Breeds in mountain areas, foothills, in trees (usually sycamores) in canyons and streamsides in extreme southeast Arizona and southwest New Mexico. Nest on a high horizontal branch, near the extreme tip (and usually with a large overhanging leaf for a roof), in deciduous trees, 25–40 ft. up, but sometimes as low as 6 ft.
Nest: A whitish cup of cottony plant down, decorated on outside with lichens. **Breeding season:** July. Double-brooded? **Eggs:** 2. Long elliptical to long subelliptical. White. 14 × 9 mm. **Incubation:** No information. **Nestling:** No information. **Nestling period:** No information.

Blue-throated Hummingbird (*Lampornis clemenciae*)
Breeds in mountain regions, frequently in rocky canyons in southern Arizona, southern New Mexico, and southwest Texas. Nest in a twig fork, usually fairly low in a shrub, or on a weed stem, or fastened to a vine on a steep slope, often overhanging water; sometimes on man-made structures, under eaves, on rafters, or placed on nail or wire. 4–14 ft. up.
Nest: A cup of fine moss, tree-blossoms and small stems, firmly and smoothly bound together with down and spiders' webs. Inner cup small and deep. *c.* $2\frac{3}{4}$ in. across by 3 in. deep, inner cup $1\frac{1}{4}$ in. across by $\frac{3}{4}$ in. deep. **Breeding season:** Begins mid-May. Double-brooded. **Eggs:** Usually 2. Long elliptical to long subelliptical. Smooth and non-glossy. White. 15 × 10 mm. **Incubation:** By female. 17–18 days. **Nestling:** Altricial and naked. **Nestling period:** Leave nest at 24–29 days.

Magnificent Hummingbird (*Eugenes fulgens*)

Breeds in mountain regions, usually in trees (either deciduous or coniferous) along streams in south Arizona, southwest New Mexico, and west Texas. Nest in a tree, often higher than those of other hummingbirds. Nest saddles a horizontal branch or twig, often overhanging a stream. 10–40 ft. up.
Nest: A cup, like a Ruby-throated Hummingbird nest, made of moss or plant fibers, bound together with spiders' webs, lined with plant down and covered outside with lichen flakes. *c.* $2\frac{1}{2}$ in. diameter by 2 in. deep, with cup $1\frac{1}{2}$ in. across and $1\frac{1}{4}$ in. deep. **Breeding season:** Usually begins by early May and ends by mid-September. **Eggs:** Usually 2. Long elliptical to long subelliptical. Smooth and non-glossy. White. 15×10 mm. **Incubation:** By female. *c.* 16 days. **Nestling:** Altricial. Not described. **Nestling period:** Little information. Nest departure estimated at *c.* 25 days.

Lucifer Hummingbird (*Calothorax lucifer*)

Breeds locally in arid canyons, dry washes, and rocky hillsides in the foothills of the Chisos Mountains of western Texas and uncommonly in southwestern New Mexico and southeastern Arizona. Nest usually fairly low, on cholla cactus stem, leafy ocotillo, or agaves, 4–8 ft. up.
Nest: A cup of vegetable fibers, bud-scales, tree-blossoms and lichen, mixed with plant down, bound together with spiders' webs and fine fibers, lined with plant down, and sometimes a few feathers, and often decorated with whitish lichen flakes or small leaves on the outside. **Breeding season:** Begins early April. Usually ends early August. Often double-brooded. **Eggs:** Usually 2. Long elliptical to long subelliptical. Smooth and non-glossy. White. 13×10 mm. **Incubation:** By female. 15–16 days. **Nestling:** Altricial and downy. Down very sparse, along mid-back only. **Nestling period:** Young tended by female only. Eyes open at 4–5 days. Feathered by *c.* 10 days. Leave nest at 20–23 days. Fed by female for another two weeks.

Ruby-throated Hummingbird (*Archilochus colubris*)   Figure 68, Plates 15, 51

Breeds over a wide variety of wooded habitats. Nest on a tree or shrub, usually on a fork of a downward sloping twig. Usually in site near, and sometimes over, water. 5–50 ft. up; usually 10–20 ft.
Nest: A neat cup saddling the nest-site. Of small fragments of plant material with a thick lining of down; bound together smoothly and tightly with spiders' webs and covered on the outside with flakes of lichens. Built by female alone in about 5 days. Outside diameter $1–1\frac{3}{4}$ in., inside diameter $\frac{3}{4}–1$ in., $\frac{3}{4}$ in. deep, 1–2 in. high. **Breeding season:** Begins late March in south to early June in north of range. 2, occasionally 3 broods a season. **Eggs:** Usually 2. Long subelliptical to long elliptical. Smooth and non-glossy. White. 13×8 mm. **Incubation:** By female only. 16 days. **Nestling:** Altricial. Nearly naked at first. Slate-blue skin, and line of yellowish down along back. Bill short and yellow. **Nestling period:** Young tended by female. Eyes open at *c.* 1 week; young leave nest at *c.* 19 days.

Black-chinned Hummingbird (*Archilochus alexandri*)   Plate 51

Breeds in drier mountain areas, in trees and shrubs along watercourses and canyons. Nest saddling a downward slanting small branch or twig; in shrubby growth 4–10 ft. up; occasionally in a creeper or on tall herbage plants; exceptionally in a tree at a greater height or on supports around buildings.
Nest: A deep rounded cup, the edge slightly incurved. Made almost entirely of plant down with occasional fragments of other material; firmly bound and felted together with spiders' webs. Colors usually shades of buff to whitish. Expands elastically as young grow. Built by female, taking several days. **Breeding season:** Begins early

Figure 68. Ruby-throated Hummingbird: *c.* 1–1¾ in. across; usually in twig fork on a downward pointing branch.

April. 2, possibly 3 broods a season. **Eggs:** Usually 2, rarely 1 or 3. Long elliptical to long subelliptical. Smooth and non-glossy. White. 13 × 8 mm. **Incubation:** By female only. 13–16 days. **Nestling:** Altricial and almost naked. **Nestling period:** Young tended by female alone. Leave nest at 21 days.

Anna's Hummingbird (*Calypte anna*)   Figure 69, Plate 51
Widely distributed in chaparral, woodlands, suburban gardens, usually in lower and less arid areas than the next species. 2–30 ft. up. Nest in a wide variety of sites, wherever a narrow support for a nest is present.
Nest: A fairly large and well-made cup, mainly of fine stems and plant down, bound with spiders' webs, lined with plant down and feathers, and often ornamented externally with lichen flakes. Egg-laying and incubation may begin before lining and outside are complete. Early nests may take *c.* 30 days to build, later nests can be built in 2 days. **Breeding season:** Begins late December. 2, possibly 3 broods a season. **Eggs:** Usually 2. Long elliptical to long subelliptical. Smooth and non-glossy. White. 13 × 9 mm. **Incubation.** Eggs laid at *c.* 2-day interval. Incubation by female alone. 16–17 days. **Nestling:** Altricial. Skin black. Smoky-gray down along mid-back. Bill short and mouth yellowish. **Nestling period:** Young tended by female only. Eyes open at 5 days. Pin feathers well sprouted at 7 days. Not brooded after 12 days. Leave nest at 25–26 days.

Costa's Hummingbird (*Calypte costae*)   Plate 51
Breeds in desert or semi-arid areas. Nest in a variety of sites, usually near water and where shrubs and trees are present. Usually in fairly open site, on a dead yucca stalk, or on the stem or leaves of tall weeds, or in shrubs or trees, usually near the extremities of twigs. Usually 4–5 ft. up, occasionally 1–9 ft. up. A number of pairs may nest close together.

Figure 69. Anna's Hummingbird: c. 1½ in. across; fairly large nest for a hummingbird.

Nest: A small cup very variable in size and material. A mixture of pieces of down, fiber, tree-flowers, bud-scales, lichen fragments, leaves, feathers, etc., bound together with fine fibers and spiders' webs. Lined with plant down and sometimes small feathers. Female continues building up shallow nest during incubation. Color of exterior distinctively gray. Outside dimensions 1½–2 in. across, 1¼–1½ in. high. **Breeding season:** Begins mid-March. Single-brooded. **Eggs:** Usually 2. Long elliptical to long subelliptical. Smooth and non-glossy. White. 12 × 8 mm. **Incubation:** By female only. 15–18 days. **Nestling:** Altricial and with skin black above and brownish below; with a double line of yellow down filaments along mid-back. Down spreads within a few days over back, wings and top of head. Bill yellowish and triangular. **Nestling period:** Young tended by female only. Pin-feathers appear at 6 days; well-feathered at 12 days. On last few days young perch on nest edge and exercise wings. Leave nest at 20–23 days.

Calliope Hummingbird (*Stellula calliope*)

Breeds on coniferous mountains, mountain meadows, and wooded hillsides. Nest usually on a horizontal or drooping twig or twig-fork of a conifer, near the end of a low branch and often partly hidden by a branch above. Sometimes built on pine cone. 2–75 ft. up. New nests may be built on old ones.

Nest: A cup of fine bark, fibers, mosses, and pine needles, mixed with plant down and bound with spiders' webs, the cavity thickly lined with down, and the outside covered with lichen flakes. c. 1½–1¼ in. diameter by ⅞ in. high, cup c. 1⅛–1⅞ in. across and ⅞ in. deep. **Breeding season:** Begins mid-May. Usually ends by early August. Probably single-brooded. **Eggs:** Usually 2. Long elliptical to long subelliptical. Smooth and non-glossy. White. 12 × 8 mm. **Incubation:** By female alone. 15–16 days. **Nestling:** Altricial. No description. **Nestling period:** Young tended by female only. Brooded and fed for 11–12 days, then only fed until young leave nest at 21–23 days.

Broad-tailed Hummingbird (*Selasphorus platycercus*)   Plate 51

Breeds in forested mountain regions, often by meadows, brushy slopes, or even gardens. Nest built on a low horizontal twig of a tree or shrub, often overhanging a stream. 3–30 ft. up, but often low.

Nest: A cup of variable plant material; fibers, rootlets, moss, and plant down, lined with plant down and bound with spiders' webs and fine fibers, the outside decorated with flakes of lichen or more rarely shreds of bark or fibers. Built by female over 4–5 days; material added during incubation. **Breeding season:** Begins early May in south to early June in north of range. Usually ends by mid-August. 1, possibly 2 broods a season. **Eggs:** Usually 2. Long elliptical to long subelliptical. Smooth and non-glossy. White. 13 × 9 mm. **Incubation:** By female alone. 14–17 days. **Nestling:** Altricial and dark-skinned. **Nestling period:** First flight at c. 23 days.

Rufous Hummingbird (Selasphorus rufus) Plate 51

Breeds over a wide range of habitats, such as chaparral, coniferous forest, brushy hillsides, and streamsides. Nest in a tree 5–50 ft. up, frequently an old conifer, or in shrub, bush, or creeper, often low down. Tree nests are usually on lower branches. Nest is usually located on a downward drooping twig or on a twig-fork or horizontal stem. A number of Rufous Hummingbirds may nest near each other.

Nest: A cup mainly made of soft cottony plant down, such as willow-seed, covered and built up outside with moss or similar material, bound with spiders' webs and covered on the outside with lichen flakes, or occasionally shreds of bark or fibers, helping to camouflage it. Diameter c. 2 in., c. 1½ in. deep, inner cup c. 1 in. × ⅞ in. deep. **Breeding season:** Begins mid-April. Usually ends by mid-July. 1, possibly 2 broods a season. **Eggs:** Usually 2. Long elliptical to long sub-elliptical. Smooth and non-glossy. White. 13 × 9 mm. **Incubation:** By female only. 17 days. **Nestling:** Altricial. Skin dark. Mainly naked with a small double line of grayish down along mid-back. **Nestling period:** Young tended by female only. Eyes open at c. 6 days. Nestling down lengthens and pin-feathers show at 6–7 days. Young leave at c. 20 days.

Allen's Hummingbird (Selasphorus sasin)

Breeds in lightly wooded areas, meadows, or thickets, often along shaded streams in coastal fog-shrouded areas. Nest on a tree, often low down, and saddling a twig or branch; on twigs or in twig forks of shrubs or bushes; occasionally on tall weed-stalks, in creepers, or on supports on buildings. At varied heights from 10 in. to 90 ft., but usually fairly low.

Nest: A cup, less deep than those of some other species; of moss, particularly in the bases of the walls, and of plant down, bound with spiders' webs and covered externally with lichen flakes or shreds of bark, pine needles or similar debris from near the site. c. 1¾–1¼ in. external diameter, and c. 1 in. deep, with cavity c. ⅞ in. across by ¾ in. deep. **Breeding season:** Begins early February. Double-brooded. **Eggs:** Usually 2. Long elliptical to long subelliptical. Smooth and non-glossy. White. 13 × 9 mm. **Incubation:** Eggs usually laid on alternate days. Incubation by female alone, beginning with first egg. 16–22 days. **Nestling:** Altricial and downy. Sparse down along mid-back only. Skin dark. Mouth bright orange-yellow. Bill short, fleshy-yellow. **Nestling period:** Young tended by female alone. Leave nest at 22 days.

Trogons (Trogonidae)

Elegant Trogon (Trogon elegans) Plates 14, 52

Found in pinyon, juniper and oak woodlands, often nesting in sycamores in mountain canyons in southeast Arizona. Nest in a natural cavity in a tree, or in an old woodpecker (Northern Flicker) hole, 12–40 ft. up.

Nest: A bare cavity, but later regurgitated seeds may be present. Cavities average 5½ in. wide, by 19 in. (in sycamore) or 12 in. (in oak or pine) deep. **Breeding season:**

Late April to late June, though sometimes into late August. Single-brooded, though may occasionally replace lost clutch. *Eggs:* Usually 2, uncommonly 3, rarely 4. Short to very short subelliptical. Smooth and non-glossy. Dull white or bluish-white. 28 × 23 mm. *Incubation:* By both sexes, with female probably incubating through the night. 17–22 days. *Nestling:* Altricial and naked. Pink skin. Eyes closed at first. Heel-joint of leg with pad of projecting papillae to protect it from abrasion. Two toes point backwards from the first. *Nestling period:* Young tended by both parents. No nest sanitation appears to occur. During first week all feathers grow as sheathed pin-feathers. Eyes open at *c.* 1 week and feathers break from sheaths. Young leave nest at 20–23 days (though also reported as 14–20 days). Stay with parents 1–2 months and are fed by both.

Eared Trogon (*Euptilotis neoxenus*)

Found rarely in conifer or mixed conifer–oak dominated mountain canyons, at *c.* 6700 ft. in southeast Arizona. Nest in a natural cavity in a tree, or in an old wood-pecker hole, *c.* 35 ft. up.
Nest: A bare cavity. Cavity approximately $5\frac{1}{2}$ in. wide by 11 in. deep. *Breeding season:* Mid-July to mid-August, though sometimes later. Related to arrival of rainy season. *Eggs:* Usually 2. No description. *Incubation:* By both? Estimated at 18 days. *Nestling:* Altricial and naked? At two weeks, covered with black and yellow down. *Nestling period:* Little information. Tended by both parents.

Kingfishers (*Alcedinidae*)

Small to medium, fast-flying predatory birds, diving for food or snatching it up. Bill well developed, feet small and weak. Nest made by tunnelling with the bill; loose earth kicked out backwards with feet. Both sexes dig. No nest but debris from food castings may line cavity. Eggs white, nearly spherical. Young naked. Huddled together at first. No nest sanitation and although feces are ejected for some distance by young the nest becomes foul before the young leave. All food brought to young is turned so that the creature is presented head first for ease in swallowing. After leaving the nest young remain together nearby and are fed by parents for some time afterwards.

Ringed Kingfisher (*Ceryle torquata*)

Breeds along deeper and smoother lowland streams, and shores of lakes, dams, and lagoons, in more open sites in the lower Rio Grande Valley of Texas. Nest a burrow in a steep earth or sand bank. Usually about 4 ft. from the top of the bank face, over-looking the water or at a little distance from it.
Nest: A burrow 5–$8\frac{1}{2}$ ft. long, *c.* 4 in. high and 6 in. across, sloping upwards at the entrance, then more level. An enlarged brood chamber at the end is unlined. Excavated by both. *Breeding season:* March–May. *Eggs:* Usually 4, sometimes 3–5. Elliptical to short subelliptical. Smooth and glossy. White. 44 × 34 mm. *Incubation:* By both sexes. Each incubating for 24 hours at a time. *c.* 22 days. *Nestling:* Altricial and naked. Skin pink and transparent. Lower mandible projects beyond blackish upper mandible. A callus pad on each leg joint is covered with small papillae. Skin rapidly covered by pin-feathers in sheath. *Nestling period:* Young tended by both adults. Bill mandibles of equal length by 14 days and feather sheaths begin to break. Leaves nest at 33–38 days. At 10 days post-fledging young catch live food and are forced from parental territory.

Belted Kingfisher (*Ceryle alcyon*)   Plates 15, 52
Breeds by water – lakes, rivers, streams, or sometimes sea-coast. Nest a burrow in a bank, usually near fresh water but occasionally at some distance when other sites are not available. Usually 1–3 ft. from the top of the bank or cliff. Exceptionally may nest in hole on shallow earth slope, or in natural cavity in a tree.
Nest: Burrow usually slopes upwards from entrance. 3–6 ft. long, occasionally up to 15 ft. long, $3\frac{1}{2}$–4 in. wide, 3–$3\frac{1}{2}$ in. high. Egg chamber *c.* 10–12 in. diameter, 6–7 in. high. Excavated by both sexes in 3 days to 3 weeks. Nest hollow usually bare when eggs are laid, but becomes lined with fishbones and insect remains. **Breeding season:** Begins early April to early May. Usually ends by mid-July. Single-brooded but lost clutch may be replaced in new burrow. **Eggs:** Usually 6–8, sometimes 5–14. Elliptical to short subelliptical. Smooth and glossy. White. 34×27 mm. **Incubation:** By both sexes. *c.* 23–24 days. **Nestling:** Altricial and naked. Skin reddish. Feathers grow simultaneously in sheath, covering bird. Bill blackish. Mouth pink. No gape flanges. **Nestling period:** Young tended by both parents. Eyes open at *c.* 2 weeks. Feather quills begin to appear in first week. Sheaths break, freeing feathers, at 17–18 days. Young leave nest at 30–35 days.

Green Kingfisher (*Chloroceryle americana*)   Plate 52
Breeds by fresh water in south and central Texas, and less commonly in southeast Arizona. Nest in a vertical bank alongside river or stream; usually 6–8 ft. up.
Nest: A burrow, *c.* 2–3 ft. long, 2 in. high by $2\frac{1}{4}$ in. wide. Small chamber at end and eggs laid on bare ground, later covered with cast-up fishbones and insect remains. **Breeding season:** May begin as early as late February, and into late June. **Eggs:** Usually 4–5, sometimes 3–6. Elliptical to short subelliptical. Smooth and glossy. White. 24×19 mm. **Incubation:** By both sexes. 19–21 days. **Nestling:** Altricial and naked. Skin pink. Small young have typical callosities on heels, and lower mandible longer than upper. **Nestling period:** Young tended by both parents. Can fly at *c.* 26 days. Independent of parents in an additional 4 weeks.

Woodpeckers (*Picidae*)

Small to medium birds, gaining most of their food by climbing tree-trunks and branches. Nest bored in a hole in a tree, usually by both birds, and often in fairly firm wood. Similar holes may be made outside breeding season for roosting. A new hole is normally made each year. Eggs very smooth, white and rounded, but may become stained in damp nest cavities. Cavities are unlined and nestlings have a hard rough pad on the back of the leg joint, and rest and move on the whole tarsus when in the nest. On small young there is a sensitive swollen lump at the base of the lower mandible, on either side, and the adults touch this to induce the young to beg for food. The young are mainly fed on regurgitated food. They often keep up a harsh noise which may betray the nests.

Lewis's Woodpecker (*Melanerpes lewis*)   Plate 52
Breeds on forest edge (especially Ponderosa Pine), or in groves and scattered trees. Nest-hole in a tree-trunk, in large dead stub, or in tree limb; in deciduous or coniferous tree. 6–100 ft. up. Regularly uses old nest sites and natural cavities. Sometimes several pairs have holes in one tree.
Nest: Cavity usually bored in dead wood. Entrance hole 2–$2\frac{1}{2}$ in. diameter, usually circular. Cavity up to 30 in. deep, *c.* 4 in. across. **Breeding season:** Begins mid-April in south to late May in north of range. Ends usually in July. **Eggs:** Usually 6–7, sometimes 5–9. Elliptical to subelliptical or oval. Variable in shape. Smooth and non-

glossy. White. 26×20 mm. **Incubation:** By both sexes, with male at night and both alternating during the day? 12–14 days. **Nestling:** Altricial and naked. **Nestling period:** Young tended by both parents. Leave nest at 31 days. Each parent accompanies part of the brood, remaining in the nest vicinity for *c.* 10 days after fledging.

Red-headed Woodpecker (*Melanerpes erythrocephalus*)   Plate 52
Breeds in open and cultivated country with scattered trees. Nest-hole in a tree-trunk, large limb, or stump; occasionally in telegraph pole, fence post or roof of house. Cavity may be re-used for second brood. Nest from almost ground level to 80 ft. up.
Nest: Cavity usually bored in dead wood. Entrance hole $1\frac{3}{4}$ in. diameter. Cavity 8–14 in. deep, $3–4\frac{1}{2}$ in. across. Excavated by both sexes. **Breeding season:** Begins late April in south to mid-May in north of range. Single- or double-brooded, and lost clutches are replaced. Usually ends in August. **Eggs:** Usually 5, sometimes 4–8. Subelliptical, oval, or elliptical. Smooth and moderately glossy. White. 25×19 mm. **Incubation:** Eggs laid at daily intervals. Incubation by both adults, beginning before completion of clutch. 12–14 days. **Nestling:** Altricial and naked. **Nestling period:** Young tended by both parents. Hatch over a period, and differ in size. Leave at 27 days. Remain near nest-site but may be driven away if second brood is raised.

Acorn Woodpecker (*Melanerpes formicivorus*)   Plate 52
Breeds in open woodland or partly wooded areas, usually where oaks are present. Nest-hole in tree-trunk or larger limb, in large dead stubs, sometimes in telegraph poles, or power poles. 5–25 ft. up. Birds breed communally, in groups of 2–15 individuals, usually about 6, helping at a single nesting.
Nest: Cavity usually in dead wood. Entrance hole *c.* $1\frac{1}{2}$ in. across. Cavity 8–24 in. deep 4–5 in. diameter. **Breeding season:** Begins early April to early May. Usually ends by mid-September. Sometimes 2, possibly 3, broods. **Eggs:** Usually 4–6, sometimes up to 10. Subelliptical to oval. Smooth and non-glossy or slightly glossy. White. 26×20 mm. **Incubation:** By both sexes and most individuals in group. 11–12 days. **Nestling:** Altricial and naked. **Nestling period:** Young tended by the whole group. Fed on insects brought in the bill. Leave at 31 days, independent 1 month later.

Gila Woodpecker (*Melanerpes uropygialis*)   Figure 70, Plate 52
Breeds in desert areas with cactus, and in river bottoms and canyons with mesquite or riverine woodland in the arid southwest. Nest-hole in a cactus (usually Saguaro) or tree such as cottonwood, willow or mesquite. 15–25 ft. up. Hole may be re-used in subsequent years. Cactus cavities are not suitable for use until the walls dry out.
Nest: Cavity bored in dead wood or live cactus. Entrance hole $2–2\frac{1}{4}$ in. diameter. Cavity 12–20 in. deep, *c.* 7–10 in. across. Made by both sexes. **Breeding season:** Begins in early April. Usually ends in June. Single- or double-brooded. **Eggs:** Usually 3–4, sometimes 5. Oval to long oval, and subelliptical. Smooth and moderately to very glossy. White. 25×19 mm. **Incubation:** By both sexes. 13 days. **Nestling:** Altricial and naked. **Nestling period:** Little information. Young are fed and cared for by adults for a long time after leaving nest.

Golden-fronted Woodpecker (*Melanerpes aurifrons*)   Plate 52
Breeds in semi-arid areas, in mesquite in pure stands or mixed with larger trees in Texas and parts of Oklahoma. Nest-hole in trunk or branch of tree; occasionally in telegraph pole or nest-box. 6–25 ft. up, occasionally lower. Cavities may be re-used in subsequent years.
Nest: Cavity bored in live or dead wood. Cavity *c.* 15 in. deep. Made by both sexes. **Breeding season:** Early March to late July. Double-brooded or rarely treble-brooded.

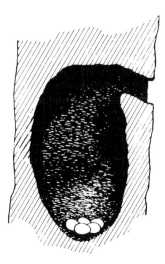

Figure 70. Gila Woodpecker: nest cavity in cross-section of Saguaro; entrance: 2–2¼ in. in diameter; cavity: 12–20 in. deep; 7-10 in. across.

Eggs: Usually 4–5, sometimes up to 7. Subelliptical to oval or elliptical. Smooth and non-glossy or slightly glossy. White. 26 × 20 mm. **Incubation:** By both sexes, beginning with first egg. 13 days. **Nestling:** Altricial and naked. Skin pink. Callus on tarsal joint of leg with prominent papillae for resting on wood. Upper mandible shorter but grows as long as lower by 8 days. **Nestling period:** Young tended by both parents. Eggs hatch over 2 days. Male broods at night while young are small. Eyes open at *c.* 9 days. Feathers grown but in sheath until 16–17 days, opening to full feathering in another 2 days. Young leave at 30 days. Remain with adults for about a month after fledging.

Red-bellied Woodpecker (*Melanerpes carolinus*)   Plate 52
Breeds in a variety of woodland habitats, including moist lowlands, mixed coniferous woods, sheltered groves, and residential areas. Nest-hole in trunk of a variety of trees and stumps; sometimes in telegraph poles or fence posts. 5–40 ft. up, or occasionally up to 80 ft. Occasionally uses old nest-holes of Red-cockaded Woodpecker.
Nest: Cavity bored in dead wood. Entrance hole slightly elliptical, 1–2¼ in. diameter. Cavity 10–12 in. deep, 5–5½ in. across. Excavated by both sexes, though mostly by male. **Breeding season:** Begins early April. Usually ends in August. Double-brooded, rarely treble-brooded. **Eggs:** Usually 4–5, sometimes 3–8. Subelliptical to long oval or elliptical. Smooth and slightly to moderately glossy. White. 25 × 19 mm. **Incubation:** By both sexes. 12–13 days. **Nestling:** Altricial and naked. **Nestling period:** Young tended by both parents. Closely brooded by either parent for first week. Leave nest at 26 days.

Yellow-bellied Sapsucker (*Sphyrapicus varius*)   Plate 52
Breeds in forest, frequently in live trees. Nest-hole in tree-trunk. Usually between 9–45 ft. up, sometimes 5–60 ft. up.
Nest: Gourd-shaped cavity, excavated about 14 in. deep by 5 in. in diameter. Exterior hole 1¼–1½ in. diameter. Chips at bottom. Excavated by both sexes over 2–4 weeks.

Breeding season: Begins late April to May. Single-brooded. **Eggs:** Usually 5–6, sometimes 4–7. Subelliptical to oval. Smooth, dull to slightly glossy. White. 22 × 17 mm. **Incubation:** By both sexes. 12–13 days. **Nestling:** Altricial and naked. **Nestling period:** Young tended by both parents. Fed directly on insects brought in bill. Climb to upper nest for feeding by 18 days, to entrance by 20 days. Leave at 25–29 days. Dependent on parents for *c.* 10 days later.

Red-naped Sapsucker (*Sphyrapicus nuchalis*)
Breeds in forest, mostly in live aspens, sometimes in live larches or dead Engelman Spruce. Usually 10–20 ft. up, but up to 70 ft. up.
Nest: Cavity, about 8 in. deep by 4 in. in diameter. Exterior hole $1\frac{1}{4}$ in. diameter. Excavated mostly by female. **Breeding season:** Begins late April. Usually ends by mid-July. Single-brooded. **Eggs:** Usually 4–5, sometimes 3–7. Subelliptical to oval. Moderately grained, moderately glossy. White. 23 × 17 mm. **Incubation:** By both sexes. 12–13 days. **Nestling:** Altricial and naked. **Nestling period:** Young tended by both parents. Leave at *c.* 27 days. Taught sapsucking upon fledging and dependent on parents for only a short additional period.

Red-breasted Sapsucker (*Sphyrapicus ruber*)
Breeds in coniferous or mixed forest in coastal ranges. Up to 45 ft. up.
Nest: Gourd-shaped cavity, 6–10 in. deep by 4–5 in. wide. Exterior hole $1\frac{1}{4}$–$1\frac{1}{2}$ in. diameter. Lined with chips at bottom. **Breeding season:** Begins May. **Eggs:** Usually 4–5, occasionally 7. Oval to long oval. Slightly to moderately glossy. White. 23 × 17 mm. **Incubation:** By both sexes. 12–14 days. **Nestling:** Altricial and naked. **Nestling period:** Young tended by both parents.

Williamson's Sapsucker (*Sphyrapicus thyroideus*)
Breeds in mountain pine forests or aspen groves. Nest-hole in tree-trunk. 5–60 ft. up. The same tree often used repeatedly over years, with new hole each time.
Nest: Cavity usually in dead wood. Entrance hole $1\frac{1}{2}$ in. diameter. Cavity 8 in. deep, 5 in. across. Excavated by male. **Breeding season:** Begins late May. Usually ends by early August. Single-brooded. **Eggs:** Usually 5–6, sometimes 3–7. Smooth. Slightly glossy. White. 24 × 17 mm. **Incubation:** By both sexes. 13 days. **Nestling:** Altricial and naked. **Nestling period:** Young tended by both parents. Leave nest at *c.* 31 days.

Ladder-backed Woodpecker (*Picoides scalaris*)   Plate 52
Breeds in open woodland of arid areas, in scattered trees, trees along stream bottoms and creeks, and in mesquite. Nest-hole in trunk of a variety of trees, in a telegraph pole or fence post, cactus, or stem of agave or yucca. At *c.* 3–30 ft. up. Usually at 5–15 ft. up.
Nest: Cavity bored in dead wood. Entrance hole *c.* $1\frac{1}{2}$ in. diameter. Cavity 7–10 in. deep. Excavated mainly by male. **Breeding season:** Begins mid-April. Single-brooded? **Eggs:** Usually 4–5, sometimes 2–7. Elliptical to subelliptical. Smooth and glossy. White. 20 × 16 mm. **Incubation:** By both. *c.* 13 days. **Nestling:** Altricial and naked. **Nestling period:** Tended by both.

Nuttall's Woodpecker (*Picoides nuttallii*)   Plate 52
Breeds in live oaks and mixed tree growth near watercourses in California. Nest-hole in a tree-trunk. 2–60 ft. up.
Nest: Cavity usually in dead wood. Entrance hole *c.* $1\frac{1}{2}$ in. diameter. Usually *c.* 12 in. deep by 5 in. across. Excavated mostly by male. **Breeding season:** Begins late March.

Usually ends by June. Single-brooded. **Eggs:** Usually 4–5, sometimes 3–6. Elliptical to subelliptical. Smooth and moderately glossy. White to creamy-white. 22 × 16 mm. **Incubation:** By both sexes. 14 days. **Nestling:** Altricial and naked. **Nestling period:** Young tended by both parents. Fly at 29 days.

Downy Woodpecker (*Picoides pubescens*)   Plate 52

Breeds in open woodland, orchards, parkland and areas with scattered trees. Nest-hole in a branch or stub, often on the underside. *c.* 8–50 ft. up.
Nest: Cavity is in dead wood. Entrance hole 1½ in. diameter. Cavity 8–12 in. deep. Excavated by both sexes in 13–20 days. **Breeding season:** Begins early April in south to late May in north of range. Double-brooded. **Eggs:** Usually 4–5, sometimes 3–6. Subelliptical to oval. Smooth and glossy. White. 19 × 15 mm. **Incubation:** By both sexes, male incubating at night. 12 days. **Nestling:** Altricial and naked. **Nestling period:** Young tended by both parents. Fed directly on food brought in bill. Climb to feed at top of cavity by 9 days, to entrance at 12 days. Leave nest at 20–22 days. Dependent on adults for up to 3 weeks after leaving nest.

Hairy Woodpecker (*Picoides villosus*)   Plate 52

Breeds in mature woodland, mainly deciduous, on woodland edge, in orchards, or parkland with scattered trees. Nest-hole in tree-trunk or large limb; occasionally in telegraph pole or nest-box. *c.* 3–55 ft. up, at average of *c.* 30 ft. up.
Nest: Cavity often in live trees. Entrance hole 2–2½ in. high by 1¼–1½ in. wide. Cavity 10–15 in. deep, *c.* 4½ in. across. Excavated by both sexes, though mostly by male, taking 17–24 days. **Breeding season:** Begins late March in south to late May in north of range. Single-brooded, but lost clutches replaced, sometimes in same cavity. **Eggs:** Usually 4, sometimes 3–6. Subelliptical to almost elliptical or oval. Smooth and glossy. White. 25 × 19 mm. **Incubation:** By both sexes, male brooding at night. 11–15 days. **Nestling:** Altricial and naked. **Nestling period:** Young tended by both sexes. Regularly brooded for first half of period, decreasing later, mostly by female. Young fed directly on food carried in bill. Nest-sanitation mostly by male. Young climb to entrance for food at *c.* 17 days. Leave nest at 28–30 days. Rely on adults for *c.* 2 weeks after leaving. May return to roost in nest.

Strickland's Woodpecker (*Picoides stricklandi*)

Breeds in lower montane woodlands of pine–oak areas of southeast Arizona and southwest New Mexico. Nest-hole in tree-trunk, 8–50 ft. up, usually about 15–20 ft. up.
Nest: Cavity usually in dead wood. *c.* 12 in. deep. Excavated mainly by the male. **Breeding season:** Begins late April. Single-brooded. **Eggs:** Usually 3–4. Subelliptical to oval. Smooth and glossy. White. 23 × 17 mm. **Incubation:** By both. 14 days. **Nestling:** Altricial and naked. **Nestling period:** Tended by both. Leave nest at 29 days. Stay with adults into summer.

Red-cockaded Woodpecker (*Picoides borealis*)   Plate 52

Breeds in open pine forest of southeast US. Usually requires old pine stands suffering from red-heart disease. Nest-hole in a tree-trunk or large limb. 18–52 ft. up, but sometimes over 65 ft. up. Some pairs may have one or more additional adult helpers.
Nest: Cavity bored in live wood. Holes (*c.* 2¼ in. diameter) made around entrance produce resin flow which hardens around the hole. Cavity 8–12 in. deep. Cavity used multiple years. **Breeding season:** Begin mid-April. Usually ends by early July. Single-brooded, but lost clutches replaced. **Eggs:** Usually 3–5. Subelliptical to oval. Smooth and glossy. White. 24 × 18 mm. **Incubation:** By both sexes, including helpers. 10–11

days. **Nestling:** Altricial and naked. Skin pink. Legs and feet white. Swollen bill base white. **Nestling period:** Young tended by both parents and any helpers. Brooded for first 4 days. Young leave nest at 26–29 days. Fed by parents and possibly helpers for up to 5 months after fledging.

White-headed Woodpecker (*Picoides albolarvatus*)

Breeds in mountain pine and pine-dominated forest. Nest-hole in a tree-trunk, often in a snag. 3–30 ft. up, sometimes to 50 ft.
Nest: Cavity usually in dead wood. Entrance $1\frac{1}{2}$–$1\frac{3}{4}$ in. diameter, usually circular. Cavity 10–15 in. deep. Width variable, wider towards base. Excavated by both. **Breeding season:** Begins in late April. Single-brooded. **Eggs:** Usually 4–5, sometimes 3–7. Subelliptical to oval. Smooth and moderately glossy to very glossy. White. 24 × 18 mm. **Incubation:** By both sexes. 14 days. **Nestling:** Altricial and naked. **Nestling period:** Young tended by both parents. Leave at 26 days.

Three-toed Woodpecker (*Picoides tridactylus*)   Plate 52

Breeds in northern woodland, in deciduous or conifer trees, may be in muskeg area, usually near or in more open places. Nest-hole in a tree-trunk. Usually 2–15 ft. up. Rarely much higher.
Nest: Cavity usually in dead wood. Entrance hole $2 \times 1\frac{1}{2}$ in., cavity 9–10 in. deep, width $4\frac{1}{2}$ in., narrower towards entrance. Excavated by both sexes but mainly by male. **Breeding season:** Begins mid- to late May. Single-brooded, but lost clutches may be replaced and cavity re-used if undamaged. **Eggs:** Usually 3–4, sometimes 5. Subelliptical to oval. Smooth and slightly glossy. White. 21 × 19 mm. **Incubation:** By both sexes. 13 days. **Nestling:** Altricial and naked. **Nestling period:** Young tended by both parents. Food brought in bill and also regurgitated. Leave at 25 days. Remain with parents for up to a month.

Black-backed Woodpecker (*Picoides arcticus*)   Plate 52

Breeds in conifer forests, often in burned areas. Nest-hole in a tree-trunk. 5–40 ft. up.
Nest: Cavity usually in dead wood. Entrance hole *c.* $1 \times 1\frac{1}{2}$ in. Cavity *c.* 8–10 in. deep, *c.* 4–5 in. wide. **Breeding season:** Begins mid- to late May. Single-brooded. **Eggs.** Usually 4–5, sometimes 3–6. Subelliptical to oval. Smooth and moderately glossy. White. 23 × 18 mm. **Incubation:** By both sexes. 13 days. **Nestling:** Altricial and naked. **Nestling period:** Young tended by both parents. Fed directly on food brought in bill. Leave at 24 days.

Northern Flicker (*Colaptes auratus* – Includes Yellow-shafted Flicker, *C. a. auratus*, and Red-shafted Flicker, *C. a. cafer*)   Plates 15, 52

Breeds in open or sparsely-wooded areas (deciduous, coniferous, or mixed) and cultivated areas with scattered trees. Nest-hole in a tree-trunk or stump; occasionally in telegraph pole, post, wooden building or in earth bank. Nest-boxes may be used. Holes usually at 8–25 ft., but may be 0–100 ft. up.
Nest: Cavity sometimes in dead wood, more often in live wood. Entrance 2–4 in. diameter, depth of cavity usually 7–18 in. but can be as deep as 36 in., width varies, usually 7–8 in. Site apparently chosen by male, excavated by both sexes but mainly by male. Excavation takes 15–28 days. **Breeding season:** Begins early March in south to early June in north of range. Probably ends by early July. Single-brooded but replaces lost clutches. **Eggs:** Usually 6–8, sometimes 3–14. Elliptical to subelliptical, long subelliptical, oval and long oval. Smooth and glossy. White. 28 × 22 mm. **Incubation:** Eggs laid daily. Incubation by both sexes, the male sitting at night. 11–13 days. **Nestling:** Altricial and naked. Skin warm brownish-orange becoming

reddish then blackish before feather quills appear. Swollen gape flanges whitish. **Nestling period:** Young tended by both parents, fed by regurgitation. Quills appear at 7 days, eyes open at 10 days. Young brooded by male for first 3 weeks. Begin climbing in nest cavity at 17–18 days, fed at entrance by 3 weeks. Leave at 25–28 days.

Gilded Flicker (*Colaptes chrysoides*)
Breeds in desert areas of southern Arizona and southeastern California with Saguaro cacti where it excavates its holes 9–30 ft. up, or in cottonwoods and willows along riverbanks 5–25 ft. up.
Nest: Cavity usually in Saguaro, sometimes in wood. In cactus the pulp hardens around cavity after excavation. Entrance $2\frac{3}{4}$–$4\frac{3}{4}$ in. diameter, depth of cavity usually 10–18 in., width varies, usually 4–7 in. **Breeding season:** Probably begins late March and ends mid-June. Single-brooded but replaces lost clutches. **Eggs:** Usually 4–5, sometimes 3, rarely 2. Elliptical to subelliptical, long subelliptical, oval, and long oval. Smooth and semi-glossy. Dull white. 28×21 mm. **Incubation:** *c.* 12 days. **Nestling:** Altricial and naked. **Nestling period:** Little information. Tended by both.

Pileated Woodpecker (*Dryocopos pileatus*)　　　　　　　　　　　　Plate 52
Breeds in forest with large trees. Nest-hole bored in tree-trunk of conifer or deciduous tree, occasionally in telegraph pole. Usually chosen site is in close stand of living trees. 15–70 ft. up, but often at about 45 ft.
Nest: Cavity bored in dead wood. Entrance hole $3\frac{1}{4}$–$4\frac{1}{2}$ in. across, usually a little taller than wide. Cavity 10–24 in. deep, 6–8 in. across. Excavated by both. **Breeding season:** Begins early March in south to mid-May in north of range. Single-brooded but replaces a lost clutch. **Eggs:** Usually 3–5. Subelliptical to elliptical. Smooth and glossy. White. 33×25 mm. **Incubation:** By both adults, male in cavity at night. 18 days. **Nestling:** Altricial and naked. **Nestling period:** Young tended by both parents. Fed by regurgitation. Eyes open at 9–10 days. Feathers break sheaths at 10–16 days. Young leave nest at 26–28 days. Family group may stay together through summer.

Ivory-billed Woodpecker (*Campephilus principalis*)
Breeds, or bred (quite possibly extinct), in forest with tall old trees in the southern US. Nest-hole bored into large tree trunk, usually 25–60 ft. up, though as low as 15 ft. and as high as 70 ft.
Nest: Cavity usually in dead wood. Entrance hole 5–6×4–$4\frac{1}{2}$ in. Entrance tunnel *c.* 5 in., and cavity 17–25 in. deep, and 6–10 in. across, elliptical, and 2–3 in. wider from side to side. Some loose sawdust and wood chips in cavity. Nest excavated by both sexes. **Breeding season:** Begins usually in March, sometimes February. Single-brooded. **Eggs:** Earlier clutches usually 1–2, later clutches 3–4. Long subelliptical to long oval. Smooth and glossy. White. 35×25 mm. **Incubation:** By both sexes, the male on the nest at night. *c.* 20 days. **Nestling:** Altricial and naked. **Nestling period:** Young tended by both adults. Brooded by the male at night, occasionally during day. Leave nest after *c.* 5 weeks. Fed by adults for an additional 2 months or more. Remain with parents until winter.

Tyrant Flycatchers (*Tyrannidae*)

Small to medium-sized insectivorous birds. Nest usually a cup, domed in one species; in a tree or shrub fork, on a branch, in a cavity, on the ground or on a ledge under an overhang. Nest a miscellaneous array of debris, usually with a soft lining. Nest of phoebes stuck to site and largely built with mud; some other small species use spiders' webs for binding and attaching nests. Eggs usually white to creamy-yellow, with sparse bold spotting, or fine streaking in crested flycatchers. Incubation usually by female. Young hatch naked and grow down within several days. Fed on insects brought in bill by adults.

Northern Beardless-Tyrannulet (*Camptostoma imberbe*)   Plate 54
Breeds usually by water in cottonwoods, mesquite thickets, or open woodlands in southeast Arizona, southwest New Mexico, and occasionally the lower Rio Grande Valley of Texas. Nest in a mistletoe clump, 25–50 ft. up (elsewhere have occurred lower in palmettos and brushy tangles). Nest globular and among the mistletoe twigs. **Nest:** A domed structure with an entrance on one side towards the top. Thick-walled, of grasses and fine weed stems, bark and fibers; the cup padded with plant down, fur and feathers. **Breeding season:** Mid-April to late July. **Eggs:** Usually 1–3. Subelliptical. Smooth and non-glossy. White, very finely speckled, mainly at the larger end, with tiny specks and spots of brown, reddish-brown, or gray. 16×12 mm. **Incubation:** By female? Period unrecorded. **Nestling:** No information. **Nestling period:** No information.

Olive-sided Flycatcher (*Contopus borealis*)   Plate 54
Breeds in open (including burned-over) conifer or mixed woodland. Nest in a tree, frequently a conifer, sometimes deciduous. Usually on a horizontal branch, among a cluster of twigs and needles, 5–70 ft. up. **Nest:** A cup with loose outer structure. Sometimes mainly of *Usnea* lichen or dead twigs, with dead grass stems, dead pine needles, and rootlets; lined with similar but finer material and hair. At times *Usnea is* lacking, and twigs and moss form the main body. **Breeding season:** Begins late May to mid-June in north of range. Single-brooded. **Eggs:** Usually 3, rarely 4. Short subelliptical. Smooth and non-glossy. Cream-colored or pinkish; spotted, and blotched with olive-brown, purplish-brown, and paler purple. Markings mostly confined to a broad wreath around larger end. 22×16 mm. **Incubation:** By female. 16–17 days. **Nestling:** Altricial and downy. Down gray. Gape flanges bright yellow. **Nestling period:** Young leave at 15–19 days.

Greater Pewee (*Contopus pertinax*)   Plate 54
Breeds in pine and pine–oak woodland on steep mountain slopes in central Arizona and southwest New Mexico. Sometimes in streamside canyon sycamore groves. Nest like that of a wood-pewee, saddling a horizontal branch or in a horizontal fork, 10–40 ft. up. **Nest:** A deep cup, bound together and to the branch with spiders' webs. Of fine grass and weed stems, weed fibers, dead leaves and flower heads, and catkins, covered on the outside with lichen flakes; lined with fine grasses and grass heads. **Breeding season:** Early May to late June. **Eggs:** Usually 3–4. Subelliptical. Smooth and non-glossy. White to creamy-white; sparsely marked, mostly at the larger end, with specks and spots of brown, blackish-brown, reddish-brown, and paler gray. 21×16 mm. **Incubation:** No information. **Nestling:** No information. **Nestling period:** No information.

Western Wood-Pewee (*Contopus sordidulus*)
Breeds in mainly coniferous and sometimes deciduous woodlands, and in trees along watercourses. Nest in a tree, like that of Eastern Wood-Pewee, usually saddling a larger branch or in a near-horizontal fork, 15–30 ft. up, or rarely up to 75 ft. **Nest:** A shallow but well-made cup, bound together and to the branch with spiders' webs and fine fibers. Of plant down, fine dry grasses, weed stems, bud-scales and

plant fibers; lined with fine grasses, hair and fibers and sometimes feathers. The outside is decorated with lichens or caterpillar cocoon. **Breeding season:** Begins early
May in south to early June in north of range. **Eggs:** Usually 3, sometimes 2, rarely 4.
Indistinguishable from those of Eastern Wood-Pewee. 18 × 14 mm. **Incubation:** By
female alone. *c.* 12 days? **Nestling:** Altricial and downy. **Nestling period:** Young
tended by both parents. Fly at 14–18 days?

Eastern Wood-Pewee (*Contopus virens*)   Plate 54
Breeds in deciduous and mixed woodland, parkland, orchard, and in scattered plantings and shade trees. Nest like that of Western Wood-Pewee, usually saddling a small
horizontal or sloping branch or in a level fork. Usually 8–20 ft. up, occasionally up to
45 ft., on a fairly open site.
Nest: A neat shallow cup, bound together and to the branch with spiders' webs and
fine fibers. Of plant fibers, weed and grass stems, bark shreds, threads, and wool;
lined with plant down, finer grasses, wool, and hair. The outside of the nest is decorated and camouflaged with lichen fibers and spider webbing. Built by female.
Breeding season: Begins mid- to late May. Probably single-brooded. **Eggs:** Usually
3, sometimes 2, rarely 4. Creamy-white to very pale yellow; speckled, spotted, or
blotched in chestnut-red, reddish-brown, and paler lilac and purple. Markings are
mainly or entirely confined to a zone around the larger end, and paler markings
often as numerous as dark ones. 18 × 14 mm. **Incubation:** By female. 12–13 days.
Nestling: Altricial and downy. Down whitish; on head and back. Gape pale yellow.
Nestling period: Young tended by both parents. Brooded by female for most of first
four days. Feathered by *c.* 7 days. Leave nest at 15–18 days.

Yellow-bellied Flycatcher (*Empidonax flaviventris*)   Plate 53
Breeds in northern spruce forests in wet or boggy places, including alder swamps.
Nest on or near ground on moss hummock, mound, tree-roots, or among the raised
roots of fallen tree. Nest sunk into a layer of moss, and usually hidden by moss or
growing herbage, or under overhanging roots, on the ground or up to 2 ft. off the
ground.
Nest: A cup of rootlets, weed stems, moss and grasses; lined with fine rootlets, black
plant fibers, and thin moss stems, occasionally fine grasses or pine needles. Built by
female. **Breeding season:** Begins early June. **Eggs:** Usually 3–4, sometimes 5.
Subelliptical to short subelliptical. Smooth and slightly glossy. White; sparsely
speckled or with occasional blotches of brown, pinkish or buffish-cinnamon, and
paler purple. 17 × 13 mm. **Incubation:** By female alone, beginning with last egg. 15
days. **Nestling:** Altricial and downy. Down brownish-olive. **Nestling period:** Young
tended by both parents. Leave nest at 13 days.

Acadian Flycatcher (*Empidonax virescens*)   Plate 53
Breeds in moist deciduous woodland, floodplain forest, and cypress swamps, and in
woodland along ravines and watercourses. Nest in a tree, suspended in a horizontal
twig fork towards the end of a branch, often over water, 8–25 ft. up.
Nest: A cup partly suspended in a twig fork, with loose material hanging down from
it. Caterpillar silk is used to bind the nest in place and plant fragments may hang
from this. Cup of slender weed stems, twigs, vine tendrils, dead leaves, grasses,
tree-blossoms and bud-scales; Spanish Moss used where available. Built by female.
Breeding season: Begins late April in south to early June in north of range. Usually
single-brooded. **Eggs:** Usually 3, sometimes 2–4. Subelliptical to elliptical. Smooth
and non-glossy or slightly glossy. Creamy-white or buffish-white. Sparsely marked
with minute specks and spots or blotches of dark brown and purplish-brown;

mainly at larger end. 18 × 14 mm. **Incubation:** Eggs laid at daily intervals. Incubation by female alone. 13–14 days. **Nestling:** Altricial and downy. Skin pink or pinkish-flesh-color. Down sparse and white. **Nestling period:** Young tended by both parents. Brooded by female only. Eyes open by 4 days. Leave nest at 13–14 days. Fed by parents for *c.* 12 more days.

Alder Flycatcher (*Empidonax alnorum*)   Plate 53

Breeds in alder swamps, low thickets along streams and lake edges in wooded areas, and open damp places with shrubs and bracken, usually near water. Nest low in a bush, shrub, or small tree, or in the fork of tall bracken, 1–6 ft. up. Nest usually in an upright fork and built around supporting stems.
Nest: A loosely built cup of weed bark, soft dead grasses, leaves, plant fibers, bracken, moss, and sometimes a few feathers; lined with finer grasses, hair, and fruiting stems of moss. Bulky and loose materials, often with an untidy tail hanging under the nest. **Breeding season:** Begins mid-May to early June. **Eggs:** Usually 3–4, sometimes 2. Subelliptical to short subelliptical. Smooth and non-glossy. White to creamy-white or tinted buff or pink. Unmarked or sparsely marked, mainly around the larger end, with fine specks, spots, and small blotches of light red, reddish-brown, and chestnut-red. 18 × 13 mm. **Incubation:** By female. 13–15 days. **Nestling:** Altricial and downy. Down pale gray, brownish-gray on the head. Mouth yellow; gape flanges deep yellow. **Nestling period:** Young tended by both parents. Eyes open at 6 days. Feathers break sheath at 5–8 days. Young leave nest at 12–15 days.

Willow Flycatcher (*Empidonax traillii*)

Breeds in dry scrub and dry overgrown upland pastures, or in low scrub by lakes and watercourses in open areas. Nest in a shrub or small tree, particularly rose and willow, usually in a vertical fork, built around supporting twigs, 5–20 ft. up.
Nest: A compact cup of weed bark, plant fibers, dry grasses, and plant down such as willow down, often giving it a cottony appearance, like that of Yellow Warbler or American Goldfinch; lined with finer grasses, plant down, and hair. Built over 5–7 days. **Breeding season:** Begins mid-April. Single-brooded. **Eggs:** Usually 3–4. Very similar to those of Alder Flycatcher, though regularly buffy with brown spots near larger end. 18 × 13 mm. **Incubation:** By female. 12–13 days. **Nestling:** Altricial and downy. Down pale olive-brown. Mouth and gape flanges yellow. Upper mandible pale pink. **Nestling period:** *c.* 14 days.

Least Flycatcher (*Empidonax minimus*)   Plate 53

Breeds in open deciduous and mixed woodland, woodland openings, orchards, lake and stream edges, parkland, and shade trees around settlement. Nest in a tree usually deciduous sometimes a conifer, often 5–20 ft. up, sometimes 2–60 ft. up. Nest on a horizontal branch, in a fork or against the trunk, or in a vertical crotch.
Nest: A small, deep and fairly compact cup; of bark fibers, shredded weed stems, fine grasses, and weed stems, dead weed and grass blossoms, plant down, cotton, and bound with spiders' webs and cocoons; lined with fine grasses, hair, plant down, and feathers. Built by female in 6–8 days. **Breeding season:** Begins mid-May to early June. Usually ends by late July. Possibly double-brooded. **Eggs:** Usually 4, sometimes 3–6. Subelliptical, short subelliptical or elliptical. Smooth and non-glossy. Creamy-white. Unmarked. 16 × 13 mm. **Incubation:** By female alone, beginning with third egg. 14–16 days. **Nestling:** Altricial and downy. Hatched naked, down appearing in 2–3 days. Flesh yellow-orange. Down light gray. Mouth yellow; gape pale yellow. **Nestling period:** Young tended by both parents. Pin-feathers appear at 8 days. Young leave at 13–16 days.

Hammond's Flycatcher (*Empidonax hammondii*)   Plate 53

Breeds in mountain conifer or mixed woodland. Nest in a tree, often a conifer, in a closed-canopy situation. From 6–60 ft. up, in a fork of a branch.

Nest: A loose cup of bark strips and fibers, rootlets, grass and weed stems, feathers, fibers, plant down, spider cocoons, lichen filaments; lined with grasses or feathers. Built by female over 4–6 days, rarely with male helping. **Breeding season:** Begins in early June. Usually ends by late July. Single-brooded, but will replace lost clutches. **Eggs:** Usually 3–4. Subelliptical. Smooth and slightly glossy. White to pale or deep creamy-white or yellow. Unmarked or with minute brown specks and larger purple spots. 17 × 13 mm. **Incubation:** By female alone, 15 days. **Nestling:** No information. **Nestling period:** Young tended by both parents. Brooded by female for first few days. Young leave nest at 17–18 days, fed by adults for *c.* 20 days more.

Dusky Flycatcher (*Empidonax oberholseri*)   Plate 53

Breeds in mountain scrub, and scrub with scattered trees. (Usually found in drier, more open situations than Hammond's Flycatcher.) Nest in a deciduous shrub or small pine, 4–7 ft. up, in a fork, along branch or resting in twigs.

Nest: A neat compact cup. Of bark fibers, fine grasses, and dead weed stems, plant fibers, etc.; lined with similar but finer material with plant down and feathers. Bound with spiders' webs. The outside and base are more loosely built with odd ends hanging down. Built mainly by female. **Breeding season:** Begins late May to mid-June. **Eggs:** Usually 3–4, sometimes 2. Short subelliptical to subelliptical. Smooth and non-glossy. White or creamy-white. Unmarked. 17 × 13 mm. **Incubation:** By female. 15–16 days. **Nestling:** Altricial and downy. White down on crown, nape, sides, thighs, back, and wings. Mouth and gape flanges bright yellow. **Nestling period:** Young tended by both parents. Leave nest at 18 days.

Gray Flycatcher (*Empidonax wrightii*)   Plate 53

Breeds in sagebrush, or semi-arid areas of pinyon-juniper, very open pine woods, and scrub. Nest usually in a shrub in a fork or low on a main stem. 2–5 ft. up. Sometimes in loose colonies.

Nest: A bulky cup with untidy exterior; of bark strips, dead weed stems, plant down, grasses and hair. Lined with wool and small feathers. Built by female, perhaps with help from male. **Breeding season:** Begins late May to early June. Double-brooded. **Eggs:** Usually 3–4. Subelliptical to short subelliptical. Creamy-white. Unmarked. 18 × 13 mm. **Incubation:** By female alone. 14 days. **Nestling:** Altricial and downy. Down sparse: on head, wings, and back. **Nestling period:** Young tended by both parents. Leave nest at 16 days, fed by adults for 14 days more.

Pacific-slope Flycatcher (*Empidonax difficilis*)   Plate 53

Breeds in deciduous woodland, mixed woodland, canyon bottoms and riparian situation. Nest in a mid-sized tree or shrub, behind loose bark, among the roots of an upturned tree, in a cavity, on a stump, or on ledges or in crevices of buildings. 0–25 ft., sometimes higher.

Nest: A cup of green moss, dry grasses, bark strips, dead leaves, lichens, lined with finer materials and hair. Sometimes will use a variety of man-made materials; other times nest mainly of mosses. Built by female. **Breeding season:** Begins mid-April in south to mid-June in north of range. Sometimes double-brooded. **Eggs:** Usually 4, sometimes 3, rarely 5. Subelliptical to short subelliptical. Smooth and non-glossy. White to creamy-white; speckled, spotted, and with small blotches usually concentrated at the larger end; of reddish-brown, cinnamon, buffish-pink, or pale purple. 17 × 13 mm. **Incubation:** By female alone. 14–15 days. **Nestling:** Altricial. Skin bright pink. **Nestling period:** Young tended by both parents. Brooded by female. Young leave nest at 15–18 days, fed by parents for 13–15 days more.

Cordilleran Flycatcher (*Empidonax occidentalis*)
Breeds in shaded woodlands (coniferous, deciduous, and mixed) in foothills and lower mountain slopes. Usually near streams or moist ravines. Nest in a sapling or shrub, in a cavity in a tree-trunk, a crevice or cavity in a rock face, a mine shaft, or on a ledge, on a stump, or among tree roots by a stream, in or under low banks of streams, or on ledges or in crevices of buildings. 0–18 ft., sometimes higher.
Nest: Often a cup of green moss with a lining of finer materials and hair. Sometimes includes bark strips, fine rootlets, and dead leaves; with a fine lining. Built by female. **Breeding season:** Begins mid-April in south to mid-June in north of range. Sometimes double-brooded. **Eggs:** Usually 4, sometimes 3, rarely 5. Subelliptical to short subelliptical. Smooth and non-glossy. White to creamy-white; usually speckled, spotted, and with small blotches most often concentrated at the larger end; of reddish-brown, cinnamon, buffish-pink, or pale purple. Sometimes slightly brighter than Pacific-slope Flycatcher. 18 × 13 mm. **Incubation:** By female alone. 14–15 days. **Nestling:** No information. **Nestling period:** Young tended by both parents. Brooded by female. Young leave nest at 14–18 days, fed by parents for 10–11 days more.

Buff-breasted Flycatcher (*Empidonax fulvifrons*)
Breeds in montane riparian forests, open pine forests or pine–oak woodlands and shrub undergrowth in southeast Arizona. Usually in wide mountain canyons between 6,400–9,300 ft. Nest in a tree, against the main trunk, saddled on a near-horizontal branch, or on a fork often high up and well out from the trunk, from 4–45 ft. up (average 25 ft. up). Most nests are built within 2 in. of an overhanging leaf or branch.
Nest: A neat, compact and deep cup, bound together and to the branch with spiders' webs. Of grasses, fine rootlets, plant fibers, leaf fragments, bark, evergreen needles, plant down, and weed heads; lined with fine grasses, plant down, hair, and some feathers. Decorated externally with lichen flakes, small gray leaves and occasional feathers. Built by female over 5–7 days. **Breeding season:** Begins mid-April. Usually ends by early August. Single-brooded, though will regularly replace lost nest. **Eggs:** Usually 3–4, sometimes 2. Subelliptical. Smooth and non-glossy. Creamy-white. Unmarked. 15 × 12 mm. **Incubation:** By female. 15–17 days. **Nestling:** Altricial. Little additional information. **Nestling period:** Originally brooded by female; fed by both adults. First flight at 13–17 days. Young may huddle together on a branch for several days after fledging.

Black Phoebe (*Sayornis nigricans*)   Plate 53
Breeds mainly around farms and human settlement. Nest on a ledge sheltered by some overhanging surface, on a beam or support in or on a building, under a bridge, in a niche in a wall, in a well or mine-shaft, or on a ledge of some other man-made structure.
Nest: A cup of mud pellets, dry grass, weed stems, plant and bark fibers and hair; lined with fine fibers, rootlets, grass-heads, hair, wool and sometimes feathers. Built by female? **Breeding season:** Begins mid-March. Double-brooded. **Eggs:** Usually 4–5, sometimes 3–6. Subelliptical. Smooth and non-glossy or slightly glossy. White, usually unmarked, an occasional egg with a few specks and spots of reddish-brown. 19 × 14 mm. **Incubation.** By female alone? 15–18 days. **Nestling:** Altricial and downy. Down sparse; gray. **Nestling period:** Young tended by both parents. Leave nest at 21 days. Male may feed young after leaving while female re-nests.

Eastern Phoebe (*Sayornis phoebe*)   Figure 71, Plate 53

Breeds usually around farms and other buildings. Exceptionally on a cliff niche or other natural site. More usually on a ledge, rafter or raised site with some over-hanging protection, in or on a building, under a bridge, or in any niche of this kind. Generally located near fresh running water.

Nest: A cup of mud pellets mixed with moss, dry grass, fibers of weeds, and vine stems; lined with fine fibers, rootlets, and hair. Built by female during 3–6 days, sometimes longer. **Breeding season:** Begins mid-April in south to mid-May in north. Usually ends by mid-July. Usually double-brooded. **Eggs:** Usually 5, sometimes 3–7, rarely 8. Subelliptical. Non-glossy or slightly glossy. White, usually unmarked, an occasional egg with a few small spots of light to dark brown. 19 × 15 mm. **Incubation:** By female alone. 14–16 days. **Nestling:** Altricial and downy. Down sparse and dark gray. Mouth orange-red; gape flanges yellow. Upper mandible pale yellow. **Nestling period:** Young tended by both parents. Leave at 15–17 days. Fed by parents for an additional 2–3 weeks.

Say's Phoebe (*Sayornis saya*)   Plate 53

Breeds in open semi-arid country where sites are available. Like other phoebes natural nest-site a sheltered ledge or crevice of cliff or cave, hole or crevice in steep bank, or cavity in tree. Now nests on ledges with some sheltered overhang in or on buildings, and bridges, or down mine-shafts and wells, or in similar man-made sites. Will also use old nests of other passerines (e.g., Cliff Swallow, Barn Swallow, Black Phoebe).

Nest: A bulky, shallow cup of weed stems, dry grasses, plant fibers, moss, wool, hair, and spiders'cocoons and webs; lined with hair. (Mud usually not used in construction.)

Figure 71. Eastern Phoebe: c. 4–5 in. across; resting on typical building ledge with obvious mud pellets.

Built by female? **Breeding season:** Begins early March in south to late May in north of range. Double-brooded. **Eggs:** Usually 4–5, sometimes 3–7. Subelliptical to short subelliptical. Smooth and non-glossy or slightly glossy. White, usually unmarked, rarely with a few brown or reddish spots. 20 × 15 mm. **Incubation:** By female alone. 12–14 days. **Nestling:** Altricial and downy. Skin deep yellow. Down very sparse and gray. **Nestling period:** Young tended by both parents. Eyes open at 6 days. Young leave at 14–16 days. The male feeds the first brood of fledged young while female re-nests.

Vermilion Flycatcher (*Pyrocephalus rubinus*)   Plate 54
Breeds in trees (often isolated groves) along watercourses in arid areas. Nest in a tree, usually in a horizontal fork, 6–20 ft. up, sometimes up to 60 ft.
Nest: A flattish, well-made cup, sunk into a fork so that only the rim is obvious. Of short dead twigs, thinner twigs, weed stems, fine grasses, rootlets, dry leaves, bark strips, lichen, spiders' cocoons. Bound together and to the fork with spiders' webs, and decorated outside with lichen; lined with plant down, hair, fur, and feathers. Built by female. **Breeding season:** Begins early to mid-March. Possibly double-brooded. **Eggs:** Usually 3, sometimes 2 or 4. Short subelliptical to short oval. Cream-colored to ivory-yellow or pale buff; spotted and blotched in light and dark olive-brown, black, and pale gray. Usually a heavy zone of markings overlapping around the larger end, and a few specks or spots elsewhere. Pale markings often a prominent part of pattern. 17 × 13 mm. **Incubation:** Eggs laid at daily intervals. Incubation by female alone. 14–15 days. **Nestling:** Altricial and downy. Skin black-ish with tufts of creamy-white down. Mouth orange; gape flanges yellow. **Nestling period:** Young tended by both parents. 14–16 days.

Dusky-capped Flycatcher (*Myiarchus tuberculifer*)   Plate 53
Breeds in scrub–oak thickets of lower mountain slopes, and dense growth along canyon streams in southeast Arizona and southwest New Mexico. Nest in a natural cavity in a tree, or in a woodpecker hole, 4–40 ft. up.
Nest: A cup of fine grasses, weed stems, various plant fragments, bark strips, dead leaves, hair, fur, or feathers; lined with finer grasses, hair and fur. **Breeding season:** Early May to mid-June **Eggs:** Usually 4–5. Subelliptical. Smooth and slightly glossy. Creamy-white or cream-colored. Markings like those of Ash-throated Flycatcher, though more likely to be finely spotted and less streaked. 20 × 15 mm. **Incubation:** 14 days. **Nestling:** No information. **Nestling period:** Fed by both. Young leave nest at about 14 days.

Ash-throated Flycatcher (*Myiarchus cinerascens*)   Plate 53
Breeds in mesquite, oak scrub and dry plains with cactus, and in open deciduous woodland. Nest in a natural cavity in tree or stump, or in cactus, or a woodpecker hole, or behind loose bark, in dry inflorescent stems of yucca or agave, or in old nest of Cactus Wren. Also nests in man-made cavities; holes in posts, pipes, nest-boxes or similar sites. Usually below 20 ft., averaging 13 ft. up.
Nest: A cup of dry grasses, rootlets, and weed stems; lined with finer grasses, hair, and fur. Cavity base may be built up with dry cow or horse dung. Entirely or mostly by female. **Breeding season:** Begins mid-April to early May. Single-brooded. **Eggs:** Usually 4–5, sometimes 3–7. Subelliptical to elliptical. Smooth and slightly glossy. Creamy-white to ivory or pinkish-white. With fine longitudinal streaking, heavier streaking, or elongated blotches and spots, or more typical spots and blotches in pur-plish-red, reddish-brown, lilac, or gray. Tending towards the pattern shown by Great Crested Flycatcher, but marking sparser, with more pale markings and more creamy

ground color showing. (See also Dusky-capped Flycatcher.) 22 × 16 mm. **Incubation:** By female alone. 15 days. **Nestling:** Altricial and naked. Skin pinkish-gray, legs gray-ish. Gape bright yellow. **Nestling period:** Young tended by both parents. Leave nest at 16–17 days.

Great Crested Flycatcher (*Myiarchus crinitus*)   Plate 53
Breeds in deciduous and mixed woodland, usually near clearings or woodland edge; in orchards, or scattered trees in cultivated regions. Nest in a cavity whether natural or a woodpecker hole in a tree, or an artificial site, such as a pipe, nest-box, or similar cavity. 10–70 ft. up.
Nest: A cavity built up at base with dead leaves, leaf stalks, twigs, and nest of stems, fibers, grass, pine needles, feathers, rootlets, hair and various debris, including pieces of snakeskin, cellophane, or smooth paper; lined with hair, fur, feathers, and fine material. Built by both over as much as 2 weeks. **Breeding season:** Begins mid-March in south to mid-June in north of range. Single-brooded. **Eggs:** Usually 4–5, rarely 6 or more. Subelliptical to short or long subelliptical or elliptical. Smooth and slightly glossy. Ivory-yellow to creamy-buff, or rarely creamy-white, pinkish or purplish-buff; heavily marked with irregular fine longitudinal streaks, sometimes thin hair lines, of purplish-red or purple, and paler gray and lavender. The lines may cross each other at times and sometimes show irregular scrawling. Usually a concentration of markings at larger end. (For similar eggs, see other *Myiarchus* fly-catchers.) 23 × 17 mm. **Incubation:** By female alone. 13–15 days. **Nestling:** Altricial. Skin dark pinkish-flesh-color. Young hatched naked, soon growing a scanty down, grayish in color. Mouth orange-yellow; gape flanges cream. **Nestling period:** Young tended by both parents. Leave nest at 14–15 days.

Brown-crested Flycatcher (*Myiarchus tyrannulus*)   Plate 53
Breeds from open deciduous woodland to mesquite and dry plains with cactus. Nest in a natural cavity or woodpecker hole in tree, Saguaro cactus, or sometimes a nest-box. 5–30 ft. up.
Nest: A cup in a cavity. Of bark and fibers, hair, wool, feathers, and usually pieces of snakeskin. **Breeding season:** Late March to late July. Single-brooded. **Eggs:** Usually 3–5. Subelliptical to short subelliptical. Smooth and slightly glossy. Creamy-white to creamy or ivory-yellow; with very fine small streaks, and more rarely heavier streaks or blotches at the larger end, of purple or purplish-red, and pale lavender or gray. Similar to those of Great Crested Flycatcher, but markings usually less profuse and ground color paler. 24 × 18 mm. **Incubation:** By female. 14–15 days. **Nestling:** Altri-cial. Developing down on upperparts dull wood-brown in front; at rear, light drab. **Nestling period:** Tended by both parents. First flight estimated at 12–18 days.

Great Kiskadee (*Pitangus sulphuratus*)   Plate 53
Breeds in trees, usually by streams, rivers, lakes, or swamps, in woodland, or in plantations and shade trees in southern Texas. Nest usually in a crotch of tree or similar site offering firm support. 10–30 ft. up.
Nest: Builds a domed structure in exposed situation, but may build an open nest in concealed place. Also, the dome may not be completed until after incubation has begun. A bulky mass of dry weed and vine stems, Spanish Moss, grasses, rags, plant fibers, feathers, etc., the shallow cup lined with finer material such as wool, feathers, and plant down. **Breeding season:** Early March to late July, occasionally to early September. **Eggs:** Usually 4, sometimes 3–5. Smooth and slightly glossy. Pale creamy-white to ivory-yellow; very sparsely marked, often only at the larger end, with specks and spots of dark brown, blackish-brown and pale gray. 28 × 21 mm.

Incubation: By female. 16 days. *Nestling:* Altricial. Down gray, gape yellow. *Nestling period:* Tended by both parents. First flight estimated at 15 days.

Sulphur-bellied Flycatcher (*Myiodynastes luteiventris*)   Plate 53

Breeds in larger trees of wooded canyons (usually with sycamores) in southeast Arizona. Nest in a natural cavity in tree, or in an old woodpecker hole, or sometimes a nest-box. 10–45 ft. up.

Nest: In a cavity which may be built up at base with twigs, bark, and other debris; with a cup of leaf stems, fine weed stems, pine needles, and an inner lining of finer stems. Built by female alone. **Breeding season:** Mid-June to mid-August. **Eggs:** Usually 3–4. Subelliptical. Smooth and slightly glossy. White to rich creamy-buff; heavily spotted and blotched with deep chestnut-red, reddish-brown, and purplish-brown, and paler purple and gray. Markings often profuse and distributed overall. 26 × 19 mm. **Incubation:** By female only. 15–16 days. **Nestling:** Altricial and downy. Skin pink at first, becoming dark gray. Down long and plentiful; dark gray. Mouth and gape flanges yellow. **Nestling period:** Young tended by both parents. Eyes open by 7 days. Young leave nest at 16–18 days.

Tropical Kingbird (*Tyrannus melancholicus*)   Plate 53

Breeds in areas of scattered deciduous trees (especially cottonwoods) near water in southeast Arizona and rarely in the lower Rio Grande Valley of Texas. Nest usually in a tree on a horizontal branch. 6–15 ft. up, but may be as high as 70 ft.

Nest: A shallow bowl-shaped structure of dry twigs, rootlets, weed stems, grasses, lined with finer materials. Built by female. **Breeding season:** May–June; probably single-brooded. **Eggs:** Usually 2–5. Subelliptical to long subelliptical. Creamy-white, boldly marked with reddish-brown spots and streaks. 25 × 18 mm. **Incubation:** By female. 15–16 days. **Nestling:** Altricial and downy? Down sparse and light gray, skin pink. Inside of mouth orange. **Nestling period:** Fed by both. Leave nest at 18–19 days.

Couch's Kingbird (*Tyrannus couchii*)

Breeds in groves and shrubs generally close to water in the lower Rio Grande Valley of Texas. Nest on a horizontal branch. Usually below 20 ft.

Nest: An untidy bowl, composed of twigs, weed stalks, and leaves, lined with rootlets and sometimes Spanish Moss. **Breeding season:** Early or mid-April to late June. **Eggs:** Usually 2–4, occasionally 5. Subelliptical to long subelliptical. Cream-colored or rich buff, spotted with dark brown and lilac over most of surface. 24 × 19 mm. **Incubation:** No information. **Nestling:** Altricial and downy? Down pinkish-buff to slightly buffy-white. **Nestling period:** No information.

Cassin's Kingbird (*Tyrannus vociferans*)   Plate 53

Breeds in dry open country with scrub, or open hillsides with scattered trees. Nests usually in tall trees along canyons, by streams, or in scattered oaks on hillsides. Nest in a tree, near the end of a horizontal branch, usually 20–40 ft. up, sometimes only 8–10 ft. up, and exceptionally on fence posts or gates.

Nest: A substantial cup of small twigs, weed stems, bark strips, rootlets, and plant fibers, with dead leaves, string, and rags; lined with finer grasses, rootlets, and sometimes some feathers and thick cottonwood down. **Breeding season:** Begins late April to early May. Double-brooded in south. **Eggs:** Usually 3–4, sometimes 2–5. Subelliptical. Smooth and slightly glossy. White to creamy-white, or faintly buff; boldly blotched, speckled, and spotted with reddish, purplish-brown or olive-brown, blackish-purple, and paler purple or gray. Markings rather sparse, usually concentrated at larger end, and often longitudinally elongated. 23 × 17 mm. **Incubation:** By female.

12–14 days. **Nestling:** Altricial and downy? Down pale pinkish-cinnamon, pale pinkish-buff, grayish-yellow, or buffy-white. **Nestling period:** Tended by both parents. *c.* 14 days.

Thick-billed Kingbird (*Tyrannus crassirostris*)   Plate 53
Breeds in cottonwood and sycamore woods (usually near streams) in lowlands in southeast Arizona and extreme southwest New Mexico. Nest usually high in trees, 50–60 ft. up, though may be as low as 5 ft.
Nest: A frail, thin cup of twigs and grasses, with ends of material projecting from edge of nest, appearing bristly and unfinished. **Breeding season:** Early May to mid-July. Double-brooded. **Eggs:** Usually 4–5, sometimes 3. Subelliptical to long sub-elliptical. Smooth and slightly glossy. Creamy-white to pale buff, spotted and blotched with brown and pale lilac. Bolder markings at larger end. 25 × 17 mm. **Incubation:** By both sexes. Period unknown. **Nestling:** No information. **Nestling period:** Fed by both sexes. Little further information.

Western Kingbird (*Tyrannus verticalis*)   Plate 53
Breeds in open country in trees by water, or shade and orchard trees around settlement. Nest in a tree, well out on a horizontal limb or occasionally by the trunk, *c.* 15–30 ft. up, or sometimes 5–40 ft. up. Nests also on shrubs, telephone poles, fence posts, buildings, or similar sites.
Nest: A large untidy cup of weed stems, thin twigs, rootlets, plant fibers, coarse grasses, wool, hair, feathers, string, plant down, scraps of paper, snakeskin, and cat-kins. Lined with similar but finer material felted together in a tight cup. Built by both over 4–8 days. **Breeding season:** Begins mid-April in south to late May or early June in north of range. Single-brooded. **Eggs:** Usually 4, sometimes 3–5, exceptionally 6–7. Like those of Eastern Kingbird in shape, color and pattern, but slightly smaller on average. 23 × 17 mm. **Incubation:** Only by female. 12–14 days. **Nestling:** Altricial and downy. White down on back. Skin pink. Mouth pink; gape flanges yellow. **Nestling period:** Young brooded by female, fed by both parents. Leave nest at 13–14 days, fly at 16–17 days.

Eastern Kingbird (*Tyrannus tyrannus*)   Figure 72, Plate 53
Breeds over a wide range, preferring open areas (e.g., farmland) with scattered trees, or forest edges. Nest usually towards the end of a horizontal branch of a tree. Often over water. Where trees are absent, post or stump may be used, sometimes standing in water. Height very variable. 2–60 ft., but often fairly low.
Nest: A large, deep cup, with loose material at outside; of thin twigs, dry weed stems, straw, twine, plant down, and hair, sometimes with feathers, string, and pieces of cloth or wool; lining of fine dry grass, rootlets, and hair. Built by both. **Breeding season:** Begins early May in south to late May or early June in north of range. Single-brooded. **Eggs:** Usually 3–4, sometimes 5. Subelliptical, to long or short subelliptical. Smooth and slightly glossy. White, creamy-white or pinkish; speckled, spotted and blotched with purplish-brown, reddish-brown and blackish-purple, and paler brown, lilac, and gray. Markings bold, often longitudinally elongated, with a concentration around the larger end. 24 × 18 mm. **Incubation:** By both sexes. 12–13 days. **Nestling:** Altricial and downy. Skin orange-yellow. Down white. Mouth orange-yellow. **Nestling period:** Young tended by both parents. Leave at 13–14 days, fly at 16–18 days. Parents continue to feed young for up to 30 days more.

Figure 72. Eastern Kingbird: c. 5½ in. across; a deep and bulky cup with rough or loose exterior.

Gray Kingbird (*Tyrannus dominicensis*)   Plate 53

Breeds near the coast in Florida and adjacent states. Nest in a tree, mangroves in the swamps and scrub oak and palmetto elsewhere, or occasionally in shade trees (e.g., in yards). Often low, c. 3–12 ft. up.

Nest: A large, loose, and flimsy cup of coarse twigs, vines, and grasses; lined with fine grass and rootlets. **Breeding season:** Early May to early August. Probably double-brooded. **Eggs:** Usually 3–4, sometimes 2–5. Subelliptical to oval. Smooth and slightly glossy. Creamy-white, ivory-yellow or very pale pink; speckled, spotted, and blotched with chestnut-red, purplish-brown, and paler lilac and gray. Bolder markings usually in a zone at larger end with sparser and smaller markings elsewhere. Markings often longitudinally elongated. 21 × 18 mm. **Incubation:** By female. 17 days? **Nestling:** Altricial and downy. Down buff to creamy-buff. **Nestling period:** Fed by both, leave nest at 18 days.

Scissor-tailed Flycatcher (*Tyrannus forficatus*)   Plate 53

Breeds in open country with scattered small trees and shrubs, open woodland edge, and shade trees around human settlement. Nest is typically on a horizontal branch or at a fork, 5–30 ft. up, in a tree or on the ledge of a man-made structure.

Nest: A loose cup of thin twigs, rootlets, weed stems, husk, twine, cotton, plant down, wool, paper, rags, and other debris. Spanish Moss if available. Lined with rootlets, hair, and cotton. Built by female alone. **Breeding season:** Begins early April in south to early June in north. **Eggs:** Usually 3–5, sometimes 6. Eggs laid at daily intervals. Subelliptical. Smooth and slightly glossy. White, creamy-white or slightly pinkish; spotted, or blotched with dark brown, chestnut-brown, or purplish-brown, and paler gray, purple, or brownish-gray. Markings sometimes very sparse or absent. 22 × 17 mm. **Incubation:** By female alone. 12–13 days. **Nestling:** Altricial and downy? Down yellowish-white or pinkish-white to buffy-white. **Nestling period:** Young tended by both parents. *c.* 14 days.

Rose-throated Becard (*Pachyramphus aglaiae*)   Plate 53
Breeds in deciduous woodlands near water in southeast Arizona, southwest New Mexico, and the lower Rio Grande Valley of Texas. Nest a rounded pendent structure at the tip of a slender branch, 15–60 ft. up, usually in cottonwood or sycamore.
Nest: A pendent, rounded, or pear-shaped structure, *c.* 12–30 in. high by 9–12 in. wide, and with walls 1½–2½ in. thick, occasionally larger if made of coarser, loose material. The entrance at one side, near the bottom and directed downwards. Nest woven and suspended with bark strips, wiry vine stems, long pine needles, long branching lichen, weed stems, grasses, and spiders' webs, and also using plant down, wool, and moss. An inner cup lined with plant down and bark fiber. Built by both, though mainly by female, sometimes for a period of over 2 weeks. Building may continue during incubation. **Breeding season:** Early April to late July. **Eggs:** 4–6. Subelliptical. Smooth and slightly glossy. White, creamy-white, or pale purplish or buffish; spotted and blotched with dull brown, olive-brown or purplish-red, and pale pinkish-cinnamon, buff, or gray. Markings frequently elongated into poorly-defined short streaks. Markings often denser at, or around, the larger end. 23 × 17 mm. **Incubation:** By female alone. Period not recorded. **Nestling:** Altricial and downy? Down white. **Nestling period:** Young brooded by female; fed by both parents. Fly after 19 days.

Larks (*Alaudidae*)

Small birds, nesting on the ground, usually in open sites. The nest is often tucked into a natural, slightly-sheltered hollow. Small stones and similar objects often gathered around part of the nest, building up or paving one side of it. Eggs usually heavily speckled in buffish or olive-brown tints. Young have long down on the back which helps to camouflage them and sometimes scanty down on underside and usually show three small dark spots in the mouth. The young may leave the nest before they can fly properly, and crouch motionless to escape predators.

Sky Lark (*Alauda arvensis*)   Plate 54
Breeds on open, treeless areas, meadows, grasslands, stony or sandy tracts. Introduced from Old World to British Columbia on Vancouver Island and has spread to the San Juan Islands in Washington (*A. a. Arvensis*). Also a rare breeder on the Pribilof Islands in Alaska (*A. a. pekinensis*). Nest in a slight depression in the ground; sometimes sheltered by a tuft of grass. Often exposed although grasses or crops may grow during the nesting period.
Nest: A shallow cup of grasses, with a lining of finer grasses and at times hair. Built by female. Occasionally small pebbles are placed around nests in more open sites. **Breeding season:** Begins in late April. Double- or treble-brooded. **Eggs:** Usually 3–4, sometimes 5, rarely 7. Subelliptical. Smooth and moderately glossy. Dull grayish-white or tinted buff or greenish, heavily spotted overall with medium brown or olive, tending to obscure ground color. 24 × 17 mm. **Incubation:** By female only. 11 days. **Nestling:** Altricial and downy. Down more scanty underneath but long and thick over upperside. Buffish-yellow. Mouth dull yellow; three spots, one at tip of tongue, two at base. Bill flanges white. **Nestling period:** Young fed by both parents, leaving the nest at 9–10 days, but unable to fly. Hide by crouching motionless, fly well at *c.* 20 days.

Color Plates

Plate 1

L O O N S . The chicks have two down coats. The second, to the tips of which the first down remains attached, is paler in color.

Red-throated Loon (*Gavia stellata*) In this species the down may be variably tinted with blackish or gray. The Pacific Loon is dark brownish-gray above with pale gray from throat and neck to upper breast. The Common Loon is blackish-brown, sometimes paler on throat, neck and upper breast and the Yellow-billed Loon is similar but paler and with a lighter bill.   **page** 45

G R E B E S . Young downy, with distinct bold striped patterns (p. 50)

Pied-billed Grebe (*Podilymbus podiceps*) This species has a more variable head pattern than other species (see p. 50). Stripes are absent on the back of Horned and Eared Grebes, and the Western Grebe has pale gray down with faint patterning.   48

S H E A R W A T E R S . These have two down coats, the second darker in color and longer, and the first clinging to the tips of the second. The young may appear larger than adults before they finally lose their down.

Northern Fulmar (*Fulmarus glacialis*) First down is whitish on head and neck, and blue-gray above; second down is gray on head, neck and back.   53

S T O R M - P E T R E L S . These are similar to shearwaters, with two successive down coats. There is usually a bare spot on the hind-crown.

Leach's Storm-Petrel (*Oceanodroma leucorhoa*) The second down is more blackish than the first. The Fork-tailed Storm-Petrel has the first down blackish-brown above and gray below; the second is gray above and paler gray below. In the Ashy Storm-Petrel both down coats are brownish-gray.   54

G A N N E T S .

Northern Gannet (*Morus bassanus*) There is sparser, longer down on a blackish skin at first. The later down is woollier.   55

P E L I C A N S , C O R M O R A N T S , and **A N H I N G A S .** These are naked when first hatched but later grow a rather woolly down coat.   56

Brown Pelican (*Pelecanus occidentalis*) Naked and reddish at first, then turning blackish and growing white down. The White Pelican is pinkish-flesh-colored on hatching, growing white down.   56

Great Cormorant (*Phalacrocorax carbo*) Naked and dark-skinned, later with dark brown down. The skin is purplish-brown to blackish, followed in the Red-faced Cormorant by dusky-brown down with white mottling below, by black down in Double-crested and Neotropic Cormorants, sooty-gray down in the Pelagic Cormorant, and gray down, mottled white below, in Brandt's Cormorant.   56

Anhinga (*Anhinga anhinga*) The naked buffish skin is later covered with buffish-brown down.   59

Red-throated Loon

Pied-billed Grebe

Northern Fulmar

Leach's Storm-Petrel

Northern Gannet

Brown
Pelican

Great Cormorant

Anhinga

Plate 2

H E R O N S . The slender head, narrow bill, and upstanding down on the top of the head are typical of nestling herons.

S P O O N B I L L and I B I S E S . Young hatched with down. Spoonbill has two down coats, the first shorter, the second longer and woollier.

S T O R K S . These usually have two down coats, but in the Wood Stork the first is limited to a little coarse down on the wings, the second thick and woolly.

Great Blue Heron

Least
Bittern

Great Egret

Black-crowned
Night-Heron

Tricolored Heron

American Bittern

Roseate Spoonbill

Glossy Ibis

Wood Stork

Plate 3

WHISTLING-DUCKS. The downy young are slimly built, boldly patterned and with a typical pale stripe on the nape.

SWANS. The downy chicks are more uniformly colored and pale.

Trumpeter Swan (*Cygnus buccinator*) The legs and bill of the Trumpeter Swan are usually pinker than shown, as opposed to yellowish. The down of the Whistling Swan is similar but extends less far laterally on the sides of the bill.

Mute Swan (*Cygnus olor*) (Gray phase shown)

GEESE. The downy young lack the more clear-cut patterns of ducklings, and show the stout and narrower goose bill.

Greater White-fronted Goose (*Anser albifrons*) The Pink-footed Goose is brown above, including the crown of the head and around the eyes, and whitish below; sometimes with a greenish-yellow tint on paler parts.

Snow Goose (*Chen caerulescens*) The figure on the left shows the downy young of the white form, the right that of the darker, 'Blue Goose' type. The Emperor Goose has pale gray down, darker above and on the head, and Ross's Goose may have down gray, white, yellow, greenish-yellow or blackish-yellow.

Brant (*Branta bernicla*)

Barnacle Goose (*Branta leucopsis*) Small white areas on back −located above wing − may also be present. (Not shown in this illustration.)

Canada Goose (*Branta canadensis*) North-western races tend to be less yellow.

Trumpeter Swan

Mute Swan

Greater White-fronted Goose

Snow Goose

Blue Goose

Canada Goose

Barnacle Goose

Brant

Black-bellied
Whistling-Duck

Fulvous
Whistling-Duck

Plate 4

D U C K S (see also Plate 5). The young of dabbling ducks in down are mostly brown above and yellow below, with a yellow face and dark eyestripe. Bay ducks of the genus *Aythya* are mostly similar but without bold face-markings.

Wood Duck (*Aix sponsa*) Foot color usually includes yellowish edges to toes. (Not in this illustration.)

Green-winged Teal (*Anas crecca*) The Blue-winged Teal is similar but with the second face streak short and narrow yellow forehead. The Cinnamon Teal is similar to the Blue-winged Teal but with the down greener and yellower, the bill grayer.

Mallard (*Anas platyrhynchos*) The American Black Duck has similar but darker down and the darker mark below the eyestripe may merge with it. The Gadwall resembles the Mallard but with upperparts browner and lighter parts paler, the eyestripe narrow, dorsal patch larger and bill edges pinkish-flesh-colored.

American Wigeon (*Anas americana*) Yellow-faced variant has brighter face and more contrast than this brown-faced variant.

Redhead (*Aythya americana*) The Ring-necked Duck and Canvasback are similar but darker and have the back and top of the head dark brown. The Canvasback is also larger and with a longer, wedge-shaped bill.

4

Mallard

Northern Shoveler

Wood Duck

Northern Pintail

American Wigeon

Green-winged Teal

Redhead

Lesser Scaup

Plate 5

DUCKS (see also Plate 4). The downy young of these diving ducks are more boldly contrasting in color or more uniformly dark than those of dabbling ducks.

Common Eider (*Somateria mollissima*) The young of the King Eider is similar with more extensive paler buff on the face, and a pale underside. Steller's Eider has a more typical rounded head without the sloping forehead, and a small light buff ring round the eye, with a streak back toward the nape and a pale chin. The Spectacled Eider has a large dark spectacle mark around the eye and down extending on to the bill base. **page** 82

Harlequin Duck (*Histrionicus histrionicus*) 84

Oldsquaw (*Clangula hyemalis*) 84

Black Scoter (*Melanitta nigra*) The Black Scoter is usually darker on the cheeks than illustrated. The Surf Scoter is similar to this but generally darker overall and the down extends on to the upper bill as a wedge. 85

White-winged Scoter (*Melanitta fusca*) 85

Common Goldeneye (*Bucephala clangula*) Barrow's Goldeneye is very similar, though with a smaller bill. The Bufflehead is similar again but smaller and with some pale lateral spots on the back sometimes joining to form stripes. 86

Red-breasted Merganser (*Mergus serrator*) The bill of the Red-breasted Merganser is usually lighter than illustrated. Common Merganser is less 'reddish' overall, with a larger and rounder appearing head and a dark bill with whitish nail. The Hooded Merganser is darker, less boldly marked; brown on back, head, and upper breast, pale buffish-brown on cheeks and white on throat. 88

Ruddy Duck (*Oxyura jamaicensis*) 88

5

White-winged Scoter

Black Scoter

Common Eider

Harlequin Duck

Oldsquaw

Common
Goldeneye

Ruddy Duck

Red-breasted Merganser

Plate 6

NEW WORLD VULTURES. Young downy, with two down coats on California Condor. Down usually pale in color and absent altogether on head.

HAWKS and EAGLES. Young are downy, the down usually tinged white, buff or gray (see identification key, downy young). Hooked bill and sharp claws may help identify young, but young falcons and owls also share these characters, and some species of both use old nests of other raptors. Hawk and eagle young have two successive down coats, the first shorter and thinner, the second longer, coarser and usually darker. The various species are difficult to tell apart in early stages.

CARACARAS and FALCONS. These also have two down coats like those of Hawks and Eagles. See also other comments under these species above.

6

Bald Eagle

Golden Eagle

Osprey

Cooper's Hawk

Shail Kite

Merlin

1st down

2nd down

Crested Caracara

Turkey Vulture

Black Vulture

Plate 7

GUANS. Downy young fairly large, with poorly-defined down pattern. More arboreal than most gamebirds.

GROUSE. Downy young boldly patterned when small, fairly stoutly-built, like young of domestic hen. Usually with some down on the legs.

Plain
Chachalaca

Sage Grouse

Blue Grouse

Rock Ptarmigan

White-tailed Ptarmigan

Willow Ptarmigan

Greater
Prairie-
Chicken

Sharp-tailed
Grouse

Spruce Grouse

Ruffed Grouse

Plate 8

TYPICAL GAMEBIRDS. Downy young usually boldly patterned, the pattern often differing between genera. Resembles the young of grouse but lack any down on legs. Quail chicks are usually small, and those with crests may show evidence of them at an early age.

8

Ring-necked Pheasant

Wild Turkey

Gray Partridge

Chukar

Northern Bobwhite

Mountain Quail

Scaled Quail

Montezuma Quail

Gambel's Quail

California Quail

Plate 9

R A I L S , G A L L I N U L E S , and C O O T S . The young are active, with black down and unwebbed feet with long toes, but coots' toes have flange-like lobes along them. The young can move and swim actively at an early age, but may remain at the nest for a period.

L I M P K I N and C R A N E S . Young lack any distinctive pattern on the down. There is usually darker color on top of head and back. Downy plumage may be retained until the young have grown very large and appear rather incongruous.

9

Whooping Crane

Sandhill Crane

Limpkin

American Coot

Purple Gallinule

Common Moorhen

Virginia Rail

Sora

Black Rail

Plate 10

SHOREBIRDS (see also Plate 11). These young are typically long-legged and slender-billed but their bills, although beginning to show the characters of the species, are usually shorter than those of adults. The basic down pattern of longitudinal stripes is similar on many species, but on some the darker stripes are masked by small white or buff spots formed by brush-tips to some down filaments, and on other patterns is so broken as to appear as dark mottling. The down pattern of the crown of the head may differ significantly between species.

10

Spotted
Sandpiper

Least Sandpiper

Sanderling

Red-necked
Phalarope

Short-billed
Dowitcher

Common
Snipe

American
Woodcock

Ruddy
Turnstone

Hudsonian Godwit

Willet

Plate 11

S H O R E B I R D S (see also Plate 10). These young are typically long-legged and slender-billed, but their bills, although beginning to show the characters of the species, are usually shorter than those of adults. The basic down pattern is of longitudinal streaks, but mottled, with or without a white collar, in plovers.

11

Semipalmated Plover

Wilson's Plover

Killdeer

American Golden-Plover

Black-necked Stilt

American Avocet

Northern Jacana

Upland Sandpiper

Whimbrel

American Oystercatcher

Plate 12

G U L L S (see also Plate 13). In their earlier stages these are not easily told apart from young terns (see above) but as they grow the shorter, stouter bill becomes apparent. They usually have a bold, spotted or mottled down pattern.

Bonaparte's Gull (*Larus philadelphia*) Little Gull and Black-headed Gull are similar but both have dull pink bills with dark tips and appear more dark-backed. The dorsal ground color of Mew Gull is pale buff to buffish-gray, of Laughing Gull pale drab brown with warmer tints, of Franklin's Gull pale buffish-brown mottled dark brown, and of Ring-billed Gull pinkish or reddish buff. The last two species have a gray phase, pale with dark gray markings. **page** 153

Herring Gull (*Larus argentatus*) Lesser Black-backed Gull is very similar. Great Black-backed Gull similar but with dark blackish-purple bill. Western Gull is somewhat darker. Glaucous, Glaucous-winged, and Iceland Gulls have ground color and markings paler. California Gull is pale buff with indistinct gray markings on the back. Thayer's Gull is similar to Glaucous Gull, but sometimes darker. 155

Sabine's Gull (*Xema sabini*) 160

T E R N S . In their earliest stages tern chicks may not be easy to tell apart from gull chicks, but they usually lack the very bold spotting or mottling on the head that most, but not all, gulls possess (note also that Black Tern chicks are heavily marked). They also tend to have shorter legs and more slender bills, and the adults are usually well in evidence. Young skimmers are tern-like and do not develop the characteristic bill until fledging.

Caspian Tern (*Sterna caspia*) Gull-billed and Royal Terns similar. The Gull-billed is more heavily marked in spots or streaks. The Royal Tern is very variable, some chicks being pale pinkish or buff with most markings absent and some dusky with blackish down tips. 161

Sandwich Tern (*Sterna sandvicensis*) Sooty and Roseate Terns also have the down sheathed in spiky tufts; grayer on Sooty Tern, more buff on back of Roseate Tern.
162

Common Tern (*Sterna hirundo*) Forster's Tern has the throat brown, paler than the Common Tern's, and belly almost white; the Arctic Tern is usually more heavily marked with dark throat color extending to chin and forehead; the Aleutian Tern has the black extending from throat to upper breast. 163

Least Tern (*Sterna antillarum*) 165

Black Tern (*Chlidonias niger*) 166

Brown Noddy (*Anous stolidus*) Three color forms are shown. The young may be white, brownish-black or in intermediate stages. 167

S K I M M E R S .

Black Skimmer (*Rynchops niger*) 168

12

Brown Noddy

Black Tern

Least Tern

Sandwich Tern

Caspian
Tern

Common Tern

Black
Skimmer

Bonaparte's Gull

Herring Gull

Sabine's Gull

Plate 13

J A E G E R S . The chicks, are uniform dull brown but otherwise resemble gull chicks, web-footed and tending to have short stoutish bills. They leave the nest-hollow at an early stage, but remain nearby and adults may attack or mob intruders.

Parasitic Jaeger (*Stercorarius parasiticus*) Color variable, usually warm dark brown or blackish-brown. Long-tailed Jaeger is also dark brown but a little paler and grayer, and the Pomarine Jaeger generally darker gray overall. **page** 150

G U L L S (see also Plate 12). In their earlier stages these are not easily told apart from young terns (see Plate 12) but as they grow the shorter, stouter bill becomes apparent. They often have a spotted or mottled down pattern.

A U K S . The chicks are downy, usually dark in color. The feathers appear quickly. The feet are webbed and the bird rests on the lower, tarsal part of the leg. Most remain in holes until ready for sea. Murres and Razorbill are on open cliff ledges and some murrelets on open, inland sites. The young usually leave for sea when only partly fledged.

Common Murre (*Uria aalge*) The Thick-billed Murre has paler brown tips on back, and is more streaked on head and neck, sometimes with a tinge of buff. Belly more mottled. 169

Black Guillemot (*Cepphus grylle*) The Pigeon Guillemot is similar. 171

Xantus's Murrelet (*Synthliboramphus hypoleucus*) The Ancient Murrelet is black, tinted blue-gray, with whitish patch on ear-coverts, and belly white tinged yellow. 132

Cassin's Auklet (*Ptychoramphus aleuticus*) Crested and Least Auklets are brown above, pale grayish-brown below; the Rhinoceros Auklet is grayish-brown, and the Parakeet Auklet blackish-brown above, paler below. 173

Atlantic Puffin (*Fratercula arctica*) The Horned Puffin is similar or more grayish; the Tufted Puffin sooty-black above, sooty-gray below. 174

13

Ivory Gull

Black-legged
Kittiwake

Parasitic Jaeger

Cassin's
Auklet

Kittlitz's Murrelet

Dovekie

Xantus's Murrelet

Black Guillemot

Atlantic Puffin

Common Murre

Razorbill

Plate 14

D O V E S . Nestlings are covered with a coarse, sparse stringy down, the bare skin showing through. The base of the bill is swollen.

White-winged Dove (*Zenaida asiatica*) Band-tailed and Mourning Doves have white down, yellowish skin; White-crowned Dove has pale buff down, blackish skin; Rock and Eurasian Collared-Doves have yellowish down, sometimes reddish in the former; Common Ground-Doves have gray down, and the Red-billed Pigeon dark down and a reddish-brown skin. **page** 177

C U C K O O S . Nestlings hatch naked or with sparse, coarse down; the feathers grow rapidly, remaining in sheath until well grown, then breaking out in a short time when young are about to fledge.

Black-billed Cuckoo (*Coccyzas erythropthalmus*) The mouth, which has a pattern of white papillae, is also shown. The Yellow-billed Cuckoo is similar. 180

Greater Roadrunner (*Geococcyx californianus*) The mouth, which shows a pattern of white markings, is also shown. 181

Smooth-billed Ani (*Crotophaga ani*) This is naked when hatched and the plate shows the later stage when the quills are growing. The Groove-billed Ani is similar. 181

B A R N and T Y P I C A L O W L S . The nestlings have thick down extending down the legs to the claws in most species.

Barn Owl (*Tyto alba*) Unlike the other species, this has two down coats: the first short, white and sparse, the second a thicker, buffish-cream coat. 183

Snowy Owl (*Nyctea scandiaca*) The Long-eared, Flammulated, Screech, Pygmy, Barred, and Saw-whet Owls also have white down. 187

Short-eared Owl (*Asio flammeus*) The down is buffish-white, white below in the Boreal Owl, white with yellowish-buff tint in the Hawk Owl; sooty-white in Elf Owl, grayish-white in Burrowing Owl, pale gray above, white below in Great Gray Owl.

190

T R O G O N S . Young naked. Feathers grow in sheath and then break over a very short period.

Elegant Trogon (*Trogon elegans*) 202

14

Elegant Trogon

White-winged Dove

Smooth-billed Ani

Greater Roadrunner

Black-billed Cuckoo

Snowy Owl

Short-eared Owl

Barn Owl

Plate 15

G O A T S U C K E R S . The young remain at the rather exposed nest site, the mottled down aiding concealment. Mottling is mostly due to the difference in color between tips and bases of down filaments, but the Pauraque shows a more distinct pattern.

Common Nighthawk (*Chordeiles minor*) The Antillean Nighthawk has finer, more dispersed, gray markings interspersed with buff areas. The Lesser Nighthawk is mottled in buff and brown with buff on the underside.

Pauraque (*Nyctidromus albicollis*)

Whip-poor-will (*Caprimulgus vociferus*) Chuck-will's-widow is tawny-brown on the back, yellowish tawny to buff on head and underside, and the Poor-will is warm buff, paler on underside.

S W I F T S . The young are hatched naked but later may grow down in some species. The feathers grow in quill and break rapidly at a late stage.

Chimney Swift (*Chaetura pelagica*) As with the Belted Kingfisher the early naked stage and later stage with feathers in quill are shown. Vaux's Swift is similar, but the Black Swift is naked at first with bluish-black skin, later has long soft blackish-brown down.

H U M M I N G B I R D S . Young usually nearly naked, with a narrow line of down along the middle of the back.

Ruby-throated Hummingbird (*Archilochus colubris*) Down yellowish on Costa's Hummingbird, gray on Anna's and Rufous Hummingbird.

K I N G F I S H E R S . The young are hatched naked, grow the feathers in quill and these break rapidly at a late stage.

Belted Kingfisher (*Ceryle alcyon*) The early naked stage and the later stage with feathers in quill are shown here.

W O O D P E C K E R S . Young have large swollen and sensitive gape flanges projecting on either side of the head, and the lower mandible is longer than the upper at first. The young of different species are not easily told apart.

Northern Flicker (*Colaptes auratus*)

15

Common Nighthawk

Whip-poor-will

Pauraque

Belted Kingfisher

Chimney Swift

Northern Flicker

Ruby-throated
Hummingbird

Plate 16

S O N G B I R D S . A selection of typical passerine nestlings is shown here. The colored pattern by each bird shows a simplified diagram of the colors of open mouth and gape flanges. A key to the mouth colors of songbird nestlings is given on p. 41. It should be noted that bills which are distinct in shape or length in adults are less obvious in the nestlings

Horned Lark (*Eremophila alpestris*) The long down of back and head helps to conceal the huddled young in the nest, but usually sparse or absent on the underside.

page 233

American Crow (*Corvus brachyrhynchos*) 233

Brown Creeper (*Certhia americana*) The down is confined to the head. On nuthatches it extends over the back. Titmice have down confined to the head and shoulders. 241

Cactus Wren (*Campylorhynchus brunneicapillus*) Other wrens show dark to whitish-gray down. 243

Bohemian Waxwing (*Bombycilla garrulus*) 264

Brown-headed Cowbird (*Molothrus ater*) with young of the **Red-eyed Vireo** (*Vireo olivaceus*) The former is a brood-parasite of a family which has down varying from white through gray and brown, rarely buff, to blackish. The vireos have usually pale gray down. 316

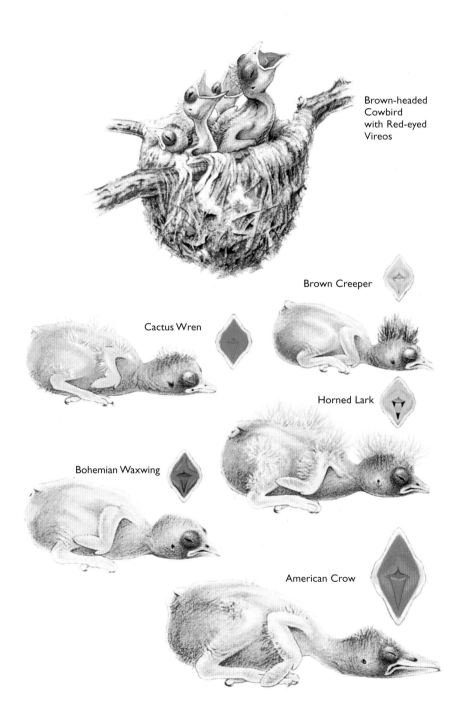

16

Brown-headed
Cowbird
with Red-eyed
Vireos

Brown Creeper

Cactus Wren

Horned Lark

Bohemian Waxwing

American Crow

Plate 17 Approx. ¾ life-size

L O O N S . The eggs are large, rather elongated and blunt-ended. They have a slightly granular or rough texture. They are usually olive-brown but may vary to more buff or greener tints, and the markings, although usually small, may sometimes be large or rarely absent. The usual clutch is 2 eggs, laid in a hollow scrape or on a pile of nearby material pulled together, by the water's edge.

1. Red-throated Loon (*Gavia stellata*) Eggs smaller and often more buff than others.

2. Arctic Loon (*Gavia arctica*)

(**Pacific Loon**, not shown, has eggs similar to those of Arctic Loon, though sometimes less olive-brown.)

3. Common Loon (*Gavia immer*) The markings are often sparse and eggs at times unmarked.

(**Yellow-billed Loon**, not shown, has eggs similar to those of Common Loon, but often lighter in color and more buff than brown.)

S H E A R W A T E R S . The eggs are usually blunt-ended but may show a more distinct taper in larger species. The eggs are usually white, smooth, and non-glossy, and only a single one is laid, usually in a burrow or crevice by the sea, the Fulmar being exceptional in nesting on an open cliff ledge. Nest material usually sparse or absent, but burrow-nesters may gradually accumulate nearby material.

4. Northern Fulmar (*Fulmarus glacialis*)

(**Manx Shearwater**, not shown, has smaller, but similar white eggs than those of the Northern Fulmar.)

G A N N E T S . The egg has an uneven white surface, thin enough in places to show the bluish shell underneath, and liable to scratch or flake away during incubation. The nest is a pile of seaweed and debris and the outer shell may be stained buff or brown by rotting nest material. Nests are in colonies, a bill-stab apart.

5. Northern Gannet (*Morus bassanus*)

(**Masked Booby**, not shown, has eggs that are chalky pale blue or white.)

17

Plate 18 Approx. ¾ life-size

G R E B E S . The eggs tend to be biconical, wider towards the middle and tapering to both ends. They are smooth but not glossy and almost white when new-laid. Usually a clutch of 3–6 eggs on a nest of waterweed, often floating. The birds cover the eggs with weed when they leave the nest, and eggs soon become stained buff or brown.

(**Clark's Grebe**, not shown, has similar eggs to those of the Western Grebe.)

S T O R M - P E T R E L S . The eggs are usually blunt-ended and may be almost elliptical in smaller species. They are white and may show tiny reddish or violet specks at the larger end. They are smooth and non-glossy and only a single egg is laid, usually in a burrow or crevice by the sea. Nest material is often sparse or absent) but burrow-nesters may gradually accumulate nearby material over a period.

(**Fork-tailed Storm-Petrel**, **Black Storm-Petrel**, and **Ashy Storm-Petrel**, not shown, have very similar eggs, all usually having a zone of fine reddish specks around the larger end.)

C O R M O R A N T S and A N H I N G A . Eggs are rather elongated and blunt-ended. The pale blue or greenish-blue shell has an outer surface layer of irregular thickness, the under shell often showing through. A clutch of *c.* 3–6 eggs is laid in a cup of twigs in a tree or pile of seaweed and debris on rocks. Eggs may become stained.

(Eggs of **Red-faced Cormorant,** not shown, are similar in appearance and size to those of Brandt's Cormorant.)

(**Magnificent Frigatebird**, not shown, has similar-looking eggs to the Anhinga, but larger.)

18

Plate 19 Approx. $\frac{3}{5}$ life-size

PELICANS. The eggs are large and blunt-ended. They have a rough uneven chalk-like layer which may become scratched and stained during nesting. The shell beneath is white. The nest is a hollow on the ground with a variable amount of material, or a stick platform in a bush or low tree.

HERONS (see also Plate 20). Eggs always greenish-blue. Smooth but non-glossy and rather blunt-ended, Usually a clutch of 3–7, in a twig nest in a tree or shrub, or on the ground or on rock ledge.

IBISES and SPOONBILLS. The eggs are subelliptical to elliptical. Smooth and non-glossy or, in the Glossy Ibis, slightly glossy. Usually a clutch of 2–4 in a rough nest of sticks, usually with leaves in lining, in a tree, shrub, or on the ground. Nests usually in colonies.

(**White-faced Ibis**, not shown, has eggs similar to those of Glossy Ibis.)

STORKS. The eggs are smooth with a finely granular texture. Usually a clutch of 3–4 laid in a large stick nest with a finer lining, in a tree.

19

Plate 20 Approx. $\frac{9}{10}$ life-size

BITTERNS and HERONS. The eggs are elliptical to subelliptical smooth and non-glossy, greenish-blue except in the American Bittern. Usually a clutch of 3–5 eggs in a stick nest in tree or shrub, plants by or in water, or on the ground. Normally a shallow structure in smaller species, sometimes massive in larger ones. Often nests in colonies.

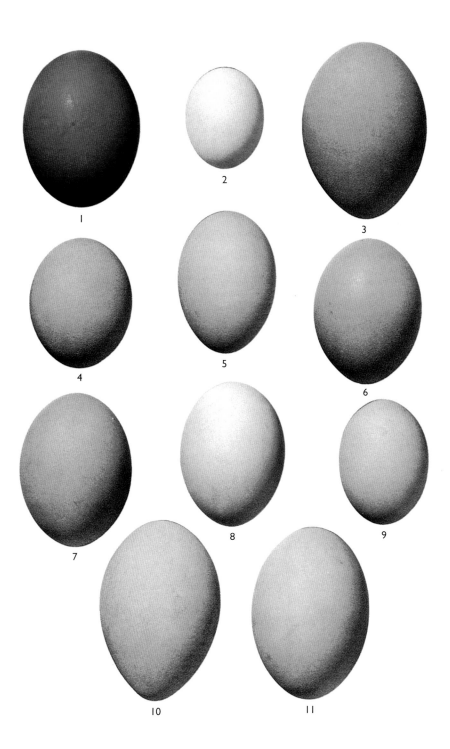

20

Plate 21 Approx. ¾ life-size

S W A N S . The eggs are large, smooth, and slightly glossy, usually with a fine granular surface texture. The clutch usually of about 5 eggs is laid in a nest formed of a large heap of plant material just in or by water; with a shallow central hollow usually containing a small amount of white down.

(**Whooper Swan**, not shown, has eggs similar to those of Trumpeter Swan.)

21

1

2

3

Plate 22 Approx. ¾ life-size

BRANTA GEESE and GRAY GEESE. The eggs are smooth with a fine granular texture, and non-glossy to slightly glossy. Usually a clutch of 3–6 eggs laid in a large nest which may be a shallow scrape or low mound of material, lined with plant fragments, down, and some feathers. Down tufts are grayish-brown with white centers and pale tips in Canada Goose, brownish-gray with whitish centers in Brant, and dark gray with whitish centers in Barnacle Goose.

22

Plate 23 Approx. ¾ life-size

GRAY GEESE. The eggs are smooth with a fine granular texture, and non-glossy to slightly glossy. Usually a clutch of 4–6 eggs is laid in a shallow scrape or low mound of plant material, lined with plant fragments, down, and a few feathers. Down tufts pale gray in Greater White-fronted Goose, and Snow Goose gray with pale tips in Pink-footed Goose, and white in Ross's Goose.

(**Ross's Goose,** not shown, has similar but smaller eggs)

WHISTLING-, WOOD, and DABBLING DUCKS (see also Plates 24–26). Eggs are smooth and vary from non-glossy to fairly glossy or with a waxy surface, and subelliptical to elliptical or oval. A clutch usually of 8–12 eggs is laid in a tree cavity or hollow among vegetation on the ground, and lined with down; except in the Whistling-Ducks which use no down lining. Down tufts white in Wood Duck, brown with paler centers and tips in Mallard, similar but with less conspicuous pale centers in American Black Duck, and dark with small pale center and distinct pale tips in Gadwall.

(**Mottled Duck,** not shown, has eggs similar to those of Mallard.)

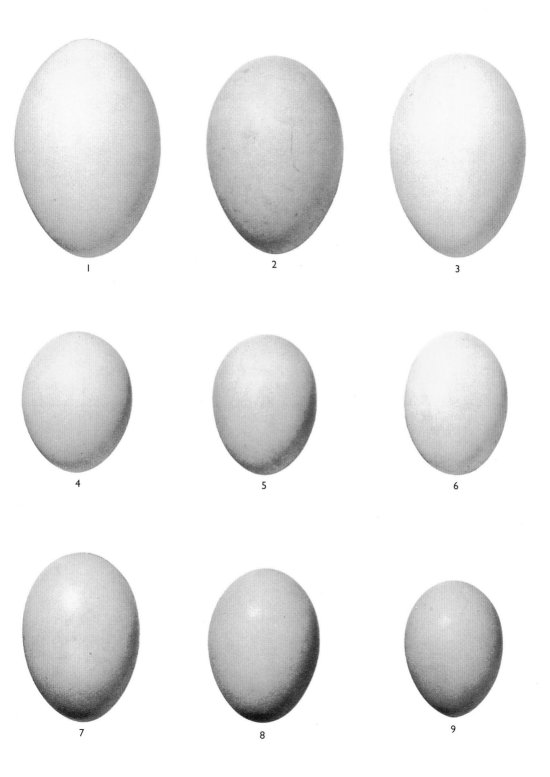

23

Plate 24 Approx. $\frac{9}{10}$ life-size

D A B B L I N G and **D I V I N G D U C K S** (see also Plates 23, 25, and 26). The eggs are smooth with a waxy rather than a glossy surface. A clutch usually of 7–12 eggs is laid in a hollow on the ground in vegetation usually near water. The hollow is lined with down. Down tufts are small and very dark with white centers in the Green-winged Teal, dark brown with large whitish centers in Blue-winged and Cinnamon Teals, dark sooty-brown with indistinct pale centers in the Greater Scaup, dark with indistinct pale centers and pale tips in the American Wigeon, warm medium brown with white centers in the Ring-necked Duck, brown with light centers in the Northern Shoveler, light brown and longish with pale centers in the Northern Pintail, and very pale grayish-white in the Redhead.

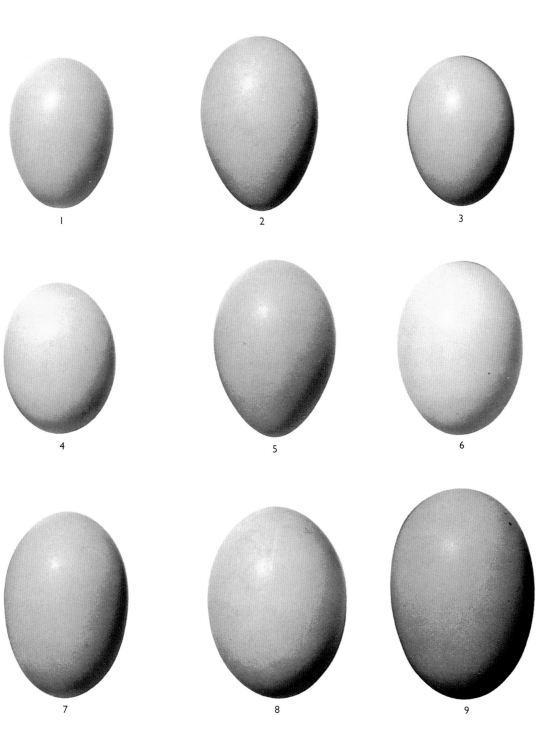

24

Plate 25 Approx. ¾ life-size

D I V I N G and **S E A D U C K S** (see also Plates 23, 24, and 26). Eggs smooth and non-glossy to slightly glossy. Elliptical to subelliptical or oval. A clutch usually of 5–12 eggs is laid in a tree cavity or hollow among vegetation on the ground near salt or fresh water. The nest is lined with down. Down tufts are dark brown with indistinct pale centers in Lesser Scaup, Black and White-winged Scoters, dark brown with whitish centers and tips in the Surf Scoter, dark grayish-brown with paler centers in Oldsquaw, light gray-brown with indistinct paler centers in Canvasback, pale gray tinted brown with indistinct pale centers in Bufflehead, grayish-white in Common Goldeneye, and white in Barrow's Goldeneye.

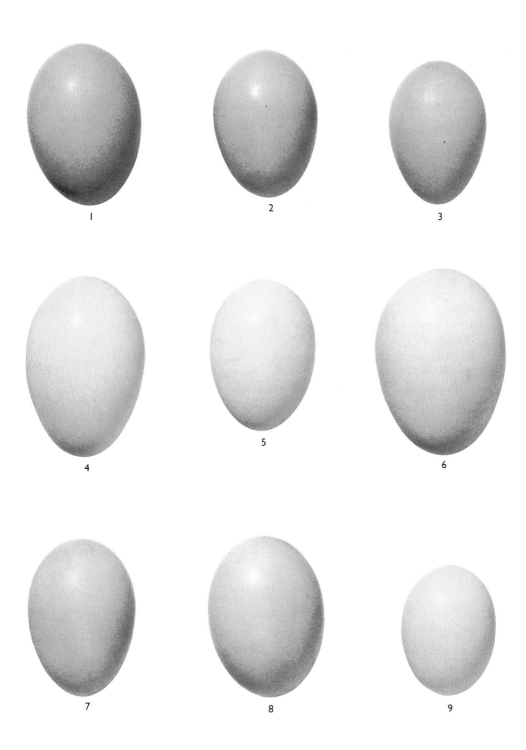

25

Plate 26 Approx. ¾ life-size

SEA DUCKS, STIFFTAIL, and MERGANSERS (see also Plates 23–25). The eggs are smooth and slightly glossy, subelliptical to elliptical. A clutch of 5–8 eggs in sea ducks, 5–12 in sawbills, in a hollow on the ground in vegetation by salt or fresh water, and in tree cavities, hollows in banks, among stones or under bushes in sawbills. Nests lined with down except in the Ruddy Duck and the Masked Duck. Down tufts are very dark brown with occasional white tufts in Steller's Eider, sooty-brown with indistinct pale centers and occasional white tufts in the King Eider, medium brown with indistinct pale centers in the Spectacled Eider, light brown with pale centers in the Harlequin Duck, light grayish-brown with indistinct pale centers and palish tips in the Common Eider, large and pale gray in the Common Merganser, darker gray tinged brown with pale centers and palish tips in the Red-breasted Merganser, and very pale gray with slightly paler centers in the Hooded Merganser.

1. **Common Eider** (*Somateria mollissima*) Egg color varies from pale green to olive, grayish, bluish or rarely buffish. **page** 82

2. **King Eider** (*Somateria spectabilis*) 82

3. **Spectacled Eider** (*Somateria fischeri*) Egg color varies from green to bluish-green or olive-buff. 84

4. **Steller's Eider** (*Polysticta stelleri*) Egg color varies from yellowish-olive to greenish or olive-buff. 84

5. **Harlequin Duck** (*Histrionicus histrionicus*) Egg color varies from pale creamy to buff. 84

6. **Hooded Merganser** (*Lophodytes cucullatus*) 87

7. **Common Merganser** (*Mergus merganser*) 87

8. **Red-breasted Merganser** (*Mergus serrator*) 88

9. **Ruddy Duck** (*Oxyura jamaicensis*) 88

(**Masked Duck**, not shown, has eggs similar to those of Ruddy Duck, though smoother and may tend to be bluish-white.)

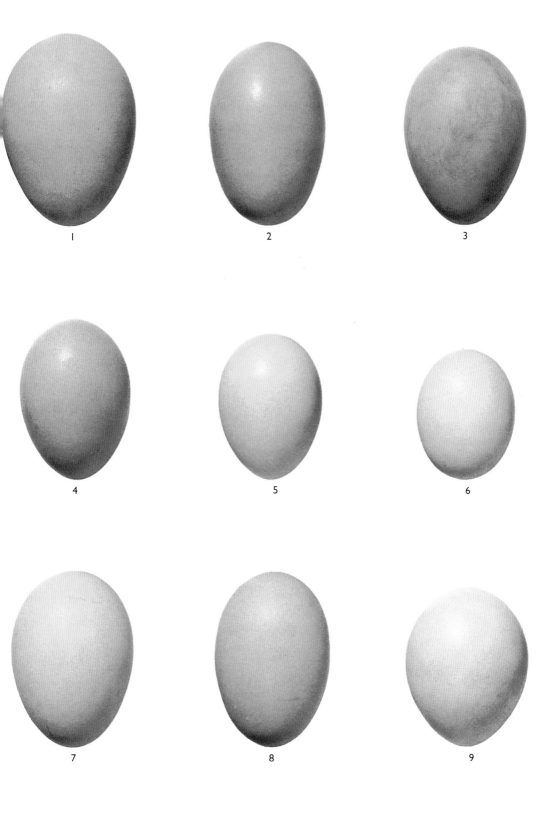

Plate 27 Approx. $^{9}/_{10}$ life-size

A M E R I C A N   V U L T U R E S . Eggs smooth and slightly glossy, and that of California Condor finely pitted. Long subelliptical to subelliptical and blunt oval. Clutch of 1 or 2 eggs laid in a bare cavity or sheltered site with no nest.

1. **Black Vulture** (*Coragyps atratus*) Color varies from pale gray-green to creamy-white or buff. Markings variable. **page** 89

2. **Turkey Vulture** (*Cathartes aura*) Markings very variable, usually a combination of fine small markings and larger irregular markings, but rarely large blotches. 90

3. **California Condor** (*Gymnogyps californianus*) 90

27

1

2

3

Plate 28 Approx. $^9\!/_{10}$ life-size

K I T E S and H A W K S (see also Plates 29–31). The eggs are smooth and non-glossy, sometimes slightly glossy in the kites. Short subelliptical to elliptical, generally rather rounded. Clutch of 2–4 eggs laid in a stick nest, usually in a tree, sometimes on the ground in marshy areas in the Snail Kite.

Plate 29 Approx. life-size

H A W K S (see also Plates 28, 30, and 31). The eggs are smooth and non-glossy, usually rather rounded. A clutch usually of 2–4 eggs, is laid in a stick nest usually with green leaves in lining. Nest in a tree, shrub, cactus, or on rock ledge, exceptionally on ground.

1. Broad-winged Hawk (*Buteo platypterus*) Markings vary in color from buff and brown to reddish or purplish brown.   **page** 99

2. Swainson's Hawk (*Buteo swainsoni*)   100

3. White-tailed Hawk (*Buteo albicaudatus*) Markings may be absent or if present are fairly faint and sparse.   100

(**Short-tailed Hawk**, not shown, has eggs bluish-white, dull white or buffish; unmarked or variably marked with speckling, scrawls or sparse to heavy blotching in light to dark brown. Similar in size to previous species.)

4. Ferruginous Hawk (*Buteo regalis*) Markings vary from almost absent to sparse specks, spots and blotches, in various brownish tints.   101

5 (a–b). Rough-legged Hawk (*Buteo lagopus*) The markings are very variable and two examples are shown here.   101

(**Zone-tailed Hawk**, not shown, has white or bluish-white eggs, usually unmarked, exceptionally with a few fine brown spots, of similar size to those of Rough-legged Hawk.)

29

1

2

3

4

5a

5b

Plate 30 Approx. ¾ life-size

E A G L E S (see also Plates 28, 29, and 31). The eggs are non-glossy with a finely granular texture, and rounded in shape. A clutch usually of 2 eggs is laid in a large nest of sticks and other debris with softer lining and leafy twigs regularly added. Nest in a large tree, on a rock ledge or outcrop, or sometimes on the ground.

3 (a–c). Golden Eagle (*Aquila chrysaetos*) The eggs vary from unmarked to spotted and blotched patterns in brown chestnut-red or purplish-red. The three examples shown indicate common varieties, and typical clutches of two eggs may show distinct differences in markings, one egg sometimes being unmarked.   102

1

2

3a

3b

3c

Plate 31 Approx. life-size

O S P R E Y and **H A W K S** (see also Plates 28–30). The eggs are smooth or slightly granular in texture, non-glossy or slightly glossy. A clutch of 2–4 eggs is laid in a stick nest in a tree, or shrub, or in the case of the Osprey sometimes on a low rock outcrop, or on the ground, in the Northern Harrier always on the ground.

1 (a–b). Osprey (*Pandion haliaetus*) The eggs are usually heavily but variably marked and two examples are shown here. **page** 91

2. Northern Harrier (*Circus cyaneus*) Eggs usually unmarked, infrequently blotched with light brown. 95

3. Common Black-Hawk (*Buteogallus anthracinus*) Markings vary from small specks to indistinct smudging. 97

4. Harris's Hawk (*Parabuteo unicinctus*) Often unmarked. Sometimes with small markings of pale brown or lavender gray. 97

5. Gray Hawk (*Buteo nitidus*) The eggs are usually unmarked, rarely with a few tiny pale brown marks. 98

1a

1b

2

3

4

5

Plate 32 Approx. life-size

C A R A C A R A and **F A L C O N S .** The eggs are rather rounded, non-glossy and often heavily freckled overall with reddish or red-brown. No nest is made but a clutch of 2–4 eggs is laid on a rock ledge, in a cavity in cliff or broken tree, on the ground or in large nests of other birds.

I N T R O D U C E D   G A M E B I R D S (see also Plates 33 and 34). The eggs are smooth and glossy, and usually subelliptical. A clutch, usually of 5–15 eggs, is laid in a hollow in the ground, usually concealed in herbage and sparsely lined with nearby vegetation.

32

1

2

3

4

5

6

7

8

9

Plate 33 Approx. life-size

G A M E B I R D S (see also Plates 32 and 34).

G U A N . Eggs smooth but with finely granular surface, non-glossy or slightly glossy, and often nest-stained. A clutch usually of 3 eggs in a nest of twigs in a tree.

T U R K E Y and G R O U S E . The eggs are smooth, subelliptical to oval, and slightly glossy to moderately glossy. A clutch of 4–12 eggs, usually a smaller clutch in ptarmigans, in a scrape nest on the ground, often concealed in vegetation, lined with a little plant material.

33

Plate 34 Approx. life-size

G R O U S E and **T Y P I C A L   G A M E B I R D S** (see also Plates 32 and 33)

The eggs are smooth and glossy, usually subelliptical to oval. A clutch of 7–14 eggs is laid in a shallow scrape, usually on the ground and concealed in herbage, lined with some plant material.

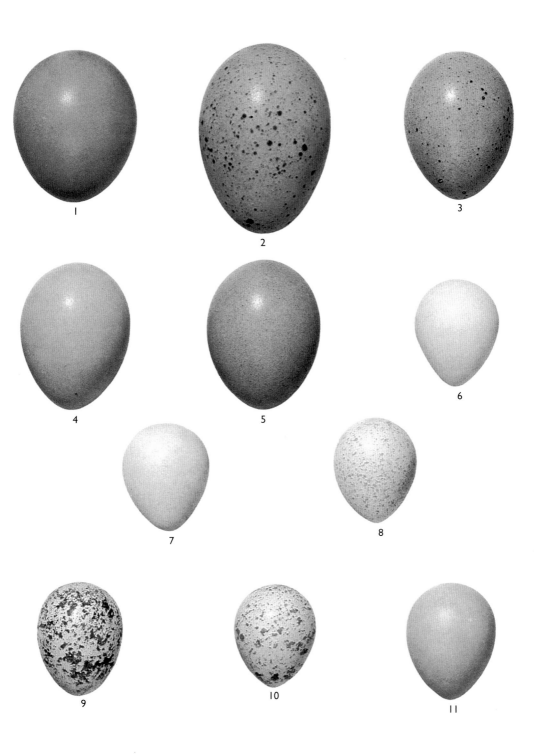

34

Plate 35 Approx. ¾ life-size

R A I L S (see also Plate 35). The eggs are smooth and moderately glossy. A clutch, usually of 6–12 eggs, is laid in a nest which is usually a substantial mound or cup of plant material hidden in marsh or waterside vegetation.

L I M P K I N and C R A N E S . The eggs are large, smooth, and slightly glossy or non-glossy. A clutch, usually of 2 eggs, is laid in a nest on the ground in an open site, sometimes in very shallow water; a large heap of vegetation with a shallow central hollow.

J A C A N A S . The eggs are smooth and highly glossy. A clutch of 3–4 eggs is laid in a scanty nest lying on floating plants.

35

Plate 36 Approx. $\frac{9}{10}$ life-size

R A I L S (see also Plate 35).

P L O V E R S . The eggs are smooth and non-glossy or slightly glossy, varying from oval to pyriform, but less pyriform than those of most other shorebirds. The clutch, usually of 3–4 eggs, is laid in a shallow hollow on open ground, sparsely lined or unlined.

(**European Golden-Plover**, not shown, has eggs similar to those of American Golden-Plover, but slightly larger and occasionally tinted reddish-brown or olive.)

(**Pacific Golden-Plover**, not shown, has eggs similar to those of American Golden-Plover, but may be paler.)

(**Mongolian Plover**, not shown, has cinnamon to olive-buff eggs, with small dark brown spots.)

(**Eurasian Dotterel**, not shown, has eggs somewhat like those of Killdeer, though slightly larger and tending to be darker.)

O Y S T E R C A T C H E R S . The eggs are smooth and glossy, less pyriform than those of most shorebirds. Usually a clutch of 3 in a bare hollow in a variety of open sites, unlined or lined with various debris.

36

Plate 37 Approx. ¾ life-size

S H O R E B I R D S (see also Plates 38 and 39). The eggs are smooth and glossy usually pyriform and cryptically patterned. A clutch, usually of 4 eggs, is laid in a shallow hollow lined with vegetation, in a variety of sites, exposed or set against a stone, log, or plant tuft, or concealed in vegetation sometimes pulled together over the nest.

(**Surfbird**, not shown, has eggs buff to pale buff, with spots and small blotches of buffish, reddish or dark brown.)

37

Plate 38 Approx. life-size

S H O R E B I R D S (see also Plates 37 and 39). The eggs are smooth and glossy usually pyriform and cryptically patterned. A clutch, usually of 4 eggs, is laid in a shallow hollow lined with vegetation, in a variety of sites, exposed or set against a stone, log, or plant tuft, or concealed in vegetation which may be pulled together over the nest. The Solitary Sandpiper nests on a raised site, an old bird nest in a tree.

38

Plate 39 Approx. life-size

STILTS and AVOCETS

1 (a–b). Black-necked Stilt (*Himantopus mexicanus*) Two varieties are shown here.

2. American Avocet (*Recurvirostra americana*)

SANDPIPERS (see also Plates 37 and 38). The eggs are smooth and glossy usually pyriform and cryptically patterned. A clutch, usually of 4 eggs, is laid in a shallow hollow lined with vegetation in a variety of sites, exposed, or set against a stone, log, or plant tuft, or concealed in vegetation sometimes pulled together over the nest.

3. Sanderling (*Calidris alba*)

4. Semipalmated Sandpiper (*Calidris pusilla*). The egg color varies from very pale olive to buff, marked with reddish, dark or purple-brown.

5. Western Sandpiper (*Calidris mauri*) The egg color varies from creamy-white to buff or brownish.

(**Red-necked Stint**, not shown, has eggs yellowish-buff, heavily speckled and spotted with reddish-brown or reddish-buff.)

6. White-rumped Sandpiper (*Calidris fuscicollis*)

7. Dunlin (*Calidris alpina*). The egg color varies from pale olive to green or blue-green, marked with dark or olive-brown.

(**Curlew Sandpiper**, not shown, has eggs light olive-green, marked in olive-brown, blackish-olive or reddish-brown.)

8. Stilt Sandpiper (*Calidris himantopus*)

9. Buff-breasted Sandpiper (*Tryngites subruficollis*)

10. Short-billed Dowitcher (*Limnodromus griseus*) The egg color varies from pale greenish to buff.

11. Long-billed Dowitcher (*Limnodromus scolopaceus*)

(**Ruff**, not shown, has eggs somewhat similar to those of the Long-billed Dowitcher.)

12. Wilson's Phalarope (*Phalaropus tricolor*)

13. Red-necked Phalarope (*Phalaropus lobatus*) Egg color varies as in Red Phalarope.

14. Red Phalarope (*Phalaropus fulicaria*) The egg color varies from greenish to buff.

1a   1b   2

3 4 5 6

7 8 9 10

11 12 13 14

Plate 40 Approx. ¾ life-size

J A E G E R S and G U L L S (see also Plates 41 and 42). The eggs are smooth and non-glossy or only slightly glossy, with a slightly granular surface evident on the larger eggs. A clutch, usually of 2–3 eggs, is laid in a nest formed from accumulated plant material, seaweed, and debris, large at times, but usually sparse in warmer climates. Nest site on a rock ledge, stack, or small island, on coastal sand or shingle, or on marshland, grassland or tundra by water.

1. **Pomarine Jaeger** (*Stercorarius pomarinus*) The egg color varies from buff to warm brown.

2. **Parasitic Jaeger** (*Stercorarius parasiticus*) The egg color varies from olive to deeper buff or brown.

3. **Long-tailed Jaeger** (*Stercorarius longicaudus*)

4. **Herring Gull** (*Larus argentatus*) The egg color varies through pale olive, greenish and buff, exceptionally pale whitish-blue or deep buff.

(**Thayer's Gull**, not shown, has eggs pale olive to buff, marked with olive-brown, brown or black.)

5. **Iceland Gull** (*Larus glaucoides*)

6. **Lesser Black-backed Gull** (*Larus fuscus*) The egg is normally colored much like that of Herring Gull. This abnormal specimen is lacking almost all blue and buff pigments (see pp. 22–23).

7. **Western Gull** (*Larus occidentalis*) The egg color varies from very pale olive to olive-buff.

8. **Glaucous-winged Gull** (*Larus glaucescens*) The egg color varies from very pale olive to buff.

9. **Glaucous Gull** (*Larus hyperboreus*) The egg color varies from light or creamy olive to buff, exceptionally bluish-white; with very variable markings.

10. **Great Black-backed Gull** (*Larus marinus*) The egg color varies from pale greenish to olive-buff, exceptionally whitish-blue or deeper buff.

40

Plate 41 Approx. ¾ life-size

G U L L S (see also Plates 40 and 42). The eggs are smooth and non-glossy or only slightly glossy, with a slightly granular surface evident on larger eggs. A clutch, usually of 2–3 eggs, is laid in a nest formed from accumulated plant material, seaweed or debris, large at times but usually sparser in warmer climates. Nest site on a rock ledge, stack, or small island, on coastal sand or shingle or in or by water in marshlands, grassland, or tundra. Bonaparte's Gull nests in spruce trees.

41

Plate 42 Approx. life-size

G U L L S (see also Plates 40 and 41). The eggs are smooth and non-glossy or only slightly glossy. A clutch, usually of 2–3 eggs, is laid in a nest formed from accumulated plant material, seaweed, or debris, large at times. Nest site on a rock ledge, stack, or small island, coastal sand or shingle, or in or by water on tundra, marsh, or tall grasses.

1. Black-legged Kittiwake (*Rissa tridactyla*) The egg color varies from cream to pale greenish, yellowish, stone, buff, or olive, exceptionally yellow or pinkish-buff. The markings are very variable. **page** 159

(**Red-legged Kittiwake**, not shown, has eggs similar to Black-legged Kittiwake, though usually lighter-colored and less heavily spotted.)

2. Ross's Gull (*Rhodostethia rosea*) 160

3. Sabine's Gull (*Xema sabini*) 160

4. Ivory Gull (*Pagophila eburnea*) The egg color varies from light olive to buff. 160

T E R N S (see also Plates 43 and 44). The eggs are smooth and non-glossy. A clutch, usually of 2–3 eggs, is laid in a shallow hollow, sparsely lined or unlined, on an open site usually on sand or shingle by water. The nests are usually close together in colonies, sometimes of several species nesting together.

5. Gull-billed Tern (*Sterna nilotica*) The egg color varies from pale yellowish to creamy-buff. 161

6. Common Tern (*Sterna hirundo*) The egg color varies from creamy and pale yellowish through greenish tints to deep buff or olive; very variably marked with shades of black and brown. 163

7 (a–c). Arctic Tern (*Sterna paradisaea*) The egg color varies through shades of pale greenish, olive or buff, exceptionally from bluish-white or creamy to deep brown. The markings are variable. Three examples are shown here. 164

8. Forster's Tern (*Sterna forsteri*) The egg color varies from very pale olive or greenish to light or olive-buff, marked with dark brown and black. 165

1

2

3

4

5

6

7a

7b

7c

8

Plate 43 Approx. life-size

T E R N S and **S K I M M E R** (see also Plates 42 and 44). The eggs are smooth, non-glossy, and cryptically patterned. The clutch usually of 2–3 eggs, or one in species of warmer climates, is laid in a shallow hollow on an open site with little or no nest material, usually on sand, shingle, or dry mud; or a nest of plant material floating on water plants for the Black Tern; and a more substantial nest in a shrub or on a ledge for the Brown Noddy. Nests are usually close together in a colony.

1 (a–b). Roseate Tern (*Sterna dougallii*) The egg color may vary to yellowish, buffish or olive, occasionally of deeper tint, and with markings very variable, but often fine and profuse. Two examples are shown here.   **page** 163

2 (a–b). Least Tern (*Sterna altillarum*) The egg color varies through pale olive, buff and cream. Markings are variable. Two examples are shown here.   165

3. Aleutian Tern (*Sterna aleutica*) The egg color varies from yellowish or olive to yellowish or olive-buff.   165

(**Bridled Tern**, not shown, has eggs that are pinkish-white or creamy-white with small spots of varied shades of brown, gray, lavender, or violet, not unlike those of Roseate Tern – example b.)

4 (a–c). Sooty Tern (*Sterna fuscata*) The egg color may vary from white to pale pinkish or buff, markings are variable and often small and profuse. Three examples are shown here.   166

5. Black Tern (*Chlidonias niger*) The egg color varies from light buff to brown, pale yellowish or cream, with irregular heavy marking.   166

6. Brown Noddy (*Anous stolidus*) The color is usually white, but may be tinted buff or pink.   167

7. Black Skimmer (*Rynchops niger*)   168

43

1a

1b

2a

2b

3

4a

4b

4c

5

6

7

Plate 44 Approx. $\frac{9}{10}$ life-size

T E R N S (see also Plates 42 and 43). The eggs are smooth and non-glossy, and cryptically patterned. The clutch, usually of 2–3, sometimes 1 only, is laid in a shallow hollow, usually on shingle, sand, or dry mud. The nests are usually close together in colonies, sometimes of several species.

1. Caspian Tern (*Sterna caspia*)   **page** 161

2. Royal Tern (*Sterna maxima*) The egg color varies from creamy-white to ivory-yellow, pale buffish or greenish, or buff and pinkish-buff. Markings are variable. 162

3 (a–f). Sandwich Tern (*Sterna sandvicensis*) Some tern species show considerable variation in egg color. This might be of value in helping birds to recognize eggs where nests are scantily lined and very close together, but the amount of variation differs from one species to another. The 6 eggs shown here illustrate the amount of variation occurring in one species.   162

(**Elegant Tern**, not shown, has eggs that are pinkish-buff to white with blotching or spotting of gray or brown, not unlike eggs of Sandwich Tern – especially examples d and e.)

44

1

2

3a

3b

3c

3d

3e

3f

Plate 45 Approx. ¾ life-size

T H I C K - B I L L E D   M U R R E and **R A Z O R B I L L**. The eggs of these two larger auks are large, usually long and pyriform, although those of the Razorbill are a little shorter and rounder. The surface is finely granular and roughened, lacking gloss. Apart from this there is little consistency, the eggs showing a great individual variation in color and markings, some examples being shown here. It is thought that the variations may enable birds to recognize their own eggs in sites where no nest is made, where one egg is laid, and where a number of birds may be crowded close together.

1 (a−c). Thick-billed Murre (*Uria lomvia*) The egg color may vary through shades of whitish, cream, buff, reddish, greenish, or blue; and markings may be buff, brown, purplish, or black.   **page** 170

2 (a−c). Razorbill (*Alca torda*) The egg color may vary from white, through yellow, buff, brown, reddish or greenish tint; variably marked with dark brown or black, the markings including scribbling and banding.   170

1a

1b

1c

2a

2b

2c

Plate 46 Approx. ¾ life-size

C O M M O N   M U R R E . The eggs of this larger auk are large, usually long and pyriform, occasionally more oval. The surface is finely granular and roughened, lacking gloss. Apart from this there is little consistency, since the eggs show great individual variation in color and markings. The group shown here indicates the range of variation with some types of color and markings. It is thought that these variations enable birds to recognize their own eggs, and since this species makes no nest and single eggs are laid on bare rocky ledges or the flatter tops of rock stacks closely crowded with birds, there would be an exceptional need for this.

Common Murre (*Uria aalge*) The egg color may vary from white through shades of brown, buff, reddish, cream, blue, or green. Markings may be brown or black, and some larger markings show a mixture of both colors. Markings are sometimes in the form of continuous zones of pigment, or sometimes absent altogether. **page** 169

46

Plate 47 Approx. $\frac{9}{10}$ life-size

A U K S (see also Plates 45, 46, and 48). The eggs are smooth and non-glossy to moderately glossy, subelliptical to long elliptical, sometimes with bluntly rounded ends. The eggs of most species are concealed in crevices or burrows near the sea, but Kittlitz's Murrelet breeds on bare places in mountains some miles inland and the Marbled Murrelet uses a platform of moss and twig debris in a forest tree near the shore.

47

Plate 48 Approx. ¾ life-size

A U K L E T S and P U F F I N S (see also Plates 45–47) The eggs are smooth and non-glossy, sometimes with a finely granular surface texture; and subelliptical to oval. The nests are burrows or rock crevices or cavities, on the coast or offshore islands.

(The **Parakeet Auklet** not shown, has eggs of white, bluish-white or pale blue, of similar size to those of the Crested Auklet. **Whiskered Auklet**, not shown, has eggs like Crested Auklet, though slightly smaller.)

3. Rhinoceros Auklet (*Cerorhinca monocerata*) The eggs are white and unmarked or sparsely marked with scrawls and spots of gray or light brown.   174

4. Tufted Puffin (*Fratercula cirrhata*) The egg markings vary from pale gray to pale brown.   174

5 (a–d). Atlantic Puffin (*Fratercula arctica*) The eggs may be unmarked, or may show faint brown or purplish blotches, or exceptionally be more heavily marked and tinted pale to deep buff.   174

6. Horned Puffin (*Fratercula corniculata*)   175

48

Plate 49 Approx. $^9/_{10}$ life-size

B A R N and **T Y P I C A L O W L S .** The eggs are rounded or blunt-ended, but those of the Barn Owl are more elongated. They are smooth, but occasionally show small, pimple-like excrescences; and are non-glossy or slightly glossy. They may become slightly stained in the nest. The clutch is usually of 2–6 eggs, but in some species may be larger, of 10–15 eggs in seasons when food is plentiful. Usually no nest is built, the clutch being laid in a hollow tree or large cactus, hollow on the ground in herbage or in the open, on a ledge or the old nest of another bird, or in a burrow.

(The **Northern Pygmy-Owl** and **Flammulated Owl**, not shown, have small eggs; similar to and slightly larger than those of the Elf Owl.)

(The **Whiskered Screech-Owl**, not shown, has eggs of similar shape and size to those of the Boreal Owl.)

14

15

16

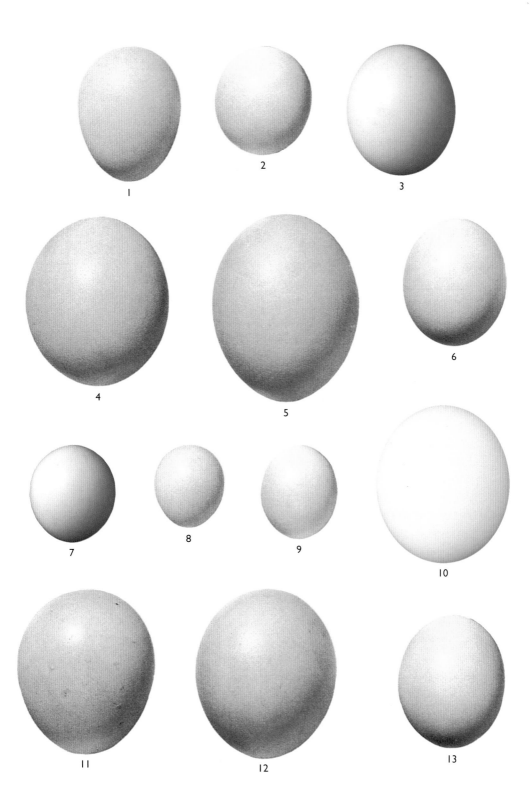

Plate 50 Approx. life-size

49

PIGEONS. The eggs are smooth and slightly to moderately glossy, and when freshly laid may have a faint pink tint that soon fades. The clutch is usually of 2 eggs, but only 1 in some larger species. The nest is a thin platform of twigs in a tree or shrub, or on a ledge, rarely on the ground.

(**Eurasian Collared-Dove**, not shown, has eggs that are similar to those of Mourning Dove.)

PARROTS. No parrot or parakeet eggs are shown. Three established species are included in the book. They are Budgerigar, Monk Parakeet, and Canary-winged Parakeet. All three species have eggs that are white and elliptical, usually 2–5 per clutch, laid in a cavity, or in the case of Monk Parakeet, in a bulky stick nest with compartments.

CUCKOOS (see also Plate 51) The eggs are smooth and non-glossy, elliptical to subelliptical. The clutch, usually of 2–4 eggs, is laid in a loose and poorly made nest of twigs in a tree or shrub.

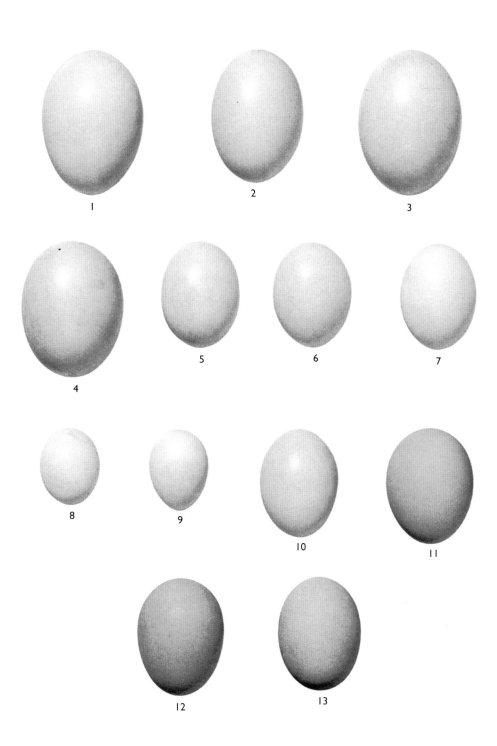

50

Plate 51 Approx. life-size

C U C K O O S (see also Plate 50). The eggs are smooth and slightly or fairly glossy. Ani eggs are blue with a white outer layer of varying thickness with the underlying color showing through at times. The Roadrunner has a clutch of 3–6 eggs in a well-made cup of plant material in a tree or shrub. Anis build loose cups of twigs, lined with fresh leaves, and a number of females lay eggs in one nest.

G O A T S U C K E R S . The eggs are elongated, biconical and blunt-ended, showing little evidence of a taper towards the narrow end. They are smooth and moderately glossy, and cryptically patterned. Usually 2 in a clutch, laid on a bare, open site with no nest.

(**Antillean Nighthawk**, not shown, has eggs that are paler and more finely marked than those of Common Nighthawk.)

H U M M I N G B I R D S . The eggs are smooth and non-glossy, long elliptical to long subelliptical, blunt-ended. A clutch, normally of 2, is laid in a small tight neat cup with a deep cavity, fixed on a twig or branch of a tree, shrub or more rarely a ledge or support on a building. All eggs are very similar and only a selection is shown here.

51

Plate 52 Approx. life-size

S W I F T S . The eggs are elongated, smooth and non-glossy. A clutch, usually of 4–5 eggs, but only 1 in the Black Swift, is laid in a nest of plant debris or small twigs, glued together with saliva; on a ledge or crevice of cliffs or rocks or glued to an upright surface in a hollow tree or chimney.

(**Vaux's Swift** and **White-throated Swift**, not shown, have similar eggs to those of the Chimney Swift.)

T R O G O N S . The eggs are smooth and non-glossy. A clutch, usually of 3–4 eggs, is laid in a natural cavity, old woodpecker hole, or possibly hole excavated by the bird itself on rotten wood.

(The eggs of the **Eared Trogon**, not shown, are reportedly white.)

K I N G F I S H E R S . The eggs are smooth, very glossy, and sometimes almost spherical. A clutch, usually of 4–7 eggs, is laid in an unlined tunnel in a bank or natural cavity, but may gradually become surrounded by food castings such as fish bones.

(**Ringed Kingfisher**, not shown, has similar but larger eggs.)

W O O D P E C K E R S . The eggs are smooth, rounded and glossy. A clutch, usually of 3–7 eggs, is laid in an unlined cavity in a·tree, pole or cactus. (A number of woodpeckers' eggs are not shown: Red-naped Sapsucker, Red-breasted Sapsucker, Williamson's Sapsucker, Strickland's Woodpecker, White-headed Woodpecker, Gilded Flicker, Ivory-billed Woodpecker.)

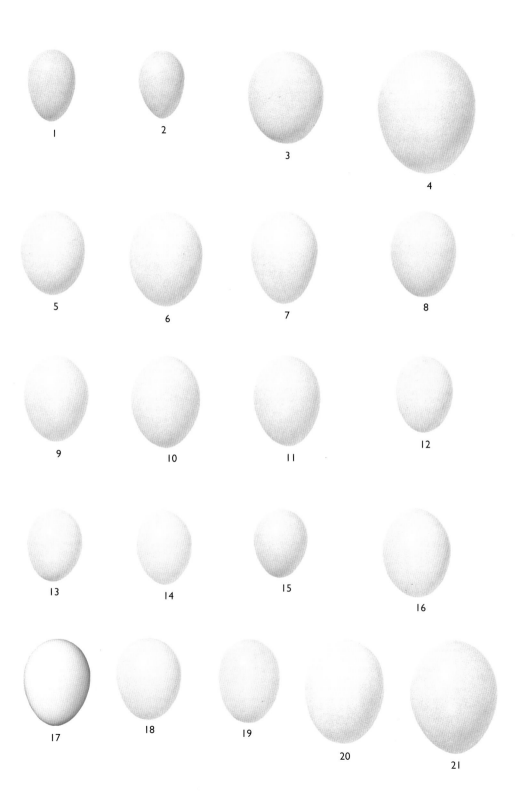

52

Plate 53 Approx. life-size

TYRANT FLYCATCHERS (see also Plate 54). The eggs are smooth and slightly glossy. A clutch, usually of 3–6 eggs, is laid in a nest, usually a cup, domed or pendent in a few species, on a tree or shrub, in a cavity, on the ground or on a ledge.

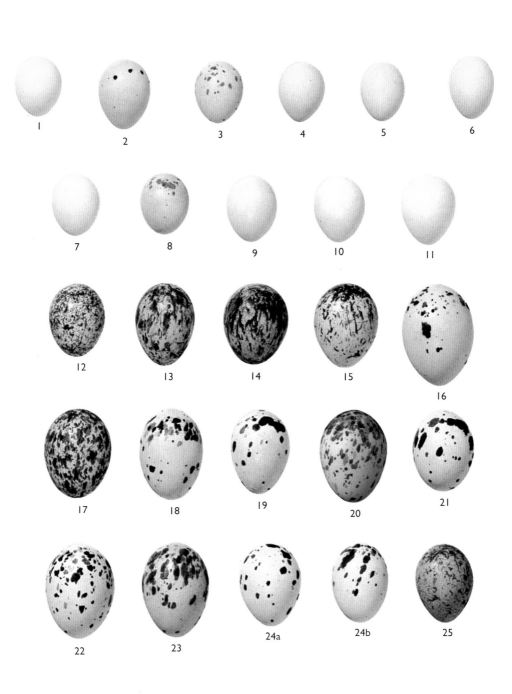

53

Plate 54 Approx. life-size

TYRANT FLYCATCHERS (see also Plate 53). The eggs are smooth and slightly glossy. A clutch, usually of 3–6 eggs, is laid in a nest, usually a cup, domed in a few species, on a tree or shrub.

LARKS. The eggs are smooth and glossy and cryptically patterned. A clutch, usually of 3–5 eggs, is laid in a cup nest on the ground.

SWALLOWS and **MARTINS.** The eggs are smooth and non-glossy or slightly glossy, and often elongated. A clutch, usually of 2–5 eggs, is laid in a cup nest in a tree cavity or earth tunnel, or in a mud nest fixed to rocks or walls.

TITMICE, VERDIN, and **BUSHTIT.** Eggs smooth and often rather rounded. Non-glossy or slightly glossy. A clutch, usually of 5–8 eggs, is laid in a pendent domed nest in the Bushtit, rounded domed nest in the Verdin and in a natural or excavated tree cavity in other species.

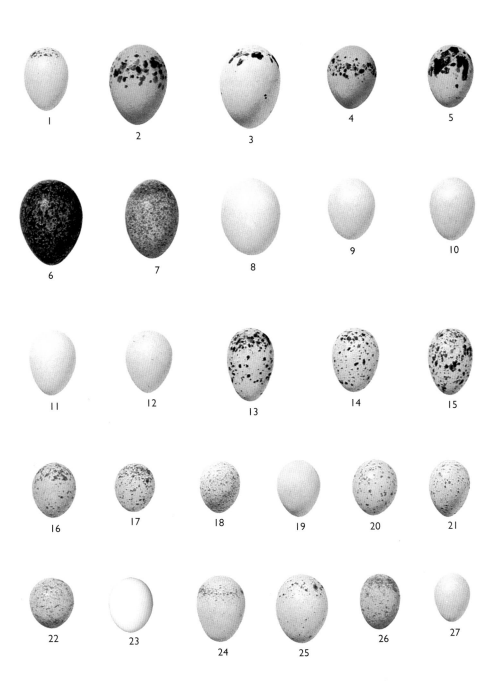

54

Plate 55 Approx. life-size

JAYS, MAGPIES, and **CROWS** (see also Plate 56). The eggs are smooth and glossy. A clutch, usually of 3–4 eggs, is laid in a largish stick nest with soft lining in a tree or shrub, or on a ledge.

1. Green Jay (*Cyanocorax yncas*) The egg color varies from creamy-white to pale greenish, buff or olive.

2. Brown Jay (*Cyanocorax morio*)

3. Florida Scrub-Jay (*Aphelocoma coerulescens*)

4. Island Scrub-Jay (*Aphelocoma insularis*)

5. Western Scrub-Jay (*Aphelocoma californica*) The egg color varies from blue to pale olive-green, sometimes washed with pink, rarely whitish, pale buff or light green; marked in olive-brown or reddish.

6. Mexican Jay (*Aphelocoma ultramarina*) The egg color varies from greenish-blue to yellowish-green. Sometimes unmarked.

7. Pinyon Jay (*Gymnorhinus cyanocephalus*) The egg color is bluish, greenish or bluish-white.

8. Clark's Nutcracker (*Nucifraga columbiana*)

9. Black-billed Magpie (*Pica pica*) The egg color varies from greenish-blue to grayish, blue, buff, and olive.

10. Yellow-billed Magpie (*Pica nuttalli*) The eggs are similar to those of the Black-billed Magpie.

11 (a–b). American Crow (*Corvus brachyrhynchos*) The egg color varies from greenish-blue to pale blue, with variable markings. Two examples are shown here.

12. Northwestern Crow (*Corvus caurinus*) The egg color varies from blue to green with variable markings.

13. Mexican Crow (*Corvus imparatus*)

14. Fish Crow (*Corvus ossifragus*) The egg color varies like those of other crows.

15. Chihuahuan Raven (*Corvus cryptoleucus*)

16. Common Raven (*Corvus corax*) The egg color varies from light blue to pale green.

14

15

16

55

Plate 56 Approx. life-size

J A Y S (see also Plate 55). The eggs are smooth and glossy. A clutch, usually of 3–4 eggs, is laid in a stick nest in a tree or shrub.

3 (a–b). Blue Jay (*Cyanocitta cristata*) The egg color varies from pale olive to green, bluish-green, buff, pinkish-buff, or whitish. Two examples are shown here.   228

N U T H A T C H E S and B R O W N C R E E P E R . Eggs are smooth and slightly glossy, non-glossy in the creeper, and rather rounded. A clutch, usually of 4–9 eggs, is laid in a cup nest in a cavity in a tree, or in a crevice in the case of the creeper.

7. Brown-headed Nuthatch (*Sitta pusilla*) The egg color varies from white to buff.
     240

B U L B U L . Eggs are smooth and glossy. A clutch of up to 4 eggs is laid in a cup nest, low in a tree or shrub.

(**Red-whiskered Bulbul**, not shown, has eggs which are white with purplish-red markings.)

W R E N S and D I P P E R . The eggs are smooth and glossy. A clutch usually of 4–8 eggs, is laid in a domed nest – in the American Dipper sited by and overlooking water, in wrens in a tree, shrub, grasses, cavity, or crevice.

14 (a–c). House Wren (*Troglodytes aedon*) Egg color may vary from white to pinkish or brown. Three examples are shown.   245

M O C K I N G B I R D S and T H R A S H E R S (see also Plate 57). The eggs are smooth and glossy. A clutch, usually of 3–5 eggs, is laid in a cup nest in a tree, shrub, or cactus.

20. Northern Mockingbird (*Mimus polyglottus*) The egg color varies from pale to greenish-blue.   258

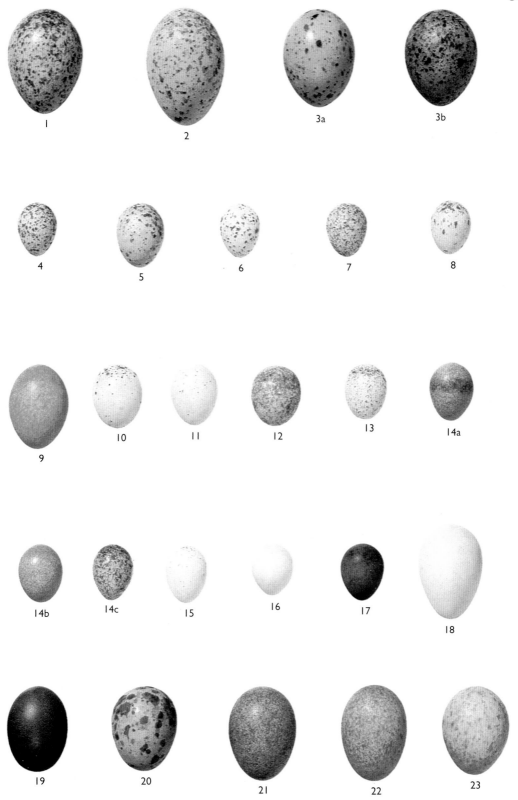

56

Plate 57 Approx. life-size

THRASHERS (see also Plate 56). The eggs are smooth and glossy. A clutch, usually of 3–5 eggs, is laid in a cup nest in a tree, shrub, or cactus.

OLD WORLD WARBLERS, GNATCATCHERS, OLD WORLD FLYCATCHERS, THRUSHES, and WRENTIT

(The eggs of the **Black-capped Gnatcatcher**, not shown, are similar to those of Blue-gray Gnatcatcher, though paler.)

(**Redwing**, not shown, has eggs similar to those of Fieldfare, though usually with finer markings.)

57

Plate 58 Approx. life-size

WAGTAILS and PIPITS. Eggs glossy. 4–6 eggs laid in a cup nest on the ground among herbage or in a cavity or crevice.

WAXWINGS and SILKY-FLYCATCHER. Eggs slightly to moderately glossy. 2–5 eggs, laid in a cup nest in a tree or shrub.

SHRIKES. The eggs are smooth and glossy. A clutch, usually of 4–7, is laid in a bulky cup nest in a tree or shrub.

VIREOS. Eggs smooth and non-glossy to moderately glossy. 3–4 eggs laid in a pensile cup nest suspended between horizontal twigs.

OLD WORLD SPARROWS. Eggs slightly glossy. 3–6 laid in a domed nest or untidy cup, usually in a hole or crevice, rarely in a more open site.

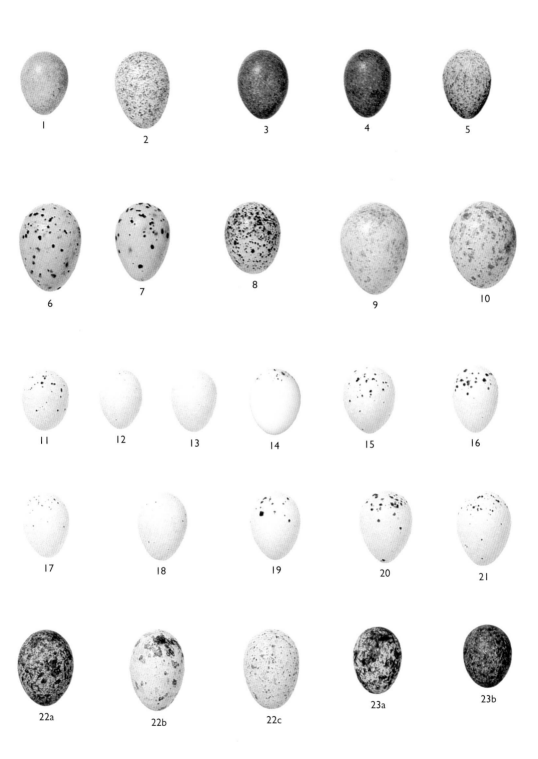

58

Plate 59 Approx. life-size, but nos. 2, 12, 14, 15, 16 and 22 are approx. ¾ life-size

A M E R I C A N   W O O D   W A R B L E R S (see also Plate 60). The eggs are smooth and slightly glossy; sometimes rather rounded. 3–5 eggs laid in a cup or sometimes a domed nest, in a tree or shrub, on the ground or in a cavity.

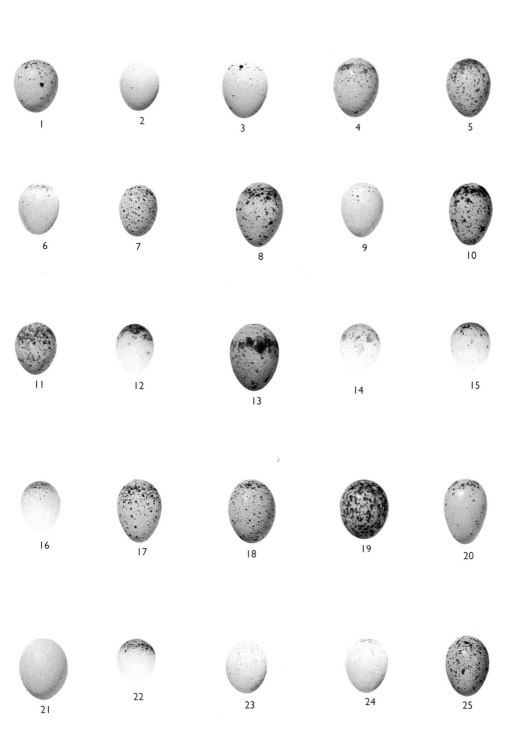

59

Plate 60 Approx. life-size, but nos. 5, 18 and 19 are approx. ¾ life-size.

AMERICAN WOOD WARBLERS (see also Plate 59). The eggs are smooth and slightly glossy; sometimes rather rounded. A clutch, usually of 3–5 eggs, is laid in a cup or sometimes a domed nest, in a tree or shrub, on the ground, or in a cavity.

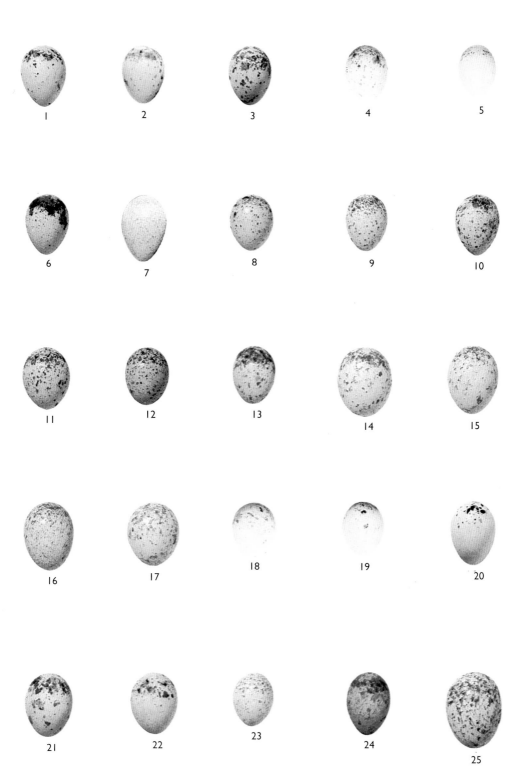

60

Plate 61 Approx. life-size

BLACKBIRDS and ORIOLES. The eggs are smooth and glossy, varying in different species from elongated to rather round. A clutch, usually of 3–5 eggs, is laid in a bulky cup in a tree, shrub, or herbage, in a deep cup among waterside plants, a domed nest on the ground in grasses, or a pensile cup or long pensile bag suspended from a twig. Cowbirds are brood parasites, laying single eggs in other birds' nests.

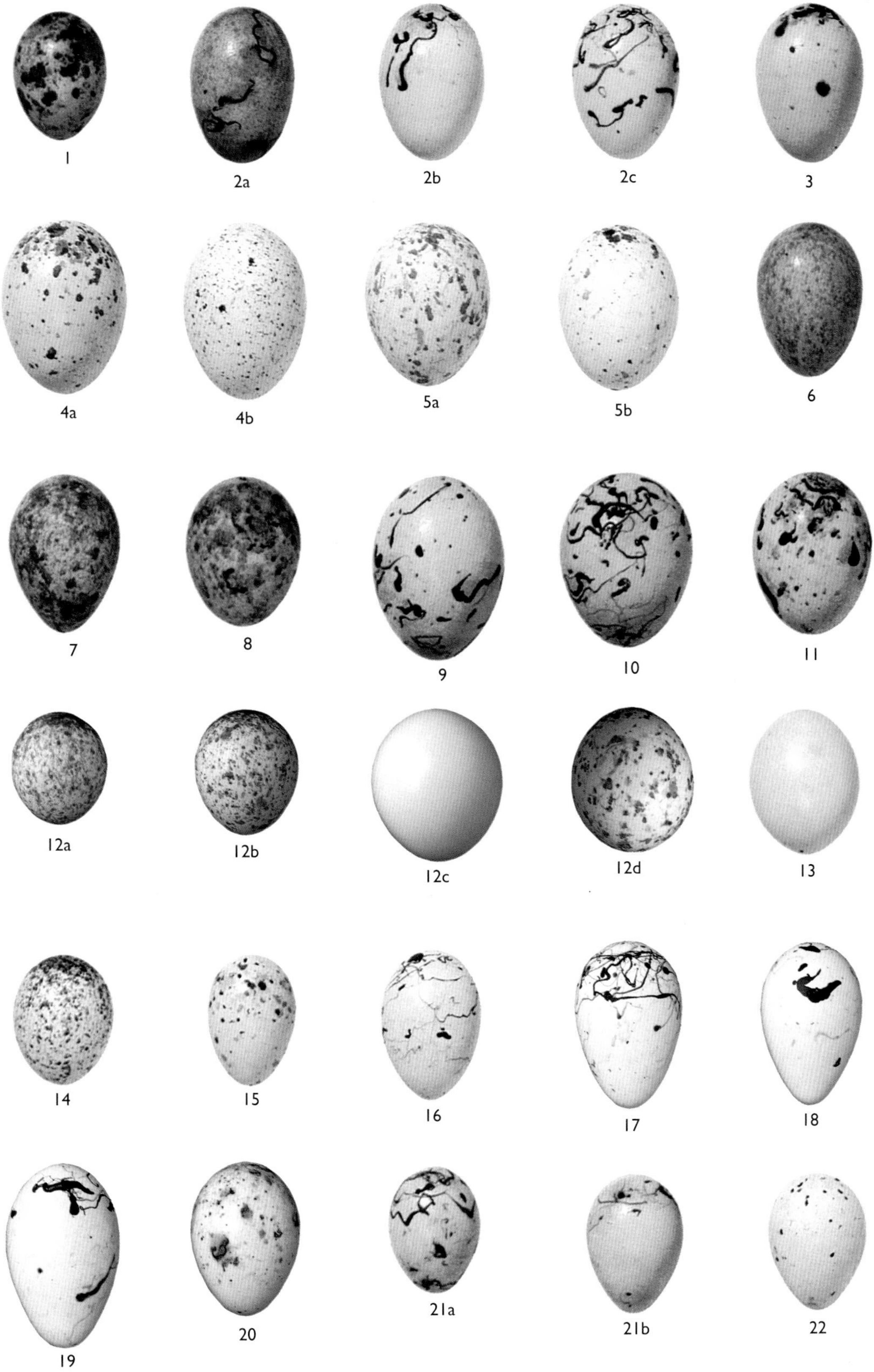

61

1 2a 2b 2c 3

4a 4b 5a 5b 6

7 8 9 10 11

12a 12b 12c 12d 13

14 15 16 17 18

19 20 21a 21b 22

Plate 62 Approx. life-size

STARLINGS. The eggs are smooth and glossy. A clutch, usually of 4–7 eggs, is laid in a cup nest in a cavity.

SPARROWS and BUNTINGS (see also Plates 63 and 64). The eggs are smooth and slightly to moderately glossy. A clutch, usually of 3–5 eggs, is laid in a cup nest, or rarely a domed structure, on the ground among herbage, or in a shrub or low tree.

(**Eastern Towhee**, not shown, has eggs similar to Spotted Towhee.)

(**California Towhee**, not shown, has eggs similar to those of Canyon Towhee, though less heavily marked.)

FINCHES. The eggs are smooth and non-glossy to moderately glossy. A clutch, usually of 3–5 eggs, is laid in a cup nest in a tree, shrub, or ground herbage.

(The eggs of **Black Rosy-Finch** and **Brown-capped Rosy-Finch**, not shown, are similar to those of the Gray-crowned Rosy-Finch.)

(**Brambling**, not shown, has eggs similar to those of Pine Siskin, though markings not confined to larger end.)

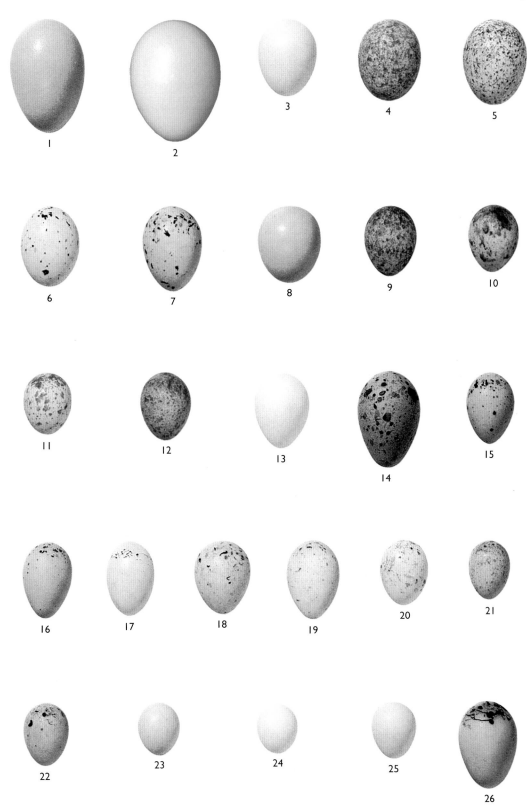

62

Plate 63 Approx. life-size

S PA R R OW S (see also Plates 62 and 64). The eggs are smooth and slightly to moderately glossy. A clutch, usually of 3–5 eggs, is laid in a cup nest on the ground among herbage, or in a shrub or low tree.

(The eggs of the **Five-striped Sparrow**, not shown, are dull white.)

(The **Nelson's Sharp-tailed Sparrow**, not shown, has eggs similar to those of Saltmarsh Sharp-tailed Sparrow.)

(**Harris's Sparrow**, not shown, has white to pale greenish-white eggs marked with brown to reddish-brown.)

63

Plate 64 Approx. life-size

TANAGERS, CARDINALS, GROSBEAKS, SPARROWS, and BUNTINGS (see also Plates 62 and 63). The eggs are smooth and slightly to moderately glossy. A clutch, usually of 3–5 eggs, is laid in a cup nest, on the ground among herbage, or in a shrub or low tree. (In the case of some tanagers and grosbeaks, the nest may be found considerably higher.)

(Eggs of **Flame-colored Tanager**, not shown, are pale blue, speckled with reddish-brown and dark lavender, mainly at the larger end.)

(**McKay's Bunting**, not shown, has eggs that are similar to those of Snow Bunting.)

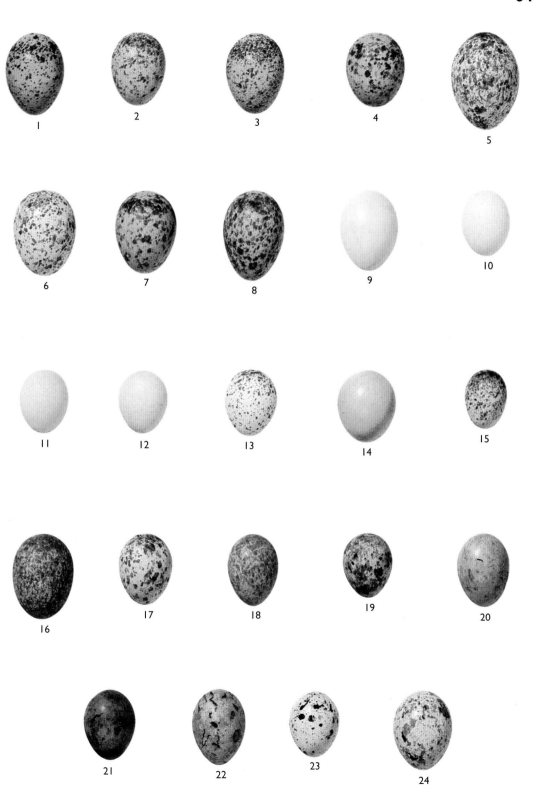

64

Horned Lark (*Eremophila alpestris*)   Plates 16, 54
Breeds in a variety of open habitats, including tundra or barren higher ground; bare, sandy, and stony terrain, and also in sparse grasses. Farther south occurs in prairies, drier grasslands, and larger treeless areas of cultivation. Nest on the ground in a small hollow, usually in the shelter of a plant-tuft or stone.
Nest: A cup of dry grass and plant stems, loosely put together, with a finer inner lining of plant down and hair. In a small hollow made by female. Small pieces of peat, dung, or pebbles may be assembled around the nest or on one side of it. Built by female over 2–4 days. **Breeding season:** Late February in south to mid-June in north of range. Will replace lost clutch. Double-brooded, and sometimes treble-brooded. **Eggs:** Usually 4, sometimes 2–7. Subelliptical. Smooth and glossy. Pale greenish-white, heavily speckled with fine buffish-brown; often with a blackish hair-line, at times with sparse bolder spots or dark zones. 23 × 16 mm. **Incubation:** Eggs laid at daily intervals. Incubation by female alone. 10–14 days. **Nestling:** Altricial and downy. Skin brown. Down long and pale creamy-buff, covering much of upper surface of head and body. Mouth bright orange-yellow; three dark spots on tongue. Gape flanges yellow. **Nestling period:** Young are tended and fed by both parents. Eyes open at 3–4 days. Leave nest at 9–12 days. Can fly poorly 3–5 days later.

Swallows (*Hirundinidae*)

Small birds, taking their food on the wing. The nest is usually a mud structure, varying in shape with the species, fixed to rocks or walls, and sheltered by an overhang; or a more typical nest in a tree cavity, nest-box, or earth tunnel. The eggs are often elongated, white or finely spotted. Young are downy on head, back and sometimes thighs; with yellowish, unspotted mouths.

Purple Martin (*Progne subis*)   Plate 54
Breeds widely where human settlement occurs. Natural nest-site appears to be a cavity or crevice in rocks, tree, or cactus, including old woodpecker holes. Now extensively uses artificial sites, nest-boxes, or gourds. Usually found in open areas near water above 5 ft. and usually nests in colonies varying in size according to site. Male sometimes polygamous.
Nest: An accumulation of loose plant material, grass, leaves, stems, twigs, straws, feathers, rags, and bark shreds. Built by both sexes. **Breeding season:** Begins late March in south to late May or early June in north of range. Single-brooded, possibly double-brooded at times. **Eggs:** Usually 4–5, sometimes 3–8. Oval to long oval. Smooth and non-glossy. White and unmarked. 24 × 17 mm. **Incubation:** Only by female, beginning before last egg is laid. 15–17 days. **Nestling:** Altricial and naked. Flesh pink. Gape flanges pale yellow. **Nestling period:** Young tended by both parents. Blue-black feathers on back and wings emerge at *c.* 10 days. Leave nest at 26–30 days. Roost in nest after leaving.

Tree Swallow (*Tachycineta bicolor*)   Plate 54
Breeds over a wide variety of habitats, often preferring open woodlands or farmlands near water. Nest in a natural cavity or woodpecker hole in tree, also in cavity or crevice in building or wooden structure, and nest-box, occasionally sign-posts, pipes, and cutbanks. Height varies from 3–25 ft. up, but usually closer to 13 ft. Can be semi-colonial. Occasionally an additional adult assists the pair.
Nest: A collection of dry grasses, pine needles, etc., with a cup lined with feathers. Built by female, rarely with help by male, from 3 days to 2 weeks. **Breeding season:** Begins late April in south to mid-May in north of range. Usually ends early July.

Single-brooded. **Eggs.** Usually 4–6; larger clutches may be from two females. Subelliptical to oval. Smooth and non-glossy or slightly glossy. White and unmarked. 19 × 13 mm. **Incubation:** By female, usually beginning at completion of clutch. 13–16 days. **Nestling:** Altricial and downy. Skin pale pink. Down whitish. Mouth pale yellow; gape flanges creamy-white. **Nestling period:** Young brooded by female; fed by both. Young leave nest at 16–24 days.

Violet-green Swallow (*Tachycineta thalassina*) Plate 54

Breeds in open forests and around human settlement. Nest in a crevice or hole in cliff surface or rocky outcrop, or in old woodpecker hole, natural cavity in tree, old nest of Cliff Swallow or Bank Swallow, crevice or cavity in building, or in nest-box. Small colonies of up to 25 pairs are common. Usually 9–17 ft. up, but can be much higher. **Nest:** An accumulation of dry grasses with a cup lined with feathers and sometimes hair or fine fibers. Built by both sexes, but mainly by female. **Breeding season:** Begins early May in south to late May in north of range. Usually ends by early August. Single-brooded. **Eggs:** Usually 4–5, sometimes 6. Subelliptical to oval. Smooth and non-glossy to slightly glossy. White and unmarked. 18 × 13 mm. **Incubation:** By female, beginning before completion of clutch. 13–15 days. **Nestling.** Altricial and downy. Skin pale pink. Down cream-colored; on head, shoulders, and back. Gape flanges whitish. **Nestling period:** Young tended by both parents (though mainly by female). Eyes open at 10–11 days. Feathers break sheaths at 10–13 days. Leave nest at 23–25 days. Young remain near nest for a few days when fed by both adults. After leaving may be fed on the wing at times.

Northern Rough-winged Swallow (*Stelgidopteryx serripennis*) Plate 54

Breeds over a wide range of open country, especially near water; nesting usually in solitary or scattered pairs. Nest a burrow dug in a steep-faced earth, sand, or gravel bank. Banks may be from 2–50 ft. high. Burrows of variable length and old kingfisher burrows also used. Also crevices and holes in buildings and man-made structures, drainpipes, and, exceptionally, a hole in a tree. May be semi-colonial in the western part of its range. **Nest:** Usually in burrow, 1–6 ft. long. Nest an accumulation of grasses, weeds, and loose plant material; the cup lined with fine grasses and rootlets. Built by female, with limited help by male over 3–7 days, sometimes much longer (20 days). **Breeding season:** Begins late-April in south to mid-June in north of range. Single-brooded. **Eggs:** Usually 6–7, sometimes 4–8. Subelliptical to oval. Smooth and glossy. White and unmarked. 18 × 13 mm. **Incubation:** By female. 15–16 days. **Nestling:** Altricial and downy. Down very pale gray. Flesh pink. Mouth and gape flanges yellow. Bill, legs, and feet pink at first. Bill tip dark. **Nestling period:** Young tended by both parents. Female broods by day for first 5 days, by night for first 9. Eyes open at 7–8 days. Feathered at c. 12–13 days. Leave at 18–21 days.

Bank Swallow (*Riparia riparia*) Plate 54

Breeds in open country, usually near water. A colonial nester. Nest in a burrow in a vertical bank, natural or artificial, quarry or cliff. Located above 3 ft. and often high up. However, in extreme north of range where sites are scarce may nest almost at ground level. Existing artificial holes may be used. **Nest:** A tunnel bored by both adults. Opening: 1 × 2 in.; depth: 10–60 in. (average 16 in.). The terminal chamber lined with plant stems, feathers, and similar material. **Breeding season:** Begins late April in south to mid-June in north of range. Usually double-brooded. **Eggs:** Usually 4–5, sometimes 3–7. Subelliptical. Smooth and slightly to moderately glossy. White. 18 × 13 mm. **Incubation:** By both adults.

12–16 days. **Nestling:** Altricial and downy. Down, on head and back, short; pale gray. Skin pink. Mouth and gape flanges pale lemon-yellow. **Nestling period:** Young tended by both adults. Fed in nest cavity at first but later come to mouth of burrow. Leave nest at *c*. 19 days. Can already fly at 17–18 days.

Cliff Swallow (*Hirundo pyrrhonota*)   **Figure 73, Plate 54**
Breeds in places where rock outcrops or cliff faces or buildings provide sites. Nest a rounded mud structure fixed to a vertical surface and protected by an overhang. Most frequently on rock faces or under eaves of buildings; but nests have been recorded on very large tree-trunks, just below projecting limbs. Nests usually in crowded colonies, often large. Located above 3 ft.
Nest: A rounded structure of mud pellets with some plant fiber or hair added; usually with a projecting and slightly downward-directed neck, 5–6 in. long. Cavity thinly lined with grasses and dry stems with an inner cup of feathers and finer fibers. Built by both over 1–2 weeks. **Breeding season:** Begins mid-April in south to late May in north of range. Double-brooded. **Eggs:** Usually 4–5, occasionally 3–6. Long subelliptical to long oval, or subelliptical. White, creamy-white or tinted pink; speckled, spotted, or blotched in shades of light to dark brown, reddish-brown, purplish-brown, and paler brownish-gray or gray. Markings often concentrated at or around the larger end and sparser elsewhere. 20 × 14 mm. **Incubation:** By both adults. 12–14 days, sometimes to 16 days. **Nestling:** Altricial and downy. Skin light pink. Down light gray. Mouth pinkish-flesh-colored; gape flanges pale flesh. **Nestling period:** Young tended by both parents. They fly first at 23 days but may return to the nest for 2–3 days.

Figure 73. Cliff Swallow: nest *c*. 6–7 in. across; opening 1¾ in. diameter; colony on cliff face.

Cave Swallow (*Hirundo fulva*)   Figure 74, Plate 54

Breeds in the partially dark zones of large caves, caverns, and cave-like highway culverts in west-central Texas and southeast New Mexico, rarely southeast Arizona and in Florida. Nest attached to upper wall or irregularities of roof, or on a ledge, often at eye-level in a culvert. Colony nests usually more scattered than those of Cliff Swallows, but clustered where the site permits. Located above 3 ft.

Nest: A half-cup of mud pellets with some plant fiber or rock chips added; stuck to a steep surface under a partial overhang, and somewhat similar to that of a Barn Swallow in appearance though usually closer to a ceiling and with fewer fibers involved. Lined with feathers, plant fragments and similar debris. Nests may be added to and re-used in subsequent years. Built by both sexes. **Breeding season:** Early March to early September (Texas); early April to mid-July (Florida). Usually double-brooded, sometimes treble-brooded. **Eggs:** Usually 4, and 3 in second brood. Oval. Smooth and moderately glossy. White, finely speckled and spotted in reddish-brown or purplish-brown. 20 × 14 mm. **Incubation:** By both. 15–18 days. **Nestling:** Altricial and downy. Light pale gray down on head and back. Pink skin, yellow gape. **Nestling period:** Young tended by both parents. Fly at 22–26 days. Young may return to nest for several days where they are cared for by parents.

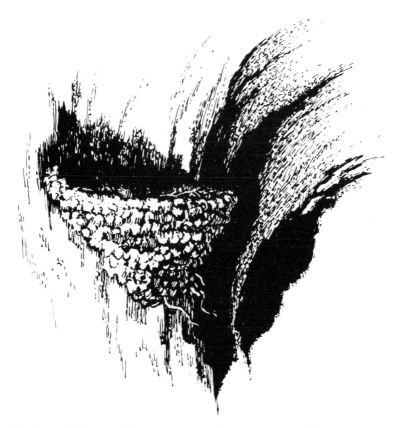

Figure 74. Cave Swallow: c. 4–5 in. across; nest plastered to cave wall.

Barn Swallow (*Hirundo rustica*)   Figure 75, Plate 54
Breeds in a variety of habitats, but more particularly near water and in open country.
The nest is usually stuck against a vertical surface, but requires some support
although often slight. The natural site probably a cave roof, but more often occurs
on upper ledges such as rafters or girders in buildings of all kinds (e.g., farm buildings) and under bridges or culverts. Exceptionally on a tree. From 6–40 ft. up. Often
in colonies.
Nest: An open shallow cup of mud pellets mixed with vegetable fibers and plant fragments; sparsely lined with feathers. Built by both adults. **Breeding season:** Begins
early April in south to early June in north of range. Season prolonged. Double-
brooded. **Eggs:** Usually 4–5, at times 3–8. Long subelliptical to long oval. Smooth
and glossy. White, sparingly marked with variable spotting of reddish-brown, lilac,
or pale gray. 20 × 14 mm. **Incubation:** By both. 14–16 days. **Nestling:** Altricial and
downy. Down on head and back, long and sparse; gray. Mouth lemon-yellow; gape
flanges whitish. **Nestling period:** Young tended by both adults. Food brought by
parents in the throat. Nest left after 17–24 days. Young return to roost on nest at first.
May be fed by adults in mid-air.

Jays, Magpies, and Crows (*Corvidae*)

Medium to large perching birds, nesting in trees or bushes, or on rock ledges. In most
species nests are made mainly of twigs and muddy earth is added to these, helping to
bind the structure. There is a soft inner lining. The eggs are mostly blue or green
with olive-green and blackish markings. In the true crows there are frequently one
or two pale, atypical eggs in a clutch. Young are downy or naked, the mouth usually
red or pink, and gape flanges pink or yellowish. Food is brought to the young

Figure 75. Barn Swallow: *c.* 4–5 in. across; nest against inside roof with a beam foundation.

pouched in the throat, and regurgitated. In a few of these species, the young may be cared for by helpers as well as the parents.

Gray Jay (*Perisoreus canadensis*) — Plate 56

Breeds mainly in conifer forests, sometimes in mixed woodland. Nest usually in a conifer, often hidden in the crown or out towards the end of a branch sometimes exposed. Usually 5–12 ft. up, sometimes up to 30 ft.

Nest: Usually a thick-walled cup, of twigs, bark-strips, grass stems, moss, lichens, and other soft materials, with spiders' webbing and cocoons on the outside; the inner lining thickly padded with fine dry grasses, moss, plant down, catkins, hair, feathers, and fur. Built by both sexes, sometimes over a period of over 3 weeks. **Breeding season:** Begins March. Usually ends by mid-May. Single-brooded. **Eggs:** Usually 3–4, sometimes 2–5. Subelliptical to short subelliptical. Smooth and fairly glossy. Very pale greenish or gray-green; speckled, spotted, and blotched fairly thickly with olive and paler gray. Markings tend to be concentrated at the larger end. 29 × 21 mm. **Incubation:** By female alone, beginning with first egg. 16–18 days. **Nestling:** Altricial with sparse down on head and back. Flesh pale pinkish. **Nestling period:** Young tended by both parents. For first few days female broods and male brings all food. Young leave at 22–24 days.

Steller's Jay (*Cyanocitta stelleri*) — Figure 76, Plate 56

Breeds in woodland, coniferous or mixed, usually near an open space, or in open woodland, parkland, or cultivated areas with trees. Nest in a tree, usually a conifer, sometimes in shrub or bush, occasionally in a tree hollow or cavity, or in a building. Nest usually 8–16 ft. up, exceptionally from 2–100 ft. up.

Nest: A cup of twigs, usually with dead leaves (and often paper) in base, lined with mud, and with an inner lining of fine rootlets, and sometimes pine needles, hair, or grasses. Built by both sexes. **Breeding season:** Begins early to mid-April in south to early May in north of range. **Eggs:** Usually 4, sometimes 2–6. Subelliptical to short sub-elliptical. Smooth and fairly glossy. Similar to the bluish and greenish types of Blue Jay eggs. 31 × 22 mm. **Incubation:** Almost always by female only, fed by male. *c.* 16 days. **Nestling:** Altricial and naked. **Nestling period:** Young tended by both parents. Fly at *c.* 18 days. Dependent on parents for *c.* 1 month after leaving nest.

Blue Jay (*Cyanocitta cristata*) — Figure 77, Plate 56

Breeds in woodland, particularly mixed woodland, cultivated areas with trees, and parkland. Nest in tree, shrub, or bush, at varying heights, usually 10–40 ft. up; rarely in or on buildings.

Nest: A cup of twigs, strips of bark, rootlets, grass and weed stems, paper, rags, and feathers. Mud may be built into the structure. Thinner lining of fine rootlets or similar material. Built by both sexes. **Breeding season:** Begins mid-March in south to early May in north of range. Single-brooded in north of range, but lost clutches replaced. Occasionally double- or treble-brooded in south. **Eggs:** Usually 4–5, sometimes 2–6. Subelliptical to short subelliptical. Smooth and fairly glossy. Very variable. Pale olive, buff, pinkish-buff, green bluish-green, or rarely greenish-white; spotted, speckled, or with small blotches of various shades of brown, olive, and sometimes dark brown, with paler gray and purple. Markings tend to be small and generally distributed. 28 × 20 mm. **Incubation:** By female alone, fed by male. 16–18 days. **Nestling:** Altricial and naked. Mouth red. No distinct gape flanges; thin and cream-colored or even pale yellow. **Nestling period:** Young tended by both parents. Brooded by female only. Eyes open at *c.* 5 days, feathers break sheaths at 8–9 days. Young leave nest at 17–21 days, probably independent after *c.* 3 weeks more, but may be partly fed for the further period.

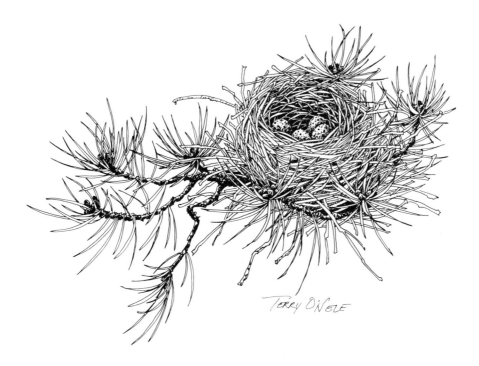

Figure 76. Steller's Jay: c. 10 in. across; typical nest in conifer.

Figure 77. Blue Jay: c. 15 days old.

Green Jay (*Cyanocorax yncas*)   **Plate 55**
Breeds in forest and thick scrub in south Texas. Nest usually well hidden in thicker shrubs and trees, often low, at 5–25 ft. up.
Nest: A cup, often of slight construction. Of twigs, sometimes thorny, with a shallowish inner cup of vine tendrils, fine rootlets, and sometimes dry grasses, moss, or dead leaves. Built by both. **Breeding season:** Late March to mid-July. Single-brooded. **Eggs:** Usually 4, occasionally 3–5. Subelliptical to short subelliptical. Smooth and slightly glossy. Creamy-white, or very pale greenish, or pale buff or olive; finely and profusely speckled and freckled, or more sparsely marked with small spots or blotches of olive, brown or buffish-brown, and pale gray or purple. 27 × 20 mm. **Incubation:** By female alone, fed by male. 15–17 days. **Nestling:** Altricial. Dark-skinned and naked at hatching. Greenish-gray down along back and on head at 4 days. **Nestling period:** Young tended by both parents, at first brooded by female while male brings food. Begin feathering at *c.* 12 days. Leave nest at 19 days, but not able to fly properly. Independent in *c.* 2 weeks more.

Brown Jay (*Cyanocorax morio*)   **Plate 55**
Breeds in small numbers in woodlands and mesquite along the lower Rio Grande in Texas. Nest in a tree or shrub often far out on a long, slender branch; usually 20–70 ft. up.
Nest: A bulky platform made of long rough sticks, with smaller sticks filling the center portion, and finished with a shallow cup lined with fibrous roots, fine twigs, or vines. Up to 6 birds of both sexes may build the nest. **Breeding season:** April–May; 1, occasionally 2 broods. **Eggs:** Usually 3–5, sometimes 2–6, rarely 1–8. Subelliptical to long subelliptical. Smooth and moderately glossy. A pale chalky grayish-white to light bluish-white, thickly speckled and blotched with brown. 35 × 25 mm. **Incubation:** By female (may be assisted by helpers from previous years' broods), fed by male and/or helpers. 18–20 days. **Nestling:** Altricial and naked. Skin yellow, darker on upper surface. Bill and feet are yellow. Inside of mouth is red. **Nestling period:** Young brooded by female, leave nest at 23–24 days. Young broods of previous year (up to 5 per nest) assist parents in feeding the nestlings and guarding them.

Florida Scrub-Jay (*Aphelocoma coerulescens*)   **Plate 55**
Breeds in oak scrub in sandy soil, including thickets of shrubby oaks, sand pine, wild olive, and palmetto in central Florida. Nest in a short tree or shrub, 4–12 ft. up. May nest in a loose colony of up to 6 nests.
Nest: A substantial, thick-walled cup of oak twigs of varying shapes and thickness; lined with fine rootlets. Built by both sexes. **Breeding season:** Early March to late June. Generally single-brooded. **Eggs:** 2–5, though usually 3 or 4. Subelliptical to long subelliptical. Smooth and slightly glossy. Pea-green to pale glaucous-green or pale grayish, blotched and spotted with irregularly shaped markings of cinnamon-rufous, typically heavier at the larger end with pinkish lilac underlying markings. 28 × 20 mm. **Incubation:** By female, fed by male. 17–19 days. **Nestling:** Altricial and naked. Reddish-pink skin. Bill and legs pale yellow. **Nestling period:** Young brooded by female, fed by both parents, with up to 6 (though usually 1 or 2) other birds present as helpers (mostly yearlings) at half the nests. Back feathers emerge at 4 days. Eyes open at 4–7 days. Young leave nest at 17–20 days. Cannot fly for many days. Feed themselves at *c.* 110 days.

Island Scrub-Jay (*Aphelocoma insularis*)   **Plate 55**
Breeds in the wooded, scrub oak-dominated canyons of Santa Cruz Island off the California coast. Nest in oak or ironwood trees, or dense bushes. Usually 8–12 ft., though may be 40 ft. up.

Nest: A large and bulky cup of mainly live-oak twigs; lined with finer twigs, coiled rootlets, and a mixture of grasses and, rarely, hair. Built by both. **Breeding season:** Early March to late April. Single-brooded, though lost clutch will be replaced. **Eggs:** 3–4, rarely 5. Short-subelliptical to subelliptical. Smooth and slightly glossy. A light bluish-green, lightly spotted with faint olive dots. 29 × 22 mm. **Incubation:** By female, fed by male. *c.* 18 days. **Nestling:** Altricial and naked. **Nestling period:** Brooded by female; leave at *c.* 21 days. Fed by both for 2 months.

Western Scrub-Jay (Aphelocoma californica)   Plate 55

Breeds in scrub woodland and low scrub, in arid and other areas; and open and broken woodland, shrubby forest edge, mangrove swamp, orchards, and cultivated areas with many low trees. Nest in a tree, shrub, bush, or vine tangle, usually fairly low, *c.* 3–10 ft. up.
Nest: A cup of twigs mixed with moss, weed stems and grasses; lined with fine roots, plant and bark fibers, and occasionally hair. Built by both sexes. **Breeding season:** Begins early April. Single-brooded but lost clutches replaced. **Eggs:** Usually 2–3, sometimes up to 6. Clutches smaller in arid areas. Subelliptical to short subelliptical or oval. Smooth and fairly glossy. Blue, greenish-blue to pale olive-green, or blue with a pinkish wash; speckled, spotted, and sometimes with blotches of light or dark drab or olive-brown, purplish-brown or reddish-brown, and paler gray and lilac. Rarely eggs are whitish, pale buff, or light green with reddish markings. 28 × 20 mm. **Incubation:** By female alone, beginning before completion of clutch, fed by male. 15–17 days. **Nestling:** Altricial and naked. **Nestling period:** Young tended by both parents. Leave nest at *c.* 18 days?

Mexican Jay (Aphelocoma ultramarina)   Plate 55

Breeds usually in oak or pine–oak woodlands of montane areas of south-central Arizona, southwest New Mexico, and Big Bend area of Texas. Nest in a tree, usually in rock areas with steep slopes, or where the woodland canopy is broken by tall pines. Nest in a tree, usually a live oak, 6–50 ft. up, usually 15–25 ft. up. Breeds in small loose colonies or solitary pairs. Pairs in a breeding colony may assist members of other pairs in some breeding activities.
Nest: A cup of coarse twigs and sticks broken off trees, lined with smaller twigs, grass, and weed stems and with an inner lining of vine tendrils, fine rootlets, and hair. Built by both sexes. **Breeding season:** Begins early March. Usually ends by mid-June. **Eggs:** Usually 4, sometimes 3–7. Subelliptical to long subelliptical. Smooth and fairly glossy. Pale greenish-blue to yellowish-green, speckled, spotted, and blotched with light to dark brown and paler gray; but usually unmarked in the Arizona subspecies. 30 × 22 mm. **Incubation:** By female alone, fed by male or by other members of breeding flock. 18 days. **Nestling:** Altricial and naked. Skin purplish-pink or purplish-flesh color. Mouth pink; gape flanges ivory or pale yellow. Bill pinkish. **Nestling period:** Young tended by both parents, and other members of flock may help to feed young. Young brooded by mother during most of first 2 weeks, feather between 10–20 days, leave nest at 24–28 days. Older young are fed by any adults.

Pinyon Jay (Gymnorhinus cyanocephalus)   Plate 55

Breeds in hilly and mountain regions, often where Pinyon Pines occur. Nest in a tree or shrub, usually pine, live oak or juniper. Nest usually in a fairly open site 3–80, but usually 5–30, ft. up. Nest in a loose scattered colony.
Nest: A large cup of twigs, weed stems, and similar material (rarely pine needles), well lined with rootlets, bark strips, vegetable fiber, grasses, hair, and wool. Built by both. **Breeding season:** Within a prolonged potential period, apparently dependent

on pinyon seed supplies. Records from February to October. Single-brooded. **Eggs:** Usually 3–4, sometimes 5. Elliptical to short elliptical. Smooth and slightly glossy. Pale bluish, greenish, or bluish-white; finely speckled and spotted with reddish-brown or, purplish-brown, and occasionally larger spots and blotches, usually concentrated about the larger end. 29 × 22 mm. **Incubation:** By female alone, fed by male. 17 days. **Nestlings:** Altricial, naked at first. Skin pink at first, later purplish-blue. Mouth orange-red. **Nestling period:** Young tended by both parents. Eyes open at 7 days. Leave nest at *c.* 3 weeks, forming creches with other young. Older nestlings sometimes fed by adults other than parents.

Clark's Nutcracker (*Nucifraga columbiana*)   Plate 55
Breeds in mountain conifer forest. Nest in a juniper or conifer, sheltered by foliage, 8–45 ft. up, often towards the end of a branch.
Nest: A large cup of twigs, sticks, and sometimes bark strips, lined with bark fiber and wood pulp, and with an inner lining of dry grasses, and plant and bark fibers. There may be a layer of soil or mud in the base of the cup between the two linings. Built by both sexes, but mainly by female. **Breeding season:** Begins early March. Single-brooded. **Eggs:** Usually 2–3, sometimes 4, rarely 5–6. Subelliptical to elliptical. Smooth and slightly glossy. Pale green, grayish-green or greenish-white; spotted and speckled with brown, olive and paler gray. Markings usually small and sparse. 32 × 23 mm. **Incubation:** By both sexes. 16–18 days. **Nestling:** Altricial. Naked at first, then with sparse white down. **Nestling period:** Young tended and brooded by both parents; leave nest at *c.* 22 days. Fed by adults for some time after leaving nest.

Black-billed Magpie (*Pica pica*)   Plate 55
Breeds in canyons and valleys near water, wherever tall shrubby growth and scattered trees occur with open spaces. Nest usually in the top of a tall shrub often thorny, or in trees where they are usually fairly low, up to 25 ft. Nest usually firmly set in a twig fork or among thick twigs. A number of pairs usually nest in the same locality.
Nest: A large, bulky cup of thick, often thorny twigs, with a heavy lining of mud or dung; and an inner lining of rootlets, thin weed or grass stems, and hair. The cup is covered with an openwork, sketchy-looking dome of twigs (diameter of *c.* 3 ft.), with one or more openings. Nest built by both sexes, the male bringing material, over as much as 6 weeks. **Breeding season:** Begins late March in south to late May in north of range. Single-brooded. **Eggs:** Usually 5–9, rarely up to 12. Subelliptical, short sub-elliptical, or oval. Pale greenish-blue, grayish-blue, blue, buff, or olive; heavily spotted, and speckled or, more exceptionally, blotched, with olive-brown and gray. Markings sometimes heavier at one end. 33 × 23 mm. **Incubation:** By female only beginning with first egg. 17–22 days. **Nestling:** Altricial and naked. Skin pink at first, then yellowish and grayish. Mouth deep pink; gape flanges pale pink. **Nestling period:** Young tended by both adults. 22–28 days in nest. Independence at 60–70 days.

Yellow-billed Magpie (*Pica nuttalli*)   Plate 55
Breeds in more open hilly country with scattered trees, cultivated areas with trees, or parkland in central and coastal valleys of California. Nest usually in a tall or medium-sized tree, usually high up (40–60 ft.) and well out on a branch. A number of pairs usually nest close together.
Nest: Similar to that of Black-billed Magpie, though somewhat smaller. Built by both over several weeks. **Breeding season:** Begins early March. Probably ends late June. Single-brooded. **Eggs:** 6–7, sometimes 5–8. Spherical to subelliptical. Olive-green to pale olive-buff, finely speckled with brown or olive. 31 × 22 mm. **Incubation:** By

female only, in part fed by male. 16–22 days. **Nestling:** Altricial and naked. Skin pink. Mouth deep pink; gape flanges pale pink. **Nestling period:** Young tended by both parents. After leaving nest young remain near nest for an additional 5 days, and are fed to some extent for up to 7 weeks more.

American Crow (*Corvus brachyrhynchos*)   Plates 16, 55

Occurs in a wide range of country where some trees or scrub are present; from open woodland and woodland edge to parkland and cultivation. Nest in a tree, shrub, or bush (10–70 ft. up); exceptionally on telegraph poles, or on the ground. Usually nests in single pairs, but sometimes several near each other.

Nest: A large cup of sticks and coarse stems, lined with bark strips and fibers and sometimes mud or earth, and with an inner lining of rootlets, grasses, fur, hair, moss, etc. Built by both adults over *c.* 12 days. **Breeding season:** Begins late January in south to early May in north of range. Single- or double-brooded. **Eggs:** Usually 4–5, sometimes 3–6. Subelliptical to oval and short to long. Smooth and slightly glossy. Greenish-blue to pale blue; very variably spotted, speckled and with small blotches of olive, olive-brown, or blackish-olive, and a few paler gray or purplish markings. Markings vary from sparse to overall, usually small, and with markings often concentrated at the larger end. 41 ×29 mm. **Incubation:** By female. 18 days. **Nestling:** Altricial and downy. Skin pink or pinkish-flesh-colored, becoming brownish-gray. Down sparse and grayish-brown, on head and upperparts. **Nestling period:** Young tended by both parents. Young of previous years may assist in caring for young. Feather between 20–30 days, leave nest at *c.* 35 days.

Northwestern Crow (*Corvus caurinus*)   Plate 55

Breeds in coastal areas and on offshore islands. Nest in a tree, shrub, or bush. Occasionally on ledge or recess of rocky outcrop or bank, or on the ground under an overhanging boulder. Usually 8–20 ft. up, sometimes to 70 ft. Sometimes semi-colonial.

Nest: A large cup of twigs and sticks, mixed with mud, and lined with bark fibers and strips and grasses: with an inner lining of dead grasses, bark and plant fibers, hair, etc. Built by both sexes. **Breeding season:** Begins in May. **Eggs:** Usually 4–5. Very similar to those of Fish Crow and other crows. 40 ×28 mm. **Incubation:** By female? *c.* 18 days. **Nestling:** Altricial and downy. Grayish-brown down on head, back, and wings. Flesh pink. **Nestling period:** Little information. Fed by both?

Mexican Crow (*Corvus imparatus*)   Plate 55

A rare breeder in arid, open country, semi-desert scrub, open riparian habitat, towns, or farming country in extreme south Texas lowlands. Nest semi-colonially in a low bush, tree, or man-made object.

Nest: A stick nest lined with leaves, grasses or reeds. Built by both sexes. **Breeding season:** Late February to mid-June. **Eggs:** 4 or 5. Subelliptical to oval. Smooth and slightly glossy. 35 ×25 mm. Greenish or pale blue eggs blotched and streaked with pale olive-buff and brown. **Incubation:** By female. 17–18 days. **Nestling:** No information. **Nestling period:** Little information. Fed by both. Leave at 30–35 days?

Fish Crow (*Corvus ossifragus*)   Plate 55

Breeds by marshes, rivers, and lakes, coastal or inland. Nest in a tree, usually high (20–80 ft.), but sometimes as low as 6 ft. Usually in small colony of a few well-spaced pairs.

Nest: A large cup of sticks and twigs, lined with bark strips and fibers and sometimes with mud or dung; and with an inner lining of bark fibers, hair, grasses, pine needles, and similar material. Built by both. **Breeding season:** Begins early April in south to early May in north of range. Single-brooded but lost clutches replaced.

Eggs: Usually 4–5. Subelliptical to oval. Smooth and slightly glossy. Bluish-green, or pale green, rarely whitish or buffish-green; speckled, spotted, blotched, or streaked with olive, olive-brown, blackish-olive, or paler gray. Larger markings tend to be bolder and sparser than on eggs of American Crow, and often concentrated towards the larger end. 37 × 27 mm. *Incubation:* By both sexes? 16–18 days. *Nestling:* Altricial, soon acquiring grayish-brown down. *Nestling period:* Fed by both. First flight at 21 days or more.

Chihuahuan Raven (*Corvus cryptoleucus*)   Plate 55

Breeds in deserts, open plains and dry foothills, and around cultivation. Nest in a tree, shrub, or on old building. Low scrub trees often used. 4–40 ft. up.
Nest: A large cup of sticks and twigs, with a softer inner lining of hair, fur, wool, and rags. Built mostly or entirely by female. *Breeding season:* Usually begins mid-May, exceptionally earlier. Single-brooded. *Eggs:* Usually 5–7, sometimes 3–8. Subelliptical to long oval. Smooth and slightly glossy. Pale to very pale blue, greenish-blue or grayish-blue; marked with black, dark olive-brown, and shades of gray, the markings being usually fine and longitudinally elongated lines and scrawls forming a fine, rather poorly-defined lacy pattern, with paler markings predominating. 44 × 30 mm. *Incubation:* By both sexes. *c.* 21 days. *Nestling:* Altricial and downy? Tan or buffy-white to yellowish-white or pinkish-white. *Nestling period:* Fed by both. First flight at *c.* 30 days.

Common Raven (*Corvus corax*)   Plate 55

Breeds mostly in hilly and mountainous regions and on coasts, but also in forests. Nest on a sheltered rock ledge, or on a large fork of a tree. 45–80 ft. up.
Nest: A large mass of twigs, and larger sticks and coarser vegetable matter, bound with earth and moss, well lined with grass tufts, leaves, and moss; and inner lining of wool and hair. Built by both sexes. *Breeding season:* Begins February and early March in south to mid-April in north of range. Single-brooded. *Eggs:* Usually 4–6, rarely 3–7. Subelliptical. Smooth and glossy. Very variable in markings. Light blue, greenish-blue, or pale green; with specks, spots, irregular blotches, streaks, or scribblings of light olive, olive-brown, or dark or blackish-brown, and light gray. Markings vary from sparse to very heavy, and sometimes show irregular patches of olive or greenish washes over more distinct markings. Often variations within a clutch, with one sparsely-marked blue egg. 50 × 33 mm. *Incubation:* Eggs laid at 1–2-day intervals. Incubation by female alone, fed by male, and beginning before clutch is complete. 20–21 days. *Nestling:* Altricial and downy. Down, on head, back, and thighs, short and thick, dull brown. Mouth purplish-pink; gape flanges yellowish-flesh. *Nestling period:* Young tended by both parents. Young leave nest at 5–6 weeks.

Titmice (*Paridae*)

Small insectivorous birds, nesting in a variety of habitats but usually in association with trees. Nest in a hole in a tree, wall, or bank, one or two species excavating their own in soft or rotten wood. Most will use artificial nest-boxes. Nest a cup within the cavity, usually on a base of moss, leaves, or earth, lined with hair and sometimes some feathers. Nest usually made by female; both sexes may excavate, or enlarge cavity. Eggs are white, variably patterned with small reddish markings. Incubation is by female, fed by male. Nestlings have grayish down, orange to yellow mouths, and pale yellowish gape flanges. Broods are often large. Young fed by both adults on insects brought in the bill. After leaving nest the family party tend to remain together for some time after young become independent.

Black-capped Chickadee (*Parus atricapillus*)   Plate 54
Breeds in deciduous and coniferous forests, and in more open areas with scattered
trees. Nest a cavity often excavated by the birds themselves in rotten wood. Often in a
decayed birch or pine stump, but an existing cavity may also be enlarged, or an old
woodpecker hole or nest-box used. At almost any height but often at only a few feet
up, typically 4–10 ft.
Nest: A cavity made by both birds, 8–9 in. deep and 2–3 in. wide, with a moss base
and cup of plant down, fibers, hair, wool, feathers, and spiders' cocoons, in the
bottom of it. Excavation 7–10 days, nest-building 3–4 days. **Breeding season:** Begins
early April in south to mid-May in north of range. Usually single-brooded. **Eggs:**
Usually 6–8, sometimes 5–13. Short subelliptical. Smooth and non-glossy. White to
creamy-white; very finely speckled and spotted with reddish-brown or purplish-
brown, sometimes with a heavier wealth of markings at the larger end. 15 × 12 mm.
Incubation: Incomplete clutches are covered with nest lining. Incubation by female
alone, beginning with last or next-to-last egg. 12–13 days. **Nestling:** Altricial and
downy. Down pale brownish-gray; sparse, on head, wings, and back. Mouth pale
yellow; gape flanges ivory. **Nestling period:** Young tended by both parents. Leave
nest at 16 days. Young remain with adults 21–28 days.

Carolina Chickadee (*Parus carolinensis*)   Plate 54
Breeds in woodland, mainly deciduous, and in scattered trees in cultivated areas or
around buildings. Nest in a cavity in a tree or fence-post; and woodpecker holes,
artificial cavities, and nest-boxes may also be used. Natural sites with decayed wood
usually excavated by the birds themselves. At 1–36 ft. up, but usually 4–15 ft. up.
Nest: A cavity in decayed wood excavated by both sexes may take up to 2 weeks.
About 5 in. deep and 2 in. wide at top, to 3 in. wide at base. Within a base of moss
and a cup of plant down, feathers, hair, and plant fibers. **Breeding season:** From mid-
February in south to early April in north. Usually single-brooded. **Eggs:** Usually 6,
sometimes 5–8. Very like those of Black-capped Chickadee. 15 × 11 mm. **Incubation:**
By female alone, beginning with last or next-to-last egg. 11–14 days. **Nestling:** Altricial and downy. Skin pale pinkish. Down dark gray. Mouth light yellow; gape flanges
ivory. **Nestling period:** Young tended by both parents. Leave nest at 17 days.

Mexican Chickadee (*Parus sclateri*)   Plate 54
Breeds in trees in mountains of extreme southeastern Arizona and southwestern
New Mexico. Nest in a tree cavity excavated by the birds, 36–58 ft. up, though sometimes as low as 1 ft. Will use nest-boxes at 13–16 ft. up (sometimes to *c.* 20 ft.).
Nest: A cavity in dead wood excavated by the birds, *c.* 8 in. deep. Cavity sometimes
located on underside of large dead limbs, well out from trunk. Contains a cup of
wool, fur, hair, and plant down. Built by female. **Breeding season:** Begins early April.
Ends mid-July. **Eggs:** Usually 5–6, rarely up to 9. Short subelliptical. Smooth and
slightly glossy. White; profusely and finely speckled and spotted with reddish-brown
and brown, and some paler purple. Often a concentration at larger end. 15 × 12 mm.
Incubation: By female, often fed by male. Period unknown. **Nestling:** No
information. **Nestling period:** Brooded by female; fed by both. Little further
information.

Mountain Chickadee (*Parus gambeli*)   Plate 54
Breeds in coniferous mountain forest. Nest in a natural cavity in tree stump, tree-
trunk, or branch, woodpecker hole, nest-box, or under rock in bank or hole in
ground. Possibly does not excavate its own hole. Site usually low, but at times up to
80 ft.

Nest: A cavity in dead wood or soil containing a cup of fur, hair, feathers, and plant fibers. **Breeding season:** Variable, early April to mid-May. Possibly double-brooded. **Eggs:** Usually 6–12. Short subelliptical. Smooth and non-glossy to slightly glossy. White, usually unmarked, or with some very fine speckling of reddish-brown or light brown; or a ring of spots around the larger end which may be bolder reddish-brown or light red. 16 × 12 mm. **Incubation:** By female. 14 days. **Nestling:** No information. **Nestling period:** Young tended by both parents. Leave nest at 21 days.

Siberian Tit (*Parus cinctus*)   Plate 54

Breeds usually in conifer woods, occasionally in mixed woods of spruce and willow bordering tundra in northern Alaska, northern Yukon and northwest Mackenzie. Nest a hole in a tree; a natural cavity or often an old woodpecker hole. (Uses nest-boxes in Scandinavia.) In conifers, or in birch, alder or aspen. Nest often low, 2–15 ft. up.

Nest: Female will partly excavate hole in rotten wood. Nest of moss with a cup lined with hair. Built by female. **Breeding season:** Begins late May to early June. Probably ends by late July. Single-brooded. **Eggs:** Usually 6–10. Subelliptical. Smooth and glossy. White; speckled, spotted, or finely blotched with light red or reddish-brown; fairly evenly distributed but tending to form poorly-defined zone at larger end. 16 × 13 mm. **Incubation:** Eggs laid at daily intervals. Incubation by female alone, fed by male, beginning with last egg. 14–15 days. **Nestling:** Altricial and naked. No additional information. **Nestling period:** Young tended by both parents. Female broods for first few days while male brings food, insects carried in the bill. 19 days in nest.

Boreal Chickadee (*Parus hudsonicus*)   Plate 54

Breeds in moist conifer forests, or mixed conifer and deciduous forest, often near bogs or muskegs. Nest in a natural cavity or woodpecker hole, in a tree, or dead stump, from ground level to *c.* 10 ft. up.

Nest: A natural cavity or one excavated by both birds in dead wood with a moss, lichens and bark base and a cup of hair and fur. **Breeding season:** Begins mid-May to early June. **Eggs:** Usually 4–9. Short subelliptical. Smooth and non-glossy. White; speckled or finely spotted with light reddish-brown, evenly distributed or concentrated in a ring around the larger end. 16 × 12 mm. **Incubation:** By female. 13–14 days. **Nestling:** Altricial and downy. Down very sparse. **Nestling period:** Young tended by both parents. Fly at 18 days.

Chestnut-backed Chickadee (*Parus rufescens*)   Plate 54

Breeds in conifer forests. Nest a cavity in the trunk of a tree or a dead branch usually excavated by the birds in rotten wood, exceptionally in a woodpecker hole or artificial cavity. Usually low, up to 10 ft., but rarely very much higher in dead trees.

Nest: A cavity in dead wood excavated by the birds. Contains a base of thick moss and a cup of fur, hair, feathers, and fibers. **Breeding season:** Begins mid-March to early April. **Eggs:** Usually 6–7, sometimes 5–9. Short subelliptical. Non-glossy and white. Speckled or finely spotted with light red, reddish-brown or brown. Markings evenly distributed or irregular, sometimes wreathing the larger end, sometimes absent altogether. 15 × 12 mm. **Incubation:** By female. *c.* 11–12 days. **Nestling:** No information. **Nestling period:** Young tended by both parents. First flight at *c.* 13–17 days.

Bridled Titmouse (*Parus wollweberi*)   Plate 54

Breeds in oak and pinyon–juniper woodland from central Arizona to southwest New Mexico. Nest in a natural cavity in a tree-trunk or stump. Will use nest-box. 3–30 ft. up.

Nest: A cavity in dead wood, containing a base of weed stems, leaves, and grasses; and a lining of fur, plant down, cotton, and spiders' cocoons. **Breeding season:** Early April to mid-June. **Eggs:** Usually 5–7. Subelliptical to short subelliptical. Smooth and non-glossy or slightly glossy. White and unmarked. 16 × 13 mm. **Incubation:** No information. **Nestling:** Little information. Gape pale yellow. **Nestling period:** No information.

Plain Titmouse (*Parus inornatus* – Includes Oak Titmouse,
P.i. inornatus, and Juniper Titmouse, *P.i. ridgwayi*)   Plate 54
These two forms may actually be distinct species. Breeds in oak woodland, mixed riparian, and wooded suburban areas (Oak Titmouse); also breeds in pinyon–juniper and mixed woodland (Juniper Titmouse). Nest a natural cavity in tree-trunk or branch, an old woodpecker hole or nest-box, 3–11 ft. up, sometimes up to 32 ft. up; exceptionally an earth bank.
Nest: A cavity, usually altered or further excavated by both birds, containing a base of grasses, bark strips, moss, and earth; and a cup of hair, fur, and some feathers. The base built mainly or entirely by female. **Breeding season:** Begins mid-March. Single-brooded. **Eggs:** Usually 6–8. Short subelliptical to elliptical. Smooth and non-glossy or slightly glossy. Often white and unmarked. Sometimes with some minute speckling of very pale reddish-brown. 17 × 13 mm. **Incubation:** By female only. 14–16 days. **Nestling:** No information. **Nestling period:** Young tended by both parents. Leave nest at *c.* 17 days and remain with adults for 3–4 weeks.

Tufted Titmouse (*Parus bicolor* – Includes Black-crested Titmouse,
P. b. atricristatus)   Plate 54
Breeds in and around deciduous or coniferous woodland. Nest in a natural cavity in a tree, or in old woodpecker hole or artificial cavity, such as pipe, or nest-box. 3–90 ft. up.
Nest: A cavity in wood; containing a base of moss and dead leaves; and a cup of hair, fibers, fur, wool, cotton, and similar material. Sometimes pieces of snakeskin. Entrance: $1\frac{3}{4}$–$2\frac{1}{4}$ in. **Breeding season:** Begins mid-March in south to late April in north of range. Usually ends by early July. Double-brooded. **Eggs:** Usually 5–6, sometimes 4–8. Short subelliptical. Smooth and non-glossy or slightly glossy. White to creamy-white; finely speckled or spotted in chestnut-red, purplish-red or brown, and sometimes paler purple or lilac. Markings evenly distributed or with some concentration at larger end. 18 × 14 mm. **Incubation:** By female alone. 12–14 days. **Nestling:** Altricial and downy. Skin flesh-pink. Down scanty, dark bluish-gray; on head and back. **Nestling period:** Young tended by both parents. Brooded by female. Eyes open at 5–7 days. Well-feathered by 10 days. Leave nest at 15–18 days.

Verdin (*Remizidae*)

Verdin (*Auriparus flaviceps*)   Figure 78, Plate 54
Breeds in arid regions with sparse thorny scrub, bushy mesquite or dry chaparral. Nest in a shrub, low tree, or cactus; fixed into a twig fork, usually towards the end of a branch, 2–12 ft. up, but more often *c.* 5 ft. up. Nests are built and used for roosting also at most times of year.
Nest: A rounded prickly mass (6–8 in. in diameter) of small thorny twigs with many ends projecting; lined with spiders' webs, then fine grasses and dead leaves, and with a thick inner layer of feathers and plant down. Entrance at side. Built by both sexes, with male building multiple structures and female finishing one off.

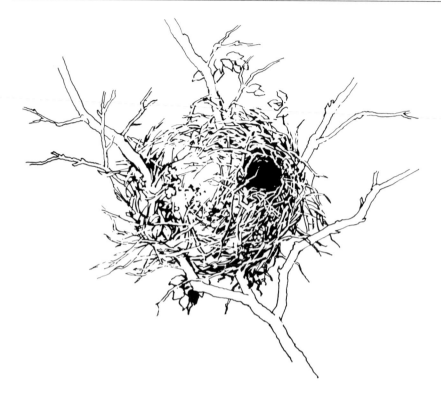

Figure 78. Verdin: c. 6–8 in. across; a rounded mass of small thorny twigs.

Breeding season: Begins late February. Possibly double-brooded. **Eggs:** Usually 4, sometimes 3–6. Subelliptical to short subelliptical. Smooth and moderately glossy. Very pale blue or greenish-blue; very finely speckled with reddish-brown, the markings often concentrated at or around the larger end. 15 × 11 mm. **Incubation:** By female alone. 14 days. **Nestling:** Altricial. Naked at hatching. **Nestling period:** Young fed by female at first, later by both parents. Leave at *c*. 3 weeks but roost in nest.

Bushtits (*Aegithalidae*)

Bushtit (*Psaltriparus minimus* – Black-eared Bushtit
included in this species)   Figure 79, Plate 54
Breeds in open deciduous and coniferous woodland, scrub and areas with scattered trees and shrubs. Nest in a tree or shrub, 4–50 ft. up, suspended from a twig fork or from two or more adjacent twigs.
Nest: An elongated, pendent structure, with an entrance to one side of the top, the whole widening towards the base. 6–12 in. from top to bottom, and 3–4 in. wide at base. A ring of material between two twigs form the entrance and the structure is held together by spiders' webs. Material very variable, twigs, rootlets, lichens, moss, grass, blossoms of trees and shrubs, plant down, small dry leaves, spider cocoons, etc.; thickly lined with feathers, fur, and down. Built by both, over 13 to as much as

Figure 79. Bushtit: c. 6–12 in. long; 3–4 in. wide at base; nest suspended and supported by two or more twigs.

51 days. **Breeding season:** Begins late February in California; early April elsewhere. Probably double-brooded. **Eggs:** Usually 5–7, rarely up to 15, possibly from two females. Subelliptical. Smooth and non-glossy to slightly glossy. White, unmarked. 14 × 10 mm. **Incubation:** By both sexes. 12–13 days. **Nestling:** Altricial. Hatched virtually naked, then develops a scanty hair-like grayish-white down. **Nestling period:** Young tended by both parents. Eyes open at 8 days. Young leave at 14–15 days, independent c. 8 days later.

Nuthatches (*Sittidae*)

Small birds, feeding over trunks and branches of trees. Nest in a cavity in dead wood, natural or excavated by birds themselves, or woodpecker hole. Hole sometimes surrounded by resin, smeared, or exuded by tree after pecking. Additional adults, usually single, may help pair in nest-making and rearing young. Nest usually a cup of hair or softer plant material in cavity. Eggs white with small reddish or brownish specks or spots. Incubation by female, usually fed by male. Young have grayish down on head and back, mouth usually yellow and gape-flanges creamy-white. Young tended by both parents and any helpers. Fed on insects brought in bill.

Red-breasted Nuthatch (*Sitta canadensis*)   Plate 56
Breeds in mixed or coniferous woodland. Nest in a natural cavity of deciduous or coniferous tree, or in old woodpecker hole, or bird excavates its own. Will also use nest-box. Nest may be 5–40 ft. up, usually about 10–15 ft. up.

Nest: A cavity in dead wood, with cup of grasses, rootlets, hair, and fur. Resin from pines, firs, or balsams is smeared around the entrance hole of the nest. Building and resin-smearing by both sexes. **Breeding season:** Begins late April to early May. Single-brooded. **Eggs:** Usually 5–6, sometimes 4–7. Subelliptical to short sub-elliptical. Smooth and slightly glossy. White, creamy-white, or pinkish-white; usually speckled or spotted with reddish-brown, chestnut-red, purplish-red, or brown. 15 × 12 mm. **Incubation:** By female, fed by male. 12 days. **Nestling:** Altricial and downy. Down dark gray. **Nestling period:** Young tended by both parents. Leave nest at 18–21 days.

White-breasted Nuthatch (Sitta carolinensis)   Plate 56

Breeds in deciduous woodland, and in conifer woodlands of mountain regions, also in orchards, and trees in cultivated areas and around houses. Nest in a natural cavity, deciduous or coniferous, or old woodpecker hole, often high but at times almost to ground level from as much as 50 ft. up. Nest-boxes are also used.
Nest: A cavity in dead wood. Cavity floored with bark flakes and strips and lumps of earth; with a cup of finer bark shreds, grasses and rootlets, but mainly lined with fur, wool, hair, and feathers. Built by female. **Breeding season:** Begins mid-March in south, to late April in north of range. Usually ends by mid-June. Usually single-brooded. **Eggs:** Usually 5–9, sometimes 10. Subelliptical to short subelliptical. Smooth and slightly glossy. White, sometimes tinted creamy or pink. Speckled and spotted with light red, reddish-brown, brown, and purplish-red, and sometimes paler gray and purple. 19 × 14 mm. **Incubation:** By female, fed by male. 12–14 days. **Nestling:** Altricial and downy. Skin light pink. Mouth cream-colored; gape flanges yellow. **Nestling period:** Young tended by both parents. Fledge at 14–16 days. Fed for 2 weeks after leaving nest.

Pygmy Nuthatch (Sitta pygmaea)   Plate 56

Breeds in mountain conifer woodland, often in open woodland with large trees. Nest a cavity, usually more than 20 ft. up. An additional adult may aid pair during breeding season.
Nest: A cavity in dead wood, excavated by both birds, or a partial cavity enlarged or an old one re-used. Entrance 1⅞ × 1½ in., cavity about 9 in. deep, and 2–4½ in. wide. Contains a cup, mainly of feathers, with bark shreds, plant fibers, moss, fur, hair, wool, plant down, leaves, and sometimes bits of snakeskin. May take 3–6 weeks. Additional bird may help. **Breeding season:** Begins mid-April to early May. Usually single-brooded. **Eggs:** Usually 5–9, rarely 10. Short subelliptical to short oval. Little or no gloss. White; variably speckled or spotted with chestnut-red, reddish-brown, or purplish-brown, the heavier markings often concentrated at the larger end. 15 × 12 mm. **Incubation:** Eggs laid at daily intervals. Incubation by female alone, fed by male on or off nest. 15–16 days. **Nestling:** Altricial and downy. Skin brownish-pink. Down pale smoky-gray; on head, back and shoulders. Mouth yellow; gape flanges creamy-white. Legs and feet light pink at first. Bill yellowish. **Nestling period:** Young tended by both parents and any helpers. Brooded by female only. Eyes open at 7–8 days. Feathers break sheaths at 7–10 days. Young leave nest at 20–21 days. Fed for 23–28 days after leaving nest.

Brown-headed Nuthatch (Sitta pusilla)   Plate 56

Breeds in open pinewoods, often in clearings or burnt-over areas with stumps remaining, and also in mixed woodland, and occasionally cypress swamp. Nest a cavity in dead wood, usually less than 10 ft. up, and less deep and dark than those of Pygmy Nuthatch. May use nest-boxes. One or more additional birds may help pair.

Nest: A cavity in dead wood or a partial cavity enlarged, or an old one re-used. Entrance $2 \times 1\frac{1}{2}$ in, cavity *c.* 7 in. deep, 2–4 in. wide. Cup mainly of pine-seed wings, with cotton, feathers, wool, bark shreds and strips, pine needles, weed stems, and rootlets. Hole excavated by both sexes, may take 1–6 weeks, and additional adult may help. **Breeding season:** Begins early March in south to early April in north of range. Usually single-brooded. **Eggs:** Usually 4–7, rarely 3–9. Short subelliptical to short oval. Smooth and moderately glossy. White, creamy-white or buffish; with bold profuse speckling, spotting, and some blotching in purplish-red, chestnut-red, and paler purple. Larger markings may be concentrated at large end with speckling elsewhere. 15×12 mm. **Incubation:** Eggs laid at daily intervals. Incubation by female alone, fed by male on or off nest. 13–15 days. **Nestling:** Altricial and downy. Skin brownish-pink. Down light brownish-gray; on head, back, and shoulders. Mouth yellow; gape creamy-white. Bill yellowish becoming gray. Legs and feet light pink at first. **Nestling period:** Young tended by both parents, and by any helper. Brooded by female only. Eyes open at 7 days. Feathers break sheaths at 7–10 days. Young leave nest at 18 days. Fed by parents and helper for 24–26 days more.

Creepers (*Certhiidae*)

Brown Creeper (*Certhia americana*)   Figure 80, Plates 16, 56
Breeds in woodland, usually in coniferous woodland of northern or mountain regions, parkland or areas with scattered large trees. Nest is concealed in the narrow space behind loose bark on a tree, in a crevice in a tree, or where ivy or accumulated debris offers a similar site. Rarely in a crevice in a wall. 5–15 ft. up.
Nest: A loose cup of twigs, roots, wood fibers, moss, and grass; lined with feathers, fine bark, and wool. The base may be built up with twigs. Built by both sexes, though mainly by female, taking 6–7 days, but sometimes over as long as 4 weeks. **Breeding season:** Begins early April in south to late May in north. Sometimes double-brooded. **Eggs:** Usually 6, occasionally 3–9. Subelliptical. Smooth and non-glossy. White, very finely speckled or spotted with pink or reddish-brown, the markings mostly or entirely confined to a cap at the larger end or a narrow zone around it. 15×12 mm. **Incubation:** By female alone (fed by male), beginning with last egg. 14–15 days. **Nestling:** Altricial and downy. Flesh pink. Down on head, thick and long; grayish-black. Mouth yellow; gape flanges yellowish-white. **Nestling period:** Young tended by both parents. 14–17 days. On leaving nest young fly weakly but climb well. Young are fed for at least $2\frac{1}{2}$ weeks.

Bulbuls (*Pycnonotidae*)

Red-whiskered Bulbul (*Pycnonotus jocosus*)
An introduced species breeding in one area of southeastern Florida. In gardens, parkland, and shrubberies. Nest in a shrub, small tree, or creeper, usually in a twig fork, 2–8 ft. up.
Nest: A shallow cup of fine twigs, dead leaves, and needles (from *Casuarina*), bound with spiders' webs, and incorporating a variety of papery debris (such as *Malaleuca* bark). Lined with fine rootlets and grass, sometimes with hair. **Breeding season:** Begins early February and ends early August. Probably double-brooded. **Eggs:** Usually 3, sometimes 2–4. Subelliptical to short subelliptical. Smooth and glossy. Ground color pale gray or tinted pink or purplish; speckled, spotted, or blotched with purplish-red, chestnut-red, or darker purple, and with paler lilac markings.

Figure 80. Brown Creeper: c. 3 in. across; concealed behind loose bark.

Markings often profuse and fine; sometimes with a heavier zone around the larger end. 23 × 16 mm. **Incubation:** By both sexes. 12–14 days. **Nestling:** Altricial and naked. Skin mostly pink, gray on wings and head. **Nestling period:** Young tended by both parents. Eyes open at *c.* 3 days. Young leave nest at *c.* 13 days, independent *c.* 12 days more.

Wrens (*Troglodytidae*)

Small birds, usually skulking in low cover, feeding on insects. Nest often a domed structure, in a tree and large and conspicuous with an entrance tunnel in the Cactus Wren; or small in a niche, crevice or cavity, in tree, shrub, bank, rocks, cliff, building, or long grass of marshes, or bound to stems of tall waterside plants. Nests in cavities may lack a domed top. Males may be polygamous, and often build a number of rough nests, a female lining one for nesting. Eggs vary from white with reddish or brown specks or spots, or unmarked, to pinkish-buff or brown with indistinct dark zones. Females incubate. Young have scanty down, yellow or red mouths and yellowish gape flanges, and are tended by both parents. The male feeds young of an earlier brood that have left the nest while the female re-nests.

Cactus Wren (*Campylorhynchus brunneicapillus*)　　　　Figure 81, Plates 16, 56

Breeds in arid regions with low scrub growth and cacti. Nest a bulky conspicuous mass on a cholla cactus, in low twiggy tree or shrub, often thorny, or on top of a yucca; occasionally in buildings. Usually 4–9 ft. up. Usually well supported by twigs on site. Nest relined and used as winter roost, and additional nests built by male may be used by female for later broods.

Nest: A large domed structure about 12 in. in diameter, the cavity with a side entrance near top opening into an entrance tube, horizontal or sloping down into nest, and often curved to one side. Cavity *c* 6 in. in diameter and entrance tube 5–6 in. long, the nest appearing horizontally elongated, the whole 12–18 in. long. Nest woven of dry grasses, fine twigs, dead leaves, and rootlets, thick-walled but untidy on the outside. Cavity lined with feathers, plant down, and fine grasses. **Breeding season:** Begins early to mid-March. Double- or treble-brooded. **Eggs:** Usually 4–5, sometimes 3–7. Long to short subelliptical or oval. Smooth and slightly glossy. White, or pale pinkish or buffish; very finely speckled, spotted, or mottled overall with purplish-red, buffish-brown, buffish-pink, pink, and paler purple and lilac. Markings may be indistinct and sometimes tint or swamp ground color. Usually a denser wreath or cap at larger end. 24 × 17 mm. **Incubation:** By female only. Partial incubation from first egg onwards. 15–18 days. **Nestling:** Altricial and downy. Down sparse and whitish. Mouth orange-red; gape flanges yellow. **Nestling period:** Young tended by both parents. Eyes open at 6–8 days. Feathers begin to break sheaths at 8 days. Leave nest at *c.* 21 days. Young return with parents to roost in nest for a period after leaving. Become independent *c.* 30 days after leaving nest. Young of earlier broods sometimes help tend young of later broods.

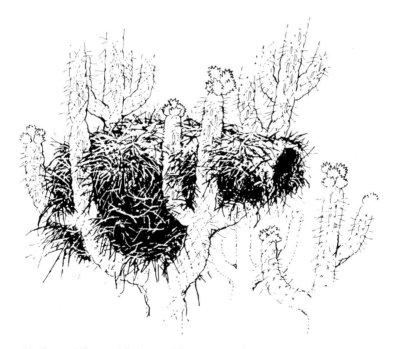

Figure 81. Cactus Wren: *c.* 1 ft. long, with entrance tube.

Rock Wren (*Salpinctes obsoletus*)   Plate 56

Breeds on bare rocky slopes and hillsides, rock outcrops, quarries, and erosion gullies, occasionally in crevices in stone or adobe walls. Also breeds on the rocky slopes of some offshore islands.

Nest: A cup in a cavity. The foundation of the nest and its surroundings are paved with small stones which may be built up in front of the nest, reducing the size of the entrance, or may form a paved approach to it. Nest of fine dry grasses, lined with hair or wool. Built by both sexes. **Breeding season:** Begins early February in south to early May in north of range. Double- or treble-brooded. **Eggs:** Usually 5–6, sometimes 4–8, rarely 9–10. Subelliptical to short subelliptical. Smooth and glossy. White; speckled, spotted, and with a few small blotches of dark reddish-brown or lighter buffish-brown, and pale purple. Markings very sparse, mostly minute and mainly around or at the larger end. 19 × 15 mm. **Incubation:** By female, occasionally fed by male. 12–14 days. **Nestling:** Altricial and downy. Down yellowish-white. Flesh pinkish-yellow. Mouth pinkish-yellow. **Nestling period:** Young tended by both parents. Leave nest at 14–16 days.

Canyon Wren (*Catherpes mexicanus*)   Plate 56

Breeds on steep rocky walls of canyons, also around buildings and in cavities of man-made structures. Nest an open cup usually placed on a ledge or in a crevice, in a cave or recess in rocks, or in similar sites under, in or on buildings; the sites often similar to those used by phoebes.

Nest: A cup with a base of twigs, and coarser material, of moss, dead leaves, lichens, and a few weed stems, bark strips, and similar material. Lined with plant down, wool, feathers, or other soft material. At times a very considerable range of small debris may be incorporated. Built by both. **Breeding season:** Begins early March in south to early May in north of range. Probably ends by early August. Probably double-brooded. **Eggs:** Usually 5–6, sometimes 4. Subelliptical. Smooth and moderately glossy. White; with very fine and minute dark speckling mostly in an indistinct zone around the larger end. 18 × 13 mm. **Incubation:** By female. 12–18 days. **Nestling:** Altricial and naked. Flesh pink. Developing down yellowish-white, pinkish-white, pale tan, or drab. Mouth and gape flanges yellow. **Nestling period:** Young tended by both parents. Depart *c.* 15 days. Cared for by parents to day 20–25.

Carolina Wren (*Thryothorus ludovicianus*)   Plate 56

Breeds in woodland with low cover in the form of thickets, brushpiles, or broken rocky areas, and along banks of streams or in overgrown swamps. Nest in a small niche or cavity in tree-trunk or stump, in a crotch, among roots, in a bank, or among low undergrowth. Usually up to 10 ft., exceptionally higher. Also in almost any cavity or niche around buildings and man-made structures, including nest-boxes.

Nest: A bulky and usually domed structure, but dome may be missing in cavity nests. Of plant material – grasses, weed stems, bark strips, leaves, moss, and rootlets, lined with fine grasses and rootlets, hair and feathers. Fragments of a wide variety of other materials may also be incorporated. Built by male with female adding lining. **Breeding season:** Begins mid-March to early April. Usually ends by mid-September. Double- or possibly treble-brooded. **Eggs:** Usually 4–6, sometimes 7–8. Short subelliptical to subelliptical or short elliptical. Smooth and moderately glossy. White; very finely speckled, spotted, or mottled in reddish-brown, purplish-brown, and paler purple or gray. Heavier markings mainly in a zone capping or wreathing the larger end, with usually profuse speckling elsewhere. 19 × 15 mm. **Incubation:** By female only. 12–14 days. **Nestling:** Altricial and downy. Down slate-gray. Scanty. Mouth yellow; gape flanges pale yellow. **Nestling period:** Young tended by both parents. Leave nest at *c.* 12–14 days.

Bewick's Wren (*Thryomanes bewickii*)   **Plate 56**
Breeds in generally open woodlands and drier thickets, orchards, fencerows, and gardens and shrubby growth around houses, replacing the House Wren in some areas. Nest a small natural cavity in tree or post, woodpecker hole, crevice in tree, wall or building, or between rocks or in brush pile, hole in a bank, or any kind of hollow object, including nest-box. Located up to 20 ft. up.
Nest: A bulky deep and irregular cup in a mass of varied material; plant material, bark and wood chips, rootlets and sticks; lined with feathers, moss, wool, hair, fur, and similar material; and like the House Wren, liable to incorporate almost any material into the nest, including spiders' webs and caterpillar webs, and sometimes snakeskin. Both sexes take part in building. **Breeding season:** Begins late March to early April. Double- or possibly treble-brooded. **Eggs:** Usually 5–7, sometimes 4–9, exceptionally 11. Short subelliptical. Smooth and slightly glossy. White; very finely speckled, spotted, and sometimes with a few small blotches in purplish-red, purplish-brown, reddish-brown, and pale purple. The heavier markings mainly in a zone at or around the larger end. The finer spotting more widely distributed. 16 × 13 mm. **Incubation:** By female alone; fed wholly or partly by male. *c.* 14 days. **Nestling:** No information. **Nestling period:** Young tended by both parents. Leave nest at *c.* 14 days. Fed by parents *c.* 2 weeks more.

House Wren (*Troglodytes aedon*)   **Plate 56**
Breeds over a wide range of country, from open woodland to cultivation and human settlement, wherever there is a low shrubby cover and thickets, with holes or niches for nesting. The typical nest-site is a natural cavity, hole, or crevice in tree or rocks; but virtually any structure offering a cavity (including nest-boxes) with restricted entrance, or a ledge or corner within a building, may be used. The male may build a number of rough nests and is sometimes polygamous, different nests being taken and lined by different females.
Nest: A cavity filled with a mass of material to leave an entrance and cavity. Basically of plant material, twigs, stems, leaves, and fibers, lined with softer material such as feathers, hair, wool, etc., but an incredible variety of debris has been recorded as nest material. **Breeding season:** Begins early April in south to late May in north of range. Double-brooded. **Eggs:** Usually 6–8, sometimes 5–12. Sub-elliptical to short subelliptical or oval. Smooth and glossy. White, or frequently tinted warm pink or buff, very finely and profusely speckled with purplish-red or purplish-brown, the markings so minute and numerous as to produce an overall mottling, or markings indistinct and tiny, producing an almost uniform tint. Often a band of denser markings around the larger end and these may be duller, more purplish or grayish. Sometimes pinkish tints replaced by medium brown. 16 × 13 mm. **Incubation:** Eggs laid at daily intervals. Incubation by female only. 13–15 days. **Nestling:** Altricial and downy. Skin dark gray. Down dark gray and scanty; on head and back. Mouth pale yellow; gape flanges whitish. **Nestling period:** Young tended by both parents. Leave nest at 12–18 days. Male may feed fledged young while female re-nests. Young begin feeding themselves at 13–19 days.

Winter Wren (*Troglodytes troglodytes*)   **Figure 82, Plate 56**
Breeds usually in thick woodland, deciduous or coniferous, at varying altitudes, and mostly in moister places, but also on rocky islands and coasts of the northwest in a wide range of sites which provide low cover. The nest is built into almost any type of hollow, cavity, or hole available from ground level upwards, but most often on the side of a tree, upturned tree root, wall, or steep bank from about 0–10 ft. up. The male is often polygamous, building a number of nests within the territory and installing several females in succession in different nests.

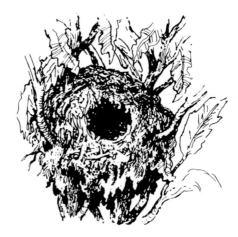

Figure 82. Winter Wren: c. 7 in. across; entrance diameter 1 in.; a more typical nest would be worked into a hollow, side of tree, or steep bank.

Nest: A stout domed structure of leaves, moss, grass, and other plant material lined with feathers. The male builds the outer nest, the female selecting one of the several he builds and lining it. The mass is *c.* 7 in. in diameter, with an entrance of *c.* 1 in. diameter. **Breeding season:** Begins late March in the south to mid-May at the north of its range. Single-brooded. **Eggs:** Usually 5–8; up to 16 have been recorded. Subelliptical. Smooth and glossy. White, at times immaculate, or with a limited area of minute speckling or tiny spots of black or reddish-brown at the larger end. 18 × 13 mm. **Incubation:** Eggs laid at daily intervals. Incubation by female alone. 14–17 days. **Nestling:** Altricial and downy. Down, on head and back, short and sparse dark gray. Mouth bright yellow; gape flanges very pale yellow. **Nestling period:** Fed by both parents. Polygamous males usually have broods which hatch at intervals, the male helping with first one, then another. 15–20 days in nest.

Sedge Wren (*Cistothorus platensis*)   Plate 56
Breeds in wet meadows or drier areas of marshes and bogs dominated by grasses and sedges. Nest is low in sedge, grass, or similar herbage, very near the ground, or over shallow water. Nest is globular and well hidden in bases of growing vegetation, or rarely 1–2 ft. up. The male is sometimes polygamous.
Nest: A rounded ball (*c.* 6 in. diameter) with entrance at the side. Of dry grasses and sedges; lined with fine grass, hair, feathers, and plant down. The male builds a number of nests. **Breeding season:** Begins late May to early June. Double- sometimes treble-brooded. **Eggs:** Usually 6–7, sometimes 4–8. Short subelliptical to short oval. Smooth and moderately glossy. White and unmarked. 16 × 12 mm. **Incubation:** By female alone. 12–14 days. **Nestling:** No information. **Nestling period:** Young tended by both parents but mainly by female. Leave nest at 12–14 days.

Marsh Wren (*Cistothorus palustris*)   Figure 83, Plate 56
Breeds in tall rushes and marsh grasses along brackish estuaries, inlets and rivers, and in tall growth of cat-tails, bulrushes, sedges, and rice of large inland freshwater marshes. Nest a domed structure raised on several stems of tall herbage over or by

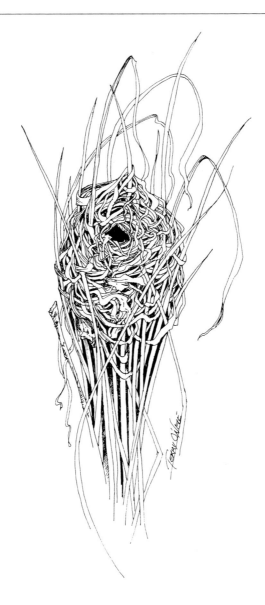

Figure 83. Marsh Wren: *c*. 7 in. high, 3 in. across, diameter of opening slightly over 1 in., worked into standing reeds.

water. Height varies with growing herbage, 1–3 ft. for earlier nests, up to 6 ft. later. Exceptionally in mangroves 5–15 ft. up. Male may often be polygamous.

Nest: A rounded oblong structure secured to two or more upright stems. Usually taller than wide with a rounded entrance on the side towards the upper end (*c*. 7 × 3 in.). Lower edge of entrance forms a thickened, inward-projecting sill, leaving the inner cavity retort-shaped with an upper entrance tube. Made of grass and sedge stems and long leaves woven around supports, filled in with leaves and small stems, plant fragments, rootlets, down, and feathers; lined with fine plant fibers and feathers. Males build a series of unlined dummy nests, nest is lined by female. Building takes 5–8 days. **Breeding season:** Begins late March in south to late May in north of range. Double- sometimes treble-brooded. **Eggs:** Usually 4–5, sometimes 3–8, rarely to 10. Subelliptical or short subelliptical to oval. Smooth and moderately glossy. Very dark in color with a general dark brownish appearance. Dull buff, pinkish-buff or light brown ground color, very finely and heavily scribbled with minute freckling of dark purplish-brown or grayish-brown, the markings often indistinct and tinting the ground color but usually with a darker wreath or cap at larger end. 16 × 12 mm. **Incubation:** Eggs laid at daily interval. Incubation by female alone, beginning with third or fourth egg. 12–14 days. **Nestling:** Altricial and downy. Down whitish; on head and back only. Mouth deep yellow; gape flanges yellow. **Nestling period:** Young tended by female alone, or by both parents, but male helps to feed older young. Young leave nest at 13–15 days. Male may feed them for an additional *c.* 7 days or so, while female re-nests.

Dippers (*Cinclidae*)

American Dipper (*Cinclus mexicanus*)   Plate 56
Breeds by mountain and hill streams. Nest built on a raised site overlooking and often overhanging water; on a bank, rock face, roots of waterside tree or fallen trunk, in a crevice or on a ledge under a bridge or culvert; sometimes behind a waterfall. Nest often tucked into a crevice or hole, or on a ledge or support, more rarely built on to top of a bank, or on a rock or stump or upturned root by a stream. Some males polygamous, with two females.
Nest: A bulky domed structure (*c.* 12 in. diameter) of moss, with an internal cup of moss and grasses, lined with dead leaves. The canopy of the dome tends to overhang the edge of the cup to form a downward-pointing entrance, directed towards the water. Exceptionally a nest in a small cavity may lack the canopy. Built by both sexes. **Breeding season:** Begins late March in south to mid-April in north. Double-brooded. **Eggs:** Usually 4–5, sometimes 3–6. Subelliptical to oval. Smooth and glossy. White and unmarked. 26 × 18 mm. **Incubation:** By female alone. 16 days. **Nestling:** Altricial and downy. Down long and thick, on head and back. Flesh pink above, orange below. Mouth orange-yellow; gape flanges yellow. **Nestling period:** Young tended by both parents. Leave nest at 18–25 days, and can dive and swim before they can fly. Fed by parents for *c.* 12 days more, and brood may be divided between parents.

Old World Warblers, Gnatcatchers, Old World Flycatchers, Thrushes, and Wrentit (*Muscicapidae*)

Small to medium-sized insect and fruit-eating birds. Breed in various habitats from thick undergrowth of woodlands to bush or isolated tree in open places. Nest in a fork or on a branch of a tree or shrub, on a ledge or in a cavity, or on the ground. Nest a stout cup in open sites, domed nest, or a loose, shallow structure in a cavity. Many species incorporate a cup either of mud or of leaf-mold into the nest structure, strengthening it. Some species regularly use lichen on the exterior or throughout. Eggs blue or whitish, unmarked or variably marked, often with reddish-brown. Incubation usually by female. Young downy or naked. They are fed by both adults on insects and invertebrates brought in the bill. The male may feed young which have left the nest if female re-nests.

Arctic Warbler (*Phylloscopus borealis*)   Plate 57
Breeds in willow scrub in Alaska. Nest on the ground at base of shrub or among
herbage, moss, tree-roots, or other cover. Usually built into dead vegetation so that
only the entrance shows. Occasionally in shrubby growth. 2–3 ft. up.
Nest: A domed structure with side entrance. Of moss, dry grass, and dead leaves; lined
with fine grass, and rarely with hair. **Breeding season:** Begins late June. Single-
brooded. **Eggs:** Usually 5–6, sometimes 3–7. Short subelliptical. Smooth and glossy.
White; finely speckled and spotted with light reddish-brown or darker brown. Markings often rather sparse; finer specklings usually profuse but sometimes faint. 16 × 13
mm. **Incubation:** By female alone. Estimated at 13 days. **Nestling:** No information.
Nestling period: Young tended by both parents. Leave nest at *c.* 12 days.

Golden-crowned Kinglet (*Regulus satrapa*)   Figure 84, Plate 57
Breeds in conifer woodland, often in dense stands of old spruce. Nest in a tree,
suspended from stems or in a twig fork, under foliage near the end of an evergreen
branch. 6–50 ft. up.
Nest: A deep, thick cup, bound together and to its supports with spiders' webs and
hair, mainly of moss and *Usnea* lichen, with some plant fibers, dead grass, and pine
needles; lined with fine rootlets, fibers, hair, and feathers. Built by female in 9 days
or longer. **Breeding season:** Begins early April in south to early June in north of
range. Double-brooded. **Eggs:** Usually 8–9, sometimes 5–10. Short elliptical to short
subelliptical. Smooth and non-glossy. Creamy-white to yellowish or buffish-cream;
speckled or spotted with drab brown and paler gray. Markings tend to form a wreath
around larger end and may be indistinct and merge together. 13 × 10 mm.

Figure 84. Golden-crowned Kinglet: *c.* 3–4 in. across; suspended from stems of old spruce.

Incubation: By female alone. 14–15 days. **Nestling:** Altricial and downy. Down fine and gray. Mouth orange-red; gape flanges pale yellow. **Nestling period:** Young tended by both parents. Leave nest at *c.* 17 days.

Ruby-crowned Kinglet (*Regulus calendula*)   Plate 57
Breeds in northern conifer woodland. Nest in a coniferous tree, usually suspended in a similar site to that of Golden-crowned Kinglet, but occasionally nest saddles a branch. 4–100 ft. up.
Nest: A thick, deep cup of green moss and *Usnea* lichen, with plant fiber, grasses, plant down, and bark shred, bound together and to supports with spiders' webs and hair; and thickly lined with feathers. Built by female over 5 days. **Breeding season:** Begins late May to early June. Usually ends by mid-July. Single-brooded. **Eggs:** Usually 7–8, sometimes 5–11. Short elliptical to short subelliptical. Smooth and non-glossy. White, to drab or buffish-white; spotted or speckled with dull brown or reddish-brown, often poorly-defined and usually capping the larger end or forming a wreath around it. 14 × 11 mm. **Incubation:** By female alone. Estimated at 12–14 days. **Nestling:** Altricial and downy. Mouth bright red; gape flanges yellow. **Nestling period:** Young tended by both parents. Leave at *c.* 16 days.

Blue-gray Gnatcatcher (*Polioptila caerulea*)   Figure 85, Plate 57
Breeds widely where there are trees, from sparse scrub to heavy woodland, but more often near water, particularly in north of range. Nest in a tree, or shrub, saddling a branch or in a fork. From 3–80 ft. up.
Nest: A deep, rounded cup, neat and compact, narrowing slightly at the rim. Of plant down, bark and plant fibers, fine grasses, catkins, feathers, and hair; bound together and to the support by spiders' webs; the outside covered with lichen flakes; and lined with plant down or feathers. Built by both sexes over 1–2 weeks. **Breeding season:** Begins early to mid-April. Usually ends by late July. Double-brooded. **Eggs:** Usually 4–5. Short elliptical to short subelliptical. Very pale to pale blue. Speckled, spotted, or blotched with chestnut-red, purplish-red, or reddish-brown and paler purple. Markings very variable, larger markings sometimes concentrated towards larger

Figure 85. Blue-gray Gnatcatcher: *c.* 2–2½ in. across; saddled on a branch and well covered with lichen flakes.

end. 14 × 11 mm. *Incubation:* By both sexes. 15 days. *Nestling:* Altricial and naked. Mouth bright yellow, with two black spots on tongue; gape flanges yellow. *Nestling period:* Young tended by both parents. Eyes begin opening at 5 days. Feathers break sheaths at 6–7 days. Leave nest at 12–13 days. Fed by adults for up to 19 more days.

Black-tailed Gnatcatcher (*Polioptila melanura*)   Plate 57
Breeds in arid regions. In mesquite, saltbush, and pinyon–juniper woodland. Nest in a low tree or shrub, 2–4 ft. up.
Nest: A deep, compact cup, narrowing slightly at the rim; of plant fiber, bark, and grasses, bound with spiders' webs; but lacking the external lichen covering. Lined with plant down, feathers, and fur. Built by both sexes. *Breeding season:* Begins mid-March to early April. Double-brooded. *Eggs:* Usually 4, sometimes 3–5. Similar to those of Blue-gray Gnatcatcher. 14 × 11 mm. *Incubation:* Eggs laid at daily intervals. Incubation beginning with the first or second egg; by both sexes. 14 days. *Nestling:* Altricial and naked. Mouth yellow; gape flanges yellow. *Nestling period:* Young tended by both parents. Leave nest at 9–15 days. Fed for an additional *c.* 3 weeks.

California Gnatcatcher (*Polioptila californica*)   Plate 57
Breeds in southern California in coastal sage scrub among slopes and low rolling hills and arid washes with low and scattered growth of shrubs. Nest in a low tree or shrub, 2–3 ft. up.
Nest: Cone-shaped, in a fork. Materials well quilted and compact. Binding materials (bark, grasses) and spiders' webs used externally, with small curled-up leaves of white sage. Deep cup-like interior, lined with finer fibers and a few feathers. Built by both. *Breeding season:* Late February to mid-July (uncommonly into August). Double-brooded. *Eggs:* Usually 4, sometimes 3–5. Similar to those of Blue-gray Gnatcatcher, though less likely to have dots concentrated on larger end. 14 × 12 mm. *Incubation:* By both sexes. 14 days. *Nestling:* Altricial and naked. *Nestling period:* Young leave nest at 16 days. Fed for 3 weeks by both parents.

Black-capped Gnatcatcher (*Polioptila nigriceps*)
An occasional breeder in dry canyons and riparian woodlands with mesquite, sycamore, and hackberry in southeast Arizona. Nest in a low bush or small tree, in a crotch of branches. 5–14 ft. up.
Nest: A neat, cup-shaped structure, not as high or as deep as Black-tailed Gnatcatcher, but with same diameter, of tightly woven spiders' webs, hair, herbaceous twigs, and bits of leaves. Built by both. *Breeding season:* Begins mid-March to early April, extends into August. Double-brooded. *Eggs:* Usually 4, sometimes 3–5. Similar to those of Blue-gray Gnatcatcher, though paler. 14 × 11 mm. *Incubation:* By both sexes. *Nestling:* No information. *Nestling period:* Young tended by both parents.

Bluethroat (*Luscinia svecica*)   Plate 57
Breeds in willow thickets and tundra streamsides in north and west Alaska, often in hilly country with little cover. Nest on the ground, usually hidden in a hollow on a slight bank, in a dense bush, or dead vegetation, or at base of a shrub.
Nest: A cup of plant stems, dead grass, roots, and moss; lined with fine grass, hair, and rarely feathers. Built entirely by female? *Breeding season:* Probably June–July. *Eggs:* Usually 5–7, sometimes 9. Subelliptical. Smooth and only slightly glossy. Pale green, bluish-green or blue, very finely speckled, mottled, or tinted with light reddish-brown, the markings often poorly defined and giving a general rusty tint to some or all of shell. Occasionally more obviously marked. Markings sometimes concentrated at the larger end. 19 × 14 mm. *Incubation:* By female. 14–15 days.

Nestling: Altricial and downy. Down, on head and back, fairly long and plentiful; dark gray. Mouth orange; gape flanges whitish-yellow. **Nestling period:** Young tended by both parents. 14 days. Usually unable to fly when they leave.

Northern Wheatear (*Oenanthe oenanthe*)   Plate 57

Breeds on barer mountains and hillsides, in areas where broken rock occurs, and around settlements in Alaska, northernmost Canada, and Greenland. Nest in a hole in rocks, walls, heaps of stones and other debris.
Nest: Large, loosely-constructed heap of grass, moss, plant stems, roots, and leaves; with a shallow cup lined with grass, hair, wool, and feathers. Built mainly by female but male may assist. **Breeding season:** Probably begins late May. Probably single-brooded. **Eggs:** Usually 5–6, sometimes 3–8. Subelliptical. Smooth and non-glossy. Very pale blue. Unmarked; or rarely with a few fine dark specks at larger end. 21 × 16 mm. **Incubation:** By both sexes but mainly by female. 14 days. **Nestling:** Altricial and downy. Down, on head, shoulders and upper back, long and fairly plentiful; dark gray. Mouth pale orange; gape flanges very pale yellow. **Nestling period:** Young tended by both parents. 15 days in nest. Parents divide brood as early as 3 days after fledging and continue to feed their respective group for 10–12 days.

Eastern Bluebird (*Sialia sialis*)   Plate 57

Breeds in open woodland, orchards, and in trees or man-made sites around farms and buildings. Nest in a natural cavity in a tree or post, old woodpecker hole in tree or post, old Cliff Swallow's nest, nest-box, or similar site. 3–20 ft. up.
Nest: A loosely built cup in a cavity. Of dry grass and weed stems and fine twigs; lined with finer grasses, and sometimes hair or feathers. Built mainly by female, usually over 4–5 days. **Breeding season:** Begins mid-March to early April. Double- or sometimes treble-brooded. **Eggs:** Usually 4–5, sometimes 3–7. Subelliptical to short subelliptical. Smooth and glossy. Pale blue, unmarked. Rarely white. 21 × 16 mm. **Incubation:** By both sexes but mainly by female. 12–15 days. **Nestling:** Altricial and downy. Skin pink. Down dark gray; on head, wings, and lower back. Mouth deep yellow; gape flanges pale yellow. **Nestling period:** Young tended by both parents. Eyes open at 4–6 days. Young leave nest at 15–18 days. Male tends fledged young while female re-nests.

Western Bluebird (*Sialia mexicana*)   Plate 57

Breeds in woodland clearings (usually coniferous, but also mixed and deciduous) and open areas, particularly where dead trees are present. Nest in a natural cavity in a tree, or old woodpecker hole. Will use nest-boxes. 5–40 ft. up.
Nest: A slight cup in a cavity. Of dry grasses and a few feathers. Built by female. **Breeding season:** Begins early April to early May. Usually double-brooded. **Eggs:** Usually 4–6, sometimes 3–8. Subelliptical to short subelliptical. Like those of Eastern Bluebird, though usually darker than those of Mountain Bluebird. Blue and unmarked. 21 × 16 mm. **Incubation:** By female. 13–14 days. **Nestling:** Altricial and downy. Down dark bluish-gray. **Nestling period:** Young tended by both parents. Leave nest at *c.* 20 days. Male tends fledged young while female re-nests.

Mountain Bluebird (*Sialia currucoides*)   Plate 57

Breeds in open woodland, forest edges, and in scattered trees of higher altitudes. Nest in a natural cavity in tree, or old woodpecker hole. Sometimes hole in earth bank, or old mammal burrow, crevice, or cavity in cliff or among rocks, or old swallow's nest. Will use nest-box. 2–50 ft. up.
Nest: A loose cup in a cavity. Of weed and grass stems, rootlets, and bark. Built by

both sexes. *Breeding season:* Begins early April in south to late May in north of range. Double- or possibly treble-brooded in south. *Eggs:* Usually 5–6, sometimes 4–8. Subelliptical. Smooth and glossy. Pale blue to bluish-white; paler than those of other bluebirds. Unmarked. 22 × 17 mm. *Incubation:* By both sexes, but mainly by female, beginning with the last egg. 13–14 days. *Nestling:* Altricial and downy. Hatched naked, skin pinkish-gray. Mouth, orange-yellow; gape flanges yellow. Thin down by second day on back and head, spreading gradually. *Nestling period:* Young tended by both parents. Eyes open at 5–6 days. Leave nest at 18–21 days.

Townsend's Solitaire (*Myadestes townsendi*) — Plate 57

Breeds in mountain conifer woodland, more often in open woodland, on steep or rocky slopes. Nest low, in a cavity or crevice in rocks, in tree-stump (usually below 8 ft.), or among tree-roots, at foot of tree on a steep slope, or in hollow or on ledge of steep earth bank.
Nest: A cup with a loose basal structure tailing off into material hanging down. Of weed stems, dry grasses, sticks, twigs, pine needles and rootlets; with a finer lined cup of shredded grass stems and blades, moss and long pine needles. *Breeding season:* Begins late April in south to late May in north of range. *Eggs:* Usually 4, sometimes 3, rarely 5. Subelliptical, sometimes longer or shorter subelliptical, or oval. Smooth and slightly glossy. White, bluish-white, or pale blue, or white tinted yellowish, greenish, or pinkish. Heavily speckled, spotted or with small blotches or scrawls of varying shades of brown, reddish-brown, or paler gray or purple. Markings sometimes concentrated at or around the larger end. 23 × 17 mm. *Incubation:* By female alone? Estimated at 12 days. *Nestling:* Altricial and downy? Flesh pinkish-orange. Down grayish. Gape flanges pale yellow. Feathered young appear spotted overall with rust on wing. *Nestling period:* Tended by both parents. Leave at *c.* 13 days.

Veery (*Catharus fuscescens*) — Figure 86, Plate 57

Breeds in deciduous woodland, usually but not invariably in a moist or marshy area. Nest near or on the ground, in the base of a sapling or shrub, in shoots, fallen branches, briers, vines, on a stump, or bank, or on the ground on a moss hummock or in a weed clump or grass-tussock, can be up to 6 ft. up, occasionally to 25 ft.
Nest: A stout cup, often with a base of dead leaves. Of grass and weed stems, bark fibers, small twigs, moss, and decayed leaves; lined with decayed leaves, rootlets, bark strips, and pine needles. Built by female over 6–10 days. *Breeding season:* Begins early to late May. Single-brooded. *Eggs:* Usually 4, sometimes 3–6. Subelliptical to short subelliptical. Smooth and glossy. Medium blue. Unmarked, or very rarely with some brown spots. 22 × 17 mm. *Incubation:* By female. 10–14 days. *Nestling:* Altricial and downy. Down gray; on head and back only. Flesh pinkish. Mouth pink; gape flanges pale yellow. *Nestling period:* Young tended by both parents. Eyes open at 5–7 days. Leave nest at 10–12 days.

Gray-cheeked Thrush (*Catharus minimus*) — Plate 57

Breeds in northern woodland and at woodland edge, in stunted spruce, and willow and alder thickets near water. Nest near the ground in the basal fork of a low shrub, or a few feet up in a small conifer. Usually *c.* 6 ft. up, sometimes 1–20 ft., occasionally on the ground.
Nest: A compact and firm cup of fine shriveled grass blades, sometimes with small twigs, bark, and mosses, incorporated with a small amount of mud. The lining is of fine dry grasses. The outside may be decorated with moss and lichens. Built by female. *Breeding season:* Begins late May. Single-brooded, but will replace lost

Figure 86. Veery: c. 9 in. across; on ground with a base of dead leaves, usually adjacent to live plants.

clutch. **Eggs:** Usually 4, sometimes 3–5. Subelliptical. Smooth and semi-glossy. Light to medium greenish-blue; speckled, spotted, blotched, or mottled, often indistinctly and sometimes sparsely with reddish-brown or purplish-brown. 23 × 17 mm. **Incubation:** By female alone. 12–14 days. **Nestling:** Altricial and downy. Down gray. Mouth and gape flanges bright yellow. **Nestling period:** Young tended by both parents. Young leave nest at 11–13 days?

Bicknell's Thrush (*Catharus bicknelli*)   Plate 57
Breeds in the northeast US and adjacent Canada in high woodlands, usually above 3,000 ft., in spruce–fir habitat, but sometimes in lower transitional or second growth hardwood–conifer vegetation. Nest in a small or medium-sized evergreen (usually in Balsam Fir or Red Spruce, though sometimes in a birch) near the ground where two or more horizontal branches join the main stem. Usually 3–12 ft. up, sometimes to 25 ft.
Nest: A cup of fresh green moss and supporting evergreen twigs, with the minor addition of non-coniferous twigs, flower stalks, fern stems, dried leaves, bark, and occasionally lichens. The inner lining is filled with partially decomposed organic debris and a lining of fine black rootlets with some occasional dry grasses or leaves. **Breeding season:** Begins late May, extending into late July. Single-brooded. **Eggs:** 3–4. Subelliptical. Smooth and semi-glossy. Bluish-green, variably spotted with brown.

22 × 17 mm. **Incubation:** By female alone. 12–15 days. **Nestling:** Altricial and downy. Down dark gray or blackish; on head, shoulders and back. Mouth bright orange; gape whitish-yellow. **Nestling period:** Young tended by both parents. Feathers break sheaths at 7–10 days. Young leave nest at *c.* 10–12 days.

Swainson's Thrush (*Catharus ustulatus*)   Plate 57
Breeds in northern coniferous and mixed woodlands, usually in moist and denser areas, or in thickets along watercourses. Nest in a small tree, close to trunk and well hidden in foliage; usually low, 2–7 ft. up, exceptionally up to 30 ft. Often in a conifer, occasionally in deciduous tree or shrub.
Nest: A compact cup of fine twigs, mosses, lichens, weed stems, decayed leaves, and mud, and bark shred, with inner lining of decayed leaves, rootlets, grasses, and other materials. Built by female over *c.* 4 days. **Breeding season:** Begins mid-April in south to early June in north of range. Double-brooded. **Eggs:** Usually 3–4, sometimes 5. Subelliptical. Smooth and glossy. Light to medium blue; speckled, spotted, and blotched with reddish-brown to purplish-brown, and paler lilac. Markings vary from profuse to very sparse, often with some concentration at larger end. 22 × 17 mm. **Incubation:** By female only. 10–13 days. **Nestling:** Altricial and downy. Down dark blackish-brown. Mouth deep orange; gape flanges pale yellow. **Nestling period:** Young tended by both parents. Brooded by female only for first few days. Eyes open at 2–3 days. Feathers break sheaths at 7–10 days, young leave nest at 10–12 days.

Hermit Thrush (*Catharus guttatus*)   Plate 57
Breeds in moist coniferous and mixed woodlands. Nest on the ground, usually in a small depression under a conifer with low branches, or hidden by low plants. Occasionally nests a few feet up (2–4 ft.) – particularly in the west – in conifer, sometimes higher up.
Nest: A compact but bulky cup. Of coarse grass, bark strips and fibers, ferns, moss, and weeds, with a middle layer of mud, and a lining of fine grasses, rootlets, pine needles, or plant fibers. Built by female. **Breeding season:** Begins early to mid-May. Double-brooded. **Eggs:** Usually 4, sometimes 3–6. Subelliptical. Smooth and glossy. Light blue and unmarked. 22 × 17 mm. **Incubation:** By female only. 12–13 days. **Nestling:** Altricial and downy. Skin dark pinkish-flesh-color. Down scanty and dark gray, on head, wings, and lower half of back. Mouth orange-yellow; gape flanges yellow. **Nestling period:** Young tended by both parents. Eyes open at 4 days. Young leave nest at 12–13 days.

Wood Thrush (*Hylocichla mustelina*)   Figure 87, Plate 57
Breeds in moist woodland (usually deciduous), often near water. Nest in a sapling or shrub, or in a tree, *c.* 10 ft. up, but occasionally 6–50 ft. Nest in a fork or saddling a small branch.
Nest: A substantial cup of grass and weed stems, usually with a middle layer of mud and dead leaves, lined with fine rootlets and dead leaves. Paper, leaves, or similar material may be present in base. Built by female over *c.* 5 days. **Breeding season:** Begins late April to early or mid-May. Sometimes double-brooded. **Eggs:** Usually 3–4. Subelliptical to oval. Smooth and glossy. Light blue and unmarked. 25 × 19 mm. **Incubation:** Eggs laid at daily intervals. Incubation by female alone, beginning with second or third egg. 12–14 days. **Nestling:** Altricial and downy. Down dark gray; on head, wings, and rear half of back only. Mouth yellow; gape flanges pale yellow. **Nestling period:** Young tended by both parents. Eyes open at 5–7 days. Feathers break sheaths at 6–7 days. Young leave nest at 12–13 days. Adults divide brood between them. Young begin to feed themselves at *c.* 20 days.

Figure 87. Wood Thrush: c. 5½ in. across; a substantial cup with a base with dead leaves, middle layer of mud, grass, and dead leaves, and a lining with rootlets.

Fieldfare (*Turdus pilaris*)   Plate 57

Breeding in southwest Greenland where it breeds in areas of short (under 6 ft.) willows and birches in hills and broken terrain (with rocks) near coast. Nest usually in a fairly open site, in a fork on a tree or among twigs (3–6 ft. up), or on the ground (on slope or cliff). Nests are usually in colonies, often in a number of adjacent trees. **Nest:** A bulky cup of dry grass, moss, twigs, and roots, lined with a layer of mud forming a cup, lined in turn with fine grass. Built by female. **Breeding season:** Begins in late May. Double-brooded at times in Europe. **Eggs:** Usually 4, sometimes 5–6. Subelliptical. Smooth and glossy. Light blue with reddish-brown markings. Markings often very small and profuse, covering much of the shell and partly obliterating ground color, sometimes markings sparse, or with heavier blotching, more sparingly distributed and at times capping the larger end. 30 × 21 mm. **Incubation:** By female alone. 11–14 days. **Nestling:** Altricial and downy. Down, on head and back, fairly long and sparse; pale buffish-gray. Mouth yellow; gape flanges yellowish-white. **Nestling period:** Young tended by both parents. 12–16 days in nest.

Redwing (*Turdus iliacus*)

A rare breeder in southwest Greenland in birch and shrub willow areas near coast. Nest usually in a tree, shrub, on a rock or on the ground. 0–10 ft. up.

Nest: A thick cup of dry grass, fine twigs, moss, and lichen, usually with an inner cup of mud, and lined with fine grass. Built by female. *Breeding season:* Begins in late May? Double-brooded in Europe. *Eggs:* Usually 4–5, rarely 2–8. Subelliptical. Smooth and glossy. Light blue or greenish-blue; marked overall with fine speckling or mottling in reddish-brown. The markings are often small and indistinct. 30 × 19 mm. *Incubation:* By female alone. 11–15 days. *Nestling:* Altricial and downy. Down, on head and back, long and fairly thick; buff. Mouth yellow; gape flanges yellowish-white. *Nestling period:* Young tended by both parents. 10–15 days in nest.

Clay-colored Robin (*Turdus grayi*)   Plate 57

An occasional breeder in dense thickets and woodlands in southernmost Texas. Nest in dense cover of tree or small bush. Usually 5–12 ft. from the ground, rarely 30 ft. or higher.

Nest: An open bowl, with an inner shell of mud mixed with fibrous material, an outer bulky wall of various plant material, a lining of rootlets, softer fibers and grasses. Built by female. *Breeding season:* Begins late March into June. *Eggs:* Usually 2–3, occasionally 4. Subelliptical to long subelliptical. Smooth and glossy. Pale gray-blue, blue, or blue-green, thickly covered with fine rusty-brown dots. 29 × 21 mm. *Incubation:* By female. 12 days. *Nestling:* Altricial and downy. Down long but sparse. Skin pink. Mouth orange-yellow. *Nestling period:* Young tended by both parents. Leave nest at 15 days.

American Robin (*Turdus migratorius*)   Plate 57

Breeds over a wide range where nest-sites occur, such as forest openings, open woodlands, farmlands, yards, and grasslands with scattered trees. Nest in a tree or shrub, in a fork or on a branch, on a ledge of a building, or occasionally on a post, or a cliff ledge, or on the ground. Usually 3–25 ft. up.

Nest: A bulky, untidy structure of twigs, coarse grass, weed and grass stems, and sometimes string, rags, and other debris; with a smooth inner cup of mud with a thin lining of fine dry grasses. Built mainly by female. *Breeding season:* Early April in south to mid-May in north of range. Double-, possibly treble-brooded. *Eggs:* Usually 4, sometimes 3–5, rarely 6–7. Subelliptical to oval. Smooth and glossy. Light blue. Unmarked. 28 × 20 mm. *Incubation:* By female alone. 11–14 days. A few records exist of apparent 8–9 day periods. *Nestling:* Altricial and downy. Skin pale pinkish-flesh-color. Down whitish at first, becoming creamy, then gray. Down on head, back, and wings. Present right along back. Mouth rich yellow; gape flanges pale yellow. *Nestling period:* Young tended by both parents. Leave nest at 14–16 days. Male may care for young while female starts new nest. Young can find their own food by *c.* 28 days.

Varied Thrush (*Ixoreus naevius*)   Plate 57

Breeds in moist coniferous woodland. Nest in a tree, usually a small conifer, sometimes a deciduous tree. In a conifer usually against the trunk, hidden in foliage. 4–20 ft. up.

Nest: A bulky cup of twigs, mosses, dead leaves, bark shreds, weed and grass stems, with an inner layer of decayed leaves and mud, grasses and moss; lined with fine dry grasses. Built by female. *Breeding season:* Begins mid-April in south to mid-May in north. Probably double-brooded. *Eggs:* Usually 3, sometimes 2–5. Subelliptical. Smooth and glossy. Light blue. Unmarked. 30 × 21 mm. *Incubation:* By female only. *c.* 14 days. *Nestling:* Altricial and downy. Down scanty and grayish. Mouth orange; gape flanges pale yellow. *Nestling period:* Little information. Tended by both parents.

Wrentit (*Chamaea fasciata*)   Plate 57
Breeds in low scrub and chaparral of coastal southwest Oregon and California. Nest
in a shrub or low tree, usually on the edge of a clearing or break in the thickets. Nest
usually very low, 1–4 ft. up. Usually in a twig fork. Nest built around supporting
stems, and well concealed by foliage.
Nest: A compact cup. Spiders' webs form the base and bind material together. Of
coarse bark fibers, fine bark strips, weed stems, and grass blades; lined with finer
fibers, grasses, and hair. Small lichen fragments may ornament the outside. Built by
both sexes. **Breeding season:** Begins late February to early March. Sometimes two
broods. **Eggs:** Usually 4, sometimes 3–5. Subelliptical. Smooth and non-glossy to
slightly glossy. Uniform greenish-blue. 18 × 14 mm. **Incubation:** By both sexes,
female incubating at night. Begins with next-to-last egg. 15–16 days. **Nestling:**
Altricial and naked. **Nestling period:** Young tended by both parents. Leave nest at
15–16 days.

Mockingbirds and Thrashers (*Mimidae*)

Small to medium-sized songbirds; arboreal or partially terrestrial, feeding mainly on
insects and fruit. Nest usually a bulky or loose cup set fairly low in thick cover. Both
sexes build the nest, incubate eggs, and rear the young. Eggs are blue or whitish-
blue, sometimes unmarked, or often profusely marked in fine speckling or spots
and blotches of reddish-brown. Young are downy, with yellow or orange-red mouth,
gape flanges whitish. They are fed on insects brought in the bill.

Gray Catbird (*Dumatella carolinensis*)   Figure 88, Plate 56
Breeds over a wide range in low thick vegetation. Often bordering woodland
marshes or watercourses; or in hedgerows, orchards, or shrubberies. Nest usually
low, 3–10 ft. up, in a small tree, shrub, or bush; sometimes much higher, up to 60
ft. in trees, or rarely on the ground or in a tree cavity.
Nest: A bulky and thick cup of coarse sticks, weed stems, grapevine, leaves, and
grasses; lined with fine rootlets, bark shreds, decayed leaves, and pine needles, and
sometimes hair. Other material, string, cotton, or rags may be incorporated. Built by
both sexes, but construction mainly by female over 5–6 days. **Breeding season:**
Begins early May. Usually ends by early August. Sometimes double- or treble-
brooded. **Eggs:** Usually 4, sometimes 3–5, exceptionally 6. Subelliptical. Smooth
and glossy. Uniform deep blue or greenish-blue. Unmarked; or rarely with a few
small reddish spots. 23 × 17 mm. **Incubation:** By female alone. 12–13 days.
Nestling: Altricial and downy. Mouth orange-yellow; gape flanges creamy-white.
Some black on tip of tongue. Skin blackish gray on upper parts. Down dark blackish
gray; on head, back, wings, and thighs. **Nestling period:** Young tended by both
parents. Closely brooded by female for first few days. Leave nest at *c.* 11 days. Fed by
adults to *c.* 24 days.

Northern Mockingbird (*Mimus polyglottos*)   Plate 56
Breeds in open woodland, scattered trees and bushes in more open country, and
especially shade trees, shrubbery, and plantings around buildings. Nest in a small
tree, shrub, vine tangle, thicket, or large cactus; or exceptionally on a stump or fence
post. Usually low, 3–10 ft. up, rarely up to 25 or 50 ft., or even higher.
Nest: A bulky cup of coarse dead twigs, sometimes thorny grasses, weed stems,
decayed leaves, rags, string, cotton, etc.; lined with fine grasses, rootlets, and sometimes hair or plant down. Built by both sexes. **Breeding season:** Begins mid-February
in southwest and Florida to late April in north of range. Usually ends by early

Figure 88. Gray Catbird: c. 5½ in. across; usually low in a bush and built from such elements as sticks, bark strips, and grapevine.

September. Double- or treble-brooded. **Eggs:** Usually 3–5, very rarely 6. Subelliptical to elliptical. Smooth and glossy. Pale blue to greenish-blue, or with additional pinkish wash; speckled, spotted, and blotched with light red, chestnut-red, or reddish-brown and paler lilac. Tends to have concentration of markings at larger end. Large blotches sometimes with indistinct edges. 25 × 18 mm. **Incubation:** Eggs laid at daily interval. Incubation by female alone. 11–14 days. **Nestling:** Altricial and downy. Down pale gray. Mouth yellow; gape flanges yellow. Irides dark gray. **Nestling period:** Young tended by both parents. Brooded by female only. Eyes open at 3–5 days. Leave nest at 12–14 days.

Sage Thrasher (*Oreoscoptes montanus*) Plate 57

Breeds in semi-arid sagebrush regions, and in shrubby or open woodland growth on foothills. Nest usually very low in a fork of a shrub from ground level to 2–3 ft. up. Sometimes on the ground in brush.
Nest: A large cup, of coarse plant stems, twigs, and bark shreds; lined with fine rootlets, hair, and fur. Probably built by both sexes. **Breeding season:** Begins mid- to late April. Double-brooded. **Eggs:** Usually 4–5, sometimes 6, rarely 7. Subelliptical. Smooth and glossy. Medium to light blue; boldly speckled, spotted, and blotched with

chestnut-red, or reddish-brown, usually with a concentration at or around the larger end. 25 × 18 mm. *Incubation:* By both sexes. 15 days. *Nestling:* Altricial and downy. Down blackish. *Nestling period:* Tended by both. Fly at 11–14 days.

Brown Thrasher (*Toxostoma rufum*)   Plate 56
Breeds over a wide range in low, thick cover, on woodland edge, in overgrown patches and secondary growth, hedgerows, dry scrub, shrubberies, and garden growth in open areas. Nest very low in a shrub or bush, near the ground, or on the ground under a bush, shrub, or small tree. Rarely more than 7 ft. up, usually under 3 ft. *Nest:* A cup with a loose outer layer of twigs, then dead leaves, bark, small twigs, and grass stems, lined with rootlets or fine grasses. Built by both sexes over 5–7 days. *Breeding season:* Begins late March in south to mid-May in north of range. Sometimes double-brooded. *Eggs:* Usually 4–5, exceptionally 2–6. Subelliptical to long subelliptical or long oval. Smooth and glossy. White, or tinted pale blue or pale greenish-blue; minutely and very heavily speckled overall with tiny reddish-brown markings, often with a denser zone at or around the larger end. Markings occasionally larger and bolder. 26 × 19 mm. *Incubation:* By both sexes. 11–14 days. *Nestling:* Altricial and downy. Skin dark pinkish-flesh-color. Down dark gray; on head, back, wings, and thighs. Mouth creamy-yellow, orange towards throat; gape flanges white. *Nestling period:* Young tended by both parents. Leave nest at 9–12 days.

Long-billed Thrasher (*Toxostoma longirostre*)   Plate 56
Breeds in dense woodland along watercourses, in mesquite thickets and in undergrowth with cactus in south Texas. Nest in a low thick shrub or thicket. Resembles that of Curve-billed Thrasher. Usually 4–10 ft. up. *Nest:* A compact layer of thorny twigs; lined with dry grasses. Probably built by both sexes. *Breeding season:* Begins early April. Sometimes double-brooded. *Eggs:* Usually 4, sometimes 2–5. Similar to those of Brown Thrasher. 27 × 20 mm. *Incubation:* By both. 13–14 days. *Nestling:* Altricial and downy. Down grayish-black. Skin pinkish-red on top, pale whitish-red on top. *Nestling period:* Tended by both. Fly at 12–15 days.

Bendire's Thrasher (*Toxostoma bendirei*)   Plate 56
Breeds in dry scrub and cacti of desert areas in slightly more fertile areas than Le Conte's Thrasher occupies, with more vegetation; and around ranches. Nest in a low tree, shrub, or cactus clump; usually 2–4 ft. up, occasionally up to 12 ft. *Nest:* A smallish cup of fine twigs, with an inner lining of grass, weeds, bark fibers, hair, rootlets, thread, wool, and cotton; lined with softer material. Usually a smaller nest than that of other thrashers. *Breeding season:* Begins late February. Usually ends by mid-June. Sometimes double-brooded. *Eggs:* Usually 3, sometimes 4, rarely 5. Subelliptical to short subelliptical. Smooth and glossy. White or tinted very pale bluish, grayish, and greenish; speckled, spotted, and blotched with poorly defined markings in light red, pale buff, and pale purple and gray. 26 × 19 mm. *Incubation:* No information. *Nestling:* Altricial. *Nestling period:* Tended by both parents. Departure estimated at 11 days.

Curve-billed Thrasher (*Toxostoma curvirostre*)   Plate 57
Breeds in arid places with sparse scrub growth and cacti, open areas in chaparral with prickly pears, and around settlements in arid areas. Nest frequently in cholla cactus, 3–5 ft. up, or in low trees where it may be up to 12 ft. *Nest:* A cup of thorny twigs; lined with grasses and hair. Built by both over as few as 3 days, but often longer. *Breeding season:* Begins early March to early April.

Protracted. Double-brooded, and lost clutch replaced. **Eggs:** Usually 3, sometimes 2–4, rarely 1. Subelliptical to oval. Very pale blue to light blue; profusely and minutely speckled with reddish-brown, the markings so fine that color may not be obvious. Sometimes a dense cup or zone of markings at the larger end. 29 × 20 mm. **Incubation:** By both sexes. 13 days. **Nestling:** Altricial and downy. Dull grayish above, white on chin and below? Flesh pinkish-red above, pinkish below. Mouth yellow; gape flanges yellow. **Nestling period:** Young tended by both parents. Eyes open at 6 days. Feathers break sheaths at 6–8 days. Young leave nest at 14–18 days, begin to feed themselves in 12 days more.

California Thrasher (*Toxostoma redivivum*) Plate 57

Breeds in California in chaparral, scrub of lower mountain slopes, and along watercourses. Nest in a low tree or shrub, usually 2–4 ft. up, but occasionally up to 9 ft. **Nest:** A cup of coarse twigs; lined with rootlets, fibers, and grasses. Built by both. **Breeding season:** Prolonged. November to July. Double-brooded. **Eggs:** Usually 3, sometimes 4, rarely 2. Subelliptical to long subelliptical. Smooth and glossy. Light to medium blue; very finely speckled, or more sparsely spotted or blotched with light to dark reddish-brown and paler lilac. Markings sometimes profuse minute speckling, occasionally indistinct, sometimes bolder sparser spots or few blotches with a tendency to concentration at larger end. 30 × 21 mm. **Incubation:** By both sexes. 14 days. **Nestling:** Altricial. Flesh pink. **Nestling period:** Young tended by both parents. Young leave nest at 12–14 days. Male feeds fledged young while female re-nests.

Crissal Thrasher (*Toxostoma crissale*) Plate 57

Breeds on the edge of desert regions, in areas of low bushy scrub and small trees, along watercourses and valleys, and on hillsides. Nest in the fork of a low tree or shrub (2–8 ft. up), often well concealed and among close twiggy growth. **Nest:** A cup with a rough, bristling outer layer of twigs, usually thorny, and within this a compact cup of dry grasses, plant stems, plant fibers, and bark shreds, with sometimes a few feathers. Built by both sexes. **Breeding season:** Begins early to mid-February. Double-brooded. **Eggs:** Usually 2–3, sometimes 4. Subelliptical. Smooth and glossy. Light blue or greenish-blue. Unmarked. 27 × 19 mm. **Incubation:** By both sexes. 14 days. **Nestling:** Altricial and downy. **Nestling period:** Young tended by both parents. Leave nest at 11–12 days.

Le Conte's Thrasher (*Toxostoma lecontei*) Plate 57

Breeds in desert with scattered shrubby growth, creosote, and cacti; and in arid sagebrush. Nest in cholla cactus, thorn-covered brush, or low tree. 2–8 ft. up. **Nest:** A loose foundation of coarse twigs, with inner cup of slender twigs and grass stems; with inner lining of fibers, rootlets, small leaves, grasses, and sometimes a few feathers. Built by both sexes over 3–12 days. **Breeding season:** Prolonged. Begins late January to February. Double- or possibly treble-brooded. **Eggs:** Usually 3, sometimes 2–4. Subelliptical. Smooth and glossy. Pale blue with a few specks, spots, and small blotches of reddish-brown, mostly at the larger end. 28 × 20 mm. **Incubation:** By both sexes. 14–20 days. **Nestling:** Altricial and naked. Developing down dull white. Skin pink. Mouth orange-yellow; gape yellow. **Nestling period**. Young tended by both parents. Leave nest at 14–17 days. Fly 5–7 days later. Young leave parents' territory at about 4 weeks.

Wagtails and Pipits (Motacillidae)

Small insectivorous birds, mainly of open country. Ground-nesting, usually in a well-concealed cup nest. The eggs are usually cryptically colored, finely spotted in brown or gray. Young are downy, with yellow, orange, or red mouths without spots. They are fed on insects carried by adults in the bill.

Yellow Wagtail (Motacilla flava)   Plate 58
Breeds on tundra and grassy areas near water from western and northern Alaska into northwest Yukon Territory. Nest on the ground in a hollow, or in thick herbage, or under a twig of a low-growing shrub.
Nest: A cup built into a hollow, of grasses, plant stems, and roots; thickly lined with hair and occasionally fur or feathers. Probably built by female alone. **Breeding season:** Begins early June. **Eggs:** Usually 5–6, rarely 7. Subelliptical. Smooth and glossy. Ground color pale buff or grayish, heavily and finely speckled with yellowish-buff and appearing uniform, or mottled with buffish-brown. Often a dark hair streak present. 19 × 14 mm. **Incubation:** Chiefly by the female, beginning with last egg. 12–14 days. **Nestling:** Altricial and downy. Down fairly long and thick; on head and back. Sandy-buff or buffish-white. Mouth reddish-orange, while some populations may show two brown spots at base of tongue; gape flanges pale yellow. **Nestling period:** Young tended by both parents. Leave nest at 10–13 days; fly at c. 17 days.

White Wagtail (Motacilla alba)   Plate 58
An uncommon breeder in northwestern Alaska and breeder in southeast Greenland. Breeds in a variety of habitats, usually with open stretches of level grass, often near water, frequently associated with human activity. Nest a cavity or hole in a great variety of sites – walls, buildings, pipes, drains, banks or old cup nest of other birds, from ground level upwards, sometimes up to 10 ft. (The closely-related Black-backed Wagtail, *Motacilla lugens*, has been reported nesting in the outer Aleutians. Its breeding biology in North America is assumed to be very similar to that of White Wagtail.)
Nest: A cup of stems, twigs, leaves, roots, and moss; lined with grasses, hair, and feathers. Built by both sexes. **Breeding season:** Begins early June. Single-brooded, but will replace lost clutches. **Eggs:** Usually 5–6, occasionally 7. Subelliptical. Smooth and glossy. Ground color gray or bluish-white; evenly and finely freckled with gray-brown and gray spots, occasionally with brown blotches, but predominantly of gray type. 18 × 14 mm. **Incubation:** By both. 12–14 days. **Nestling:** Altricial and downy. Down dark gray; very scanty on underside. Mouth orange-yellow; gape flanges very pale yellow. **Nestling period:** Young tended by both parents. Leave nest at 13–16 days. Fed an additional 14–18 days.

Red-throated Pipit (Anthus cervinus)
Breeds in the Bering Strait area of Alaska in more open habitats, usually where block-fields and dwarf shrub meadows are juxtaposed, often where exposed to the open coast. Nest on the ground, usually tucked into the sides of grassy mounds or sheltered by plants.
Nest: A cup of drier grasses, lined with finer grasses, fibers, and hair. Built by both. **Breeding season:** Begins mid-June. Single-brooded. **Eggs:** Usually 5–6, rarely 4–7. Subelliptical. Smooth and glossy. Variable in color, grayish, buffish, olive, or pinkish; finely speckled, spotted, or indistinctly blotched with gray, buff, brown, or reddish-brown. Lighter eggs may show fine black hair streaks. Similar to eggs of American Pipit. 19 × 14 mm. **Incubation:** By female alone; may be fed by male. 12–14 days?

Nestling: Altricial and downy. Down long and thick, dark grayish-brown. Mouth red; gape flanges pale yellow. **Nestling period:** Young brooded by female, fed by both adults. Leave in 11–13 days.

American Pipit (Anthus rubescens)   Plate 58

Breeds on alpine meadows and rocky slopes, or more level ground along water-courses at high altitudes, to cliffs and rocky coastlines, extending to level marshy coasts with occasional boulders or earth cliffs, and in extreme north on swamps and tundra near coast. Nest in a recess or shallow hole in bank or cliff, or on the ground concealed in a hole or under plants.

Nest: A cup built into a hollow, of plant stems and grasses and some moss; lined with finer grasses, fibers, or hair. Built by both sexes. **Breeding season:** Begins early to mid-June. Usually ends by early August. Single-brooded. **Eggs:** Usually 4–6. Sub-elliptical. Smooth and glossy. Ground color whitish-gray, heavily spotted in brown and pale gray. Occasionally with a thin black hair streak, or with accumulated dark markings wreathing or capping the larger end. 21 × 15 mm. **Incubation:** By female alone. c. 14 days. **Nestling:** Altricial and downy. Down long and fairly thick. Brown-ish-gray; shorter and whiter on underside. Mouth reddish-orange; gape flanges very pale yellow. **Nestling period:** Young tended by both adults. Eyes open at 4–5 days. Feathers break sheaths at 8–9 days. Young leave nest at 14–16 days. Become inde-pendent at c. 29 days.

Meadow Pipit (Anthus pratensis)   Plate 58

Breeds uncommonly in open country, in grassy areas along the coast in southeast and northeast Greenland. Nest on the ground, in herbage, usually well concealed from view, at times some distance under cover, occasionally just at edge of plant tuft.

Nest: A cup of dry grasses and plant material; lined with finer material, plant fiber, and hair. Built mainly by female. **Breeding season:** Begins early June. Probably ends mid-August. **Eggs:** Usually 3–5, sometimes to 7; clutches larger in north. Subellipti-cal. Smooth and glossy. Variable in color, but with several distinct types – brownish, grayish, or reddish. Ground color pale gray, buff, or pink; spotted or mottled with brown and pale gray, or so finely marked as to appear almost uniform dark gray or buff. Occasional blackish hair streaks. 20 × 15 mm. **Incubation:** By female only. 11–15 days. **Nestling:** Altricial and downy. Down long and thick, brownish-gray. Mouth red with whitish rear spurs on tongue; gape flanges light yellow. **Nestling period:** Young tended by both adults. Eyes open at 4–5 days, feathers break sheaths at c. 12 days. Leave nest at 10–14 days, before they can fly well.

Sprague's Pipit (Anthus spragueii)   Plate 58

Breeds on short-grass prairie. Nest on the ground in growing herbage, usually set in a slight hollow and concealed by overhanging grasses.

Nest: A cup of fine grasses, with a canopy and sometimes with a covered entrance-way. **Breeding season:** Begins mid-May to early June. **Eggs:** Usually 4–5, rarely 3–6. Subelliptical to oval. Smooth and moderately glossy. Grayish-white to pale buff; finely speckled and spotted, or heavily mottled with buff, olive-brown, or purplish-brown and paler gray or purplish-gray. Markings usually fairly evenly distributed. Thin dark hair streaks sometimes present. 21 × 15 mm. **Incubation:** By female. c. 13 days. **Nestling:** Altricial and downy. Down long and thick; light gray; on head and upperparts. **Nestling period:** May be tended only by female. Young leave nest about 10–11 days after hatching.

Waxwings (*Bombycillidae*)

Bohemian Waxwing (*Bombycilla garrulus*)   Plates 16, 58
Breeds in coniferous and birch forests. Nest in a tree, usually a conifer, 5–20 ft. up.
Nest tree often on forest edge, or by lake or stream, or in a swamp.
Nest: A cup of conifer twigs, reindeer moss, and grass; lined with hair and down.
Built by both. **Breeding season:** Begins variably in late May to late June. Single-
brooded. **Eggs:** Usually 5, sometimes 4–6. Subelliptical to oval. Smooth and glossy.
Pale blue or grayish-blue, rarely slightly buffish; sparsely marked with spots of black
and gray, spots occasionally showing blurred brownish edges. 25 × 17 mm.
Incubation: By female alone, fed by male. 13–14 days. **Nestling:** Altricial and naked.
Mouth bright red with violet-blue bands down either side, tongue purplish. **Nestling
period:** Young tended by both parents. Fed on regurgitated insects and berries. Leave
nest at 15–17 days.

Cedar Waxwing (*Bombycilla cedrorum*)   Plate 58
Breeds over a wide variety of habitats, generally woods and orchards. Nest in a tree,
usually fairly high, from 5 ft. upwards; frequently well out on a horizontal branch.
Usually a number of pairs nest fairly near each other.
Nest: A bulky cup of twigs, dry grasses, and weed stems, or *Usnea* lichen; lined with
wool, pine needles, rootlets, plant down, or fine grasses. Built by both in 5–7 days.
Breeding season: Begins early June, but variable and possibly dependent on food
supply. Double-brooded. **Eggs:** Usually 3–5, rarely 6. Subelliptical to oval. Smooth
and moderately glossy. Very pale blue or grayish-blue; spotted and speckled with
black and pale gray. Markings rather sparse, sometimes more numerous towards
larger end, and sometimes with blurred brownish edges. 22 × 16 mm. **Incubation:**
Probably by female alone. 12–14 days. **Nestling:** Altricial and naked. Mouth bright
red; gape flanges creamy-yellow but not swollen. **Nestling period:** Young tended by
both parents. Eyes open at 7–8 days. Feathers break sheaths at 8–14 days. Young
leave nest at 16–18 days.

Silky Flycatchers (*Ptilogonatidae*)

Phainopepla (*Phainopepla nitens*)   Plate 58
Breeds in desert scrublands, dry oak woodland, and trees bordering watercourses in
arid areas. Nest in a tree usually in a stout fork or on a horizontal branch. Usually
6–11 ft. up, sometimes 4–50 ft. up.
Nest: A shallow cup, compactly made of fine material. Small twigs, stem fragments,
tiny leaves, and oak blossoms, and plant down; bound together with spiders' webs
and lined with hair, wool, and plant down. Built by male at first but completed by
female. **Breeding season:** Begins late February through July. Two broods, possibly
three. May nest early in desert, then move to moist habitat to re-nest. **Eggs:** Usually
2–3, rarely 4. Subelliptical to short subelliptical. Smooth and slightly glossy. Grayish-white or very faintly pinkish; finely and profusely speckled and spotted with
black, and paler shades of lavender and gray. Markings becoming denser towards
larger end. 22 × 16 mm. **Incubation:** By both sexes but possibly mainly by male.
14–15 days. **Nestling:** Altricial and downy. Skin purplish-black. Down white, in long
tufts; on head, back, wings, and tail, but center of crown bare. Mouth pinkish-flesh-
colored; gape flanges yellow. **Nestling period:** Young tended by both parents. Pin-
feathers appear at *c.* 7 days, crest begins to appear at 10–11 days. Young leave nest at
18–19 days.

Shrikes (*Laniidae*)

Northern Shrike (*Lanius excubitor*)   Plate 58
Breeds in open forest and forest clearings, open country with scattered trees, tundra
edge, and scrubland. Nest-sites vary from fairly low sites in thorn bushes and small
trees, to sites high in taller trees. 5–20 ft. up.
Nest: A bulky cup of dry grass and moss on a foundation of twigs, greater use being
made of twigs in more arid areas; lined with roots, wool, hair, and feathers. **Breeding
season:** Begins mid- to late May. Single-brooded. **Eggs:** 5–7, occasionally 8–9. Subelliptical. Smooth and glossy. White, tinged greenish or buffish, usually heavily
marked with spots and small blotches of brown, light reddish-brown, olive, buff, or
pale purplish-gray; the markings present over most of the surface but also tending to
concentrate in a wreath about the larger end. 26 × 19 mm. **Incubation:** Chiefly by
female, fed by male. 15 days. **Nestling:** Altricial and naked. Skin pinkish-flesh-
colored, becoming darker after few days. Mouth pink; gape flanges yellow. **Nestling
period:** Young tended by both parents. Female broods for first day or two, male bringing food. Young leave nest *c.* 19–20 days, independent at *c.* 35 days.

Loggerhead Shrike (*Lanius ludovicianus*)   Plate 58
Breeds in open country with scattered trees or shrubs (such as shelterbelts), or open
scrub or woodland. Nest in a thick shrub or low tree, usually 3–15 ft. up, occasionally higher in tall trees (to 30 ft.). Usually among twigs, sometimes well out in a fork
of a branch, but concealed by foliage. Occasionally a number of pairs nest near each
other.
Nest: A bulky cup of long twigs, weed stems and rootlets; lined with plant down,
bark, hair, rootlets, and feathers. Built mostly or entirely by female over 6–11 days.
Breeding season: Begins mid-February in south to late April in north of range.
Double-brooded, sometimes treble-brooded. **Eggs:** Usually 4–5, sometimes 6–7.
Subelliptical. Smooth and moderately glossy. White, creamy-white or faintly tinted
buff or gray; speckled, spotted, and blotched in light to dark brown, or purplish-
brown, and paler buff, purple, or gray. Larger markings often concentrated at or
around larger end; and paler markings may form a distinct band. 24 × 19 mm.
Incubation: By female alone, beginning with next-to-last egg, and fed by male.
14–16 days. **Nestling:** Altricial and downy. Skin bright orange. Down very sparse,
white; on body only. Bill buffish-yellow. Mouth yellow; gape flanges yellow. **Nestling
period:** Young tended by both parents. For several days female broods and male
brings food. Young usually feathered by 15 days, leave at 17–21 days, become independent at 40–45 days.

Starlings (*Sturnidae*)

European Starling (*Sturnus vulgaris*)   Plate 62
Introduced from Europe. Breeds in a range of habitats where nest-site holes occur
with open areas of herbage. Nest in hole in tree, rocks, buildings, creepers on trees,
or nest-box. 2–60 ft. up.
Nest: An untidy accumulation of stems, leaves, and other plant material, with cup
lined with feathers, wool and moss. Male begins nest before pairing, female com-
pletes nest. **Breeding season:** Begins mid-April, exceptionally at other times. Single-
or double-brooded. **Eggs:** Usually 5–7, rarely 4–9. Subelliptical. Smooth and slightly
glossy. Pale light blue, varying in tint. Very exceptionally a few brown spots. 30 × 21
mm. **Incubation:** By both sexes, beginning at completion of clutch. 12–15 days.

Nestling: Altricial and downy. Down fairly long and plentiful; grayish-white, darker on head. Mouth bright yellow; gape flanges pale yellow. **Nestling period:** Young fed by both sexes. 20–22 days. Dependent on parents (4–5 days) for food after leaving nest, following them and food-begging.

Crested Myna (*Acridotheres cristatellus*)   Plate 62
Introduced from Asia into Vancouver, British Columbia area. Breeds around cultivation and buildings, or open parkland, in natural cavities in trees, old woodpecker holes, or new ones taken over, crevices and holes in buildings, or any similar site. Usually 10–25 ft. up, though as low as 2 ft. and as high as 60 ft. up.
Nest: Cavity lined with grasses and weeds, dead leaves, feathers, pieces of paper, rootlets, and various debris and rubbish, to form a rough cup. Built by both sexes. **Breeding season:** Begins early April. Usually ends by mid-August. Double-brooded. **Eggs:** Usually 4–5, sometimes 6–7. Subelliptical to oval. Smooth and glossy. Light blue or greenish-blue, normally unmarked, very rarely with a few dark spots. 31 × 22 mm. **Incubation:** By both sexes. 12–15 days. **Nestling:** Altricial. Grayish down is shorter than that of European Starling. **Nestling period:** Young leave nest at *c.* 22 days; and are fed by parents for *c.* 1 week longer.

Vireos (*Vireonidae*)

Small insectivorous and arboreal birds. Nest a pensile cup suspended in a thin twig fork. Nest bound together and the upper rim bound to the twigs with plant fibers, hairs and spiders' webs. Nest rounded, sometimes drawn in towards the mouth, and lined with fine grasses or fibers. Eggs usually 3–5, white and very sparsely speckled. Incubation and care of young usually by both sexes. Young altricial and downy. Fed on insects brought in the bill.

White-eyed Vireo (*Vireo griseus*)   Plate 58
Breeds in lower shrub growth, thickets, woodland edge, hedgerows, and scrub, usually near water. Nest usually suspended in a horizontal twig fork, 3–6 ft. up, or sometimes 2–25 ft. up.
Nest: A deep pensile cup, attached to twigs at the rim. The outer layer of coarse, looser material tapering away at the bottom. Outer layer dead or green leaves, wasp nest fragments, and bark flakes; cup of finer bark strips, fibers, spiders' cocoons, wool, plant down, lichen, and moss, bound with spiders' webs; lined with fine grasses and hair. Built by both sexes. **Breeding season:** Begins late March in south to mid-May in north of range. Usually ends by mid-July. Probably double-brooded. **Eggs:** Usually 5, sometimes 3–4, Subelliptical to elliptical. White; very sparsely marked with minute speckling and spotting in black, sometimes with blurred edges to marks. 19 × 14 mm. **Incubation:** By both sexes. 12–15 days. **Nestling:** Altricial and downy. Flesh orange-pink; down grayish. Mouth and gape flanges light yellow. **Nestling period:** Tended by both parents. Leave at 9–11 days.

Bell's Vireo (*Vireo bellii*)   Figure 89, Plate 58
Breeds in dense shrubby growth and woodland edge, riparian thickets, scattered cover and hedgerows of cultivated areas, and in mesquite. Nest in a shrub or low tree, usually at *c.* 3 ft., or between 1–10 ft., and rarely up to 25 ft. Suspended usually from a horizontal twig fork.
Nest: A deep rounded cup, often with material hanging from bottom, bound to twigs at the rim. Of bark strips, feathers, grass and leaf fragments, and plant down, bound

Figure 89. Bell's Vireo: c. 2–2½ in. across; the cup, suspended from a twig fork, often has material hanging from the bottom (not shown here).

with spiders' webs and cocoons; lined with fine grasses, or thin weed stems, and hair. Built by both sexes, over 4–6 days. **Breeding season:** Begins early April in south to late May in north of range. Usually ends by early July. Double-brooded. **Eggs:** Usually 4, sometimes 3–5. Subelliptical. Smooth and non-glossy. White, with a few specks of dark brown or black, or spots of reddish-brown or brown. Sometimes unmarked. 17 × 13 mm. **Incubation:** By both sexes, before clutch is complete. 14 days. **Nestling:** Altricial and downy. Skin pinkish to reddish. Mouth and gape flanges yellow. Legs pale yellow. **Nestling period:** Young tended by both parents. Leave nest at 10–12 days. Remain with adults for 25–30 days more.

Black-capped Vireo (*Vireo atricapillus*)   Figure 90, Plate 58
Breeds in scrub–oak woodland and shrubby growth in arid, hilly regions, often on steep hillsides near water in Texas and central Oklahoma. Nest in a twig fork of small tree or shrub, or in tangle of shrubby growth, usually c. 2–6 ft. up, rarely up to 15 ft. **Nest:** A pensile cup, slung between horizontal twigs to which the rim is bound. Rather rounded and thick-walled; of leaves, coarse grasses, bark strips, catkins, and spiders' cocoons, bound together and to supports with long plant fibers, spiders' webs and wool; and lined with finer grasses. Built by both, though mainly by female, over 6–9 days. **Breeding season:** Begins mid-April. Usually ends early August (later in Oklahoma). Sometimes double-brooded. **Eggs:** Usually 4, sometimes 3–5. Subelliptical to long subelliptical. Smooth and non-glossy. White and unmarked. 18 × 13 mm. **Incubation:** By both sexes. 14–17 days. **Nestling.** Altricial and naked. Yellowish-pink skin, bill, and feet. Mouth orange-yellow; gape flanges yellow. **Nestling period:** Young leave nest about 10–12 days after hatching.

Gray Vireo (*Vireo vicinior*)   Plate 58
Breeds in thorn scrub or pinyon–juniper woodland. Nest fairly low, 2–8 ft. up, in thorny or twiggy shrubs or trees, or in juniper. Nests often with several supporting twigs around, although basically pensile like those of other vireos. **Nest:** A cup, bound to twigs at its rim. Of dry grasses, plant fibers, stems, shredded weed stems, and spiders' cocoons. Bound together with spiders' webs and often decorated

Figure 90. Black-capped Vireo: c. 3 in. across; a thick-walled vireo nest slung from supporting horizontal twigs.

with sagebrush leaves externally. Lined with fine, hair-like fibers. Built by both sexes. **Breeding season:** Begins late April to May. **Eggs:** 3–4. Subelliptical. Smooth and moderately glossy. Pure white; with sparse minute specks at the larger end, of dark brown or black. 18 × 13 mm. **Incubation:** By both. 13–14 days. **Nestling:** Altricial and downy? Down dull white. **Nestling period:** Tended by both, fly at 13–14 days.

Solitary Vireo (*Vireo solitarius* – Includes Blue-headed Vireo, *V. s. solitarius* and *V. s. alticola*, Plumbeous Vireo, *V. s. plumbeus*, and Cassin's Vireo, *V. s. cassinii*)   Plate 58

These forms may actually be three distinct species. Blue-headed Vireo breeds in deciduous or mixed woodland; Plumbeous Vireo breeds in pinyon–juniper, Ponderosa pine, aspen, cottonwood, or oak woodland; Cassin's Vireo breeds in oak, oak–coniferous, or mixed riparian woodland. Nest in a tree or shrub, in a twig fork, 6–15 ft. up, exceptionally as low as 3 ft. and as high as 40 ft.

Nest: A rounded cup, less deep than some other vireo nests and more loosely constructed than other vireo nests, bound to twigs at its upper edges. Of bark strips, plant fibers, rootlets, threads, grasses, lichen, moss, fur, wool, plant down, cotton, and feathers; bound together with spiders' webs and lined with finer grasses or moss stems, and some hair or fur. Paper, pale wasp nest elements, or pale birch bark strips often on the exterior. **Breeding season:** Variable, beginning mid-April to mid-May. Probably double-brooded. **Eggs:** Usually 4, sometimes 3–5. Subelliptical to short oval. White or creamy-white; sparingly speckled or spotted in brown, chestnut-red, or blackish. Markings mainly at the larger end. 20 × 14 mm. **Incubation:** By both. 15 days. **Nestling:** Altricial and downy? Down buffy-white. Bill, legs, and feet pinkish-buff. Mouth yellow-orange; gape flanges pale ivory (*V.s. plumbeus?*) or pale yellow. **Nestling period:** Tended by both parents. Fly at 13 days.

Yellow-throated Vireo (*Vireo flavifrons*)   Plate 58

Breeds in deciduous or mixed forest, by clearings or near water (e.g., river bottoms), and in scattered or shade trees elsewhere. Nest in a tree, usually deciduous, in a

horizontal twig fork towards the end of a branch; usually more than 20 ft. up, sometimes 3–60 ft. up.
Nest: A deep rounded cup with thick walls and an incurved rim. Of plant fibers and very large amounts of spiders' webs, the outside and supports covered with flakes of lichen; the cup lined with fine grass-heads or thin pine needles. Built by both sexes, but mostly by female, over *c.* 7 days. **Breeding season:** Begins late April in south to late May in north of range. **Eggs:** Usually 4, sometimes 3–5. Subelliptical to oval. Smooth and slightly glossy. White, creamy-white or pale pinkish-white; spotted or with very small blotches, mostly at the larger end, of black, brown, reddish-brown, and pale gray or purple. Larger spots may show blurred edges. 21 × 15 mm. **Incubation:** By both sexes. 14–15 days. **Nestling:** Altricial and downy. Down gray. Mouth and gape flanges yellow. **Nestling period:** Tended by both. Fly at 14 days.

Hutton's Vireo (*Vireo huttoni*)   **Plate 58**
Breeds in live oaks and other trees along mountain streams and canyons. Nest in a deciduous or coniferous tree, suspended from a twig fork, 5–35 ft. up.
Nest: A deep rounded cup, bound to twigs at the rim. *Usnea* lichen, Spanish Moss or plant down are extensively used where available, the structure bound with fine grasses, hair, and spiders' webs, and incorporating small amounts of a wide range of other plant materials; lined with fine grasses or grass-heads, and sometimes a little hair. Built by both over 4 days, sometimes longer. **Breeding season:** Begins late February to early May. Usually ends by mid-July. Possibly double-brooded. **Eggs:** Usually 4, sometimes 3–5. Subelliptical to long subelliptical or oval. Smooth and moderately glossy. White; very sparsely marked with a few specks or spots of brown or reddish-brown at the larger end. Occasionally unmarked. 18 × 13 mm. **Incubation:** By both parents. 14–16 days. **Nestling:** Altricial and naked. Flesh pale pink. Developing down pale yellowish-white or pinkish-white to very pale drab gray. **Nestling period:** Young tended by both parents. Leave at *c.* 14 days.

Warbling Vireo (*Vireo gilvus*)   **Plate 58**
Breeds in large deciduous trees, roadside tree belts, mature riparian woodlands, orchards, scattered trees in cultivated areas, on hillsides, by lakes and streams, and along canyons. Nest in a tree, usually high up in a horizontal twig fork, well out on a branch in the canopy. Usually 20–60 ft. up, occasionally lower, and in the west frequently lower, sometimes in shrubs down to 4 ft.
Nest: A rough, rounded pensile cup bound to twigs at its rim. Of hair, long grasses, threads and string, bark strips, plant down, and lichen. Bound with spiders' webs and lined with fine shredded weed stems. Built by both in about a week. **Breeding season:** Begins mid-May. Double-brooded. **Eggs:** Usually 4, sometimes 3–5. Long subelliptical or oval. Smooth and non-glossy. White; with a few specks and spots of black, brown or reddish-brown mostly at the larger end. 19 × 14 mm. **Incubation:** By both sexes. 12–13 days. **Nestling:** Altricial and downy. Skin dark yellow. Down pale brown. Mouth orange; gape flanges yellow. **Nestling period:** Young tended by both parents. Eyes open at 9 days. Young leave nest at 14 days?

Philadelphia Vireo (*Vireo philadelphicus*)   **Plate 58**
Breeds on woodland edge, in deciduous scrub, cutover areas in regeneration, and open secondary growth, in trees along streams and rivers, and on lake islands. Nest in a horizontal twig fork 10–40 ft. up in a deciduous tree, usually near the upper canopy.
Nest: A pensile rounded cup, narrowing at the rim where it is bound to twigs. Of bark fibers and strips, shreds of *Usnea*, grass-blades, twine and spiders' webs lined

with pine needles, fine grass-stems, and sometimes a few feathers. Built by female? over *c.* 6 days. **Breeding season:** Begins early to mid-June. Usually ends by early August. **Eggs:** Usually 4, sometimes 3–5. Long subelliptical. Smooth and non-glossy. White; sparsely speckled and spotted in black and brown. Larger spots sometimes with blurred edges. Markings often confined to the larger end. 19 × 14 mm. **Incubation:** By both sexes. 13–14 days. **Nestling:** Altricial and downy. Skin light orange-yellow. Down pale gray and short. Mouth yellow. **Nestling period:** Young tended by both parents. Leave nest at 13–14 days. Remain with parents until at least 24 days old.

Red-eyed Vireo (*Vireo olivaceus*)   Plates 16, 58
Breeds widely in deciduous woodland with dense undergrowth, or scattered groups of trees in open or cultivated areas. Nest suspended in a horizontal fork, usually of a shrub or low tree branch, 5–10 ft. up, exceptionally 2–60 ft. up.
Nest: A pensile rounded cup, bound to twigs at its rim. Of vine-bark strips, thin grasses, rootlets, and birchbark, bound with spiders' or caterpillar webs. Occasionally ornamented outside with lichen. Built by female in 5 days. **Breeding season:** Begins mid-May in south to mid-June in north of range. Occasionally double-brooded. **Eggs:** Usually 4, sometimes 3–5. Subelliptical to long subelliptical or oval. Smooth and non-glossy. White. Sparsely and finely speckled, spotted, or rarely blotched with reddish-brown, brown, or black. Rarely unmarked, or with larger light brown spots. Markings mostly at the larger end. Larger marks may show blurred edges. 20 × 14 mm. **Incubation:** By both sexes. 11–14 days. **Nestling:** Altricial and downy. Down pale gray. Skin yellowish-flesh-color. Mouth pale yellow; gape flanges pale cream. **Nestling period:** Young tended by both parents. Eyes open at 4–5 days. Young leave nest at 12 days.

Yellow-green Vireo (*Vireo flavoviridis*)
An occasional breeder in wooded resacas and shade trees, edges of forests and brushy pastures in extreme south Texas. Nest suspended in a horizontal fork, in a tree or shrub, 5–40 ft. up, though not usually over 10 ft. up.
Nest: A suspended cup of grasses, leaves, bark, and fibrous plant parts, fastened with spiders' webbing to branch. Built by female. **Breeding season:** Mid-May to mid-July. **Eggs:** Usually 3–4. Short subelliptical to oval. White, rather sparsely dotted with browns, orange-rufous and black. 21 × 15 mm. **Incubation:** By female. 13–14 days. **Nestling:** Altricial and downy. Down short and drab gray. Mouth yellow. **Nestling period:** Young tended by both parents. Almost fully feathered by 10 days. Leave at 12–14 days.

Black-whiskered Vireo (*Vireo altiloquus*)   Plate 58
Breeds in Florida in mangroves (usually Red Mangrove). Nest usually in mangrove tree on the edge of a group of trees, *c.* 7–10 ft. up, sometimes higher. Suspended in the fork of a horizontal twig, overhanging the water.
Nest: A pensile cup, bound to twigs at its rim; of grass-blades, plant down, dead leaves; bound with long plant fibers and spiders' webs; and lined with palm threads and fine grasses. Built by female. **Breeding season:** Begins late May. Ends early September. **Eggs:** Usually 2–3. Subelliptical to oval. Smooth and non-glossy. White with a few sparse specklings of black and purplish-brown; mostly at the larger end. 21 × 15 mm. **Incubation:** By female. Period unknown. **Nestling:** No information. **Nestling period:** No information.

Wood Warblers, Tanagers, Cardinals, Grosbeaks, Sparrows, Buntings, Blackbirds, and Allies (*Emberizidae*)

This is a large and varied family composed of small to medium-sized seed-eating, insect-eating, and fruit-eating birds. Nest in a tree or shrub, on the ground and well concealed in vegetation, or rarely in a cavity. Usually a cup, sometimes pensile or a domed structure. Nest usually built by female. (Three species are brood parasites, laying eggs in the nests of other birds which hatch them and rear the young.) Eggs with pale ground color, sometimes spotted and blotched, but more often marked with intricate scrawling and scribbling; or blue, pinkish or purplish, boldly marked, often with heavy scrawling or scribbling. Incubation is usually by female alone. Male's role varies from help with nest-building and feeding of young to none at all. Nestlings downy. Mouths usually pink or red, and gape flanges yellow or creamy-yellow. Young fed mainly on insects brought in the bill.

Bachman's Warbler (*Vermivora bachmanii*)
Extremely rare and almost extinct breeder in southern US in thick swampy decid-uous woodland, possibly associated with cane. Nest in a fork, in vines or on palmetto leaf. 2–5 ft. up.
Nest: A cup of dead weed and grass stalks, decayed and skeletonized leaves, and sometimes Spanish Moss; lined with finer weed and grass stems, and black lichen fibers. **Breeding season:** Begins late March. Ends in early June? **Eggs:** Usually 3–4, sometimes 5. Subelliptical. Smooth and glossy. White and unmarked. 16 × 12 mm. **Incubation:** By female. Estimated at 11 days. **Nestling:** No information. **Nestling period:** Little information. Young tended by both parents. Assumed to leave nest at 10 days.

Blue-winged Warbler (*Vermivora pinus*)   Plate 59
Breeds in overgrown old pastures with secondary growth, woodland edge and clear-ings with low or shrubby cover, on hillsides or low, swampy areas. (Usually in older overgrown fields and moister habitat than preferred by Golden-winged Warbler.) Nest on the ground or a little above ground (up to 1 ft.) concealed among ferns, in a grass tuft, or low plant growth. Multiple pairs may nest in close proximity.
Nest: A cup, usually narrow and deep, of coarse grass, dead leaves, and vine bark strips; lined with finer grass stems, fibers, and hair. Built by female. **Breeding season:** Begins mid- to late May. Probably ends in July. **Eggs:** Usually 5, sometimes 4–7. Short subelliptical to subelliptical. Smooth and slightly glossy. White; finely speckled or sparsely spotted with shades of brown, reddish-brown and paler gray. Markings often concentrated at larger end. Rarely unmarked. 16 × 12 mm. **Incubation:** Eggs laid daily. Incubation by female alone, beginning with last egg. 10–11 days. **Nestling:** Altricial and downy. Almost naked at hatching. Skin pinkish-flesh-colored. Down grayish; on head and shoulders. Mouth pink; gape flanges cream. **Nestling period:** Tended by both. Eyes open at *c.* 5 days. Young leave nest at 8–10 days.

Golden-winged Warbler (*Vermivora chrysoptera*)   Plate 59
Breeds in openings deciduous woodland, usually in areas of thick undergrowth or on woodland edge with low cover, or in hillside scrub and overgrown pastures. (Habitat occupied is usually earlier-successional and drier than that preferred by Blue-winged Warbler.) Nest usually on or occasionally above the ground, in a grass-tuft, fern or weed clump or concealed in herbage at the base of a shrub or tree. Multi-ple pairs may nest in close proximity.

Nest: A loosely built cup, often on a base of dead leaves, grasses, vine tendrils, and bark fibers; lined with finer material and hair. Built by female in 1–3 days. **Breeding season:** Begins mid- to late May. Usually ends by early July. Probably single-brooded. **Eggs:** Usually 4–5, sometimes 6–7. Short subelliptical to subelliptical. Smooth and slightly glossy. White or creamy-white; speckled, spotted, or blotched with shades of brown or reddish-brown, and with paler gray or purple, and occasionally blackish spots or hairlines. Markings usually concentrated at larger end. 17 × 13 mm. **Incubation:** By female only. 8–10 days. **Nestling:** Little information. Gape pale yellow. **Nestling period:** Young tended by both parents. Leave nest at 10 days.

Tennessee Warbler (*Vermivora peregrina*)   Plate 59
Breeds in northern coniferous and deciduous forests in a variety of sites, including thickets, openings, and second-growth. May prefer spruce/aspen forests. Nest on the ground, usually set in a hollow in moss and concealed by grasses and dead herbage. Multiple pairs may nest in close proximity.
Nest: A cup of thin grasses; lined with finer grasses and hair. Built by female. **Breeding season:** Begins late May to early June. Probably ends July. **Eggs:** Usually 4–6, sometimes 7. Subelliptical to short subelliptical. Smooth and slightly glossy. White to creamy-white; speckled and spotted with chestnut-red, reddish-brown, or pale purple. Markings sometimes concentrated at the larger end. 16 × 12 mm. **Incubation:** By female. Estimated at 11–12 days. **Nestling:** Altricial and downy. Mouth orange; gape flanges pale yellow. After 5 days, olive-brown feathers become obvious on back. **Nestling period:** Tended by both parents. First flight at *c.* 11 days.

Orange-crowned Warbler (*Vermivora celata*)   Plate 59
Breeds over a wide variety of habitats. In shrubby growth along rivers and low, tangled growth at woodland edge, and overgrown clearings with shrubs and weeds, north to the tree-line; and in similar places on mountains at higher levels. Nest on the ground or in a bush, up to *c.* 2 ft. (On Channel Islands off California coast that subspecies will regularly nest off the ground.)
Nest: A fairly bulky cup of coarse grasses, bark strips, plant down, and finer grasses; lined with fur, hair, and feathers. Built by female over 2–4 days. **Breeding season:** Begins early to mid-April. (Earlier on Channel Islands.) Usually ends by late June. Single-brooded, but will replace clutch. **Eggs:** Usually 5, sometimes 4–6. Short subelliptical. Smooth and moderately glossy. White; speckled, spotted or occasionally blotched, with light red to purplish-red, reddish-brown, brown, and paler lilac, and gray, with occasionally blackish-brown scrawls. Markings often mainly or entirely around the larger end. 16 × 13 mm. **Incubation:** By female. 12–14 days. **Nestling:** Altricial and downy. Mouth red; gape flanges yellow. **Nestling period:** Fed by both. First flight at 12–13 days.

Nashville Warbler (*Vermivora ruficapilla*)   Plate 59
Breeds in saplings and thickets, on woodland edge, in shrubby areas of open woodland, and secondary growth in open spaces; and in the north on boggy forest edge. Nest on the ground, set in a hollow in moss, or against and concealed by shrubby growth, weeds, or dead bracken.
Nest: A small, compact cup of rootlets and fibers; lined with hair. Built by female in 7–9 days. **Breeding season:** Begins early May in south to late May in north of range. Probably ends late July. **Eggs:** Usually 4–5. Subelliptical to short subelliptical. Smooth and slightly glossy. White to creamy-white; speckled, spotted, and blotched or scrawled with chestnut-red to reddish-brown. Markings usually confined to a wreath at the larger end. Sometimes unmarked. 15 × 12 mm. **Incubation:** By female,

rarely with help from male. 11–12 days. **Nestling:** Altricial and downy. Down dark brown. Mouth reddish; gape yellow. Bill and feet pinkish-buff. **Nestling period:** Young tended by both parents. Leave nest at *c.* 11 days.

Virginia's Warbler (*Vermivora virginiae*)   Plate 59
Breeds on steep slopes in mountain scrub–oak and pine–oak woodlands. Nest on the ground, in dead leaves or earth, sunk into a small hollow, the rim at or near ground level (usually below 1 ft.), and concealed against an overhanging grass-tussock.
Nest: A shallow cup of shreds of weed and grass stems, bark strips, dry leaves, moss, and lichen; lined with finer fibers. Probably built by female. **Breeding season:** Begins mid-May to early June. Single-brooded. **Eggs:** Usually 4, sometimes 3–5. Short subelliptical to subelliptical. Smooth and slightly glossy. White; finely speckled, and spotted with chestnut-red, reddish-brown, and paler lilac. Markings vary from profuse to a concentration at the larger end. 16 × 12 mm. **Incubation:** By female. 12–14 days. **Nestling:** Altricial and downy. Mouth reddish; gape yellow. **Nestling period:** Young tended by both parents. Leave at 11–12 days. Age of independence estimated at 3 weeks.

Colima Warbler (*Vermivora crissalis*)
Breeds in the Chisos Mountains of Texas between 5700 and 6500 ft. in oak–pinyon–juniper woodlands. Nest on the ground in dead leaves, concealed by low plants and shrubs.
Nest: A cup of grasses, dead leaves, moss, and bark strips; lined with fine grasses, fur, and hair. Built by both sexes. **Breeding season:** Mid-April to mid-July. **Eggs:** Usually 4. Creamy-white; speckled or blotched, usually in a wreath at the larger end, in shades of dull brown and buff. 18 × 14 mm. **Incubation:** Eggs laid at daily intervals. Incubation by both. 9–12 days. **Nestling:** Little information. Mouth orange; gape yellow. **Nestling period:** Tended by both. Leave at 11 days. Little attention is given young after a few days of leaving.

Lucy's Warbler (*Vermivora luciae*)   Plate 59
Breeds in desert areas especially among mesquites, especially close to main watercourses. Nest in a natural cavity in a tree, behind loose bark, in a woodpecker hole, or in old Verdin's nest; exceptionally in a bank. Usually below 6 ft., but also up to 15 ft.
Nest: A small cup of bark, leaves and leaf-stems, and plant fibers; lined with hair, feathers, and fur. Built by female? **Breeding season:** Begins late April. Usually ends June. Double-brooded. **Eggs:** Usually 4–5, sometimes 3–7. Short subelliptical to subelliptical. Smooth and slightly glossy. White or creamy-white; finely speckled, with chestnut-red to reddish-brown, or light red and paler gray. Markings often concentrated at the larger end. 15 × 11 mm. **Incubation:** By female, possibly with help from male. **Nestling:** Altricial and naked? Down pale yellowish-white to pinkish-white. **Nestling period:** Tended by both parents.

Northern Parula (*Parula americana*)   Plate 59
Breeds mainly in woodland with pendent *Usnea* tree-lichen in north, and trailing Spanish Moss in the south. Nest built into hanging tufts of lichen or moss, but occasionally in more normal sites in conifers or deciduous trees. 5–15 ft. up.
Nest: A cup, built into pendent *Usnea* or Spanish Moss which may form the major part of it, elsewhere of thin grasses and bark shreds; lined with plant down and fine rootlets. Built by female over *c.* 4 days. **Breeding season:** Begins mid-April in south to mid- to late May in north of range. Usually ends by late July. Probably single-brooded. **Eggs:** Usually 4–5, sometimes 3–7. Subelliptical to short subelliptical. Smooth and slightly glossy. White to creamy-white; variably speckled and spotted with chestnut-

red, purplish-red, reddish-brown, dull brown, paler gray, and purple. Markings often mainly confined to larger end; paler markings may be prominent. 16 × 12 mm. **Incubation:** By female alone. 12–14 days. **Nestling:** Altricial and downy. Down smoke-gray, but may appear whiter at first on head and along mid-dorsal area. Skin yellowish-pink. **Nestling period:** Young tended by both parents. Leave nest at 10–11 days, though unable to fly.

Tropical Parula (*Parula pitiayumi*)   Plate 59

Breeds in woodland in epiphytic growth on trees in southernmost Texas. Nest built into the pendent mass. 8–40 ft. up.

Nest: A cup built into pendent epiphytic growth. In Spanish Moss little material may be added. Entered from one side, though there may be a top entrance also; may create a covered nest. Nest-cup of fine grasses, moss, rootlets, bark shreds, and tree blossoms; lined with fine fibers, hair, plant down, and some feathers. Probably built by female. **Breeding season:** Mid-April to mid-July. **Eggs:** Usually 3–4. Subelliptical to short subelliptical. Smooth and slightly glossy. White or creamy-white; speckled and spotted overall or in a wreath around the larger end with brown, cinnamon-brown and gray, and sometimes reddish-brown. 16 × 12 mm. **Incubation:** No information. **Nestling:** No information. **Nestling period:** No information.

Yellow Warbler (*Dendroica petechia*)   Figure 91, Plate 59

Breeds in shrubby growth bordering swamps or watercourses, in wet scrub, mangroves, and tree growth, also in gardens, shrubberies, and berry patches. Nest in an upright twig fork of shrub or tree, usually low, 2–12 ft. up, and occasionally up to 40 ft. Males sometimes polygamous.

Nest: A neat and compact cup of dry weed-stem fibers, fine grass stems, wool, and plant down; lined with fine plant fibers, cotton, plant down, and sometimes feathers.

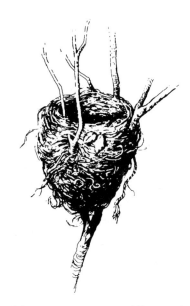

Figure 91. Yellow Warbler: c. 3 in. across; a neat cup of fibers and plant down in an upright twig fork; often with cottony appearance.

Built by female in *c.* 4 days. **Breeding season:** Begins mid-April in south to mid-June in north, extending into July. Sometimes double-brooded. **Eggs:** Usually 4–5, rarely 3–6. Subelliptical to short or long subelliptical. Smooth and slightly glossy. White, or tinted grayish or greenish; speckled, spotted, or blotched in dull brown, olive-brown, or purplish-brown, and paler gray, purple, or olive-buff. Markings mostly confined to a ring around larger end, often with bold spotting; and with paler markings prominent. 17 × 13 mm. **Incubation:** Eggs usually laid at daily intervals. Incubation by female only, beginning before completion of clutch. 11 days. **Nestling:** Altricial and downy. Down scanty and light cream colored; on head, wings, thighs, and back. Mouth red; gape flanges yellow. **Nestling period:** Young tended by both parents. Female broods for most of first few days. Eyes open at 4–5 days. Young leave nest at 9–12 days.

Chestnut-sided Warbler (*Dendroica pensylvanica*)   Plate 60
Breeds in deciduous secondary growth of open woodlands, clearings, woodland edge, and cut-over areas, particularly on mountain slopes, and in overgrown pastures and roadsides. Nest low in a sapling, shrub, thicket, or vine tangle usually 1–3 ft. up.
Nest: A compact cup of fine grasses, bark fibers, shredded weed stems, and plant down; lined with fine grasses and hair. Built by female in *c.* 5 days. **Breeding season:** Begins late May. Usually ends by mid-August. Possibly double-brooded. **Eggs:** Usually 4, sometimes 3–5. Smooth and slightly glossy. Subelliptical to long subelliptical. White, creamy-white, or very pale greenish; speckled, spotted, and blotched with light and dark reddish-brown, purplish-brown and dull brown, and paler gray and purple. Markings usually largely confined to a narrow ring around the larger end, but fine speckling may be more dispersed. 17 × 12 mm. **Incubation:** By female only. 12–13 days. **Nestling:** Altricial and downy. Down fine and sparse, dark gray. Mouth red; gape flanges yellow. **Nestling period:** Young tended by both parents. Eyes open at 3–4 days. Feathers break sheaths at 6–8 days. Young leave nest at 10–12 days.

Magnolia Warbler (*Dendroica magnolia*)   Plate 59
Breeds in small conifers in bogs, and overgrown clearings and woodland edge, usually in lowlands. Rarely in drier oak–hickory–chestnut woodland. Nest on a branch out among twigs and foliage, or by trunk. Usually 1–15 ft. up, sometimes higher.
Nest: A loose cup of fine twigs, coarse grasses, moss stems, pine needles, and fine rootlets, sometimes bound with spiders' webs; lined with fine black rootlets and sometimes hair. Built mostly by female in 4–6 days. **Breeding season:** Begins late May to early June. Usually ends by mid-August. Single-brooded, but will replace lost clutch. **Eggs:** Usually 4, sometimes 3–5. Subelliptical to short subelliptical. Smooth and slightly glossy. White, creamy-white or faintly tinted greenish; variably speckled, spotted, and blotched or smudged in shades of brown, reddish-brown, and olive-buff, with paler purple and gray. Markings may vary from dispersed speckling to a wreath or cap of overlapping brown and gray blotches at larger end. **Incubation:** Eggs laid at daily intervals. Incubation by female only, sometimes beginning with second egg. 11–13 days. **Nestling:** Altricial and downy. Down dark brown. Mouth pinkish; gape flanges pale yellow. **Nestling period:** Young tended by both parents. Brooded by female for first few days. Eyes open at 3–4 days. Feathers break sheaths at 6 days. Young leave nest at 8–10 days.

Cape May Warbler (*Dendroica tigrina*)   Plate 59

Breeds in conifer woodlands with mature spruces either in open woodland or scattered through canopy. Nest high in a spruce, 30–60 ft. up, near the trunk on short branches at the top of trees.

Nest: A bulky cup of twigs, stems, grass, and moss; lined with hair, fur, feathers, and some rootlets. Built by female. **Breeding season:** Begins early June. **Eggs:** Usually 5–6, sometimes 4–9. Subelliptical to short subelliptical. Smooth and very slightly glossy. Creamy-white; spotted, and blotched, mainly at larger end, with brown, reddish-brown, occasional blackish scrawls and paler buff, grayish-brown, and gray. 17 × 13 mm. **Incubation:** By female. **Nestling:** Little information. Flesh pinkish. Mouth orange; gape flanges yellow. **Nestling period:** Tended by both parents. Little further information.

Black-throated Blue Warbler (*Dendroica caerulescens*)   Figure 92

Breeds in deciduous or mixed woodlands, preferring areas of saplings and secondary growth, or thick shrub layers for nesting. Nest in a small tree or sapling, or in a shrub, sometimes preferring evergreen or rhododendron. Nest low, *c.* 1–3 ft. up, in a twig fork.

Nest: A fairly bulky cup, with a base of bark and twigs. Of bark strips, moss, dead leaves, and rotten wood fragments, partly bound together with spiders' webs, lined with hair, black hair-like rootlets and similar fibrous material. Built mostly by female in 3–5 days. **Breeding season:** Begins late May to early June. Usually ends by early August. Up to 3 broods recorded in the north. **Eggs:** Usually 4, occasionally 3–5. Subelliptical to short subelliptical. Smooth and slightly glossy. White to creamy-

Figure 92. Black-throated Blue Warbler: c. 3½ in. across; nest low in a twig fork; a fairly bulky cup, with a base of bark and twigs.

white, speckled, spotted, blotched, and clouded with shades of brown, cinnamon-brown, reddish-brown, brownish-gray, gray, and pale purple. Markings very variable, sometimes indistinct and often concentrated at the larger end. 17 × 13 mm. *Incubation:* By female alone. 12 days. *Nestling:* Altricial and downy. Skin yellowish-flesh color. Down dark gray; on head, back, wings, and thighs. Mouth pink; gape flanges pale yellow. *Nestling period:* Young tended by both parents. Brooded by female only. 10 days.

Yellow-rumped Warbler (*Dendroica coronata* – Includes the Myrtle Warbler, *D. c. coronata*, and Audubon's Warbler, *D. c. auduboni*)   Plate 59

Breeds in conifer woodland over an extensive area, sometimes in deciduous woodland (e.g., aspen) often in more open areas or woodland edge, or in scattered conifers in open country. Nest on a branch at varying heights 4–50 ft. up. Nests in twigs, on a fork, saddling a branch, or in foliage.
Nest: A cup of twigs, bark strips, moss, lichen, fibers, parts of weeds, grasses, rootlets, and hair; lined with hair and obvious feathers. *Breeding season:* Variable, beginning from mid-April to mid-June in various areas. Sometimes double-brooded. Built by female. *Eggs:* Usually 4–5. Subelliptical to short subelliptical. Smooth and slightly glossy. Light buff, speckled, spotted, or blotched with shades of brown, chestnut-red, reddish-brown, and pale gray or purplish-gray. The paler markings often prominent. Sometimes a few scrawls of blackish-brown present. Markings vary but often almost entirely concentrated in a wreath around, or a cap at, the larger end. 17 × 13 mm. *Incubation:* By female alone. 12–13 days. *Nestling:* Altricial and downy. Down dark brown. Mouth reddish; gape flanges yellow. *Nestling period:* Young tended by both parents. Brooded by female only. Young leave at 12–14 days.

Black-throated Gray Warbler (*Dendroica nigrescens*)   Plate 59

Breeds mainly in mountain areas, in open woodlands, pinyon–juniper, shrubby growth with scattered tall trees, or scrub, coniferous or deciduous. Nest in a tree or shrub, usually low, 3–10 ft. up, but occasionally up to 50 ft.
Nest: A cup of dry weed and grass stems, plant fibers, and dead leaves; bound with spiders' webs, sometimes decorated with spiders' cocoons; usually lined with feathers, sometimes with fur and hair. Built by both? *Breeding season:* Begins early May in south to late May in north of range. Usually ends in July. Usually single-brooded. *Eggs:* Usually 4, occasionally 3–5. Subelliptical to short subelliptical. Smooth and slightly glossy. White to creamy-white; speckled, spotted, and occasionally blotched with chestnut-red, reddish-brown, brown, and paler brownish-gray and purple. Markings usually a wreath at larger end, with paler markings prominent. 16 × 12 mm. *Incubation:* By female alone. Period unknown. *Nestling:* Altricial and downy? Down drab gray to pale drab gray. Mouth dull red; gape flanges pale yellow. *Nestling period:* Young tended by both parents. Little further information.

Townsend's Warbler (*Dendroica townsendi*)   Plate 59

Breeds in conifer woodland, sometimes in mixed forest. Nest often in an old coniferous tree, 7–15 ft. up to 100 ft. or more and well out on a branch.
Nest: A compact, but rather large and shallow cup. Of plant fibers, slender twigs, bark strips, moss, lichens, and plant down; lined with moss fruiting stems and hair. Built by both? *Breeding season:* Begins late May to early June. *Eggs:* Usually 3–5. Subelliptical. Smooth and slightly glossy. White; speckled and spotted with chestnut-red, brown, and brownish- or purplish-gray. Spotting may be denser at the larger end. 17 × 13 mm. *Incubation:* By female alone? 12 days. *Nestling:* No information. *Nestling period:* Tended by both. Fly at 8–10 days?

Hermit Warbler (*Dendroica occidentalis*)   Plate 60
Breeds in conifer woodland, preferably of a more open type with scattered large firs.
Nest in a conifer, often high up, usually 20–40 ft., but sometimes to 70 ft. or higher.
Often well out on a branch.
Nest: A cup of weed stalks, fine twigs, lichen, pine needles, and plant fibers; bound
with spiders' webs; lined with fine grasses, plant fibers, and hair. Built by female.
Breeding season: Begins mid-May in south to early June in north of range. **Eggs:**
Usually 3–5. Subelliptical. Smooth and slightly glossy. Creamy-white or faintly pink;
finely speckled or spotted, or sometimes heavily blotched in reddish-brown, brown,
and pale purple or brownish-gray. Markings usually concentrated at larger end.
17 × 13 mm. **Incubation:** By both? 12 days? **Nestling:** Altricial and downy. Down dull
brown. **Nestling period:** Tended by both. Fly at 8–10 days.

Black-throated Green Warbler (*Dendroica virens*)   Plate 59
Breeds in conifer woodland or mixed woodland where conifers predominate, over a
wide range and at various altitudes. Nest often in conifers but also in deciduous
trees, shrubs, and vine tangles, from almost ground level up to *c.* 70 ft., but usually
fairly low.
Nest: A compact deep cup, of twigs, bark strips, moss, grasses, and plant fibers, lined
with hair and feathers. Built mostly by female in *c.* 4 days. **Breeding season:** Begins
mid-May to early June. Usually ends by late July. Possibly double-brooded. **Eggs:**
Usually 4–5. Subelliptical to short subelliptical. Smooth and slightly glossy. Grayish-white to creamy-white. Speckled, spotted, blotched, or with small scrawls of
chestnut-red, reddish-brown, purplish-brown, and paler brownish-gray or purple.
Variably marked, usually with a heavy wreath at larger end. 17 × 13 mm.
Incubation: By female alone? *c.* 12 days. **Nestling:** Altricial and downy. Skin dark
orange. Down dark brown. Mouth pink; gape flanges pale yellow. **Nestling period:**
Young tended by both parents. Eyes open at 3–4 days. Young leave nest at 8–10 days,
and parents divide the young.

Golden-cheeked Warbler (*Dendroica chrysoparia*)   Plate 59
Breeds in shrubby hill country of central Texas. Closely associated with mature Ashe
Juniper; nesting in thick scrubby juniper breaks or scattered clumps of junipers.
Nest in mid-canopy in juniper or deciduous tree, usually low, 4–20 ft. up, in a twig
fork.
Nest: A compact but large cup of juniper bark strips, fine grasses, rootlets and fibers,
bound with spiders' webs; lined with hair and feathers. Built by female. **Breeding
season:** Mid-May to mid-July; single-brooded. **Eggs:** Usually 4, sometimes 3–5. Subelliptical to short subelliptical. Smooth and slightly glossy. White to creamy-white;
finely speckled and spotted in red, purplish-red, or brown, and pale lilac and gray.
Markings scattered or concentrated in dense mass at larger end. 18 × 13 mm.
Incubation: By female, after laying last egg. *c.* 12 days. **Nestling:** Altricial and
downy? Down light brown. **Nestling period:** Young leave nest 9 days after hatching,
and remain with parents for at least 4 weeks.

Blackburnian Warbler (*Dendroica fusca*)   Plate 60
Breeds mainly in conifer woodland, but also in hickory–oak woodland on mountains farther south. Nest usually in a conifer, 5–85 ft. up, well concealed in foliage
or *Usnea* lichen.
Nest: A large compact cup of fine twigs, lichens, moss, and rootlets; lined with plant
down, hair, fine grasses, and rootlets. Built by female over 3–6 days. **Breeding season:**
Begins late May to early June. Usually ends by mid-July. Probably single-brooded. **Eggs:**

Usually 4, sometimes 5. Subelliptical to short subelliptical. Smooth and slightly glossy. White or very pale greenish-white; spotted and blotched with chestnut-red, brown, occasionally blackish-brown scrawls, and pale brownish-gray and purple. Paler markings may predominate. Markings vary from even spotting to a heavy wreath around the larger end. 17 × 13 mm. **Incubation:** By female alone. 12–13 days. **Nestling:** Altricial and downy. Down dark brown. Mouth and gape flanges yellow. **Nestling period:** Young tended by both parents, which divide brood after fledging.

Yellow-throated Warbler (*Dendroica dominica*)   Plate 60
Breeds in areas of live oaks with Spanish Moss, in pine woodland and in deciduous woodland along watercourses. Where Spanish Moss occurs the nest is built into a moss clump, but elsewhere is built on to a horizontal branch. Nest from 3–120 ft. up; but usually 15–60 ft.
Nest: A cup of fine grasses, weed stems, bark shreds, plant fibers, and down, hair or dead leaves, bound with caterpillar webs; lined with plant down and sometimes feathers, or with Spanish Moss strands and flowers. Built mostly or entirely by female. **Breeding season:** Begins early to mid-April. Usually ends early July. Sometimes double-brooded. **Eggs:** Usually 4, rarely 5. Subelliptical to short subelliptical. Smooth and slightly glossy. Pale greenish- or grayish-white; speckled, spotted, and blotched in purplish-red, reddish-brown, blackish- or grayish-purple, and paler purple and gray. Pale markings numerous. 17 × 13 mm. **Incubation:** By female. 12–13 days? **Nestling:** Altricial. Down brownish-gray. Mouth pinkish; gape flanges cream to pale yellow. **Nestling period:** Tended by both. Fledge at *c.* 10 days.

Grace's Warbler (*Dendroica graciae*)   Plate 60
Breeds in mountain pine and pine–oak woodlands. Nest typically in a pine tree, usually high up, *c.* 20–60 ft., and well out on a branch, usually concealed in foliage.
Nest: A compact cup of hair, vegetable fibers, plant down, catkins, and bud-scales, wool, and caterpillar webs; lined with feathers and hair. Probably built by female alone. **Breeding season:** Begins early May. Probably ends June. Usually double-brooded. **Eggs:** Usually 3–4. Subelliptical. Smooth and slightly glossy. White or creamy-white; finely speckled and spotted, or sometimes blotched, with chestnut-red, reddish-brown, light olive, brown, grayish-brown, and a few blackish-brown marks, with paler purple and gray. Markings often limited to a wreath at the larger end; sometimes speckled overall. 17 × 13 mm. **Incubation:** No information. **Nestling:** Altricial. Down grayish. Mouth pink; gape flanges pale yellow. **Nestling period:** Tended by both. Little further information.

Pine Warbler (*Dendroica pinus*)   Figure 93, Plate 60
Breeds in open pine woodland. Nest in a pine tree, on a horizontal branch or among the foliage at the branch tip, usually 15–80 ft. up.
Nest: A compact cup of weed stems, bark strips, pine twigs and needles, and plant fibers bound with caterpillar or spiders' webs; lined with fern-down, pine needles, hair, and feathers. Built by female. **Breeding season:** Begins early April in south to late May or June in north of range. Double-brooded, perhaps sometimes treble-brooded. **Eggs:** Usually 4, sometimes 3–5. Subelliptical to short subelliptical. Smooth and slightly glossy. White, grayish- or greenish-white; speckled, spotted, or blotched with shades of reddish-brown to brown, or paler brownish-gray or purplish-gray, and sometimes a few dark brown or blackish scrawls. Markings usually in a cap or wreath at the larger end. 18 × 13 mm. **Incubation:** By both sexes? 12–13 days. **Nestling:** Altricial and downy. Down dark brown. **Nestling period:** Young tended by both parents. Leave at *c.* 10 days.

Figure 93. Pine Warbler: c. 3 in. across; saddled to a pine branch, often at or near the branch tip.

Kirtland's Warbler (*Dendroica kirtlandii*)   Plate 60

Breeds only in thick stands of small pines in the Michigan Jack Pine plains. Nest on the ground very close to a pine-trunk and concealed under ground vegetation. Male sometimes polygamous.

Nest: A compact cup of dry grasses and plant fibers; lined with finer grasses, fruiting stems of moss, and some hair. Built by female in 2–4 days. **Breeding season:** Begins late May. Usually ends by late July. Single-brooded or sometimes double-brooded, but lost clutch replaced. **Eggs:** Usually 4–5. Subelliptical to short subelliptical. Smooth and slightly glossy. Creamy-white or faintly pink; speckled, spotted, and blotched with buffish-brown or brown. Variably marked, often a concentration at larger end. 18 × 14 mm. **Incubation:** By female. 13–15 days. **Nestling:** Altricial and downy. Down grayish-brown. Mouth red; gape flanges cream. **Nestling period:** Young tended by both parents. Female broods for first few days while male brings food. Young leave nest at 9 days, sometimes longer. Fed by parents until 26–44 days old.

Prairie Warbler (*Dendroica discolor*)   Plate 60

Breeds in low scrub and secondary growth, in clearings, woodland edge, open woodland with low undergrowth, and roadside thickets. The southern subspecies nests in mangroves, bordering coastal marshes. Nest in a shrub, sapling, thicket, or fern clump, usually 1–10 ft. up, occasionally up to 25 ft. in pines. Males sometimes polygamous.

Nest: A compact cup of plant fibers, small dead leaves, fine grasses, bud-scales, fern and seed down, bound with spiders' webs; lined with hair and feathers. Built by female. **Breeding season:** Begins late April in south to late May in north of range. Occasionally double-brooded. **Eggs:** Usually 4, sometimes 3–5. Subelliptical to short subelliptical. Smooth and slightly glossy. White, creamy-white or with faint greenish tint; spotted and speckled with reddish-brown, chestnut-red, and brown, with paler purple and gray. Spotting forms a denser band at larger end. 16 × 12 mm. **Incubation:** By female alone. 11–15 days. **Nestling:** Altricial and downy. Skin yellow-orange. Down dark gray. Mouth and gape flanges pale yellow. **Nestling period:** Young tended by both parents. Leave nest at 8–10 days. Dependent on parents until 33–35 days of age.

Palm Warbler (Dendroica palmarum) Plate 60

Breeds in northern areas of scattered trees around wet or dry muskeg or conifer areas. Nest on the ground, on a small hummock, in moss, concealed under a tuft of grass or other herbage or at the base of a spruce sapling. Occasionally up to 4 ft. up in spruce sapling. Multiple pairs may nest in close proximity.
Nest: A cup of plant fibers, bark shreds, dry grasses, and shredded weed stems; lined with finer grasses and feathers. Built by female? **Breeding season:** Begins mid- to late May. Single-brooded. **Eggs:** Usually 4–5. Short to long subelliptical. Smooth and slightly glossy. White or creamy-white; speckled, spotted, and blotched in chestnut-red, reddish-brown, or brown, with paler brownish-gray or gray. Sometimes a few blackish scrawls. Markings often in a wreath at larger end. 17 × 13 mm. **Incubation:** By female, fed by male. 12 days. **Nestling:** Little information. Developing down brown or dark reddish-brown. **Nestling period:** Young brooded by female, fed by both parents. Leave nest at 12 days, cannot fly for several days and hide in herbage. Remain with parents until 20 days old.

Bay-breasted Warbler (Dendroica castanea) Plate 60

Breeds in northern conifer woodland, or mixed woodland. Nest in a tree, usually on a horizontal branch, 5–20 ft. up, sometimes up to 50 ft.; exceptionally on a shrub.
Nest: A bulky cup of fine twigs, dead grasses, bark strips, and caterpillar webs; lined with fine black rootlets and hair. Built by female, assisted by male. **Breeding season:** Begins late May. Probably ends early August. **Eggs:** Usually 4–5, sometimes 3–7. Subelliptical to long subelliptical. Smooth and slightly glossy. White, creamy-white or very pale bluish or greenish; boldly speckled, spotted, and blotched with shades of reddish-brown or brown, and paler gray and lilac. 18 × 13 mm. **Incubation:** By female alone, fed by male. 12–13 days. **Nestling:** Altricial and downy. Flesh pink. Down brown. Mouth red; gape flanges pale yellow. **Nestling period:** Fed by both. Leave at 11–12 days. Parents continue to feed young for several days.

Blackpoll Warbler (Dendroica striata) Plate 60

Breeds in northern spruce woodland, or in deciduous thickets beyond the tree limit. Nest in a small tree, 1–10 ft. up, usually well hidden in foliage; rarely on the ground concealed in a grass-tuft. Males sometimes polygamous.
Nest: A cup of small twigs, spruce shoots, bark fragments, dead grasses, weed stems, moss, wool, and Usnea lichen; lined with plant fibers, fine rootlets, hair, and feathers. Built by female. **Breeding season:** Begins mid-June. Sometimes double-brooded. **Eggs:** Usually 4–5, sometimes 3. Subelliptical. Smooth and slightly glossy. White, pale creamy-buff, or very pale greenish; speckled, spotted, and blotched with reddish-brown and brown, or paler purple and purplish-gray. Markings often concentrated at larger end. 18 × 13 mm. **Incubation:** By female alone, sometimes beginning before completion of clutch, fed by male. 11 days. **Nestling:** Altricial and downy. Down gray;

on head, back, wings, and thighs. Mouth dull pink; gape flanges pale yellow. **Nestling period:** Young tended by both parents. Eyes open at 4–5 days. Feathers break sheaths at 5–8 days. Young leave nest at 10–11 days.

Cerulean Warbler (*Dendroica cerulea*)   Plate 60

Breeds in wooded swamps and moist bottomlands. Nest in a tall tree, often well out on a branch and high up, 15–100 ft., in a fork.
Nest: A neat cup of bark fibers and shreds, lichen, moss, and fine grasses; bound with spiders' webs; lined with hair and fruiting moss stems. Probably built by female alone. **Breeding season:** Begins mid-May to early June. Usually ends July. Single-brooded. **Eggs:** Usually 4, occasionally 3–5. Subelliptical to short subelliptical. Smooth and slightly glossy. Creamy-white, grayish-white or very pale greenish-white; speckled, spotted, and blotched with chestnut-red, reddish-brown, or purplish-brown and paler brownish-gray. Markings sometimes overall, often concentrated at larger end, varying from fine to heavy. 17 × 13 mm. **Incubation:** By female. 12–13 days? **Nestling:** Altricial and downy? Down light mouse-gray to light drab. Bill, legs, and feet light pinkish-buff. Irides blackish. **Nestling period:** Little information. Tended by both.

Black-and-white Warbler (*Mniotilta varia*)   Plate 59

Breeds in deciduous or sometimes mixed woodland. Usually but not invariably on moist hillsides or ravines. Nest usually on the ground, in a hollow, against the foot of a tree or shrub, among roots, by a log, in a crevice or under an overhanging rock. Occasionally raised above ground in a cavity in a stump.
Nest: A stout cup of grasses, dead leaves, bark strips, rootlets, and pine needles lined with finer grasses, rootlets and hair. Built by female. **Breeding season:** Begins mid-April to early May. Usually ends by mid-July. Single-brooded. **Eggs:** Usually 4–5. Short subelliptical to subelliptical. Smooth and slightly glossy. White or creamy-white; speckled, spotted, or less frequently blotched; in light red, reddish-brown, purplish-brown, or dark brown, with paler lilac, purplish, or olive spots. Markings often concentrated at or around the larger end, with a fine sprinkling elsewhere. 17 × 13 mm. **Incubation:** By female. 11 days. **Nestling:** Altricial and downy. Skin pink. Down very dark gray; on head, lower back, wings, and thighs. Mouth pink; gape flanges pale yellow. **Nestling period:** Young tended by both parents. Leave nest at 8–12 days.

American Redstart (*Setophaga ruticilla*)   Figure 94, Plate 60

Breeds in open deciduous woodland, or mixed woodland, orchards, secondary growth, trees in clearings, cultivated areas, and bordering water, shade trees, and shrubberies. Nest usually in a vertical fork of a sapling, shrub, or tree; occasionally in vine tangle, or in old nest of a vireo. Nest usually 5–10 ft. up, sometimes 2–20 ft. up, or exceptionally much higher in big trees.
Nest: A firm, compact cup of grasses, bark fibers, and strips, small rootlets, and vine tendrils; bound with spiders' webs and ornamented externally with lichen flakes, birch bark, seed heads, and plant down; lined with fine grasses, plant and bark fibers, and often hair. Built by female in 7 days or more. **Breeding season:** Begins late May to early June. Single-brooded. **Eggs:** Usually 4, sometimes 3–5. Subelliptical to short subelliptical. Smooth and slightly glossy. White to creamy-white, or tinted grayish or greenish; speckled, spotted, and blotched with shades of brown and reddish-brown, and with paler brownish-gray, gray, and purple. Heavier markings often concentrated at larger end forming wreath, with finer speckling elsewhere. 16 × 12 mm. **Incubation:** By female alone. *c.* 12 days. **Nestling:** Altricial and downy. Down brown; on head and upperparts. Mouth red; gape flanges yellow. **Nestling period:** Young

Figure 94. American Redstart: c. 3 in. across; nest usually in a vertical fork.

tended by both parents. Eyes open at 4 days. Feathers break sheaths at 6–8 days. Young leave nest at 9 days.

Prothonotary Warbler (*Protonotaria citrea*)   Plate 59
Breeds along streams, and in flooded or swampy woodland areas of all kinds (often preferring shaded area with little understory). Nest in a cavity, usually near water, often low, sometimes up to 10 ft., occasionally to *c.* 35 ft. Nest in natural cavity in tree, woodpecker hole, hole or crevice in building or bridge, or post, or in any small artificial cavity, including a nest-box.
Nest: A cup of small twigs, decayed leaves, moss, lichens, bark, and plant down; lined with rootlets, fine grasses, or sedge. Built mainly by male in 6–10 days.
Breeding season: Begins mid-April in south to mid-May in north of range. Often double-brooded. **Eggs:** Usually 4–6, sometimes 3–8. Short elliptical to elliptical. Smooth and moderately glossy. Pale creamy, yellowish, white, or tinted pale pink; spotted, or blotched with reddish-brown, purplish-red and dark brown, with paler lilac and purplish-grays. Markings are variable, often distributed overall, but sometimes a partial concentration at the larger end. 18 × 15 mm. **Incubation:** By female alone. 12–14 days. **Nestling:** Altricial and downy. Skin orange-red. Down brownish-grey on head, back, wings, and thighs. Mouth orange-red; gape yellow.
Nestling period: Young tended by both parents. Eyes open at *c.* 3 days. Feather sheaths break at 5 days. Young leave nest at 10–11 days. Young said to remain in the immediate nest area for at least a week, fed by both parents.

Worm-eating Warbler (*Helmitheros vermivorus*)   Plate 59
Breeds in deciduous woodland, usually in the leaf-litter on a bank, hillside, or steep
slope. Nest on the ground, among and partly hidden by dead leaves, usually at the
base of a shrub or sapling, among roots, or in a slight cavity.
Nest: A cup of skeletonized and decayed leaves; lined with fungi filaments (*mycelia*),
hair moss stems (*Polytrichium*), fine grasses, and hair. Built by female. **Breeding season:** Begins mid- to late May. Single-brooded. **Eggs:** Usually 4–5, sometimes 3–6. Short
subelliptical to subelliptical. Smooth and slightly glossy. White, unmarked, or marked
with fine speckling and spotting in reddish-brown. 17 × 14 mm. **Incubation:** By female
alone. 13 days. **Nestling:** Altricial and downy. Down brownish-gray; on head, back,
and wings. Mouth orange; gape flanges yellow. **Nestling period:** Young tended by both
parents. Leave nest at 10–11 days.

Swainson's Warbler (*Limnothlypis swainsonii*)   Plate 59
Breeds typically in floodplain swamps, thickets and tangles, and in canebrakes, in
lowland regions of the southeastern US; but also nests up to 3000 ft. in Appalachian
areas of rhododendron thickets, fern, and evergreen shrubs. Nest in canes, shrubs,
vine tangles and similar sites. 2–10 ft. up. Usually in a fork where dead leaves have
lodged.
Nest: A bulky cup often based on lodged debris, of dead leaves of trees and bamboos,
lined with pine needles or cypress leaves, moss fibers, rootlets, grass stems, and
sometimes hair. Built by female over 2–3 days. **Breeding season:** Begins late April.
Usually ends by late June. Usually single-brooded. **Eggs:** Usually 3, rarely 4–5. Short
subelliptical to subelliptical. Smooth and slightly glossy. White, sometimes faintly
tinted bluish-greenish, pinkish, or buffish. Unmarked or rarely with very sparse
spotting. 19 × 15 mm. **Incubation:** By female alone, beginning with last eggs. 13–15
days. **Nestling:** Altricial and downy? Down dark, brownish drab. Bill, legs, and feet
pale pinkish-buff. Mouth pinkish; gape flanges pale yellow. **Nestling period:** Young
tended by both parents. Leave nest at 10–12 days, accompanying parents for 2–3
weeks more.

Ovenbird (*Seiurus aurocapillus*)   Plate 60
Breeds in deciduous woodland with scanty secondary growth or thickets, where
ground is covered in leaf-litter. Nest on the ground, in the open or partly hidden by
plant growth; set in a small hollow and domed, covered with leaves and debris, with
a side entrance invisible from above.
Nest: A rounded, domed structure set in a small hollow made by the birds; of dead
leaves, pine needles, grass, and weed stems, rootlets, and moss, the inner cup lined
with hair and fine rootlets. Built by female in *c.* 5 days. **Breeding season:** Begins mid-
May. Usually ends by late July. Usually single-brooded. **Eggs:** Usually 4–5, sometimes
3, rarely 6. Subelliptical to short subelliptical. Usually smooth and slightly glossy.
White; speckled and spotted and with small blotches of reddish-brown, brown, and
paler reddish-buff, lilac, and gray. Markings usually in a wreath around the larger
end, with a very fine speckling elsewhere. 20 × 15 mm. **Incubation:** By female alone,
beginning with completion of clutch. 11–14 days. **Nestling:** Altricial and downy.
Down medium gray; on head, back, wings, and thighs. Mouth pink; gape flanges
pale yellow. **Nestling period:** Young tended by both parents. Leave nest at 8–10 days.
Parents divide the brood once young leave the nest. Continue to feed young up to
another 3 more weeks.

Northern Waterthrush (*Seiurus noveboracensis*)   Plate 60
Breeds in northern woodland in swamps or boggy areas, by streams or pond edges;
particularly where fallen timber occurs. Nest in a cavity or hollow among roots of a
fallen tree base, or in a bank, among tree-roots, or in the side of a decayed stump; the
site normally raised and often over water.
Nest: A cup of moss, decayed leaves, bark strips, rootlets, small twigs, and pine
needles lined with fine grasses, hair, or fruiting moss stems. Built by female.
Breeding season: Begins late May in south to early June in north of range. Probably
ends by late July. Single-brooded. **Eggs:** Usually 4–5, sometimes 3–6. Subelliptical to
short subelliptical. Smooth and slightly glossy or non-glossy. Creamy-white, buffish
or yellowish-white; speckled, spotted, or blotched with reddish-brown, brown or
cinnamon-brown, and paler purplish-gray or brownish-gray. Occasionally clouded
or scrawled with brown. Usually heavier markings concentrated at larger end with
fine speckling elsewhere. 19 × 13 mm. **Incubation:** By female, starting with next-to-
last egg. 12–13 days. **Nestling:** Altricial and downy. Down dark olive-brown. Mouth
red; gape flanges yellow. **Nestling period:** Tended by both. Young leave nest at 10
days. Continue to be fed by parents for at least another 2 more weeks.

Louisiana Waterthrush (*Seiurus motacilla*)   Plate 60
Breeds in swampy woodland and along wooded watercourses, but differs from the
Northern Waterthrush in preferring running water. Nest-site, like that of previous
species, in a crevice or raised site in tree-roots, banks of streams, and cliffs or ravines
over water.
Nest: A cup of moss, decayed leaves, grasses, and rootlets; lined with finer grasses,
rootlets, hair, and fruiting moss stems. Built by both sexes in 4–6 days. **Breeding
season:** Begins early April in south to early May in north of range. Usually ends in
late June. Single-brooded. **Eggs:** Usually 4–6. Subelliptical to short subelliptical.
Smooth and slightly glossy. White to creamy-white; speckled, spotted, and blotched
with reddish-brown to brown, and paler purple and purplish-gray. Variably marked
and sometimes with heavy overall mottling. Paler markings sometimes prominent.
20 × 15 mm. **Incubation:** By female alone. Beginning with next-to-last egg. 12–14
days. **Nestling:** Altricial and downy. Down dark gray. Mouth red; gape flanges
yellow. **Nestling period:** Young tended by both parents. Leave nest at *c.* 10 days. Can
fly at 6 days after leaving nest and begin feeding themselves after *c.* 7 days.

Kentucky Warbler (*Oporornis formosus*)   Plate 60
Breeds in moist, deciduous woodland with heavy undergrowth, thickets, and
ground vegetation. Nest on or just above the ground at the foot of a tree or shrub, or
in a weed clump, or patch of weeds; usually hidden by overhanging vegetation or
fallen branches.
Nest: A loose, bulky cup of dead leaves, with grass and weed stems, bark strips, and
rootlets; and a lining of rootlets and hair. Built by both. **Breeding season:** Begins
early to mid-May. Usually single-brooded. **Eggs:** Usually 4–5, sometimes 3–6. Subelliptical to long or short subelliptical. Smooth and slightly glossy. White or creamy-
white; speckled, spotted, or blotched with chestnut-red, reddish-brown, and pale
gray. Fine speckling and spotting more typical, often denser at the larger end.
19 × 14 mm. **Incubation:** By female alone. 12–13 days. **Nestling:** Altricial and
downy? Down olive-brown. Bill, legs, and feet pinkish-flesh-color. **Nestling period:**
Young tended by both parents. Brooded by female only. Eyes open at 5 days; young
leave at 8–10 days, before they can fly. Fed by adults for up to 17 days more

Connecticut Warbler (*Oporornis agilis*)   Plate 60
Breeds in woodland, often in moist areas (e.g., damp Black Spruce and Tamarak bogs), with low shrubby growth, thick undergrowth, or sapling thickets. Nest on the ground, in a small hollow, on a moss mound, or in grasses or weeds, or at the base of a shrub. Usually concealed by overhanging herbage or shrubby growth.
Nest: A deep compact cup, though somewhat frail, of fine dry grasses and rootlets; lined with grasses, fine rootlets, or hair. **Breeding season:** Begins mid-June. **Eggs:** Usually 4–5. Subelliptical. Smooth and slightly glossy. Creamy-white; speckled, spotted, and blotched with reddish-brown, chestnut-red, and paler purple, gray, and brownish-gray. Occasionally streaked with brown. Markings usually concentrated at the larger end but do not form a distinct wreath. 19 × 14 mm. **Incubation:** By female. Period unknown. **Nestling:** Altricial. Mouth orange; gape yellow. **Nestling period:** Little information. Tended by both parents.

Mourning Warbler (*Oporornis philadelphia*)   Plate 60
Breeds in northern woodland where heavy undergrowth occurs, on edges of swamps, on steep slopes, regenerating clearcuts, and in bushy thickets. Nest on or near the ground in thickets, thorny briers or similar growth, in fern or weed clumps, grass-tussocks, or sometimes up to 3 ft. in thickets.
Nest: A bulky but compact cup of dead leaves, vine stems, and with inner cup of grasses, weed stems, and leaves; lined with fine grasses and hair. Probably built by both sexes. **Breeding season:** Begins late May to early June. **Eggs:** Usually 4, sometimes 3–5. Subelliptical to short subelliptical. Smooth and slightly glossy. White to creamy-white; speckled, spotted, and blotched with chestnut-red, reddish-brown, and paler purple, brownish-gray and gray. Sometimes a few spots or specks of black. 18 × 14 mm. **Incubation:** By female alone, sometimes before clutch is complete. 12–13 days. **Nestling:** Altricial and downy. Down dark gray. Mouth red; gape flanges yellow. **Nestling period:** Young tended by both parents. Leave nest at 7–9 days, unable to fly. Begin to fly in second week out of nest. Remain with adults for *c.* 3 weeks.

MacGillivray's Warbler (*Oporornis tolmiei*)   Plate 60
Breeds in low moist thickets in or around woodland, often on hill slopes, and in secondary growth or early successional cut-over areas, and moist hillside scrub. Nest low in a thick shrub, conifer sapling, weed clump or fern clump; 1–5 ft. up.
Nest: A small compact cup of fine blades and stems, dead grasses, weed stems, and bark shreds; lined with fine grasses, rootlets, and hair. Built by female. **Breeding season:** Begins early May in south to late May in north of range. Usually ends by early August. Double-brooded. **Eggs:** Usually 4, sometimes 3–5, rarely 6. Subelliptical. Smooth and slightly glossy. White or creamy-white; speckled, spotted, and blotched with chestnut-red, reddish-brown, and paler brownish-gray, gray, or purple. Occasionally clouded with brown or with small blackish spots or scrawls. 18 × 14 mm. **Incubation:** Eggs laid at daily intervals. Incubation by female only, beginning with last or next-to-last egg. 11–13 days. **Nestling:** Altricial and downy. Scanty down on head, back, and wings. Mouth orange; gape flanges yellow. **Nestling period:** Young tended by both parents. Eyes open at 4–5 days. Feathers break sheaths at 7–8 days. Young leave nest at 8–10 days.

Common Yellowthroat (*Geothlypis trichas*)   Plate 60
Breeds in low undergrowth by water, in sloughs, on islands, and by creek and swamp edges. In tangled thickets of shrubs, weeds, and vines, along hedgerows, woodland edge, and similar sites. Nest just above the ground, or over water, in weeds, reeds,

cat-tails, tule, grass-tussocks, brier bushes, or similar situations; often at base of shrub or sapling, sometimes higher in weeds or shrubs up to 3 ft.
Nest: A bulky cup of dead grasses and leaves, ferns, weed stems, bark strips, grass-blades, and moss; lined with fine grasses, vine tendrils, bark fibers, and often hair. Loose material is occasionally built up above the rim of the cup, forming a partial hood. Built by female in as few as 2 days. **Breeding season:** Begins late April in south to early June in north of range. Double-brooded. **Eggs:** Usually 4, sometimes 3–6. Subelliptical. Smooth and slightly glossy. White or creamy-white; speckled, spotted, and blotched with occasional dark scrawls, of reddish-brown, black, and paler reddish-buff, lilac, and gray. Markings often form a wreath about the larger end. Pale markings may predominate. 17 × 13 mm. **Incubation:** By female only. 12 days. **Nestling:** Altricial and downy. Skin light orange. Down dark gray; on head, back, and wings. Mouth red; gape flanges bright yellow. **Nestling period:** Young tended by both parents. Eyes open at 4–5 days. Feathers break sheaths at 6–7 days. Young leave nest at 9–10 days.

Gray-crowned Yellowthroat (*Geothlypis poliocephala*)   Plate 59
A former breeder in the lower Rio Grande Valley of Texas in grasslands or pastures with scattered thickets and low trees, or dry hillsides with scattered shrubs. Nest on a grass-tussock.
Nest: A stout cup of dry grasses and dead leaves; lined with finer grasses and hair. **Breeding season:** Late April to late June. **Eggs:** Usually 4, sometimes 3. Subelliptical. Smooth and slightly glossy. Creamy-white; speckled, spotted, and blotched with chestnut-red, reddish-brown, brown, and paler brownish-gray or buffish-gray. Sometimes a few small scrawls of blackish-brown. 18 × 14 mm. **Incubation:** No information. **Nestling:** No information. **Nestling period:** No information.

Hooded Warbler (*Wilsonia citrina*)   Plate 60
Breeds in moist deciduous woodland, where shrubby growth or thick undergrowth is present. Nests low in sapling, shrub, palmetto, cane clump, or vine tangle. Often about 2 ft. up, sometimes 1–6 ft. up. Usually in a twig fork, often resembling lodged dead leaves.
Nest: A compact cup with a loose outer layer of dead leaves; a main cup of vine-bark strips, plant fibers, weed stems, down, and dry catkins; lined with plant fibers, fine rootlets, and moss fibers. Built by female over 2–6 days. **Breeding season:** Begins late April in south to late May in north of range. Usually ends by early July. Double-brooded, and lost clutches replaced. **Eggs:** Usually 3–4, rarely 5. Subelliptical, sometimes short or long subelliptical. Smooth and slightly glossy. Creamy-white; speckled, spotted, or blotched with reddish-brown, brown, and paler purplish-brown or brownish-gray. Markings often concentrated at the larger end, forming a wreath. 18 × 14 mm. **Incubation:** By female. 12 days. **Nestling:** Altricial and downy. Down pale brownish-gray or olive-brown. Bill, legs, and feet pinkish-buff. Gape flanges pale yellow. **Nestling period:** Young tended by both parents. Leave at 8–9 days; fly 2–3 days later. Brood divided between parents.

Wilson's Warbler (*Wilsonia pusilla*)   Plate 60
Breeds in open areas of northern forest, in willow and alder thickets, edge between willow and meadow, bogs with scattered small trees, and wet clearings with secondary growth. Nest on the ground, in moss or soil, at the base of a shrub or sapling, or hidden in herbage, in a grass-tussock, hidden in dry grass under low willow branches, or in a hollow in a bank with overhanging plants. Multiple pairs may nest in close proximity. Males sometimes polygamous.

Nest: A bulky cup of dead leaves, bark shreds and strips, thin dead weed stems, grass blades, and stems; lined with fine dry grasses, rootlets, and hair. Built by female in 4–5 days. *Breeding season:* Begins late April in south to early June in north of range. Single-brooded. *Eggs:* Usually 5, sometimes 4–6. Subelliptical to short subelliptical. Smooth and slightly glossy. White or creamy-white. Finely speckled, and spotted with chestnut-red, reddish-brown, and paler brownish-gray. Often a wreath of speckling at the larger end. 16 × 12 mm. *Incubation:* By female alone, beginning with last egg. 11–13 days. *Nestling:* Altricial and downy? Down brownish-gray or olive-brown. *Nestling period:* Young tended by both parents. Brooded by female only. Eyes open at 5–6 days; feathers break sheaths at 6–8 days. Young leave nest at 10–11 days.

Canada Warbler (*Wilsonia canadensis*)   Plate 60
Breeds in moist mixed woodland, usually where the canopy is broken by streams, bogs, or gullies. Nest on or near the ground, in the roots of a fallen tree, in a cavity of a bank, or on the side of rocks, on a ledge, on a hummock, stump, or fallen log, or on the ground under a shrub. Often concealed by overhanging plants.
Nest: A bulky cup of dry or decayed leaves, bark shreds, dead grass and weed stems, fern leaves, pine needles, and plant fibers; lined with plant fibers, fine rootlets, and hair. Built by female. *Breeding season:* Begins late May. Single-brooded. *Eggs:* Usually 4, sometimes 3–5. Subelliptical to short subelliptical. Smooth and slightly glossy. White to creamy-white. Speckled, spotted, and blotched with chestnut-red, reddish-brown, and paler purple or gray. Sometimes marked in duller brown and black. Markings tend to form a wreath round larger end. 17 × 13 mm. *Incubation:* By female, perhaps with help from male. Estimated at 12 days. *Nestling:* Altricial and downy. Down dark brown. Mouth and gape flanges bright yellow. *Nestling period:* Little information. Young tended by both parents.

Red-faced Warbler (*Cardellina rubrifrons*)   Plate 59
Breeds in streamside canyons and mountain forests of south-central Arizona and west-central New Mexico, coniferous or deciduous (up to 9,000 ft.). Nest on the ground, on a bank or slope, against and concealed by a shrub, sapling, log, rock, or herbage.
Nest: A cup sunk in a small hollow made by bird. Of dead leaves and grasses, pine needles, and cedar bark strips; lined with fine grasses and hair. Built by female. *Breeding season:* Begins early May. Usually ends late June. Single-brooded. *Eggs:* Usually 5, sometimes 3–4. Long to short subelliptical. Smooth and slightly glossy. White; finely speckled, rarely spotted or with small blotches, of brown and pale gray. Often speckled overall with a slight concentration at larger end. 16 × 13 mm. *Incubation:* By female. *c.* 13 days. *Nestling:* Altricial and downy. Down about the head pale smoke-gray. Mouth deep orange-yellow; gape flanges yellow. *Nestling period:* Tended by both parents. Flight feathers break sheaths *c.* 6 days. Fledge at 12 days. Depend on parents for additional 3–7 days.

Painted Redstart (*Myioborus pictus*)   Plate 59
Breeds in canyon oakwoods in the highlands of Arizona, southwest New Mexico, sporadically to southeast California, and Big Bend area of Texas. Nest on the ground, on a slope or rocky face, under a tree or shrub root, or under a projecting rock, against an overhanging grass tuft, or among grasses, ferns, or vines which hide it. Male may be polygamous.
Nest: A bulky, rather shallow cup of bark strips, weed-stem fibers, dead grasses, and leaves; lined with finer grasses and hair. Built by female. *Breeding season:* Mid-April

to late July. Often two broods. **Eggs:** Usually 4, sometimes 3–5. Subelliptical. Smooth and slightly glossy. Creamy-white; finely speckled with chestnut-red or reddish-brown, and paler brownish-gray or buffish-gray. Markings concentrated towards larger end. 16 × 13 mm. **Incubation:** By female. 13–14 days. **Nestling:** Altricial. Mouth deep orange-yellow; gape flanges yellow. **Nestling period:** Tended by both. Fly at 9–13 days.

Yellow-breasted Chat (*Icteria virens*)   Plate 60
Breeds in thick tangled shrubby growth on woodland edge, old pastures; stream, pond, and swamp edges, hedgerows, and scrub country. Nest in a dense shrub or tangle, from about ground level to 5 ft., sometimes to 8 ft. up.
Nest: A cup of coarse grasses, dead leaves, weed and grass stems and bark strips; lined with finer grasses and weed stems. Built by female. **Breeding season:** Begins early April in south to mid-May in north of range. Double-brooded. **Eggs:** Usually 3–5, sometimes 6. Subelliptical. Smooth and slightly glossy. White or creamy-white; speckled, spotted, and occasionally blotched with chestnut-red, reddish-brown, brown, and paler gray and purple. 22 × 17 mm. **Incubation:** By female. 11–12 days. **Nestling:** Altricial and naked. Skin dull yellow. Mouth red; gape flanges creamy-white. **Nestling period:** Young tended by both parents. Leave nest at 8–11 days?

Olive Warbler (*Peucedramus taeniatus*)   Plate 59
Breeds in mountain conifer woodland (up to 12 000 ft.) in southeast Arizona and southwest New Mexico usually dominated by Ponderosa Pine. Nest often high up, 30–70 ft., usually out in the foliage and smaller twigs.
Nest: A neat compact cup of rootlets, moss, lichens, bud and flower scales, fibers, and spiders' web; lined with fine rootlets and soft white plant fibers. The outside is decorated with reddish-brown bracts of pine needles. Built by female alone. **Breeding season:** Begins late May. **Eggs:** Usually 3–4. Subelliptical to short subelliptical. Smooth and slightly glossy. Very pale bluish or grayish, or pale blue; heavily speckled, spotted, or blotched with shades of olive-brown to olive, olive-gray, gray, and grayish-brown. The markings vary from bold to indistinct; often denser towards larger end. 17 × 13 mm. **Incubation:** Little information. By female alone? **Nestling:** Altricial and downy. Mouth orange-pink; gape yellow. **Nestling period:** Tended by both? Prior to leaving nest the young will soil the nest rim, cup, and nearby needles with excrement. (This is a trait of many cardueline and Old World estrildine finches.)

Hepatic Tanager (*Piranga flava*)   Plate 64
Breeds in trees of mountain canyons of the southwest US (5000–7000 ft.). Nest on a conifer or deciduous tree, usually high up and well out on a branch at a fork. 18–50 ft. up.
Nest: A rather shallow cup of grass, weed stems, and flower stalks; lined with finer grasses. Built mostly by female. **Breeding season:** Early May to late August. Single-brooded. **Eggs:** Usually 4, sometimes 3–5. Subelliptical to short subelliptical. Light blue or greenish-blue; speckled and spotted with chestnut-red, reddish-brown and brown, and paler lilac. Markings usually fine and profuse, but often with a concentration at or about the larger end. 24 × 18 mm. **Incubation:** By female. Estimated at 13 days. **Nestling:** No information. **Nestling period:** Tended by both. Little further information.

Summer Tanager (*Piranga rubra*)   Plate 64
Breeds in open deciduous woods, orchards, oak–pine woodland, and bottomland forests. Nest in a tree, usually well out on a horizontal lower branch. 10–35 ft. up.

Nest: A flimsy-looking shallow cup of grasses and weed stems, and sometimes Spanish Moss; lined with finer grasses. Built by female. **Breeding season:** Begins late March in south to mid-May in north of range. Usually ends by late August. Single-brooded. **Eggs:** Usually 4, sometimes 3–5. Subelliptical to short subelliptical. Light blue or greenish-blue; speckled, spotted, and blotched with chestnut-red or purplish-red, and paler lilac. Markings often sparse with a concentration at the larger end. 23 × 17 mm. **Incubation:** By female. 11–12 days. **Nestling:** Altricial and downy. Down buffy-gray. Skin pink. Gape flanges yellow. **Nestling period:** Young tended by both parents. Fly at 10 days; cared for another 19 days.

Scarlet Tanager (*Piranga olivacea*)   Plate 64
Breeds in deciduous and sometimes mixed woodland, in wooded parks, and roadside shade trees. Nest in a tree, usually well out on a branch at a twig fork and shaded from above. 15–60 ft. up.
Nest: A rather shallow and loose cup of twigs, grass, weed stems, and rootlets; lined with finer grasses, weed stems, and rootlets. Built by female in 2–7 days. **Breeding season:** Begins late May. Probably ends mid-August. Single-brooded. **Eggs:** Usually 4, sometimes 3–5. Subelliptical to short subelliptical. Smooth and moderately glossy. Light blue or greenish-blue; finely speckled and spotted, and sometimes with small blotches of chestnut-red or purplish-red and paler lilac. Markings often finer than those of Summer Tanager. 23 × 16 mm. **Incubation:** By female alone. 13–14 days. **Nestling:** Altricial and downy. Down plentiful, light gray; on head, back and wings, becoming yellowish on belly. Mouth orange-red; gape flanges yellow. **Nestling period:** Young tended by both parents. Leave nest at 15 days. Fed by parents until *c.* 25 days old.

Western Tanager (*Piranga ludoviciana*)   Plate 64
Breeds in conifer and sometimes mixed forests, primarily in mountains. Nest in a tree, usually a conifer, rarely deciduous; at varying heights, 8–60 ft. up, usually well out on a branch, often at the fork of a horizontal limb.
Nest: A stout cup of conifer twigs, rootlets, and moss; lined with finer rootlets and hair. Built mostly by female? **Breeding season:** Begins early May in south to early June in north of range. Usually ends by early August. Probably single-brooded. **Eggs:** Usually 3–5, clutches smaller in south. Subelliptical to short subelliptical. Smooth and moderately glossy. Light blue or greenish-blue; finely speckled and spotted with brown, dark brown and paler gray. 23 × 17 mm. **Incubation:** By female alone. 13 days. **Nestling:** Altricial and downy. Down pale gray, on head, back, and wings. Mouth orange-red; gape flanges yellow. **Nestling period:** Young tended by both parents. Leave nest at 10–11 days.

Flame-colored Tanager (*Piranga bidentata*)
Breeds rarely in oak and pine–oak highlands in southeastern Arizona. Nest found in a tree, usually 16–35 ft. up (with a low of 4 ft. and a high of 75 ft. in the Neotropics). **Nest:** A loosely built cup of rootlets, twigs, and vine branches; lined with fine grass. Built by female. **Breeding season:** Begins mid-May to early June? Built by female. **Eggs:** Usually 2–3. Pale blue, or greenish-blue, speckled with reddish-brown and dark lavender, mostly at larger end. 24 × 18 mm. **Incubation:** By female alone? Period unknown. **Nestling:** No information. **Nestling period:** Little information. Fed by both?

Northern Cardinal (*Cardinalis cardinalis*)   Plate 64
Breeds in a wide variety of sites but usually in a shrubby thicket or vine tangle, overgrown clearing, woodland edge or other secondary growth, open woodland with

undergrowth and cane thickets, and in mesquite and thickets along streams in drier regions. Nest usually in a shrub or vine tangle, 1–20 ft. up, usually 4–6 ft. up.

Nest: A cup of thin twigs, weed stems, grasses, bark fibers, vines, and rootlets, mixed with large dead leaves, rags, paper, and other debris; lined with rootlets, fine grasses, and sometimes hair or Spanish Moss. Usually built by female alone in 3–9 days. **Breeding season:** Begins late March to early April. At times 3–4 broods. **Eggs:** Usually 3–4, sometimes 2–5. Subelliptical to short subelliptical. Smooth and slightly glossy. White or very slightly greenish; speckled, spotted, and with small blotches of medium to dark brown, rarely reddish-brown, and paler purple or gray. Markings often profuse and usually present overall but with some concentration at larger end. 25 × 18 mm. **Incubation:** Usually by female alone, beginning with third egg. 11–13 days. **Nestling:** Altricial and downy. Skin orange. Down blackish-gray. Mouth red; gape flanges cream. **Nestling period:** Young tended by both parents. Young leave nest at 9–11 days, fly well at 19 days, become independent at 38–45 days.

Pyrrhuloxia (*Cardinalis sinuatus*)   Plate 64

Breeds in more arid regions, on mesquite edge and in more open sites in shrub growth than the Northern Cardinal uses. Nest in a shrub, 5–7 ft. up, in a twig fork or against the trunk.

Nest: A small and fairly compact cup, but with loose outer layer of dry twigs, weed stems, coarse grass, bark fibers, and spiders' webs; lined with fine grasses, fibers, rootlets, and hair. Built by female. **Breeding season:** Begins mid-March to early April. Prolonged, but birds probably single-brooded. **Eggs:** Usually 2–3. Short subelliptical to subelliptical. Smooth and slightly glossy. White or very pale greenish; speckled, spotted, and blotched with brown and pale purple and gray. Very like those of Northern Cardinal, but markings often a little finer. 24 × 18 mm. **Incubation:** By female alone, fed by male. 14 days. **Nestling:** Altricial and downy? Crown drab gray, remaining upperparts pale drab gray or very pale smoke-gray. Mouth orange; gape flanges yellow. **Nestling period:** Young tended by both parents. Leave nest at *c.* 10 days.

Rose-breasted Grosbeak (*Pheucticus ludovicianus*)   Figure 95, Plate 64

Breeds in scrub woodland and shrubby growth by streams and woodland edge, and in parkland shrubbery. Nest in a shrub or small tree. Usually in a twig fork, 4–20 ft. up, occasionally much higher in trees.

Nest: A loose cup of small twigs, coarse grasses, weed stems, and decayed leaves; lined with fine twigs, rootlets, and hair. Built by female with help from male. **Breeding season:** Begins mid- to late May. Double-brooded. **Eggs:** Usually 4, sometimes 3–5. Subelliptical to short subelliptical. Smooth and slightly glossy. Light blue to greenish-blue; blotched, spotted, and speckled with reddish-brown or purplish-red, the markings being sparse at the narrow end, increasing in density towards the larger end. 25 × 18 mm. **Incubation:** By both sexes. 12–14 days. **Nestling:** Altricial and downy. Skin orange. Down white but grayish on head. Mouth reddish-orange; gape flanges yellow. **Nestling period:** Young tended by both parents. Leave nest at 9–12 days. Male may feed fledged young while female re-nests. Young dependent on adults for *c.* 3 weeks more.

Black-headed Grosbeak (*Pheucticus melanocephalus*)   Plate 64

Breeds in thickets and in trees along streams and floodplains; or in open woodlands, orchards, or parkland. Nest in a tree or shrub usually 6–12 ft. up, in a twig fork.

Nest: A loose, bulky cup, of thin twigs, weed stems, and rootlets; lined with finer grasses, stems, and rootlets. Built by female in 3–4 days. **Breeding season:** Begins

Figure 95. Rose-breasted Grosbeak: c. 4 in. across; a loose cup of small twigs.

late April in south to early June in north. Usually ends by early July. Usually single-brooded. **Eggs:** Usually 3–4. Short subelliptical to subelliptical or oval. Smooth or slightly glossy. Pale blue; speckled, spotted, or blotched with light to medium brown, and scarcer pale gray. Markings tend to be more concentrated at larger end. 28 × 18 mm. **Incubation:** By both sexes, beginning with next-to-last egg. 12–13 days. **Nestling:** Altricial and downy. Down grayish-white, sparse. Mouth red; gape flanges yellow. **Nestling period:** Young tended by both parents. 12 days.

Blue Grosbeak (*Guiraca caerulea*)   Figure 96, Plate 64
Breeds in shrubby growth, weedy pastures, thickets, tall herbage, vines, and low trees. Nest from *c.* 6 in. to 15 ft. up. Nest in a twig fork or among stems.
Nest: A cup of stems, thin twigs, bark strips, rootlets, dead leaves, corn-husks, and occasionally cotton, paper, or cast snakeskins; lined with fine rootlets, tendrils, hair, and fine grasses. Probably built by both. **Breeding season:** Begins mid-April in south to mid-May and early June in north of range. Double-brooded in south of range. **Eggs:** Usually 4, sometimes 2–3, rarely 5. Subelliptical to short subelliptical. Smooth and slightly glossy. Very pale blue. Unmarked. 22 × 17 mm. **Incubation:** Eggs laid on successive days. Incubation by female alone. 11–13 days. **Nestling:** Altricial and downy? Skin pinkish. Down brownish mouse-gray. Bill (with gray lower mandible), legs, and feet dull brownish-pink. Gape flanges yellow. **Nestling period:** Young tended by both parents. Leave nest at 9–13 days. Male feeds fledged young while female re-nests.

Figure 96. Blue Grosbeak: *c.* 4 in. across; a compact cup, finely lined, and often incorporating a cast-off snakeskin.

Lazuli Bunting (*Passerina amoena*)   **Figure 97, Plate 64**
Breeds in trees and shrubby growth along streams, or on nearby hillsides. Nest in low thick shrubby growth, vine tangle, sapling, or small tree, 1–10 ft. up, but usually low. In twig fork or similar site.
Nest: A cup of coarse dry stems and leaves of grass, bark strips, and rootlets; lined with hair and fine grasses. Nest is bound to supporting stems. Built by female.
Breeding season: Begins early April in south to early June in north of range. Usually two broods. **Eggs:** Usually 4, sometimes 3–5. Subelliptical to oval. Smooth and slightly glossy. Very pale bluish or greenish white, or very pale blue. Unmarked. 19 × 14 mm. **Incubation:** By female. 12 days. **Nestling:** Altricial and downy. Flesh orange-yellow. Down gray; on head and back. Mouth orange; gape flanges yellow.
Nestling period: Young tended by both parents or female alone. Leave nest at 10–15 days. Male feeds fledged young, possibly while female re-nests.

Indigo Bunting (*Passerina cyanea*)   **Plate 64**
Breeds in scrub, on forest edges and clearings, and in hedgerows and orchards. Nest in a shrub, low bush, tree sapling, vine tangle, or on tall weeds; usually in a twig fork *c.* 5–15 ft. up, sometimes lower. Male sometimes polygamous.
Nest: A well-made cup of dry grass and weed stems, dead leaves, Spanish Moss, etc., lined with fine grasses, rootlets, hair, wool, cotton, feathers, and occasionally pieces of snakeskin. Built by female. **Breeding season:** Begins mid-May to early June. Ends by mid-September. Sometimes double- or treble-brooded. **Eggs:** Usually 3–4, sometimes 2. Subelliptical to oval. Smooth and slightly glossy. Very pale bluish to greenish-white. Unmarked. 19 × 14 mm. **Incubation:** Mainly by female. 12–13 days.

Figure 97. Lazuli Bunting: c. 4 in. across; a cup of coarse grasses bound to supporting stems.

Nestling: Altricial and downy. Skin pinkish-orange. Down sparse and gray. Mouth red; gape flanges yellow. **Nestling period:** Young tended almost entirely by female. Eyes open at 4–5 days; feathers break sheaths at 5–6 days. Young leave nest at 9–13 days. Male may feed fledged young, possibly while female re-nests.

Varied Bunting (*Passerina versicolor*)   Plate 64
Breeds in arid and semi-arid scrub and thorny brushes along much of US–Mexican border, from Arizona through Texas. Nest in a low tree, shrub, or vine tangle, 1–12 ft. up.
Nest: An untidy cup of dry grasses, small weed stems, plant fibers, plant down, and other debris (occasionally with snakeskin); lined with rootlets, fine grasses, and hair. Built by both sexes. **Breeding season:** Mid-April to mid-July. Double-brooded. **Eggs:** Usually 3–4. Subelliptical to oval. Smooth and slightly glossy. Pale blue to white. 18 × 14 mm. **Incubation:** By female. 12–13 days. **Nestling:** Altricial. Skin pink; down grayish. Gape yellow. **Nestling period:** Tended by both. Young leave at 12 days. Parents divide young and tend for them separately. When almost independent, male may care for all of them while female begins re-nesting.

Painted Bunting (*Passerina ciris*)   **Plate 64**
Breeds in low shrubby growth, hedgerows, and rank herbage. Nest in a bush or vine
tangle, usually 3–6 ft. up. Sometimes in a tree in thick Spanish Moss at much greater
height. Males may often be polygamous.
Nest: A neat, deep cup, partly woven around its supports. Of grasses, finer weed
stems, and leaves; lined with hair and fine grasses. Built by female in as few as
2 days. **Breeding season:** Begins late March in southwest, to early to mid-May elsewhere. Usually double-brooded, sometimes up to four. **Eggs:** Usually 3–4, sometimes
5. Subelliptical to short subelliptical. Smooth and slightly glossy. White; very finely
speckled with chestnut-red and purple, often with a wreath or cap of heavier spotting at the larger end. 19 × 14 mm. **Incubation:** By female alone, often before last egg
is laid. 11–12 days. **Nestling:** Altricial and downy. **Nestling period:** Young tended by
female. Leave nest at 8–9 days. Male may feed fledged young, while female re-nests.

Dickcissel (*Spiza americana*)   **Plate 64**
Breeds on prairies, agricultural fields, and meadow grassland, with or without
scattered shrubs. Nest on the ground in grass or rank herbage, or raised a little above
ground, in grass tufts or tall weeds, or in low shrubs or trees, up to about 6 ft., but
usually low. Males may often be polygamous.
Nest: A loose cup of coarse grass and weed stems, plant fibers, and leaves; lined with
finer grasses, rootlets, and hair. Nest built by female alone in *c.* 4 days. **Breeding
season:** Begins late April in south to mid-May in north of range. Sometimes double-
brooded. **Eggs:** Usually 4, sometimes 3–5. Light blue, unmarked. 21 × 16 mm.
Incubation: By female alone. 11–13 days. **Nestling:** Altricial and downy. Down
white; on head, wings, and body, but absent from underside. **Nestling period:** Young
tended by female alone. Brooded for most of first 6 days. Feathers break sheaths at *c.*
6 days. Young leave nest at 7–10 days, unable to fly until *c.* 11–12 days.

Olive Sparrow (*Arremonops rufivirgatus*)   **Plate 62**
Breeds in shrubby thickets, tall second growth, and undergrowth at forest edge in
southernmost Texas. Nest low in a bush, 2–5 ft. up.
Nest: A domed structure with a large entrance; of fine twigs, grass and weed stems,
pieces of bark, and leaves; the cup lined with finer grasses and hair. **Breeding season:**
Early March to late September. Double-brooded. **Eggs:** Usually 4–5, sometimes 3. Subelliptical. Smooth and glossy. White and unmarked. 22 × 16 mm. **Incubation:** No
information. **Nestling:** Altricial and downy. Bare skin pinkish-flesh-colored. Down
dark gray. Mouth red; gape flanges yellow. **Nestling period:** No information.

Green-tailed Towhee (*Pipilo chlorurus*)   **Plate 62**
Breeds in scrub and brush of dry foothills to montane areas, often close to sagebrush. Nest on or near the ground in the base of a bush, up to *c.* 2 ft., usually well
concealed.
Nest: A large, deep and thick-walled cup. Of twigs, grasses, weed stems, and bark.
Lined with fine stems, rootlets, and hair. **Breeding season:** Begins mid- to late May.
Double-brooded. **Eggs:** Usually 4, sometimes 2–5. Subelliptical to short subelliptical. Smooth and moderately glossy. White, finely speckled and spotted, and occasionally blotched in reddish-brown to dull brown, with paler gray or purple
markings. Larger markings often concentrated at the larger end. 22 × 16 mm.
Incubation: By female. 12 days. **Nestling:** Altricial and downy. Down gray. Mouth
bright red; gape flanges yellow. **Nestling period:** Young tended by both parents.
Young leave nest at 11–12 days.

Eastern Towhee (*Pipilo erythrophthalmus*)
Breeds in low shrubby growth, thickets, or undergrowth of forest woodlands or woodland edge. Nest hidden in or under undergrowth or tangled brush; or occasionally sheltered by a large plant tuft. Some nests built a little above ground in brushwood piles, dense bushes, or vine tangles. Usually 1–5 ft. up. Occasionally on ground. Rarely in sites up to 18 ft.
Nest: A stout cup of grasses, bark shreds, rootlets, and bits of dead leaves; sometimes lined with finer grasses and hair. Built by female alone in *c.* 5 days. **Breeding season:** Begins early April in south to late May in north. Double-brooded, occasionally treble-brooded in southern part of range. **Eggs:** Usually 3–4, sometimes 2–6. Subelliptical to short subelliptical. Smooth and moderately glossy. Grayish or creamy-white, occasionally greenish-white; evenly speckled with dark brown spots and other markings of chestnut-red, purplish-red, reddish-brown or brown, and paler purple or gray. Markings usually profuse, sometimes with a concentration at the larger end. 23 × 17 mm. **Incubation:** By female only. 12–13 days. **Nestling:** Altricial and downy. Skin pinkish-flesh-colored. Sparse gray down on head, wings, back, and thighs. Mouth pink; gape flanges pale yellow. **Nestling period:** Young tended by both parents. Brooded by female only. Fed by regurgitation at first. Young leave nest at 8–10 days. After young learn to fly, the family often stays together for some time.

Spotted Towhee (*Pipilo maculatus*)   Plate 62
Breeds in low shrubby growth, medium-sized bushes, sagebrush, or undergrowth. Usually on ground. Sometimes 1–5 ft. up.
Nest: A well-built cup of dried leaves, grasses, bark strips, or pine needles; lined with finer dry grasses and rootlets. Set in a small hollow made by bird, the rim at ground level. Built by female alone. **Breeding season:** Begins late April to early May. Double-, occasionally treble-brooded. **Eggs:** Usually 3–4, sometimes 2–5. Subelliptical to short subelliptical. Smooth and moderately glossy. Grayish or creamy-white, occasionally pale greenish-white; speckled with dark brown, chestnut-red, purplish-red, reddish-brown or brown, with undermarkings of paler purple or gray. Markings often with a concentration at the larger end. 24 × 18 mm. **Incubation:** By female only. 12–13 days. **Nestling:** Altricial and downy. Sparse gray down on head and back. **Nestling period:** Young tended by both parents. Brooded by female only. Young leave nest at *c.* 9 days?

California Towhee (*Pipilo crissalis*)
Breeds in brushy-covered areas of California, chaparral. Nest in a small tree or shrub. Found in the densest part of the foliage and supported by several branches. Usually between 4–12 ft. up, though may be 1–35 ft. up.
Nest: A frail or loosely constructed cup of twigs, weed stems, flower-heads, lined with fine thin stems, dried rootlets, grasses, and hair. Built by female. **Breeding season:** Begins mid-April. Double-brooded, though sometimes three or four broods. **Eggs:** Usually 4, sometimes 3. Smooth and slightly glossy. Subelliptical to long subelliptical. Pale bluish- or creamy-white, similar to, but less heavily marked than Canyon Towhee. 25 × 19 mm. **Incubation:** By female only. 14 days. **Nestling:** Altricial and downy. Down gray, skin dark gray. **Nestling period:** Tended by both. Young leave at *c.* 10 days. May stay with both adults for 4–6 weeks.

Canyon Towhee (*Pipilo fuscus*)   Plate 62
Breeds in areas of shrubby thickets, edges of dry scrub, in shrubby growth and low trees of arid slopes, canyons, and gullies, and in cover around buildings. Nest in a

small tree or shrub, often against the trunk or in a strong twig fork, well hidden by cholla cacti, mesquite, elderberries, or other foliage. Usually 3–12 ft. up sometimes higher in large trees.
Nest: A solidly-constructed cup of small twigs, dry composite stems, and grass leaves. Lined with fine leaves, small stems, and fine strips of bark. **Breeding season:** Mid-February to mid-September. Double-, rarely treble-brooded. **Eggs:** Usually 3, sometimes 4, Smooth and moderately glossy. Short subelliptical to subelliptical. White to pale blue, occasionally with a pinkish wash; very sparsely marked, mostly in a zone at or around the larger end, with some specks, spots, small blotches, and scrawls of black, purplish-black, or purplish-brown, and pale gray or lilac. Larger markings sometimes have blurred reddish edges. 23 × 18 mm. **Incubation:** By female only c. 11 days. **Nestling:** Altricial and downy. Down brown. **Nestling period:** Young tended by both parents. Fly at c. 10 days.

Abert's Towhee (*Pipilo aberti*)   Plate 62
Breeds in short trees and desert scrub, especially along creeks and watercourses, and in mesquite, and occasionally orange groves. Nest usually in a low bush or tree, but may be as high as 25–30 ft. up.
Nest: A bulky cup of weed stems, bark strips, vines, and green leaves; lined with finer bark strips, dry grasses, and hair. Built by female over 6–8 days. **Breeding season:** Begins mid-February. Usually ends by late September. Rains may encourage second brood. **Eggs:** Usually 3, sometimes 2–4. Subelliptical. Smooth and slightly glossy. Very similar to those of California Towhee. 24 × 18 mm. **Incubation:** By female, c. 14 days. **Nestling:** No information. **Nestling period:** Tended by both. Fledge at 11–13 days. Independent at 28–35 days.

White-collared Seedeater (*Sporophila torqueola*)   Plate 64
Breeds in open grassy areas with some shrubs or tall herbage uncommonly in the lower Rio Grande Valley of Texas. Nest 3–5 ft. up in a low bush or tall weed. Nest in a fork.
Nest: A thin, delicate cup of fine stems or rootlets; lined with a little very fine dry grass and hair. Built by female. **Breeding season:** Early March to mid-September. **Eggs:** Usually 3–4. Subelliptical. Smooth and moderately glossy. Very pale blue to greenish-blue; speckled, spotted, and blotched in shades of brown and sometimes paler purple. Markings bold, often profuse, sometimes concentrated at the larger end. 16 × 12 mm. **Incubation:** By female alone. 13 days. **Nestling:** No information. **Nestling period:** Young tended by both parents. Leave nest at 10–11 days.

Bachman's Sparrow (*Aimophila aestivalis*)   ·   Plate 63
Breeds in open pinewoods with shrubby secondary growth, or in open grassland overgrown with tall weeds. Nest on the ground, partly concealed, against a grass-tuft or under a low shrub or palmetto frond.
Nest: A cup of weed stems and grasses; lined with finer grasses and hair. In some instances the nest sides are built up high, with the opening deflected to one side, producing a virtually domed nest. Built by female. **Breeding season:** Begins mid-April to early May. Double-, possibly treble-brooded. **Eggs:** Usually 3–5. Subelliptical. Smooth and slightly glossy. White and unmarked. 19 × 15 mm. **Incubation:** By female only, beginning with third egg. 13–14 days. **Nestling:** Altricial and downy. Down light drab, skin orange-pink. Mouth red; gape flanges yellow. **Nestling period:** Young tended by both parents. Leave nest at 10 days, unable to fly properly.

Botteri's Sparrow (*Aimophila botterii*)   Plate 63
Breeds in drier grassland with tall grass, scattered shrubs, and small trees, or small
bushes or cacti in southeast Arizona, southwest New Mexico, and southernmost
Texas. Nest on or near the ground (up to 1 ft. up in a grass clump).
Nest: Rather roundish and flat; made of grasses and stems of grass. Lined with finer
grasses and a few finer grass stalks. **Breeding season:** Late May to late August. (In
Arizona, timed to coincide with rainy season.) Ends by mid-September. **Eggs:** Usually
4, sometimes 2–5. Subelliptical. Smooth and glossy. White and unmarked. 20 × 15
mm. **Incubation:** By female. *c.* 12 days. **Nestling:** Altricial and downy. Down buffish-
gray on crown and nape; whitish on back, wings, and sides of rump. Irides dark
brown. Bill yellowish-pink to yellowish-flesh. Feet pinkish-flesh to yellowish-flesh.
Nestling period: Tended by both parents, fly in *c.* 10 days. Independent at 28–35 days.

Cassin's Sparrow (*Aimophila cassinii*)   Plate 63
Breeds in short-grass plains with scattered shrubs, cacti, or yuccas, or scrub areas
broken by open grassy spaces. Nest usually on the ground in cover, either against or
under a shrub or low bush, or grass-tuft; or in tall grasses. Sometimes raised in a low
bush or cactus up to 1½ ft.
Nest: A deep cup of dead grasses, weed stems, bark and plant fibers and sometimes
grass flowers; lined with finer grasses and grass flowers, rootlets, and sometimes
hair. **Breeding season:** Begins early April, extending to mid-September. Probably
double-brooded. **Eggs:** Usually 4, sometimes 3–5. Subelliptical. Smooth and slightly
glossy. White and unmarked. 19 × 15 mm. **Incubation:** Estimated at 10 days.
Nestling: Altricial and downy. Down sparse and very dark. **Nestling period:** Young
tended by both parents. Leave at *c.* 9 days.

Rufous-winged Sparrow (*Aimophila carpalis*)   Plate 63
Breeds in drier areas with grass and shrubby growth, usually in low-lying areas or
by watercourses in south-central Arizona. Nest in a low thick bush or cactus, 1–6 ft.
up. Nest in a twig fork.
Nest: A deep stout cup of dead weed stems, coarse grasses, bark strips, or fine twigs,
lined with finer grasses and hair. Built by female. **Breeding season:** Begins mid-April
(depending on rainfall) into late September. Double-brooded, though sometimes
treble-brooded. **Eggs:** Usually 4, rarely 2–5. Subelliptical. Smooth and slightly
glossy. Very pale bluish-white and unmarked. 19 × 14 mm. **Incubation:** By female
alone. 11 days. **Nestling:** Altricial and downy. Down sparse and brown. Mouth reddish; gape flanges yellow. **Nestling period:** Young tended by both parents. Leave nest
at 9–10 days. Remain dependent on parents for 3 weeks after fledging.

Rufous-crowned Sparrow (*Aimophila ruficeps*)   Plate 63
Breeds on dry, rocky areas with sparse undergrowth, low shrubs and grasses, or
widely-spaced shrubs or trees. Nests on the ground, usually at the base of a grass
clump or sapling, sometimes up to 1½ ft. above the ground.
Nest: A loosely-constructed, thick-walled nest of coarse dry grasses, grassroots,
twigs, fibers; lined with hair or fine dry grasses. Sunk in a small hollow made by
the bird, the rim level with the ground. **Breeding season:** Begins mid-March
(depending on rainfall) into August. Sometimes two broods. **Eggs:** Usually 3–4,
rarely 2–5. Subelliptical. Smooth and slightly glossy. Very pale bluish-white and
unmarked. **Incubation:** By female only, beginning with last egg. Period not
recorded. **Nestling:** Altricial and downy. Skin orange. Down blackish. **Nestling
period:** Young tended by both parents. Leave at *c.* 9 days. Will accompany parents
for some time.

American Tree Sparrow (*Spizella arborea*)   Plate 63
Breeds in low shrubby growth along northern tree limit, tundra edge, and river flats
of north. Nest on the ground, at the base of a small tree, shrub, grass-tuft, or dead
branch which hides it; or in a grass tussock, or occasionally in dwarf willow at
height of up to 4 ft.
Nest: A cup of coarse grass and weed stems, bark shreds, rootlets, moss, and lichen;
lined with fine dry grasses and moss and with an inner lining of feathers, hair, and
fur. Built by female over 7 days. **Breeding season:** Begins early June. Usually ends by
late July. Single-brooded. **Eggs:** Usually 3–5, occasionally 6. Subelliptical to short
subelliptical. Smooth and slightly glossy. Very pale blue or greenish, sometimes with
dull buffish or pinkish wash; speckled, spotted, blotched, or indistinctly mottled
with chestnut-red, purplish, or reddish-brown, and pale lilac. Marking often more
concentrated at larger end. 19 × 14 mm. **Incubation:** Eggs laid at daily interval. Incubation by female alone, beginning with last egg. 12–13 days. **Nestling:** Altricial and
downy. Skin pinkish-yellow. Down dark grayish-brown. Mouth pinkish-orange.
Nestling period: Young tended by both parents. Eyes open at 4–5 days; feathers
break sheaths at 6–8 days. Young leave nest at 9–10 days, unable to fly for 5–6 days,
fed by parents for *c.* 2 weeks more.

Chipping Sparrow (*Spizella passerina*)   Plate 63
Breeds in open woodland, on woodland edge and in clearings, in parkland, cultivation with trees, and in gardens. Nest in a tree, usually a conifer, a shrub, or a vine,
occasionally in other sites. From 3–60 ft. up, but mostly between 3 and 20 ft. up.
Nest in a twig fork or among foliage.
Nest: A cup of dead grasses, weed stems and rootlets; lined with finer grasses and
hair. Built by female, accompanied by male, over 3–4 days. **Breeding season:** Begins
mid-March in south to late May or early June in north of range. Double-brooded.
Eggs: Usually 4, sometimes 3–5. Subelliptical to short subelliptical. Smooth and
moderately glossy. Light blue; very sparsely marked, mostly at larger end, with irregular spots, small blotches and specks in black, blackish-brown, and paler purple
and lilac. 18 × 13 mm. **Incubation:** Eggs laid at daily intervals. Incubation by female
alone (fed by male), beginning with next-to-last egg. 11–14 days. **Nestling:** Altricial
and downy. Skin dark red. Down fairly thick, dark gray. Mouth pinkish-red; gape
flanges pale yellow. **Nestling period:** Young tended by both parents. Female broods
young for most of first 4–5 days. Young leave nest at 9–12 days, can fly at 14 days.

Clay-colored Sparrow (*Spizella pallida*)   Plate 63
Breeds on prairies and upland plains where some shrubby cover is present, and on
scrubland by cultivated areas, on hillsides or bordering swamps and woodland. Nest
a little above ground level in the base of a shrub, weed clump, or grass tuft, or in the
lower branches of a shrub. From almost ground level to *c.* 5 ft. up. Usually well-hidden.
Nests tend to be higher up in taller herbage.
Nest: A cup of thin twigs, weed stems, grasses, and rootlets; lined with finer grasses
and rootlets, and hair. Built by female over 2–4 days. **Breeding season:** Begins late
May to early June. Usually ends by late July. Sometimes double-brooded. **Eggs:**
Usually 3–4, occasionally 5. Short subelliptical to subelliptical. Smooth and moder-
ately glossy. Eggs very similar to those of Chipping Sparrow. 17 × 13 mm. **Incubation:**
By both sexes, beginning with third egg. 10–12 days. **Nestling:** Altricial and downy.
Skin pinkish-flesh-colored. Down very sparse and dark gray, on head and back only.
Mouth bright orange-red; gape flanges white becoming yellow. **Nestling period:**
Young tended by both parents. Both sexes brood. Young leave at 7–9 days. Adults
continue feeding for at least 8 days more.

Brewer's Sparrow (*Spizella breweri*)   Plate 63
Breeds in arid sagebrush, with a northern subspecies in exposed scrub of mountain tree-lines. Nest low in a small shrub, in a twig fork, a few inches to *c.* 4 ft. up, but usually very low.
Nest: A cup of dry grass stems, dead weeds, and rootlets; lined with dried grasses, rootlets and hair. **Breeding season:** Begins mid-April in south to late May or early June in north of range. Sometimes double-brooded. **Eggs:** Usually 3–4, occasionally 5. Subelliptical. Smooth and moderately glossy. Similar to those of Chipping Sparrow. 17 × 13 mm. **Incubation:** 11–13 days. **Nestling:** Altricial and downy. Down light to dark gray. **Nestling period:** Young tended by both parents. Fly at 8–9 days.

Field Sparrow (*Spizella pusilla*)   Plate 63
Breeds in old pastures and clearings overgrown with low scrub and bushes. Early nests are on or near the ground in weed clumps or grass tufts, later ones may be higher in small thick shrubs as leaves grow. Nests a few inches to *c.* 1 ft. up, later to 4 ft.
Nest: A cup of coarse grasses and leaves; lined with finer grasses, rootlets, and hair. Built by female, accompanied by male, in *c.* 5–7 days. **Breeding season:** Begins late April in south to early May in north of range. Usually ends by late July. Probably treble-brooded, and in addition lost clutches are replaced. **Eggs:** Usually 3–5, rarely 6. Subelliptical. Smooth and slightly glossy. White or tinted very pale bluish or greenish; finely speckled, spotted, or with small blotches of medium brown, reddish-brown, or purplish-brown, and paler purple or gray. Markings usually minute or very sparse except at the larger end where they form a cap or wreath. 18 × 13 mm. **Incubation:** Eggs laid at daily intervals. Incubation by female alone. Usually 10–11 days, exceptionally up to 17 days in cold weather. **Nestling:** Altricial and downy. Skin pinkish to orange. Down light to dark gray. Mouth bright red; gape flanges yellow. **Nestling period:** Young tended by both parents. Brooded by female for most of first few days. Young leave at 7–8 days, can fly only short way 5 days later. (Male may care for fledged young while female re-nests.) Independent 18–26 days later.

Black-chinned Sparrow (*Spizella atrogularis*)   Plate 63
Breeds in sagebrush, brushy mountainsides, and chaparral. Nest in a shrub, 1–3 ft. up, in a twig fork. May nest in loose colony.
Nest: A cup, often of loose construction, of dry grasses and weed stems; lined with finer grasses, plant fibers, hair, or feathers. **Breeding season:** Begins late April. **Eggs:** Usually 2–4, occasionally 5. Subelliptical. Smooth and moderately glossy. Light blue, unmarked or with a few scattered specks or spots of black or dark brown. 18 × 13 mm. **Incubation:** By female? *c.* 13 days. **Nestling:** Altricial and downy? Down drab or buffy drab. **Nestling period:** Little information. Young tended by both parents.

Vesper Sparrow (*Pooecetes gramineus*)   Plate 63
Breeds in drier grassland on upland or well-drained soils, in sagebrush flats, in pastures or cultivated land, or in open or burned-over forest clearings where vegetation is scanty in places. Nest on the ground, often near patches of scanty or absent herbage. In a small hollow against the base of a weed or grass tuft, concealed or exposed.
Nest: A cup in small depression made by bird. A loose structure of grass and weed stems and rootlets; lined with finer grasses, rootlets, and hair. Sometimes with pine needles. **Breeding season:** Begins mid-April in south to late May in north of range. Double- or treble-brooded at times. **Eggs:** Usually 3–5, sometimes 6. Subelliptical to oval. Smooth and slightly glossy. White, with fine speckling or indistinct mottling of

paler purplish or pinkish-buff; and very sparse bold markings, chiefly towards the larger end, of reddish-brown, brown, or blackish-purple in irregular blotches or scrawls. 21 × 15 mm. **Incubation:** By both sexes, usually by female. 11–13 days. **Nestling:** Altricial and downy. Skin pinkish-flesh-colored. Down gray. Mouth deep pink; gape flanges pale yellow. **Nestling period:** Young tended by both parents. Brooded and shaded by female. Leave nest at 9–13 days, unable to fly. Dependent on adults for 20–22 days more. Male feeds fledged young while female re-nests.

Lark Sparrow (*Chondestes grammacus*)   Plate 63

Breeds on open grassland, weed-grown or old pastures, and in areas of low scrub or scattered trees. Nest usually on the ground, sometimes low in a shrub or tree, up to 7 ft., rarely up to 25 ft. When on the ground, often sheltered by a weed or grass tuft, exceptionally in a low rock crevice.
Nest: On the ground, a hollow made by the bird containing a thin cup of grasses; above ground, a stouter cup with a base of small twigs and walls of thicker grass and weed stems, lined with finer grasses and rootlets, and rarely hair. Built by female. **Breeding season:** Begins early April in south to early June in north of range. Double-brooded. **Eggs:** Usually 4–5, sometimes 3–6. Short subelliptical to subelliptical. Smooth and glossy. White; sparsely marked with specks, spots, scrawls, or scribbles of black or purplish-black and paler gray and lilac. Markings irregular, often very sparse and sometimes with a scribbled wreath around the larger end. Paler markings often conspicuous. 20 × 16 mm. **Incubation:** By female alone. 11–13 days. **Nestling:** Altricial and downy. Down sparse, brownish-gray. **Nestling period:** Young tended by both parents. Eyes open at 4 days, feathers grow at 3–4 days, break sheaths at 6–7 days. Young leave nest at 9–10 days, only able to fly short distances. (If disturbed will leave nest at 6 days.) Young are led to more brushy areas upon fledging.

Black-throated Sparrow (*Amphispiza bilineata*)   Plate 63

Breeds on arid or desert areas with sparse cover of shrubs or cactus. Nest low in small bush or cactus, about 6–18 in. up, in a fork; occasionally higher.
Nest: A cup of fibers, blades and stems of grasses, weed stems, small twigs; lined with fur, hair, wool, fine grasses, and plant down. The lining is usually pale in color. **Breeding season:** Begins mid-April to early May. Probably double-brooded. **Eggs:** Usually 3–4, larger in the north. Subelliptical. Smooth and slightly glossy. Bluish-white to white and unmarked. 17 × 14 mm. **Incubation:** *c.* 12 days. **Nestling:** Altricial and downy. Down buffish-white with slight gray tint. Mouth pinkish; gape flanges ivory. **Nestling period:** Tended by both parents. Fly at *c.* 10 days.

Sage Sparrow (*Amphispiza belli*)   Plate 63

Breeds in chaparral sagebrush, and other low arid scrub. Nest low in a thick bush, 3–17 in. up; sometimes higher or sometimes on the ground in a small hollow.
Nest: A cup of dry twigs, sticks, and weed stems; lined with shreds of bark and grass stems; and with inner lining of finer bark fiber, grasses, with fur, hair, wool tufts, and sometimes feathers. **Breeding season:** Begins late March in south to late May in north of range. Double-brooded. **Eggs:** Usually 3–4, rarely 5. Subelliptical. Smooth and moderately glossy. White or faintly greenish or bluish; speckled, spotted, and with a few small blotches of reddish, purplish-brown, or brown, and paler purple. Markings mostly fine, with heavier markings confined to larger end. Occasionally brown or blackish scrawls or spots present. Paler markings may be conspicuous. 19 × 15 mm. **Incubation:** 13–16 days. **Nestling:** Altricial and downy. Down pale. Bill grayish; gape flanges yellow. **Nestling period:** Tended by both? Fly at 9–10 days.

Five-striped Sparrow (*Amphispiza quinquestriata*)
Breeds occasionally in southeast Arizona in canyons with tall dense shrubs, and rocky, steep, semi-desert slopes. Nest low in shrub, of grass clump, from ½–4 ½ ft. up. **Nest:** A deep cup of grass stems and blades, lined with fine grass and hair. Built by female. **Breeding season:** Begins early June. Probably ends by mid-September. Usually double-brooded, sometimes treble-brooded. **Eggs:** 3–4. Subelliptical. Dull white. 20 × 16 mm. **Incubation:** By female only. 12–13 days. **Nestling:** Altricial and downy. Down dark gray on back and head. Mouth bright red; gape flanges yellow. **Nestling period:** Eyes open by 4 days. Fed mostly by female until 4–5 days when both participate. Depart at 9–10 days; fed by both (unless female re-nesting) for 18 more days.

Lark Bunting (*Calamospiza melanocorys*)   Plate 62
Breeds in short-grass prairie, though also in taller grasses, sagebrush, cultivated fields, or roadsides with weeds. Nest on the ground in growing grass, sometimes against a grass tuft or weed clump, or under a low shrub or cacti. In a slight hollow with the rim a little above or level with the ground. Rarely in a raised site. May nest in loose colonies. Male may often be polygamous.
Nest: A cup in a small hollow made by the bird. Of dry grass stems and blades; with an inner lining of fine grasses, rootlets, and hair. **Breeding season:** Begins mid- to late May. Probably double-brooded at times. **Eggs:** Usually 4–5, sometimes 3–6, rarely 7. Short subelliptical to subelliptical. Smooth and slightly glossy. Light blue and unmarked. 22 × 17 mm. **Incubation:** By female alone, with possible assistance by male. 12 days. **Nestling:** Altricial and downy. Down dark blue-gray. **Nestling period:** Young tended by both parents. Fly at 8–9 days.

Savannah Sparrow (*Passerculus sandwichensis* – Includes the
Ipswich Sparrow, *P. s. princeps*)   Plate 62
Breeds in open areas with grass or short vegetation, including meadows, dunes, tundra, sedge, bogs, prairie, salt marsh, and grass islands. Nest on the ground, sunk in a small hollow and usually concealed by a tuft of vegetation overhanging it. Male sometimes polygamous.
Nest: A hollow scratched out by the bird in soft soil, nest rim level with the ground. Lined with a cup of coarser grasses, sedges or *Salicornia* and similar material, depending on habitat; lined with fine grasses, rootlets, and hair. Does not usually use feathers. Built by female over 1–3 days. **Breeding season:** Begins mid-March in southwest to late May or early June in north of range. Double- or sometimes treble-brooded. **Eggs:** Usually 4–5, sometimes 3–6. Second clutches usually smaller. Subelliptical. Smooth and slightly glossy. Very pale greenish or bluish, or dull white; speckled, spotted, and blotched with brown, purplish-brown, or chestnut-red, and paler lilac or gray. Markings often heavy, often concentrated at the larger end. Markings sometimes indistinct on eggs with general reddish or brownish wash. 19 × 15 mm. **Incubation:** By female. 8–12 days. **Nestling:** Altricial and downy. Down grayish-brown to dull brown. Mouth pink; gape yellow. **Nestling period:** Tended by both. Age of reported first flight is variable, from 8 to 14 days. Young may stay with one parent for *c.* 15 days.

Baird's Sparrow (*Ammodramus bairdii*)   Plate 62
Breeds in open grassland, preferring taller grasses. Nest on the ground, concealed under a grass tuft or a small shrub, among a tangle of grasses, or occasionally in grass but exposed from above. Nest sunk in a small hollow. May nest in loose colony. **Nest:** A poorly-made and short-lived cup. Nests in tangled grasses may be deep thin

cups of dead grasses with raised entrances. Where nest is sunk in a hollow made by the bird it may be a thicker cup. The lining is of finer grasses or rarely with hair. Built by female. *Breeding season:* Begins early June. Usually double-brooded. *Eggs:* Usually 3–5, rarely 6. Subelliptical. Smooth and slightly glossy. White, speckled, spotted, and blotched with chestnut-red or brown, and with pale gray, and exceptionally black spots. Markings in general similar to those of Savannah Sparrow. 19 × 15 mm. *Incubation:* By female alone. 11–12 days. *Nestling:* Altricial and downy. Skin reddish-flesh. Down pale smoky-gray. Longest and thickest on head, present on back, wings, and thighs. Irides brown. Bill pale to pinkish-gray, brown along culmen. Legs and feet pink. *Nestling period:* Young tended by female alone for first few days. Later male helps. Young fed on insects. Daytime brooding stops at *c.* 5 days, eyes open at 3–4 days, young leave nest at 8–10 days and hide in grass, begin to fly at 13 days and wander at 19 days.

Grasshopper Sparrow (*Ammodramus savannarum*)   Plate 62
Breeds on grasslands, prairie, cultivated fields, and large grassy forest clearings; in Florida in stunted and sparse palmettos and burnt-off places. Nest on the ground, sunk in a small hollow at the base of a tuft of overhanging grass or weeds. A number of pairs may nest within a limited area.
Nest: A hollow made by the bird, with a cup of stems and blades of grass, the rim level with or slightly above the ground; the inner lining of fine grasses, rootlets, and hair. Built by female over 2–3 days. *Breeding season:* Begins early April in south to late May or early June in north of range. Double- or treble-brooded. *Eggs:* Usually 4–5, sometimes 3–6. Short subelliptical to subelliptical. Smooth and moderately glossy. White. Speckled, spotted, or blotched with brown to reddish-brown. Markings usually concentrated at larger end, sparse elsewhere. 19 × 14 mm. *Incubation:* By female alone. 11–12 days. *Nestling:* Altricial and downy. Down grayish-brown; on head, wings, and body. *Nestling period:* Young tended by female alone, but male reacts to predators near nest. Young begin feathering at 4 days, leave nest at 9 days, unable to fly, run through grass if disturbed.

Henslow's Sparrow (*Ammodramus henslowii*)   Plate 63
Breeds on rough meadows and grassland with taller weeds or scattered small shrubs; often in damp, low-lying areas. Nest well hidden in grass, either at the base of a tuft under overhanging grass, or raised in the stems of growing herbage up to 20 in. above ground. A number of pairs usually nest within a limited area.
Nest: Usually a deep cup, of coarse grasses and dead leaves; lined with finer grasses and occasionally hair. Partial roof is often formed over nest using nearby vegetation as arch. Built mainly or entirely by female in 4–6 days. *Breeding season:* Begins mid- to late May. Double-brooded. *Eggs:* Usually 3–5. Subelliptical. Very pale greenish or creamy-white; speckled, spotted, and with some blotching in chestnut-red, reddish-brown, and brown and paler purple and gray. Markings like those of Grasshopper Sparrow, tending to be very sparse except at larger end. 18 × 14 mm. *Incubation:* By female alone. 11 days. *Nestling:* Altricial and downy. Down smoky-gray to brownish-gray; on head, back, wings, and thighs. *Nestling period:* Young tended by both parents. Leave nest at 9–10 days.

Le Conte's Sparrow (*Ammodramus leconteii*)   Plate 62
Breeds in herbage of drier edges of marshes or in moist grasslands. Nest on or a little above the ground, concealed in a thick and tangled growth of rushes, sedges, or tall grasses. Varies from a sunken cup to a site about 9 in. above ground.
Nest: A compact cup of grasses, the outermost layer of grasses and rushes woven

around supporting stems; inner lining of finer grasses. Built by female. **Breeding season:** Begins late May to early June. Ends by mid-August. **Eggs:** Usually 4, sometimes 3–5. Subelliptical. Smooth and moderately glossy. White, faintly bluish, greenish, or grayish, very heavily speckled, spotted, or blotched with reddish-brown or brown. Markings usually concentrated at larger end. 18 × 14 mm. **Incubation:** By female alone. 11–13 days.**Nestling:** Altricial and downy. Down sparse and dull brown. **Nestling period:** Little information. Young tended by female alone at first, male helps later?

Saltmarsh Sharp-tailed Sparrow (*Ammodramus caudacutus*)   Plate 63

Breeds on coastal saltmarsh (e.g., *Spartina, Puccinellia,* and *Salicornia*). Nest is in the taller, drier grasses and sedges bordering creeks and pools; built among the stems and raised a few inches from the ground (though sometimes on the ground, up to 2 ft. up, or just above the high-tide mark). Usually concealed by overhanging vegetation. Semi-colonial. Males mate promiscuously.

Nest: A loosely-woven cup of coarse, dry grasses, seaweed, and other plant material, built up around supporting stems often high-sided and almost as deep as wide with the opening slightly to one side as though tending towards a domed structure. The inner lining of finer grasses is at the bottom of the cavity. Built by female over *c.* 4 days. **Breeding season:** Begins early May in south to mid-June in north of range. Usually ends by early August. Double-brooded. **Eggs:** Usually 3–5, sometimes 6, rarely 7. Subelliptical to short subelliptical. Smooth and slightly glossy. Very pale greenish-white; speckled, spotted, blotched, or finely mottled with shades of brown or reddish-brown, the markings often fine and profuse. 19 × 15 mm. **Incubation:** By female alone. 11–13 days. **Nestling:** Altricial and downy. Down grayish-brown. Skin yellowish-orange. Mouth pinkish-orange; gape flanges yellow. **Nestling period:** Young tended by female alone. Eyes open at 3 days, feathers break sheaths at 7 days, leave at 10 days. Young dependent on female for *c.* 20 days after leaving nest.

Nelson's Sharp-tailed Sparrow (*Ammodramus nelsoni*)

Breeds on coastal saltmarsh, and on the edges of freshwater prairie lakes, pools, and marshes. Nest is built among the reed-stems and raised a few inches from the ground, or is placed on the ground. Semi-colonial. Males may mate promiscuously.

Nest: A neat, round cup of dry coarse or fine grasses with an inner lining of finer grasses or hair. Built by female. **Breeding season:** Begins late May to mid-June. Probably ends by mid-August. Probably double-brooded. **Eggs:** Usually 4–5. Subelliptical to short subelliptical. Smooth and slightly glossy. Very similar to Saltmarsh Sharp-tailed Sparrow. 19 × 14 mm. **Incubation:** By female alone. *c.* 11 days. **Nestling:** Altricial and downy. Down gray to brownish-black. **Nestling period:** Little information. Young tended mainly by female.

Seaside Sparrow (*Ammodramus maritimus* – Includes Dusky Seaside Sparrow, *A. m. nigrescens*, and Cape Sable Seaside Sparrow, *A. m. mirabilis*)   Plate 63

Breeds on saltmarshes (though Cape Sable Seaside Sparrow breeds in freshwater habitat). Nest in wetter parts in tufts of rushes, cord-grass and similar growth, 7 in. to 3 ft. above ground level; or in *Salicornia,* marsh shrubs or low mangrove, in twig forks up to 5 ft., or at times to 14 ft. above ground level.

Nest: Simple open cup of rush stems, or grass stems and blades; lined with finer grasses; apparently built up at the sides to an almost semi-domed structure in some instances. **Breeding season:** Begins mid-April to early May, sometimes with second brood late June to early July. (Cape Sable Seaside Sparrow may begin mid-March or a little earlier. It is treble-brooded.) **Eggs:** Usually 4–5, sometimes 3–6. Subelliptical to short subelliptical. Smooth and slightly glossy. Very pale greenish-white, grayish-white or white; speckled, spotted, and blotched with purplish-brown, reddish-brown, or dull brown, and some paler purple or gray. Markings very variable, often bold, and with some concentration at larger end. 21 × 16 mm. **Incubation:** By female alone. 11–12 days. **Nestling:** Altricial and downy. Skin pink, darkening to blue-gray. Down smoky-gray on head, back, wings, and thighs, whiter on legs and flanks. Mouth red; gape flanges yellow. **Nestling period:** Young tended by both parents. Eyes open at 3–6 days, feathers break sheaths at *c.* 7 days, young leave nest at 9–10 days. Can run well but cannot fly at first. Dependent on parents for an additional 3 weeks.

Fox Sparrow (*Passerella iliaca*)   Plate 64
Breeds over a wide variety of habitats where thick shrubby growth is present, ranging from the stunted northern trees of conifer tree-line to western chaparral; and including smaller areas in cultivated and cleared regions. Nest frequently on the ground in thickets, or above ground in shrubs or low branches of trees up to *c.* 7 ft. **Nest:** A bulky and deep cup of twigs, bark shreds, grass and weed stems, wood chips, or moss; lined with fine rootlets, fur, and sometimes feathers. Built by female over 2–3 days. **Breeding season:** Begins early to mid-May. Double-brooded at times? **Eggs:** Usually 3–5. Subelliptical. Smooth and slightly glossy. Pale blue or greenish-blue; heavily speckled, spotted, or mottled with chestnut-red or purplish-brown. Markings sometimes evenly distributed or with concentration at or around larger end. 23 × 16 mm. **Incubation:** Mostly by female. Beginning with first egg? 12–14 days. **Nestling:** No information. **Nestling period:** Young tended by both parents. Fly at 9–11 days.

Song Sparrow (*Melospiza melodia*)   Figure 98, Plate 64
Breeds in low shrubby growth and thickets in a variety of habitats, but most often in moist or swampy places. Earlier nests mostly on the ground under a tuft of grass or weed clumps. Later nests often in shrubs or trees, usually up to *c.* 4 ft., exceptionally in trees up to 30 ft., usually in a twig fork. Rarely in a cavity. **Nest:** A cup, with a rough outer layer, of dead grasses and weed stems, with some rootlets and bark shreds; lined with finer grasses and sometimes hair. Built by female in 5–10 days. **Breeding season:** Usually begins in April and ends in August. Often treble-brooded and lost clutches replaced. **Eggs:** Usually 3–5, rarely 2–6. Subelliptical to short subelliptical, or oval. Smooth and slightly glossy. Very pale blue or greenish-blue, rarely pale buff; finely speckled, spotted or mottled, or with some blotching in purplish-red or purplish-brown, reddish-brown or dark brown, and some pale lilac. Markings often more concentrated towards larger end. 22 × 17 mm. **Incubation:** By female alone. 12–14 days. **Nestling:** Altricial and downy. Skin yellowish. Down is dark gray; on head, back, wings, and thighs. Mouth red; gape flanges bright yellow. **Nestling period:** Young tended by both parents. Brooded by female for most of first 5–6 days. Eyes open at 3–4 days. Young leave nest at *c.* 10 days, can fly well at 17 days, and independent in 18–20 days more. Young may be fed by male while female re-nests.

Lincoln's Sparrow (*Melospiza lincolnii*)   Plate 64
Breeds in shrubby growth on forest edge, clearings, borders of bogs and water-courses in forest and secondary growth; often on the edge of wet areas. Nest on the ground hidden by plant growth or shrubs, or in wet places usually on drier raised mounds. **Nest:** A cup of dry stems and blades of grass, and dead leaves; lined with finer grasses and a little hair. Built by female in 2–3 days. **Breeding season:** Begins late

Figure 98. Song Sparrow: c. 7 in. across; a typical nest among grasses on the ground.

May in south to mid-June in north. Usually ends by mid-August. Possibly double-brooded. **Eggs:** Usually 4–5, sometimes 3–6. Very similar to those of Song Sparrow, but markings often browner. 19 × 14 mm. **Incubation:** Eggs laid at daily intervals. Incubation by female only. 13–14 days. **Nestling:** Altricial and downy. Skin dark reddish-buff. Down dark blackish-gray; on head, back, wings, and thighs. Mouth bright red; gape flanges creamy-white at hatching, becoming yellow. **Nestling period:** Young tended by both parents. Eyes open at 5–6 days. Young leave nest at c. 10–12 days. Stay with parents an additional 2–3 weeks.

Swamp Sparrow (Melospiza georgiana)   Plate 64
Breeds in marsh vegetation of freshwater swamps, marshes and bogs, marshy edges of lakes and streams, and wet meadows, or sometimes brackish tidal marshes. Nest in large grass or sedge tussock, or suspended in tall plants such as cat-tails growing in water, or in shrub growing in water; but usually with foliage concealing the nest from above. Usually c. 1 ft. above ground or water. Male polygamous at times.
Nest: A cup, often with bulky foundations of coarse stalks and leaves, supporting a neater cup of coarser grasses; lined with fine grass stems. Built by female. **Breeding season:** Begins early or mid-May. Double-brooded. **Eggs:** Usually 4–5, sometimes 3–6. Subelliptical. Smooth and slightly glossy. Very pale blue or greenish-blue; speckled, spotted, or blotched in purplish-red, purplish-brown, or reddish-brown, and paler lilac or purple. Markings often concentrated at or about the larger end. Occasionally with very sparse, bold spots or blotches. 19 × 15 mm. **Incubation:** By

female alone. 12–13 days. **Nestling:** Altricial and downy. Skin pink. Down blackish-brown, with some white on undersides. Mouth reddish-orange; gape flanges pale yellow. **Nestling period:** Young fed by both parents. Young leave nest at 11–13 days.

White-throated Sparrow (*Zonotrichia albicollis*)   Plate 63
Breeds on forest edge, in partly open areas, clearing with scrub, shrubby growth on bog edge, and open woodland on mountain slopes. Nest on the ground at the edge of clearing, usually by or under low shrubs, tree branches, grass tufts, weed clumps, and ferns. Exceptionally above ground (to 3 ft.) in thick bushes or low in trees.
Nest: A cup of coarse grasses, wood chips, twigs, pine needles, and rootlets; lined with fine grasses, rootlets, and hair. Built by female over 4–6 days. **Breeding season:** Begins mid- to late May. Ends by late July. Usually single-brooded. Lost clutches are usually replaced. **Eggs:** Usually 4–6. Subelliptical or long subelliptical. Smooth and slightly glossy. Very pale blue or greenish-blue; speckled, spotted, or blotched in purplish-red, or chestnut-red, and paler lilac. Markings variable, sometimes fine and profuse, sometimes concentrated about the larger end. 21 × 15 mm. **Incubation:** Eggs laid at daily intervals. Incubation by female alone. 11–14 days. **Nestling:** Altricial and downy. Almost naked at hatching. Down on head, back, and wings, sparse and brown. **Nestling period:** Young tended by both parents. Usually brooded by female. Eyes open at 3–4 days. Young leave nest at 7–12 days, usually 8–9. Can fly 2–3 days later. Stay with parents until 22–24 days old.

Golden-crowned Sparrow (*Zonotrichia atricapilla*)   Plate 63
Breeds in willow and alder scrub and herbage along the tree-line of northern mountains; and in similar types of growth near sea level. Nest on the ground at the base of a small shrub or in a bank under overhanging plants. Rarely on a low branch of a shrub within thick cover.
Nest: A thick cup of small twigs, bark flakes, fern leaves and stems, dry grasses and dead leaves; lined with fine grasses, and hair and feathers. **Breeding season:** Begins late May to early June. **Eggs:** Usually 3–5. Subelliptical to long subelliptical. Smooth and slightly glossy. Very similar in color and markings to those of White-crowned Sparrows. with less of a bluish background and slightly more and darker markings. 23 × 16 mm. **Incubation:** By female. 11–13 days. **Nestling:** Altricial and naked. Developing down gray. Mouth red; gape flanges yellow. **Nestling period:** Fed by both. Eyes open at 3 days. Leave nest at 9 days and fly short distances 4 days later.

White-crowned Sparrow (*Zonotrichia leucophrys*)   Plate 63
Breeds in open, stunted woodland and scrub in the north, similar habitat on western mountains and in cleared, cultivated, or burnt-over areas in forest. Nest on the ground, partly concealed in moss and low shrubby growth, or in or under a grass tuft or fern, or at the base of a shrub. Or a few feet above the ground in a bush, or low tree branch, exceptionally much higher in trees. Males sometimes polygamous.
Nest: A cup of grass stems, dead leaves, thin twigs, pine needles, bark shreds, and some moss; lined with fine rootlets, hair, and feathers. Built by female. **Breeding season:** Varies in different populations. May begin early March to April in west to early June in north. Ends by August or later if rainfall was plentiful previous winter. Lost clutches usually replaced. Some populations may produce up to four broods. **Eggs:** Usually 2–5, rarely 6. Subelliptical. Smooth and slightly to moderately glossy. Very pale blue or greenish-blue; spotted, speckled, or mottled in light red, reddish-brown, or purplish-red. The markings usually fine and profuse. 21 × 16 mm. **Incubation:** By female alone, beginning at or just before completion of clutch. 11–15 days. **Nestling:** Altricial and downy. Down brownish-gray; on head, back, wings,

and thighs. Mouth bright red; gape flanges yellow. **Nestling period:** Female broods for first 2 days fed by male. Young tended by both parents. Eyes open at 4 days. Leave nest at 9–11 days. Young still fed to some extent for 25–30 days more. Male may feed fledged young, possibly for a shorter period, if female re-nests.

Harris's Sparrow (*Zonotrichia querula*)

Breeds in stunted trees of forest along the northern tree-line, and along woodland edge, by clearings or in burnt-over areas. Nest on the ground on a hummock among trees, usually sheltered by a low shrub or small tree.
Nest: A bulky cup in a hollow made by the birds; of coarse rootlets, dead grass stems, and sometimes mosses; lined with finer grasses. Built in 2–3 days, probably by female. **Breeding season:** Begins early June. Usually ends by late July. Single-brooded but a lost clutch may be replaced. **Eggs:** Usually 4, sometimes 3–5. Subelliptical. Smooth and slightly glossy. White to pale greenish-white; speckled, spotted, blotched, and scrawled with brown or reddish-brown. Markings usually heavy and sometimes with a concentration at the larger end. 22 × 17 mm. **Incubation:** By female only. 12–14 days. **Nestling:** Altricial and downy. Flesh pink. Down gray on wings and back area. Mouth red; gape flanges yellow. **Nestling period:** Fed by both. Eyes open at 3 days. Leave nest at 9 days and fly short distances 4 days later.

Dark-eyed Junco (*Junco hyemalis* – Includes Slate-colored Junco, *J. h. hyemalis*, Gray-headed Junco, *J. h. caniceps*, and Oregon Junco, *J. h. oreganus*)
Plate 63

Breeds in open woodland, woodland clearings, and forest edge. Nest on the ground among tree-roots, or partly hidden by brushwood, stump, or rock, often in ferns or herbage on a bank or rocky slope, or in more open site against a plant tuft. Exceptionally in low shrubs or on conifer branches, in tree cavities or on raised sites on ledges and niches of buildings, to 8 ft., rarely higher.
Nest: In a small hollow made by bird where site is soft. A cup, often substantial, of thin twigs, fine stems, dry grasses, bark strips, rootlets, and moss; lined with finer stems, grasses, and hair. Built by female, though male may carry some material. **Breeding season:** Begins mid-March in south to mid-May in north of region. Double- or treble-brooded in some areas. **Eggs:** Usually 3–5, rarely 6. Short subelliptical to subelliptical. Smooth and slightly glossy. White or slightly greenish or grayish; speckled, spotted, and blotched in reddish-brown, chestnut-red, and purplish-brown. Markings usually very sparse except as a cap or wreath at larger end. 19 × 14 mm. **Incubation:** Eggs laid at daily intervals. Incubation by female alone, beginning with next-to-last egg. 12–13 days. **Nestling:** Altricial and downy. Skin dark reddish-orange. Down dark gray. Mouth deep pink; gape flanges pale yellow. **Nestling period:** Young tended by both parents. Eyes open at *c.* 5 days, feathers showing at 7 days. Young fed on insects, regurgitated at first, fed directly later. Young leave nest at 10–13 days, partly dependent for *c.* 3 weeks more.

Yellow-eyed Junco (*Junco phaeonotus*)
Plate 63

Breeds in mountain conifer forest in southeast Arizona and southwest New Mexico. Nest on the ground hidden under plant tuft or grass tuft, log, fallen branch, or rock. Exceptionally in conifer tree to 9 ft. up.
Nest: In small hollow made by bird in soft site. A cup of coarse grasses and moss; lined with finer grasses, hair, and fur. Usually built by female alone. **Breeding season:** Mid-April to mid-August. Double-brooded. **Eggs:** Usually 3–4, sometimes 5. Subelliptical. Smooth and slightly glossy. Similar to lightly spotted eggs of Dark-eyed Junco. 20 × 15 mm. **Incubation:** By female alone. 13–15 days? **Nestling:** Altricial and downy. Down

sparse and gray; on head and body. Irides dark brown. *Nestling period:* Young tended by both parents. Eyes open at 4–5 days, feathers break sheaths at 6–8 days, young leave nest at 10 days. Young evicted from breeding territory by parents at 32–38 days.

McCown's Longspur (*Calcarius mccownii*)   Plate 64
Breeds on more arid short-grass prairie often on nearly bare ground. Nest on the ground, often at the base of a grass tuft, weed clump, or small shrubby growth.
Nest: A cup in a small hollow made by the bird, its rim at or near ground level. Of coarser stems and blades of grass; lined with finer grasses and sometimes plant down, fur, hair and wool. Built by female. *Breeding season:* Begins early to mid-May. Usually ends by early August. Often double-brooded. *Eggs:* Usually 3–4, occasionally 5. Very pale buffish or olive, grayish-white, or pinkish, or with a wash of buff or purplish; blotches and scrawled with olive-brown, brown, blackish, or paler lilac; the markings sometimes sparse and faint. 20 × 15 mm. *Incubation:* Eggs usually laid at daily intervals. Incubation by female only. 12–13 days. *Nestling:* Altricial and downy. Skin pale reddish. Down long and pale buff; on head and back. Mouth deep pink. *Nestling period:* Young tended by both parents. Female broods for first 3 days. Eyes open at 4–5 days; feathers break sheaths at 6–7 days. Young leave nest at 10 days; can fly short distances at 12 days.

Lapland Longspur (*Calcarius lapponicus*)   Plate 64
Breeds on open tundra or on similar habitat on northern mountain tops, often in moist places. Nest on the ground in a depression; may be in the side of a bank or hummock, usually well hidden by surrounding vegetation.
Nest: A cup of grasses, moss, and roots; lined with finer grass, hair, and feathers. Built by female over *c.* 3 days. *Breeding season:* Begins end of May to June. Single-brooded. *Eggs:* Usually 5–6, sometimes 2–7. Clutches may be small in cold seasons. Subelliptical. Smooth and glossy. Pale greenish, buffish, or grayish; usually largely obscured by indistinct mottling of dull reddish-brown or purplish-brown, and with some sparse dark spots or scrawls of black or purplish-black, the darker markings sometimes absent. 21 × 15 mm. *Incubation:* Eggs laid at daily intervals. Incubation by female, beginning with completion of clutch. 10–14 days. *Nestling:* Altricial and downy. Down light brown. Mouth red; gape flanges yellow. *Nestling period:* Young brooded and fed by both parents, leave nest at 8–10 days. They leave 3–5 days before they are able to fly.

Smith's Longspur (*Calcarius pictus*)   Plate 64
Breeds on moister, grassy tundra. Nest on the ground, on slightly raised hummock or grass tussock, often sunk into small hollow probably made by bird. Female mates with 1–3 males; these males in turn mate with 1–3 different females.
Nest: A cup of dry grasses; lined with finer grasses, hair, down, and feathers. Built by female over 3–4 days. *Breeding season:* Begins early June. Usually ends by late July. *Eggs:* Usually 3–4, sometimes 5. Subelliptical to short subelliptical. Smooth, non-glossy or slightly glossy. Very pale olive, bluish, or greenish, sometimes with a purplish wash; spotted, blotched, or mottled in pale dull purplish-brown, or lilac; and with sparse dark scrawls and specks in dark brown, purplish-black, or black. 21 × 15 mm. *Incubation:* By female only, beginning before completion of clutch. 11–14 days. *Nestling:* Altricial and downy. Down buff with dark gray tips; on head, back, wings, and thighs. Skin orange. Mouth pink, becoming red. *Nestling period:* Young tended by both parents. Eyes open at 3–4 days. Feathers break sheaths at 4–6 days. Half the nests may have more than one male feeding the young. Young leave nest at 7–9 days. Can fly when 12 days old. Fed for *c.* 3 weeks after leaving nest.

Chestnut-collared Longspur (*Calcarius ornatus*)   Plate 64

Breeds on prairie where grass is short and sparse. (Grass is taller than that favored by McCown's Longspur.) Nest on the ground in short grass.

Nest: Nest built in a small hollow made by the bird, the rim level with the ground. A cup of dry grass blades and stems, with a lining of finer grasses and some feathers and hair. Built by female. **Breeding season:** Begins May. Double-brooded. **Eggs:** Usually 3–5, sometimes 6. Short subelliptical to elliptical. Smooth and slightly glossy. Creamy-white, or usually tinted faintly blue or gray, with very minute speckling in purplish or blackish, and sparse irregular spots and blotches of reddish-brown, purplish-brown or black, and pale purple or lilac. 19 × 14 mm. **Incubation:** Eggs laid at daily intervals. Incubation by female alone, beginning at completion of clutch. 11–13 days. **Nestling:** Altricial and downy. Down buffish-gray; mainly on head and back. Legs and feet pale pinkish-flesh color. Bill pinkish-flesh-colored with dark tip. **Nestling period:** Young tended by both parents. Brooded by female for first *c.* 5 days. Eyes open at 5–6 days; leave nest at 9–11 days. Independent at 25 days.

Snow Bunting (*Plectrophenax nivalis*)   Plate 64

Breeds on bare rocky areas and screes, from sea level to mountain. Nest on the ground, concealed in a crevice among rocks and boulders, or hole in a wall or old building. Many pairs may nest in proximity. Male sometimes polygamous.

Nest: A cup of dry grass, moss, and lichens; lined with finer grass, hair, wool, and feathers. Built by female, often accompanied by male. Old nests may be re-used. **Breeding season:** Begins late May to mid-June. Varying with locality and altitude. Probably ends early August. Single-brooded. **Eggs:** Usually 4–6, rarely 3–9. Subelliptical. Smooth and glossy. Very pale blue or greenish-blue, very variably blotched, spotted, or speckled with light reddish-brown, dark brown, purplish-brown, light purplish-gray, and occasionally purplish-black. Markings may be sparse and concentrated at the larger end, or heavier and more widely distributed. 23 × 16 mm. **Incubation:** By female alone. 10–15 days. **Nestling:** Altricial and downy. Down fairly long and plentiful but absent from underside; dark gray. Mouth deep red; gape flanges yellow. **Nestling period:** Young brooded by female for *c.* 5 days while male brings food. Later both parents bring food. Young are active at 8 days and may leave nest and return. Finally leave at 10–14 days. Fed by parents to day 18–26.

McKay's Bunting (*Plectrophenax hyperboreus*)

Breeds only on islands in the Bering Sea. Nest on the ground, hidden under vegetation, in deserted vole holes especially along stream banks, far back in rock crevices in cliff faces above the ocean, or deep in mountainside rock rubble. Often in hollow drift logs along the wreck line on shingle beaches.

Nest: Built of grasses. **Breeding season:** June–July. Possibly double-brooded. **Eggs:** 3–5. Subelliptical. Smooth and moderately glossy. Light greenish-white, dotted with pale greenish-brown. 23 × 17 mm. **Incubation:** By female alone. Estimated at 14 days? **Nestling:** No information. **Nestling period:** Little information. Young tended by both parents.

Bobolink (*Dolichonyx oryzivorus*)   Plate 61

Breeds in open grassland, preferring moist, lusher areas, meadows, and cultivated clovers and grain. Also in grassy marshland. Nest on the ground, in a small hollow. Semi-colonial. Male may often be polygamous.

Nest: A shallow hollow, sometimes made by the bird, containing a thin, shallow cup of dead grass and weed stems; lined with finer grasses. **Breeding season:** Begins mid-to late May. Usually single-brooded. **Eggs:** Usually 5–6, sometimes 4–7. Subelliptical to oval. Smooth and glossy. Very pale blue or greenish, sometimes tinted by a brownish or purplish wash; boldly but sometimes sparsely blotched, mottled, and scrawled, and sometimes with finer speckling and spotting of medium to deep brown, purplish-brown, or blackish-brown. 22 × 16 mm. **Incubation:** By female. 11–13 days. **Nestling:** Altricial and downy. Flesh pink. Down buffish. Mouth yellowish; gape flanges cream. **Nestling period:** Young tended by both parents. Leave nest at 10–14 days. Cannot fly for some days.

Red-winged Blackbird (*Agelaius phoeniceus*)   Figure 99, Plate 61

Breeds usually by or over water in marshes, swamps, or wet meadows, or in tall herbage bordering open water or slower streams; in cat-tails, rushes, sedges, large grass tussocks, waterside shrubs, or low trees. Occasionally in shrubs, bushes, and tall herbage some distance from water. Exceptionally in trees. Up to 14 ft. Semicolonial. Male may often be polygamous.

Nest: A deep cup of long leaves and stems woven tightly around the upright supports, with a layer of broken plant material and fibers, roots, decayed leaves, and some mud, firmly shaped; and lined with fine dry grasses or thin rushes. Built by female in 3–6 days. **Breeding season:** Begins late March in south to late May in north of range. Usually ends by early August. Double-brooded. **Eggs:** Usually 4, sometimes 3–5. Subelliptical to long subelliptical. Smooth and glossy. Very pale blue, sometimes tinted pinkish or purplish; sparingly scribbled, scrawled or with a few blotches or spots of black, blackish-brown, or blackish-purple, and paler purple and gray. Larger markings sometimes superimposed on pale brown or purple marks. Sometimes indistinct blotching or clouding of brown or purple. Markings tend to be concentrated towards the larger end. 25 × 18 mm. **Incubation:** By female alone. 10–12 days. **Nestling:** Altricial and downy. Skin scarlet. Down whitish, scanty; on head,

Figure 99. Red-winged Blackbird: c. 4½ in. across; a cup woven around upright supports.

lower back, wings, and thighs. Mouth red; gape flanges yellow. **Nestling period:** Young tended by both parents. Feather sheaths break at 6–8 days. Young leave at 10–11 days. Present around nest area for 10–14 days longer.

Tricolored Blackbird (*Agelaius tricolor*)   Plate 61

Breeds in sloughs, swamps, marshes where tall growth of water plants – cattails, tule, and the like – is present in California and southern Oregon. Sometimes breeds in cultivated fields. Nesting usually occurs in dense and sometimes enormous colonies. Nests may be very close together and colonies may extend into shrubs and trees in the area, or into grain or similar crops nearby, or tall herbaceous growth on dry ground. Nest may be almost at ground level ($\frac{1}{2}$ ft.) or several feet up (to 5 ft. or occasionally to 12 ft.). Male may often be polygamous.

Nest: A deep cup, bound to upright stems of growing plants, the outer layer of long leaves and stems woven tightly around supports, and long coiled leaves inside. There is a middle layer of broken and decayed leaves, roots, and muddy plant material, compacted together; and an inner lining of fine grasses. Built by female. **Breeding season:** Late March to mid-June. Double-brooded. **Eggs:** Usually 4, rarely 5–6. Similar to those of the Red-winged Blackbird. 28 × 20 mm. **Incubation:** By female. 11 days. **Nestling:** Altricial and downy. **Nestling period:** Young tended by female alone or by both parents. Young leave at *c.* 13 days, but may leave much earlier if disturbed.

Eastern Meadowlark (*Sturnella magna*)   Figure 100, Plate 61

Breeds in open grassland, meadows, and pastures, and in similar low herbage such as clover, alfalfa, or young corn. Will also use areas such as orchards, with scattered trees. Nest on the ground in growing herbage, concealed by a domed top and overhanging grasses. Male may often be polygamous.

Nest: A large domed structure, nests usually having a roof of grasses woven into the growing herbage around the nest, leaving a fairly large side entrance. Of dry grasses, the cup lined with finer grasses and sometimes hair. Nest set into a small hollow which may be made by bird. Built by female only in 3–8 days. **Breeding season:** Begins late March in south to early May in north of range. Double-brooded, and lost clutches may be replaced. **Eggs:** Usually 3–5, sometimes 2–7. Short subelliptical to short oval. Smooth and glossy. White; speckled, spotted, or with small

Figure 100. Eastern Meadowlark: c. 6–7 in. across; a domed roof is interwoven with surrounding grasses.

blotches of reddish-brown, purplish-brown, chestnut-red, light red, light brown, and pale lilac and purple. The markings tend to be sparse and largely concentrated at larger end with fine speckling elsewhere. 28 × 20 mm. *Incubation:* By female only. 13–15 days. *Nestling:* Altricial and downy. Skin orange-red. Down abundant, pale gray; on head, back, wings, and thighs. Mouth red; gape flanges ivory. *Nestling period:* Young tended by both parents, but mainly by female. Eyes open at 5 days. Young leave nest at 11–12 days. Male may take over feeding of young out of nest while female re-nests.

Western Meadowlark *(Sturnella neglecta)*   Plate 61
Breeds on open grassland of prairies and river valleys, in mountain areas of open and broken woodland, in more open sagebrush, in pastures, and in cultivated areas with clover, alfalfa, and grain or similar crops. Male may often be polygamous.
Nest: A domed structure like that of Eastern Meadowlark. In both species the birds' visits to the nest entrance through tall grass may result in a small tunnel being formed. Built by female over 4–8 days. *Breeding season:* Begins late February in south to mid-June in north of range. Usually ends by early August. Double-brooded, and lost clutches may be replaced. *Eggs:* Usually 5, sometimes 3–7. Similar to those of Eastern Meadowlark. 28 × 21 mm. *Incubation:* Eggs laid at daily intervals. Incubation by female only. 13–15 days. *Nestling:* Like that of Eastern Meadowlark. *Nestling period:* Young tended by both parents. Leave nest at 10–12 days, before being able to fly. Fed by parents for *c.* 2 weeks more.

Yellow-headed Blackbird *(Xanthocephalus xanthocephalus)*   Plate 61
Breeds in tall herbage growing in water on the edge of lakes and open waters, and on deeper marshes or sloughs. Nest in a thick growth of tall vegetation – tule, reeds, bulrushes, or cat-tails – over water of reasonable depth. The nest is bound to several stems, usually 2–3 ft. up, occasionally ½–6 ft. up. Pairs nest in colonies, often very large, with nests fairly close together. Males may often be polygamous.
Nest: A deep cup of long stems and blades of wet, partly decayed grasses, woven around supporting stems to form a tight cup, lined with dead leaves of plants, coarse grasses, roots, and decayed plant material, firmly packed and with an inner lining of narrow leaves, leaf strips, or fine grasses. Occasionally fine material built above rim to form a partial canopy. Built by female in 2–4 days. *Breeding season:* Begins late April in south to early June in north. Usually ends by mid-July. Usually single-brooded. *Eggs:* Usually 4, occasionally 3, rarely 5. Long subelliptical to long oval. Smooth and glossy. Very pale bluish-white; profusely and finely speckled and mottled with brown, purplish-brown or reddish-brown, usually with denser markings at the lower end. Markings occasionally coalescing to form heavier but poorly-defined overall spotting or blotching. 26 × 18 mm. *Incubation:* By female alone. 10–13 days. *Nestling:* Altricial and downy. Down sparse, buff; on head and back. *Nestling period:* By female alone or by both parents. Young feather by 8–9 days, leave nest unable to fly at 9–12 days, and can make short flights by *c.* 20 days.

Rusty Blackbird *(Euphagus carolinus)*   Plate 61
Breeds usually by open waters with swampy shores, in woodland areas, where trees mix with swamp. Nest in a tree or shrub usually growing in or by water, frequently in conifers. 2–20 ft. up.
Nest: A stout bulky cup of twigs, lichens, including *Usnea*, and sometimes long grasses. A middle layer is a firmly molded bowl of decaying plant material smoothed and lined with dry grasses, fibers, and sometimes thin twigs. Bult by female. *Breeding season:* Begins early to mid-May. Usually ends by mid-June. *Eggs:* Usually

4–5, sometimes 6. Eggs similar to those of Brewer's Blackbird. 26 × 19 mm. **Incubation:** By female alone, beginning with first egg. 14 days. **Nestling:** Altricial and downy. Down long and thin, dark brown. **Nestling period:** Young tended by both parents. Eyes open at 5–6 days. Young leave nest at *c.* 13 days.

Brewer's Blackbird (*Euphagus cyanocephalus*)　　　　　　　　　Plate 61

Breeds in a variety of habitats and sites, but more particularly in trees or shrubs adjoining open water or marshy areas or along watercourses. Also in shade trees and shrubs of cultivated or urban areas. Nests in a variety of sites, in trees or shrubs, in a fork or on a branch, often in conifers, usually between 18–30 ft. (but also up to 150 ft.), in bushes, tall sedges in wet marshes, or on the ground in plant tufts on the top of a steep bank or growing in water. Nest sometimes in cavity or broken tree. Usually in small colonies or groups or pairs. Males often polygamous.
Nest: A stout cup of fine twigs and grasses with a middle layer of grasses, pine needles, and fibers mixed with mud and dung and forming a firm cup, with an inner lining of rootlets and hair. Built by female. **Breeding season:** Begins late March in south to late May in north of range. Often double-brooded. **Eggs:** Usually 5–6, sometimes 3–7. Subelliptical to short subelliptical or oval. Smooth and glossy. Very pale blue or greenish-blue, sometimes suffused by a pink, brown or purple wash; speckled, spotted, blotched, or mottled in purplish-brown, brown, or purple, and paler purple and purplish-brown or buff. Markings are frequently poorly defined and additional spots or scrawls of blackish-brown may be present. Occasionally markings are sparse and largely confined to the larger end. 25 × 19 mm. **Incubation:** By female alone. 12–13 days. **Nestling:** Altricial and downy. Down blackish. **Nestling period:** Young tended by both parents. Leave nest at 13 days and fed for an additional 12–13 days

Great-tailed Grackle (*Quiscalus mexicanus*)　　　　　　　　　Plate 61

Nests most frequently in vegetation by or over water, in rushes, reeds and canebrakes, shrubs and trees; in trees or thickets along watercourses in drier regions; in mesquite; in coastal cactus, yuccas, and grasses; and shade trees around houses. On Texas coast nests in large numbers in heron colonies, with some nests in herons' stick nests. Usually breeds in colonies, often very large with nests close together. Height usually 5–15 ft., though as low as 2 ft. (above water) to as high as 50 ft. (above ground). Male takes no part in nesting other than defence against predators. Male may often be polygamous.
Nest: A bulky cup of weed stems, coarse grasses, strips of bark, plant fibers, or sometimes Spanish Moss, lined with mud and cow dung to form a firm structure with an inner lining of fine grasses and rootlets, feathers and other soft material. Built by female alone. **Breeding season:** Begins early April. Sometimes double-brooded. **Eggs:** Usually 3–4, sometimes 5. Long subelliptical to subelliptical or long oval. Smooth and glossy. Pale blue or tinted to varying degrees with pink, purple, or brownish. Boldly scribbled or scrawled and with occasional blotches or spots of black, and pale purple or gray. Dark markings may have blurred purplish edges or pale purple suffusions around them, less widely dispersed than in the Boat-tailed Grackle and more apparent at the larger end. Markings often sparse. 33 × 22 mm. **Incubation:** Eggs usually laid at daily interval. Incubation by female alone. 13–14 days. **Nestling:** Altricial and downy. Skin salmon-colored. Down long and sparse; gray; on head, back, wings, and thighs. Mouth bright red. **Nestling period:** Young tended by female alone. Eyes open at 3–5 days. Young feathered at *c.* 14 days. Leave nest at 20–23 days.

Boat-tailed Grackle (*Quiscalus major*)   Plate 61
Nest usually in vegetation by or over water, in sawgrass, bulrushes, shrubs, and trees. Nest usually low, 3–12 ft. up, but sometimes up to 50 ft. in trees. Usually breeds in colonies. Male takes no part in nesting other than defence against predators. Male may often be polygamous.
Nest: A bulky and compact cup of rushes, flags, coarser grasses, and stalks, with an inner lining of bark strips and fibers, grass stems and decayed waterplant material bound with rotted plant material and mud to form a firm cup, lined with fine rootlets and dry grasses. Built by female alone in 4–5 days. **Breeding season:** Begins early March in south to late April in north of range. Breeding in November–December has occurred in Florida. Double- or sometimes treble-brooded. **Eggs:** Usually 3–4, sometimes 5. Long subelliptical to subelliptical or long oval. Smooth and glossy. Pale blue or tinted to varying degrees with pink or purple. Boldly scribbled or scrawled and with occasional blotches or spots of black, and paler purple or gray. Dark markings may have blurred purplish edges or pale purple suffusion around them. Markings often sparse. 32 × 22 mm. **Incubation:** By female alone. 13–14 days. **Nestling:** Altricial and downy. Down long and sparse, gray; on head, back, wings, and thighs. Mouth bright red. **Nestling period:** Young tended by female alone. Eyes open at 3–5 days. Young feathered at *c.* 14 days. Leave nest at 20–23 days.

Common Grackle (*Quiscalus quiscula*)   Plate 61
Breeds through open and cultivated country, especially in wetter areas. Nests in trees, particularly conifers, in low shrubs and bushes, on dry land and in marshes and in tall swamp vegetation. Also in shade trees around houses, and in niches and ledges on or in buildings. Sometimes in holes in large dead trees and stumps, in nest-boxes (e.g., for Wood Duck), or in stick nests of large birds. Nests from ground level to *c.* 45 ft. up, but often low. Nests singly or in loose colonies. Male sometimes polygamous.
Nest: A bulky, externally loose cup, of twigs, weed stems, coarse grasses, *Usnea* lichen, Spanish Moss, pine needles, or seaweed in some areas, and inner cup of mud or dung; lined with fine dry grasses and rootlets, a few feathers, or hair, and sometimes paper, string, or rags. Built by female. **Breeding season:** Begins mid-March in south to mid-May in north of range. Sometimes double-brooded. **Eggs:** Usually 4–5, sometimes 6, rarely 7. Long to short subelliptical. Smooth and glossy. Pale blue, sometimes tinted pinkish; with bold scrawls or scribbles, spots or blotches, and a little fine speckling or spotting in black, blackish-purple or blackish-brown. Markings often show blurred purple or brown edges; and paler parts of shell may show variable clouding or suffusion with brown or purplish-brown. 28 × 21 mm. **Incubation:** By female alone, beginning with next-to-last egg. 12–14 days. **Nestling:** Altricial and downy. Down pale brown. Irides brown. **Nestling period:** Young tended by both parents. Brooded by female only. Leave nest at 10–17 days; usually at *c.* 12 days, and only remain in vicinity of nest for 2–3 days.

Shiny Cowbird (*Molothrus bonariensis*)   Plate 61
A recent arrival to Florida from the Caribbean (where it parasitizes over 100 species). It breeds over a wide range of habitats. It is probable that each female cowbird lays only 1 egg in a nest, but several females may each deposit an egg, with up to 14 being recorded in a nest in the Neotropics.
Breeding season: Probably April to July. **Eggs:** It is estimated that each female may lay 1 egg in 5 different nests in a season. Elliptical to short subelliptical, though varies in shape and coloring. Smooth and semi-glossy. It may be white, yellowish, pale green, pale pink, light brown, or blue, and there may be markings or spots or blotches in brown, pale violet, reddish, or black. Though size varies, the egg averages 21 × 16 mm. **Incubation:** 11–13 days. **Nestling:** Altricial and downy. Skin orange-

pink. Down gray, with scattered tufts of black. Mouth reddish; gape pale yellow to orange-yellow. Bill grayish-yellow, and feet orange to yellow. **Nestling period:** Young develop very rapidly. Young of host sometimes survive with young cowbird, but are often unable to compete. Young cowbird leaves at *c.* 12 days.

Bronzed Cowbird (*Molothrus aeneus*)   Plate 61

Breeds in open areas and farmland. Like the Brown-headed Cowbird a brood parasite. The typical hosts for this species are the various oriole *(Icterus* species) but occasionally eggs are laid apparently at random in almost any nest of birds of moderate size, some of which might rear young, but some wholly unsuitable. Includes grosbeaks, sparrows, thrashers, wrens, warblers, flycatchers, and even ground-doves among hosts. Normally only 1 egg laid in a nest, but several females may lay in the same nest.

Breeding season: Begins mid-April. **Eggs:** Usually 4–5 eggs laid by each female. Subelliptical or tending to biconical. Smooth and glossy. Very pale blue or greenish-blue. Usually unmarked, but sometimes with a few scattered pale specks of brown. 23 × 18 mm. **Incubation:** 10–13 days. **Nestling:** Altricial and downy. Skin pinkish-orange becoming brownish. Down gray; on head, back, wings, and thighs. Mouth reddish; gape flanges cream or white. Bill, legs, and feet yellowish. **Nestling period:** Young develop very rapidly. Young of host sometimes survive with young cowbird, but are sometimes unable to compete. Eyes open at 5 days. Feathers break sheaths at 6–7 days. Young cowbird leaves at *c.* 11 days. Fed by hosts for an additional *c.* 2 weeks.

Brown-headed Cowbird (*Molothrus ater*)   Plate 16, 61

Breeds over a wide range on and around grasslands, farmland, brushy thickets, forest edge, and suburban areas. Promiscuous and a brood parasite, eggs being laid in the nests of other bird species and the young reared by these hosts, sometimes at the expense of the host's young. The principal hosts are various species of finches, vireos, warblers, and flycatchers; but eggs appear to be laid at times in almost any available nest of birds of moderate size, some of which might rear young, but some wholly unsuitable. Usually only 1 egg is laid in a nest, but several eggs may be laid by different cowbird females. Occasionally eggs are ejected or built over by the host.

Breeding season. Begins early April in south to mid-May in north of range. **Eggs:** Up to *c.* 30 laid by a female in one season. Short subelliptical to elliptical, or subelliptical. Smooth and glossy. White or faintly bluish or greenish; profusely and finely speckled or mottled with brown, purplish-brown, or reddish-brown, and paler gray or purple. Markings sometimes show longitudinal elongation. Usually finely marked overall but sometimes greater concentration at larger end. 21 × 16 mm. **Incubation:** 11–12 days. Often hatching a little sooner than eggs of host. **Nestling:** Altricial and downy. Skin pinkish-flesh-color. Mouth deep pink; gape flanges cream. **Nestling period:** Young develop very rapidly. The young of the host often survive with the cowbird but sometimes fail to compete successfully for food. Cowbird leaves nest at 10 days. Host continues to feed it for an additional *c.* 2 weeks.

Orchard Oriole (*Icterus spurius*)   Plate 61

Breeds in tree belts and riverine woodland along watercourses, in orchards, in shade trees around farms and settlements, or in scattered trees in cultivated areas. Nest in a tree, less frequently in a shrub, 4–50 ft. up. Has also been found nesting in *Phragmites* reeds down to 2–3 ft. Nest usually suspended in a twig fork at the tip of a branch, but may be built into a vertical fork, or a hanging tuft of Spanish Moss. Sometimes in loose colonies.

Nest: A pensile or semi-pensile rounded cup, *c.* 4 in. long, attached to supports at the rim and sometimes at the sides. Of long fine stems and fibers woven around to form a thick cup, lined with some plant down. Built mostly if not entirely by female in 3–6 days. **Breeding season:** Begins late April in south to early June in north of range. Usually single-brooded. **Eggs:** Usually 4–5, sometimes 3–7. Long subelliptical to long oval. Smooth and glossy. Very pale blue; with scrawls, small blotches, spots, and specks of black, blackish-brown, blackish-purple, and paler gray and purple. Markings often sparse and mainly around or at the large end. 20 × 15 mm. **Incubation:** By female, fed by male. 12–15 days. **Nestling:** Altricial and downy. Down sparse; on head and back. **Nestling period:** Young tended by both parents. Leave nest at 11–14 days.

Hooded Oriole (*Icterus cucullatus*)   Plate 61

Breeds in woodland along watercourses and in shade trees, palms, and shrubs around houses. Nest a cup in a tree or shrub, 10–45 ft. up, suspended between twigs, or in a fork and attached at sides as well as rim, or sewn by fibers to the underside of a palm or palmetto leaf, the bird entering between nest-rim and the leaf above. At earlier periods nest recorded in, and of, Spanish Moss.

Nest: A cup a little deeper (4 in.) than wide. Woven of fine grasses and long plant fibers to form a strong, firm, fibrous cup; lined with some plant down, or occasionally a little wool, feathers, or hair. Built by female with possible help from male in 5–6 days. **Breeding season:** Begins early April to early May. 2 or sometimes 3 broods. **Eggs:** Usually 4, sometimes 3–5. Long subelliptical to long oval. Smooth and glossy. Very pale blue, sometimes with a slight pink or purple wash. Finely scribbled and scrawled or with a few elongated blotches or specks of black, usually with the markings concentrated at the larger end. Sometimes almost unmarked. 22 × 15 mm. **Incubation:** Eggs laid at daily intervals. Incubation by female alone. 13 days. **Nestling:** Altricial and downy. Down sparse; on head and back. **Nestling period:** Young tended by both parents. Leave nest at *c.* 14 days.

Streak-backed Oriole (*Icterus pustulatus*)   Plate 61

Breeds rarely in southeastern Arizona in cottonwood-dominated riparian areas or perhaps mesquite. Nest suspended from a branch in a tree, *c.* 20–25 ft. up, under tree canopy in an exposed position.

Nest: A very elongated, loosely constructed, pear-shaped bag, 1¼–2 ft. long. Woven of tree bark, grasses, and other available materials. Loose ends of fibers may hang down around and below the nest. Lined with downy vegetation and a few feathers. Suspended from a twig fork usually at the end of a branch, with a loop of materials forming a narrow entrance at the top. Built by female. **Breeding season:** Begins early June. Possibly double-brooded. **Eggs:** Usually 5. Long subelliptical to long elliptical. Smooth and glossy. Very pale bluish-white with dark brown and lavender scrawlings and a few spots confluent around the larger end. 26 × 17 mm. **Incubation:** By female. Estimated at 12–14 days. **Nestling:** No information. **Nestling period:** Young tended by both parents. Age at first flight estimated at 14 days.

Spotted-breasted Oriole (*Icterus pectoralis*)   Plate 61

Introduced on southeastern coast of Florida. Breeds in tall trees, up to 60 ft. Nest an elongated pensile bag suspended from a twig fork or tip, at the end of a branch.

Nest: An elongated pear-shaped bag, 10–18 in. long by 6 in. wide at the bottom end. Suspended from forked twigs which form part of the rim of the entrance. Shallower, cup-shaped nests have been built by introduced Florida birds. Nest of long plant fibers (often of palms) and fine aerial roots of epiphytic plants woven together. Some of the material ends may hang down below the bottom of the nest. Nest cavity with a thick lining of fine plant fibers. Built by female alone in 6–7 days. **Breeding season:** Begins mid-March. Ends late August. Double-brooded. **Eggs:** Usually 3–4. Long sub-elliptical. Smooth and slightly glossy. Pale bluish-white, scribbled and scrawled with black and pale lilac. 26 × 18 mm. **Incubation:** By female. Period unknown. **Nestling:** No information. **Nestling period:** Fed by both. Age of first flight estimated at 13 days.

Altamira Oriole (*Icterus gularis*)   Plate 61
Breeds in lower Rio Grande Valley in groves of tall trees, willows, or mesquite. Nest suspended from a twig near the tip of a branch in a tree, usually 15–30 ft. up, some-times 7–50 ft. up, in an exposed position, over edge of water, open space, or road. **Nest:** A very elongated, pear-shaped bag, 1–2 ft. long and *c.* 6 in. wide at the basal nest cavity. Woven mainly or entirely of aerial roots of epiphytic plants and long plant fibers. Loose ends of material may hang down around and below the nest. Sus-pended from a twig fork or a loop of material bound to a twig and forming an entrance at the top. The entrance may be widened and the side torn open during the nestling period. Nest cavity lined with plant fibers and plant down. Built by female in 18–26 days. **Breeding season:** Begins late April. Probably ends by late July. Usually single-brooded in US. **Eggs:** Usually 3–4. Long subelliptical to long elliptical. Smooth and glossy. Pale bluish-white; scribbled, scrawled, and with irregular spots and small blotches of black and paler lilac. 29 × 19 mm. **Incubation:** By female. *c.* 14 days? **Nestling:** No information. **Nestling period:** Young tended by both parents. Male feeds young of fledged first brood while female re-nests.

Audubon's Oriole (*Icterus graduacauda*)   Plate 61
Breeds in dense thickets with scattered taller trees near forest edge or along water-courses in southern Texas. Nest usually in a tree or shrub, 5–15 ft. up (though as high as 45 ft.), suspended in an upright fork of a terminal branch. Attached at both rim and sides to twigs, like that of Orchard Oriole. **Nest:** A semi-pensile structure (about 4 in. long). A smallish, rounded cup of fibers of palmetto plants or of fine long grasses woven, often while green, around the supports and twigs to form a firm cup lined with finer grasses or grass heads. **Breeding season:** Begins late March to mid-July. **Eggs:** Usually 3–5. Long subellipti-cal to subelliptical. Smooth and slightly glossy. Very pale bluish or grayish-white, sometimes with a purple wash. Scribbled, scrawled, blotched, or sometimes spotted or speckled with brown, purplish-brown, blackish-purple, purplish-red, or paler purple or gray. Sometimes with only a few spots or fine scribbles at the larger end; sometimes clouded or blotched with lighter reddish-brown and with darker speck-ling of the same. 26 × 19 mm. **Incubation:** By female. **Nestling:** No information. **Nestling period:** Fed by both. Little further information.

Baltimore Oriole (*Icterus galbula*)   Plate 61
Breeds in open woodlands, in shade trees, orchards, wooded residential areas, and similar sites. Nest suspended in a twig fork, usually at the end of a branch, mostly about 25–30 ft. up, sometimes 6–90 ft. up. **Nest:** A deep pensile pouch (about 6 in. long), bound to forked twigs at its rim and with twigs sometimes extending down and bound to the sides. Of long plant fibers, vine bark, hair, string, yarn, and other similar human-made products when avail-able, and other long material including Spanish Moss in some locations, woven into a deep cup; lined with hair, plant down, wool, and fine grasses. Built mostly by female in 4–8 days. **Breeding season:** Begins in May in north. Single-brooded. **Eggs:** Usually 4, sometimes 5, rarely 6. Long oval to long subelliptical. Smooth and

glossy. Very pale grayish-white, sometimes bluish-white or with a faint purplish tint. Scribbled and scrawled with black or blackish-purple and paler purple or gray. Markings usually around larger end. Sometimes the markings form an irregular wreath, occasionally eggs are entirely unmarked. 23 × 15 mm. *Incubation:* By female alone. 12–14 days. *Nestling:* Altricial and downy. Skin pink. Mouth reddish; gape flanges yellow. *Nestling period:* Young tended by both parents. Young can fly at 12–14 days.

Bullock's Oriole (*Icterus bullockii*)   Figure 101
Breeds in scattered trees in more open areas, along streamsides, in shade trees, orchards, farmlands, and similar sites. Nest suspended in a twig fork, often on ascending twigs. Often fastened to supporting twigs at sides as well as at top; in a tree or shrub, sometimes in a mistletoe bunch 6–15 ft. up, sometimes to 50 ft.
Nest: A pensile pouch, often not quite as deep as that of Baltimore Oriole, bound to forked twigs at its rim and with twigs sometimes extending down and bound to the sides. Of long plant fibers, flax, juniper or willow bark, and similar long materials, woven into a deep cup; lined with hair, plant down, wool, fine grasses and moss. Built by both sexes but mostly by female. *Breeding season:* Begins late April in south to late May or June in north of range. Single-brooded? *Eggs:* Usually 4–5, sometimes 3–6. Long subelliptical, sometimes biconical. Smooth and slightly glossy. Very pale grayish-white or bluish-white, sometimes with faint purplish tint. Markings similar to Baltimore Oriole but usually less coarse and fine hair lines around the larger end may be more prevalent. 24 × 16 mm. *Incubation:* By female alone. *c.* 14 days. *Nestling:* Altricial and downy. Skin pink. Down long and scanty, white; on head and back. Mouth red or orange; gape flanges pale yellow. *Nestling period:* Young tended by both parents. Young can fly at *c.* 14 days.

Scott's Oriole (*Icterus parisorum*)   Figure 102, Plate 61
Breeds by semi-arid and desert areas, on the edges of dry plains and in open pinyon – juniper woodland on foothills and mountains. Nests are frequently in yuccas where these are present but elsewhere in trees 4–20 ft. up. A typical site is in dead leaves under a yucca crown. Nest a semi-pensile cup attached to the edges of yucca leaves or bound to supporting twigs in trees.

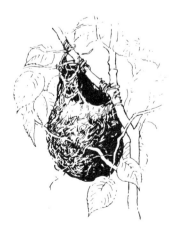

Figure 101. Bullock's Oriole: 2½ × 4 in. wide; *c.* 5½ in. deep; a pensile pouch bound to twigs at top and often at sides.

Figure 102. Scott's Oriole: 4 in. wide; 4 in. deep; nest is bound to leaves of yucca.

Nest: A semi-pensile or pensile cup (about 4 in. long), strongly woven of fine grasses and plant fibers and attached to supports at its rim and sometimes at its sides. Lined with fine grasses and down. Built by female? **Breeding season:** Begins late April to mid-May. Double-brooded. **Eggs:** Usually 3, sometimes 2–4. Long subelliptical to subelliptical. Smooth and slightly glossy. Very pale blue; blotched, streaked, and spotted with black, purplish-brown, chestnut-red, and paler brownish-gray, gray, or purple. 24 × 17 mm. **Incubation:** By female alone. 14 days. **Nestling:** Altricial and downy? Pale gray down. Mouth dull pinkish; gape flanges grayish. **Nestling period:** Young tended by both. Leave nest at *c.* 14 days.

Fringilline and Cardueline Finches, and Allies (*Fringillidae*)

Small, seed-eating birds. Nests in trees, shrubs, or terrestrial herbage. Nest a cup, usually substantial and well made; varying from the neat downy cup of the American Goldfinch to the looser stick nest of the Evening Grosbeak. Nest usually built by female. Eggs usually very pale blue, variably but often sparsely marked in purplish or red, the markings largely confined to the larger end. Often several broods. Sometimes a number of pairs nest near each other in a social group. The female incubates alone and may be fed by the male. Young are downy, with reddish mouths and yellowish or white gape flanges. Both adults tend them, but if successive broods overlap the male may care for fledged young while the female begins re-nesting. Young are usually fed on regurgitated seeds and plant material. Parents may fail to remove droppings of the young for most or all of nestling period, and these may accumulate on the edge of the nest. Young rely on parents for food for a while after leaving the nest and may follow them, noisily begging for food.

Brambling (*Fringilla montifringilla*)
Normally breeds in forests, usually conifers, though in our area (as a very rare breeder in the Western Aleutians) has been found among willow. Nest usually 5–30 ft. up, but in our area has only been found on the ground.
Nest: A neat deep cup of moss, grass, and hair, decorated with lichens and lined with hair, down and feathers. Built by female. **Breeding season:** Begins mid-June.

Usually single-brooded. **Eggs:** Usually 5–7, sometimes 4–8. Subelliptical to short oval. Light blue, variably tinged or blotched with pink or light red, sparsely marked with spots or small blotches. 20 × 15 mm. **Incubation:** Eggs usually laid at daily intervals. Incubation by female alone. 11–12 days. **Nestling:** Altricial and downy. Down white. **Nestling period:** Young tended and fed by both parents. Leave nest at 11–13 days.

Gray-crowned Rosy-Finch (*Leucosticte tephrocotis*)   Plate 62

Breeds on mountains at high altitudes around glaciers and melting snow, also breeds on rocky islands in Alaska. Nest in a cavity or on ledge of rocky tundra outcropping. Sometimes in buildings on Alaskan islands, using beams and cracks.
Nest: Bulky; built of rootlets, mosses, lichens, grasses, and pine needles, when available; lined thickly and firmly with fine grasses and occasionally feathers (often from ptarmigan) and hair. Built by female. **Breeding season:** Mid-June to August. May be double-brooded. **Eggs:** Usually 5, often 4 or 6, sometimes 3. Oval to pyriform. Glossy. White or light creamy-white, and usually unmarked, although sometimes with reddish or yellowish-brown specks. 22 × 16 mm. **Incubation:** By female alone. *c.* 14 days. **Nestling:** Altricial and downy. Down sparse, long and grayish-white, on head and back. Gape flanges yellow. **Nestling period:** Young tended by both parents. Eyes open by 6 days. Young leave nest at *c.* 15 days.

Black Rosy-Finch (*Leucosticte atratus*)

Breeds in the central Rockies on high rocky tundra slopes above timberline (e.g., 11,000 ft.). Nest in a crevice, hidden among boulders, or in a cavity in a vertical cliff.
Nest: A bulky cup of mosses, grasses, feathers, and hair, lined with finer grasses and hair. Built by female, accompanied by male in *c.* 3 days. **Breeding season:** Mid-June to early August. Single-brooded. **Eggs:** 4–5. Oval to pyriform. Slightly glossy. Pure white and unmarked. 22 × 16 mm. **Incubation:** By female alone. 12–14 days. **Nestling:** Altricial and downy. Mouth bright red; gape flanges yellow. **Nestling period:** Young tended by both parents. Eyes open at 4 days; feathers break sheaths at 7–11 days. Young leave nest at *c.* 20 days, fed by adults for 2 weeks more.

Brown-capped Rosy-Finch (*Leucosticte australis*)

Breeds in southern Rockies on mountains at high altitudes (e.g., above 12 000 ft.) in rocky alpine tundra. Nest on rock shelves, talus slides, or in cavities of precipitous cliffs, sometimes several feet back in a narrow fissure. Sometimes on rafters and beams in abandoned mine buildings high in Colorado mountains.
Nest: A cup of dry grasses, flower stems, compactly woven together with fine moss; lined with fine yellow grass, sometimes a few feathers (often from a ptarmigan or finch), fur, or hair. Built by female in 2–3 days. **Breeding season:** Late June to August. Double-brooded. **Eggs:** 3–4, sometimes 5. Oval to pyriform. Slightly glossy. White. 23 × 16 mm. **Incubation:** By female alone. 12–14 days. **Nestling:** Altricial and downy. Down white. Mouth orange; gape flanges pale yellow. **Nestling period:** Young tended by both parents. Young leave nest at *c.* 18 days. Remain with adults until fall.

Pine Grosbeak (*Pinicola enucleator*)   Plate 62

Breeds in coniferous or mixed forest. Nest in birch, conifer, or juniper, fairly low, about 2–10 ft. up.
Nest: A loose structure of twigs; with an inner cup of fine roots, grass, and moss. Built by female. **Breeding season:** Begins late May to early June. Single-brooded. **Eggs:** Usually 4, sometimes 2–5. Subelliptical. Smooth and moderately glossy. Deep light blue; sparsely spotted and blotched with bold black and purplish-brown spots

or small blotches, and more profusely marked with pale lilac or purplish speckling or spotting. Often most heavily marked at the larger end. 26 × 18 mm. **Incubation:** By female only, fed by male. 13–14 days. **Nestling:** Little information. Mouth orange; gape flanges pale yellow. **Nestling period:** Young fed by both parents. Food regurgitated. *c.* 14 days?

Purple Finch (*Carpodacus purpureus*)   Plate 62

Breeds in open woodland, parkland, cultivation with trees, and areas of scattered trees and shrubby growth; favoring conifers in the east part of the range. Nest in a tree, in conifers usually fairly high up and well hidden in foliage, elsewhere in deciduous trees and in lower sites. 5–60 ft. up.

Nest: A cup of fine twigs, grasses, and rootlets; lined with moss, hair, or wool. Built by female over 3–8 days. **Breeding season:** Begins early to mid-May. Usually single-brooded, but may be double-brooded in the west. **Eggs:** Usually 4–5, sometimes 3–6. Subelliptical to oval. Smooth and slightly glossy. Pale light blue, finely speckled, spotted and with, occasionally, scrawls in black and paler purple; the markings small and sparse, often concentrated at the larger end, the purple markings often larger and more numerous. 20 × 15 mm. **Incubation:** By female only, fed by male. 13 days. **Nestling:** Altricial and downy. Pink skin. Developing down, dark gray. **Nestling period:** Young tended by both parents. Leave nest at *c.* 14 days.

Cassin's Finch (*Carpodacus cassinii*)   Plate 62

Breeds in mountain conifer forests. Nest usually in a conifer, high up and usually well out on a branch. Also occurs at lower levels and in deciduous trees. Usually 30–40 ft. up, though sometimes 15–60 ft.

Nest: A loose cup of thin twigs, weed stems, rootlets, and lichen; with a finer lining of rootlets, hair, wool, and bark fiber. Probably built by female over just a few days. **Breeding season:** Usually begins mid-May. Probably double-brooded at times. **Eggs:** Usually 4–5, sometimes 3–6. Subelliptical to long subelliptical. Smooth and slightly glossy. Light blue, finely speckled and spotted in black and pale purple, the markings sparse and often concentrated at the larger end. Purple spots tend to be larger and more numerous. Eggs sometimes unmarked. 20 × 15 mm. **Incubation:** By female only, often fed by male. 12–14 days. **Nestling:** Altricial and downy? **Nestling period:** Young tended by both parents. Fed by regurgitation. Age of first flight estimated at 14 days.

House Finch (*Carpodacus mexicanus*)   Plate 62

Breeds in cultivated areas and around buildings. More rarely in trees, near water, in montane country. Nests in a variety of sites, where a raised ledge or cavity is available. On branches of trees or shrubs, on cacti, in cavities of trees or walls, old nests of other birds, from grosbeaks to cliff swallows, very exceptionally on the ground. Usually 5–7 ft. up, sometimes lower or much higher. Nests may be re-used for second broods and in subsequent years. Will use nest-boxes.

Nest: Cup of fine weed and grass stems, leaves, rootlets, thin twigs, string, wool, and feathers, with similar but finer material as lining. Built by female in as few as 2 days, but can also take up to 21 days. **Breeding season:** Begins late February in south to mid- or late April in north of range. Often double-brooded, sometimes treble-brooded. **Eggs:** Usually 4–5, sometimes 2–6. Subelliptical to long subelliptical. Smooth and slightly glossy. Very pale blue, with or without some very fine but scanty black and pale purple speckling, usually confined to the larger end; or a wreath of very fine scrawls around the larger end. 19 × 14 mm. **Incubation:** Eggs laid at daily intervals. Incubation by female (sometimes before last egg is laid), fed by male. 12–14 days. **Nestling:** Altricial and downy. Down long and grayish-white. **Nestling period:** Young tended by both parents. Brooded mainly by female. Fed by regurgitation. Droppings are not removed after first 3 days and nest-edge becomes soiled. Eyes open at 4 days. Main feather growth at 3–6 days. Young leave nest at 14–16 days.

Red Crossbill (*Loxia curvirostra*)   Plate 62

Breeds in conifers on edges of woodland, or in scattered groups of trees. Nest at varying heights, 6–60 ft. up, usually high and well out on a branch, among twigs and foliage.

Nest: A basal cup of pine twigs, built up with grasses, moss, lichen, and wool; and with a finer inner cup of fine grass, moss, hair, fur, and feathers. Built by female. **Breeding season:** Very variable, usually beginning in January or February, but at times earlier, and extending sometimes to July. Single-brooded. **Eggs:** Usually 3–4, sometimes 2–5. Subelliptical. Smooth and glossy. Very pale blue or bluish-white, variable and sparsely marked with specks, spots, and short scrawls of purple or purplish-black, and fainter pale pink and lilac, mostly limited to the larger end. 22 × 16 mm. **Incubation:** Eggs laid at daily intervals. Incubation by female only (beginning with first egg), fed by male. 13–16 days. **Nestling:** Altricial and downy. Down dark gray. Mouth deep red; bill flesh-red; gape flanges pale yellow or yellowish-pink. **Nestling period:** For about a week the female broods the young while the male brings food, later both parents bring food. Eyes open and feathers break sheaths at 5 days. Young leave nest at 17–22 days, but depend on adults for 3–4 weeks afterwards, until crossed bill-tips have developed.

White-winged Crossbill (*Loxia leucoptera*)   Plate 62

Breeds in conifer forests. Nest in a tree, usually a conifer, built on branches, at varying heights (usually 8–15 ft., sometimes 5–70 ft.) and well hidden in foliage.

Nest: A cup built on a foundation of twigs, of grass, lichens, moss, and leaves; with inner lining of roots, lichen, moss, wool, hair, and feathers. Built by female, with some help by male. **Breeding season:** Begins early February. Usually single-brooded, but may be double- or treble-brooded. **Eggs:** Usually 3–4, rarely 5. Subelliptical. Smooth and glossy. Like the eggs of Red Crossbill. Pale bluish or greenish-white, spotted or variably marked in dark purple and sometimes pale lilac at the larger end. 21 × 15 mm. **Incubation:** By female, fed by male. 14–15 days. **Nestling:** Altricial and downy. Mouth bright purplish-red. Mandibles not crossed. **Nestling period:** Brooded by female for first *c.* 10 days. Leave nest at 22–24 days, and can fly well about 1 week after leaving nest. Independent 3–5 weeks later, when crossed bill-tips have developed.

Common Redpoll (*Carduelis flammea*)   Plate 62

Breeds in mixed conifer and birch woodland, cultivation with plantations and shrubberies; birch scrub, dwarf trees of semi-barrens and tundra. Nest in a tree, shrub, or bush, often high in trees, but at times down to ground level. Usually 3–6 ft. up. Pairs often nest near each other in loose associations.

Nest: A small, untidy cup of fine twigs, grass, and plant stems; lined with plant down, feathers, and hair. In arctic areas old nests may be relined and re-used in subsequent years. Built by female. **Breeding season:** Begins late April in west to June in east. Single- or double-brooded. **Eggs:** Usually 4–5, sometimes 3–7. Subelliptical. Smooth and slightly glossy or non-glossy. Pale blue, marked with fine specks, spots, small blotches, and scrawls; many of them in pale pink or lilac, and sparser reddish-brown and purple marks. Markings mostly concentrated at larger end. 17 × 13 mm. **Incubation:** By female alone. 10–13 days. **Nestling:** Altricial and downy. Down fairly long and thick; dark gray. Mouth red with two pale spots on palate; gape flanges yellow. **Nestling period:** Young tended by both parents. Eyes open at 5 days. No removal of dropping by adults during most of period. Young leave at 11–14 days.

Hoary Redpoll (Carduelis hornemanni)   Plate 62

Breeds in northern scrub and tundra. Nest in a low tree or shrub, or on the ground sheltered by a rock. Usually 1–7 ft. up.

Nest: A cup of grasses and twigs, sometimes rootlets; lined with feathers, hair, and plant down. Old nests may be relined and re-used in subsequent years. Built by female over 3–4 days. **Breeding season:** Begins late May to late June. Single-brooded. **Eggs:** Usually 4–5, rarely 3–6. Similar to those of Common Redpoll but larger and a little paler in ground color. 18 × 13 mm. **Incubation:** By female alone, beginning with second or third egg. 14–15 days in all. **Nestling:** No information; probably similar to Common Redpoll. **Nestling period:** Young tended by both parents. Brooded by female only for c. 10 days. Young leave nest at 10–14 days.

Pine Siskin (Carduelis pinus)   Plate 62

Breeds in forests, usually conifers. Nest in a tree or shrub, usually at medium height but sometimes 3–50 ft. up. Frequently in a conifer out on a branch, well hidden in foliage; usually resting in or on a twig fork. May nest in loose colony.

Nest: A fairly large cup of twigs, rootlets, and grass; with a finer lining of feathers, hair, fur, fine rootlets, and fibers. Built by female, accompanied by male. **Breeding season:** Begins late March to early April. Possibly double-brooded. **Eggs:** Usually 3–4, sometimes 2–6. Subelliptical to short subelliptical. Very pale blue or greenish-blue; speckled, spotted, blotched, or scrawled with purplish-black and pale lilac. The markings usually sparse and confined to a wreath around the larger end. 17 × 12 mm. **Incubation:** Eggs laid at daily intervals. Incubation by female alone, fed by male. 13 days. **Nestling:** Altricial and downy. **Nestling period:** Young tended by both parents. Fed by regurgitation. Brooded for first c. 9 days by female with male bringing food. No droppings removed after c. 9 days. Young become active at c. 11 days. Leave nest at 14–15 days.

Lesser Goldfinch (Carduelis psaltria)   Plate 62

Breeds in more arid open country, in trees and shrubs close to water. Nest in a twig fork, usually well hidden in foliage, and in larger trees may be well out in canopy. 2–30 ft. up, more usually 5–10 ft. up. Usually nest in solitary pairs, though sometimes in loose colony.

Nest. Fairly compact cup of fine grass stems, plant and bark fiber, and moss or wool; lined with very fine fibrous material or plant down. Built mostly or entirely by female. **Breeding season:** Begins late March in south to early May in north of range. Double-, sometimes treble-brooded. **Eggs:** Usually 4–5, sometimes 3–6. Subelliptical to oval. Smooth and slightly glossy. Very pale blue or greenish-blue. Unmarked. 15 × 12 mm. **Incubation:** By female alone, fed by male. 12 days. **Nestling:** Altricial and downy. Mouth orange; gape flanges pale yellow or cream. **Nestling period:** Young tended by both parents. Fed by regurgitation. Nest sanitation ceases about halfway through period. Departure estimated at 11 days.

Lawrence's Goldfinch (Carduelis lawrencei)   Plate 62

Breeds in drier regions with scattered trees or open woodland. Usually near water. Nest often, but not always, in conifers from 3–40 ft. up, but usually 15–20 ft. up; in a twig fork. Pairs nest singly or with a number nesting near each other.

Nest: A small cup, usually of coarser material; stems, grasses, and lichen towards the outside, but including grass and flower heads, wool, hair, and feathers. Built by female, rarely helped by male. **Breeding season:** Begins late March to early April. **Eggs:** Usually 4–5, sometimes 3–6. Subelliptical to oval. Smooth and slightly glossy. White and unmarked. 15 × 12 mm. **Incubation:** 12–13 days. By female alone, fed by male. **Nestling:** Altricial and downy. **Nestling period:** Young tended by both parents. Leave at *c.* 11 days.

American Goldfinch (*Carduelis tristis*)   Figure 103, Plate 62

Breeds over a wide variety of habitats with openings and where trees and shrubs are present. Nest in a tree or shrub, usually 3–10 ft. up, occasionally 1–33 ft. or higher in trees; sometimes low on tall weeds. Nest often near water or in swampy area. Nest placed on twigs or in fork or between uprights with nest material bound around supports.

Nest: A neat and firm compact cup of plant fibers and strips of bark, with catkins, plant down, cotton and wool; lined with plant down. Nest edges and probably elsewhere bound with spiders' and caterpillar webs and strengthened with long fibers. Built by female in 4–6 days. **Breeding season:** Begins April or May in southwest to mid-June or early July in east. Double-, sometimes treble-brooded. **Eggs:** Usually 5, sometimes 4–6. Smooth and slightly glossy. Subelliptical to oval. Very pale blue or greenish-blue, unmarked. 16 × 12 mm. **Incubation:** By female alone, fed by male. 12–14 days. **Nestling:** Altricial and downy. Pale grayish down on head and body. Mouth pinkish-red; gape flanges pale creamy-yellow. **Nestling period:** Young tended by both parents. Brooded by female during first week and all food brought by male. No droppings removed after *c.* 1 week. Young leave nest at 11–17 days.

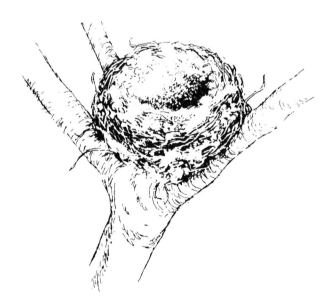

Figure 103. American Goldfinch: c. 3½ in. across; a deep cup of fine plant fibers, often with an overall cottony appearance.

Evening Grosbeak (*Coccothraustes vespertinus*)   Plate 62

Breeds in northern spruce forest, and in montane conifer forest elsewhere. Nest usually high in a tree, coniferous or deciduous, in a crotch, or close to the trunk, or well out towards the end of a conifer branch, where foliage offers concealment. 20–60 ft. up.

Nest: A loosely constructed cup of sticks, untidily put together and elliptical in shape, with some moss, lichens, and rootlets woven into it, and an inner cup of finer material; rootlets and some hair and fibers. Built mostly, if not entirely, by female. **Breeding season:** Begins mid-May in south to late June in north of range. **Eggs:** Usually 3–4, sometimes 2–5. Subelliptical. Smooth and glossy. Light blue or greenish-blue, speckled, spotted, and with blotches and large scrawls of dull purplish-brown, olive-brown, or purplish-gray; the markings very sparse and bold and mainly concentrated at the larger end. Resembles egg of Red-winged Blackbird in color and pattern. 24 × 17 mm. **Incubation:** Eggs laid at daily intervals. Incubation by female only (sometimes before last egg is laid), fed by male. 12–14 days. **Nestling:** Altricial and downy. Skin dark. White down on head, wings, back, and thighs. Bill yellow. Mouth violet and red; gape flanges white. **Nestling period:** Young tended by both parents. Fed on regurgitated insects. Eyes open at 4–6 days. Young leave nest at 13–14 days.

Old World Sparrows (*Ploceidae*)

House Sparrow (*Passer domesticus*)   Figure 4, Plate 58

Introduced to North America. Breeds around or near human habitation, usually in association with cultivation. Nest in a hole or crevice of any kind in or near a building. In creepers growing on buildings, or occasionally among twigs in trees. Height variable from 1–75 ft. up, though usually between 10–20 ft. Will use nest-box. May nest in loose colony.

Nest: In trees a neat rounded domed structure with side entrance, in creepers or crevices an untidy domed structure, or in holes may be a cup. Of straw, plant stems and any appropriate trash such as paper, string, or cloth; lined with feathers, hair, and wool. Built by both sexes, but mainly by the male. **Breeding season:** Usually begins about May, but variable, and exceptional nests have been recorded in most months. Double- or treble-brooded. **Eggs:** Usually 3–5, rarely up to 8. Subelliptical. Smooth and only slightly glossy. White, or faintly tinted greenish or grayish; very variably marked with spots, speckling, or small blotches of gray, blue-gray, greenish-gray, purplish-gray, black, brown, or purplish-brown. Eggs may vary within a clutch, usually one being much more sparsely marked and appearing whiter. Rarely unmarked. 23 × 16 mm. **Incubation:** Chiefly by the female, beginning with the completion of the clutch. 11–14 days. **Nestling:** Altricial and naked. Mouth pinkish-yellow; gape flanges pale yellow. **Nestling period:** Young brooded by female, who roosts in nest for first *c.* 7 days. Young fed by both parents, mainly on insects brought in the bill. 15 days in nest.

Eurasian Tree Sparrow (*Passer montanus*)   Plate 58

Introduced in the vicinity of St. Louis, Missouri. Breeds in sites offering nest-holes in regions of cultivation or wasteland. Nest a hole in a tree, cliff, quarry, wall, thatched roof, haystack, thick creepers on walls or rocks, pipe, or mammal hole. Often just 4–8 ft. up. Will use nest-box.

Nest: A domed structure or untidy cup of plant stalks and twigs; lined with down and feathers. Built by both sexes. **Breeding season:** Begins April, extending to early August. Double- or treble-brooded. **Eggs:** Usually 4–6, rarely 2–9. Subelliptical.

Smooth and slightly glossy. Variable, but less so than those of the House Sparrow, being darker, browner and smaller. Ground color white to very pale gray; heavily marked with spots, small blotches or speckling, usually in dark brown sometimes purplish or grayish. Markings often heavy enough to obscure ground color. At times very fine speckling makes eggs appear uniform in color but usually darkening towards the larger end. Markings tend to concentrate towards the larger end. Many clutches show one or two pale, sparsely-marked eggs, 19 × 14 mm. **Incubation:** By both sexes. 11–14 days. **Nestling:** Altricial and naked. Mouth pink, sometimes with dark spot at tongue tip; gape flanges pale yellow. **Nestling period:** Young tended by both parents. 12–14 days in nest.

A Selected Bibliography

Anyone studying the habits of North American birds must acknowledge the vision and stamina of Arthur Cleveland Bent who compiled the life histories of these birds published by the Smithsonian Institution for over five decades in the *Life Histories of North American Birds*. We are grateful not only to A. C. Bent but also to the multitude of individuals who over the last half-century have made their contributions, large and small, in various books and ornithological journals, and steadily increased our knowledge of North American birds.

Space prevents us from listing all the individual journal articles and authors, from which we culled material on the nests, eggs, and nestlings of North American birds. The major journals, however, were *The Auk*, *The Condor*, *The Journal of Field Ornithology* (formerly *Bird-banding*), *Western Birds*, and *The Wilson Bulletin*.

Moreover, the life histories of these birds are currently being compiled in the *Birds of North America* (BNA) species' accounts. This expanding series of modern, authoritative references is designed to replace the classic Bent series. BNA is the project of the Academy of Natural Sciences and the American Ornithologists' Union and currently numbers about 240 species' treatments.

If you are a researcher wishing to know our sources of information on a particular species, you should write to Paul J. Baicich, P.O. Box 404, Oxon Hill, MD 20750, USA.

Though we could not include the myriad of source articles from journals, the one hundred most important books that we used are listed below. (This listing does include a number of works that might be considered 'more than journals, but probably less than books,' for example, lengthy pamphlets, monographs, or conference proceedings.)

Ainley, D. and R. J. Boekelheide. 1990. *Seabirds of the Farralon Islands*. Stanford.

American Ornithologists Union. 1983. *The A.O.U. Check-list of North American Birds*. AOU.

Andrews, R. and R. Righter. 1992. *Colorado Birds, A Reference to Their Distribution and Habitat*. Denver Museum of Natural History.

Atwood, J. L. 1990. *Status Review of the California Gnatcatcher* (Polioptila californica). Manomet Bird Observatory.

Baily, A. M. and R. Niedrach. 1965. *Birds of Colorado* (Vol. 1 and 2). Denver Museum of Natural History.

Bellrose, F. C. 1967. *Ducks, Geese, and Swans of North America*. Stackpole.

Birkhead, T. R. 1991. *The Magpies: the ecology and behaviour of Black-billed Magpie and Yellow-billed Magpie*. T. & A. D. Poyser.

Brown, L. and D. Amadon. 1968. *Eagles, Hawks, and Falcons of the World*. Country Life Books.

Burton, J. A. (ed). 1973. *Owls of the World*. E. P. Dutton.

Byers, C., J. Curson, and U. Olsson. 1995. *Sparrows and Buntings: A Guide to the Sparrows and Buntings of North America and the World*. Houghton Mifflin.

Cadman, M. D., P. F. J. Eagles, and F. M. Helleiner. 1988. *Atlas of the Breeding Birds of Ontario*. University of Waterloo Press.

Campbell, R. W., N. K. Dawe, I. McTaggart-Cowan, J. M. Cooper, G. W. Kaiser, and

M. C. E. McNall. 1990. *The Birds of British Columbia* (Vol. 1 and 2). Royal British Columbia Museum.

Clapp, R. B., R. C. Banks, D. Morgan-Jacobs, and W. A. Hoffman. 1982. *Marine Birds of the Southeastern United States and Gulf of Mexico* (Part I, Gaviiformes through Pelecaniformes). USF&WS.

Clapp, R. B., D. Morgan-Jacobs, R. C. Banks, and W. A. Hoffman. 1982. *Marine Birds of the Southeastern United States and Gulf of Mexico* (Part II, Anseriformes). USF&WS.

Clapp, R.B., D. Morgan-Jacobs, and R. C. Banks. 1983. *Marine Birds of the Southeastern United States and Gulf of Mexico* (Part III, Charadriiformes). USF&WS.

Collias, N. and E. Collias. 1984. *Nest Building and Bird Behavior.* Princeton.

Cramp, S. (ed). 1983. *Handbook of the Birds of Europe, the Middle East and North Africa* (Vol. III waders to gulls). Oxford University Press.

Curson, J., D. Quinn, and D. Beadle. 1994. *Warblers of the Americas.* Houghton Mifflin.

DeGraaf, R. M. and J. H. Rappole. 1995. *Neotropical Migratory Birds.* Cornell University Press.

Ehrlich, P. R., D. S. Dobkin, and D. Whye. 1988. *The Birder's Handbook.* Simon and Schuster.

Farrand, J. Jr. (ed.). 1983. *The Audubon Society Master Guide to Birding* (Vol. 1–3). Knopf.

Ffrench, R. 1973. *A Guide to the Birds of Trinidad and Tobago.* Livingston Publishing.

Fjeldså, J. 1977. *Guide to the Young of European Precocial Birds.* Skarr Nature Publications.

Foss, C. R. (ed). 1995. *Atlas of Breeding Birds of New Hampshire.* Audubon Society of New Hampshire.

Forshaw, J. M. 1973. *Parrots of the World.* Doubleday & Co.

Friedman, H. 1929. *The Cowbirds.* Thomas Pub. Co.

Gabrielson, I. N. and F. C. Lincoln. 1959. *Bird of Alaska.* Stackpole.

Gaston, A. J. 1992. *Ancient Murrelet. A Natural History in the Queen Charlotte Islands.* Poyser.

Godfrey, W. E. 1986. *Birds of Canada.* National Museum of Natural History.

Goodwin, D. 1976. *Crows of the World.* Comstock.

Griscom, L. (ed). 1979. *The Warblers of America* (revised and updated by E. M. Reilly, Jr.). Doubleday.

Hancock, J. and H. Elliott. 1978. *The Herons of the World.* Harper and Row.

Hancock, J. and J. Kushlan. 1984. *The Herons Handbook.* Harper and Row.

Harrison, C. 1975. *A Field Guide to the Nests, Eggs and Nestlings of British and European Birds.* Collins.

Harrison, H. 1975. *A Field Guide to Birds' Nests.* Houghton Mifflin.

Harrison, H. 1979. *A Field Guide to Western Birds' Nests.* Houghton Mifflin.

Hayman, P., J. Marchant, and T. Prater. 1986. *Shorebirds, An Identification Guide.* Houghton Mifflin.

Howell, S. N. G. and S. Webb. 1995. *A Guide to the Birds of Mexico and Northern Central America.* Oxford University Press.

Isler, M. L. and P. R. Isler. 1987. *The Tanagers.* Smithsonian.

James, R. D., P. J. McLaren, and J. C. Barlow. 1976. *Annotated Checklist of the Birds of Ontario.* Royal Ontario Museum.

Johnsgard, P. A. 1975. *Waterfowl of North America.* Indiana University.

Johnsgard, P. A. 1983. *Hummingbirds of North America.* Smithsonian.

Johnsgard, P. A. 1988. *North American Owls.* Smithsonian.

Johnsgard, P. A. 1990. *Hawks, Eagles, and Falcons of North America.* Smithsonian.

Johnson, S. R. and D. R. Herter. 1989. *Birds of the Beaufort Sea.* BP Explorations.

Kale, H. W. II. 1978. *Rare and Endangered Biota of Florida* (Vol. II – birds). Univ. Presses of Florida.

Kaufman, K. 1996. *Lives of North American Birds.* Houghton Mifflin.
Low, R. 1972. *The Parrots of South America.* John Gifford.
Marzluff, J. M. and R. P. Balda. 1991. *The Pinyon Jay: Behavioral Ecology of a Colonial and Cooperative Corvid.* T. & A. D. Poyser.
Morse, D. H. 1989. *American Warblers.* Harvard University Press.
Murphy, R. C. 1936. *Oceanic Birds of South America* (Vol. I and II). Macmillan/AMNH.
Nelson, C. H. 1995. *The Downy Waterfowl of North America.* Delta Station Press.
Nelson, J. B. 1978. *The Sulidae.* Oxford University Press.
Newton, I. 1979. *Population Ecology of Raptors.* Vermillion: Buteo Books.
Oberholser, H. C. and E. Kincaid (ed.). 1974. *The Bird Life of Texas* (Vol. I and II). University of Texas.
Ogilvie, M. A. 1976. *The Winter Birds.* Praeger.
Orians, G. H. and T. Angell. 1985. *Blackbirds of the Americas.* Univ. of Washington.
Palmer, R. S. 1962, 1976, 1976, 1988, and 1988. *Handbook of North American Birds* (Vol. I, II, III, IV and V). Yale University Press.
Poole, A. F. 1989. *Ospreys: A Natural and Unnatural History.* Cambridge University Press.
Pough, R. H. 1951. *Audubon Water Bird Guide.* Doubleday.
Pough, R. H. 1957. *Audubon Western Bird Guide.* Doubleday.
Portenko, L. A. 1972. *Birds of the Chuchi Peninsula and Wrangel Island* (Vol. I). Amerind.
Proctor, N. S. and P. J. Lynch. 1993. *Manual of Ornithology.* Yale University Press.
Pulich, W. M. 1976. *The Golden-cheeked Warbler.* Texas Parks and Wildlife.
Ralph, J. C., G. L. Hunt, Jr., M. G. Raphael, and J. F. Piatt. 1995. *Ecology and Conservation of the Marbled Murrelet.* U.S. Dept of Agri. (USFS).
Reed, C. A. 1904. *North American Bird Eggs.* Doubleday.
Ripley, S. D. 1977. *Rails of the World.* Godine.
Rising, J. D. and D. D. Beadle. 1996. *A Guide to the Identification and Natural History of the Sparrows of the United States and Canada.* Academic Press.
Scott, S. L. (ed.). *Field Guide to the Birds of North America.* National Geographic Soc.
Short, L. 1982. *Woodpeckers of the World.* Delaware Museum of Natural History.
Salomensem, F. 1950. *Grønlands Fugle, The Birds of Greenland.* Bording.
Skutch, A. F. 1960. *Life Histories of Central American Birds* (Vol. 2 – Pacific Coast Avifauna). Cooper Ornithol. Soc.
Skutch, A. F. 1972. *Studies of Tropical American Birds.* Nuttal Ornithological Club.
Skutch, A. F. 1976. *Parent Birds and Their Young* . Texas University Press.
Skutch, A. F. 1989. *Life of the Tanager.* Cornell University Press.
Skutch, A. F. 1996. *Orioles, Blackbirds, and Their Kin: A Natural History.* The University of Arizona Press.
Smith, S. M. 1991. *The Black-capped Chickadee: Behavioral Ecology and Natural History.* Cornell University.
Smithe, F. B. 1966. *Birds of Tikal.* Natural History Press.
Stiles, F. G. and A. F. Skutch. 1989. *A Guide to the Birds of Costa Rica.* Cornell University Press.
Stokes, D. and L. Stokes. 1990. *The Complete Birdhouse Book.* Little Brown.
Sowls, A. L., S. A. Hatch, and C. J. Lensink. 1978. *Catalog of Alaskan Seabird Colonies.* U.S. Fish and Wildlife Service.
Tacha, T. C. and C. E. Braun. (eds.). 1994. *Migratory Shore and Upland Game Bird Management in North America.* International Association of Fish and Wildlife Agencies.
Taylor, R. C. 1993. *Trogons of the Arizona Borderlands.* Treasure Chest Publications.
Terres, J. K. 1980. *The Audubon Society Encyclopedia of North American Birds.* Knopf.
Turner, A. and C. Rose. 1989. *Swallows and Martins.* Houghton Mifflin.
Tyrell, E. Q. and R. A. Tyrell. 1985. *Hummingbirds, Their Life and Behavior.* Crown.

Veit, R. and W. Petersen. 1993. *Birds of Massachusetts*. Massachusetts Audubon Society.

Verner, J. and M. F. Willson. 1969. *Mating Systems, Sexual Dimorphism, and the Role of Male North American Passerine Birds in the Nesting Cycle*. AOU Monographs.

Wallace, G. J. 1939. *Bicknell's Thrush, its taxonomy, distribution, and life history*. Boston Soc. Nat. Hist.

Wauer, R. H. 1973. *Birds of Big Bend National Park and Vicinity*. Univ. of Texas Press.

Wetmore, A. 1984. *Birds of the Republic of Panama* (Part 4). Smithsonian.

Winkler, D., D. A. Christie, and D. Nurney. 1995. *Woodpeckers: An Identification Guide to the Woodpeckers of the World*. Houghton Mifflin.

Walkinshaw, L. H. 1983. *Kirtland's Warbler: The Natural History of an Endangered Species*. Cranbrook Institute of Science.

Warham, J. 1990. *The Petrels*. Academic Press.

Woolfenden, G. E. and J. W. Fitzpatrick. 1984. *The Florida Scrub Jay: demography of a cooperative breeding bird*. Princeton.

Index of common and scientific names

Note: numbers in **bold** refer to nestling plate number and numbers in *italic* refer to egg plate number.

DATE DUE